The
Neo-Tech
World

The
Neo-Tech
World

Mark Hamilton

NEO-TECH BOOKS

Published by Integrated Management Associates
850 S. Boulder Highway, Henderson, Nevada 89015, U.S.A.

First published in the United States of America by
Integrated Management Associates

2   4   5   3

LIBRARY OF CONGRESS
CATALOGING-IN-PUBLICATION DATA
Hamilton, Mark
The Neo-Tech World
ISBN 911752-90-0

Printed in the United States of America
March 2002 [KNI-TNTW] [5,000]

Table of Contents

Part One
The Twelve Visions

i

Table of Contents

Part One

The Twelve Visions

Vision Prologue
Witness the Approaching Neo-Tech World

I observe people. Their behaviors are very predictable. Most people, however, have no idea how predictable (and controllable) they are. Let's take a look:

Our behaviors descend directly from nature's original design of the human brain. That original design can be understood by observing the behavior of man and the structure of his society 150 generations ago.

So, let's go back in time.

If we could send ourselves back in time 150 generations ago, people would seem really weird. They would seem to be in a trance, walking around seemingly with no soul, functioning automatically, systematically to the world around them, sometimes hearing and reacting to imagined voices of their gods, or waiting for directions from oracles or God-Kings who hallucinated voices of the higher gods. The strange people around you would have no sense of self, merely empty-shell automatons with no internal thoughts.

Scientists have learned that man had a completely different mentality 3000 years ago. He did not have the linguistic tools yet to separate from the world around him, to turn inward and think internally as we do today. He had no inner mind space of thoughts and judgements. He went through life reacting as all animals to the world around him.

If you could suddenly go back 150 generations, you would find that civilization functioned smoothly and people communicated through a simplistic language prior to the development of the much more sophisticated metaphor. The metaphor and the analogy use something to describe something else, which enabled man to finally separate from the world directly before him, to step back into an inner mind space from where he could view the world around him, think about it, about himself, to judge and analyze and to introspect. That vast inner mind space, which did not exist in man 150 generations ago, is known as *human consciousness*. The metaphor was the big bang that opened up the universe of our minds. Before human consciousness, the human race smoothly functioned as well-programmed automatons.

If those people void of human consciousness 150 generations ago talked to you, you would find the communication bizarre, for they could only report scenes of action like news flashes, but never express internal thoughts or judgements whatsoever, as though nothing existed in their minds. Again, as they simply reported the action, you would be filled with an eerie sense that those people had no soul...as though there was no one *inside* those bodies. Are they all, you would wonder, under some kind of hypnotic spell? It would seem to you as though they all had undergone some kind of mind-altering lobotomy that removed their individuality. In fact, going back from the 21st century, those identity-void automatons would act and talk sort of like data processors, not unlike computers. And, in a sense, their spiritless mentality was just that — sophisticated computers processing the data from the world around them and acting accordingly, just as their brains were programmed from mimicked and learned reactions.

The smoothly functioning civilization around you would appear to be filled with well-programmed but mindless beings. As you stood close to some of those automatically functioning beings, you would begin to think they were schizophrenic as you would hear them talking to themselves or answering imagined voices and obediently obeying hallucinated audio commands from their "gods". The voices in their heads came from neurological impulses in their brains not unlike nature's guidance system for any animal, but man's brain was larger, more intelligent, and had evolved a simplistic language. So, nature's neurological guidance system that made animals act, functioned in man not through impressions in the mind, but through hallucinated voices of the "gods". He would audio hallucinate the voices of different gods telling him how to live and survive, especially when under stress and forced to make a decision. Through today's eyes, looking back, his every action was as predictable as a computer program.

The First Insight in Part Two of this book, goes into detail about that different mentality 150 generations ago, shortly before human consciousness opened the vast universe of our minds. The First Insight describes the hallucinated voices — man's neurological survival mechanism prior to human consciousness. That different mentality is known scientifically as the *bicameral mentality* from the Bicameral Age three thousand to ten thousand years ago.

The bicameral civilizations were structured into effective Theocracies. The higher position in the hierarchy of power one was, the more powerful gods he could "hear" and, in turn, give direction to the trancelike masses of automatons waiting to be led.

On the other hand, if you went back and spoke with authority to those automatons 150 generations ago, they would obey your commands. You would be looked upon as a god, more powerful than their own God-Kings, because *you* alone could make decisions. Therefore, you would have to be a god, one who gives direction to the automatons waiting for a voice to tell them how to act. You could easily take over an entire civilization just as the small band of conscious European "white gods" easily conquered the wealthy and massive bicameral Inca civilization in South America without any resistance. (The American Indians were still bicameral when the European explorers arrived.)

That same behavioral pattern of obeying those who speak with authority can be found throughout modern-day politics. Furthermore, although most Western governments today are not theocracies, the same dynamic of leaders and those waiting to be led exists in society's structure and in our own behavioral patterns. Indeed, we would be lost without leaders. In short, society's structure of governments and religions telling man how to live descends directly from the Bicameral Age. Even in the 21st century, society's structure is strikingly similar to ancient times.

Man's behavior and society's structure today, although much more sophisticated, still follow the original patterns. By understanding the original behavioral patterns from our early development as an animal of nature and the remnant effects on our behavior today, we can get some amazing understandings about ourselves, which includes easily predicting how we (and others) will act in different situations. Moreover, we can accurately project how things will be as those ancient behavioral patterns wear off. Indeed, those behavioral patterns from our distant past have been slowly wearing off, generation after generation. The 21st-century world of super rapidly advancing knowledge and technology will wipe off those old behavioral patterns more quickly than ever before, giving rise to the Twelve Visions.

In time, the bicameral behaviors will wear off completely, which will happen most dramatically in the first half of the 21st century as all knowledge since the beginning of time multiplies a hundredfold.[1] Society's structures will change. By understanding the bicameral behaviors and their coming demise, the Twelve Visions into the 21st century become quite apparent...and lucrative.

Instead of a ruling class sitting atop society, a new paradigm will unfold as the mind loses its bicameral longings for leaders. As politics become less and less popular, federal and local governments will shrink to military, police, and court protection only. Without massive bureaucratic regulations, millions of entrepreneurial geniuses will rise easily and quickly and will bring society spectacular new technologies that we cannot even imagine now, at lower and lower prices, which will drive up our standards of living and eradicate most diseases.

The fully evolved mentality in that approaching world, an extraordinarily powerful mentality in which man's mind ceases to seek external authority, is called the *Neothink mentality*. And with that Neothink mentality, man needs no hallucinated voices of the gods or modern-day vestiges, no external authorities telling him how to live, no voices of politicians or clergymen. He becomes his own god, so to speak, his own authority, his own *God-Man*.

God-Man has no traces of bicameral man. God-Man is our final evolution. He will affect the world in amazing ways...amazingly positive ways.

So, let's explore what happens when humanity leaves behind the vestiges of its bicameral past and its modern-day mutations such as the ruling class of politicians and regulatory bureaucrats

---

[1]The Futurist Society estimates that all known knowledge on Earth will multiply a hundredfold by 2050 AD.

6

— that hierarchy of authorities who rule over us in the name of the "social good". What happens when man's mind becomes its own authority? The answer is: man releases his full, human potential. We know the breathtaking knowledge that rose during the Golden Age of Greece 2400 years ago just two dozen generations after the Bicameral Age and its world of powerless, bicameral automatons. The amazing Greeks were discovering the authority of man's own mind, thus unleashing its awesome power.

What could that power lead to in today's world of high technology? The answer is: to a Golden Neo-Tech World — a world of super rapidly advancing new technologies and super rapidly falling prices. Before long, we will afford all the luxuries of life in the Neo-Tech World.

In describing that Golden Neo-Tech World, you will read about a non-authoritarian government that will open the starting gates to a great Technological Revolution that will make everyone as wealthy as millionaires; you will read about millions of geniuses who replace a few hundred politicians to convincingly take care of us and all our needs beyond our wildest imaginations...such as bringing us perfect health and perfect bodies as we live with vitality well into our hundreds; you will read about a world where there are not only no diseases, but no violence, crime or terrorism. Also, you will read about a job revolution that will change our boring routine ruts into exciting entrepreneurial jobs with major profit sharing; you will even read about ordinary people having spectacular romances with sexy spouses of their dreams with slim and sensuous bodies; and, of course, you will read about a new way of using the mind called Neothink and about someday becoming a genius yourself.

Those fortunes will occur in the 21st century because of one phenomenon: man sheds his bicameral behaviors and longings for higher "authorities" as man makes his final evolutionary "jump" into God-Man. When that begins, civilization will enter a paradise on Earth...our Golden Neo-Tech World.

Neo-Tech means: *super rapidly advancing new (Neo) technologies (Tech).*[1] The Neo-Tech World will become a supercivilization of computerlike, technological revolutions in all

---

[1]The deeper treatment of Neo-Tech and its deeper meaning resides in The First Insight in Part Two of this book.

industries, including the medical industry, which will make us wealthy and vigorous with nearly perfect health. Let us look at what the Neo-Tech World will do for us:

The Gifts

For two decades I have explored removing my bicameral behaviors and have even personally jumped into the realm of Neothink on several occasions. The power is enormous and has brought me personal success. I have written several books on the subject, but it was not until my Twelve Visions, when I temporarily experienced God-Man, that I connected all the dots into one succinct picture of our Neo-Tech World to occur as mankind begins evolving into God-Man. The Twelve Visions showed me that in tomorrow's Neo-Tech World, we lived like millionaires, enjoyed passionate romantic relationships, and enjoyed very long, healthy lives. And, as you will see, *you* have a very good chance to experience that Neo-Tech World in *your* lifetime.

The story about to be told, by the way, offers a benefit even beyond a look at our future. Perhaps just as important, the New (Neo) Techniques (Tech) — a second definition of Neo-Tech — used in the future actually deliver to the reader significant wealth and love, *right now,* perhaps validating the soundness and probability of the hypothesis. The Twelve Visions show us the Gifts in the Neo-Tech World enjoyed by tomorrow's multitudes, gifts that, with these New Techniques (Neo-Tech), I now personally enjoy, too...as you can, too, such as:

- being surrounded by geniuses who help make your every wish come true

- becoming a millionaire without lifting a finger

- living with extraordinary health, happiness, and longevity

- enjoying the exciting career of your dreams

- soaring to the top of the company you always wanted to work for

- becoming the person you were meant to be

- living the life you were meant to live
- making love to the person of your dreams
- becoming slim and sexy with a more satisfying diet than those who are obese
- rising with superior intelligence using 21st-century Neothink

After my Twelve Visions, I automatically went through a *personal renaissance* that delivered the Gifts to me, *today*. (The gift of health and longevity still depends on the Technological Revolution that has just begun.) In short, the knowledge in this book hastens your destiny of becoming a romantic millionaire in the 21st century.

The Twelve Visions

So, if you want to become a millionaire, keep reading. How about living to be 130 years old? Are you searching for romantic love? It's all possible.

One Sunday afternoon, I was in my home office going over some financial papers. Outside my sliding glass door, the day was winding down into dusk when I suddenly and involuntarily started remembering back over my life. I was pulled back in my chair as memories raced through my mind and somehow took me all the way back into my infancy. After my life had rewound back to my first year, suddenly I *knew* my life and others *had* to rise to a higher level. I had no idea at the time that the higher level would be man's next evolutionary jump. In fact, at that moment I felt lost...as if every ambitious idea I ever thought of had been relatively ineffectual. I needed some kind of insight on *how* our lives would be lived radically for the better. I had no clue beyond the life I had always lived.

After watching all those memories in my mind's eye, I now started slipping into visions of my future. I knew a lot about Neo-Tech and Neothink, which started integrating into those visions of my future. Gradually, something incredible happened: I could see mankind and our world in a whole new light — like an unexplainable new color. I did not know then that I was

9

seeing man after his next evolutionary jump or that I was witnessing his magnificent Neo-Tech World.

Specifically, I was able to see well into the 21st century through Twelve Visions. My mind kept snapping together twelve different puzzle pieces into one brilliant puzzle picture of our future. I knew that most of the puzzle-pieces did not yet exist, but they snapped so perfectly into the puzzle that I knew they would someday exist. I was aware that this puzzle-building phenomenon was how Neothink worked, but it all happened so fast that I knew I had gone to some level I had never reached before. Later, I realized I had my first experience as God-Man.

I witnessed the glorious way we lived...in a place where we routinely filled our greatest desires and enjoyed daily the Gifts. When mankind's bicameral mentalities collapsed, our money, our health, our romantic relationships were on entirely new levels. I was so overwhelmed by the prosperity and sheer honesty of what I saw in just one Vision, I laid my head down on my desk and reveled in euphoria. Since I did not know at the time that I had just experienced my first encounter with God-Man, I had no clue what had just happened to me or why I could so quickly and clearly see into the future...not until much later did I learn that my years of experimenting with Neothink finally enabled me to experience God-Man. (As you will learn, the God-Man can see into the future, even create the future.)

As the phenomenon ended during the middle of the night, something told me the time had come as we entered the third millennium to tell the world. So, here are bare abbreviations of half my Visions with enough insights to give you an initial glance at our fast approaching Neo-Tech World that begins when man begins switching over to Neothink and evolving into God-Man:

Vision

One Vision showed me unbelievable *security*. Millions of geniuses rose throughout all industries to take care of our needs and wants. In recent years, geniuses have had the freedom to rise quickly only in the computer industry, and look what they have done: They have brought us cheap home computers with the power of million-dollar mainframes of a decade ago. And for our kids? They play video games at home that would have cost millions a few years ago. In tomorrow's Neo-Tech (New Technology) Era, Bill Gates-like geniuses "spoiled" us and allowed us to spoil our children and grandchildren with incredible yet affordable goods. Geniuses took care of our personal needs and wants in every industry (not just the computers) as the external authorities and their massive regulations came down. The geniuses were the first to switch over to the Neothink mentality, and they took wonderful care of us. The new code of living meant that genuine geniuses, not pretentious politicians, took extraordinary care of us. That was a Gift in the Neo-Tech World.

Vision

In another Vision, I saw unbelievable *wealth*. The cost of raw technology moved towards zero. For example, take the technology of fiber optics today. For one person or thousands of persons to talk over that fiber optic cable costs the same — zilch, which by the way is why the telecommunications revolution has begun...watch the prices fall. That explains why in tomorrow's Neo-Tech Era of super rapidly advancing new technologies in all industries, our costs for all those new technologies and resulting consumer products moved towards zero. Thus, similar to the computers, our buying power multiplied hundreds, sometimes thousands of times for most consumer products, raising our buying power toward that of millionaires. The new way meant that ordinary people were abundantly prosperous, not fighting over their finances month to month. That was a Gift in the Neo-Tech World.

Vision

A Vision showed me unbelievable *health*. As technology soared ahead in all industries, the medical industry was no exception. The geniuses of society quickly answered our needs, especially our cries for help. So the geniuses teamed up with super technologies to aggressively go after and eradicate diseases.

In that disease-free world, most people lived vigorously, well into their hundreds. The new way meant that people did not get sick, and they lived a lot, lot longer. That was a Gift in the Neo-Tech World.

Vision

In another Vision, I saw unbelievable *jobs*. In tomorrow's super rapidly advancing Neo-Tech Era, businesses had to change to keep up and remain competitive. For the first time, businesses had to bring out their greatest assets — the buried creativity in their employees. Things got really exciting at work as we broke the chain of stagnation and soared into the exhilarating new world of creation. With a little help from management, we shocked ourselves at what we could do. We loved to go to work as we achieved things tomorrow we never even dreamed about today. The new way meant that we were now dream builders, not daydreamers. That was a Gift in the Neo-Tech World.

Vision

In another Vision, I saw unbelievable *love*. Today we know what that love is like, for we already experienced it when we were first falling in love — those exciting initial few weeks. But the excitement faded over time. That's because we stagnate financially and emotionally in this suppressed society, and we soon have little energy or love left to give. But tomorrow, we were rich, healthy, successful and happy. We escaped from our stagnation-traps, and we suddenly had lots of energy and love to give. Those initial falling-in-love feelings returned and never faded. The new way meant that we felt the exhilaration of falling in love for our entire lives. That was a Gift in the Neo-Tech World.

Vision

A Vision showed me unbelievable *intelligence*. Our minds developed an entirely new way of thinking to deal with the information explosion. They called the new way of using the

12

mind: Neothink (New Think). Neothink took the endless bits of information and interlocked them by common denominators into a few bigger, more manageable thought clusters or concepts. As those endless bits of floating information snapped together into solid units, they became easy to handle and easy to build upon, sort of like puzzles. So, with bicameral tendencies behind us now and no longer waiting for external guidance, our minds aggressively snapped together more and more knowledge and power to guide itself. We became widely knowledgeable and extremely smart. This new integrated thinking lifted our intelligence to a whole new level. The new way meant that even the dullest people today naturally became geniuses tomorrow. That was a Gift in the Neo-Tech World.

After my night of Visions, ending a restless decade and a half of tossing and turning, I finally knew a better life indeed existed. Until now, I was a belabored businessman confronting corruption in politics and difficult regulations. Furthermore, I often faced unrest in my personal life. I was always searching, but I could not get to the better life I somehow knew existed. That Sunday night, everything changed. I received those Twelve Visions from some higher power — I did not know from where it came, perhaps some people would call it God, although later I learned it was my first encounter with God-Man — but the experience was so honest and truthful that the answers to everything that ever bothered me fell into place, and so did my dreams of a better world. The Gifts would be mine!

Vision One
Discover the Person You Will Become

Are you looking for *immediate* results? The Twelve Visions are built upon a spiral of techniques. You will acquire the tools to make man's final evolution into a superior being called the **God-Man**. The God-Man enjoys several Gifts including extraordinary health and longevity, millionaire wealth, an exhilarating livelihood, romantic love, and superior intelligence called *Neothink*.

"But," you may be thinking, "to read through the Twelve Visions and become the God-Man seems overwhelming and would take such a long time." Vision One will get you started on this journey immediately. This chapter will give you *immediate results* so you can start your journey toward the prosperous God-Man tomorrow morning, bringing you instant energy, enthusiasm, *and payoffs* as you discover the life you were meant to live.

Before you begin, let me ask you: how much is it worth to you to discover what you would have done best in life? $250, $500, $1000? I know I would pay five-thousand dollars to know. ...Over the next twenty-four pages, you have the opportunity to see, via the proven Neo-Tech techniques, *your* best path in life. It will cost you an hour of your time to read those pages that open the door to the life you were meant to live. Some people just like to know, out of curiosity, what they would have done best in life. But, even more go on to travel that life they were meant to live, and they become deeply happy and motivated, wealthy and powerful, and often discover a rare and lasting romantic love. Men and women are equally invited to take the journey.

When you finish reading the next twenty-four pages, as prosperous as those pages are for you, remember that your exciting journey will just be starting.

Therefore, let us begin. The Gifts can start filling your life as early as tomorrow morning. The Gift of extraordinary health and longevity still relies on the Technological Revolution. But you do not have to wait for the other Gifts: profound security,

15

millionaire wealth, a dream career, a dream lover, and superior intelligence. Follow the step-by-step instructions in this chapter today to open the door tomorrow to the life you were meant to live.

Opening the Door to the Person You Were Meant to Be

What motivates *you* into making the evolutionary leap into God-Man? Perhaps, the idea of success and power sounds exciting.

Success and power come from something I call *downstream focus*. Downstream focus happens when your thoughts naturally flow back to your work, even in the evenings and weekends. If thinking about your work, especially in the evenings and on weekends, is an upstream battle (as it is for most), you will not be a major success because, for those elite few who make it to the top in your field, thinking about work is a natural downstream rush. They pass right by you to the power positions.

Do you feel the tug to get back to your livelihood — after work and on weekends? I'm not talking about external deadlines, but internal desires? If not, then you are swimming upstream, and I can guarantee you will not experience major success...because there are people in your line of work who are pulled back to it. They may be the owners, or they may be your peers who will rise beyond you. Is watching TV or listening to a ball game or bowling or hanging out with friends hard to pull away from in your evenings? Those are indicators that you have not experienced what I call a *downstream focus* to success.

Every person has a door inside that opens to the person he or she was meant to be. That person, once the door opens, lives every moment with natural downstream focus and soars to major success. Today, you will open that door within you.

Without discovering and opening that door, you will never soar. It is a depressing thought to have lived but never soared.

Let me give you an example, using a person who works for me. Dave was a high-energy guy, but in business he would never be big. He could do a good job, and he rose into management. But one day, I discovered that for him to be formulating thoughts and pulling together integrations outside of his designated duties, for example during the evenings and weekends, was an upstream battle for Dave. Business simply was not his element.

At first, I was frustrated because I really wanted and needed Dave to become my right-hand man, and I was counting on him to be focussed on the business all the time, evenings and weekends. We live in a very competitive world, and to rise to the top, downstream focus is essential. I needed and wanted Dave to have downstream focus on the business.

But over time, I knew Dave had other interests in the evenings and weekends, pulling his thoughts and integrations — his focus — away from the business. I reluctantly realized he would not rise in the business world to the top with me. About this time, I was learning about that one door inside a person that opens to the person he or she was meant to be. Although disappointed that the door to my expectations of Dave was closing, I began pondering: "What if I opened not the door *I* had planned for Dave, but that one door that exists in him that would open to the life he was meant to live?" Although one opportunity was closing for both of us, could even a bigger opportunity be opening?

As owner of my company, I took on the challenge to unleash Dave's human potential by discovering the person he was meant to be and creating a job that would offer him the life he was meant to live. The results are just being realized now. They look so profitable for both Dave and my business that I predict the most competitive companies in the 21st century will learn to hire people differently: based on who they were meant to be.

The job revolution of the 21st century, as explained in Vision Five, will change our routine-rut jobs of labor into exciting entrepreneurial jobs of the mind. Adding to that job revolution, companies will set us up as entrepreneurs soaring ahead not just on any job of the mind, but specifically on the path we were meant to travel. Some companies, as I have done for Dave, will even *create* new entrepreneurial jobs of the mind that open the doors of their best employees to the person they were meant to be.

Dave now lives his career 24 hours a day with downstream

focus, which I will describe in a moment. He is deeply happy, living the life he was meant to live and rising toward major success. By focussing on his livelihood and integrating his thoughts in the evenings and weekends, he is beginning to build Neothink puzzles and is on his way toward making the jump into the Neothink mentality and becoming the prosperous God-Man.

In short, Dave discovered his downstream focus. I have never seen him so happy with so much energy. He is soaring toward something big...enthusiastically building his competitive creations at nights and on weekends, well beyond his daytime duties. That ongoing drive is the only way to put time and thought enough to rise into the top 1% success in any field. My experiment with Dave taught me that by finding and opening his door to the person he was meant to be, I had someone who would rise to the top in that field working for me — a powerful asset to my company. I knew other companies will discover how to unleash the human potential of their employees in the 21st century and then put them into the new, entrepreneurial living jobs (Vision Five) and watch them soar.

Dave was not meant to be a businessman per se, although he functioned competently as such. After some deep searching on my part and honesty on his part, we discovered he was meant to be an artist. He was an artist, a performer, and performing brought forth natural downstream focus. So, I started a seminar circuit with Dave at the helm as the performer. I could not believe my eyes as Dave flowed into integrated thinking and onto building Neothink puzzles. He became happy, dedicated, and focussed. He has made it possible for me to seriously look at the next level of film, where he will become a valuable asset to me.

Dave went through a personal renaissance via profitable downstream focus, which as we'll see brings:
1) wealth,
2) happiness, and
3) romantic love to one's existence.

To not discover the person you were meant to be is a personal tragedy. I know this from personal experience. I witnessed my mother, like most people, not identify thus not assertively pursue the life she was meant to live. This caused her, like many people, a hard life, including lost love, disillusionment, and poverty. Then, just a few months before she died, with my help she began to make the self-discovery of the person she was meant to be. Those last few months were by far the happiest in her life. She opened the door to the life she was meant to live as she discovered and pursued her downstream focus. The adventure, as it knows no other way, got more and more involved and exciting with each day. The great tragedy for my mom was that her adventure had just begun: after a hard life, she had discovered immense happiness at the end. She died early and with no warning at sixty-six years old of a congenital cerebral aneurysm, right when she was finally discovering the life she was meant to live. In those few months, she produced an eternal contribution to the world, an invaluable Neo-Tech Book titled *No More Lies*. ...I often wonder, because of her death so soon after getting on the path she was meant to journey, what great values she would have produced...values the world will never know. I know her brilliant mind had put together an immensely valuable Neothink puzzle in *No More Lies* based on her lifetime of experiences. What that Neothink puzzle could have grown into, well, the world will never know. Both my mother and the world really missed out.

Our mortality makes it imperative for you to discover the life you were meant to live *right now*, without missing another day. How will *you* discover and open the door to the person *you* were meant to be to release *your* downstream focus? Everyone is different with a different set of life experiences, upbringings, environments, talents and tastes. Today you will discover your unique downstream focus, which may be quite different than your current job. It may not seem practical to pursue. But with special techniques that make it safe and practical to pursue your downstream focus, you will open the door today to *your* path to major success and, in turn, happiness and love.

To *open that door* to success, happiness, and love is the first objective. The next objective is to show you *how* to get that success, *how* to soar after opening that door. Without opening the door first, though, you are blocked from the life you were meant to live. Every human being was meant to live a motivated, exciting life of wealth, happiness, and love...the life of the God-Man.

Let's now work on opening the door to the life you were meant to live.

Fill out the chart on the next page. Write down what you did Monday though Friday in the evenings after work and what you did on your weekends. Try to remember. If you cannot, then write in what you think you did or typically do. Do not try to impress yourself. This chapter is for you to dig in and discover your downstream focus that has been waiting to be discovered all your life. You will miss that opportunity if you are not brutally honest today. I am not looking for comrades. You are not trying to impress me or yourself. Instead, you must honestly observe your frustrations and stagnation. This chapter is your tool to break free from that stagnation and this anticivilization. So, write down what you do in the evenings and weekends. The more humdrum or boring it is, the more value this chapter will be to you today. Okay, get to work.

When you finish, read out loud what you wrote down for your evenings and weekends. Now, prepare yourself for this fact: people who have major success, their evenings and weekends look different than yours. And, here's the key: their evenings and weekends looked different than yours *before* they were very successful. Now, that's nothing for you to be ashamed of. Those super successful people had merely made a self-discovery that you have not. Their self-discovery sent their lives into an exciting adventure that *naturally* changed their schedules. Realize, they made their self-discovery of the person they were meant to be *first*; they did not change their schedules first. And so will you. When you make that self-discovery today of the person you were meant to be, then your schedule will naturally change. Most self-improvement programs try to put the cart before the horse by changing the schedule first. But the upstream battle will always lead to failure.

In the weeks following your self-discovery today, your evenings and weekends will begin to look different, too...like the very successful. You need your evenings and weekends to look like theirs. You need to have focus. But it has to be downstream focus, or it will never last and major success will

Evenings-and-Weekends Chart	Monday	Tuesday	Wednesday	Thursday	Friday	Saturday	Sunday

never happen.

This self-discovery is of something you are magnetically drawn to — that unique something you are meant to be. As you become that person, you are naturally pulled away from TV and sports and from other entertainment...from those things that fill your evenings and weekends now. You lose interest in them. The real values stick, however, such as time spent with your children and spouse, but you really have to schedule that time, and the quality of that time multiplies many times for two reasons:

1) you are deeply happy, and

2) that time goes from passive to active planned time.

How do you discover that person you were meant to be? How do you make that self-discovery that is unique for each person? How do you discover what you have unknowingly longed for? How do you open the door to the one path that is uniquely yours that can take you to major success...to the life you were meant to have?

Every person who ever became a major success discovered the life he or she was meant to live. Many if not most of those people simply got lucky. As a matter of circumstances, they got on the unique paths on which they were meant to be. They were victors of circumstances.

As a matter of circumstances, you did *not* get on your unique path. You and most others are victims of circumstances, and you are here today to change that fact.

Now, to discover your unique path is not so easy because your mind will not open the door to it. Your unique path has been buried by falling leaves of resignation over time, and you might not recognize it even if you were looking at it. The life you were meant to live has been filed away somewhere in your mind, perhaps permanently shut off in some closed section called "The Impractical Section". But, when combined with the techniques in the Twelve Visions, there is nothing in life more practical than opening that door to downstream focus.

For now, we will not argue practicality. We are only going to open our minds — or at least stretch our minds — to discover your unique path and the person you were meant to be. The "how to do it" part will come later. I must say, you will be

pleasantly surprised with the "how to do it" techniques I have developed over the past seventeen years that will rapidly change your long-lost "impractical" dream into a highly practical adventure that will do three things:
1) Make you deeply happy like never before (good-bye stagnation)
2) Lead you to *major* success and wealth
3) Make you a romantic lover like never before

The motivational drive found today only in toddlers will become nourished and begin to grow inside you again from the combination of those three points above. The return of your deep motivational drive will release your human potential for the first time since your preschool days. Those dynamics will take you to the edge of an evolutionary leap, into integrated thinking (Vision Nine) and then into Neothink puzzle building and eventually into the new mentality of the God-Man.

The techniques to travel your unique path are found later in this chapter. But right now, we must open the door to that path, before you walk the path. I must let your mind know, however, that no matter what, even if your path has been buried and lost in the impractical section of your mind, we will make your new journey very practical...even if you are in your golden years, I might add.

Now, what I want you to do is to look over your weekday evenings and your weekends that you filled in earlier, and then remember back over the past year. Was there ever a weekday evening or weekend in which you would have filled in something of a different nature than what you have written on your Evenings-and-Weekends Chart...something different that you did — not because of some external demand or deadline, rather because you *wanted to*? Is there something different that was not a chore, not something you had to force yourself to do...rather something you just did? Now, I'm not saying like going to a football game or to the theatre; I'm saying something other than passive entertainment or sports, something that took initiative on your part? Take five minutes and think hard...

First, clear your mind. Clear your mind. Take a deep breath. Again. Okay, I want you to think back over your last year or two. Can you remember moments in your life when you broke from your normal evenings and weekends? It may have happened only once. It may have happened more than once. Again, I want you to exclude passive entertainment such as watching movies, playing arcades, watching ball games, going to a park or amusement park. And I want you to exclude active sports such as golfing, playing basketball, bowling, playing tennis. You are looking for some activity, project, or interest that pulled you away, on your own will, from the environment that normally surrounds you. Take a few minutes to reminisce. Put your hands in your lap or on your desk and just remember. After five minutes, you'll write down an episode or two you might remember. If you do not remember any such event, then you'll write nothing. ...Do this now.

Assuming five minutes have passed, write down what you thought of. Now, ask yourself two questions:
    1) Take a moment and try to remember and describe to yourself how you felt while doing it?
    2) After remembering how you felt, ask yourself why you did not continue to pursue it more aggressively?
    Answering the first question potentially sheds light inside your psyche on a tiny cell of motivation that is uniquely yours. That cell is the germ of success within you and can multiply and rapidly take over your psyche and your life if able to reproduce.
    Answering the second question potentially sheds light on why that tiny cell of success never reproduced. Whatever cut off the growth of that cell of success — the reasons you did not pursue it — can quickly be removed through the techniques later in this chapter.
    The most common reason the cell of success never multiplied is lack of opportunity or circumstances combined with an emotional disbelief that it would practically succeed. Usually what happens is: one's livelihood must come first, and so most people never know how to start the cell growing while still making a living. The livelihood is too demanding and enveloping. One never fully recognizes and goes right by his unique cell of success. Later, I will show you how to grow that cell while not sacrificing your livelihood. Right now, you are trying to recognize and come back to your unique success cell

24

lost within your psyche.

Okay, if you were able to write something down above, consider it a potential clue for the next and final step to open your door to the person you were meant to be. Before you do this final step, let me tell you that at first the results may seem hazy. It's not easy to recognize your tiny success cell since it never grew after all these years. It is so tiny and inconspicuous, lost within a lifetime of complexities.

But, you will write something or some things down. In the next few days, your focus on that image will sharpen and, like looking through a microscope, will focus on your cell of success. So, here's the final step:

Look at the chart you filled out earlier. Specifically, look at what you wrote down for Friday night. In many if not most cases, Friday night is the "shut-down" night. Our minds travel furthest away from active responsibility such as work. It all started back in our school days: Friday night was the furthest time away from our next class, further away than Saturday night, and much further away than Sunday night or any other weeknight. So, our minds did not even think about our homework. The first thoughts about homework did not even surface, at the soonest, until sometime Saturday afternoon. Friday night was the party night...time to turn off and tune out.

So, Friday night becomes our litmus test for downstream focus. Once you discover your true *Friday-Night Essence*, then you have opened the door to *your* path to the life you were meant to live. Your Friday-Night Essence is that one thing (minus passive entertainment or sports) you would enjoy doing on a Friday night.

For example, my employee Dave would enjoy teaching or taking an acting workshop on Friday night — that is *his* Friday-Night Essence.

I, myself, would enjoy writing on a Friday Night — that is *my* Friday-Night Essence.

What about you? What would you enjoy doing on a Friday night? Your Friday-Night Essence always exists in you — even before you become successful and rich. You just need to identify it.

For example, Henry Ford would have enjoyed taking apart

and putting together an engine on Friday night, well before he had any business success. In fact, he did that for fun as a child.

Steven Jobs would enjoy working on software applications on a Friday night before he had success. He did so often.

I frequently worked on my literature, drawn to it even on Friday nights, long before I had major success.

You need to discover *your* Friday-Night Essence — it's in you. Look now at your previous clue...at what you wrote down, that something you previously did in the evenings or weekends that broke your normal routine. If you did not write anything down, don't worry about it. Those of you who did, take one minute now to just think about that project or interest. Let's pause while you reflect on that project or interest for a minute before moving on.

Now, I want you to do something: Forget about everything you've read here today and what we're trying to discover. Just relax your mind. It's getting a little intense here, so let's take a moment to relax. Take a deep breath and hold it for 3 counts. Ready: Take a deep breath — hold it...one, two, three...okay, breathe out slowly. Again, deep breath — hold it...one, two, three...okay, breathe out slowly.

Okay now...think about the present and the past. What is something that you are drawn to...and perhaps have always been drawn to? Something that genuinely interests you. Take a couple of minutes to think about this. Sometimes a clue is something you like to read about. Put out of your mind any form of judgement such as, "Oh, that's silly; that's impractical to pursue," or "I couldn't possibly pursue that because I have no educational background on it," or "...there's no money in it, at least for a long time to come." Forget any kind of judgement for now; just think about something that naturally attracts you and has done so over your life. Try to finally see that recurring interest — try now to see the trend over your life to pay attention to a particular interest. Take five full minutes to do this.

I purposely did not give you the four categories in which I see these persistent attractions falling into so as not to sway your thoughts. But now that you have thought about what attracts you, here are the four categories I see people's attractions falling under. Pick which one yours falls under:

1) Business
2) Science
3) Arts
4) Professions

Let me say that the category of arts is usually the easiest to spot...such as Dave and his acting; myself and my writing.

Business can be a little more complex, for a lot falls under business. For example, a person attracted to machinery or mechanics would fall under business, for machinery is the product of business. Business is easier to spot if one has an obvious lifelong attraction to business. For example, I actually have two Friday-Night Essences: business and writing, both being guided by my ultimate goal of creating the sociopolitical conditions for achieving biological immortality. All my life, I was drawn to business. As a child I was very entrepreneurial, trying several different business ventures and door-to-door selling. As I grew up, I idolized, read about, and listened to tapes on the great businessmen and women. Business and its values created out of the blue always fascinated me.

People who like to read about a particular subject — actually enjoy learning about it — have a pretty good sign of a natural attraction...be it in the arts or in business or in a specific profession such as psychology or medicine, or in the sciences.

I did not say anything previously about sports because, first of all, every man enjoys watching some form of sports, so it can easily block out what one's real Friday-Night Essence is. But, occasionally, and only occasionally, sports can be one's Friday-Night Essence, especially when we get beyond the fantasies about competition. Competitive sports is so physically based and linked to youth that either you know you have a shot at the top or you don't. At this point, assuming you are not a teenager or in your early twenties, no one is going to leave this page and go into competitive sports to become a multi-millionaire basketball star, for example. But there is, as with every legitimate value, the business side of sports. It is possible, although unlikely, that your true Friday-Night Essence lies there. Of course, that falls under the sweeping category of business.

Okay, now that I gave you the four general categories that Friday-Night Essences fall under, select a *category* based on all the reminiscing and pondering you have done today. I'll give you a minute to do this.

Okay, write down that category: business, sciences, arts, professions, sports. And if you were able to define earlier a more specific attraction, write it under the general category. For instance, my employee Dave would write down Arts — acting. I would write down Arts — writing...as well as Business — marketing God-Man/Neo-Tech.

I *live* my two Friday-Night Essences. You, most likely, do not live your Friday-Night Essence, not yet. In the less common event that you try to live your Friday-Night Essence, the format of your job and your techniques might be all wrong for you to soar along that path of the exciting life you were meant to live, which we will fix today.

Now, I want you to look at what you have just written down: either a general category or a general category with a specific next to it. Look at what you wrote down, and then imagine yourself spending a Friday night pursuing that interest. Take a moment and imagine that. I'm not saying that you will never go to the movies again on Friday night and will only do this. I am saying, picture yourself on <u>one</u> Friday night pursuing this attraction you wrote down.

Does the thought excite you? If so, you have discovered something that brings you passion and deep motivation. You have discovered an interest that is *downstream focus* for you to pursue. You have discovered your Friday-Night Essence. That means, you have opened the door to the path that will be an exciting adventure to you — *the* life you were meant to live.

The self-discovery you just made may or may not hit you just right now. After all these years, discovering your Friday-Night Essence is sort of like holding your first newborn child. Although you feel love and protectiveness, it takes a few days to get used to and to get to know the little one. Over those few days, your love for the little one just seems to blossom.

You need a few days to get used to and get to know your Friday-Night Essence. Over the next few days, do not be surprised if your excitement for life and enthusiasm and, yes, *love* for your newborn Friday-Night Essence just blossoms.

Today if you picked a general category but not a specific interest, that is perfectly okay. You can have a broad-based Friday-Night Essence such as business or arts. In fact, that generality can give you flexible advantages.

Also, let me add that the general categories can cross over. A good example is myself whose Friday-Night Essence could be termed Business-Arts. I'm a businessman disseminating as much of my writings as I can. (In fact, Business will more and more cross over into a natural marriage with our Friday-Night Essences in the 21st century as the coming job revolution changes the nature of jobs into entrepreneurial mini-companies, as shown in Vision Five. I said *a natural marriage* because, of course, artists and scientists and professionals will be motivated to get their creations out into the world for maximum exposure and use. They will do that through *business*.)

Hold onto what you have written down. Over the next few days, your love for your Friday-Night Essence will blossom, especially as you discover the techniques that send you along the path that you have now opened the door to...no matter how "impractical" and without sacrificing your livelihood or the other values in your life.

Without your Friday-Night Essence and the techniques to make it happen, you will die unfulfilled without experiencing wealth, prosperity, and romantic love. You will never evolve into the prosperous God-Man. You will go on in your routine, silently suffering in stagnation. With upstream focus, you will never break free to the wealthy, prosperous, romantic life you were meant to live.

But that's not what you want, for that's why you're here today — to break free from your routine rut into the spectacular life of wealth, power, and love. So, I want you to carry around with you your Friday-Night Essence.

The Twelve Visions give you the effective techniques and

advantages to take you practically along your unique path without disrupting anything you have now. Let me tell you what happens immediately upon stepping through the door you opened here today...onto your unique path to major success:

Suddenly, you discover the power and *joy* of downstream focus. Whereas the wealth is not overnight, the joy, excitement and passion is. When you become a motivated, happy person, suddenly you have lots of feelings for love and you become romantic. Flames that flickered out long ago suddenly rekindle. It's an amazing experience that I personally went through.

There is nothing better than travelling through life on the path you were meant to travel and doing what truly impassions you. Suddenly, you are where you belong, and you *know it*! The journey is an adventure; it is the opposite of a stagnant routine rut, and you love the feeling! It is *the love* for the journey that will bring you to major success. Once you're on your way, you know it, and nothing can stop you.

But you will not know that journey if you do not have my techniques that take you along your path. You are standing before your path. You have opened the door to it. You know you want to start your journey and the exciting adventure. You *know it*. Let's take the journey:

Journeying The Life You Were Meant To Live

Starting tomorrow morning, you will be walking along the path of the life you were meant to live. This time tomorrow, I guarantee you will be another person, the person you were meant to be. You will instantly feel the joy and power of becoming the person you were meant to be — tomorrow.

Before you start your journey, let me make clear that the leap of power in the Twelve Visions comes from the new mind space that will open — something called *Neothink*. Your journey into the life you were meant to live will bring you to the edge of making the evolutionary leap into Neothink. When you make that leap, you will become the God-Man.

Now, let me show you a little diagram that demonstrates our approaching evolutionary leap:

Discover the Person You Will Become

Man's Evolvement Over Past 3000 Years

1) Bicameral "Animal" Mentality: No mind space. Automatic reactions
   (who man was)   to external stimuli.

    Leap of Power

2) Conscious "Human" Mentality: A new mind space opened through
   (who man is)   sophisticated language, metaphors and
                      analog models that let man think and
    Leap of Power   make decisions and control his own life.

3) Neothink "God-Man" Mentality: A new mind space opens through
   (who man will be)   Neothink puzzle building that snaps
                      together never-before-seen pictures —
                      puzzle pictures — that let man contin-
                      ually jump to the next level at
                      everything he does in all fields of
                      knowledge.

Through a very simple how-to technique, today you will get started, in a very practical way, along your path. Your deep motivational drive will reactivate and re-release your human potential. For, through the constant downstream focus on your great adventure, you will gather more and more experiences and will start seeing and pulling together common denominators over time. You will experience increasing integrated thinking (Vision Nine), which will eventually take you into Neothink puzzle building. Immensely enjoying yourself with each step you now take in life, you will not stop taking those steps. You will discover new experiences along your journey that snap into your growing Neothink puzzle. Before long, you will see a puzzle-picture forming that has never been seen before...your first leap into the new, Neothink mind-space of the God-Man.

To learn the technique to get started along your path, I want you to read through pages 101-119 (in Vision Five) first, starting at the heading "Your Money-Generating Factory". Those pages show you how the technique works. Those pages, however, show

31

you how the technique works for your job of the future. Starting tomorrow, you will use the technique not for your job per se, but for your Friday-Night Essence. So, as you read through pages 101-119 in Vision Five, keep in mind that the technique (known as the mini-day system) will be used somewhat differently when you return to this chapter. Go now, and read pages 101-119 in Vision Five, starting at "Your Money-Generating Factory".

Now, I am assuming you read pages 101-119 in Vision Five. I want you to pull out your piece of paper upon which you wrote down your Friday-Night Essence. Think about it, and imagine it either as a commercial or professional venture. Take a minute to do that. The image of making a living doing your Friday-Night Essence is, whether you realize it or not, your *ambition in life*.

So, you are going to now "mini-day" your ambition in life and put those mini-days around your livelihood. You are going to determine the physical movements *necessary to accomplish your life's ambition*. Whereas on pages 101-119 in Vision Five that you just read, I had determined the physical movements of my living job of the mind (which you can do when you read Vision Five), right now to live the life you were meant to live, you must determine the physical movements needed to accomplish your life's ambition. And you must structure those mini-days to either side of your income mini-day, which is your current job. This will pull you out of your rut and send you along your unique path toward exciting success, happiness, and romantic love. Let me give you an example:

An American hero pulled himself out of an impossible stagnation-trap. Yes, it can be done; it has been done. He was a laborer at the turn of the century, a dock worker among the roughest ports of early nineteen-hundred America. That dock breed spoke illiterate English, crude, unrefined. This lowly laborer had dropped out of school at fourteen. He lived on the streets. He survived. He never had an opportunity. Like millions of others, he was headed for a cruel life. A desire burned inside, though. He desired to pull himself out of the abyss. He desired to become a successful writer. In the early 1900s, an illiterate dock worker had essentially no chance to ever sell a piece of literature. But that man became the highest paid author in history! And if we adjust for inflation today, he is the highest paid author of all time. That man was Jack London. He wrote many adventure stories and best-selling novels including *Call of the Wild, The Sea Wolf, Martin Eden*.

Exactly how did Jack London do it? He established four physical movements, four mini-days that would achieve his desire of becoming a writer: (1) reading, (2) intense grammar study, (3) self-education (a library-study program), and (4) writing. Those four mini-days were divided before and after his full-day income mini-day and on weekends. Even after he pulled himself out of his trap and off the docks, he never stopped the mini-day system. He stayed on the mini-day system through his fame and glory to the last days of his life.

Jack London merely discovered his Friday-Night Essence and broke it into mini-days. Now, talk about impractical — imagine an illiterate dock worker at the turn of the century dreaming of being a professional writer! But, using this simple technique combined with downstream focus, he became the richest writer of all time (when adjusting for inflation). As I said before: there is nothing more practical than downstream focus. He wrapped his mini-days around his job in the evenings and weekends. ...I recommend reading his autobiographical novel *Martin Eden* that demonstrates the drive, excitement, motivation when one gets on his Friday-Night Essence using the mini-day system.[1]

Do this now: What are the <u>physical</u> <u>movements</u> to achieve your ambition in life — your forgotten dream? Take five

---

[1]Jack London (1876-1916) fought an internal battle, ostensibly between individualism, which he lived through and through, versus socialism, which he believed in. On a larger scale, however, he fought the battle between the Civilization of God-Man, which he lived, versus the anticivilization, which he was inescapably surrounded by. The conflict led to turmoil and suicide for both Jack London and his autobiographical hero Martin Eden. If Jack London had access to the Twelve Visions, he would have seen the route out of the anticivilization and easily averted suicide.

minutes to do this.

Now, assuming you have done this, you will do the same as Jack London — put the mini-days of your life's ambition, your Friday-Night Essence, in the evenings and weekends.

Let me point out something important: before if you tried to put work or tried to study in the evenings or weekends, sticking to it would frankly become a <u>bitch,</u> excuse my layman's term. Words cleaned up a little: to work or study in the evenings or weekends was always an upstream battle — your focus was what we've been calling an <u>upstream</u> <u>focus.</u>

But pursuing your Friday-Night Essence changes everything. It tugs you away from other things, back to it...back to the deep excitement inside you. For the first time, you've opened the door to the path you were meant to walk. This "work" becomes motivating, just as it was for Jack London and every other great success throughout history. You have discovered downstream focus.

On the next page is the same weekly chart you filled out earlier. Fill in your evenings (you can take Friday evening off), and fill in a portion of your weekends — perhaps Saturday morning — with your new, Friday-Night-Essence mini-days. Take a few minutes to do this, now.

Alright, have you done that? Now, compare what you just filled out on the next page to the same chart you filled out on page twenty-one. Flip back and forth and notice the contrast.

Okay, I want you to stop and think hard about two things:

1. Now your evenings and weekends look the same as the Bill Gates, Sam Waltons, Henry Fords, Jack Londons, and Mark Hamiltons.

—and—

2. Now, with downstream focus, you are not deluding yourself. You can <u>keep up this schedule</u> — because it's <u>your</u> <u>essence</u> — the person you were meant to be!

Evenings-and-Weekends Chart	Monday	Tuesday	Wednesday	Thursday	Friday	Saturday	Sunday

The self-discovery is complete. I want you to go out there and <u>enjoy</u> your life, which I guarantee you will with your new weekly schedule that opens the door and takes you along the life you were meant to live. You will feel exhilarated the first day you start. And the beauty of your new adventure in life is: it gets more and more exhilarating the further you go. Your adventure is the opposite of what most people experience, sinking in miserable stagnation. Each day, each week, gets you more and more involved in the person you were meant to be. And, that's fun!

As you go along, new experiences will begin linking together. That is the beginning of integrated thinking that will grow like a puzzle. As the puzzle grows, you will eventually see a never-before-seen picture forming, a new creation built by you. That creation goes beyond the normal capacity of your mind. That creation takes you into the new mind space of Neothink.

If you have not already done so, tomorrow read the next few pages in Vision Five, pages 119-124, starting at "The RNA Phenomenon" about power thinking, the first small step into the new leap of power that opens the new mind space called Neothink. Today, you opened the door to the exciting life you were meant to live; now you can soar using the mini-day/power-thinking team.

No More Suffering in Silent Resignation

Let me tell you a little story about something that recently happened to me: I was having an interesting conversation with a religious man, a very nice man. He had a lot to say. Somewhere along the line, I started going into the history of man and Christianity, sort of scientifically explaining where religions came from, as I do in the Second Insight in Part Two of this book. To my surprise, he put up his hand as if to say, "Stop now." So I stopped. He took a deep breath and nervously said, "I must have HOPE."

HOPE...let's talk about that. What was he hoping for? He, like so many, was hoping for a better life in the afterlife. What does that hope really mean? It means he, like so many, is *not getting the life he wants now*. Today you opened the door to that life, and with the techniques in the Twelve Visions, you are on your way to getting the life you want *now*.

As explained in Vision Three, *deep-rooted motivation* or lack of it determines man's success. Anyone who stays focussed long enough will rise to the top of the field. Anyone. He will go *beyond* competition and onto creation...unique *creation* of values people want.

To stay focussed, such a successful person erases laziness out of his life. How? Realize that laziness comes from backing off from hard upstream focus, and everyone has laziness written into his life...except for that one out of thousands who discovered his or her natural downstream focus. Today, with your Friday-Night Essence, you discovered your downstream focus.

What do I mean by, "Everyone has laziness written into his life"? And is that why big-time success is so rare and so unlikely in your life? Deep-rooted motivational drive is <u>what makes</u> big-time success eventually. Of course, laziness kills deep-rooted motivational drive. But everyone has that root — that <u>one</u>, deep motivational root. You have one deepest root, but there are thousands of different jobs and careers. What are the odds you (or a loved one or anyone) has the job that is fed directly by that <u>one</u>, deep motivational root in you? The odds are thousands to one against you. Therefore, the odds are thousands to one that you will succumb to this term called laziness...since we realized laziness happens by struggling against and finally succumbing to *upstream focus*. And that is why there are thousands of people to every one rich man on the hill.

Today, you experienced a godsend: you found your one, deepest motivational root inside you, perhaps never known before or long forgotten before today and given up on. Now, with natural *downstream focus*, laziness will, for the first time in your life, just seem to vanish. In its place, fed by your deepest root of motivation, *energy* and *excitement* will come rushing into your life, just as it did for my employee, Dave.

What about discipline and effort needed to be successful? Sure — that's all there, and the more of that you exert, the further you'll go in any field. But your Friday-Night Essence and its downstream focus and your new source of energy and excitement will let it happen and finally release your human potential.

Now, back to HOPE. What if I say to you that I want to, first, unearth...and then, second, wipe out all your suppressed hope? What if I say I think suppressed hope is the greatest epidemic of all time?

When you get down to it, doesn't suppressed hope, as seen in my gentleman friend, mean that people are not getting the life they want — the life they were meant to have? And since there are thousands of people wasting their lives this way to every one person who is living that exciting life he was meant to live...isn't that a horrific epidemic?

As more and more people discover their Friday-Night Essences, they will get reacquainted with hope...and then they will harvest that hope. They will enjoy that elusive life they once silently hoped for and then forgot about.

What this Vision and the Twelve Visions does is: make suppressed hope resurface and happen. Over the years, youthful hope gets deeply suppressed, and most people like my gentleman friend silently surrender to resignation. Our deep motivational root shrivels up and dies as we lose our motivational drive. Hobbies, sports, entertainment, and routines take over. In most cases, our suppressed desire for a better life shows up in our religious beliefs — in some kind of vague <u>hope</u> for a blissful afterlife. We silently hold <u>hope</u> for something better...better than what? Better than <u>now</u>.

Hope is a desire, often an unspoken desire, for something in the future...something better than the present. That hope can be for any number of things: <u>wealth</u>, <u>health</u>, <u>love</u>.

Let's use an example: if a person is in great pain, say, suffering from cancer, he holds hope for the future...for a cure.

Anything that pains you — physical pain, emotional pain (as in financial or love difficulties) causes hope for the future...for a cure. The same applies for the <u>painful</u> state of stagnation.

As the cure never comes, we become disillusioned. The feeling of hope in most of us has long ago been buried beneath recognition. I ask you, now that you have opened the door to the person you were meant to be, can you feel your hope in <u>this world</u> again...not just hope there's something good out there in heaven, but hope right here for tomorrow when you wake up and take your first steps into the life you were meant to live? Can you feel it? I guarantee you that over the next few days you will feel your youthful hope resurfacing. It's a good feeling, a feeling synonymous with *youth*. But feeling those youthful feelings is only the beginning, because before long, you will begin to harvest that hope, which will increasingly happen as you read the rest of the Twelve Visions.

The person pursuing his Friday-Night Essence with the tools in the Twelve Visions is not wasting his life. He is not suppressing his hope; he is instead busy fulfilling his hope, living his dreams.

Here is what you can expect will happen to you as you read further into the Twelve Visions: Your resurfacing hope becomes part of *a process* to wealth, love, and happiness. (You will never again sink to disillusionment, pain, and resignation.) Your resurfacing hope will take the form of energy and enthusiasm, looking forward to specific accomplishments...mapping out a course for your internal motivational drive. Through resurfacing hope, you will set new goals that you will achieve quickly with the techniques throughout the Twelve Visions.

Now, take a moment to acknowledge some of your resurfacing feelings of hope. I'll give you a couple of minutes to get in touch with some feelings of hope. Anything goes — any feelings of hope...for better security, wealth, health, love — anything...and it can be one thing or several. Write them down. Take a couple of minutes to do this.

From experience, I have found that hope usually breaks into a handful of common denominators. The seven most common denominators of hope are for:

1) Comfortable Security
2) Better Health and Longevity
3) More Wealth
4) Stimulating Career
5) Romantic Love
6) Superior Intelligence
7) Fulfilling Happiness and Spiritual Harmony

Six of those seven points of hope will happen through your self-discovery today of your Friday-Night Essence combined with your techniques here and in Visions Two through Nine. One of those points of hope — health and longevity — still largely depends on the advancement of technology.

But through your Friday-Night Essence and the techniques in the Twelve Visions, the other six — security, wealth, career, romance, intelligence, happiness — will happen the way they were supposed to happen in your life: in large abundance! As you will discover, they come to you as Gifts.

Vision Seven explains the exciting relationship between success and love — the psychological/physical relationship between value creation (success) and value reflection (love). Also, as you will discover, your Friday-Night Essence will lead you into *Neothink*, which is a new way of using the mind beyond the smartest people today.

Thousands of different jobs and paths through life exist, but of those thousands of paths, there is *one* path, in particular, that *you* can travel to a better life. The key to your future is to find *your* path and then get on the mini-day system to take the adventure.

You have done that today. Tomorrow, your adventure begins.

Vision Two

Yes, There Is "Something More" to Life...*For You*

This is your week...

Sat.	Sun.	Mon.	Tues.	Wed.	Thur.	Fri.

...and therein lies the secret of life. I'm going to unlock that secret today that has eluded man since the beginning of time.

Mankind has searched for the missing element in his life since the beginning. His restless quest for "something more" is responsible for all religions, mythologies, and spiritual paths. What he is searching for is harmony with himself, the world around him, and with the Universe, harmony he knows he does not have now. The endless search travels through generation after generation, without the answer ever found.

When you do find the secret of conscious life, you are filled with a feeling that becomes everlasting and omnipresent. It does not come and go, wax and wane. It just fills and fulfills you. I know, because I have found it...through my Second Vision.

The closest I can come to explaining that feeling is: *growing exhilaration.*

41

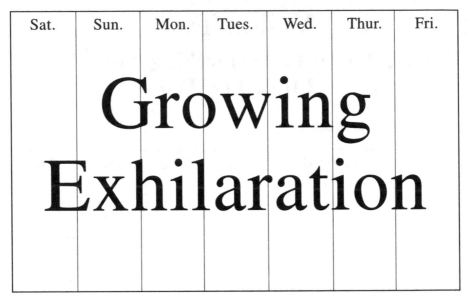

Sat.	Sun.	Mon.	Tues.	Wed.	Thur.	Fri.

Growing Exhilaration

But it is much more than that.

Here's what it really is: you discover harmony with the world around you, with the Universe, and with yourself. Every man and woman's life-long search for "something more" comes to completion, for he or she has found it.

Before I uncover humanity's most sought after secret to end the great search that leads people in many frustrating directions, first realize that by not knowing the secret, not knowing harmony with ourselves and with the Universe, well, that means we are living *without* harmony...we are living *a contradiction*. And we are; almost everyone is.

In fact, that is why we have religions, none of which get to the answer. They exist because of that elusive search for "something more", for harmony with the world around us, with the Universe, and with ourselves.

You will discover what the contradiction is upon discovering the secret. But before we do that, let me describe the manifestation of the contradiction almost everyone has endured:

The Contradiction

To live — the act of self-reliant living — requires certain

responsibilities. Those responsibilities require energy and effort. And what does that energy and effort get you...besides a life of stagnation? To describe this properly, I will jump into a real-life example:

My friend is a pilot who flies all over the world. He does a good job for his company. He does a good job as a husband and provider. And he does a good job raising his daughter. He puts a lot of effort and energy into his life. Seven years ago when I met him, to the present, and ten years into the future, my friend was and always will be a good worker, husband, and father. He will always fly airplanes. And that's an admirable, even a glamorous livelihood.

But after I read a special issue of *Business Week* that predicted super life-preserving technologies in the twenty-first century, I talked to my friend about those very real possibilities of immortality around the corner. I guess I half expected his reaction when he honestly answered he would *not* want to live forever.

That answer was the litmus test for living a contradiction. For, when one achieves harmony with oneself, with the world around him, and with the Universe — as we suppose we do in heaven — then he or she will honestly want to live forever, just as we suppose we do in heaven.

As I said, my friend puts a lot of energy and effort into his responsibilities for self-reliant living. But, those responsibilities do not go anywhere. Seven years ago flying planes...ten years, twenty years, thirty years from now, flying planes...just like his father.

If one is putting out energy and effort, and those responsibilities are not going anywhere significant, then doing those responsibilities is...*a burden.*

Sat.	Sun.	Mon.	Tues.	Wed.	Thur.	Fri.
		\

Burden

Now, that's not to say that life's not worth living. Let's make that clear right now:

Life has very nice, enjoyable experiences that can make one very happy. For example: finding and doing well in an admirable career, falling in love and getting married, having children and raising a family, buying that dream home, perhaps traveling and seeing the world in retirement. Those are all major experiences of happiness.

But those wonderful experiences do not remove the subtle but persistent burden underneath it all. As one puts forth energy and effort, yet those responsibilities do not go anywhere, the burden is always there. Those wonderful experiences of life...*mask the burden.*

Sat.	Sun.	Mon.	Tues.	Wed.	Thur.	Fri.

Burden

Mask

the Burden

The ordinary person does not want to live forever, for when the wonderful experiences run out, living forever with the burden would become torture. And *that's why* we do not have biological immortality today. Down deep, people do not want it!

Now, we must uncover the secret for eternally happy conscious life — a secret buried deep within the Universe. So, bear with the next section that lasts about a page, even if it seems a little over your head.

The Secret For Eternal Happiness

Albert Einstein said mass and energy were the fundamental components of existence that make up the cosmos. The Third Insight in Part Two of this book identifies Einstein's one oversight: his paradigm did not recognize consciousness as the third fundamental component of existence. As you will see in the Third Insight, consciousness is a fundamental component of existence just as mass and energy are fundamental components. With the recent discoveries of the availability of water throughout the Universe (the key substance for sustaining life), and on the size-and-time scale of the Grand Cycle of the Universe, consciousness easily and quickly evolves within innumerable mass/energy systems. Those conscious beings quickly take control of nature, just as we are doing on Earth. Recent understandings of the abundant availability of water throughout the Universe and its older-than-thought age and massive size...come together to scientifically conclude that conscious beings not only exist throughout the Universe, but have for many millions, perhaps billions of years before conscious beings ever appeared on Earth. As consciousness takes control of nature, of mass and energy, it eventually takes over. Consciousness eventually takes over the mass/energy system in which it lives including its solar system, eventually its galaxy...ultimately its Universe. As you will see in the Third Insight, consciousness is more than just a third and fundamental component of existence — it's the *controlling component*.

To understand ourselves and our relationship with the Universe and the world around us, we must look at the role of consciousness throughout the Universe. When you read the Third Insight, you will clearly see the nature of consciousness and how its accelerating acquisition of knowledge quickly takes over and controls the dynamics of the solar system, galaxy, and Universe in which it lives. As you will see in the Third Insight, consciousness takes over mass and energy for the most ideal living conditions. Of course, as shown in the Third Insight, the death of the Universe through entropy death or the collapse and rebirth through the big bang on both sides of the Grand Cycle of the Universe never happen because consciousness would never let itself perish. The Universe is the house; consciousness is the housekeeper.

When you understand how consciousness quickly, permanently, and completely takes control of nature, you then realize that consciousness quickly, on the time scale of the Grand Cycle of the Universe, takes over the creation cycle of existence. In fact, *creation* is how consciousness controls the cosmos: creating, for example, new mass/energy systems wherever it benefits the house consciousness lives in. Consciousness controls the universe through creating galaxies, black holes, formats of energy or mass to keep its house in perfect order.

Consciousness does not *just* control through creation, but it brings values to its house through creation. For example, the greatest value creation of conscious beings is creating new realms of existence with the conditions to evolve new realms of conscious life. For, new, evolving conscious beings eventually create and add more values to the house...to our Universe. Creating new realms of consciousness puts ever growing new values into our Universe. Ultimately, as explained in the Third Insight and described in my novel *The First Immortals*, conscious beings work in beautiful harmony throughout the Universe, creating wonderful values for each other that make conscious life better and better. That universal Neo-Tech World is the *Civilization of the Universe.*

The *role* of consciousness in the Civilization of the Universe is *creation*: to be *the creator*. The nature of consciousness is *creation...value creation.*

When going as far as we can extrapolate at this time, to the most advanced conscious being Dr. Frank R. Wallace calls *Zon*, powerful logic seen in the Third Insight tells us consciousness, a Zon, created our Universe. Zon is *THE Creator*. Within this house he built for consciousness, conscious beings control it through being *the creators* at their levels and add to it through being the *value creators* at their levels.

You becoming *the value creator* at your level on Earth puts you in harmony with the role of consciousness throughout the Universe. Your becoming *the creator* on Earth puts you in harmony with yourself, the world around you, and the Universe...and is *the* secret for eternally happy conscious life.

Become the Creator

Okay, coming back down to Earth: to be in harmony with the secret for eternal happiness, to be filled with everlasting exhilaration, you must become *the creator*, which means creating values that never existed before. And I'm going to show you how to do that.

Before I do that, however, let me point out *the contradiction* we almost all live with today. That is: we are *value producers*, like my friend who flies planes. He is producing a value when he goes to work. But ten, twenty, thirty years from now, he will be producing the same values. Those values will not build and grow as value creation does. Therefore, his life, underneath, is a burden.

Human consciousness was not designed to be stagnant, which causes our living contradiction. Human consciousness was designed to be always growing...expanding and exhilarated. Therefore, we must leap from value producers to *value creators* to end the stagnation and the burden of life. And when we do, we will honestly want to live forever.

Now, I can tell you not only how to do that, but how to do it practically. The amazing thing is, you do not have to be a Bill Gates or Ray Kroc to do this. *Anyone* can do this.

You may ask yourself, how can *I* create new values for the world that have never been built? Actually, being *the creator* is better described this way: you will go on a vector of value creation that forever grows to the next level and the next, like building a bigger and bigger puzzle-picture that's never been seen before.

Human consciousness *is designed* to build those ever growing creative puzzles to new levels of knowledge, which is called *Neothink*. Your mind is already designed to be *the creator*. Every mind, every person, has the mental faculty to be a *value creator*. Once we know that, then knowing the key to being a value creator is not so difficult: I call it *downstream focus*.

Almost all people, when they leave work at the end of the workday, don't like to think about it until they have to clock in again. Very rarely, a person is drawn back to his work in the evenings and on weekends, not because it's a duty, but because his mind and heart — his focus — is drawn to it. For most, to be focussed on work in the evenings is an upstream battle. But for that rare person, his focus on work is a downstream flow. If *any* person is focused all day and drawn back in the evenings and on weekends to a particular interest, his natural mental faculty will eventually take him on a vector of open-ended value creation called Neothink.

How do we capture downstream focus? Every person has a *deepest motivational root* inside that would bring him downstream focus.

In children, we can spot those deepest motivational roots. I

48

can see them in my two-year-old son and six-year-old daughter. My son is fascinated with the world around him in the way a scientist or perhaps an engineer would be. For instance, if we go to play miniature golf, and we come upon one of those two-tier holes where the ball goes in a hole and disappears as it travels down a PVC pipe to the lower tier, my two-year-old son will be transfixed with that hole for a long time, going up and down between the two levels, examining the hole and the ball's journey through it. His deepest motivational root — his Friday-Night Essence — seems to gravitate toward physics/engineering. My six-year-old daughter has a strong trait I've picked up on. Ever since she was a year old, she would not leave a project until she finished it. Whereas most children her age or much older could not focus their attention that long on something, my daughter would focus for hours, if needed, until she finished the project. She displays mental endurance, which is a sign of a deep thinker/writer. Her deepest motivational root — her Friday-Night Essence — points toward some form of a deep thinker and writer.

That deepest, motivational root, easily spotted from a young age, is the person *you were meant to be.* Living as that person you were meant to be, you would enjoy every day, for all your life, downstream focus which would take you onto a vector of being *the creator.*

Become the Person You Were Meant To Be

As adults, we cannot so easily identify our deepest motivational roots — the persons we were meant to be. The reason the person we were meant to be becomes so elusive to adults is because we have been so preoccupied with making a living; we have no idea of what we passed over and filed away in the *impractical section* of our minds. We have no idea of just how practical and powerful our deepest motivational root would have been had we pursued it.

My employee Dave (whom you read about in Vision One) put together a seminar that takes people off the streets — people who have never seen Neo-Tech literature — and goes through exercises to discover the person they were meant to be; that is, we discover their deepest motivational roots that would bring them downstream focus. Then, we go through a set of exercises to send them along that path they were meant to travel. They travel just a little at first. Before long, however, they can make their livings doing what they were meant to do in life, which means they discover downstream focus and go on to become *the creator*. This is every person's ambition in life.

To match your livelihood to your deepest motivational root is your life ambition. To become the creator and experience the secret for eternal happiness is done through a self-discovery: discovering the person you were meant to be. Once you pursue that path, you suddenly possess downstream focus. In time, your mind will be building puzzles of new knowledge. Through Neothink, you will become *the creator*.

Remember, pay attention to a few things:

• notice any particular subject you tend to be drawn to — say something you consistently like to read about,

• notice any particular interest besides passive entertainment or active sports that you tend to do in the evenings or weekends,

• and think back across your life to any interests that consistently attracted you.

Being on the lookout for things that seem to motivate you can help give you some clues to your deepest motivational root. In time, you will make the full self-discovery. (Go back to Vision One to make the self-discovery.)

Once you make the self-discovery, set up a mini-day schedule (Vision Five) in the evenings and on the weekends to start taking a few small steps along the path you were meant to travel. To your pleasant surprise, downstream focus will kick in and your journey along that path will take on a life of its own. Before long, your deepest motivational root will take over and grow into your livelihood. You will go on to become the *value creator*. ...By being on the lookout for your deepest motivational root, you will discover it in the next few weeks or less.

Now, let's summarize what we have uncovered today:

1) We have uncovered the elusive secret for eternal happiness that puts us in harmony with the Universe, with the world around us, and with ourselves. Again, we must leap from the value producer to the value creator.

2) In the process, we have uncovered the contradiction almost everyone lives with. Again, we are value producers, not value creators, which causes our lives, underneath all the wonderful experiences, to be a burden. Most of us could not live that way forever.

3) We have uncovered how to make the leap from the value producer to the value creator: We must make the self-discovery of our deepest motivational root, which would bring us downstream focus, which is all that is needed for our minds to switch in time to puzzle-building Neothink as we become *the creators*.

In short, I've shown you how the individual gets out of the *anticivilization* (i.e., today's limited civilization). In today's anticivilization, to live for eternity would be intolerable. When you join the Civilization of the Universe (i.e., tomorrow's limitless civilization), when you jump from the value producer to the value creator, to *die* for eternity becomes intolerable.

(See chart on the next page.)

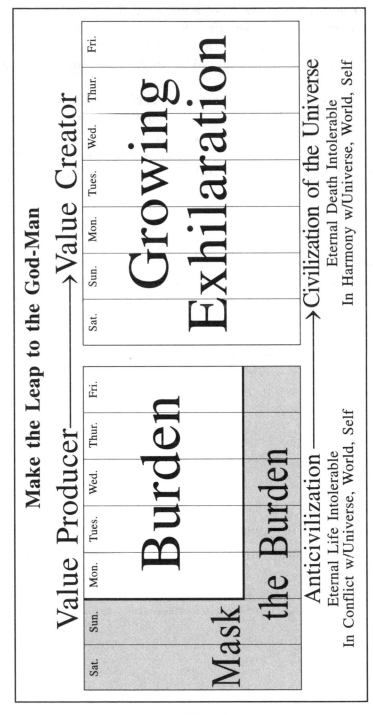

Make the Leap to the God-Man

Value Producer →Value Creator

Sat.	Sun.	Mon.	Tues.	Wed.	Thur.	Fri.

Burden

Mask the Burden

Anticivilization
Eternal Life Intolerable
In Conflict w/Universe, World, Self

Growing Exhilaration

→Civilization of the Universe
Eternal Death Intolerable
In Harmony w/Universe, World, Self

Vision Three

You Will Feel
Extraordinary Stimulation

How Neothink Will Save Civilization

Now I'll show you how our *entire* civilization, which includes *you,* will get out of the limited anticivilization.

This is the route most people will take out of the anticivilization, *not* the individual route just covered in Vision Two. So, for most, what follows is their leap into God-Man.

Let's start by asking, "What holds us in the anticivilization?" The answer, as you will see, is: *external authorities.*

Here are three examples of external authorities:

1) The political paradigm: politicians and bureaucrats control how we spend our money and run our businesses through their ever growing laws and regulations that suppress our minds and society's progress.

2) The religious paradigm: the church subjugates the mind into subservience, and

3) The business paradigm: routine-rut value-producing jobs stifle the mind (versus exhilarating value-creating jobs described in Vision Five).

Those are three major examples of external "authorities", vestiges of the bicameral mentality when external authorities told us how to live. Such external guidance today blocks our own internal guidance and takes away the potential of our minds to be self-guiding value creators. Those external "authorities" suppress society into a sea of value producers.

Now, let me rhetorically ask this question: Do you believe that those external "authorities" such as politicians exist and suppress us in an anticivilization because of the clever illusions they craft of doing "social good" or "spiritual good"?

Well, surprise: although they craft masterful illusions, that's *not* why or how they exist.

To learn why external authorities exist, I must tell you a little something about severe drug addicts: they *know* they will die if they cannot get off the habit. They know. But it's almost impossible to stop because of the stimulation they receive. To go back to the nonstimulating, boring world of being sober is nearly impossible for them.

Stimulation is the key word. A milder example is the cigarette smoker: he knows smoking is bad for him, but he does it for the *stimulation*. And the more a person tries to show him the harm, show him how smoking will cause clogged arteries, high blood pressure, lung cancer, the more the smoker *pushes him away*.

That *pushing away* is what you might experience when you try to reveal the dishonest illusions of external "authorities" to others. You see...external "authorities" provide *stimulation*, and *that's why* we have them. They are society's cigarettes. Belief in heaven, life hereafter...well, that's invigorating! Following politics...that's invigorating.

People implicitly know reality, and they don't want you showing it to them anymore than the smoker does. People already know and accept the harm, which is why, for example, a former president could jeopardize national security for personal power-advancing campaign contributions ...yet not be removed from office.

The illusions of doing "social good" are there only so everyone can save face. People implicitly know the harm, but they want the external "authorities" for the stimulation they provide. That stimulation helps the people *mask the burden of life*...right to the point of being led into stimulating war...even to their deaths.

Now, stay with me here, for this is important: those stimulating external "authorities" are actually part of something larger called: *the forces of nature.*

External "authorities" come from a mutation of our bicameral mentality of the ancient past. The bicameral mind was, 3000 years ago, part of nature. External authorities, in that primitive nature-controlled mind, formed the crucial individual and political fabric for civilizations to survive. But we no longer should be controlled by nature. Remember, consciousness is supposed *to control nature.*

Other forces of nature we are trapped in include:

Forces of Nature

Forces of Nature...	Their Destructive Stimulations Control Us
We were driven to mate with symmetrically superior specimens (i.e., beautiful lovers).	**Animalistic lust** (disregards human, psychological needs in romantic love)
We developed strong, competitive drives.	**Preying on weaknesses in others** (disregards human love for his fellowman)
We harbored a strong drive for moment-to-moment prosperity.	**Pursuing immediate financial gratification** (disregards human need of pursuing one's deep motivational root)
We needed the "Silverback" to lead the clan.	**Political leaders** (disregards the human ability to lead oneself)
Followers needed to be led.	**Followers** (disregards human integrating powers of the mind)
Advantages came from group acceptance and popularity.	**Attention seeking** (disregards human route to happiness and success, which is *value creation*)
External authorities were part of bicameral man's nervous system (i.e., the voices of the gods) and survival system (i.e., directives from King-Gods and oracles)	**External authorities** (disregards human consciousness and prevents leap into Neothink)

Forces of Neothink

We're trapped in the forces of nature; we're addicted to their destructive stimulations (including external authorities) in order to relieve the burden of life. In this anticivilization, revealing all the illusions in the world isn't going to change that.

So, what will?

On an individual basis, *the feeling* from becoming *the creator* frees us (Vision Two). That feeling, living the life every human being was meant to live, is far, far more stimulating than the life of a value producer, the life no one was meant to live for more than a few decades. But as I've said, that initial leap from a value producer to a value creator will at first be a small, albeit growing percentage of people. So, what will free civilization *as a whole* from the forces of nature and our addiction to the spiral-of-death stimulations?

The answer is: something so stimulating that it outdoes stimulations from the forces of nature to pull civilization free from them. That something so stimulating is: the forces of Neothink in the developing *supersociety* (i.e., society in the approaching Neo-Tech World). Those *supersociety stimulations* will pull us free from the spiral-of-death stimulations.

Supersociety Stimulations Pull Us from the Anticivilization

For example, in the supersociety of the Neo-Tech World, everyone becomes wealthy through a Technological Revolution. The computer revolution, in which buying power multiplied thousands of times, is a forerunner to a much larger, universal Technological Revolution to come. That Technological Revolution, as we enter the supersociety, will make us wealthy. Our buying power will multiply many times over in all industries, from genetic construction to home construction.

If everyone is wealthy from this one force of Neothink, then people will leave behind the force of nature that seeks immediate financial gratification, for they are wealthy already. Instead, they will now pursue their deepest motivational root and go on to become the *value creator*.

That is an example of just one force of Neothink that pulls people free from one, very powerful force of nature, out of the anticivilization and into the Civilization of the Universe. Next, I will show you several other forces of Neothink and the resulting supersociety stimulations.

As the supersociety stimulations start to build momentum, they will obsolete the spiral-of-death stimulations. Put them head-to-head, and there's no contest (explained next). The external "authorities" will no longer be needed for their spiral-of-death stimulations.

Without external "authorities", all the properties of civilization change, as explained throughout the Twelve Visions and demonstrated in my novel *The First Immortals*. And with those changed properties, everyone easily, naturally becomes the person he or she was meant to be — *the creator* filled with growing exhilaration.

Then, with the demand for eternal life and with the freedom for industries to pursue it, biological immortality will naturally follow.

Now, the *big question*: WHEN?

When supersociety stimulations supplant the spiral-of-death stimulations, we will have non-aging immortality (Vision Four).

Supersociety Stimulations Supplant Spiral-of-Death Stimulations

The Way Things Are

Let's begin with the beautiful woman married to a tall and handsome broad-shouldered MAN who looks as though he was born a man (no traces of "boy" or those days before body hair). That pretty lady, in time, will begin to look with a curious eye at the rich man, even if he's not as physically endowed (and even if she sees him, physically, as a "boy"). Nevertheless, she will look at him and wonder what life must be like as a rich man's wife, for she could have that life, and she knows it.

On the other hand, the beautiful woman with the rich man, in time, will start looking at the physically superior "hunk" MAN, even if he's not nearly as financially endowed. Nonetheless, she will look at him and wonder what life must be like with a stud, for she could have that, and she knows it.

Now, the beautiful woman with a *rich* "hunk" MAN has it all, so it seems. She has it all for only a little while, though, for *he* starts looking at other beautiful women. He could have them, and he knows it.

"None of this applies to me," you might think. Oh, but it does — it all does. Whether or not you are or are not rich or a hunk or do or don't have a beautiful spouse — and whether or not such actions (i.e., sleeping with others) take place, these are the forces constantly at work on relationships. For, these are the forces of nature, from which there is no escape. Those constant forces, more often than not, win out.

Nature instilled women with a deep drive to mate with the physically superior man. Nature also instilled women with the deep drive to mate with the prosperous man. Nature instilled men with a deep drive to mate with the physically symmetrical (i.e., beautiful) woman. Those are the forces of nature from which no individual human being can escape, no matter how intellectual or moral that human being may be. Whether or not he or she *acts* on those forces is up to the individual. But the forces are there, always there, in everyone.

Those constant forces quietly push the happy couple toward becoming *distrustful, unfaithful, anxious, insecure,* and *unhappy.*

Let us shift from romantic relationships to plutonic relationships. Do we really feel love and compassion for our fellowman? To the contrary, down deep we hope for faults, errors, weaknesses in others. No matter how much we deny it or hate it in ourselves or suppress it...we do secretly applaud weaknesses in others because that lessens the competition for us and our survival. That competitive drive to better our peers is a fundamental force of nature...for our survival.

That constant force of nature quietly pushes happy friends, neighbors, and co-workers toward *hate, spite, and envy.*

What are we saying here about the world we live in? The problem gets even more complicated. Consider that our lifelong relationships with our livelihoods most often exist for the money and not for the love of one's work or accomplishments. In fact, most people go through life despising work, never knowing what they would love doing or that they could even love their work. Seeing work only for financial survival — that powerful force of nature from which there is no escape — results in quiet dislike for work, where we spend a large percentage of our lives. On the grand scale of life, the inescapable forces of nature steadily push us into *unhappiness* and *camouflaged failure.*

Looking further into the forces of nature, consider that in a society of animals living together, nature produces leaders. Those leaders, say the Silverbacks of the gorilla clans, get treated to the best life, the best food, the best females.

Likewise, in our society, the forces of nature produce political leaders. Some individuals are driven to seek power through politics. Others file in, looking toward the political leaders for an economic advantage. In any case, this force of nature that dominates our society — this need for political leaders — pushes society toward *oppression, corruption, illusions,* and *gullibility.*

How deep do the forces of nature affect us? In our personal lives, we seek attention — everyone does. Watch toddlers, years before they ever have a romantic or monetary thought: they seek attention! It is the most basic human desire, from the toddler to the teenager...to the senior citizen. Seeking attention is also a raw force of nature: the animal that gets more attention and approval — the popular one — does best in its society. However, this force of nature pushes humans toward *egotism* and *terribly immature decisions.*

In conclusion, the civilization in which we live is an anticivilization that pushes us toward distrust, unfaithfulness, anxiety, insecurity, unhappiness, hate, spite, envy, failure, oppression, corruption, illusions, gullibility, egotism, and immaturity. And we cannot escape those forces of nature because we are still, unnaturally part of nature.

Why are the forces of nature so destructive to man and civilization...creating this anticivilization in which we are trapped? The answer is: the *conscious* man, as you will learn in the First Insight, does **not** belong to nature. Human consciousness transcends nature, left behind with the bicameral man 3000 years ago. Nature could evolve no further than bicameral man. Human consciousness was a man-made leap *beyond* nature. The forces of nature were valuable and vital in a system designed by nature. But the forces of nature, as you can see, wreak havoc on a system outside of nature.

In many respects, without fully knowing why, original spiritual leaders such as Lao-Tzu, Buddha, and Jesus sensed this and sensed forces that transcended nature, meant for conscious man, such as love and compassion obsoleting hate, spite and envy.

As those spiritual leaders learned, it is almost impossible for an individual to escape the forces of nature and leave this destructive anticivilization that continues to wear us down. An individual can intellectually know the way things should be, say, in marriage, business, politics, and personal relationships. He or she can even intellectually see and acknowledge what is wrong with the way things are now. But for that individual to *emotionally* escape the forces of nature is, well, nearly if not impossible. He is trapped.

Tomorrow: Freed by a Supercivilization and its Forces of Neothink

The Supercivilization answers the ancient spiritual leaders and explains exactly where we're going, why we're going there, and how it will be when the forces of tomorrow's *supersociety* save us and lift us from the forces of nature.

There is a way out of the anticivilization. In fact, we are the first generation with a way out ever since civilization veered off course between 2400 and 1600 years ago with the Plato/St. Augustine mutation of the bicameral mind (explained in the Second Insight), which prevented Neothink and enslaved us to the forces of nature, trapping us in the anticivilization. Indeed, the bicameral mentality is a mentality designed by nature. The Plato/St. Augustine mutation of the bicameral mentality (the Second Insight) took the conscious mentality and infected it with a powerful mutation of the obsolete bicameral mental structure dependent on external authorities as designed by nature, enslaving the conscious man to the forces of nature. The supersociety and its forces of Neothink could not rise within the bicameral mentality or its powerful mutation.

Although no individual can emotionally escape the forces of nature in the anticivilization, we can leap beyond nature by riding upon the coming supersociety that will shrink the forces of nature to nothing. To nothing? Feeling lust for a beautiful woman, for instance, is an automatic and unstoppable urge! And it is also void of any values; it is based solely on instant gratification...it is so animalistic in nature, not human. When we ourselves feel our strings of nature being pulled and look eagerly at a beautiful woman, for instance, it seems only natural. But observe as a pretty woman sits alone at a cafe. You, as a third party, watch the men, one after the next, as they walk past her. Watch where their eyes go, where their minds go. Like you, they cannot really help it, but where is the value there? Where is the value structure that separates us from the other animals and makes us human? There is nothing human about our indiscretionary lust. But we cannot stop it. We may not act on that lust, but the forces of nature are always there pushing and pulling us. The forces of nature work to destroy our happy, romantic relationships, and the forces of nature do not stop there. The forces of nature work to destroy our livelihoods, our plutonic relationships, our freedom, and more. What's worse, we cannot stop those forces of nature within us. They are always there, working against us and society.

But something beyond ourselves can overwhelm those forces of nature within us. The *supersociety* is the inevitable destiny of *Neothink*, a new way of using the mind based on creating new knowledge through building puzzles of knowledge, adding one puzzle piece after another until a never-before-seen puzzle-picture forms. The supersociety is bigger than any one person's mind; it is a growing puzzle that can be built by hundreds at first, then by thousands, millions, or the entire human race snapping in parts to the superpuzzle. The supersociety gave us a glimpse of its power in the computer field, bringing us spectacular breakthroughs of knowledge, bigger than any single individual, at fantastic speeds. And, as we will see in a moment, the supersociety not only is bigger than our individual minds, but is bigger than the forces of nature within us that push us toward destruction.

As individuals put in vital Neothink puzzle pieces into the

61

overall superpuzzle, the Neothink puzzles in the supersociety take our knowledge and power to levels unreachable before. We have seen glimpses of the supersociety during the Industrial Revolution and even more so during the computer revolution and now during the communications revolution. However, those are only gentle tremors compared to the great Technological Revolution that will rock the world as Neothink geniuses rise, a few at first, then thousands, then by the millions to build the superpuzzles that will eradicate disease, bring us immortality, and great wealth.

The capacity for the supersociety has existed since man leapt from the bicameral mind to human consciousness 3000 years ago. But the Plato/St. Augustine mutation of the bicameral mentality infected human consciousness and prevented the supersociety, for we cannot have a supersociety built upon Neothink superpuzzles without Neothink. The Plato/St. Augustine bicameral mutation prevented Neothink for 2400 years, as shown in the Second Insight.

As explained throughout the Twelve Visions, the Technological Revolution will have breathtaking effects on civilization. Let us see how the superpuzzles of super-technological progress will carry us right out of the clutches of the destructive forces of nature:

The Way Things Will Be

Let's begin with the most basic biological drive — mating. Trapped by the forces of nature, a person may look at his or her spouse and secretly wonder, "Can I possibly go through my entire life, having sex only with this one person?" The forces of nature work and work and work on that person until, under great anxiety, he or she weakens and has that one affair, usually with a less-than-ideal willing partner, which usually leads to havoc and turmoil.

Now, let's compare what the forces of nature get you compared to the forces of the supersociety. First, you have to free your mind to a whole different level to even begin to imagine the supersociety of Neothink geniuses. The best way to think about the supersociety is: anything that is valuable, anything beneficial to man, will be done, often sooner than later (anything that is possible within the laws of science).

That being said, people will, sooner than later through cloning and other technologies, be able to experience different body parts, even different bodies. Instead of going through the enormous upheaval for that one affair (with a less-than-ideal partner) when corrupted by the forces of nature, spouses can happily enjoy entirely different bodies — their dream bodies — in the supersociety, yet always stay with the person they love...in perfect harmony. However, most would discover in the Neo-Tech World they prefer their spouses' original, yet perfected and enhanced bodies. (Now, if they were to sleep with another, they would do so because of *human* reasons — for reasons based on psychological decisions for changing to an improved value structure — and *not* for animal urges to "screw another piece of ass".) Instead of "risking it all for a lousy lay", we will add excitement to our happy marriages by enjoying our fantasy bodies with our spouses. ...You can get an idea, at this most fundamental biological level, how the man-made forces of the supersociety will shrink the destructive forces of nature to nothing[1].

Just in this area of romantic relationships, the forces of the supersociety will lift happy couples to *trust, security, faithfulness, eternal love,* and *happiness.*

The supersociety is beyond anything humanity has known, so it is beyond anything we have ever perceived. You will understand the supersociety as you read the Twelve Visions, and you will emotionally experience the supersociety by reading my descriptive novel *The First Immortals.* For thinking purposes now, assume that in the supersociety, *everyone* will automatically live with enormous wealth. The best analogy in today's world would be the computer industry. During the rapid advancement of computer technology, prices fell to fractions making the ordinary person "rich" at buying computer power. That dynamic will occur many times over in the supersociety advancing through

[1]Conscious man lives in a man-made system, not a system designed by nature as the bicameral man. That is why the forces of nature damage today's civilization so dramatically with high divorce rates, widespread boredom and depression, violence, and war.

superpuzzles of technology in every aspect of man's life, from medicine to education to marriage. Costs for just about everything will drop to fractions as we become rich at just about everything we buy.

Now, assuming everyone is rich, what does that do to us in regards to our livelihoods? Well, it immediately breaks the force of nature to have our livelihood dictated by money/prosperity. The physical, psychological, and emotional properties completely change in regards to our careers. Now rich and secure, we will search for and discover our Friday-Night Essences...what we *love* to do! As explained in Vision Two, your livelihood will now bring you pride and happiness as you enthusiastically build your creations for the world. The forces of the supersociety, in the area of business alone, will lift people to *pride, happiness,* and *success* versus miserable stagnation, unhappiness, and camouflaged failure in the anticivilization.

The supersociety will fill people with the love and compassion for their fellowman that great spiritual leaders Lao-Tzu, Buddha, and Jesus tried to harness. Remember, in the anticivilization trapped by the forces of nature, people inherently desire weakness in their fellowman in both love and in business, for the competitive survival pressures of nature dictate our emotions. But in the supersociety, spouses are secure and everyone is rich. And people are pursuing their Friday-Night Essences with great love and enthusiasm, bringing wonderful values to the supersociety. Down deep, we will cheer them on, for their creations will bring irreplaceable values to us. Think about the feeling of love you would have for a doctor who saved your child's life or who eradicated a disease that threatened you or a loved one. That is a close analogy of the love that will fill you toward your fellowman who is contributing major values to the supersociety. ...Again, the man-made forces of the supersociety will lift you from the destructive forces of nature and out of the anticivilization. Toward your fellowman, you will feel *love, compassion, admiration.*

The forces of nature, always vying for attention for survival advantages, push us toward egotism in the anticivilization. But the forces of the supersociety supersede those forces of nature. Getting attention, say through buying the biggest diamond or most expensive car or boat or home, will no longer have any significance. Everyone will be rich. The ego-desperate drive for getting attention, which satisfies temporarily but leaves one feeling empty in the end, will be replaced with something much more permanent and fulfilling. Remember, in the supersociety, people will pursue what they *love* to do — their Friday-Night Essences. By doing that, they will create important values for society, from which comes love and admiration from your fellowman, pride and happiness within. Those forces of the supersociety lift you to *maturity, self-control,* and *modesty.*

As you will see in the First Insight, there will be no more political roles in the supersociety. No one will be looking to be led; there will be no need for an economic edge. The forces of the supersociety will lift us to *freedom, productivity, creativity* and *knowledge.*

In conclusion, the supersociety, in which we will someday live, will lift us out of the anticivilization, from the destructive forces of nature, to trust, security, faithfulness, eternal love, happiness, pride, success, compassion, admiration, maturity, self-control, modesty, freedom, productivity, creativity and knowledge.

Why are the forces of the supersociety so constructive to man, creating a Supercivilization (also described as the Civilization of the Universe)? The reason is: the supersociety can come only from man at a level not touched by nature, possible only through puzzle-building Neothink. Soon, we will head into the supersociety of extraordinary prosperity, driven by Neothink superpuzzles of knowledge to which each person can snap into and build. We are headed into the supersociety because mankind has reached the jumping-off point to Neothink, and the Twelve Visions deliver the tools to replace the forces of nature with the forces of Neothink. (The forces of the supersociety are the forces of Neothink.)

Evil, Evil Everywhere

To understand the enormous evil around the world from school shootings to war, one only need to realize we are trapped in an anticivilization dominated by the forces of nature, which should have been obsoleted 2000-3000 years ago with our man-made leap into human consciousness. With teenage boys and world leaders, for example, still struggling to be the Silverbacks, we will have school shootings and wars. In the Supercivilization, though, there will be no more misplaced forces of nature as love and compassion fill the world, for good.

Indeed, every evil event that occurs in our anticivilization from school shootings to war can be explained as conscious human beings being destructively driven to action by forces of nature...say, for example, for attention, dominance, leadership. In bicameral civilizations, such forces were necessary for advancing the species and society. Today, outside the system of nature, such actions destroy society.

Our anticivilization is filled with hatred. The coming Supercivilization is filled with love — the pure love expressed in the First Insight.

The Culminating Moment

During the first half of the twenty-first century, we will be leaving behind the anticivilization where we are now trapped by the forces of nature. Aging and death are forces of nature. When man jumped past nature into human consciousness 3000 years ago, we should have jumped past the forces of nature, including aging and death. But we did not. Why not?

Before 3000 years ago, our mentality was bicameral — a mentality designed by nature. Between 2000 and 3000 years ago, under enormous survival pressures, mankind jumped past nature into human consciousness — a mentality designed by man. At that point, mankind should have quite rapidly advanced and, in a few hundred years or less, advanced into the supersociety that is forming today. Then, the supertechnologies would have quickly overpowered the forces of nature...such as eliminating human aging and death (Vision Four).

The bicameral mentality was dependent on external authorities, which worked well within a system designed by nature. But, external authorities destroy a system beyond nature. During the early times of human consciousness, 2400 years ago, the Greek philosopher Plato (427-347 B.C.) developed a seductive philosophy that would preserve a world of external "authorities".

For many reasons, Plato's philosophy gradually infected the newly conscious world and became even more virulent with St. Augustine and the Church in 400 A.D. (the Second Insight). The Plato/St. Augustine mutation of the bicameral mentality trapped us in a societal structure of external "authorities", meant for nature, not man.

The result? Three thousand years after humanity shifted from the bicameral man to human consciousness, we are still aging and dying. But that is about to change, which we will witness in the years ahead as we travel to the other shore. The shore we are travelling to is the Supercivilization, also called the Civilization of the Universe, where we are freed from the spiral of death by the forces of Neothink.

To best understand where we are coming from and where we are going, let us remember the forces of nature that trap us in the anticivilization with its spiral-of-death stimulations. The supersociety will make you rich, romantic, and immortal...where you will become the God-Man.

Vision Four
Soon, You Will Cease Aging

Let's start at the beginning to really understand the cure to aging. Realize, once we say "curing aging", then we are actually saying something much further. We are saying "curing death" or biological *immortality*. Curing aging also means properly preparing oneself and civilization for immortality, which causes much greater resistance to curing this 100% fatal disease. Curing death, for instance, is simply not desired by the average person who feels the burden of life lurking beneath his happy experiences of life. That vast, added dimension to the phrase "curing aging" will help you understand what follows:

Cure Aging / Eradicate Death

The goal of Neo-Tech, of our company, of my life and Dr. Wallace's[1] life has always been, for over thirty years...biological immortality.

Yet, not until recently has Dr. Wallace or I taken an interest in a single biomedical approach.

Seems strange, doesn't it? Not when you understand that curing aging and death is a *dynamic process* that breaks into three parts:

The first part is *political*: a virulent part of the disease of aging is the politicization of society, which holds back progress to curing aging. We must depoliticize civilization.

The second part of the dynamic process to curing aging and death is *psychological*: a virulent part of the disease of aging is the burden of life people feel, which blocks the desire to cure aging. We must replace the burden of life with exhilaration for life.

The third part of the dynamic process to curing aging is *physical*: the final and ironically least difficult part of the disease of aging is the cellular degeneration itself. When the first two

---

[1]Dr. Frank R. Wallace is the discoverer of Neo-Tech and author of *The Neo-Tech Discovery*.

69

parts of curing aging succeed, then the technology, drug, or procedure to cure aging will rise almost overnight.

By now into the Twelve Visions, Parts One and Two above probably seem somewhat obvious to you:

Part One: yes, we say, we must depoliticize America to free business and entrepreneurs to race forward as they did in the relatively nonpoliticized computer industry of the 70s, 80s, and 90s.

Part Two: yes, we say, we must discover our Friday-Night Essences and make the leap from value producers to value creators to become motivated individuals who feel great about ourselves and desire longer and longer lives.

But, as you have gathered, those first two parts of the three-part dynamic process to curing aging sit upon major Neothink puzzles. Those Neothink puzzles took entire lifetimes to build, and they consist of the large bodies of work of Wallace and myself. Those puzzles grew to the point where they became effective, obvious, and were able to get traction.

An analogy would be the expression <u>existence</u> <u>exists</u>. As obvious as that sounds, that statement took entire lifetimes and the large bodies of work of Aristotle and Rand to develop the meaning behind the expression to the point that it now seems obvious.

The obvious sounding first two parts to the dynamic three-part process to curing aging and death are large Neothink puzzles, but to begin analyzing this process to curing aging, let's start with the root behind each part.

Part One, depoliticizing civilization, the root underneath it all is leaping from the bicameral mentality to the Neothink mentality...which I'll come back to.

Part Two, replacing the burden of life with exhilaration, the root underneath it all is leaping from a value producer to a value creator...which I'll come back to.

Part Three, developing the physical cure, the root underneath it all is achieving Parts One and Two.

Why is the root to the physical cure, Part Three...achieving Parts One and Two?

Very simply, *we are dealing with a cause-and-effect process to curing aging and death.*

If we achieve Parts One and Two, here's what would happen:

People would be free of contradictions, filled with the exhilaration for life that brings on the desire, the *passion* to live forever, brings on *the demand* for biological immortality.

Remember, civilization would no longer be politicized, which brings on the supersociety with super rapid advancement of new technologies, enabling *the supply* to rise and meet the demand for biological immortality.

With Parts One and Two, there would be a world-drive greater than anything humanity has ever seen, greater than the Manhattan Project or the Moon Project. That drive would be for biological immortality or *Project Life*.

I describe this drive in my novel *The First Immortals*. Everything that's going to happen in the future from these Twelve Visions is described in that novel.

Now, let's go back and take a deeper look into this three-part, cause-and-effect process for curing aging and death.

Three-Part Dynamic Process to Curing Aging and Death

Part One: Depoliticizing civilization

There's so much more here than meets the eye. And we could *never* succeed without the deep work of understanding what's beneath this expression *depoliticize civilization*.

This is why Libertarians will not, in the end, succeed...not without Neo-Tech.

This first part of the dynamic process of curing aging and death requires the whole body of work of Neo-Tech including my work, Dr. Wallace's work, and Dr. Julian Jaynes' work, and the decades behind those works.

The root beneath depoliticizing civilization, as I've said, is leaping from the bicameral-like mentality that needs authorization from outside to the Neothink mentality that integrates knowledge into puzzles or maps, which guide oneself, independent of authorization from outside.

Let's take a brief look at the bicameral mentality:

Three thousand years ago man, as all other animals, reacted automatically to external stimuli. As any other animal, he could not separate from the world immediately before his eyes. He had no inner mind space as we do today. He had no way to turn inward into his thoughts to think, analyze, judge, introspect, or make decisions.

Bicameral man had the largest brain, a huge two-chamber (i.e., bicameral) brain. Bicameral man had the most advanced mind that could be developed by nature. He even developed spoken languages and was the only animal with a mind sophisticated enough to do so.

As all animals, he was guided by his nervous system. It was so sophisticated, though, that the guidance came through his language. His guidance system came in the form of neurological impulses from the right-chamber brain, fired to the left-chamber brain, and "heard" as hallucinated voices of the gods.

Physically, the bicameral brain was identical to today's brain. It simply did not have the inner mind space to step back from the world to look at it, think about it, judge it, and make decisions.

Those decisions came from the voices of the imagined gods. Here's a quick way to understand how the bicameral brain worked. Have you ever had a "Eureka!" experience or an "I've got it!" experience...where all at once you see the big picture to something? Here's how that happened:

Your right brain is not conscious of what audio/visual data it absorbs, but it absorbs all day long, and it holds a lot of data we are not aware of. One day, your left brain suddenly sees a big picture to something. That logical left brain pulled information from that stored-up data in the right brain and snapped it together like a puzzle.

That big-picture "Eureka!" is essentially how bicameral voices guided bicameral man: His right brain stored up data...then under stress, the left brain processed the relevant data into the best action that fired from the right brain to the left *as a voice of god.*

Bicameral man's nervous system, his guidance mechanism, was the most advanced by nature. For example, in a forest fire a deer might smell smoke and run; whereas the bicameral man,

72

under stress, would hear the voice of his god command, "Danger. Run, flee!"

Bicameral commands from the gods mostly happened under stress when forced to make decisions.

As bicameral man's language grew more and more sophisticated, eventually came the development of the metaphor, which uses something to describe something else. The metaphor gave the bicameral man the stunning ability to separate from the outside world, to turn inward, analyze it, judge it, and make decisions.

Suddenly, man could make decisions — he gained the power *of the gods.*

This new power to make decisions, which today is no big deal, back then was stunning — it was the power of God. It changed man from trance-like unconscious beings with no soul into thinking conscious beings with an inner world rich in thoughts, judgements, decisions. This stunning power of God is called *consciousness.*

In the Second Insight, I show how the non-biblical Jesus was a peasant with this new power of God, bringing this powerful new mind space, the new consciousness, to the powerless bicameral peasants. (That breakthrough about Jesus' teachings was first made by the late Tracey Alexander.) Through Jesus, the powerless peasants began gaining the power of consciousness. They started becoming one with God. After Jesus's death, the powerful educated elite who were already conscious and enslaving the bicameral peasants, discovered a way to continue to enslave the masses...by taking away this new unity with God — splitting apart this ancient God-Man. Those early neocheaters did this by recreating a separate supreme being, as explained in the Second Insight. That way, man remained subservient to that supreme being and continued to be controlled by the leaders of the Church in the name of God. Those leaders led civilization into the Dark Ages just when civilization should have soared with the new power of consciousness.

In other words, the religions, the Theocracies, became mutations of the bicameral mentality...the authorization from outside. The newly conscious mind, instead of guiding itself, continued to be guided by external authorities.

Governments today are mutations of the bicameral mentality...the authorization from outside. The conscious mind, instead of guiding itself, continues to be guided by external authorities. The bicameral mutations get programmed into our psyches like a computer virus via learned and mimicked reactions from the moment a child starts becoming conscious — learned from his parents first, then from society.

Not until getting down to this level of understanding the mind can we begin to know what to do to remove those bicameral mutations such as government controlling and guiding civilization, in order to accomplish Part One of the dynamic process to curing aging: depoliticizing civilization.

So, back to the mind, how do we get the man-in-the-streets' mind to jump from the bicameral mentality to the Neothink mentality that *guides itself?* For when that happens, then depoliticizing civilization by removing the external "authorities" happens automatically.

Of course, we must deprogram the bicameral programming that is in every living adult's psyche. But how do we possibly do *that?* How do we shift not just one individual, but all of mankind's mentality from bicameral-like to Neothink?

Okay, stay with this:

We must go into understanding *the lock* that the *forces of nature* have on us, as introduced in the previous Vision. Realize, if we are controlled by the forces of nature, then we are still stuck in a bicameral-like *nature-controlled* mentality, which includes external "authorities". Man's mind should be *beyond* nature, should be a Neothink man-controlled mentality.

Some forces of nature, and the Civilization-of-the-Universe's (C-of-U) reactions, include:

- The ultimate, destructive force of nature is *death* for evolution of the species. The C-of-U reaction to *conscious* death is: What! We actually have death when we advance faster than nature? Impossible!
- Another force of nature would be leaders of clans in the wild. The C-of-U reaction to that would be: What! We actually have political leaders leading *human beings* versus people leading themselves with Neothink? Impossible!

- Another force of nature is seeking instant prosperity and gratification in the wild. The C-of-U reaction to that is: What! We actually have *human beings* acting this way versus looking deeper at who they are and were meant to be? Impossible!
- Another force of nature is lust for the symmetrically superior — the beauty. The C-of-U reaction to that is: What! We actually have *human beings* acting that way versus discovering the complete physical/psychological package of lifelong "falling-in-love" romantic love? Impossible!

The forces of nature are very stimulating, and human beings seek stimulation. For example:
- Politics gives us a lot to talk about and to feel stimulated over.
- Seeking immediate financial gains stimulates everything about your life.
- Indulging in a beautiful woman, as in an affair, brings enormous stimulation to your life.
- In terms of the anticivilization in which we live, even death brings stimulation into our boring old-age.

The way to break from those destructive forces of nature is to create even greater <u>Neothink</u> or <u>supersociety stimulations</u> that outdo those spiral-of-death anticivilization stimulations. Here are eight examples, explained within this manuscript, of our rapidly developing Neothink or supersociety stimulations: 1) Get-the-people-rich political paradigm (Vision Eleven). 2) Get-the-people-creative business paradigm (Vision Five). 3) Immortality-here-on-Earth religious paradigm (the Second and Third Insights). 4) Perfect-health medical paradigm (Vision Twelve). 5) Person-you-were-meant-to-be personal paradigm (Vision One). 6) Falling-in-love-forever marriage paradigm (Vision Seven). 7) Make-the-kids-geniuses educational paradigm (Vision Nine). 8) Becoming-the-value-creator job paradigm (Vision Two).

As you might guess, each of those eight supersociety stimulations come from large Neothink puzzles. They will eventually outstimulate the anticivilization stimulations and will pull people out of their bicameral-like addictions to the stimulating forces of nature. As that happens, people will naturally make the leap into the Neothink mentality.

I'll pick just one of those eight Neothink supersociety stimulations above to demonstrate that leap from the bicameral mode to the Neothink mode: Let's see...I'll pick get-the-people-creative business paradigm. You will witness this Neothink puzzle in Visions Five and Six. I give you the next paradigm shift of the business world: from today's division of labor to tomorrow's division of essence. As I teach you in Vision Five, you will jump from a bicameral-like following mode — currently stuck in a job of labor following your boring routine rut, your same old set of responsibilities...your external authority — you will jump in the division of essence to *following nothing.* Your mind will jump to a job of the mind, from following a boring routine to *creating* exciting new values. As you will see, this is *far, far more stimulating!* Your mind jumps from the bicameral mentality to the Neothink mentality. The point is: those eight supersociety stimulations among others in this manual will pull you from the stagnant bicameral mentality into the soaring Neothink mentality.

These Neothink, supersociety stimulations will wipe out the destructive forces of nature, including external "authorities" and governments. These are major new paradigms that will bring you the new power of Neothink. Each of the Twelve Visions bring to you a major paradigm shift with awesome new power and stimulation...out of the bicameral mentality, into the Neothink mentality. Indeed, these supersociety stimulations are what will shift the man-in-the-streets from a bicameral mentality to the Neothink mentality, which is needed for the people to depoliticize America, the first part to the three-part process of curing aging and death.

Now, before I go on, you can see why speaking against the government, even with very sound ideas as the Libertarians have, for example, could never succeed. Without these Neothink puzzles that get down to the deepest problem and the solution, even the most solid political ideas in themselves could never succeed.

Depoliticizing civilization is simply so much more involved. In fact, to shift man's mentality from bicameral-like thinking to Neothink in order to properly integrate knowledge for self-leadership and to accept depoliticizing America actually requires the supersociety stimulations that arise from all Twelve Visions. Here is a list of the twelve paradigm shifts from the anticivilization to the Neo-Tech World that will come from the Twelve Visions. You can imagine the supersociety stimulations you will harvest from the twelve paradigm shifts:

The Twelve Paradigm Shifts
(And Their Self-Explanatory Supersociety Stimulations)

Tomorrow's Neo-Tech World Paradigm
<u>Outstimulates (os.) Today's Anticivilization Paradigm</u>

Vision One	I-love-my-work paradigm os. I-hate-my-work paradigm
Vision Two	Creator's exhilaration-for-life paradigm os. Producer's burden-of-life paradigm
Vision Three	Supersociety-stimulations paradigm os. Spiral-of-death-stimulations paradigm
Vision Four	Youth-and-immortality paradigm os. Aging-deterioration-and-death paradigm
Vision Five	Entrepreneurial jobs-of-the-mind paradigm os. Routine rut jobs-of-labor paradigm
Vision Six	Living creative-based-companies paradigm os. Lifeless labor-based-companies paradigm
Vision Seven	Falling-in-love-forever paradigm os. Drifting-apart-toward-indifference paradigm
Vision Eight	Slim-and-sexy paradigm os. Chubby-and-undesirable paradigm
Vision Nine	Brilliant-creator paradigm os. Bored-producer paradigm
Vision Ten	Geniuses-filling-your-life-with-Gifts paradigm os. Politicians-stripping-your-life-of-values paradigm
Vision Eleven	Live-like-a-millionaire paradigm os. Live-paycheck-by-paycheck paradigm
Vision Twelve	Free-of-diseases-anxieties-unhappiness paradigm os. Plagued-with-diseases-anxieties-unhappiness paradigm

Those twelve paradigm shifts are needed to send people from bicameral-like mentalities into Neothink mentalities as they are drawn to the supersociety stimulations. Make no mistake: the supersociety stimulations that arise from those twelve paradigm shifts are what will shift people's mentality from the forces of nature to the forces of Neothink, from a nature-controlled bicameral-mutant mentality to the man-controlled Neothink mentality, which will result in depoliticizing America, the first part to the dynamic three-part process to curing aging and death.

Now that I've introduced you to the Neothink superpuzzle that first had to be set in place to depoliticize civilization, let's go on to Part Two of this three-part process to curing aging and death:

Part Two: Replacing the Burden of Life with Exhilaration

The root beneath replacing the burden of life with exhilaration for life is to leap from the value producer to the value creator.

Let me give you a brief background on the burden of life:

In Vision Two, I explained why underneath all our happy experiences of life exists *a burden.*

Our happy experiences include:
• Getting a good education
• Landing a good job after our schooling
• Falling in love
• Getting married
• Having children, raising a family
• Retirement, perhaps travel, seeing the world

But when those happy experiences are all used up, then the burden rises to the surface like the static on an old record when the song ends. The burden that rises between and after the happy experiences, *allows us to accept death.*

Why do we have that burden? That understanding comes by understanding the nature of consciousness.

That understanding of consciousness grows as you begin to gain an understanding about the Universe...an understanding as presented in the Third Insight that goes beyond the bicameral explanation that God created everything.

Ever since bicameral times to the present, whenever nature

went beyond man's realm of comprehension, the explanation always, *always* jumped to God (or other mystical being). But as science moved in and explained nature, the role of God became less and less. For example, Darwin used science to show us how we got here; his scientific evidence moved in and replaced the idea of God's Majestic Creation and His Divine Plan...with Natural Selection *and chance*. At the time, Darwin's sound scientific evidence was extremely hard for people to accept.

Wallace uses science to show us how the Universe got here (the Third Insight). His science explains that God is really Zon — the name given to the very, very advanced God-Man (the Third Insight). Wallace's sound scientific reasoning might be extremely hard for people to accept. Nevertheless, as you study the Third Insight, you begin to see that, indeed, science explains *all of* nature. You begin to see how science moves in and explains the most incomprehensible realms of nature, including the creation of the Universe itself. Wallace's scientific reasoning moves in and replaces the idea of God's Majestic Creation and His Divine Plan...with Zon's creation and orchestration. As you read the Third Insight, you begin to see that, indeed, advanced conscious beings throughout the cosmos, advanced God-Men whom Dr. Wallace named Zons, orchestrate creation cycles of mass and energy throughout the Universe, very possibly the big-bang creation of our Universe itself. You also begin to see that conscious beings *always* evolve into *value creators*, and that the *supreme value* in the Universe is conscious life. As you read the Third Insight, you begin to realize Zons have taken exclusive control of the *creation cycle* in nature to create new realms of existence that will ultimately evolve the supreme value — conscious life.

In other words, Zons — conscious beings — create Universes and galaxies by controlling mass and energy.

As you read the Third Insight, you come to realize the role of conscious beings throughout the Universe is *creation*, whether a Zon creating a galaxy or Universe out there in the cosmos...or you and I *creating* — as opposed to *producing* — values here on Earth.

Consciousness is meant to *create the new*, not produce the old. Producing — yeah, that routine rut...producing the same values over and over — leads to stagnation. Consciousness will, does, *and must* die from stagnation.

But consciousness thrives *forever* from creation.

The world's whole business structure is set up for value production and, therefore, human stagnation...and acceptance of our deaths. It's set up by the physical division of labor and its jobs of labor, which yield *value producers*.

Vision Five, next, shows us the next paradigm of business — the *division of essence* and its *jobs of the mind*, which yield *value creators*. My Twelve Visions give people two fundamental ways to leap from value producers to value creators:

1) By showing you how to form a mini-company within the company you work for to advance from a cog-in-the-wheel job of labor to an entrepreneurial job of the mind (Vision Five, next).

2) By showing you how to discover your Friday-Night Essence — the person you were meant to be, living the life you were meant to live. If you do this and set up mini-days in your evenings and weekends, then your downstream focus, as I call it, will lead you eventually into making a living doing what you love to do...and eventually that downstream focus will lead you onto *creating* magnificent values for the world (Vision One).

Once you are *creating* values — once you are a value *creator* — then you are fulfilling the role of consciousness. You will be filled with exhilaration, and you will feel an omnipresent harmony within yourself, with the world around you, and with the Universe, a feeling you never knew existed. You will have found that "something more" to life that nearly everyone yearns for but never discovers.

That daily *feeling* within you — that harmonious, happy feeling of a value *creator* — is void of the burden of life. The thought of dying becomes intolerable, as it is now for the toddler who does not yet know the burden of life.

Pure exhilaration replaces the burden, and you will *want* more than anything the achievement of biological immortality, which completes Part Two of the three-part process to curing aging and death.

With the Twelve Visions now in your hands, you and millions of others will discover the exhilaration of life.

Now, after introducing you to the Neothink puzzle underneath replacing the burden of life with the exhilaration of conscious life, you can see why the thousands and thousands of self-improvement books, positive thinking, and spiritual books let you feel good for awhile, but they could never accomplish the feeling that value creation can — the permanent feeling of exhilaration and harmony with yourself, the world, the Universe. And that feeling makes you *want* life forever...more than you've ever wanted anything before, which cures Part Two of the three-part dynamic process to curing aging and death.

Now, we move on to Part Three.

Part Three: The Physical Cure

The drug, the serum, the operation, the electronic transfer.

What is the root behind this? Cells? Genes? DNA? Proteins? Cryonics? Quantum computers? What *is* the root behind the physical cure?

Now remember, Dr. Wallace has been at this drive for biological immortality for over *thirty years*, back in the days when medical efforts on anti-aging were considered quackery. Of course, that's changed completely today. The majority of medical research today is connected in some way to anti-aging.

But underneath it all, which today's doctors and scientists pursuing anti-aging will not know, is the ultimate necessity of succeeding with Part One (depoliticizing civilization) and Part Two (replacing the burden of life with the exhilaration for life). Those Parts One and Two are necessary to succeed with Part Three (the physical cure). Parts One and Two not only are needed to pull off Part Three, but Parts One and Two are *the cause* and Part Three is *the effect*, making the three-part dynamic process a *cause-and-effect* process to curing aging and death:

The Cause-and-Effect Process To Curing Aging

The cause is:
- Depoliticizing civilization
- Replacing the burden of life with the exhilaration for life.

The effect is:
- The physical cure to aging.

When you understand this cause-and-effect process to curing aging and death, you realize why, until now, neither Dr. Wallace nor I ever got involved with a physical approach. We needed to set in place the first two parts of the dynamic process — *the cause* — to get civilization in position to successfully go for *the effect* — the physical cure.

For the first time in my life, I feel that Parts One and Two are set in place with the completion of *The Neo-Tech World* and its emotional counterpart *The First Immortals.*[1] It's all together now; it's all here in your hands.

On a Personal Note

The self-proof I have personally that Parts One and Two are now set in place is: Last February, I completed an in-depth, 50-page working outline of my next body of work...powerful, unique knowledge the world has never seen that comes from the broadest Neothink puzzle I have ever conceived. For the past twenty years, I would have dived head first into that crucial product development. Instead, I put it all aside for a couple of years. You see, I'm not a writer *by goal.* I'm *whatever* it takes to achieve biological immortality, which until now required writing. The leverage for my goal of immortality now shifts, however, now that Parts One and Two are set in place in *The Neo-Tech World* and demonstrated in *The First Immortals.* My leverage shifts from product development to the marketing — mass marketing. For, my goal has always been to get immortality as quickly as possible.

Although my next body of work will be immensely valuable, I have judged it not necessary to the three-part process of curing aging and death. So, I have shifted my attention away from product development to mass marketing so that *millions of people* can learn about the leap into Neothink, leave behind external "authorities", and feel the exhilaration of life...from which the physical cure will rise quickly.

Moreover, now that Parts One and Two are set in place, Dr. Wallace and I are introducing ourselves to a biotech project on

---

[1] I must add here that *The Neo-Tech World* and *The First Immortals* were not possible without Dr. Frank R. Wallace's *The Neo-Tech Discovery.*

anti-aging for the first time ever. Yes, for the first time since Dr. Wallace began the quest for biological immortality over thirty years ago, we are introducing ourselves to a physical project.

Before we leave this subject, I must say there could theoretically (although unlikely) be a technological breakthrough on anti-aging that could potentially offer a cure *before* Parts One and Two — before depoliticizing civilization and before replacing the burden of life with exhilaration. But civilization would then need Parts One and Two *very quickly* as never before for survival as the old bicameral-like structures based on a seven or eight-decade human life span would break down. We simply could not live well into our hundreds and longer without depoliticizing civilization and replacing the burden of life with exhilaration. Civilization would self-destruct...and people eventually *would die,* whether from economic collapse, war, or boredom. Thus, the three-part dynamic process to curing aging and death cannot be separated, even in the very unlikely scenario that Part Three came first.

The goal of conscious life has always been the goal of Dr. Wallace and myself. Remember, the goal of conscious life — untouched by the anticivilization — is not just happiness, but happiness *forever.* It took us over thirty years to position ourselves to be able to do what will unfold next. As you will see: it's time for us *to go for the gusto* and to cure the disease itself, starting with the most virulent cause and spreader of the disease: the FDA.

Once the FDA is made impotent through our direct confrontations, essentially once the FDA is eradicated through our bait-and-switch advertisements to appear on high-profile TV, then biotech progress gets a large dose of freedom, which is Part One of curing aging and death.

Part Two will come through our mass dissemination of this how-to manual and my novel as people discover their Friday-Night Essences and discover that "something more" really does exist in life.

Mark my words: Part Three — the physical cure — will rise very, very quickly as Parts One and Two are cured. As external authorities and the burden are eradicated through these New Techniques (Neo-Tech), you will soon experience deep and permanent happiness...*forever!*

Summary

Non-aging technology yields biological immortality, which unlocks a bigger, a much bigger issue than merely the fountain of youth. To live *forever*, three things MUST occur:
1) Political — bicameral-like guidance of conscious minds must be replaced by self-guiding Neothink minds.
2) Psychological — burden of life must be replaced with exhilaration for life.
3) Physical — developing the technology must have enormous demand and freedom to dwarf all other historical medical efforts such as the Polio effort or other national efforts such as the Moon Project or Manhattan Project.
Curing Parts One and Two — those *mind diseases* — will bring on the *physical* cure, Part Three. Neo-Tech (as further explained in the First Insight) cures One and Two; it is the antidote to aging because Part Three will be the automatic effect.

Neo-Tech not only is the cure to aging, it is the *only* cure. It is the only antidote sufficiently developed enough over the past thirty years to cure the most virulent problem of the disease: the shift of the mind from the bicameral-like mentality to the Neothink mentality. That shift is needed to break from the debilitating forces thriving upon that mutant mentality. Once those debilitating forces are gone, then the physical cure, such as the biotech project on the eighteen-again stem-cell serum, will rise overnight.

Those debilitating forces — the external "authorities" — will try to stop us. They are the most virulent part of the disease. They are the forces dependent on our outmoded bicameral-like mentality that accepts being led by a parasitical ruling class. Advancing mankind's mentality means the end of their parasitical livelihoods. So, they will fight us for their own parasitical survival.

We fully expect those debilitating forces to attempt to stop Neo-Tech. Some already have tried, putting the original discoverer of Neo-Tech, Dr. Frank R. Wallace, in prison. The Ninth Circuit Court of Appeals ruled his First Amendment Rights were violated, and he is now a free man.

We are writers and scientists not part of the insulated academia. We are part of the real world — the arena of providing values to society...or fail. As writers, scientists, and business people *who know*...the physical cure would be here overnight if not for debilitating forces such as the FDA, for example, a powerfully harmful force of the parasitical ruling class...the most virulent part of the aging disease. As you will learn, Neo-Tech is the antidote to those debilitating forces.

My thousand-page novel *The First Immortals* is a harbinger of what's to come. It demonstrates that the battle will begin with depoliticizing the country by introducing people to the consequences — their own millionaire phenomenon (Vision Eleven). That's where it all starts, the first of three anchors holding us back from curing aging.

We have staked our claim to having the antidote — the cure — to the disease of aging. Now will come the challenges from the FDA and FTC. But, those authorities are part of the disease itself that prevent the cure. To cure aging, humanity must be cured of those authorities as demonstrated in *The First Immortals*. Then, the supersociety will rise and quickly cure aging and death.

You have in your hands the antidote — the cure — to the disease of aging. Now, as millions of others join you, it's just a matter of time.

The First Immortals gives you an accurate feel of how quickly things can move; it answers the mysteries of how the future will unfold. The how-to nonfiction counterpart to *The First Immortals*, now in your hands, shows you how to *personally* do what you read about in my novel.

As you continue reading, you will see how, with puzzle-building Neothink, you can snap together a puzzle picture and, as with any puzzle, reach a point where you know exactly what it will look like, even before having all the pieces in place, which means you can see the future. This book teaches you how. *The Neo-Tech World* and *The First Immortals* are Neothink superpuzzles; they're accurate forecasts of our future.

Vision Five
The Job of Your Dreams Is Coming

As I watched super rapidly advancing new technologies light up more and more industries like a new dawn, I was amazed at how rapidly businesses raced forward. I then noticed how our jobs were swept up into the fervor. While watching that progressive world, I saw our jobs leap to the next level so alive and exciting that today's jobs seemed dead by comparison.

Imagine a world in which every working adult was, in essence, an energized entrepreneur building his or her own fortune. That was exactly what I saw in my Fifth Vision into the third millennium...a hundred million super entrepreneurs pouring endless energy and creativity into America alone, teaming up with super technologies and sending civilization into new wealth not measurable by today's standards.

The American enterprise system underwent a definitive job revolution. In fact, jobs at all levels became entrepreneurial. Of course, entrepreneurs use their minds every day, day after day. With such growing, stimulated minds, 21st-century working adults left behind their bicameral tendencies of automatically reacting to a set routine and surprised themselves as they grew more and more creative...until, lo and behold, they themselves became super entrepreneurs and eventually geniuses of society overflowing with exhilaration and pride...and success. In time, they made the evolutionary leap into Neothink.

As you read my Fifth Vision and begin to believe that essentially every worker will become an entrepreneur in the 21st century, you will begin to ponder the might of a hundred million entrepreneurs pouring their energy and creativity into society, uninhibited by regulations and catapulted by super technologies. You will readily believe my Tenth Vision in which many millions of geniuses took care of our every need. You will begin to grasp that the way to take care of us is *not* through big government but through freed geniuses of society. You will begin to realize that a national escalation of standards of living called the *millionaire phenomenon* just may be believable after all, despite the traditional academic arguments. After all, the power of a hundred million entrepreneurs free to race ahead will dwarf anything ever seen on our planet including the computer/ information revolution.

A Hundred Million Entrepreneurs

Here is what I saw during the Fifth Vision: Depoliticizing America in the 21st century set free a rapidly advancing Neo-Tech World in which businesses had no choice but to evolve beyond their outmoded jobs of labor, our routine ruts. To remain competitive, as in the computer business, all businesses had to tap their greatest asset — the creativity of each and every employee — causing a job revolution that metamorphosed our boring routine ruts into exciting jobs of the mind. Depoliticizing America not only set free the country's existing entrepreneurs, but set off a 21st-century revolution of business that made all jobs entrepreneurial and created a hundred million in-house entrepreneurs.

American enterprise moved beyond the old division of labor and its jobs of labor into the new division of essence and its *jobs of the mind.* You see, the *essence* of business is to BUILD WEALTH through the creation of new or improved product or marketing. The division of essence breaks down businesses into *jobs of the mind* in which each and every employee himself — not just the founder and top executives — actually builds wealth.

Each and every employee tomorrow — including today's janitors — BECAME CREATIVE AND GOT RICH in tomorrow's jobs of the mind. I saw it in the Fifth Vision: with stimulated minds, day after day, ordinary people eventually grew into irreplaceable geniuses of society!

Let's take a look at the 21st-century division of essence and its jobs of the mind...the whole new business paradigm that I witnessed in my Fifth Vision. I took what I saw in my Fifth Vision and used it to structure my own company. Using my company as the example, Diagrams One through Four over the next five pages illustrate the obvious division of essence sitting right before our eyes. Sometime in the 21st century, all jobs came to life, became unbearably exciting, and led us for the first time into the world of profits and Neothink.

The Job of Your Dreams Is Coming

(Note: Diagrams One through Four over the next four pages are specific examples of dividing Integrated Management Associates by essence into wealth-building jobs of the mind — that is, 21st-century jobs with the purpose to BUILD WEALTH.)

Diagram One

Process To Divide Business By Essence Into Wealth-Building Jobs of the Mind

FIRST: LIST THE BASIC RESPONSIBILITIES
(Example from Integrated Management Associates)

Integrated Management's Basic Responsibilities:

Buy Television Spots

Set Up TV Commercials

Buy Space (newspapers, magazines)

Set Up Space-Media Ads

Rent Mailing Lists

Set Up Mailings

Manage Computer Database

Keep Data/Statistics

Keep Books

Do Accounting

Control Order Processing

Control Shipping Products

Control Product Manufacturing

Control Customer Service

Control Computer Needs

Diagram Two
(column one)
Process To Divide Business By Essence
Into Wealth-Building Jobs of the Mind

NEXT: DEFINE THE RESPONSIBILITIES' PURPOSE
(Example From Integrated Management Associates)

The basic responsibilities all need a purpose. For, a responsibility cannot exist by itself. For example, look at the first responsibility on the list (next column): *buy television spots*. Could buying TV spots exist on its own if not for the television marketing program? Of course not. That responsibility is dependent on the television marketing program. The television marketing program is the purpose of the first responsibility on the next page, the purpose of buying television spots. The *television marketing program* is *a job with purpose* — a wealth-building job in Integrated Management Associates that thrives on creativity. Buying television spots along with nine other responsibilities integrate into the television marketing program as will become clear over Diagrams Two, Three, and Four. As we will learn, one person will handle that fully integrated job with purpose, that money-making job of the mind, the television marketing program.

Randomly running down the list: could buying ad space in newspapers exist on its own? No. It needs a purpose. Could renting mailing lists (known as list brokering) exist on its own? No. It needs a purpose. Could accounting exist on its own? No. It needs a purpose. Could order processing exist on its own? No. It needs a purpose. And so on.

Today, however, all the responsibilities on the next page are established as departments in the traditional publishing companies, existing on their own as ends in themselves instead of integrating into their purposes. That is why most jobs today are closed-ended ruts. For, no way exists to build a mere responsibility that is split from its open-ended purpose. Again, how can one build renting mailing lists without that responsibility being integrated to its purpose: the direct mail marketing program? Yet, list brokering is treated as an independent department in nearly every direct mail company today.

To determine the purpose of each basic responsibility, simply finish the sentence: "This responsibility exists due to_____." For example, "Buying television spots exists due to *the television marketing program*." Integrated Management's example of this process is done on the next column. Several of the responsibilities exist in more than one purpose. For example, accounting could not exist on its own. That responsibility is dependent on, for example, the television marketing program. The television marketing program is its purpose. Also, other accounting records exist due to other marketing programs. Therefore, that responsibility will exist in more than one purpose as seen on the next column.

Do not get tied up on technicalities if you have trouble grasping the process. By the time you get through Diagram Four, the process will become clear.

Diagram Two
(column two)
Process To Divide Business By Essence
Into Wealth-Building Jobs of the Mind

BASIC RESPONSIBILITIES:
(Example From Integrated Management Associates)

Buy Television Spots:
Responsibility exists due to: *Television Marketing Program*

Set up Television Commercials:
Responsibility exists due to: *Television Marketing Program*

Buy Space (newspapers, magazines):
Responsibility exists due to: *Space Media Marketing Program*

Set Up Space-Media Ads:
Responsibility exists due to: *Space Media Marketing Program*

Rent Mailing Lists:
Responsibility exists due to: *Direct Mail Marketing Program*

Set Up Mailings:
Responsibility exists due to: *Direct Mail Marketing Program and Neo-Tech Database Marketing Program*

Manage Neo-Tech Database:
Responsibility exists due to: *Neo-Tech Database Marketing Program*

Keep Data/Statistics:
Responsibility exists due to: *Each of the marketing programs*

Keep Books:
Responsibility exists due to: *Each of the marketing programs*

Do Accounting:
Responsibility exists due to: *Each of the marketing programs*

Control Order Processing:
Responsibility exists due to: *Each of the marketing programs*

Control Shipping Products:
Responsibility exists due to: *Each of the marketing programs*

Control Product Manufacturing:
Responsibility exists due to: *Each of the marketing programs*

Control Customer Service:
Responsibility exists due to: *Each of the marketing programs*

Control Computer Needs:
Responsibility exists due to: *Each of the marketing programs*

Diagram Three

Process To Divide Business By Essence
Into Wealth-Building Jobs of the Mind

OVERVIEW OF BASIC RESPONSIBILITIES
AND THEIR MONEY-MAKING PURPOSES
(Example From Integrated Management Associates)

Basic Responsibilities:	Money-Making Purposes:
Buy Television Spots	Television Marketing
Set Up Commercials	
Buy Space (newspapers, magazines)	Space Media Marketing
Set Up Space-Media Ads	
Rent Mailing Lists	Direct Mail Marketing
Set Up Mailings	
Manage Database	Database Marketing
Keep Data/Statistics	
Keep Books	
Do Accounting	
Control Order Processing	
Control Shipping Products	
Control Product Manufacturing	
Control Customer Service	
Control Computer Need	

Diagram Four

Process To Divide Business By Essence Into Wealth-Building Jobs of the Mind

LASTLY: PULL TOGETHER THE WEALTH-BUILDING JOBS
(Example From Integrated Management Associates)

Now, pull the basic responsibilities together by their money-making purposes as follows:

Television Marketing:
Buy Television Spots
Set Up TV Commercials
Keep Data/Statistics
Keep Books
Do Accounting
Control Order Processing
Control Shipping Products
Control Product Manufacturing
Control Customer Service
Control Computer Needs

Space Media Marketing:
Buy Space
Set Up Space-Media Ads
Keep Data/Statistics
Keep Books
Do Accounting
Control Order Processing
Control Shipping Products
Control Product Manufacturing
Control Customer Service
Control Computer Needs

Direct Mail Marketing:
Rent Mailing Lists
Set Up Mailings (purchasing, printing lettershop)
Keep Data/Statistics
Keep Books
Do Accounting
Control Order Processing
Control Shipping Products
Control Product Manufacturing
Control Customer Service
Control Computer Needs

Database Marketing:
Manage Database
Set Up Mailings (purchasing, printing lettershop)
Keep Data/Statistics
Keep Books
Do Accounting
Control Order Processing
Control Shipping Products
Control Product Manufacturing
Control Customer Service
Control Computer Needs

Observation

As you can see, the company divides into specific marketing programs — wealth-building jobs. And as the company grows, those marketing programs divide further into specific marketing projects, every job always remaining a wealth-building job. In fact, every job becomes a little company in itself — a *mini-company*...a true job of the mind.

The Coming Job Revolution

I witnessed during my Fifth Vision that a job revolution changed your place of work into these entrepreneurial jobs, whether you worked for a large or small company, regardless if you are now the janitor or the president. The Fifth Vision was clear: the essence of business was to BUILD WEALTH. The *division of essence* divided business into entrepreneurial-like wealth-building jobs.

The Fifth Vision showed me that tomorrow all employees were their own in-house entrepreneurs, motivated to build profits and success. As a result, employees eventually shared in the profits, oftentimes in the equity. As do all entrepreneurs, their minds turned on like light bulbs and started shining. They left behind their bicameral behavioral patterns of automatically reacting to set routines and eventually entered the new Neothink mentality of creating new knowledge. *Creating* values that never existed before brought enormous wealth to the creator. Creating values also brought enormous exhilaration to the creator. The transformation worked for *any* job, from the bricklayer to the Wall Street executive. Eventually, every ordinary employee became an in-house entrepreneur.[1]

In short, every responsibility in every business simply attached to its money-making purpose. All responsibilities came together into integrated chunks of essence — into wealth-building jobs. Responsibilities no longer remained detached from their money-making purposes forming routine-rut jobs such as today's jobs. Responsibilities no longer were such ends in themselves — dead ends. Instead, they became exciting means to an end — BUILD WEALTH!

Realize that each wealth-building job was a job for one person. The integrated responsibilities were never broken from their money-making purpose, not even with growth of the business. For, once a responsibility got split from its money-making purpose, then that created a specialized, routine-rut job that was not integrated with making money — a dead-end job

---

[1]For an in-depth treatment of the division of essence and its 21st-century entrepreneurial jobs of the mind, see *Neo-Tech Business Control*, Mark Hamilton, 740 pages.

with no essence.

As I watched my Fifth Vision, a question arose in my mind: "As a business grows, how could a person single-handedly handle a wealth-building job without delegating some of the responsibilities to others?" Then I saw the answer: as a business grows, the *number of responsibilities* in a wealth-building job do not grow. The *number of projects* and *volume of business* grow. More marketing projects form *within* each marketing program. Each new marketing project can potentially break off into its own wealth-building job with a very similar and complete set of responsibilities attached to its money-making purpose. Those new wealth-building projects get transferred (i.e., get replicated, as learned later) to other persons along with the similar or same group of responsibilities. That way, as the company grows, every person's job remains an exciting wealth-building job — a chunk of the company's essence. As the business grows, the wealth-building jobs continue to divide again and again into more and more wealth-building jobs, every job always remaining an exciting, wealth-building job of the mind with a marketing format to build profits as an in-house mini-company by an in-house entrepreneur.

Most jobs today merely MAINTAIN the business. Very few jobs give one the chance to BUILD WEALTH. Are *your* job responsibilities integrated means with which to build wealth? Or are they specialized ends in themselves, dead-end routine chores? Chances are you are stuck in a boring routine rut!

But that will change. My Fifth Vision showed me that you could build wealth in the Neo-Tech World. Building wealth became the ends into which your job responsibilities converged. Responsibilities then became potent integrated MEANS to build wealth, not impotent specialized ENDS in themselves to routinely turn in.

For example, you saw in Diagram One my company's basic responsibilities, a total of fifteen basic responsibilities. Traditional publishing/direct-mail companies make each of those basic responsibilities a separate job or department. Therefore, those dead-end departments and their jobs cannot build wealth and grow.

But I used my Fifth Vision of the supersociety's division of essence to break out of the anticivilization's routine-rut jobs. You saw, in Diagram Four, Integrated Management's wealth-building jobs, pulling together the basic responsibilities into their money-making purposes. Those dynamic jobs of the mind immediately started building wealth and growing without limits. They represent tomorrow's work force.

Today, under the division of labor, most people never experience building wealth. The division of labor scatters job responsibilities into specialized routine ruts. The division of essence, on the other hand, attaches those same job responsibilities to their money-making purposes. Today, in the anticivilization, job responsibilities are ends in themselves instead of integrated means to making money. Therefore, nearly all jobs today are non-growth, dead-end routine ruts in which people cannot build wealth, cannot grow, thus stagnate. They are trapped all their lives in the bicameral mentality at work – automatically reacting to their routine tasks day after day. The ordinary person quietly becomes unhappy as he or she sinks into miserable stagnation under the division-of-labor business structure. The conscious mind is not meant to stagnate, which goes against its nature. The conscious mind is meant to create. The ordinary person's routine rut becomes his prison, his creativity the prisoner.

Becoming the Person We Once Dreamed of Being

Whatever happened to the person we once dreamed about being? Most of us got trapped in a routine-rut job year after year. As the burden of life grew, the creative person we were meant to be got hopelessly buried and forgotten.

Under the division of labor, we sank in stagnation; we suffered in silent frustration, forever forgetting about the creative and wealthy person we once dreamed about. In the fascinating Fifth Vision, however, in tomorrow's division of essence, ordinary people *single-handedly* created wealth. Everyone went about making money, by creating values. Creating values is the most exhilarating, natural use of the conscious mind.

Whole families in tomorrow's Neo-Tech World, including the toddlers, got involved in what their parents were building.

Families grew emotionally closer as creating and building values became a family event. Creativity abounded among adults and children alike. You see, children grew up in that exciting entrepreneurial environment. Dinner talk was often filled with Dad's or Mom's latest venture. The idea of creating values and achieving goals excited children, which made them look forward to their futures. The culture changed; children were motivated about growing up to become creative entrepreneurs.

Of course, the workplace today simply is not set up that way. Most parents dread going to work and seldom talk about that miserable place they go to every weekday. Again, the conscious mind is not designed for stagnation.

Fortunately, as seen in my Fifth Vision, as we lost our bicameral longings for higher "authorities" telling us how to live our lives, and we consequently depoliticized America, the freed geniuses and technologies advanced so quickly the job revolution had to occur for businesses to keep up and remain competitive.

The competitive advantage is so clear: the essence of business — building wealth — demands creativity, and the essence of man is his mind, his creativity. Therefore, sitting right below our noses, the most powerful business structure imaginable divides its jobs in such a way that *every employee* uses his or her mind creatively to push the business forward. That business structure is the division of essence. As shown to me in my Vision, the division of essence will become the business structure sometime in the 21st century.

In my Fifth Vision, I could see excitement buzzing about these entrepreneurial jobs of the mind because ordinary people for the first time built profits. Therefore, they inevitably shared in those profits and ultimately in the equity. I cannot do justice to the personal excitement and motivation I witnessed. It was beyond anything we have seen. For the first time, ordinary people everywhere built profits, equity, and power for themselves. The whole family got involved and excited. Their successes were stimulating, which motivated children toward success. As ordinary people everywhere became dynamic in-house entrepreneurs, they discovered the thrill of personal-power in business and togetherness in family.

The Fifth Vision showed me the uniquely creative genius

buried inside a deep, dark corner of every ordinary person's mind. That lost person today achieved amazing accomplishments tomorrow. Companies evolved with the times beyond their stagnant jobs of labor designed for automatically reacting, bicameral mentalities. Companies evolved into dynamic jobs of the mind for creatively thinking, Neothink mentalities. In fact, people's jobs became transmission belts to Neothink. (Neothink is explored in the Ninth Vision and the First Insight.) With Neothink, ordinary people naturally generated exhilarating creative energy and contributed new values to society.

The Miracle of the New Business Paradigm

Consider that every value in society exists because someone, somewhere, sometime exerted creative energy. Moreover, society's prosperity and rising standards of living come from, originally, creative energy put into society. In other words, the more creative energy put into society, then the more values, prosperity, and higher standards of living we enjoy. With a hundred million Neothink entrepreneurs pouring enormous creative energy into society as I witnessed in my Fifth Vision, our prosperity and standards of living broke all the records in the history books and all the economic formulas in the text books. The results were a 21st-century miracle...the miracle of the new business paradigm.

Becoming in-house entrepreneurs in wealth-building jobs, our minds were stimulated, every day...from morning till night. Creative talk about each new accomplishment flowed at the dinner table. Eventually, we surprised ourselves as we evolved into geniuses in our areas of expertise. But we became more than just any geniuses: no, we became *unburdened* geniuses with no risky regulations or litigation holding us back. We rose beyond our previously most ambitious dreams.

A hundred million of us — unrestricted super entrepreneurs — poured energy and creativity into this country, and we zoomed ahead with 21st-century super technologies. The Neo-Tech World of super geniuses and super technologies taking care of us and all our needs, large and small as described in the Tenth Vision, brought everyone millionaire wealth, perfect health, and a supremely happy self...the only possible outcome of so much creative energy flowing into society.

In tomorrow's Neo-Tech World, we no longer did the same boring routines every day while a select few others got powerful and rich. Instead, we built our own businesses within the companies we worked for. We built our own personal power and riches. Our minds shed their bicameral behavioral patterns; we discovered power and creativity, and we got very enthusiastic about working and living. Moreover, our excitement happily overflowed into our romantic-love and family relationships.

Tomorrow's jobs awakened the unknown self in ordinary people everywhere as we steadily became geniuses of society. We experienced honest *power* for the first time in our lives. We became dream builders, achieving dreams in the 21st century beyond our favorite daydreams in the 20th century. We also enjoyed the new sensation of becoming admired and beloved VIPs for our accomplishments.

We traded in our boring division-of-labor routine ruts for exciting division-of-essence wealth-building jobs. Those wealth-building jobs resembled little companies — *mini-companies* run by our minds. We felt alive again and excited by our goals as the age of labor gave way to the age of the mind.

Jobs With Life

The dynamic power behind those jobs in the future was: *life.* Your non-living job today transformed into a living one tomorrow. What exactly made your job alive, dynamic, and growing versus not alive, static, and stagnant?

First had to come the discovery of the "DNA of a job". (DNA is the substance that defines life, found in living cells, causing them to grow and reproduce.) The "DNA of a job" — the substance that makes it a living job...growing and reproducing — is the *money-making purpose.* With money-making purpose (Diagrams 1-4 on pages 89-93), a job comes to life. Its responsibilities come to life and form around the money-making purpose like a living cell around DNA.

In tomorrow's Neo-Tech World, this life-force transformed *every* job as businesses in the supersociety determined the "DNA" of their jobs — the wealth-building purposes. Even the most routine jobs...even specialized construction jobs came to life as workers got involved with the numbers and profits like entrepreneurs.

In today's world, the bricklayer, for instance, knows very little about numbers and profits and is helplessly trapped in his routine rut. Similarly, most division-of-labor jobs give us wealth-building control of *nothing*, trapped in our routine ruts. But as my Fifth Vision showed me, all that changed with the job revolution soon after we depoliticized America.

As your division-of-essence job came to life, it began to "talk". That's right, it actually began to tell you exciting things to do to improve it, wooing your creativity...through the *numbers*. When the time came that you took over a wealth-building job, you paid close attention to what your living job was telling you. In other words, as with every successful entrepreneur, you paid attention to the numbers involving your living job, for improving numbers translated into profits. You made yourself aware of all the numbers, from measuring the smallest details by numbers, by their cost/efficiency...up to the marketing numbers of your living job. Remember, you now had a mini-company to run. Getting close to all those numbers told you an ongoing story. That story led you to ways of improvement, along the path to prosperity. Ironically, the logical numbers opened the window of creativity in your mind as they showed you the way to improvements and advancements. As the numbers helped you discover your creativity, your division-of-essence *job of the mind* tomorrow left your division-of-labor *job of labor* today in the dust.

Money-making purpose always existed throughout business. Not until the job revolution sometime in the 21st century, however, did companies restructure into those wealth-building living jobs. Those new, division-of-essence businesses were like growing, living organisms as their living jobs reproduced like living cells. Just as living cells generate new living cells, those living jobs generated new living jobs.

Most jobs prior to the new business paradigm, by contrast, were not living jobs. They were, in a sense, non-living substances of the business anatomy. They helped hold the business together, but they did not cause the growth of the business. They had no "DNA", no money-making purpose, thus had no life, no growth. They were specialized, ends in themselves — DEAD ends. Their job responsibilities came from delegating specialized dead-end responsibilities and not from replicating integrated living jobs with DNA-like nucleuses. They had no life substance.

Your Money-Generating Factory

Only living cells build protein; only living jobs build wealth. Looking back from my Fifth Vision, today's non-living jobs could not build anything. They just maintained the structure...static and stagnant. In short, they were not alive.

In a living cell exists the ribosome — a protein-generating factory. This protein-generating factory pours out protein to build our bodies with muscle, hair, organs, and so on. Similarly, in tomorrow's living jobs I witnessed something called *the mini-day schedule* — a money-generating factory. That money-generating factory poured out money-making projects to build our wealth-building jobs with wealth and success. Ordinary people moved forward into growing, money-making projects. They built their profits, equity, and power. Realize to do that, they first needed a division-of-essence living job with money-making purpose. They set up their days like a manufacturing factory...say like Ford Motor Company's assembly line. But instead of manufacturing cars, they manufactured success and money.

As did Henry Ford, they applied the division of labor to their "manufacturing factories". Later came the vital ingredient of creativity. But at first, they divided their work into the smooth physical movements of labor. Then, like Henry Ford's record-smashing assembly-line, they broke all conceivable records in their manufacturing of success, money, and power.

Let us compare their superior productivity to today's jobs. Say we list the tasks done in a day by a typical manager. His list would look something like this:
• Organized work for subordinates
• Called Jim Peabody of X & Y Company

- Drafted letter to supplier
- Had meeting with secretary
- Reviewed inventory report

Now if we were to also list the tasks he planned to do but did not have time to do, it might look like this:
- Wanted to write to second supplier
- Wanted to call about new quotes
- Wanted to meet with programmer
- Wanted to update marketing data
- Wanted to organize most current files
- Wanted to talk to longtime employee about friction building

Now if we were to list the tasks he scheduled for the following day, his list could look something like this:
- Will definitely write letter to second supplier
- Will make sure to get new quotes
- Will meet with programmer
- Will not leave till update marketing data
- Will finally organize files
- Will make sure I talk to that longtime employee
- Meet with staff for three-hour weekly meeting in afternoon
- Must prepare for meeting all morning

The example above reflects a common problem with today's managers: They are out of control while getting little done. Even worse, *physical* labor in today's business paradigm traps most of the working class in inescapable ruts. Most are at the mercy of their bicameral tendencies, needing to be told what to do instead of using their own minds to generate direction and build competitive creations.

Gathering Control

In my Vision of tomorrow's living jobs, on the other hand, existed the money-making "factory" that enabled ordinary people to double then triple then quadruple their productivity by dividing work into smooth physical movements. Diagram Five on the next two pages provides an example of just three days of tasks I personally did using the money-making "factory" witnessed in my Vision.

How did I easily handle that seemingly overwhelming list in just three days? Consider the task of delivering the overwhelming number of pieces of U.S. mail each day. If that mail were dumped into large piles for the mailmen to fill their bags and start delivering — the first letter to an address perhaps on the west side, the next letter perhaps to the south side, the next letter back to the west side — the physically disjointed mail-delivery system would get hopelessly behind. Similarly, the physically disjointed, traditional work schedule today gets hopelessly behind.

As the overwhelming U.S. mail must be divided into smooth physical movements — the easy-to-handle carrier-route sorts — my overwhelming job that previously never got finished was divided into smooth physical movements, into a few easy-to-handle physical movements that now always get done.

To divide my living job, my mini-company, into smooth physical movements, I wrote down and studied three days of tasks. From those tasks, I identified only six physical movements. I identified: (1) Phone Calls, (2) Letter Writing, (3) Copy Writing, (4) Accounting, (5) Meetings, (6) Operations.

Like a manufacturing factory, each movement is a raw physical act. Making phone calls, for example, like driving in rivets on the assembly line, requires a smooth physical movement — picking up the phone and dialing no matter what the call is about. Look over my three days of tasks, and notice that I make a number of phone calls. To make a phone call, I make a physical movement. The movement remains the same no matter who I call or what I call about. Go through the list and put a #1 next to all phone calls.

Next you can see that I write a number of letters. To write a letter requires a physical movement regardless who I write or what I write about. Put a #2 next to the letter-writing tasks.

I develop ads and product copy. Copy writing too is an independent movement. That is #3. Mark all copy writing tasks #3.

I spend substantial time doing finances, bookkeeping,

Diagram Five

My Three Days Of Completed Tasks

- Call Stuart to uncover lucrative French Canadian magazines for ad
- Write letter to Nightingale-Conant to rent profitable list
- Copy write revolutionary videotape production
- Call and negotiate KCI masterfile for potential European profits
- Call Jim Tegtmire, review in detail envelope quotes
- Write Stuart C. about discount on older, large mailing lists
- Write e-mail letter to British on organizing Europe mailing
- Make format corrections on new "expanding envelope" idea
- Fill out and send 2nd-class application to post office
- Meet with Keri to further organize Summit
- Meet with Helen to supervise IBM computer process
- Hold interviews for job opening
- Arrange insertion in Strategic Investing Newsletter
- Organize business trip to Europe this weekend
- Call InterMarket Magazine to negotiate "expanding envelope"
- Call around other video shops for better deal
- Write e-mail letter to Peter R. in England about lettershop process
- Study costs, set up costs, overall company costs
- Review lettershop invoices and correct problems developing
- Train new employee
- Call Data For Graphics' typesetters about ads
- Write e-mail letter to Irish Agency: business center in Ireland
- Review financial records; develop financial statement
- Meet with WW, president
- Call Better Investing and negotiate "expanding envelope"
- Write Newsletter Management about their list, negotiate their list
- Write Brian K. of Boardroom a note about discounting list
- Write Bernard letter preparing extensive meeting in Canada, Oct.
- Go through in-basket (each day)
- Organize sections in office for daily inspection
- Study job applications for customer service and accounting

(continued next page)

Diagram Five
(continued)
My Three Days of Completed Tasks

- Call Don P. about space ad
- Call Bill Levine with final Moneysworth edits
- Write two letters to authorities
- Make purchase order to Linden Computer Services
- Review Helen W.'s writing: edit, copyright new profitable product
- Review accounting procedures with HW
- Call Maclean Hunter, leads on big Canadian lists
- Call "La Opinion" to inquire about new, Spanish-speaking market
- Write letter to HUME about doing business together in Canada
- Make corrections in Andrews Printing invoice
- Meet with Melinda
- Call Blue Shield to establish new insurance policy
- Meet with Vicki
- Meet with Kay
- Call Newsletter Management to confirm deal
- Write "mass" letter for "expanding envelope" concept
- Write Canadian DMA for leads on printers
- Design brief coupon for split test on free-offer newsletter
- Make and send "expanding envelope" mock to Don Perry
- Develop outline and start copywriting report with FW, joint venture
- Review all data and effects on finances, set up new incoming data
- Meet with Shelly
- Call Lori D. of Success Magazine to run inquiry ad
- Call LA Times to run classified and get information on other ads
- Call Metro Mail, quotes in acquiring phone number, telemarketing
- Write e-mail letter to Peter R. in England about invoice
- Meet with Keri
- Call PSA computer shop for schedule to put up names
- Call the National Enquirer about ad
- Call Mega Media about inquiry ad in Globe
- Call West Coast Video about production
- Meet with WW, president

accounting, creative accounting, and invoice review. Mark all financial matters #4.

Although many approaches and techniques exist for meetings, holding meetings still is a specific physical act. Mark all meetings with a #5.

To determine the final movement, look over the tasks; all but a few are marked off. The remaining unmarked tasks do not seem to link together into a related movement. Those disjointed, leftover tasks are the culprits of nitpicking work that once shot my day to shreds. Now I could finally corner them. You see, in my Vision, all living jobs had disjointed tasks left over. Those seemingly disjointed tasks actually all fall under one physical movement — the physical movement of operating the mini-company. Now I could finally capture those problem makers into one movement to blast through in one shot. In my living job, I move forward all day long in other important movements, momentum not destroyed by nitpicking work. Number those now-harmless tasks with a #6.

Now notice the same unwieldy three days of tasks when streamlined into their physical movements (on the next page). Diagram Six shows my 21st-century mini-company divided into the smooth physical movements. Notice the assembly-line efficiency as everything moves toward simplicity.

Putting Your New Power To Work

Now I put the physical movements to work, just as I witnessed in my Fifth Vision. Consider that small personal computers years ago broke through to produce almost any image — abstract designs, quality pictures, even motion pictures. The small home computers produce those advanced images through a two-step process: First, they break down complex images to their handful of fundamental shapes. Indeed, every shape on earth comes from a handful of fundamental shapes just as all colors on earth come from three fundamental colors — red, yellow, and blue. Second, the home computers interlock little specks of that handful of fundamental shapes by the hundreds to form advanced images with incredible speed, power, and control. The ability to produce complex images has become

Diagram Six

The Rich Man's
Same Three Days Of Tasks By Physical Movements

Physical Movement #1: Phone Calls

- Call Stuart
- Call KCI
- Call Jim T.
- Call InterMarket
- Call Video Shops
- Call Data-For-Graphics
- Call Better Investing
- Call Don P.
- Call Bill L.
- Call Maclean Hunter
- Call La Opinion
- Call Blue Cross/Blue Shield
- Call Newsletter Management
- Call Lori D.
- Call LA Times
- Call Metro Mail
- Call PSA
- Call National Enquirer
- Call Stuart, Mega Media
- Call West Coast Video

Physical Movement #2: Letter Writing

- Write Nightingale-Conant
- Write Stuart
- Write e-mail to British authorities
- Write e-mail to Peter R.
- Write e-mail to Francis, Ireland
- Write Newsletter Management
- Write Brian K.
- Write Bernard M.
- Write letter for authorities
- Write HUME
- Write expanding-envelope letter
- Write Canadian DMA
- Write e-mail to Peter R.

Physical Movement #3: Copy Writing

- Script for Video Production
- Edit Helen W.'s new product
- Write outline, start writing joint book with FW

Physical Movement #4: Accounting

- Study costs
- Review invoices
- Review records
- Understand HW's procedures
- Correct Andrews invoice
- Data review

Physical Movement #5: Meetings and People

- Meet with Keri
- Meet with Helen
- Meet with WW
- Meet with Melinda
- Meet with Vicki
- Meet with Kay
- Meet with Shelly
- Meet with Keri
- Meet with WW

Physical Movement #6: Operations

- Corrections expl. envelope
- 2nd-class application
- Interviews and training
- Strategic Investing insertion
- Prepare for European trip
- Train new employee
- In-basket each day
- Sections for inspection
- Study job file
- PO to Linden
- Layout for newsletter
- Mock expanding envelope to Don

simple and efficient.

Similarly, my complex mini-company breaks down to a few fundamental movements. Just as the many colors and many shapes all reduce to a few fundamental colors and shapes, the many projects and deals in my mini-company all reduce to a few fundamental movements. I interlock all the little tasks of that handful of basic movements by the hundreds to perform advanced business moves with amazing speed, power, and control. The ability to manage my complex mini-company has become simple and efficient.

As in my Vision, after determining my basic movements, I determined the approximate activity of each movement. In other words, I estimated the percentage of my 10-hour day that I *should* devote to each movement. Recognize that I estimated what I should devote, not necessarily what I was devoting at the time. I estimated the following percentages:

(1)	Phone Calls	20%	or	2	hrs.
(2)	Letter Writing	15%	or	1.5	hrs.
(3)	Copy Writing	10%	or	1	hrs.
(4)	Accounting	20%	or	2	hrs.
(5)	Meetings	15%	or	1.5	hrs.
(6)	Operations	20%	or	2	hrs.

Then, I made a daily schedule as follows:

8:00-10:00am	Phone Calls (2 hrs.)
10:00-11:30	Letter Writing (1.5 hrs.)
11:30-1:30pm	Operations (2 hrs.)
1:30-2:30	Copy Writing (1 hrs.)
2:30-4:30	Accounting (2 hrs.)
4:30-6:00	Meetings (1.5 hrs.)

Now, look over my schedule, "Three Days Of Tasks Interlocked" on the next page. I do not schedule my *tasks* to time as does the traditional daily schedule. I schedule my *physical movements* to time (just as the assembly-line does not schedule tasks to time as in the hand-built days; it schedules the physical movements to time stations).

The Job of Your Dreams Is Coming

Diagram Seven

The Money-Making Factory
Three Days Of Tasks Interlocked

MONDAY, AUG. 7 249/146	TUESDAY, AUG. 8 220/145	WEDNESDAY, AUG. 9 221/144
Phone Calls 8:00	Phone Calls 8:00	Phone Calls 8:00
✓Stuart → Spanish & French Can. Magazines	✓Brian @ Better Inv. → expl. env.	✓Kathy @ Newsletter Mgt → deal
✓Karen Johnson, KCI ✓ letter	✓Don Perry → Money Making Mag.	✓Lori Dub → "Ticket" ad
✓Jim Tegtmire → order die cut + quotes on CS	✓Bill Levine → final Moneysworth edits	✓LA Times → Classified ad
✓Inter Market → deal	✓MacClean Hunter → leads on big lists & Canadian printers	✓metro Mail → phone #s
✓Make arrangements, video	✓"La Opinion" Irene Wangter (213) 748-2141	✓PSA → ph #s ? - Stuart
✓Data for Graphics	✓Blue Cross → Shelly 382-3302	✓National Eng. & Globe → "Ticket"
Letter Writing 10:00	Letter Writing 10:00	✓APPOINTMENT West Coast Video 9:00
✓Write Vic Conant → ✓ 8 rent list	✓Write Newsletter Mgt. → ✓ 8 list	✓Expl. Env. letter to mass mags.
✓Write similar to Stuart → ✓ 8	✓Send Orrin a note on #40M	✓Canadian DMA → printers
✓E-mail British Authorities	✓Bernard Mooney → meet in Oct	✓E-mail Peter R. → 8s
✓E-mail Peter R., England	✓Authority letters	
✓E-mail Francis L., Ireland	✓HUME Canadian	
Operations 11:30	Operations 11:30	Operations 11:30
✓Basket	✓Basket - Sections in office & in out	✓Basket - expl. envelope
✓Corrections on expl. env.	✓Study job-file applicants	✓Ad copy for test on newsletter
✓Send in 2nd Class application	for Cust. Service & Accountant	✓Design heading for newsletter
✓Interviews & training	✓Interviews & training	✓Interviews & training
✓Strategic Inv. → insertion order	✓Purchase Order Linden & PSA	✓Mock to Don Perry
✓Prepare operations for my departure to Europe	✓Prepare operations for my departure to Europe	✓Prepare operations for my departure to Europe
Copy Writing 1:30	Copy Writing 1:30	Copy Writing 1:30
✓Video tape production	✓Helen → go over, give direction quick edit → then let her	✓Prepare outline, details
✓Pre-production	work more on it	for book w/FW & turn over
Accounting 2:30	Accounting 2:30	Accounting 2:30
✓Records	✓Records	✓Records
✓Invoices	✓Cost study	✓Cost study
✓Study costs → set up cost-	✓HW procedures	✓HW procedures
study program w/HW	✓Andrews corrections	✓Review data & set up SH
Meetings 4:30	Meetings 4:30	Meetings 4:30
✓Meet w/KJ → mailing lists & Summit	✓Melinda → set up "salvage"	✓Shelly → review my outline of organization
✓Helen → finish IBM	✓Vicki → policies & fines	✓Keri → Summit
✓HW	✓Kay → collections turn over + set up mailings from home	✓WW → European plans
Evening	Evening	Evening
✓Work on NT Management	✓NT Management	✓Work on GT's brochure:
brochure	brochure	"A Day of Consultation"
✓Work on NT Mgt. book	✓Final Chapter edits	✓Personal night w/Grace

← Clip for Current Week

Driving Home Success

Indeed, the inferior traditional schedule that schedules tasks to time is like the inferior hand-built car process, the traditional way during the early 1900s that scheduled tasks to time — to the time-consuming tasks of putting in and adjusting the steering wheel, then carrying over and hand-fitting the seats, collating the rubber and rim and then putting on the wheel, and so on. Today's traditional schedule misses the interlocking integration of scheduling the physical movements to time, out of which surface intensified, streamlined, physically integrated tasks like the intensified, streamlined tasks of a rivet-man in an assembly-line.

Look closely at my three-day schedule on the previous page. I *drive home* my physically integrated tasks like the rivet man drives home rivets. Like the rivet man driving in rivet! after rivet! after rivet!...I push out phone call! after phone call! after phone call! I do not walk over and have a meeting, then pick up the phone to make a call, then try my hand at a little copy writing, then make another call, then draft a letter. Such a common scenario among businessmen could be compared to the old way of building cars by putting the seats in, then coming over and putting in the brakes, changing tools to work on the steering wheel, then stopping for a lunch break. No, I just "drive that rivet home", drive it home. In my Vision, upon integrating movements to time, the average person soared beyond all productivity records just as the development of the assembly-line soared past all productivity records.

Quadrupling Success

The new schedule first doubled, then tripled, then quadrupled my intensity. To my delight, I discovered intensity was the most leveraged time-management tool. For example, previously I tried several popular time-management courses; they offered unrealistic disciplines to find an extra hour to two hours in a day. Even if I could handle the disciplines, how much good was an extra hour? Aside from not being worth the effort, that extra hour would not make me a money/power giant.

Now consider that as I doubled my intensity, I basically doubled my capacity. Suddenly, I in a sense gained ten extra hours in my day! As I tripled my intensity, I gained twenty extra hours in my day! With a physically streamlined schedule to run my mini-company, my intensity continued to multiply up to *many times* what it once was. Suddenly, I was in businessman's heaven!

The physically streamlined schedule on page 109 deceives the reader as to just how much I really accomplished. Like observing a skillful athlete, the simplicity and ease of the new schedule tends to camouflage the significance of this money-making factory. See Diagram Eight over the next five pages, however, to get a perspective of the volume of my living job. To appreciate the intensity generated by my streamlined schedule, which I patterned after tomorrow's schedules I saw in my Fifth Vision, realize that everything on that five-page power-thinking list was done or was put into motion in *one week*. (Diagram Seven, "Three Days Interlocked" on page 109, shows Monday through Wednesday of that week.) A lot was on that list in Diagram Eight. All those money-making projects were pushed through the money-making factory in a week! That happened by creating intense pockets of time interlocked to the physical movements.

Ordinary People, Extraordinary Jobs

Most remarkable, consider that you, your neighbor, your son or daughter in high school could handle my schedule. That's no exaggeration. You could easily make phone calls, write letters, go through the in-basket and stay on my schedule. Yes, you could sit down tomorrow in the seat of a high-powered entrepreneur and orchestrate his highly complex job. With the 21st-century division-of-labor schedule, any great career could be yours. In my Fifth Vision, ordinary people orchestrated dynamic, dream-building mini-companies.

Let us look at the underlying concept that allows ordinary people to handle dynamic entrepreneurial jobs in tomorrow's living jobs. Go back for a moment to the eighteenth-century economist Adam Smith who identified that dividing labor into

Diagram Eight

Power-Thinking List
Week of 8/19 – 8/25

Europe
- Read first test results
- Determine results of British Postal Meeting; make decisions on mailing lists as a result of meeting
- Boardroom negotiate price to rent entire file
- KCI negotiate price 550M...call Karen and lower price
- Newsletter Management negotiate price...send letter to lower price
- Nightingale Conant negotiate price
- Cogan's masterfiles such as Shindler masterfile
- Then continue in big numbers from there

Expanding Envelope
- Finishing designing and typesetting
- Have first batch printed
- InterMarket arrange
- Better Investing call for test
- Design letter to ad director of several magazines
- Call Money Making and try it there

Inserts
- Send Strategic Investing order for October issue
- Print 32M brochures; print 32M remittance envelopes
- Test Newsletter Management with 300M universe

AMS Lettershop
- Test new 8-page newspaper format
- Test tabloid in larger size envelope; have Pacific Envelope print larger size envelope
- Test placing conversion notice first
- Test logo coupon vs. regular
- Put some lists through women-purge program; test repeat of 2nd quarter Shindler to increase universe
- Ticket to Success test; if looks good, go back to England test

Space Media
- Test Moneysworth; Better Living; good space deals
- Test Neo-Tech Management ad; go in all good publications that rejected Neo-Tech ad — send brochure
- Test "Ticket to Success" ad in Spanish-speaking magazine; set ad

112

Diagram Eight
(continued)
Power-Thinking List
Week of 8/19 – 8/25

through Stuart
- Test "Ticket to Success" ad in French-speaking Canadian magazine; check with Stuart if knows market
- Test 1/6 page "Ticket to Success" ad in next issue of Success to demonstrate if nature of ad can run time after time such as Mellinger's 1/6 page ads, year after year, building recognition and credibility. If so, study different magazines.
- Test "Ticket to Success" bind-in card in magazine; test versus exploding envelope in InterMarket
- Of course, pursue exploding envelope as indicated above
- Classified ad
- Pick up National Enquirer and determine best inquiry ad size
- Pick up and study different publications and ads.

Canadian Market
- Run "Ticket to Success" in several Canadian publications as a) a feeler ad, and b) good strategy for them to get used to us to accept 4-page or expanding envelope
- Set Fiduciary loose on testing Canadian lists
- Establish a Canadian mail house in October while in Montreal
- Get a huge-volume list and mail via BMI into Canada
- Test French brochure to French-Canadian names - via AMS 106
- Send Claudette letter for leads

Neo-Tech Management Book
- Finish brochure and mail from England before October 1st to best 70M Neo-Tech names
- Finish editing...to WW
- Finish final chapter
- Ongoing product development

Gary's Area
- Finish brochure and mail from England hopefully before October 1st to all Neo-Tech buyers minus RIBI names
- Provide GT with necessary information to produce "A Day of Consultation"
- Encourage and work closely with GT on developing cassette tapes on each concept — "Tape of the Month Club"
- Begin developing brochure for monthly cassettes

Diagram Eight
(continued)
Power-Thinking List
Week of 8/19 – 8/25

Keri's Area

- Encourage development and growth of Fiduciary Lists as it expands into large operation with perhaps added help
- Encourage and work closely in BMI and mailings as KJ will become in charge of those mailings and acquiring the mailing lists
- Shoot for first Neo-Tech Summit in November:
  1) Finish ad copy
  2) KJ find out best time to mail prior to Summit
  3) Mail to 3M RIBI Names
  4) My good opportunity to do our first telemarketing test. If works, do them all and MH start for Integrated Management Associates
  5) Have a blast in Las Vegas come November
- Work with KJ to write out philosophical linkages of Paradise Valley to man's nature...why different. Then will publish that in some mailing to monitor immediate interest.

Kay's Area

- Take a good list and run through "common-women names" program and pull out good select of women so Kay's mini-company can make money while testing. Great source of names once get started; can establish "core" lists as does Integrated Management and have good income while pursuing more profitable lists.
- Test three approaches; keep on 4-page format for test, for this is different ball game; after 1st test then may switch to 8-page format, depending on results of 3-way test.
- Work closely with Kay to develop "Ticket to Success" 1/6 page ad for women. Test in low-cost magazine.
- Could women be similar in nature to Japanese and other Far East cultures? Could they need to first develop trust with a company? Make 3-way test a 4-way test and test women's "Ticket to Success" as an inquiry postcard through the mail.
- Pending on British Postal Meeting, will eventually start testing from England once find substantial names to work with, which may warrant Kay traveling to England if her mailings really got rolling.
- Set up and turn over profitable decline, invalid, bad-check program to Kay's mini-company. A good sustaining income.
- Finish questionnaire and insert to go with her booklist mailing to Neo-Tech names.

Diagram Eight
(continued)
Power-Thinking List
Week of 8/19 – 8/25

Frank's Area
- Provide FW with outline idea of book
- Let FW read Neo-Tech Management book
- Start program of weekly writing with FW

Helen's Area
- Work closely with Helen guiding her writing
- Work heavily with editing as she provides me her drafts

Ruth's Area
- Develop makeshift video cassette with wedding tape, cutting, narrating, and dubbing in music and narration
- Provide Ruth and John idea and makeshift videos
- Let them do one on their own with my narration edits to their music and drama...great potential
- Eventually perhaps blend in with GT's tape-of-the-month product

Neo-Tech Newsletter/2nd-class project
- Test the newsletter concept AMS 105
- Work with FW and WW on newsletter
- Apply for 2nd-class mail
- Advertise back-end plus send out brochure to other 50% if more profitable
- Pursue with local postal authorities and those in CA

Writing Projects
- Neo-Tech Management Book
- Neo-Tech Management brochure
- A Day of Consultation brochure
- Neo-Tech Summit brochure editing
- Children's concepts, Neo-Tech
- Two chapters of "Money/Power Through Successful Love"
- Doris insert and questionnaire
- Booklist insert
- New product — Look and See
- Article about loving your work means making the most money, even if money means little to you
- Letter to Peter
- New CCL letter

Diagram Eight
(continued)
Power-Thinking List
Week of 8/19 – 8/25

- Prepare consultation on Mini-Day and Power-Thinking for in-house meeting
- Prepare consultation on Mini-Day and Power-Thinking for Summit
- Never can lie — right brain. Support structure

Internal Operations (Vicki, Helen, Shelly)

- Hard copy checks of everything
- Install long overdue fine system
- "Shake-up"
- Set up "salvage" programs as discover mistakes
- Interview job applicants
- Search job file to bring in a customer service and public relations full time, ambitious employee; will determine how to set up as self-motivated entrepreneur
- Daily organization put into office — becoming straight and tight; want to have the tightest office in the country
- Set up auditing control on everything, including bank check-in, check-out control on returns
- Bank-like control on all orders
- Bank-like control on all correspondence, computer work, and customer service with MH personal check now
- Collection to go to entrepreneurial-motivated Kay
- Fine system to clean up non-conscientious work
- Drawers and files and storage becoming a pleasure to enter, not a drag — every desk and cabinet
- Job file search — Accountant, customer service

Late Notes and Additions:

Accounting

- Search for CPA — run ad, contact RIBI customers
- Numbers man — study response

Mailing list project

- Orders 18-24 to Linden, to PSA, into 8C
- RIBI's to Linden, to PSA
- Orders 8C & RIBI's to MetroMail — phone numbers
- To Newsletter Management or Astro for telemarketing list

smaller and smaller units could build wealth at greater and greater speeds. Throughout the Industrial Revolution, society divided labor into smaller and smaller units — into the physical movements of survival — and became highly integrated. For instance, many people now worked for each individual making his clothes, farming his food, building his home, making his tools, his furniture and so on instead of each individual doing it all himself as done centuries ago.

As society became highly integrated through dividing labor, the economy became increasingly successful, and the act of living became increasingly easy. For instance, the street sweeper in the early 21st century lives with better choices of food, clothes, entertainment, travel than the aristocrats a few hundred years ago, even a few decades ago. Indeed, the division of labor changed the world forever. The division of labor caused the Industrial Revolution that eventually made America the most integrated thus the most prosperous civilization in history.

In the early 1900s, Henry Ford catapulted the power of the Industrial Revolution. Ford Motor Company divided labor into the smallest possible units — into the physical movements of production — and created the world's most integrated production method: the assembly-line.

The assembly-line integrated literally every split second of production. Dividing labor down to the precision movement of the rivet man, for instance, greatly intensified and simplified each split second for a tighter and tighter, no-waste integrated system. As Ford divided labor into smaller and smaller movements, his business went through production records with greater and greater profits. Indeed, the division of labor made Ford Motor Company the most integrated thus the most prosperous car company in the world.

My physically streamlined money-making factory captures the essence behind America's rise to power and Ford Motor Company's rise to dominance. Of course, only tomorrow's living jobs, not today's non-living routine ruts, could successfully accommodate the dynamic division-of-labor schedule, the money-making factory for manufacturing money and success. You see, without money-making purpose — the "DNA" of a living job — then the physical movements to making money could not

117

really exist; instead, we would remain bound to the same narrow set of specialized tasks day after day after day. We would continue in an automatically reacting, bicameral-like mode, powerless at making money. In tomorrow's living jobs, however, we captured the division-of-labor power in our daily schedules — the same power that lifted the world to modern prosperity — for our own fast-track to success. (Yet, as you will see, that power is just the beginning, for later in this chapter you will witness the multiplying power of the mind.)

Putting Life Under Iron-Grip Control

The key concept behind this power in tomorrow's living jobs is the *mini-day*. For example, I put life under immediate, iron-grip control by treating each of my six movements as a separate day, or mini-day. Treating each mini-day as a full day in itself, I start each mini-day on time and end each mini-day on time. When the mini-day time is up, that day is over, regardless of the amount of tasks that were or were not completed. For, the physical movements, *not tasks*, are integrated to time. Remember, I established the most beneficial relationship of those physical movements to time. Therefore, I do not let one mini-day get more time, for another would get less, which if continued for long would force the integration to get off, force the imbalance of physical movements, force missed tasks needed to complete the integration like cars with missed lug nuts coming off the production-line. By staying strict with the mini-days, I am forced to stay integrated.

I run a calculated, serious mini-company consistently building wealth week by week instead of comically chasing tasks day by day. I have my personal assembly-line of productivity in place and turn it on each day. Immediately I feel good. I negate that annoying uncertainty that some work may not get done. I rapidly move through the tightly integrated tasks of six mini-days. Again, look at my schedule on page 109. It is called the *mini-day schedule:*

Phone Calls	was	Day 1.
Letter Writing	was	Day 2.
Operations	was	Day 3.
Copywriting	was	Day 4.
Accounting	was	Day 5.
Meetings and People	was	Day 6.

The physically integrated tasks light up like a fuse racing to the powder. What took two hours rushing disjointedly before takes fifteen minutes after some experience with the straight-arrow mini-day schedule. My whole day catches fire. Each mini-day is the opposite of the overwhelming, traditional all-day schedule in which lethargy sets in as it would when hand-building a whole car. Instead, I attack each organized movement like the rivet man. Task follows integrated task at high speed with no hesitation. And knowing that once the mini-day ends, time is up for another 24 hours, adds to the intensity. Like cramming for a final-exam deadline, the mini-day deadlines throughout the day stimulate tremendous natural intensity.

Now the question arises: What money-making project do I go after next? How, exactly, do I go about building my mini-company? The answer lies in the "RNA Phenomenon". Let's bring on the power of the mind:

The "RNA Phenomenon"

A living cell contains RNA, the genetic-code messenger. RNA attaches itself to a protein-generating factory and pours in it the information of what exactly to generate. During the Fifth Vision, I witnessed a similar process in tomorrow's living jobs as *power-thinking* attached itself to and poured into the money-generating factory, the mini-day schedule, exactly what to generate. Let's take a look:

First of all, the traditional daily schedule quickly fills to its capacity and can only react day by day to the job at hand. Power-thinking could never attach itself to the traditional daily schedule. The new mini-day schedule, by contrast, rarely fills to its capacity. Power-thinking easily attaches to that money-generating factory in the living job. For example, racing through streamlined tasks, I found myself done with all my week's work by Tuesday afternoon. I was stunned. With nothing left to do, I began to think creatively. I began to uncover new money-making projects through power-thinking.

With the mini-day schedule intact, I began reaching out and quickly began pulling in future wealth, goals, projects through power-thinking. For example, I reached out and handled among other things a large, complex project overseas. I initiated major marketing programs in England and Ireland. The new programs were complex and could take many months to start. Instead, I did the following: I focused in my mind the end result. I actually saw in my head the completed project right up to the hundreds of thousands of marketing packages filling a containerized truck being lifted into the ship. In seeing that finished project, I swiftly began to see what I needed to do to achieve that full container. I began focusing on the suppliers I needed to contact, the shipping routes I needed to uncover, the postal systems I needed to work with, the schedules I needed to orchestrate.

I thought about and imaged in my mind as many steps as possible to achieve that container full of my marketing packages and wrote the steps down. I called that list of steps my *power-thinking list*. But my power-thinking list turned into so much more than just projecting ahead, for I fed the projections into the high-intensity action units — the mini-days — that quickly got done. The results pulled me up the ranks as I moved through important projects that other workers and competitors just thought about.

Indeed, I determined the task or tasks needed to complete the first step listed on my power-thinking list, then injected the task(s) into the proper mini-day(s). I then did that for each step listed on my power-thinking list. I quickly took control.

In one day I did, among several other things, the following: During my phone-call mini-day I called the major printing consultant in Ireland, contacted the marketing manager of the Irish An Post, called a printer in England and discussed a large test mailing; during my letter-writing mini-day I drafted a letter to the Irish postal authorities; during the operations mini-day I organized some data to indicate what mailing lists I would consider using; during the accounting mini-day I did a brief cost analysis on mailing abroad; during my meeting mini-day I discussed the overseas possibilities with my in-house mailing list broker to set her in action, I also reviewed with two executive officers the tentative plan with nearly a full-scale layout. I did all that among other productive tasks in one day. I did more in one day toward completing that project than most would do in a month. By the next day, people on both sides of the Atlantic were moving into action, all moving the project toward completion.

The New Dimension

My high-capacity mini-day schedule opened to me the whole new dimension of power-thinking. I could suddenly power-think large, major projects and rapidly move them into action. I left my previous self in the dust, for my previous low-capacity traditional schedule blocked me from power-thinking new money-making projects as I barely kept up with my routine job. Before, I just reacted to business. I was just an ordinary guy. Now, I controlled and built business. I had become an in-house entrepreneur for the company I then worked for. The founder of the company was so impressed that he promptly gave me a major promotion, pay increase, and bonus. ...Yet anyone could have done it. With the mini-day/power-thinking team, you or your son or daughter in high school (save for actual hands-on experience) could have done what I did that day.

The results of power-thinking just pulled me up the hierarchy. My Vision showed me that ordinary people tomorrow with power-thinking put lucrative projects through their mini-day production-lines each week that people today would not even think about in their entire lives. Those in-house entrepreneurs tomorrow dynamically cranked out several projects at a time as they compiled future projects into that week's mini-days. Tomorrow, people on the mini-day/power-thinking team running their mini-companies, as I witnessed in the Fifth Vision, built exciting success in the new business paradigm instead of just maintaining a boring job under the old paradigm.

Imagine that not long after I discovered the mini-day/power-thinking team in my Fifth Vision, I had 22 projects on my power-thinking list. Underneath those projects were 150 steps needed to accomplish those 22 projects. Within one week, every step was accomplished or moved into flowing action. Before the mini-day/power-thinking team, I had problems just keeping up with my routine work, trapped in a routine rut, sinking in stagnation with no way to even think about *just one* forward-movement project in one week. How did I go from not accomplishing one project to 22 lucrative projects a week? That was quite a leap.

Going Beyond the Capacity of Your Mind

Consider that the average person's mind can focus on only one project at a time, with its five or six thoughts. His mind certainly could not cope with 22 projects, 150 tasks, for he would be paralyzed. I, on the other hand, easily coped with 22 projects at a time, with its 150 tasks. I easily did that through power-thinking: First, I determined the steps needed to complete a project by focusing in my mind the completed project. I focused on one project at a time. I uncovered and listed the steps needed to complete the project. Then I put that project out of my mind altogether to make room for the next project. At this point, I had formed a maximum-integration puzzle piece to a success puzzle.

I then concentrated on the next project. I imagined the completed project and wrote down the steps to reach that image. Now I had formed another maximum-integration puzzle piece to the success puzzle. Then I cleared my mind and went on to the next project, and so on, each project forming another puzzle piece to the success puzzle. Those puzzle pieces snapped together into the mini-day schedule, and my growing puzzle pictures led me into Neothink.

I did my power-thinking on Sunday and injected my entire power-thinking list into my next week's mini-day schedule. The human mind can focus intensely on just one project — no more. But with the use of special tools, ordinary people tomorrow operated beyond their mental processing capacity. The mini-day/

power-thinking team was their 21st-century tool that let them go beyond the capacity of their minds — their 21st-century tool to building major Neothink success puzzles.

Power-thinking tomorrow captured vague ambitions, goals, projects into tangible steps. The steps further broke down into specific tasks when injected into the mini-days. Ambitions, goals, projects broke down, down, down to earth...down to tasks that got done. By plugging those tasks into the intense mini-days, average people tomorrow yanked in faraway dreams right away, right down to quick-action reality.

Everything You Want...In the Palm of Your Hand

Of course, only the living jobs of the future accommodated such wealth-building mini-day/power-thinking dynamics. Ordinary people tomorrow in living jobs routinely reached forward, grabbed hold of their most ambitious goals and projects with power-thinking, and brought them back to themselves right away with the mini-days. Ordinary people experienced those accomplishments not only sometime within their lifetimes, but right away and then moved on to even bigger and better accomplishments. Ordinary people like you and me discovered the exhilaration of moving through goals. Think now about *your* ambitions, your goals. With a living job and its mini-day/power-thinking team, you can bring everything you want into the palm of your hand, right now.

So, there you have it — the three main components that constitute life: the DNA, the ribosome protein-generating factory, and the RNA. Our jobs in tomorrow's new business paradigm came to life with money-making purpose ("DNA"), a money-generating mini-day schedule (a "ribosome"), and power-thinking ("RNA").

Vision Five showed me that in the new world of Neothink mentalities, sometime in the 21st century, you and your peers enjoyed a living job. Once you took over the responsibilities of a living job — that money-making purpose — then you built abundant wealth with your mini-day/power-thinking team, always listening to your mini-company, talking to you in numbers. You became the 21st-century profit-making entrepreneur of your 20th-century dreams. You realized your Fifth Gift of the Neo-Tech World: excelling in the career of your dreams.

Vision Six
The Company You Always Wanted To Work For *Can Now Be Yours*

The Living Company

Now, let me tell you how businesses looked dramatically different in my Sixth Vision, after the job revolution that shed bicameral mentalities at work. Similar to our 21st-century jobs, our 21st-century companies came to life. Business and its many Neothink geniuses took care of every need we could possibly imagine and even needs we never imagined. Breathtaking business breakthroughs became exciting topics of discussion. Instead of politics, tomorrow's front-page news media was packed full every day with the latest technological breakthroughs. People checked their computers for news sometimes two, three, or more times a day to get the latest updates on breakthroughs. People tomorrow would check the news with far greater enthusiasm than people today. Checking the latest breakthroughs was more stimulating than checking the latest football scores or the latest movie releases, for the technological breakthroughs directly boosted the reader's standard of living. Sports stars and movie stars, by the way, took a distant second in popularity and fame to business stars, for business stars brought wealth, health, and excitement directly to the people. Indeed, ordinary people became the beneficiaries of the new, living businesses with their workforces of creative Neothink geniuses. ...Let me take a moment to show you the anatomy of tomorrow's exciting living businesses making it all possible:

Physical Growth

In my Sixth Vision, I witnessed the most amazing thing: businesses were divided not like most businesses today into lifeless jobs, but into living ones. Instead of employees draining the cash flow, they actually generated cash flow! After all, the entrepreneurial employees ran mini-companies within the company. They faced their jobs with entrepreneurial intensity.

In fact, tomorrow's living companies established some form of performance pay and, eventually, equity programs to drive their employees' motivation to new heights.

More and more 21st-century businesses divided their companies into these wealth-building living jobs by transferring to employees complete, integrated wealth-building nuggets, not by turning over specialized responsibilities. Each employee got a money-making purpose with its complete chunk of attached responsibilities versus a stagnant bunch of routine responsibilities delegated without regard to their money-making purpose, their "DNA", the essence of life. The process that effectively transferred those wealth-building living jobs was called: *replicating.*

Imagine being able to reproduce a company's original entrepreneur. Say he could clone himself to fill every job in his company. Well, his company would boom. In my Vision, replicating himself came close to filling his company with himself. The companies that grew through replicating were filled with people with the same life-code as the original entrepreneurs.

Companies still under the old 20th-century paradigm, on the other hand, grew through delegating and were filled with people with no life-code in non-living jobs. Those division-of-labor companies did not last long under the new division-of-essence paradigm in the 21st century and soon had to evolve or become extinct.

Consider that every original entrepreneur, who builds his start-up company from the ground up, intimately knows the "DNA" of his business — *how to make money!* In my Sixth Vision, I witnessed that the "DNA" was preserved through replicating himself. The Neo-Tech World's division-of-essence entrepreneur did not *turn over* selected responsibilities, in other words, delegate. Instead, he took the time to transfer an entire living job with its "DNA", its money-making purpose, and all its attached responsibilities that made up the "living cell". He demonstrated to his employee, first hand, how to do each responsibility and, most importantly, all the intricacies of how to go about making money — the essence of his job.

In my Sixth Vision, tomorrow's businesses taught employees how to make money in their living jobs. Nearly everyone, for the first time, went about making money while creating exciting values and breakthroughs...sending the wealth of society beyond any description ever attempted in economic theory from the old school of thought. A hundred million creative entrepreneurs together with 21st-century super technologies in a depoliticized society created wealth faster and bigger than anything previously considered. In Adam Smith's time, for example, Neo-Tech did not even exist.

An Unbelievably Wealthy World

The new living companies in the coming Neo-Tech Era, driven forward by those in-house entrepreneurs, poured so much creative energy into society that a whole new economic model had to be written. The old models just did not apply. Indeed, when every working adult was a motivated entrepreneur putting creative energy into society, and society was free to race forward with no big-government regulations, and high technology catalyzed all efforts...our society metamorphosed into something never even theoretically conceived, not even as an academic thought. Everyone lived like a millionaire; the enormous creative energy flowing into society left no other possibility.

Traditional economic ideas and worries about inflation, deflation, money supply and wealth distribution became obsolete. Creative energy of a hundred million entrepreneurs flowing into society and lifting everyone's standard of living overwhelmed all other market dynamics and became the dominating and unstoppable factor of individual prosperity.

People's prosperity simply was buoyed by unprecedented creative energy flowing into society. You see, all that creative energy, overflowing throughout society, could go nowhere else but toward elevating everyone's standard of living. The old economic models of inflation, deflation, money supply, wealth distribution applied to the old socio-economic era and not to the Neo-Tech Era of win, win, win wealth for *everyone*. *Everyone* was rich.

Taking Your Piece of the Action

When someone decided to start a living company in

tomorrow's Neo-Tech World, here is what he would do: He would start with something he knew well, perhaps in a similar line of work as his prior mini-company. He would select something he was comfortable with, something he *knew* he could do. He would start with something that motivated him, his Friday-Night Essence. He would begin his new living company *as a lone, one-man business.* Although things seemed a bit hectic, *he did not hire others to delegate responsibilities to.* Often he would not even hire a secretary, for if he did, he would have someone to delegate to. His first solo money-making job in his new company was in itself a mini-company. He sacredly held together the living cell of responsibilities. He kept its responsibilities together around their money-making purpose. He knew that delegating would obliterate that living cell. Instead, he did all the work himself. To stay in good control, he used the mini-day/power-thinking team.[1]

When his company began to grow, he brought in a successor and replicated his *entire* wealth-building nugget, as follows: He did *all* the work in his successor's presence. He let his successor *take from him* when ready and able — not he give to his successor — the nitty-gritty details, one by one. This way, his successor would pick up the fine art of making money. The founder's genetic code would pass to his successor.

Once that original entrepreneur successfully transferred the DNA and its *entire* cell of responsibilities to his successor, then the original entrepreneur could put his mind to work again and concentrate his entrepreneurial drive on building a new wealth-

---

[1] Every mini-company consisted of both essence responsibilities and follow-through responsibilities. See on page 93: the first five responsibilities in each mini-company were essence responsibilities, the second five were follow-through, all indicated by "*control...*". With growth, follow-through responsibilities were often done by someone else who was well replicated and well tracked by the mini-company head via the "immune-system" tracking reports, described next. Moreover, the follow-through jobs were set up as "entrepreneurial units" with performance incentives to keep out stagnation. ...For full, how-to details, see Mark Hamilton's *Neo-Tech Business Control*, 740 pages, Neo-Tech Publishing Company.

building mini-company. Indeed, his business never stagnated as he and his successors all concentrated on *making money.*[1]

Some businesses tomorrow worked better if the founder kept the original wealth-building mini-company and grew through replicating new wealth-building mini-companies (i.e., new marketing projects) that grew from within his original mini-company. In any case, physical growth came through replicating "DNA" (i.e., the money-making purposes) and their attached responsibilities. The founder lived the exhilarating life of building a 21st-century living company and bringing life-lifting values to the world. All routine ruts, all bicameral mentalities, vanished in such living companies, forever.

In my Sixth Vision, we were among the first to experience the next great curve of prosperity coming to business and its workers as everything shifted with our generation from brain-dead jobs of labor to brain-stimulated jobs of the mind. And those jobs of the mind served as transmission belts that helped hundreds of millions of ordinary people around the world make the evolutionary jump into Neothink.

Full of living jobs with "DNA", tomorrow's living companies grew, on their own, as their living jobs reproduced and formed profitable new ones. In the end, original entrepreneurs of tomorrow's living companies became wonderful pillars of society as they helped make their entrepreneurial employees rich value creators. In fact, all people in those living companies became major players in life. The founder's crucially important role was to ultimately integrate and coordinate all the pieces to the big success puzzle...to best snap together the pieces into the overall puzzle picture and be sure everything stayed healthy:

The Immune System

Like a living body, the 21st-century living company had an intricate immune system. My Sixth Vision clearly showed me that immune system, which came from powerful tools called

---

[1]One's business would, sometimes gradually or sometimes rapidly, migrate towards his Friday-Night Essence until, ultimately, his business embodied his Friday-Night Essence.

tracking reports. Just as your body's immune system detects something wrong in any part of your anatomy, the tracking reports in tomorrow's living companies would detect something wrong in any part of the business. The tracking reports directly or indirectly reached each and every detail.

Each mini-company employee would fill out his tracking reports. To fill out the reports, the responsibilities all had to be done and done right or they jumped out as "ill" on the catch-everything "immune system". The mini-company employee himself caught whether or not something was wrong and, if needed, corrected it immediately before any further time passed and before it went beyond him.

With a skillfully developed "immune system", proper tracking reports, everything throughout the living company stayed healthy, even if the company grew into a multi-million-dollar business or larger, which many did.

I used these techniques that I saw in my Sixth Vision to build my own living company. I started in the business I knew well, in the same line of work as my prior mini-company. Upon replicating my first mini-company, I designed tracking reports. Remember, the living job or mini-company has a living "cell of responsibilities", as shown attached to my company's mini-companies on page 93.

The first mini-company I built and then replicated was the direct-mail mini-company. I developed the tracking reports to assure me that every one of its responsibilities was done and done right. For example, see Diagram Nine over the next eleven pages. It illustrates my direct-mail mini-company's "cell of responsibilities" followed by the tracking reports. In only a few minutes, I glance over those reports and know that everything is healthy.

As I developed a set of tracking reports for each new mini-company, those reports kept me in touch with every responsibility in my company. In a few minutes, I snapped all responsibilities together in my mind, like pieces to my success puzzle. As I sat back and snapped together the big puzzle picture in my mind, I knew the missing pieces and then turned around and gracefully, omnipotently conducted my business. I was beginning to use Neothink to build my business. Thus, I was able to bring out

Diagram Nine

Direct-Mail Marketing Mini-Company
Cell of Responsibilities

1	Rent Mailing Lists	(Page 132)
2	Set Up Mailings	(Page 133)
3	Keep Data/Statistics	(Page 134)
4	Keep Books	(Page 135)
5	Do Accounting	(Page 136)
6	Control Order Processing	(Page 137)
7	Control Customer Service	(Page 138)
8	Control Shipping Products	(Page 139)
9	Control Printing Mailers and Product	(Pg.140)
10	Control Computer Needs	(Page 141)

Note: The following ten pages illustrate the tracking reports for the Direct-Mail Mini-Company. The tracking reports directly answer each responsibility in the "Cell of Responsibilities" above. The reader may study, skim, or even skip over the tracking reports if he fully understands the concept that tracking reports directly answer each responsibility in the mini-company's "Cell of Responsibilities".

		TR-1 Rent List Report	
		Date	Aug 20
		Page	1 of 1

INTEGRATED MANAGEMENT ASSOCIATES

(Note: First eight lists are monthly; last two are quarterly. A core list cannot be missed without a big blank square staring at us.)

Core Lists Through July

List Name*	Code	Jan.	Feb.	Mar.	April	May	June	July
Proprietary	% orders	1.170	1.922	1.467	1.454	1.779	0.628	0.948
Information	Qty. Mailed	5634	13261	21055	38148	5675	51243	16238
Proprietary	% orders	1.626	1.571	1.616	1.621	1.481	1.514	1.572
Information	Qty. Mailed	13278	17432	8785	25550	23294	5348	19647
Proprietary	% orders	0.794	1.227	0.939	1.383	1.002	0.620	1.312
Information	Qty. Mailed	3400	5865	39075	3685	3590	6930	10818
Proprietary	% orders	1.543	1.587	1.107	1.056	1.532	0.860	0.792
Information	Qty. Mailed	6998	8314	3160	7289	6133	11391	3787
Proprietary	% orders	0.535	1.164	1.161	0.443	0.567	1.444	1.272
Information	Qty. Mailed	1308	3606	9214	11736	3524	3531	8971
Proprietary	% orders	1.346	2.195	2.991	3.558	2.367	2.220	2.123
Information	Qty. Mailed	13441	1776	1638	2473	7053	1171	2590
Proprietary	% orders	2.415	1.817	2.214	1.945	2.409	1.290	2.177
Information	Qty. Mailed	6997	8144	6502	3136	3071	3333	3674
Proprietary	% orders	0.433	1.099	1.510	1.188	1.614	1.179	1.214
Information	Qty. Mailed	12453	6096	1721	3533	3468	3722	2893
Proprietary	% orders	X	X	1.567	X	X	1.226	X
Information	Qty. Mailed	X	X	3253	X	X	14436	X
Proprietary	% orders	X	X	1.660	X	X	1.365	X
Information	Qty. Mailed	X	X	23915	X	X	15158	X

*Integrated Management cannot reveal its core lists.

	TR-2
	Set-Up Report
	Date May 9
	Page 1 of 1

INTEGRATED MANAGEMENT ASSOCIATES

(Note: All details are captured and organized over two weeks before mailing.)

Information for Mailing 245 Product *Neo-Tech* Mail Date 5/27 Postage Class 1st Mailing Point *Paramount*

Code	List P.O.#	List Name	Description	Input Qty.	Projected Qty.	Splits/Inserts	Notes
3990 ↓ 3993	8846X	Boardroom Book Buyers	April Names	16.7M	11Mmales 3Mfemale	In-Line Envelope < Jet-Press Envelope < ZE Brochure < ZW Brochure	
4001	89EP4	Nightingale-Conant (c)	1st Quarter	5M	5M	Control	Canadian
3994 ↓ 3995	89EC2	Real Estate Financial Opportunity	April Names	5M	3.5M	ZE Brochure < ZF Brochure	
3997	89D12	Elite Self-Improvement	April Names	2M	1M	Control	
3996	89DX2	Publisher's Choice	April Names	1.2M	1M	Control	
4002	89E02	J.E.W. Jewels (c)	April Names	3M	1M	Control	Canadian
3998	89EQ3	Passe Publications	April Names	1.2M	1M	Control	
3999 ↓ 4000		Mailing 239 Multi-Buyers	Multi-Buyers	9.5M	9.4M	Control	Canadian

133

	TR-3
	Data/Stats Report
Date	July 11
Page	1 of 1

INTEGRATED MANAGEMENT ASSOCIATES

(Note: The mailing set up on previous tracking report #2 is complete with results in tracking report #3, below.)

Results for Mailing 245

Date Mailed	May 27	Orders Update:	July 11

Code #	List	Description	Mailed	Orders	%	Inserts	Split Code
3990	Boardroom Book Buyers	April Names	5276	70	1.33	Control w/In-Line Envelope	Test 1 Side 1
3991	Boardroom Book Buyers	April Names	5275	70	1.33	Control w/Jet Press-Envelope	Test 1 Side 2
3992	Boardroom Book Buyers	April Names	1609	20	1.24	Control w/ZE Brochure	Test 2 Side 1
3993	Boardroom Book Buyers	April Names	1609	17	1.06	Control w/ZW Brochure	Test 2 Side 2
4001	Nightingale-Conant (C)	1st Quarter Names	4639	159	3.43	Control	
3994	Real Estate Financial Opp.	April Names	1671	27	1.62	Control w/ZE Brochure	Test 3 Side 1
3995	Real Estate Financial Opp.	April Names	1670	12	0.72	Control w/ZF Brochure	Test 3 Side 2
3997	Elite Self Improvement	April Names	1131	5	0.44	Control	
3996	Publisher's Choice	April Names	1072	6	0.56	Control	
4002	JEN Jewels (C)	April Names	1000	7	0.70	Control	
3998	Pase Publication	April Names	651	7	1.08	Control	
3999	Mailing 239	Multi Buyers	4717	47	1.00	Control	
4000	Mailing 239	Multi Buyers	4717	57	1.21	Control	
U245	Unidentified Orders		0	8			
Totals			35,037	512	1.461		

Split-Run Tests for Mailing 245

Split Test: 1: In Line Env. versus Jet-Press Env.

Code	3990	3991
Split #1	In-Line	Jet-Press
Orders	70	70
Percent	1.33	1.33

Split Test: 2: ZE Brochure vs ZW Brochure

Code	3992	3993
Split #2	ZE	ZW
Orders	20	17
Percent	54.1	43.9

Split Test: 3: ZE Brochure vs ZF Brochure

Code	3994	3995
Split #3	ZE	ZF
Orders	27	12
Percent	1.62	0.72

	TR-4 Cash Tracking Report
Date	July 10
Page	1 of 1

INTEGRATED MANAGEMENT ASSOCIATES

(Note: This tracking report is printed on demand covering any span of time requested: one day, one month, one quarter, one year. For illustrative ease of reviewing, only one day is printed below although this is turned in weekly.
(note continued at bottom))

Opening Balance $61,119.47

Cash In (Deposits)

Orders: Check $ Received	Orders: Credit Card $ Received	Reversed Refunds	Royalty Receipts	Reimbursement Money	Transfer In (From Other Accts.)	Miscellaneous Income
3517.95 (52 total)	2618.15 (37 total)	0	799.60	432.00	5000.00	0
3517.95	2618.15	0	799.60	432.00	5000.00	0

Total In (above) $12,367.70

Cash Out (Checks/Wires)

Operating Expenses	Wages	Marketing Postage	Marketing Expenses	Marketing Purchases	Advertisements Paid	Royalties Paid	Taxes Paid	Refunds Paid	Transfer Out (To Other Accts.)
1,312.71	0	8700	2208.15	0	1481.42	934.50	0	202.50	0
1,312.71	0	8700	2208.15	0	1481.42	934.50	0	202.50	0

Total Out (below) $14,839.28

Ending Balance $58,647.89

(note continued from above)
This report is generated automatically from the computer, tied into all the other workings of the bookkeeper. For example, the "cash out" portion gets its data straight from the bookkeeper's check register. Much of the "cash in" portion gets its data from the bookkeeper's computerized deposit slips. Those deposit slips must match the "order processing" tracking report #6 so that nothing can go wrong, no mistakes can occur, and no embezzlement can occur. This tracking report shows where every penny comes from and where every penny goes to. Thus, with that overview, every penny can be tracked and verified. No mistakes can occur. Everything can be reconciled.

INTEGRATED MANAGEMENT ASSOCIATES

[Note: Below are two completely independent accounting reports. Yet, the profit/loss of mailings (bottom left) must equal delta (i.e., the change) of cash position (bottom right). Triple control: 1) self-proofing 2) accurate profit/loss 3) location of every penny.]

TR-5
Accounting Report
Date June 16
Page 1 of 1

May Mailings Profit/Loss

Net Revenue

Mailing 242

Total Direct Costs _____ $65,229.89
    (131,935 pieces @49.4¢)
Revenue _____ $75,598.60
    (1,540 orders @$49.09)
    Net _____ $10,368.71

Mailing 243

Total Direct Costs _____ $33,805.75
    (68,530 pieces @49.3¢)
Revenue _____ $30,288.53
    (617 orders @$49.09)
    Net _____ <$3,517.22>

Mailing 244

Total Direct Costs _____ $44,249.58
    (89,552 pieces @49.4¢)
Revenue _____ $47,273.67
    (963 orders @$49.09)
    Net _____ $3,024.09

Mailing 245

Total Direct Costs _____ $17,369.51
    (35,037 pieces @49.5¢)
Revenue _____ $25,134.08
    (512 orders @$49.09)
    Net _____ $7,764.57

Expenses

Less General Overhead	$18,174
Less General Freelance	$22,628

Profit/Loss $ < 23,161 >

May Cash Location & Delta

Beginning Cash Position		**$323,280**
ASSETS		
Inventory		
Brochures	$38,552	
Coupons	$22,848	
Envelopes	$25,081	
Products	$73,703	
Total		$160,185
Cash On Hand - Accounts		
Bank of America	$(11,718)	
Valley Bank	$(10,623)	
Total		($22,341)
Cash Expected In - Receivables		
MC/Visa	$32,255	
Club Cards	$12,995	
Total		$45,250
Cash Invested - Future Mailings		
Mailing 246	$77,270	
Mailing 247	$70,010	
Total		$147,280
Total Assets		**$322,439**
LIABILITIES		
Accounts Payables		
Unshipped Orders	($1,605)	
Invoices	($15,360)	
Refunds	($13,290)	
Total Liabilities		**($30,255)**
Ending Cash Position		**$300,119**

CHANGE IN CASH POSITION
(Ending minus Beginning)

Ending	$300,119
(less) Beginning	$323,280

Delta $ < 23,161 >

INTEGRATED MANAGEMENT ASSOCIATES
(Note: Nothing can go wrong without jumping out on
this tracking report. Banking-like tracking of orders.)

TR-6
Order Processing
Date	July 10
Page	1 of 1

Order Processing Tracking

Raw Count	136

Station One: Open/Sort Mail

Raw Count Done by (Initials):
SR & RW

Checks/Money Orders	52
Cash	0
MasterCard/Visa	32
American Express/Diner's Club	8
Canadian Money Off	4

Nevada Orders	1
Collections	1
Total Orders	96
Non-Orders*	38
Total Sort	136

*Note: Non-Orders go to Customer Service
and into Tracking Report #7.

Station Two: Verifone Credit Cards

MasterCard/VISA	32
Declines	1
Invalids	1
Net MasterCard/VISA Orders	30

American Express/Diner's Club	7
Declines	0
Invalids	0
Net AmEx/Diner's Orders	7
Total Credit Cards	37

Station Three: Check/Cash Deposit

Checks	50
Money Orders	2
Cash	0
Total Check/Cash	52

Station Four: Data Entry

Total Orders Brought to #61	93
Total Orders On Summary Below	93

Total Orders On Summary (below) must
equal Total Orders brought to #61 (above)

Order Summary Sheet

Product	Cash	MO/Checks	VISA	MC	AmEx	Diners	Canadian	Totals
Neo-Tech Discovery		33 $2458.85	10 $699.50	8 $559.60	4 $279.80		4 $279.80	59 $4277.55
Neo-Tech System		14 $559.30	3 $119.85	3 $119.85	1 $39.95			21 $838.95
Neo-Tech Tapes		5 $499.80	2 $199.90	4 $399.90	1 $99.95	1 $99.95		13 $1299.40
Totals		52 $3517.95	15 $1019.25	15 $1079.25	6 $419.70	1 $99.95	4 $279.80	93 $6415.90

INTEGRATED MANAGEMENT ASSOCIATES
(Note: These 38 customer service pieces were received
from mail raw count, see Tracking Report #6. Every
piece, every action is accounted for below. Nothing can
be missed.)

TR-7	
Customer Service	
Date	July 10
Page	1 of 1

Customer Service Tracking Report

	Raw Count	38
Plus _/_ Invalid _/_ Decline	2
Total	40

Station One: Sort Customer Service Mail

Potential Cash Gain		Potential Cash Loss	
More Information Requests	16	Non-Delivery Inquires	7
Forgot To Enclose Payment	3	Help/?'s On Product	7
Invalid/Decline Credit Card	2	Refund Requests	5

Station Two A: Customer Service Profits

Potential Profits	rec'vd	# of	First Attempt 7/10	Second Attempt 7/25	Third Attempt 8/10	Total
More Information Requests	7/10	16	Attempt: 16	Attempt: 12	Attempt: 10	Attempt: 16
			Convert: 4	Convert: 2	Convert: 0	Convert: 6 (37%)
Forgot to Enlose Payment	7/10	3	Attempt: 3	Attempt: 3	Attempt: 2	Attempt: 3
			Convert: 0	Convert: 1	Convert: 0	Convert: 1 (33%)
Invalid/Deline Credit Cards	7/10	2	Attempt: 2	Attempt: 1	Attempt: 1	Attempt: 3
			Convert: 1	Convert: 0	Convert: 0	Convert: 1 (33%)

Station Two B: Customer Service Preservation

Potential Losses	Date rec'vd	# of	Processed for Mail	Spot Checked by Steve R.	Delivered to Post Office
Non-Delivery Inquiries	7/10	7	Done by: RW	Ok'd by: SR	Delivered by: KP
			Date: 7/10	Date: 7/10	Date: 7/10
Help/?'s on Product	7/10	7	Done by: RW	Ok'd by: SR	Delivered by: KP
			Date: 7/10	Date: 7/10	Date: 7/10
Refund Requests	7/10	5	Done by: RW	Ok'd by: SR	Delivered by: KP
			Date: 7/10	Date: 7/10	Date: 7/10

Total Pieces Handled and Mailed Today 7/10 : 38

+ 2 Invalid/Decline

40 Total

138

INTEGRATED MANAGEMENT ASSOCIATES
(Note: Nothing can be missed with this iron-grip control.
All orders to shipping accounted for.)

TR-8	
Shipping Log	
Date	Aug
Page	1 of 1

Shipping Summary Sheet

Order Dates	Ship Number	Ship Date	Product Quantity	No. of Int'l	Manuscript Numbers	Letter Sent	Book Ship Date	Decoy Rec'vd
5/12-5/18	S-126	Jun 13 May 22 May 22 May 22 May 22	A=1382 B=3 E=9 GT/E=5 G=1 A=-4	20	410SM-291SP 4 Labels pulled – bad payments	May 23	Jun 17 May 23 May 26 May 26	Jun 21
5/19-5/25	S-127	Jun 9 May 30 May 30	A=743 B=10 E=5 A=-1	19	292SP-34SR 1 Label Pulled – bad payment	May 30	Jun 14 Jun 2 Jun 4	Jun 29 Jun 6 Jun 14
5/26-6/1	S-128	Jun 15 Jun 5 Jun 5 Jun 5	A=573 B=3 E=1 GT/E=6	105	35SR-107SS	Jun 6	Jun 21 Jun 7 Jun 9 Jun 9	July 10
6/2-6/8	S-129	Jun 23 Jun 12 Jun 12 Jun 12	A=633 B=4 E=8 GT/E=6 A=-1	242	108SS-240ST (241ST used by RW) 1 Label pulled	Jun 12	Jun 29 Jun 14 Jun 16 Jun 16	July 17 Jun 16 Jun 23
6/9-6/15	S-130	Jun 30 Jun 19 Jun 19 Jun 19 Jun 19 Jun 19	A=304 B=2 E=1 F=1 G=1 GT/E=1	203	242ST-45SU (46SU used by RW)	Jun 19	Jul 6 Jun 21 Jun 23 Jun 21 Jun 23 Jun 23	July 24
6/16-6/22	S-131	Jul 7 Jun 23 A=-3	A=789 G=1 A=-3	108	47SU-335SV 3 Labels pulled	Jun 26	Jul 13 Jun 26	Jul 24
6/25-6/29	S-132	Jul 17 Jul 3 Jul 3 Jun 30 Jul 3	A=696 B=14 E=13 F=1 GT/E=5	71	336SV-31SX	Jul 3	Jul 20 Jul 5 Jul 7 Jul 5 Jul 7	Jul 31 Jul 6 Jul 11
6/20-7/6	S-133	Jul 21 Jul 10 Jul 21 Jul 10 Jul 10	A=953 B=399 D=1 E=306 GT/E=3	74	32SX-484SY	Jul 10	Jul 27 Jul 14 Jul 27 Jul 14 Jul 14	Aug 7 Jul 20 Jul 31
7/7	S-134	Jul 21 Jul 10 Jul 10	A=10 B=122 E=124	0	485SY-494SY	Jul 10	Jul 27 Jul 14 Jul 14	

*Product Codes: A=Neo-Tech Discovery B=Neo-Tech System E=Neo-Tech Tapes

	TR-9
	Inventory Report
Date	July 15
Page	1 of 1

INTEGRATED MANAGEMENT ASSOCIATES

(Note: Every product, quantity, and location is "in your face" with this tracking report. This report continues beyond this page to also track the mailers - brochures, envelopes, coupons, etc.)

Inventory

Code	Product	Quantity	Site	Company	As of	By
A1	Neo-Tech I, III, IV, V	1903	Doris	006	Sep 15	MF
A1	Neo-Tech I, III, IV, V	152	LV - 59	002	Jun 27	MF
A1	Neo-Tech I, III, IV, V	2420	Banta Company	009	Jul 10	MF
A1	Neo-Tech I, III, IV, V	1139	Melinda	007	Aug 2	MF
A2	Neo-Tech Discovery II	2187	Doris	006	Sep 15	MF
A2	Neo-Tech Discovery II	1124	Melinda	007	Aug 2	MF
A2	Neo-Tech Discovery II	4377	Braceland	005	Sep 15	MF
B	Neo-Tech System	1576	Braceland	005	Aug 2	MF
B	Neo-Tech System	442	Melinda	007	Aug 3	MF
BE	NTS Envelopes	6983	Braceland	005	Aug 18	MF
BJPL	Job Power List	1423	Braceland	005	Aug 2	MF
D	Neo-Tech Encyclopedia	217	Doris	006	Aug 18	MF
E	Neo-Tech Tapes	2192	Doris	006	Sep 15	MF
EA	Neo-Tech Album	6864	Magnetix	008	Jul 27	MF
EMBC	Neo-Tech/Summit Book Carton	4862	Magnetix	008	Aug 18	MF
EW	Neo-Tech Workbook	2864	Magnetix	008	Aug 18	MF
G101	Consultation Pack Vol. 1/1	50	LV - 59	002	Aug 18	MF
G102	Consultation Pack Vol. 1/2	38	LV - 59	002	Aug 18	MF
G103	Consultation Pack Vol. 1/3	25	LV - 59	002	July 19	MF
G104	Consultation Pack Vol. 1/4	50	LV - 59	002	July 19	MF
G105	Consultation Pack Vol. 1/5	200	LV - 59	002	July 19	MF
G106	Consultation Pack Vol. 1/6	150	LV - 59	002	July 19	MF
G107	Consultation Pack Vol. 1/7	175	LV - 59	002	July 19	MF
G108	Consultation Pack Vol. 1/8	50	LV - 59	002	July 19	MF
G109	Consultation Pack Vol. 1/9	200	LV - 59	002	July 19	MF
G110	Consultation Pack Vol. 1/10	30	LV - 59	002	July 19	MF
G111	Consultation Pack Vol. 1/11	75	LV - 59	002	July 19	MF
G112	Consultation Pack Vol. 1/12	50	LV - 59	002	July 19	MF
G201	Consultation Pack Vol. 2/1	200	LV - 59	002	July 19	MF
G202	Consultation Pack Vol. 2/2	150	LV - 59	002	July 19	MF
G203	Consultation Pack Vol. 2/3	150	LV - 59	002	July 19	MF
GA	Consultation Tapes Album	1100	Magnetix	008	July 19	MF
K	Philosophical Zero	420	LV - 59	002	July 19	MF
M1	Summit One Tapes	357	Magnetix	003	Jun 15	MF
M1A	Summit One Album	357	Magnetix	008	Jun 15	MF
M1W	Summit One Workbook	1452	Magnetix	008	Jun 15	MF
QA	Ultimate Battle Album	15	Magnetix	008	Jun 15	MF
T	Bible A	22	Melinda	007	Jun 15	MF
U	Bible B		Melinda	002	Jun 15	MF

INTEGRATED MANAGEMENT ASSOCIATES
(Note: The computer needs are "in your face" with description and status. The completion date adds healthy pressure and discipline to programmer for best efficiency and control over area.)

TR-10	
Computer Needs	
Date	June 15
Page	1 of 1

Computer Projects

Project	Status	Completion Date
Computerize the Accounting Tracking Report #5	I tied "mailing accounting" portion into Data Tracking Report #3 to automatically bring up direct costs and revenue. Now tying into checkbook to automatically bring up General Overhead and General Freelance. Nearly complete. This will allow entire left side, "mailing accounting" portion, to come up automatically with one command. Next I will do the same for the right side, "cash location accounting". That needs to be tied into a combination of our inventory program (Tracking Report #9) and our check register program in order to pull up the right side of Tracking Report #5, the "cash location" portion, with a single command.	July 1 (On Schedule)
Data Tracking Report #3 Advancements		
1) Compile data from same split tests among different mailings	I will tie all Data Tracking Reports from all mailings together to recognize, match up and compile data from the same tests among different mailings to give ongoing, cumulative data on major tests. Going smoothly.	July 7 (On schedule)
2) Add refund data to this tracking report	I will tie into the Customer Service Tracking Report #7 to match all refunds to the original list from which they came. I will add a new column to the Data Tracking Report #3 to show how each list performs, refund wise. Complication on Tracking Report #7, but working through it.	July 7 (1 week behind schedule. Needs more programing than anticipated. TR-7 must be revamped. New projection date is July 15.)
Demographic Project	I will break down all names mailed for six months by SCF zip locations. I will then compare that to our own mailing list. That should reveal our more favorable markets throughout the country. Simple — I let program run at night when office is down.	July 1 (On schedule)
Data Entry	Set up double entries of street address and zip code. Automatic merge upon second entry. If does not match, then reject into a purge file to be redone. This will eliminate keypunching errors. Looks easy.	July 15 (On schedule)
Merge/Purge	I will improve accuracy of our merge/purges. Not finished flow-chart thinking. Will explain and give completion date on next week's report.	

the power of the mind, just as I saw happen during my Vision:

Mental Growth

The 21st-century living companies in my Sixth Vision unleashed the power of our minds. Throughout each month, the founder or president outlined the *forward movement* he expected done by each mini-company the following month. Then, once a month, he met with the mini-company employees.

Nothing but forward-movement issues got discussed in this monthly Essence Meeting. The founder clearly outlined for each mini-company specifically what forward movement must be accomplished next month. Then, everyone in the company drove forward for the full month following the Essence Meeting.

Everyone in my Vision drove hard to meet the deadlines set by the founder. No one ever drifted into aimlessness. No one ever drifted into filling his or her day with tasks that did nothing to drive the business forward. For, the founder had determined for each mini-company the projects that specifically drove the business forward. The founder laid out what he expected done, and he set deadlines.

Thus, every month the founder sent his 21st-century living business into double-time, forward-march action. The next two pages show the outline of actions I prepared for the direct-mail mini-company before the January Essence Meeting at my company. Of course, I used the same technique I witnessed from future companies in my Sixth Vision.

The greatest payoffs in those future companies during my Vision, however, came through developing the mini-company employees to, *on their own,* initiate and carry through forward movement...to power-think money-making projects and become creative like the founder. Upon doing that, the living company had succcssfully become a 21st-century division-of-essence business.

As the in-house entrepreneurs got used to driving forward projects laid out by the founder, they began to, on their own, develop their own projects. Gradually, they provided the founder with *their list* of forward movement for the following month. They became self-perpetuating essence movers. Yes, they became *value creators.*

Diagram Ten

January Essence Meeting
for
Direct-Mail Mini-Company

1) *Testing Program*: Research and report on on at least three new mailing lists a day.

2) *Virgin List Project*: Uncover five lists not yet on the market — five per week. Suggestions: Go to library and research magazines. First try opportunity type, self-help type. Then try health, nutrition, holistic. Every weekend spend a couple hours going through magazines. Go to bookstores too. ...Also, call owners of products (much better than writing).

3) *Field Research Program*: Get on all our core mailing lists. Chase down all mailing pieces we receive. These people all have and know about mailing lists, of course.

4) *Malaysia Program*: Get into the numbers. Realize that by developing capacity to pack more in, this could be a bonanza for Bob. Here is the question and actions:
- Will this spread both programs thin? or...
- Will This thicken Bob's essence and power for both programs < U.S. / Malaysia ?
- Malaysia has same profit margin as U.S. program. Must go at .33%, must build steadily to a 500M per month quota.
- Bob do two test mailings to begin getting data.
- We must be at 500m per month if tests prompt us to continue. I know that can be done. But,

143

**January Essence Meeting
for
Direct-Mail Mini-Company**

can Bob build this? List research is his essence, maybe a natural. Not only that, by getting into may drive up his knowledge on lists to actually boost U.S. program. Will double his income if mail 500M per month (@ .33%).

• In any case, Bob must do two mailings @ 200M each this month to hang on to this lucrative new program.

5) Special List Project: I want a blitz put on acquiring the following hard-to-get lists, with verbal discussions with the lists' owners by the end of next week: HUME, Star Trek, Vietnam Vets, Black Belt, Spotlight, Scientology.

6) Demographic Program: Set up your first test this month — no if's, no but's.

7) Bob's Programs: Review Bob's essence ideas and projects. Encourge & nurture Bob's creativity.

8) List Rental Program: Use our leverage. Make deals. We have a _hot_ list. Also, we will clean lists... (good leverage for virgin lists). Every list you research, introduce to our list & try to set up swap. I expect at least one such special swap deal per week.

9) Customer Service (Essence): I want an improved tracking report in two weeks.

10) Essence Accounting: Bob must master my tracking report (TR-#5, see page 45). Must master every detail and thoroughly grasp its logic. Turn in with no mistakes two weeks from today.

Heaven On Earth

The Sixth Vision showed me that after the job revolution *ordinary people* eventually became self-perpetuating essence movers. Ordinary people became value creators. Not only did the creative energy of a hundred million value creators lift society's wealth into a whole new dimension, but the ordinary person became a deeply happy person. Ordinary people achieved dreams monthly, in the new business paradigm, that surpassed most dreams ever imagined in a lifetime under the old business paradigm. ...This exciting metamorphosis is happening in my own company since I switched to the new business paradigm.

Applying these future techniques now to build my own living company, I use the following technique to push along my company's division of essence: I have each mini-company employee submit a *weekly* forward-movement Essence Report. The weekly report gets turned in every Monday, without exception. The report is brief. It tells me what each mini-company employee did on *forward movement* the past week and what he or she will do on *forward movement* the new week. No detail work. No excuses. Simply what was done on forward movement, nothing else. (See weekly Essence Report, next page.)

Every Monday, without exception, I review the weekly forward-movement reports. The weekly reports, in a sense, "corner" my people into doing forward movement.

Again, the weekly Essence Report breaks into two brief parts: 1) the forward movement accomplished the past week, and 2) the forward movement to be accomplished that week. When I receive the next Essence Report, I see if the person was successful with his week's projection.

The weekly Essence Report sets a forward-movement goal for the week. The goal set in the weekly report forces focused concentration on forward movement each new week. When the previous company I worked for was under the old business structure dominated by bicameral mentalities, employees handled only routine responsibilities without ever a thought beyond their routines — without ever a thought of investing in their own growth and futures. Under the new business structure dominated by Neothink mentalities with the weekly forward-movement

Diagram Eleven

Weekly Essence Report
for
Direct-Mail Mini-Company

January 7
Date

Actions	Last Week	This Week
1) Testing Program	Acquired five new test lists today, and fifteen for the week.	Research fifteen new test lists.
2) Virgin List Project	Sent letter to seven small health + vitamin companies (names fax'd to you).	Research magazines for small companies. Try science field.
3) Field Research Program	Tracked down + called list manager of five businesses that solicit via our core lists.	Will get on mailing list of some of our core lists. We'll also network aggressively.
4) Malaysian Program	No movement this week. Lists are in transit to Malaysia.	Call Boardroom + KCI to negotiate price of list. Set up next mailing.
5) Special List Project	Called HUME: U.S. list – no problem. Canadian: must call Canadian office.	Research Vietnam Vets, Star Trek, Black Belt, Spotlight, Scientology, + HUME Canadian.
6) Demographics Program	Called Joe W. to set up test. I told him only if he waives $5000 charge.	Call competitors if do not hear back on $5000.
7) Bob's Programs	Tonight will work on my notes for Neo-Tech book on negotiating. Finished outline.	Write networking article for DM News + make contacts.
8) List Rental Program	No movement today, but acquired 7 new renters + $14,000 in rentals.	Will set up outbound telemarketing program to call list managers + solicit list.
9) Customer Service (Essence Progress)	Worked on developing a new tracking report for better control. See attached.	Will implement + perfect new tracking report.
10) Essence Accounting	Studied numbers we estimate on Tracking Report #5. See my notes, attached.	Meetings scheduled with computer programmer to set up computer controls.

Essence Report, however, each new week employees think about how to further advance themselves. They integrate more and more widely and become increasingly creative and exhilarated. I help them grow into the creative people they always dreamed of and were meant to be.

I learned that the most effective format for the weekly Essence Report was to integrate that report with the monthly Essence Meeting. For example, in the monthly Essence Meeting, I will, in conjunction with each mini-company, establish the forward-movement actions to be accomplished the following month. Each mini-company employee then lists those actions 1...2...3...4... on a sheet of paper with space to the right of each action to write the past week's forward-movement progress and the new week's projected progress. See the sample on the previous page, and compare its actions to the Essence Meeting on pages 143 and 144. The mini-company employee then photocopies four or five copies of that list of forward-movement actions for one full month of weekly Essence Reports. Each weekend the mini-company employee writes either his progress (or exactly when he plans to make progress) in the first column next to each essence action. And he writes what he plans to do the coming week in the second column next to each essence action.

This format keeps the mini-company employee focused *every week* on pushing through the forward movement covered in the monthly Essence Meeting. By bringing this wealth-building essence to every employee, I help unleash his or her buried creativity. My company experiences extraordinary creativity, which is the greatest power in business. I conduct a life-lifting business, and thoroughly enjoy my work, loved ones, and friends. There is something sensational about becoming the entrepreneur of a living business. I can see the whole puzzle picture by snapping together the tracking reports. Then I easily dole out omnipotent life-enhancing advice as I guide others to ultimately making themselves rich and making their best dreams come true.

So, there you have what was shown to me — the 21st-century living company with the three main components that constitute a living organism: the physical growth, the physical immune system, and the mental growth. The 21st-century living company physically grows through replicating "living cells", has an immune system through tracking reports, and grows mentally through monthly Essence Meetings with weekly Essence Reports. And that last component — mental growth — brings an unbeatable advantage to the 21st-century living company. For, through the division of essence, tomorrow's companies unlock the greatest power in business — the creativity now locked inside every employee's mind. In fact, ordinary people tomorrow will evolve, through these jobs of the mind, into Neothink. Indeed, the Fifth and Sixth Visions showed me that these essence-driven jobs were our transmission belts to the Neothink mentality.

The Secret Code

While using these new techniques (Neo-Tech) to acquire my own living job and then my own living company, right now before the coming job revolution, I kept this in mind: When I acquired a 21st-century living job at my place of work, and when I later started my own 21st-century living company, what I needed more than anything else was more and more *creativity*. In my Fifth and Sixth Visions, I discovered the window to a whole new creative world. That window to a creative new world was not easy to find at first because it was "written in code". The code first had to be broken. In time, I began breaking that code written in *numbers*.

What irony: "all that logical stuff" was the window to creativity! Whereas I once ignored "boring" numbers, I found myself chasing after the numbers. You see, the numbers began telling me a story every day — an exciting story about my new wealth-building job and then about my new living company. I began looking for that story, every day enthusiastically wanting the latest story. For, that story told me ways to advance my business and profits. When I had my mini-company, and again later when I had my full-blown living company, I established a numbers mini-day. It took awhile to "crack the code" and make use of that mini-day. But once I did, the numbers threw open the window to a whole new creative world.

Tomorrow's Living Jobs and Companies — Summary

Routine-rut jobs were left behind and then forgotten. Work became exciting as ordinary people achieved 21st-century dreams that surpassed their most ambitious 20th-century daydreams. Let us summarize the 21st-century new techniques of living jobs and living companies, which you will experience sometime in the 21st century with the changing of the old business paradigm to the new:

One of Three Exercises
To Make Your *Job* Come To Life

One: Determine Your Living Job

DNA Exercise — Capture The Elusive Life Substance:

1) List the basic responsibilities at your place of work.
2) Determine *the money-making purpose* for each basic responsibility.
3) Regroup the basic responsibilities under their money-making purposes to form on paper the wealth-building jobs of the mind — the living jobs. Target and take over *your* living job by steadily taking over the details that make up each of its responsibilities.

Two of Three Exercises
To Make Your *Job* Come To Life

Two: Set Up Your Mini-Day Schedule

Ribosome Exercise — Start Your Money-Generating Factory:

1) List three days of tasks NOT from memory but as you do them.
2) Determine from that list of tasks your job's raw physical movements.
3) Decide what percentage of your day *should be* devoted to each movement, assign time slots, and write down your first mini-day schedule.

Three of Three Exercises
To Make Your *Job* Come To Life

Three: Do Your First Power-Thinking List

RNA Exercise — Create Wealth Yourself:

1) Think of your most ambitious projects and goals.
2) Imagine them completed, and write down the steps needed to get there.
3) Put the tasks needed to complete each step into next week's mini-day schedule for super-rapid forward movement.

One of Three Exercises
To Make Your *Company* Come To Life

One: Replicate Living Jobs

Physical-Growth Exercise — Self-Perpetuating Success:

1) Define your first wealth-building mini-company and its "cell of responsibilities" to replicate.
2) List its every nitty-gritty detail, and personally *do* all the work — all those details listed — in the presence of your successor.
3) As he observes and absorbs from you those nitty-gritty details and all the nuances to making money (i.e., your life code), cross out on the list those details that he masters, and gradually cut back to crucial-detail meetings — meeting only on the details not yet crossed out. Keep up those meetings until your successor masters all the details, crossing them out as he docs.

**Two of Three Exercises
To Make Your *Company* Come To Life**

Two: Develop Tracking Reports

Immune-System Exercise — Fail-Proof Success:

1) Study your first replicated mini-company and list its "cell of responsibilities".
2) Carefully develop tracking reports on separate sheets of paper that tell you the health of each and every responsibility listed in its "cell of responsibilities".
3) Establish and enforce punctuality on turning in those catch-all tracking reports.

**Three of Three Exercises
To Make Your *Company* Come To Life**

Three: Outline Your First Essence Meeting

Mental-Growth Exercise — Corralling The Greatest Money-Making Power In Business:

1) Snap together the puzzle pieces — the tracking reports — and study the success puzzle. Think hard about how each mini-company in your company can specifically improve the puzzle picture and build wealth.
2) Write down those specifics for each mini-company.
3) Meet with each mini-company employee and give him or her those forward-movement specifics, and encourage his or her own forward-movement projects, setting a completion deadline for each. Do this monthly. (Have your mini-company employees turn in weekly Essence Reports to track progress.)

Vision Seven
You Will Embrace the Lover of Your Dreams

Imagine this: you became the most desirous attraction to the person of your dreams. Romance ensued and the flame of those passionate first few weeks just kept burning year after year. This time, your fairy-tale romance lasted a lifetime. And to add to your physical passion, both you and your lover easily acquired your most sexy and slim look, without really trying. ...This scenario was no secret wish; it actually happened tomorrow in the Neo-Tech World. I saw it happen in my Seventh Vision. And it happened to married couples, too, who fell in love all over again.

The Seventh Vision came to me in two parts: first for men and their love-lives, second for women and their love-lives.

First Part For Men
How To Love A Superwoman

Being a man myself, my Seventh Vision opened my eyes to how to love a special woman:

Before the Neo-Tech World, most men got their *source* of happiness externally from vacations, sports, entertainment, partying. Suppressed in routine ruts, they had no other choice. A few lucky men, however, got their source of happiness internally from their competitive creations and development of important values for others and society. The first group of men sometimes seemed to have more fun because they oriented their lives around high-visibility, one-shot segments of "fun". But that was the very reason why most men stagnated into increasing boredom.

In tomorrow's Neo-Tech World, men thrived on value creation, not on time off per se. They thrived on exciting value creation in their living jobs; they never stagnated. Life was inspiring. When America went Neo-Tech in the 21st century, ordinary men enjoyed the jobs of their dreams, their natural

153

source of happiness. Never stagnating in their new jobs, they enjoyed the *most* fun of all.

And with their spouses, they experienced something special beyond today's wildest imaginations. They shared with their spouses entire lifetimes of emotional celebrations with the intensity previously experienced only during the first few weeks of falling in love before sinking into increasing stagnation and boredom.

Today, in the anticivilization, stagnant and subtly suffering from the burden of life, men slowly lose their enthusiasm and energy for living. Eventually, they have nothing left for love.

But tomorrow, their exhilarating value creation in their living jobs generated a growing energy and happiness inside that fueled and fired up their lifelong celebrations of love. And then, entertainment, vacations, parties became more enjoyable than ever before as precious times spent together with loved ones.

Alive and Romantic

My Seventh Vision into tomorrow's Neo-Tech World showed me that ordinary men had a lot of romantic go-power. Accomplishing and surpassing our dreams became our ongoing source of energy and happiness. *Love* and spending time with our loved ones became our way to *feel* all that happiness.

The Seventh Vision showed me that life was a ball. The careers of our dreams awaited us every morning, full of creative projects that beckoned us...teased us...while we were with our women. And the women of our dreams awaited us, full of love and affection that beckoned us...teased us...while we were with our jobs. We felt good. Every day was like a tycoon/romance story!

Life became an indescribable treat. Nearly every man fell deeply in love with his spouse.   With her, he felt incredible during the celebrations. You see, in the entrepreneurial job of his dreams, he lived in a cornucopia overflowing with excitement and happiness. He enjoyed all that earned happiness with the woman of his dreams (and his loved ones). Now, he finally knew that building and enjoying his earned happiness was the meaning of life. Romantic love (and family love) was what he ultimately lived for.

Rediscovering the Thrill

Most men today, trapped in the anticivilization, lose their romantic selves because they have nonliving jobs. Stuck in stagnation, most men just do not feel romantic. In the end, for most couples, profound happiness is a forgotten love-struck moment of the past.

After America went Neo-Tech and the ordinary man felt the pulse of a living job, he felt alive and romantic again. He rediscovered the thrill of living.

In tomorrow's new way of living, his motto was, "Inject myself into life!" The more values he created, the more exhilarated he became. With his mini-day/power-thinking tools from the Fifth Vision, with his downstream focus from the First Vision, he eventually advanced on a unique vector of value creation. As a value creator, he discovered harmony with himself, the world around him, the Universe. He discovered power — the power of his consciousness...the power (and emotional rewards) of making a difference and creating values for mankind.

Once you use the New Techniques (Neo-Tech) in Vision Five and you start rolling along in a living job, then to stop your exciting, new value creation and spend time with your woman might, at first, cause a conflict. You might ask, how can I jump off my locomotive of value creation to "skip through the woods"? If that happens, and you have a hard time enjoying the celebrations, then you have to rethink what you are living for: *happiness*.

The inherent sadness of life, the shortness of your time to experience everything you will ever know, underscores the supreme importance of happiness. By acknowledging the shortness of life, you realize you *must* let yourself feel intense happiness during your brief time, for everything special in life you will *ever feel* happens only during your brief years alive. Indeed, the celebrations let you *feel* the happiness you earn. Building and feeling happiness is the meaning of life. Building happiness comes through value creation; feeling happiness comes

155

through the celebrations with your woman and loved ones.

Moreover, you will accomplish bigger and better dreams when motivated by *the woman of your dreams*. You will travel farther and faster in your freight train of value creation with her aboard. For, motivated by the woman *of your dreams*, your train will always be well fueled, and you will conduct that train from the highest view of life. You will be wiser because of your relationship, and you will see wider horizons. You will reach exciting destinations that before, without romantic love, were unseeable, thus unreachable.

The Celebrations

Life tomorrow, as shown to me in the Seventh Vision, was the reverse of most people's lives today in which time hangs heavy on their hands and is boring. Men on their Friday-Night Essences felt incredible and poured on the love and affection during the time they were with their women and families. With their living jobs, they had inside a bottomless well of happiness and romance because they accomplished their dreams and then built new dreams. Their women, at first, lived in disbelief at their husbands' romantic power. Every day, the time men spent with their wives was *a celebration!*

I know from first-hand experience that the deep, permanent happiness achieved by men tomorrow on their Friday-Night Essences in living jobs, creating values for the world, emits a feel-good sensation throughout their bodies and souls. I know this sensation personally because I use the New Techniques (Neo-Tech). That feel-good sensation stimulates a lot of energy. And that abundance of energy overflows into a man's love life and family life.

On the other hand, without that deep, permanent happiness, stuck in today's routine ruts, most men do not have that feel-good sensation inside. They have little energy left over after work...not enough for passionate romantic love and joyous family love.

That lack of romantic and family love occurs in most marriages and families today; they have no idea what they could have together.

156

But those few who pursue these New Techniques (Neo-Tech) prior to the Neo-Tech World and acquire a living job today, build values for society, success and happiness for themselves, and celebrations with their spouses and families, have to be aware of a threat to their celebrations. Surrounding those rare, *deeply happy* people today, prior to the Neo-Tech society, are subliminal influences against being happy. For, "how dare you indulge in large doses of happiness," the anticivilization around us says.

To overcome society's subliminal scolding, remind yourself of the sadness — the brief time you are here to experience everything in life you will ever know in all eternity. Then, as an early pioneer to the Neo-Tech World, you can go all out for super guilt-free happiness. You can let all your happiness come out with no apologies, especially during the celebrations with your woman and family.

Getting Back the Celebrations

My Seventh Vision showed me that when society went through the transition into the Neo-Tech World, getting back our emotional celebrations of our falling-in-love days long ago was not easy at first. You see, right at first men did not necessarily miss those celebrations that happened long ago in their pasts. Men were still a bit numb to love after many years under the old code of living. We simply accepted that the celebrations slowly ended...as was to be expected. Then, everything went back to "normal".

Is that what happened to you? Did the celebrations quietly die? Did you forget how you felt so incredible...so special and loved as though you were the most important man in the world and the greatest lover alive? What an exciting event it was every time she was there! Yet, you and your wife probably never looked back or felt a tug in your hearts for the passionate and precious moments once felt between you. The celebrations simply got left behind, and in the anticivilization you would never have them again.

You will, however, vividly remember them when one of you are gone. Then, like so many poor souls in the anticivilization, you will feel unforgiving sorrow that you spent your lives together *without* the celebrations.

But the fault is not yours. Saturated by the negative influences around you in our politicized society, you cannot hold onto the very purpose for living your short life — *super happiness* during your one brief moment in all eternity.

Just what is lost in the anticivilization? The goal of life is lost. You should be enjoying your brief moment in eternity with intense happiness. But, your celebrations lasted only for a few weeks or maybe months — while falling in love. ...Your brief time in all eternity brought only a miniature moment of intense happiness.

In my Seventh Vision, ordinary men, stagnant for so very long, generations long, could not bring themselves back to those celebrations until they felt the insane sadness of life. You see, in the Neo-Tech World, men and women loved life so much that it magnified the tragedy of death. The intensely happy people could barely believe that when life ended, and it ended so soon, all was gone. This sadness of life granted them the rightness of super happiness. Suddenly, they could feel the tragedy of having lost the celebrations. And only then could they emotionally rediscover the celebration.

Becoming Irresistible

In the Neo-Tech World, all ordinary men— yes, *you* naturally regained your romantic self. Here was why: Consider that, when you first fell in love, going to a movie felt wonderful regardless how the movie turned out. After a few months, however, if the movie was not good, then the whole evening was uneventful. You now needed external sources of entertainment to bring happiness and excitement into your life. Overall, life became boring.

By contrast, after the job revolution you never became bored and were never boring. The reason was: you did not need external sources of entertainment to bring happiness and excitement into your life. Your creations did. You spent time with your wife and family *to experience* that endless flow of happiness. And since *everyone* was like that in the nonpoliticized no-lose supersociety, there were no negative influences around you tearing you down.

You enjoyed being romantic and sexual. Your woman became powerfully drawn to your strength, aroused by your manliness, and she slimmed down to a sexy, desirous peach (described in Vision Eight).

Second Part For Women
How To Love A Superman

My Seventh Vision first took me a ways into the 21st century and showed me that not long after America went Neo-Tech, nearly every woman proudly showed off her man, for he was a very successful and attractive superman — a real *man*. Ladies, have you ever looked at one of those very successful and attractive men — a real *man* — and wondered how to get one of those guys for yourselves? Did you eventually shrug off the thought, resigned to dying without ever experiencing romantic love with a superman? When America went Neo-Tech, however, your husband transformed into one of those quality men. And in tomorrow's Neo-Tech World, he cherished you as if you were the only woman alive.

Whatever happened to the power of love that once overwhelmed you and your husband? Where did those wonderful celebrations go? Of course, they died in today's suppressed world. But they came back in the Neo-Tech World sometime in the 21st century. Let us look ahead at tomorrow's typical love-life as shown to me during my Seventh Vision:

What Sparked Love?

In tomorrow's Neo-Tech World, the ordinary woman was wealthy, healthy, and happy. With no more financial, physical, and emotional burdens of the anticivilization, the nature of woman flourished in the Neo-Tech World. Free of the debilitating forces of the old code of living, now when she sought her dream man, she sought a man who made her feel very proud. Of course, a man with a sense of humor, good looks, and a pleasant personality attracted her, too. But for the love to grow, a woman fell in love with a man for his real-man element —

his value creation, his accomplishments. To fall *deeply* in love, she had to see competence, strength, and success in her dream man.

Her Wish Came True

The Seventh Vision showed me every woman's deepest romantic wish came true: she married a superman. You see, in the new nonpoliticized supersociety, ordinary men became supermen. The job revolution in the 21st century brought ordinary men and women into that world of super competence and eventually Neothink. Nearly every woman looked up to and fell in love with her Neothink God-Man creating major values and building his dreams. He made her feel deeply proud; the values she upheld as important were reflected in her man. He symbolized her values in life; indeed, everything she represented was symbolically reflected in her dream man — the man she allowed to "take" her. ...He was a model of success, competence, and strength.

Women tomorrow were drawn toward strength, competence, accomplishment in men. Men zoomed ahead with natural downstream focus (Vision One) into value creation and success. Women zoomed ahead on their Friday-Night Essences too, but they also discovered a second Friday-Night Essence: contributing emotionally and tangibly toward their husbands' success. To understand this, let us look at the biological nature of a woman:

Mating and Her Biological Nature

A woman physically and psychologically "surrenders" her body and soul to her lover. Her body and soul is "taken", dominated and penetrated by her *chosen* man during lovemaking. To fall passionately in love, she has to look up to the man she gives herself to. He must be worthy of her. She has to see in him everything she upholds as important. For, he whom she chooses to "surrender herself to" symbolizes the value of her own self.

With her survival needs well met in the Neo-Tech World, my Seventh Vision showed me that every woman sought a superman

160

— a man with competence and strength...a man she could really look up to.

Because of her biological nature, a woman gained more and more happiness the more she could admire her man, his success and value creation. Therefore, I saw in tomorrow's Neo-Tech World the ordinary woman supporting her husband's value creation. The more she could do to help propel him forward in his career, the more she felt genuine pride, admiration and happiness. Supporting both emotionally and tangibly her husband's success was a source of happiness for her, too. Her contribution to his value creation was her value creation, too.

Today in the anticivilization's suppressed society, men become miserably stagnated in their careers and women become stifled in their marriages. Tomorrow, I saw the ordinary man was happy with a career he admired; the ordinary woman was happy with a man she admired. Tomorrow, men became much more successful and women became more supportive.[1]

A Woman's Emotional Nature

As we transcend today's suppressed society and rise into tomorrow's Neo-Tech World sometime in the 21st century, the ordinary woman's psyche will leave behind certain pervasive, debilitating influences of the anticivilization. For example, in today's politicized anticivilization, many women readers reject the idea that a woman "surrenders" to a man during lovemaking; they reject it as something unequal. The Seventh Vision showed me that in tomorrow's Neo-Tech World, whereas a man and a woman's similarities were recognized, so were their differences. Those differences made them unique and special to each other. For example, a woman's emotional nature brought an irreplaceable value into a man's life. He cherished that fulfilling

---

[1]This does not mean women did not have careers. In fact, a woman's career was also a very real *source* of happiness. But that woman, even as a career woman, sought the superman *she* could look up to — someone more accomplished than herself. She took great pride in her superman's accomplishments and was very supportive of his success.

dimension he could not experience without her. The woman brought out the man. The man brought out the woman.

Their private world existed for both to share and to enjoy, which included each other's differences and unique qualities as man and woman. Great pleasures and mutual value exchanges came from being different, from being woman...from being man. That private world was for each other only and had no bearing on a woman's public world including her career and interaction with other men outside her romantic-love relationship. She could go just as far as any man in any career she chose. But her lover was someone special — someone she could look up to and admire...someone she could "surrender" to.

Without acknowledging her biological and emotional nature in today's anticivilization, a woman misses the very understanding of looking up to and admiring a man for her own happiness. Thus, she forever misses her deepest happiness in life and loses the deepest pleasure and joy of being a woman deeply in love.

Tomorrow, however, in the Neo-Tech World, she did not deny her nature. She fell in love with a man she could look up to and admire. She fell in love with a superman she could "surrender" her body and soul to. She loved having such a man and discovering intense happiness and lifelong celebrations. Her chances at getting a superman (from within her own spouse if she was married) were certain when America went Neo-Tech.

In today's world, unfortunately, a woman's odds are diminished or destroyed if the wonderful differences between man and woman get obscured. Tomorrow, fortunately, the ordinary woman's psyche left behind any such denial of her nature.

His Flame Never Died

In the Neo-Tech World, your superman's flame for you never died. You see, happiness is the crucial ingredient for a love affair to last forever. Where does happiness come from? The answer that came to me in the Seventh Vision was not what you might think. To easily answer that question, the Seventh Vision provided me with an observation of the transitional period from the old world to the new world: During the transition, people who took more from society than they put in — unproductive people, from destructive thieves to prestigious politicians — had no base of happiness and no potential for happiness. People who put more into society than they took — productive people, from productive housewives to wealthy self-made entrepreneurs — had a base of happiness and a potential for unlimited happiness.

The age-old riddle was solved: what is happiness? Happiness is putting values into society, *value production* at first, *value creation* eventually, which sent people onto the entirely new dimension of *eternal* happiness — free of the burden of life.

Man is a social animal who lives together in a society. Putting values into that society gives him pride and happiness. Building more and more values for society builds more and more pride and happiness for himself. The Seventh Vision showed me, after the transition into the Neo-Tech World, unproductive and unhappy people no longer existed.

So, value creation is the key to happiness. And lifelong happiness is crucial for lasting romantic love. Today, in the anticivilization, your husband is most likely trapped in a rut at work and cannot advance into value creation. Stagnation sets in and happiness wanes. Tomorrow, after the job revolution described in the Fifth Vision, he enthusiastically soared ahead in the career of his dreams. Every day he built more happiness inside through his living job, and every day he let that feeling flow out through love and passion for the woman for whom his flame burned.

Of course, that woman was the one who fueled his flame — the woman who supported his accomplishments and goals. His work was his way to build happiness, but you were his way to *feel* all that happiness.

His Flame Burned Forever...For Only You

Tomorrow your husband, the exciting superman making his best dreams come true, was a dynamo. His bottomless enthusiasm for value creation filled big reservoirs of happiness and love. He enveloped you with a special love and tenderness that took you into a private world untouched by anyone else. And *the preciousness* of your private world was the foundation upon which romantic love was built in the Neo-Tech World.

In today's stagnant world, the sweetness and tenderness dies with time. As our happiness wanes, our love fades. Sometimes we look outside our marriages for those lost special feelings. But in tomorrow's Neo-Tech World, all that changed. As your husband filled his reservoirs of happiness, precious feelings for you grew...and grew. My Vision showed me that those happy men tomorrow such as your husband never desired any other women beyond their own spouses. *The preciousness* of their private worlds with their spouses made the relationships inseparable, even in the face of other quality women and men.

Because of the endless flow of happiness in tomorrow's Neo-Tech World, you truly celebrated your love, not for a few months, but for decades. Throughout your one moment of time, you were always filled with happiness and love.

Find Love Today

Any woman today, by the way, can use these New Techniques (Neo-Tech) now to spark love in one of today's successful supermen and enjoy a lifetime of the preciousness before it is too late. Simply do today what the women in my Seventh Vision did tomorrow: show him you are attracted to him because of his accomplishments. All focussed men love being noticed by a woman. Take a genuine, deep interest in each specific accomplishment. Show admiration for his success. Increasingly become his reward for his competence and achievement, and you will spark his love.

Your growing attraction to him will reflect his competence and ability to draw such a wonderful woman. Your growing love and admiration for him will reflect his success as a man; your desire to contribute to his life will make him feel spectacular; Cupid's arrow will strike. Indeed, true love happens to a successful man through this reflection of his value creation and competence.

Remember, if you are married, I witnessed that in tomorrow's

Neo-Tech World, after the job revolution sometime in the 21st century, most men soared ahead in living jobs (Fifth Vision), enthusiastically accomplishing their dreams and beyond. Your husband will become one of those supermen.

As your husband transforms into your dream man, making your dream love come true, you will find yourself motivated to fuel his flame. As your husband becomes a successful superman in tomorrow's living jobs, he will eventually bring values to the world he could never even imagine today in his routine rut. With all that value creation, he will become wonderfully happy and passionately romantic. His value creation will steadily fuel his flame of love. Motivated to help fuel his flame, you will emotionally and often tangibly support his value creation. His brightly burning flame will always warm his precious, supportive woman.

True To Your Heart

The bottom line in every person's life is: *happiness.* You must be true to what brings you happiness in life. A lifelong, passionate romantic-love relationship with a superman brings a woman happiness in life. Down deep, all women want that. Tomorrow, in the Neo-Tech World, all women had that. My Seventh Vision showed me fairy-tale love and happiness that, before, women only dreamed about.

Tomorrow the ordinary woman loved to make her husband, her superman, feel special. He came to her to *feel* life's greatest attraction: happiness. He built his happiness through his competitive creations; he *felt* his happiness through you. It mattered not what you did together. Like the first few weeks of falling in love, even walking through a grocery store together was wonderful.

In the Neo-Tech World, the ordinary man was extraordinary. He had a living job and built values and dreams and happiness; and when he was with his woman, no matter where they were or what they were doing, he celebrated his happiness with her. On his own, he seldom left his living job just "to have something to do" or for the entertainment itself. But he did take substantial time from his living job to be with her and with his family and closest friends.[1]

Tomorrow, love stayed as pure as the first few beautiful weeks. Impurities, from financial worries to emotional worries, did not intrude into the love affair. Nearly every ordinary man turned into a superman, and he cherished his woman for the feelings she brought to him...for an *entire lifetime.*

Today, any woman who uses these 21st-century love techniques can sweep the rare superman off his feet. Leona Helmsley did it back in the 20th century. For, once a superman gets a taste of real romantic love, then he lets himself go and rediscovers *the celebration.* Romantic feelings rise from the innermost depths of his happy soul as he rediscovers the celebration of true love.

Looking forward into the Seventh Vision, women put out a conscious effort to bring happiness into their supermen's lives every day. Realize that a man's effort into the relationship was different than a woman's. You see, a man in a living job tomorrow drove forward broader value creation than his woman.[2] He moved forward with her a joint journey toward exciting goals. He drove aggressively on his work and built a base of happiness for both himself and his wife...and his family. His effort was for her, too.

Describing Your Husband

Of course, we are describing your husband *after* the job revolution. Your future superman will enthusiastically look forward to the celebration — to the affection and romance —

---

[1]Man tomorrow celebrated his happiness with his woman and family; he built that happiness through his value creation, *his essence.* Woman tomorrow had *dual* essences: her value creation *and* her man and family, which were also a woman's value creation. (The technical explanation of woman's *dual essences* was not included here, but you can get a sense of it. The technical treatment can be found in Mark Hamilton's *Happiness Forever*, 240 pages, Neo-Tech Publishing Company.)

[2]This did not mean women were less capable than men. But when they paired up after the job revolution, women sought men who were more accomplished in business than themselves.

with you, every day. He will discover a whole new dimension to life as the time celebrated with you becomes a major event of happiness. With you, life will become a luscious treat, an almost unbearable tease. You see, anticipation will play on him all day long at work. Then, when he sees you, he will become very romantic as he covers you with love and affection; he will *really feel* and celebrate his happiness with you. Unlike today's anticivilization in which your husband more than likely passively receives or perhaps brushes off whatever love and affection you send his way, tomorrow in the Neo-Tech World your husband will really pour it on!

Turning Him On

In turn, you will really turn him on! You see, the *psychological emotion* — love — is *physically captured* through affection. Indeed, the emotions of love are sent back and forth physically between two people through affection; so physical affection captures and shares physically what the mind and heart feel emotionally. You will realize, as a woman, the importance of being physically desirable. You will become sexier than you have ever been through a 21st-century slim-and-sexy secret (revealed in the Eighth Vision). With such a nice body, the physical affection will come very easily. If the physical affection is enhanced, then the feelings inside are enhanced.

Now, you will pour on the affection each and every day as you did once before, during the first few falling-in-love weeks. No matter what you and your superman do together in the new world, from entertainment to clothes shopping — you will always be very affectionate. Again, affection is the way you *feel* your love for each other. And you really will be in love! Your husband will discover, with you, *the celebration* of life...the very meaning of life. Both of you will look forward to that celebration, every single day. ...Only a fairy-tale? I saw it all happen in my Seventh Vision.

Love-Life — Summary

Section One For Men:

1) Pursue a Living Job (Value Creation): Your biological nature dictates that your essence is your thrust into your career success. Deep happiness comes not from hobbies, vacations, or sports, but from value creation. Put your focus in life on your career and pursue a living job.
2) Open Your Heart (Value Reflection): As you pursue your essence and build your happiness, you must discover how to *experience* that earned happiness. You must open your heart and soul to your woman and children and discover the celebrations. Take time every day for your love.

Section Two For Women:

1) Spark the Superman's Love: Show your attraction to his real-man element — his value creation. A superman who is not yet in love cannot help falling in love with an attractive woman drawn to and turned on by his competence.
2) Fuel the Superman's Flame: Emotionally support and, wherever possible, tangibly contribute to his real-man element — his value creation. A superman cannot help growing close to the woman supporting and contributing to his essence as man.
3) Pursue Your Dual Essences: A genuine source of happiness for every woman is the success of her husband. So, while you pursue your career in business or at home, also pursue your superman; emotionally and tangibly support his career — a source of happiness for you, too.

A Love Tip

For those trying the love techniques, keep a list of things to do together for the upcoming week. Also, decide in the morning what you will do together that evening. Then you look forward to it all day long. Otherwise, deciding at the last moment turns the celebration into a chore.

The list, in a sense, acts as a power-thinking list (see Fifth Vision) for your celebrations. You should also establish a consistent, designated time you will spend together each day. That designated time together, in a sense, is a sort of mini-day. Because of the free-flowing nature of this time, the mini-day and power-thinking are not as rigid as in a living job. The mini-day and power-thinking act as an informal guide to facilitate the celebrations. ...Now, put it all together, and go out and enjoy life!

Vision Eight
A Beach-Model Body Will Emerge In You...and In Your Spouse

How To Have A Super Body

In the midst of the Seventh Vision, suddenly I noticed images of ordinary people's bodies in the Neo-Tech World. They all looked so beautiful or handsome — like models! Could that really be, I wondered. Tomorrow's world was so romantic...and sexy. My Eighth Vision shifted to our bodies. In today's anticivilization, we tend to put on weight because we live in a suppressed society and become bored. Food breaks the boredom; food is stimulation. In tomorrow's world, however, everything changed. In my Eighth Vision of the Neo-Tech World, our lives were not boring. We no longer looked toward food to break the boredom. Eating was looked at more as a chore and was done with efficiency in mind. Our bodies naturally trimmed down to our optimum, most sexy weights. I witnessed the essence behind our slim and sexy bodies tomorrow; which I personally used to get a slim body today:

The Secret of Slim

Three powerful evolutionary forces have always dictated our eating patterns:
- *hunger* dictated when we ate,
- *craving* dictated what we ate,
- *fullness* dictated how much we ate.

Throughout the 20th-century, the struggles we went through while trying to lose weight were very intense because we were fighting those powerful multi-million-year-old evolutionary forces. *The secret* of the gorgeous bodies tomorrow, as shown to me, was to not fight those unbeatable forces, but to instead join them and make them work for us. Then, the 21st-century eating pattern became so in line with our nature that it was the most satisfying diet; it was downright "addicting"!

171

In fact, the 21st-century eating pattern was much more rewarding, satisfying, and fulfilling than a chubby person's diet today and much easier to stay on. In fact, when I tried the 21st-century eating pattern, *Neo-Tech Eating*[1], it was downright hard to ever stop, for it was in natural accord with our evolutionary forces.

The endless diets in the 20th century and early 21st century fought the three most powerful evolutionary forces in our physiological makeup — the three forces of eating: craving, hunger, fullness. The magic in tomorrow's Neo-Tech Eating was that it not only embraced the three forces of eating but actually intensified their satisfaction. Craving, hunger, fullness actually felt more intensely rewarded as Neo-Tech Eating reconditioned us away from infinitely diverse desires for endless different foods, eating times, and quantities to intensified, targeted foods, eating times, and quantities. Going from many foods, eating times, and quantities to one food, eating time, and quantity intensified craving, hunger, and fullness to such a level that we experienced "a fix" with each meal — "a fix" that ironically became more powerful and more "addicting" as we lost weight! Nothing in this world could give you the uniquely wonderful feeling that came from Neo-Tech Eating. I know, because I *enjoyed* taking off 30 pounds!

I personally tried tomorrow's Neo-Tech Eating, as shown to me during my Eighth Vision. Here, I put it together into a diet and named it Neo-Tech Eating (because it was the fundamental eating pattern of people in the Neo-Tech World). Let us start with two secrets and twelve facts about tomorrow's Neo-Tech Eating:

---

[1]In the Neo-Tech World, after the nationwide division of essence in business when people raced forward on their Friday-Night essences, Neo-Tech Eating described here naturally turned into our 21st-century eating pattern. But in the anticivilization's suppressed world in which food breaks the boredom, Neo-Tech Eating is still...a diet.

Two Secrets/Twelve Facts

Secret One: Fullness Level

1) You cannot be afraid to eat — the resulting fear or nervousness causes the desire to eat for calmness. With Neo-Tech Eating, you will eat, you will also <u>fill your desire</u>. So, unlike tough 20th-century diets, there is no need to be nervous or to fear this 21st-century diet.

2) Your body knows a "fullness level". It will prompt you to eat until that fullness level is complete.

3) People who are overweight, that fullness level is too high. We will adjust that fullness level.

4) The same concept applies to average-weight people who want to be slim — we will simply adjust your fullness level, too.

5) The reason most diets fail is that they do not deal with fullness level. They deal with reducing caloric intake, putting the cart before the horse. If your body is struggling or craving more food, you will eventually give in.

6) Neo-Tech Eating is designed around your fullness level. In fact, the first week of Neo-Tech Eating is designed to locate your fullness level, not to lose weight.

Two Secrets/Twelve Facts

Secret Two: Replace Overwhelming, Infinite Struggles with an Easy-To-Handle, Solo Struggle

7) When you reduce calories, your body craves more food.

What multiplies the problem is the infinite choices of food making infinite triggers to set off cravings. The many struggles add up and become overwhelming.

8) Infinite, endless temptations cannot be beaten.

9) Neo-Tech Eating conditions the body to crave <u>one thing only</u>. Then, when fullness-level adjustments occur, your body has only one struggle to overcome — its one craving. The struggle is far from overwhelming and the body quickly adjusts.

10) After the fullness-level adjustment is made, one can eat diversely again. Simply go back to Neo-Tech Eating whenever the need arises.

11) This approach works <u>permanently</u> for overweight people.

12) Also, this is the one and only diet that can enable people without a weight problem to get a new look — the model-slim look.

The Hidden Key: Eat What You Crave

Have you ever been so involved in some project so exciting that you forgot to eat? Finally, when your stomach hurt, you probably grabbed whatever, maybe a quick burger or pizza so as to least distract your focus from your prized project. If you were ever so lucky to enjoy such a motivating event, you got a glimpse of how your life was every single day in the Neo-Tech World. My Eighth Vision showed me that you were so motivated by your competitive creations that you forgot about food. In fact, you pretty much grabbed the same thing each day for breakfast and lunch out of convenience. As the days went by, eating the same breakfast, lunch and often grabbing the same dinner simply out of convenience while not losing momentum

174

or focus on your exciting creations...an odd thing happened: you stopped craving your favorite foods. In fact, the only thing you could now classify as a "craving" was for those very same foods you had been eating out of convenience over and over again.

Your new "big-shot" lifestyle dramatically affected your eating pattern. Eating was now an afterthought only. Ironically, you now preferred the same old thing, "the usual", for breakfast, lunch, even dinner. If someone brought you something different, although you would smile and say "thanks," you probably would have rather had "the usual".

Having witnessed this unusual new eating pattern in my Eighth Vision, I realized we could adopt that Neo-Tech eating pattern (less the exciting lifestyle, of course) today. A powerful diet could be patterned after the eating habits of people in tomorrow's Neo-Tech World.

I realized, the master key to this 21st-century diet was: you could now eat what you craved! Therefore, it would work now and always.

"But if I ate what I craved, I'd become a blimp," you say? Well, did you know that you can get your body to crave certain foods and certain quantities at certain times of the day? When those particular foods and quantities are consumed, you will become relaxed and satisfied until your next scheduled craving.

The master key is you can now develop your own cravings. And so be it: you can now eat what you crave.

I further realized you could develop your own dynamics of hunger and fullness once you got used to eating at set times and set quantities. The three evolutionary forces that dictated our eating patterns not only could be custom made for us, but could for the first time be made to work *for* losing weight instead of against it. Of course, you could imagine the "new you" that would come from this new diet.

In today's world, if you are normal, you crave just about everything all the time. That problem creates ongoing struggles in your life. Since the choices of foods are almost infinite, the odds are overwhelming that your cravings will win. And they do. The ongoing struggles against "giving in" wear people down, and they eventually give in. Every evening from dinner to bedtime, for instance, the poor dieter has to go through a dozen or so struggles just to keep from biting into one of the dozens of available foods in the average pantry. In time, most people lose the endless battle and eventually become overweight.

The only way to effectively and permanently lose weight is to remove *the struggles* — the cause of becoming overweight. Trying to reduce intake per se does a temporary job at best because the struggles still exist. Those struggles occur every day and every evening. Such persistency eventually prevails.

You see, in today's world, we tend to get bored with lots of time on our hands, especially in the evenings. During those uneventful evenings, the desire to snack is persistent; the struggles to keep from snacking are relentless. But the Eighth Vision showed me that in the Neo-Tech World, we were wrapped up in such exciting projects at work and such exciting celebrations with our spouses and families at home, we seldom thought about eating and almost never desired to snack. So, the struggles to keep from snacking did not even exist. Your cravings for the endless foods in your pantry were gone.

Adopting the magic behind tomorrow's slim and sexy looks, let us get to the reason — *no struggles*. The struggles, of course, are your natural cravings for the endless different foods in your pantry and refrigerator. So, to eliminate those struggles, we will start this Neo-Tech Eating by dealing with the physical cravings:

Eliminating sweets, think of your favorite breakfast, your favorite lunch, your favorite dinner, and your favorite evening snack. Ask yourself: "What breakfast, lunch, dinner, evening snack do I like enough to have over and over again every single day for the next two months?" Think about this, because for at least the next month or two you will eat the very same breakfast, lunch, dinner, and evening snack each day.

At first, this may seem boring. But you will find that your body becomes conditioned to those foods and begins craving those foods and, eventually, only those foods. When you eat, your body becomes much more intensely satisfied because its one and only exact craving is hit — bull's-eye. And as we begin to gradually adjust your fullness level down, your body's craving goes up. Its craving will be for these specific foods only. When your craving intensifies, your satisfaction level intensifies when you eat your next meal. Neo-Tech Eating actually becomes addicting to where you never want to leave it even after getting the model look.

After my Eighth Vision, I tried the Neo-Tech eating pattern myself and became Neo-Tech Eating's prototype. After losing thirty pounds, I had to eventually force myself off the diet and from my intensely targeted cravings to eat more diverse dinners with the family. In short, Neo-Tech Eating *felt good.*

The First Week: Establish Fullness Level And Cravings

The first week of Neo-Tech Eating will be spent determining what you like to eat, excluding sweets, and the amount that makes you full. Eat your selected foods at about the same time each day, always the same food. Find the level where you feel comfortably full and have no additional hunger cravings.

Hone in on that evening snack. Eating in the evenings is where the most damage is done to weight control. We more or less eat what our bodies need during the day. The evening eating is the unneeded excess food that causes us to gain. For this evening snack, select a food that is not sweet but is satisfying in taste and fullness. I personally chose unsweetened frozen blueberries and poured evaporated milk on them. The thick milk froze into a creamy substance, as if I were eating blueberry ice cream. (You may prefer to mix the blueberries and evaporated milk in a blender and then freeze a little longer if you really want to give it a blueberry ice cream consistency.) I'd sprinkle the blueberries with a packet or two of Equal or Sweet'n Low. That satisfied both my sweet tooth and my fullness level. And that blueberry ice cream concoction took a long and satisfying time to eat every evening.

One substantial evening snack that does not change night after night begins to condition your body to crave that one food. You look for that one food, that same amount, at about the same time. As the craving grows, so does the satisfaction when fed. Soon, you desire no other foods or feedings in the evening at all. ...You are now on your way to controlling your weight, all while feeling more and more satisfied! This magical Neo-Tech Eating becomes more satisfying and far easier than a chubby person's diet or even a normal person's diet, for they are always fighting their cravings.

The Second Week: Weight Reduction Begins

Now you have been eating the exact same breakfast, lunch, dinner and evening snack — always at about the same time — every day for one full week. You have been eating the same amount each day — an amount that leaves you satisfied. Now, you will reduce one of those four feedings — the evening snack. You will cut that evening snack in half.

When this happens, your diet actually increases in satisfaction. Here's why: Instead of completely satisfying your fullness level now, you are slightly below it. That immediately intensifies your targeted cravings, which intensifies the satisfaction when servicing those cravings — bull's-eye. Suddenly, when you cut that evening snack in half, you will find yourself craving your next feeding — in this case, your breakfast. You will enjoy that breakfast and feel exceptionally good after eating it.

Remember, you have established one set food at a set time and quantity for each meal. When you cut your evening snack in half and fall below your fullness level, suddenly those "boring" set foods you have been loyally eating each day after day take on a life of their own. You see, now you begin to really *crave those foods*. Before long, you not only crave them, but you crave *only* those set foods and those set quantities!

At first, you will experience a struggle — one solo struggle — in the evening now that your evening snack is half. But that one solo struggle will not last long — a few days — before your body adjusts. Your body will never adjust when fighting infinite struggles, but a solo struggle subsides quickly. When that solo struggle subsides, you have permanently reformed your fullness level. You will acquire a new look at that reformed fullness level. Congratulations!

Again, a nice benefit about this diet is: as you reduce or eliminate one craving/feeding, you intensify the other cravings/feedings, which intensifies your satisfaction throughout the day while servicing those cravings. Neo-Tech Eating creates a powerful and unique physical satisfaction you can get no other way.

As your fullness level adjusts downward, you *will not* experience an increased appetite during your other set feedings, just a more intense craving for those set foods and quantities, and a more intense satisfaction at each feeding. ...After the second week, you begin feeling very healthy and in control.

The Third Week: Noticeable Weight Loss

Before we go on, let me make a point: You are on your way to losing weight that can finally stay off for the rest of your life. So, you have no reason to push this along. Take your time. If this schedule brings up a sense of panic, then *double* the timetable. If, going into this third week, you feel anxieties about dropping the evening snack altogether, then wait another week *or longer* until you truly *feel* ready. Feelings of fear or anxiety or panic are not only common but totally natural when losing weight. We emotionally fight a fear of failure. Moreover, our bodies are so private and important to us that we simply tend to get nervous when dieting. All those feelings hurt your progress and are unnecessary. If you feel nervous or seem afraid to take the next step, then don't. Wait until your body tells you it's ready. Your body will tell you when it's right — both physically *and* emotionally — for *you.*

That being said, now you will eliminate the evening snack altogether. Most dieters strive to achieve this goal, for this accomplishment is when major weight loss occurs. But those dieters eventually fail at this point. Moreover, they subconsciously know they are going to fail, leaving them nervous and anxious, wanting to eat even more.

Our secret here is: We have reduced the evening struggles from overwhelming infinite struggles to one solo struggle — our *one* craving — that we can overcome.

Just as you conditioned your body from infinite cravings at feeding times to one set craving, you will soon condition your body from one set craving for your evening snack to *no* craving at all. Your other cravings will intensify, especially breakfast. But your evening craving will go away. Now, here is an important tip: Until then, go to bed early in the evenings. That is the easiest and quickest way to beat your one solo struggle before it goes away forever. Also, I enjoyed sipping on a 16-ounce bottle of caffeine-free diet pop. It just kept my mouth occupied in the evenings.

Once that evening craving is gone, you have again successfully adjusted your daily fullness level downward. Now you have a whole new fullness level. With it will come a whole new look — a substantially slimmer look. Your new fullness level is permanent because the struggles have left. Congratulations.

The Fourth Week: Going For It

Let me reiterate: This may be the eighth week (or longer) for you, and that is perfectly fine. You do not even need to think about this step until you and your body say, "It's time." In fact, I suggest holding off on this step until you see just how slim you become first with your new fullness level that eliminates the evening snack. Then and only then, if you still want to go slimmer, here's what you do:

Realize that every *successful* diet ultimately reduces to rationing. But the rationing process fails because of the infinite cravings (i.e., struggles). Our secret to success here is reducing infinite random cravings to one targeted craving. Whereas people cannot overcome infinite cravings bombarding them at many different times throughout the day, they can overcome one craving that arises at one set time during the day. First we reduce infinite cravings to one craving; then we reduce that one craving to no cravings. At this point, we have permanently reformed our fullness level.

Now, if we want to become slimmer still, we permanently reform our fullness level again. Realize that only by *eliminating* our craving (for a full feeding or for a particular quantity) do we forever keep off the weight. Other diets eliminate some intake, but the cravings remain in full force (or are amplified by hunger, nervousness, and anxieties). Therefore, the dieter loses in the end. Neo-Tech Eating, by contrast, eliminates the craving by systematically reforming the fullness level.

After eliminating all desire for an evening snack (or simply cutting it in half if that brings the desired results), you must target one of your other feedings to reduce the quantity if you want to go slimmer still. For me, that was breakfast. My body simply has little appetite in the morning, so I cut my breakfast in half. Of course, that made my set lunches much more satisfying. Soon, I cut out breakfast altogether and simply stopped craving it. Again, I reformed my fullness level.

All my body wanted now was lunch and dinner. And, wow, did I ever enjoy those two set cravings...or, perhaps more descriptively, two set "addictions" that left me feeling really good, like a "fix" — the most satisfying diet I have ever tried. Although I never would have believed it when I was heavier, I now only craved two meals a day and was far more satisfied than when I was heavier and always watching what I ate to keep from getting fat. When I was heavier, my diet was a constant struggle. Now, it was no struggle at all, yet more intensely satisfying! I really liked the unique feeling from Neo-Tech Eating. ...I actually miss it.

Today, I have no more struggles. I am thirty pounds lighter and have been this weight for years. I had to leave this diet of one set food for my two meals as a father who eats dinner with his family. But my reformed fullness level never left me. Now and then I go back to Neo-Tech Eating when I feel my appetite going up. I easily lasso it back. I have told my wife over and over how happy I am to look so young and slim when so many of my peers have unfortunately lost their youthful looks to weight gain.

A Final Comment: Use Any Combination Best For You

Neo-Tech Eating harnesses the two essentials to permanently losing weight: 1) Reduce the infinite struggles to one struggle, by establishing set cravings. 2) Then, eliminate the solo struggle to no struggle, permanently reforming fullness level.

Every person has different psychological and physical needs or desires. For some, it is simply a psychological (not a physical) *must* to have an evening snack to help relax and, perhaps, accompany watching TV. If that is your situation, DO NOT WORRY. After all, we are still in an anticivilization and just may have that need until the Neo-Tech World makes our

The Neo-Tech World

lives more exciting. Instead, follow this diet and its two secrets
to merely reduce the evening snack and another feeding. In fact,
any combination that reduces intake is perfectly fine. The key
is to always put the horse before the cart — to reduce then
altogether eliminate the struggles, which *permanently* reforms
fullness level.

For instance, many people doing this Neo-Tech Eating prefer
to target breakfast, first, not the evening snack. Some people
have less appetite in the morning and feel "safer" targeting
breakfast. That is PERFECTLY FINE. Moreover, for many
working people, they are so busy in the morning, their minds
are less on food than they may be in the evening at home when
relaxed. Being busy makes overcoming the solo struggle that
much easier. If you feel this way, then by all means target
breakfast. Cut your breakfast in half. Then next, either cut out
breakfast altogether, or cut your evening snack in half, too.
Others, by contrast, like a substantial breakfast and target other
feedings, perhaps lunch. In any case, the result is the same —
as you permanently reform your fullness level, you permanently
reduce intake and acquire a new look.

A potent little tip: Since the evening snack and breakfast
seem to be the most targeted feedings to reduce, I found it
helpful to eat my lunches earlier. Remember, I eventually
eliminated both my evening snack and breakfast, so I really
craved and looked forward to my lunches. As my craving
intensified for lunch, my satisfaction soared while eating lunch.
Setting my lunch time at 10:30 or 11:00 instead of noon or later
helped me get over my solo struggle when cutting out the
evening snack and then breakfast. ...Remember, the whole idea
behind Neo-Tech Eating is to reduce your infinite struggles to
a solo struggle, and then to reduce that manageable solo struggle
to no struggle. Then, you have permanently reformed your
fullness level. Of course, then you can go out for dinner and
eat whatever you wish without worrying about a thing, for now
your new fullness level rations your intake for you. You will
not even have to think about it!

182

Summary

Your Body:

1) Determine Foods & Fullness Levels: The first week is spent determining the foods you will eat steadily for a month and the quantities that make you full. Eat the same meal, same quantity, at about the same time every day. You are building cravings to work on your behalf during this diet.

2) Adjust Fullness Level: The second week is spent eating a reduced feeding of your choice — perhaps cutting the evening snack in half. Satisfying your other cravings throughout the day help you overcome the solo struggle. By the end of the week, your body will feel satisfied eating the reduced quantity as the solo struggle fades away and fullness level permanently adjusts.

3) Adjust Fullness Level: The third week is spent eating another reduced feeding of your choice — perhaps cutting out the evening snack or cutting breakfast in half. Your other cravings immediately go up and so does their satisfaction when fed, once again helping you to overcome the solo struggle. Fullness level permanently adjusts downward.

4) Watch Results: The fourth week can be spent merely observing the results while remaining under total control. By contrast, most other diets often leave us feeling unsure, even out of control; Neo-Tech Eating puts us under immediate control, for we know exactly how our bodies handle each feeding. We feel in control and calm. If, after that fourth week you want to lose even more weight, then merely adjust your fullness level another step downward, as stated in Steps Two and Three.

Vision Nine
You Will Become A Genius

As my mind's eye was still admiring the slim and sexy people in my Eighth Vision, I started noticing something else about them, something startling: those people with beautiful bodies also had brilliant minds! My Ninth Vision was showing me: ordinary people tomorrow were *very* smart...in fact, they were geniuses. They had both awesome bodies...and minds! A shiver of excitement went through me as I witnessed perhaps our greatest childhood wish come true tomorrow: we were extremely bright!

Even if you think you are dull today, my Ninth Vision showed me you were a genius tomorrow. In my Ninth Vision, I was there: in the Neo-Tech World, the stagnation-trap around your mind finally came off. We know now that the stagnation-trap was the mutant bicameral mentality...a disease of the conscious mind. That trap devastated your human potential.

But tomorrow, you left behind your bicameral tendencies. Through New Techniques (Neo-Tech) you cured your mind of the mutant bicameral mentality (as taught in The First Insight, Part Two). You then naturally made the evolutionary jump into Neothink. Using Neothink to make stunning wide-scope integrations of knowledge and major advancements of new knowledge, you were a genius by today's standards.

Let me tell you a little about becoming a genius:

It is well known that most people think *in words*. It is also well known that a few people — and they're all geniuses such as Einstein, for instance — think *in pictures*. By the way, for the first time in my life, my Twelve Visions all came to me *in pictures*.

Of course, you cannot control how you think. You're either a genius, or you're not. Most are not.

But in tomorrow's new mentality of Neothink, the ordinary person, such as myself when I had my Twelve Visions, will think *in pictures*. And by seeing *in pictures,* you can see the future *before it happens*.

Let me explain how:

Neothink works by building *a puzzle*, piece by piece, in any area of life a person wants to excel or know the future, say in business or love. In most areas of life, the ordinary brain subconsciously absorbs an ongoing flow of information. Whether playing poker or purchasing stock, whether watching the news or watching a sporting event, your mind subconsciously absorbs ever-flowing bits of information. Those little bits of information are little puzzle pieces.

Everyone automatically does this. Now, through common denominators, you can quickly snap together those little pieces of floating information into a solid puzzle. In fact, any ordinary person can handle *the smaller pieces* to any large, sweeping puzzle that normally goes over his head, normally well beyond his scope of knowledge...the exclusive territory of *geniuses*.

Throughout the Twelve Visions, you have learned how to begin snapping those little pieces together to build the large puzzle. Start by snapping your power-thinking list into your mini-day schedule (Vision Five). Before you know it, you can see and operate at a level that, before, was well beyond your scope of knowledge and power.

At first, when I used Neothink, it seemed to me like magic. As I learned to build my success-puzzles, unique *puzzle-pictures* would form before my eyes. I started seeing wide-scope pictures of new knowledge only geniuses could see. As I snapped together my Twelve Visions into a picture of the Neo-Tech World, I realized I was seeing and thinking *in sweeping pictures*, just like the geniuses. In fact, people who read my Twelve Visions said I *was a genius*. Yet, I knew I was no genius. I was an ordinary guy who was experiencing Neothink.

I saw how people in my Ninth Vision quickly snapped together the puzzle pieces into their puzzles of interest. I saw how ordinary people easily handled *the smaller pieces* to any large puzzle. They could easily build those smaller pieces and snap them one by one into their growing puzzles. After awhile, as they snapped their puzzles together, the *puzzle-pictures* started forming before their eyes. Now, they were seeing and thinking *in pictures*, just like the geniuses. (The Twelve Visions showing the puzzle picture of tomorrow's Neo-Tech World provides a perfect example of how this Neothink works.)

Now, here is how the ordinary people in my Ninth Vision

could see the future: As with any puzzle-picture, a point came when they could see what their puzzle-pictures were going to look like *before* all the pieces were in place. Therefore, those ordinary people already knew the future — the pictures — before a person who thinks in words even had a clue! *They knew the future before it actually happened.* With Neothink, ordinary people tomorrow instantly became *geniuses* with enormous advantages far beyond ordinary people today. Enormous advantages.

Moreover, I saw in my Ninth Vision that those missing pieces, say in business and love, were the elusive missing pieces in life...those always-missing mysterious pieces to money, power, and love not in our lives today. Through Neothink, ordinary people tomorrow knew what those pieces were, what they looked like, and they quickly snapped those pieces in place. Ordinary people not only controlled, but they created their own futures.

Almost no one today ever sees those missing pieces, and we lament that "something more" must exist to life.

With Neothink, however, we will see, snap into place, and enjoy that "something more". With Neothink, nothing will be missing in our lives.

As motivated geniuses in the Neo-Tech World, we looked back at ourselves in the anticivilization as though we were partly retarded. In a sense, we were. You see, the human mind can naturally grow forever, yet our minds had stopped growing. In the end, we were pinned down in stagnant ruts, so natural growth of our minds had been retarded or stopped in the anticivilization.

Looking back, we often wondered *why* our minds had stopped growing, for making breakthroughs and creating values seemed so natural *and rewarding* in the Neo-Tech World. We loved being so smart! And it really bothered us that we were so dull before. We finally realized *why* our minds had stopped growing in the anticivilization: they had lost their *human* potential to the forces of *nature* because of the mutant bicameral mentality (Vision Three).

Our human potential is limitless value creation, which we can go on forever. What exactly opens up our human potential, and why does it close down and die today? One's deeply rooted *motivational drive* will forever generate and rejuvenate one's creative energy (Vision One). When motivation gets replaced by resignation in today's anticivilization, however, our human potential dies.

This deep motivation comes and goes early in our lives today in the anticivilization. Of course, I am talking about one's deep, lifelong motivational drive...not surface, temporary motivations inspired by motivational tapes or self-improvement seminars. One's very deep motivational drive in life dictates his or her eventual success and happiness. To understand why, we have to go yet a level deeper to answer the question, "What constitutes human motivation?" We have to get down to the root-cause of our seemingly "inborn" motivational drives or seemingly "inborn" lack of motivational drive.

That brings us back to our infancy. There, we can observe the natural thrill felt in human babies while developing human consciousness. Humans start out mimicking reactions of those around them as do most other animals, but we humans continue developing greater and greater levels of awareness. Our minds keep developing *and developing* far beyond other animals...into human consciousness. Infants and toddlers feel a natural thrill that generates a lot of natural energy and happiness as they experience more and more control when entering human consciousness. That exhilarating thrill and power is a *natural* reaction to *human consciousness.*

Unfortunately, as we grow up in the anticivilization, the power of our human consciousness becomes diseased and badly weakened relative to our Neothink minds tomorrow. Eventually, we cannot even remember our childhood exhilaration for life.

In today's anticivilization, a world of mutant bicameral mentalities, unbeknownst to us, unnatural forces of nature (described in Vision Three) dominate our lives. The resulting burden of life (Vision Two) destroys the natural thrill of life. But the thrill exists in very young children, before the burden sets in. The thrill of life once existed in you.

That thrill for expanding awareness and control over life that exudes happiness and energy constitutes a human being's deep motivational drive in life as a toddler. To whatever degree you still have a small bit of that thrill as an adult determines your motivational drive and energy level and dictates your success and happiness in life.

By the way, the emotional experience of that thrill is *intense happiness*, which we witness frequently in young children, but seldom in adults.

If that thrill for life were not crippled with an invasive, mutant bicameral mentality during your childhood, then your motivational drive would have remained throughout your entire life as it was during your first few years of life. While enthusiastically and easily integrating knowledge to the next level and the next, you would have gone on an amazing vector of value creation and brought values to the world beyond many of today's most successful people. Indeed, driving ahead on your Friday-Night Essence (Vision One), in a living job (Vision Five), you would have become a creative genius among the world's most valuable and richest people.

Toddlers Routinely Neothink

As toddlers, we learned to talk and become conscious, easily and eagerly integrating knowledge to the next level and the next, routinely pulling together major Neothink integrations. Remember, the Neothink mentality is the disease-free, pure state of consciousness. We were naturally able to Neothink because we were still free of the unnatural, mutant bicameral mentality (studied in the First Insight). As we absorbed the unnatural mutant bicameral mentality like a bad computer virus, absorbing it through learned and mimicked bicameral reactions from the adult world around us, we lost our natural ability to Neothink.

We lost our ability to Neothink and our ability to break through to new levels in life. We lost our ability *to create*. Thus, we lost our ability to fulfill our role as conscious beings...we lost our human potential. We increasingly absorbed resignation from the world around us as we lost our deep motivational drives and our thrill for life. And, as a result, we lost the intense happiness that was in us as young children. Instead, the burden of life moved in. The contradiction of human consciousness — the trap of stagnation — sadly started closing around our minds and hearts rather early in life.

Tomorrow in the Neo-Tech World, as shown to me in this

Ninth Vision, young children were not retarded with the bicameral mind disease. They never lost their thrill for life, and they continued soaring with deep-rooted motivational drives into greater and greater value creation. They grew up keeping their puzzle-building ability, routinely breaking through with brand-new puzzle pictures. Adults around them were racing forward with puzzle-building Neothink, too, routinely breaking through with brand-new values. Natural Friday-Night Essences and downstream focuses (Vision One) swept us along and onto exciting journeys through life, just like those first few toddler years.

But today, the motivational drive is gone in nearly all adults — replaced by resignation. Children learn from adults; indeed, children learn the bicameral mentality and resignation. ...And that is how our human potential disappears. We are mentally handicapped in the anticivilization for the rest of our lives.

In the anticivilization, once one's motivational drive collapses at six or seven years old, it never comes back. But in tomorrow's Neo-Tech World, adults on their Friday-Night Essences started integrated thinking again, setting off gushers of creativity and reigniting motivational drives.

Let us look at the entirely new way of using the mind that made us very creative and motivated sometime in the 21st century:

Inner Workings of the New Mentality

Your mind tomorrow worked an entirely different way. Without bicameral behavioral patterns, your mind was not in the following mode waiting for automatic, external guidance. Void of the bicameral mind disease, your mind led itself and snapped together information into little puzzles. In other words, your mind conceptualized or thought in concepts, not percepts as it does today.

Percepts are simple events or thoughts all around you perceived through your five senses: I *smell* the stench of garbage in the streets; I *see* the run-down store fronts; I *taste* the greasy food at the neighborhood taco stand; I *feel* the jolt of potholes in the deteriorating roads; I *hear* police sirens over and over again every night. Your senses register those percepts just as the dog or any other animal registers those percepts. Concepts jumped to a whole new level of using the mind, capable only by humans. Concepts (multiple thought clusters) organize several percepts (single thoughts) into a broader level of awareness: run-down, low-income neighborhoods are not safe at night. ...A dog could never reach that level of awareness.

That concept was developed by pulling together percepts through a *common denominator*: all such low-income neighborhoods with run-down storefronts, deteriorating roads, low-end food, have something in common: frequent crime at night. Conceptualizing lifts humans to a much greater level of power.

Of course, that is a well-known anticivilization concept. Beyond the most well-known concepts, however, most people today do not think in concepts. They react to percepts only...a bicameral-like mode responding to external stimuli.

If toddlers' motivational drives and their energy/emotional levels continued beyond six or seven years of age, conceptual thinking and then Neothink would have taken over. But you can listen to almost any conversation today and, in most cases, a story is being told, percept by percept. Very few conversations occur at the conceptual level and virtually none at the Neothink level. The bicameral-like mode of just *reacting* to external stimuli, instead of *controlling* the world around us, dominates human "thinking".

Without conceptualizing, ordinary people are powerless in life and helpless in their careers, forever stuck in percepts — in routine tasks at work that control them, for instance. People can only *react* to those tasks, forever trapped in routine ruts, unable to structure those simple tasks into more powerful conceptual units to *control* their destinies.

Of course, in the Neo-Tech World with the new division of essence (Visions Five and Six), the simple tasks were pulled together by the common denominator — physical movements — into the powerful, conceptual mini-days. And the basic responsibilities at work were pulled together by the common denominator — money-making purposes — into the powerful, conceptual mini-companies (the Fifth Vision). Ordinary people's careers were structured conceptually, ready for them to advance rapidly with integrated thinking and then Neothink using power-thinking and numbers (the Fifth Vision) as their guiding tools, no longer stuck in routine ruts reacting to specialized tasks, drowning in stagnation.

Discover a Whole New World

Similar to a child who learns to read then suddenly sees a whole new world of words all around him, my Ninth Vision showed me that ordinary people tomorrow learned to conceptualize, then suddenly saw a whole new world of common denominators all around them. Once conceptual thinking kicked in and we spotted common denominators all around us, we structured our lives and careers for success. We advanced into the more powerful realm of integrated, puzzle-building thinking and then, as Neo-Tech weeded out the bicameral programming in our minds (the First Insight), motivation returned and eventually replaced resignation. We jumped into Neothink.

Today, seeing common denominators is the first step toward a creative mind. The common denominators, the first phase as shown on the chart on the next page, is a structuring phase — structuring concepts, structuring your job conceptually. Indeed, common denominators put random percepts into structured concepts, random tasks into structured mini-days, random responsibilities into structured mini-companies, random chaos into structured order.

Then, *forward-movement* integrated thinking kicks in; you will move forward and no longer stand still. You will become an essence mover, a profit builder...a value creator. That next phase to a creative mind builds upon the conceptual structure...builds knowledge steadily piece by piece like building a house, beam by beam, or like building a puzzle, piece by piece.

In your living job tomorrow (Vision Five), for example, the conceptually structured mini-day schedule enabled you to power-think the puzzles pieces, and the conceptually structured mini-company job enabled you to pursue the numbers to conceive and build your success puzzles. The mini-day and mini-company provided the conceptual structure upon which you built success with power-thinking and the story of the numbers.

THE PROCESS OF BECOMING CREATIVE

One
Forming Concepts
(By Integrating Percepts)
Conceptualizing Is First Job

↓

Two
Building Success Puzzles
(By Integrating Concepts)
Snapping Together a Puzzle Picture Is Second Job

↓

Results
Making Creative Breakthroughs
(By Completing Never-Before-Seen Puzzle Pictures)
Creating New Knowledge Is Creative Results

Specific Corollary Steps for Your Career

One
Forming Mini-Days & Mini-Companies
(By Integrating Tasks and Responsibilities)
Structuring Job Conceptually Is First Job

↓

Two
Building Money-Making Projects & Success Puzzles
(By Power-Thinking & Studying the Numbers)
Integrated, Puzzle-Building Thinking Is Second Job

↓

Results
Making Product & Marketing Breakthroughs
(By Completing Never-Before-Seen Success Puzzles)
Creating New Values Is Creative Results

In the Neo-Tech World, the Above Steps Will Eventually Lead To Neothink (and To Your Own Vector of Value Creation)

Instead of your mind following set routines or external guidance, tomorrow your mind easily integrated knowledge and snapped together success puzzles. Natural exhilaration returned and dominated your psyche and soul while unnatural stagnation left your psyche forever. Without bicameral programming, you naturally integrated knowledge to build wider and wider puzzle pictures and eventually evolve into Neothink. That is when you joined the geniuses.

The Vigorous Mind

Have you ever heard of the Hemingway Code? It came from the famous American writer, Ernest Hemingway, and his legendary youthful vigor. Using an analogy to Hemingway's legendary vigor, here is my attempt to describe my Ninth Vision and how your mind was different in the Neo-Tech World: your mental state was always in that Hemingway Code. *Every day* your mind would vigorously integrate knowledge to create values that never existed before. Your mind vigorously pressed forward, building breakthrough puzzle pictures, piece by piece. When you drove down the highway, when you took a shower, when you got ready for bed, when you ate lunch, your mind was not dormant as it is today. It was intensely churning in the Hemingway Code, putting together an exciting success puzzle, making lucrative breakthroughs, feeling exhilarated. Your mind was always in action!

After awhile, your mind performed no other way. And with your stimulating new power, integrated thinking, you never had a shortage of puzzle pieces to build. Assembling larger and larger success puzzles as your bicameral mentality vanished, your motivation, enthusiasm and energy kept expanding. Your success puzzles reached the next level and the next, and your mind evolved into Neothink. You continually made major advancements of human knowledge and lived as a proud genius.

I wanted to try this stimulating, new way of thinking that I so clearly saw in my Ninth Vision. So, I took one small step toward the Neothink mentality by waking up my mind to a higher level. Here is what happened:

194

Once a week I had to drive about 300 miles in Southern California. During one trip, I decided I was going to keep the radio off and make my mind work the whole time while driving instead of being in a blank, bicameral-like state of mind. During the long drive, I was expanding my awareness and control over the development of my accounting tracking reports in my company. I forced my mind to think about how to develop foolproof accounting tracking reports (Vision Six). I noticed my mind would "activate" for several minutes. Then, several minutes later, I would "catch" my mind dormant again in a bicameral-like state. So, I would start the process over and force myself to think. My mind would go a few minutes, then "short circuit" again. I soon discovered a useful technique: When my mind went blank, I would silently say the word "accounting" in my head over and over until my mind "activated" again. By doing that, I became aware of my "downtime" instead of being in an oblivious daze. Soon, I was able to shorten my mind's "downtime". By the end of the trip, I had discovered an entirely new, foolproof accounting system, now permanently used by my company (see Tracking Report #5, page 136). But most important, my mind would not stop thinking! It was no longer hard. Instead of being the exception, thinking had become the norm. Needless to say, that was a wildly successful trip.

Ever since that trip, my mind naturally functioned at that next level. As boring as accounting tracking reports might seem, product development and marketing breakthroughs started happening for me and filled me with exhilaration! For, creating values and marketing those values meant pride and profits for me.

Elevating my mind broke me through to the next level again and again in my living job, which lifted me to a whole new level of success. In fact, all my success today is because my mind rose to that next level.

But to many, this would seem too hard to do within today's suppressed anticivilization. But in tomorrow's Neo-Tech World, after the political and job revolutions, this exhilarating thinking and resulting big-shot success came naturally. That stimulating world reawakened our thrill for life, and creating values while making lots of money generated enormous enthusiasm.

The Neo-Tech World

The "Average Joe" Becomes "Psychic"

As the "average Joe" in tomorrow's Neo-Tech World built success piece by piece, he was in for a surprise: his growing success puzzles formed puzzle pictures not seen before. In other words, he was creating values that never existed before and was discovering Neothink. He was becoming a creative genius.

You see, as our success puzzles in life formed, we began to know what our developing puzzle pictures ultimately would look like, and therefore, well before those puzzle pictures were complete, we knew what the missing pieces would have to look like that would complete the puzzle picture. In other words, our minds became seemingly psychic to our peers at knowing exactly what to do to take success to the next creative level.

We increasingly knew the future before it ever happened, similar to these Twelve Visions that know the future through a major Neothink puzzle. Merely ordinary people in today's anticivilization, we became creative geniuses in the Neo-Tech World. Our minds became free of bicameral programming and no longer sat dormant waiting to be led. Instead, our minds churned constantly in the Hemingway code, integrating knowledge and pulling together success puzzles as we used Neothink to create the future. God-Man not only sees, but *creates* the future.

The "Average Joe" Becomes a Legend

You may not think you have a creative thought in your head, today. But creativity was never meant to be some special gift radiating from a destined few geniuses. After extensive research, I learned that most creative people today started out the same way — *without* creativity and directionless. But, often by mere coincidence, those lucky few people got a little involved with a particular interest that gradually generated more and more enthusiasm...until eventually a powerful motivational drive emerged. That powerful motivational drive, of course, was their Friday-Night Essence (Vision One). Then and only then did those people — those otherwise "average Joes" — build creative puzzles, piece by piece. By the time their lives were over, they

196

may have become legends, but their legacies were built piece by piece. Tomorrow with integrated thinking and Friday-Night Essences, all of today's directionless "average Joes" found their way, became deeply motivated, creative, and left important legacies.

I could find no appropriate words that described tomorrow's joy from becoming creative and evolving into Neothink. A deeply satisfying sense of self-importance filled us as we brought permanent values into the world that never existed before. Our deep motivational drives returned as we lived by succeeding at the very essence of man — at advancing society with our value creations. Our deep motivational drives restored both our limitless potential and our intense happiness not known since we were toddlers. Ordinary people became rich and revered.

The World of Our Minds

After the world went Neo-Tech, we loved our living jobs with their mini-day/mini-company structures, flowing forward with downstream focus into value creation on our Friday-Night Essences. In that new world, the driving force in life had become our minds. We looked at everything differently. We looked beneath the surface perceptions at work, at home, on the news, in social life. We always searched for common denominators and formed concepts.

We frequently came up with awesome marketing ideas, for great marketing ideas were simply an exercise of the mind: of finding common denominators that served a lot of people's needs. We then built success upon those structured concepts, say those great marketing ideas, through forward-movement integrated thinking.

Our creativity and energy went toward identifying then servicing society's needs. Indeed, we joined those geniuses solving people's problems and needs. As a result, enormous creativity and energy rushed into society. Prosperity reigned throughout America, then across our planet.

197

You Can Start Now

When I pursued the next level of thinking today that I saw in my Ninth Vision, I began searching beneath surface perceptions for common denominators in whatever I did. That entry level into integrated thinking introduced me to a new power in life: as I strengthened my ability to form concepts, I developed the ability to conceptualize powerful marketing ideas. I then put many of those ideas into action, using integrated thinking (which encompasses power-thinking and pursuing the story of the numbers) to steadily build those ideas into success puzzles. Those marketing projects, of course, serviced a lot of people's needs.

For instance, my Twelve Visions showed me that society's major problems in the anticivilization nearly all have a common denominator: most if not all problems are caused by politicians and bureaucrats regulating business, medicine, and science (which occurs because of our deep-rooted remnants of the bicameral mentality that seek external guidance on what to do and how to live, from higher "authorities"). So, with that common denominator in hand, I set about building this book, piece by piece, vision by vision, insight by insight, to help solve society's problems and service people's needs.

The central idea in this book of removing the external "authorities" and empowering the mind to integrate its own path could become perhaps the most leveraged common need (i.e., marketing concept) of all time. *The Neo-Tech World* will eventually cause the demise of external "authorities" to free the geniuses of society to service the people's needs, remove their many problems, and make their lives wealthy and healthy (Visions Ten and Eleven).

Indeed, my Tenth and Eleventh Visions showed me that the puzzle picture created by this book eventually caused a peaceful political revolution that eliminated the ruling class. Eliminating the ruling class set free the Technological Revolution that made us rich, caused a medical revolution that eradicated all diseases and quickly doubled the number of years in our lives, caused the job revolution that brought us exciting living jobs of the mind, sparked a love revolution that resulted in intensely happy and romantic couples, and ultimately catalyzed the worldwide evolution into Neothink.

Of course, it all started by merely pulling together a common denominator...*the* common denominator to nearly all our problems — the ruling class. After forming that concept, then came the integrated, puzzle-building thinking — building the puzzle picture...this book. By the way, I witnessed in my Visions that, sometime in the first quarter of the 21st century, this common denominator to nearly all our problems — this ruling class — came into clear focus in most people's minds after fifty million people were exposed to the Twelve Visions. That exposure sparked the inextinguishable fire beneath the Neo-Tech Party (Vision Eleven).[1]

Although I have built perhaps the most widely needed puzzle picture of our time,[2] I started small. When I first tried the creative thinking that I saw in my Ninth Vision, I did the following exercise to accompany my living job: I first pushed myself at work to think in concepts. While looking over the details at work, I looked for common denominators to recurring problems. By doing that, I surprised myself as I discovered solutions I never would have thought of before. With time, my mind became used to and shifted to this new way of thinking. By using conceptualization in my wealth-building job, I gradually discovered creativity growing in me. I steadily advanced from stagnant specialized thinking into forward-movement integrated thinking. Now, I actually started to build success in contrast to my previous routine rut. And as I came closer to thinking the way the dynamos thought in my Ninth Vision, I rediscovered my deep motivational drive previously left behind at six years old.

In today's anticivilization submerged in bicameral mentalities, we were doomed early on to dull lives and minds, even *before* our first day of school. And then, our public education

---

[1]That figure of fifty-million people is why, as I explained in Vision Four, I have shifted my personal efforts now from writing to marketing.

[2]The pieces to that puzzle picture could not have been developed without the original work of Dr. Frank R. Wallace: *The Neo-Tech Discovery*.

devastated whatever potential we still had left. We left school with dull minds, doomed to dull lives. Fortunately, when the world went Neo-Tech (the First Insight), we recaptured our potentials lost as young children. We joined the geniuses.

The Old School Versus The New School

In today's anticivilization, upon entering first grade at six years of age, the motivational drive still in the child is gradually lost. You see, the premise of public schools today is: *Prepare children to effectively integrate into society.* Now, imagine that the eager child dreams about growing up and becoming a famous person who does wonderful things...a great value creator. "I'll do great things for the world and become a millionaire!" But those dreams gradually dissipate as the child blends into the suppressed anticivilization.

In my Ninth Vision, I witnessed the premise of Neo-Tech World schools: *Prepare children to create values that many people need and are excited to buy.* My Vision showed me that on the child's first day of school, the teacher would walk in and say, "I'm going to prepare you to create great things for the world, and as a result you will become famous and rich!" Wow, the child sat up and took notice — his dreams confirmed! His motivation grew with compounding momentum as he steadily gained the ability to achieve his dreams throughout his Neo-Tech World education.

The Old School

In today's anticivilization, children have little chance to grow up and become rich with a public education. Consider the trend in public schools today concerning the three fundamentals of education (according to educator Professor Leonard Peikoff):

Structure: Increasing trend toward class discussions, free-flowing thoughts from kids and teachers, random facts about events and dates pragmatically "structured" to bring the child into "what's happening in today's social environment". The child hears all those unintegrated points (i.e., percepts), but later he forgets much of what he saw and heard in school.

Thinking: The child is not taught to *integrate*. He is not taught to integrate the many random percepts into common denominators — into a few timeless, unforgettable concepts. He never knows the power of his mind to integrate random percepts into structured concepts for everlasting knowledge. Knowledge is power, but he retains little knowledge. Instead, he absorbs then forgets unintegrated, pragmatic percepts, many regarding what's germane to the politically correct times. When he graduates, his mind is quite impotent as he settles into our suppressed society.

Motivation: He has little certainty, just a go-with-the-flow "education". The child learns to "fit in". He is trapped, at the mercy of our society, economy, national standard of living. There is nothing to be motivated over, for the child implicitly feels less and less power to rise above the suppressed state of things, above the burden of life he sees in his parents, to create new values for society and enjoy the emotional and financial rewards as an adult. Dreams become blurry and fade.

The New School

In tomorrow's Neo-Tech World, by comparison, dreams not only came true for schoolchildren and for adults, too, but those initial dreams were just the beginning. I saw it all in my Ninth Vision:

Structure: Neo-Tech World schools had a highly ordered presentation of knowledge, via class lectures, starting with bare percepts and integrating those many percepts by common denominators into a few timeless concepts for rapid absorption and permanent retention of knowledge. Knowledge was power. Through building timeless concepts, the child retained all that he learned in school. Moreover, he observed and learned *how to integrate* to build, piece by piece, onto his base of concepts — to build more and more knowledge and power throughout his life in order to someday *create great values for society*.

Thinking: The child was taught to integrate. He discovered why his mind was infinitely superior to all other animals. He integrated knowledge through common denominators from random percepts into structured concepts. He learned to form a few large concepts, not memorize many specific percepts. Thus, that child retained magnitudes more knowledge through integrated thinking. Soon, he learned how to snap a few of those concepts together into simple puzzles. Integrated, puzzle-building thinking sent thrills through the child, and it would eventually take him to great heights. The child quickly rose beyond the reach of all stagnation traps. Instead of heading toward a routine rut, he was heading toward exhilarating value creation.

Motivation: The child knew with certainty that he could make a difference, for knowledge was power. The child felt certainty and power. He naturally became motivated for more, for superchild would now grow up to become superman or superwoman. The child felt like dynamite! The thrill for life, for expanding awareness and control, gained momentum. He felt more and more power to someday do great things for society and make great wealth for himself — every child's dream. Dreams became focussed and closer. The child became highly motivated.

Our Children Lifted the World

In the anticivilization, our education does not properly teach children how *to think, to integrate and build mental puzzles* of new knowledge. In the Neo-Tech World, education and children's minds will exist at a whole different level.

The Ninth Vision showed me that toddlers' rapid learning curves did not slow down. With the same thrill for life and expanding awareness nurtured by proper education, our children and grandchildren evolved straight into Neothink and soared beyond even the smartest and richest people alive today.

Tomorrow's superchild became a genius of society who, with his peers, made us all rich through brilliant technological breakthroughs that drove prices toward zero and buying power toward infinity, a similar phenomenon to what we have already seen in the computer industry. For the most part, our children and grandchildren lifted the world after the collapse of the mystical ruling class.

On the Path to God-Man

Obviously, tomorrow's superchild needed a lot of knowledge. The discussion method that dominated public schools in the late 20th century and early 21st century vanished. The original idea behind that popular, discussion method was that children taught each other in order to help develop their social and communication skills — to better integrate into society. However, *tomorrow's superchild needed knowledge.* Neo-Tech World education used the old-fashioned lecture method in which the teacher did the teaching and filled the child with knowledge.

Now, the superchild rapidly built upon that base of knowledge as he grew up. Unlike us, he was taught conceptual thinking and integrated thinking. To perceive surroundings — see, hear, feel, smell, taste — was automatic and present in most animals. Man's superiority came from his ability *to integrate.* Tomorrow, starting as children, mankind integrated those percepts by common denominators into concepts to generate reason and knowledge. That process was called conceptual thinking. Soon thereafter, the human mind could build concept upon concept into puzzles of knowledge. That process was called integrated thinking. Without bicameral programming tomorrow blocking our children's integrated thinking, they reached out more and more widely and onto Neothink as they made the next and final evolution into God-Man.

Leaving Behind the Old Way

As researched by renowned Professor Leonard Peikoff and detailed in his *Philosophy of Education,* public schools (and most private schools) in the latter 20th century and early 21st century did not teach children how to integrate the endless percepts into a few simplified concepts. For example, instead of teaching children the simple concepts of phonetics (e.g., a "p" makes a "pa" sound), public schools in the late 20th century taught the look-say or whole-language method. Phonetics required understanding 44 simple concepts (i.e., sounds); look-say required memorizing how to read *every single word* the child ever saw (i.e., perceived) with no simplifying common denominators such as phonics (i.e., no concepts).

Indeed, children in *all* subjects — history, math, science, literature — were taught impotent perceptual thinking and not potent conceptual thinking. History, for example, was taught by unintegrated specific events (i.e., by percepts) and not grouped together by common denominators into concepts. For example, the wrath of human destruction over the centuries was touched on fact by fact (i.e., percept by percept) but not grouped into the basic underlying concept of tyranny. Thus, children did not make connections of logic and, instead, lived their lives in a somewhat helpless "airhead state". They retained very little knowledge since they never learned how to *integrate* percepts by common denominators into interlocked concepts of logic — the very capacity that separated man from the other animals. In short, children never learned *to think*. ...Was it not to be expected that essentially all children in the anticivilization grew up to a life of stagnation? Was it any surprise that smart politicians ran things the way *they* wanted to?

In the Neo-Tech World, as I saw in my Ninth Vision, children grew up to be geniuses with powerful motivational drives. They were intensely happy, for, they did not experience the tragedy of their dreams fading as we did. Moreover, as those children tomorrow grew up, they used Neothink to not only make their own dreams come true, but ours as well.

Our Transition Today

Even with an old-school education, I saw in my Ninth Vision we still grew rich in the Neo-Tech World when our deeply grooved-in bicameral behavioral patterns were broken apart by Neo-Tech (learn how in The First Insight, Part Two), and we evolved into Neothink.

As we broke apart our deeply grooved-in bicameral behavioral patterns with Neo-Tech, we first discovered integrated thinking, the precursor to Neothink. Integrated thinking quickly made us creative, for integrating lots of existing knowledge eventually generates new knowledge. That *new knowledge* — new products, new marketing — made us rich.

To get a sense of the power of integrated thinking, imagine, for a moment, a large boulder sits near the edge of a cliff. We find the strongest man in the world and ask him to push that boulder over the cliff. He braces his shoulder against the boulder and pushes with all his might. The boulder does not even budge. Well, we could find the next thousand strongest men in the world, line them up, and watch them one by one push the boulder with all their might. But the boulder never budges. ...That is a metaphor for how we are taught to use our minds through school and at work — to helplessly push our thoughts one by one against the big boulder to success. The big boulder to success never budges.

Now, imagine this: you and I and ten average guys brace our shoulders against the big boulder and, all together, give it one big heave. That boulder would roll right over the cliff! ...That is a metaphor for how our minds will work tomorrow in our living jobs — continually bringing together many thoughts into one powerful force to easily push over the big boulder to success. Through this powerful *integrated thinking* tomorrow, we pushed through all the money-making barriers of today that even the thousand smartest men today could never move through.

More Creative Than Today's Smartest People

My Ninth Vision clearly showed me that integrated thinking gave us more creative power tomorrow than the smartest men in the world today. That was why we — yes, humdrum people like us — actually became creative geniuses, even with our average IQs!

Our education today in our suppressed anticivilization gives us powerless perceptual or specialized thinking that leaves us stranded as adults in routine-rut jobs with specialized tasks. Even if someone today is very good at what he does, he is usually powerless at fulfilling his deepest dreams, sort of like those world's strongest men powerless at pushing over the big boulder. In the Neo-Tech World, however, we learned to snap thoughts together into an integrated force that easily pushed over the big boulder to major success.

When citizens of Earth went Neo-Tech, we left behind our mutant bicameral mentality and evolved from mental weaklings reacting automatically to our routine ruts into mental giants integrating major success puzzles.

In the anticivilization, the same forces that held back super entrepreneurs and super technologies held back our own creativity. You see, career politicians and regulatory bureaucrats increasingly controlled our educational system. The ordinary person graduated from our public schools with severe short circuits; he or she could not put together the connections needed to be creative. He or she, in short, could not integrate.

Going For It, Now

In trying these techniques now, I overcame many of my own short circuits. I actually knocked out of my mind the passive acceptance of settling into a specialized routine. You too can escape the stagnation-trap:

Imagine your most ambitious dream, and daydream about it for a few minutes. In your mind's eye, block out the obstacles that hold you down in a stagnant routine rut. Instead, see yourself leading your way to exhilarating success.

With all that you know now, that daydream strikingly demonstrates to you (as it did for me) that, under anticivilization dynamics, you are in a terminal rut. As simple as it may seem, that striking snapshot of your lifelong stagnation-trap can set off an act of self-preservation: as happened to me, you might automatically start seeking broader thought clusters at your work. And now, with the Ninth Vision, you know what to do: tie together the stagnant simple thoughts (impotent specialized thinking) into growing thought clusters (potent integrated thinking). When I did that, I went from very limited to limitless.

How To Do It — The First Step

Let me review how I did that, starting with the first of my two steps to creativity: *structuring my thoughts and my work with common denominators*. In *The Philosophy of Education*, Professor Peikoff used the following example to explain common denominators: Consider a drunk takes a stroll on the beach. He perceives many things — the wave breaking and rumbling onto the shore then sliding back into the ocean, the pebbles rolling down the wet sand toward the sea, the fish jumping and splashing back into the water, the sea gull landing. To the drunk, like to a dog or cat, all such events are like new and unique experiences. The events seem to come at him at random, with no structure or sense. Each event happens, then is gone. He retains no logic or memory. He does not integrate events by common denominators. For instance, he does not link together the concept that the wave breaks, the pebbles roll down, the jumping fish splashes back into the water, and the sea gull lands because of gravity. The drunk never sees that common denominator, and neither do ordinary people with today's public education.

That common denominator — that concept of gravity — begins integrating those random events into some sort of structure, making them sensible and retainable in one's memory. But to the drunk, to the dog, to the ordinary person today, the events make no particular sense; they just happen and are just as quickly forgotten as other events are perceived. That "drunken stupor" is not so bad when strolling along a beach; but it is tragic when strolling through one's life, one's career, one's marriage and family life.

In the anticivilization, most people live their lives in this impotent "drunken stupor". We never stop to realize: we comprehend only the most surface spur-of-the-moment events as they randomly come at us — just like the drunkard, just like the dog, just like bicameral man, just like people graduating from public educational systems.

For example, to the amusement of people tomorrow in the Neo-Tech World, people today schedule their work as the tasks randomly come at them instead of by common denominators — by physical movements...the mini-days (the Fifth Vision). And to the amusement of business managers tomorrow in the Neo-Tech World, business managers today structure their companies from automatic reactions and surface perceptions, not deep integrations. Many of today's managers come from a generation never taught to think conceptually. Those managers often structure their departments and jobs in a somewhat "drunken" see-react manner: the manager sees he is busy, so the manager automatically reacts by delegating responsibilities not attached to their money-making purpose (the Fifth Vision). Our money-making lives are about as directionless as the drunkard. Worst of all, *our jobs* are part of that "drunken stroll" and become our terminal stagnation-traps.

In the Neo-Tech World, all that changed. Our living jobs became our transmission belts to Neothink. Until then, I decided to personally restructure my company — regrouping job responsibilities by common denominators...by their money-making purposes — into powerful growth-oriented jobs...the mini-companies (the Fifth Vision).

How To Do It — The Second Step

Once I did that conceptual structuring for both my schedule and job, then I moved on to the second step to creativity: *forward-movement integrated thinking.* Now, I could *build* my way to new levels, piece by piece, beam by beam, always building upon and snapping or nailing together my progress. I did this forward-movement integrated thinking through power-thinking, studying the numbers, and lifting my mind to the next level, through the Hemingway Code. ...To become a genius of society today at first takes hard work. Before long, however, it becomes easy, for you become loaded with an exhilarating motivational drive and inspired by the monetary and emotional rewards. I speak from experience.

With my mini-days and mini-companies intact, I could handle vast amounts of growth. Remember, in the Fifth Vision, I handled 22 new projects and 150 dynamic tasks in one week alone by contrast to no projects and a handful of routine tasks previously. I easily handled new projects and new money-making experiments generated by power-thinking, the guiding numbers, and my newly discovered high-powered mind. While pursuing new directions and, in doing so, integrating lots of knowledge each week, at times new knowledge sprang forth with no warning. I was beginning to experience Neothink.

Knowledge is power. But creating *new knowledge* is *super power.* The richest people today *created* something new. Through forward-movement integrated thinking, they integrated lots of existing knowledge. While steadily putting together existing knowledge, they hit a critical point that broke through into new knowledge. While steadily building their success puzzles piece by piece, they reached a point when they had snapped together a creative new puzzle picture. At that point, they experienced Neothink. Tomorrow, we all evolved into the Neothink mentality, all the time.

Realize, those geniuses today were not necessarily gifted with creativity. Not until they built a certain size success puzzle did they begin springing into creativity. You see, as they built their success puzzles piece by piece, they began to see "puzzle pictures" gradually forming. As they saw their puzzle pictures coming together, they broke into new knowledge while seeing how their unique pictures and their missing pieces must look like. Then they began *creating* by completing those unique puzzle pictures.

Forming Your Bridge to Money and Power

Sometimes we wonder how a money/power giant got from point A in school to point B at the top of the world. Building success puzzles, piece by piece, formed his bridges to money and power. To build those success puzzles, piece by piece, though, requires integrated thinking. Tomorrow, under the new code of business, that happened automatically to ordinary people. Today, under the old code of business, I used all the techniques given to me in my First, Second, Fifth, Sixth, and Ninth Visions as well as the powerful insights in the First Insight in Part Two of this book.

I observed in my Ninth Vision that it was integrated thinking that eventually enabled the entire human race to mentally cross the bridges to a whole new way of orchestrating our minds in the Neo-Tech World, something they called the *Neothink Mentality*. Neothink was so superior that once it got started, its natural advantages quickly engaged people everywhere.

Neothink comes from compilations of complex concepts that, when pulled together, reveal startling, synergistic advancements of human knowledge.

Let us look at a Neothink compilation of complex concepts: the mini-day, mini-company, power-thinking, replicating, tracking reports, essence meetings (Visions Five and Six) are each, in themselves, complex conceptual advancements of knowledge, discovered one by one through integrated thinking, but not in themselves Neothink breakthroughs. However, pull the integration string and those conceptual breakthroughs interlock with synergy and suddenly become a whole new paradigm of business, as presented in the Fifth and Sixth Visions. Indeed, the *division-of-essence* archetype will advance the entire world of business, as we know it, beyond the long-standing division-of-labor tradition. That major advancement of human knowledge could only be made through Neothink.

Very rare today, Neothink became our normal mentality in tomorrow's Neo-Tech World. With Neothink, ordinary people contributed huge, life-lifting values to mankind.

Are you ready to take your first step?

Becoming A Genius — Summary

The breakdown of the bicameral mind and its societal structures three thousand years ago generated the survival pressures for mankind to cross over to human consciousness. The increasing breakdown of the mutant-bicameral mind and its societal structures today will increasingly generate survival pressures for the human race to cross over to Neothink.

When that happens, we will discover our unknown selves: our buried genius...our God-Man within. The measurement for intelligence will change from intelligence tests or IQ to the efficacy of one's integrated thinking. IQ will no longer matter (save for subnormal, mental retardation, of course). In time, the superior Neothink mentality will sweep across our planet. Even babies will naturally grow into and stay in the Neothink mentality.

The geniuses of society will be the first to cross over to Neothink. Thereafter, ordinary people will join the geniuses. In exhilarating mini-companies at work instead of boring routine ruts, we will become entrepreneurial geniuses and create wonderful values for the world.

First Feat: Get Back Your Motivational Drive

First, learn to conceptualize. Search for common denominators around you...particularly at work. Start small with the everyday details. Conceptualizing gives them structure and makes them efficient, such as the mini-day schedule (the Fifth Vision). Then advance to the job responsibilities and pull them into their common denominators to form your mini-company. From that conceptual structure, begin forward-movement integrated thinking using power-thinking and the numbers as your tools, pushing ahead with the Hemingway Code to build your success puzzles. As you discover your creativity, you will eventually build puzzle pictures the world has never seen. You will then experience a motivational drive not known since you were a toddler, replenishing your limitless potential...and happiness.

Second Feat: Tap Your Potential

With the return of your motivational drive, your potential will soar and so will your mental and physical energy. You will easily stay forever in the Hemingway Code of the mind. With your motivational drive back, you will think a lot again about ambitious dreams, as you used to early in your youth. But you will be no daydreamer now — you will be a dream doer. You will accomplish those dreams. You will feel the contrast between your newborn potential versus your old hopelessness. That new feeling will nourish your motivational drive, at which point you will permanently make the "jump" into integrated thinking. Now, without the burden of life to drain energy from your new creation/motivation/creation cycle, you will permanently build success puzzles. You will build larger and larger puzzles of knowledge with integrated thinking. With that integrated, puzzle-building thinking, surpassing your best dreams becomes natural and fun. You will finally live the way man is supposed to live. Highly motivated and making more and more conceptual advancements, you will learn how to pull the integration string. That is when you will see your first puzzle picture. Pulling together your conceptual advancements into one interlocked, synergistic advancement of knowledge, one clear puzzle picture of new knowledge, you will experience the ecstasy of Neothink. Soon, you will cross over to the Neothink mentality and continue to pull together those synergistic advancements of knowledge in your line of work or interests. Of course, you will be greatly rewarded with prestige, wealth, happiness, and love.

My Ninth Vision showed me that sometime in the 21st century, putting together synergistic advancements of knowledge became the norm for ordinary people as mankind completed his final evolutionary jump into God-Man. The resulting Neo-Tech World was beyond any conception by today's scope of knowledge. Let us just say, despite what some critics might say, the Gifts described in this book are not simplistic, optimistic projections; they are understatements. ...Our Neo-Tech World awaits us at the end of the long road of bicameral behavioral patterns deeply grooved into the minds of mankind. As the First Insight in Part Two of this book shows you, only Neo-Tech can break apart those bicameral behavior patterns.

Vision Ten
Geniuses Will Surround You and Bring You the Gifts

"Another sign of a healthy, competitive industry is lower prices. The statistics show that the cost of computing has decreased ten million fold since 1971. That's the equivalent of getting a Boeing 747 for the price of a pizza."

— Bill Gates

My Tenth Vision showed me why we so loved our geniuses: they brought us the Gifts.

Stepping through the doorway into the Neo-Tech Era in my mind's eye, our geniuses made us rich, made us healthy, made everything good for us. The geniuses of society, who first evolved into Neothink, led the Technological Revolution that raised our standards of living towards that of millionaires. Then, when our fellowman joined the geniuses, they swept civilization into the extraordinarily prosperous Neo-Tech World. We, the yesterday's victims, became tomorrow's victors.

At first, in the late 20th century, the geniuses freely rose in the computer world and brought ordinary children cheap video game machines that, just a few years before, only the children of millionaires could enjoy. My Tenth Vision showed me that sometime in the first quarter of the 21st century, the geniuses freely rose throughout the rest of the business world and brought us cheap products that a few years before only the millionaires could enjoy. Indeed, this computerlike *millionaire phenomenon* came to more and more industries beyond the computer industry, making ordinary people such as you and me essentially millionaires without lifting a finger.

Looking back over the 20th-century, the millionaire phenomenon had already happened in the computer industry because it was uniquely free of big-government regulations. The computer industry gave us a look ahead at what life would be like in the Neo-Tech World.

My Tenth Vision showed me that, to the amazement of the

213

people, the millionaire phenomenon came to more and more industries as we universally removed big-government regulations. After our Neo-Tech World's get-the-people-rich government (Vision Eleven, next) removed most big-government regulations, technologies in all industries raced ahead like the computers. As in the computer industry, where buying power multiplied thousands or millions of times, our buying power in more and more industries multiplied hundreds, sometimes thousands of times or more. That was because the geniuses were now able to rise and evolve into Neothink.

Freeing The Geniuses

Simply put, America's falling out with big government freed all the potential geniuses of society to drive our costs toward zero and our buying power toward infinity. Fantastic products and services never before imagined suddenly came into existence and then became cheap and affordable. What happened in the computer/communication world was a harbinger of what happened in my Vision of tomorrow. When Neo-Tech spread beyond the computers, we lived in increasing wealth and luxury. People became economically driven to end the anticivilization's big government and to embrace the Neo-Tech World's get-the-people-rich government.

The Neo-Tech World's get-the-people-rich political party was called the Neo-Tech Party (Vision Eleven). The Neo-Tech Party ushered in get-the-people-rich government, a completely new political paradigm of entrepreneurs and market-driven business leaders in which your every need, no matter how extraordinary or how small, was taken care of. You and your problems were never alone; help was always on the way for every need.

To achieve that never-alone, always-taken-care-of state, the get-the-people-rich government shifted the responsibility of taking care of you — i.e., social well-being — from a few hundred phony career politicians interested in ruling over you...to a hundred million geniuses in entrepreneurial jobs (the Fifth Vision) with rapidly expanding creativity and multiplying genius, very interested in taking care of all your needs and wishes.

Millions of unrestricted geniuses, aggressively seeking out our needs, very rapidly answered our every cry for help. That was the new code of living in the Neo-Tech World. Even your slightest problem had you immediately surrounded by quality people, by geniuses of society, wanting to help you. Just one cry for help sent out from your home over the Internet, for instance, ever so quickly led to its cure.

The job of looking out for your well-being and the social good shifted from impotent government and its corrupt ruling class to the miraculous might of an unrestricted Neo-Tech Society and its unleashed creativity and multiplying geniuses of society. Your problems were the geniuses' problems to solve. In short, geniuses were hard at work taking care of you.

Today in the anticivilization, big-government career politicians do not care about your problems, no matter how real, unless your problems fall into their self-aggrandizing schemes to rule. That is the old code of living in the anticivilization. All other good working people have to fight for their survival. If you contract an obscure disease, you are doomed. In tomorrow's Neo-Tech World, however, geniuses using Neothink squeezed forth a cure *before* the disease destroyed you. I saw it all in my Tenth Vision. Tomorrow, you were always safe. Looking back at today's anticivilization, if you are not happy with your job and pay or with the direction of your career and income, you are trapped. In tomorrow's Neo-Tech World, genius-driven businesses brought you exciting opportunities including the lucrative career of your dreams, namely your Friday-Night Essence. Today in the anticivilization, if you are not happy with your wealth, you are rather helpless. Tomorrow, the multiplying wealth of society rescued your plight. Today, if you are not happy with love, you grow more and more apathetic. Tomorrow, the happiness available from living the life you were meant to live helped you activate a new, superlove. If you felt lonely, the enhanced networking of society brought you quality friends, especially as your own value to the world soared. If you were having hard times, the curing nature of society took care of you in every way. Geniuses were there for you, in minutes. Money was no longer an issue. A hundred million geniuses in this country alone took care of your every need.

They Brought Us Fortunes

The Neo-Tech Party simply freed the geniuses of society, who became the first to evolve into Neothink. We sat back and collected the rewards from society's most gifted people. It was a nice exchange: we gave them freedom, and they gave us fortunes. We certainly were at a unique place in history.

In the late 20th century when conversations at cocktail parties developed about computers and the Internet and how we could access for free computing power that would have cost millions a few years before, usually some attractive yuppie said something like, "Can you believe that amazing technology!" Everyone then shared looks of astonishment. Little did we stop to realize that *the geniuses of society* brought us that soaring technology and buying power. And those geniuses would do so in every industry if free to do so...making ordinary people rich and completely healthy.

Sometime in the first quarter of the 21st century, after fifty million of these Twelve Visions were disseminated, all the connections were made. Ordinary people began to admire and love those geniuses who brought them new technologies at lower and lower prices. The feeling grew despite political rhetoric that traditionally caused Americans to envy and dislike the geniuses of society. As the geniuses improved everyone's life in so many ways, the ordinary person developed a warm fondness for the geniuses of society not unlike one would for a highly competent doctor who saved his child's life, for instance.

Indeed, imagine if your own child or grandchild were terminally ill and the heroic efforts of a highly competent doctor saved your child. You would forever feel a warm affection for that doctor who saved your child's life. Or imagine a wealthy person gave you and your family a cashier's check for a million dollars. You would forever feel a very warm closeness to that person who made your life so rich and wonderful.

Once fifty million copies of *The Neo-Tech World* were disseminated, the people felt similar feelings towards the geniuses of society, for those geniuses eradicated diseases and lifted us into a wealthy and wonderful world. The hoodwinking by the media that made us envy and dislike the geniuses of society subsided. The forces of Neo-Tech were now too great to be stopped. Sure the geniuses were rich, because they were geniuses! But they made *us* rich, too. Furthermore, they brought us the Gifts, which fulfilled our greatest desires. The entire population, sometime in the first quarter of the 21st century, felt a warm closeness to those geniuses who brought us and our families into an increasingly wealthy and wonderful life.

We also felt growing contempt toward those big-government career politicians who blocked the geniuses and Neo-Tech. They blocked the Gifts and the wonderful lives we were meant to live. Most productive Americans in the 21st century disliked career politicians, and soon thereafter they understood why. Once the people made the connection and felt a warm admiration and fondness for the geniuses of society, then the Neo-Tech Era irreversibly took off.

We sat back and watched in awe as the geniuses of society took care of our needs, fixed our problems, made our dreams come true, and made us rich.

Of course, career politicians would not let go of their ruling power as we entered the Neo-Tech Era. They hung on, but they were part of the old world of bicameral mentalities on its way out. Being labeled "career politicians" ended their political careers as the new world of no more higher "authorities" moved in. *The Great Replacement Program*, replacing career politicians with market-driven businesspeople, happened like an unstoppable wave. Across the country, then the world, the big wave washed away career politicians and replaced them with entrepreneurs and market-driven businesspeople. They, in turn, freed the geniuses of society whose life ambitions were to solve any and all of our problems and needs, large or small.

Example of a Genius Evolving Into Neothink

Just how effective were those geniuses of society at taking care of our every need or problem? Instead of me impossibly trying to describe what I saw in my Tenth Vision, which overwhelmed me to the point of euphoric collapse, let me take you into the life and times of an obscure genius of society who already lived, as first told to me by my brother. That way, I can show you already *proven facts*. Now, since some people say the computer revolution was unique — an anomaly based on the invention of the silicon chip — let us go outside the computer industry. In fact, let us go back in time before high technology altogether to see the universal life-lifting power of the geniuses of society *on their own*, even before their catalytic reaction with modern technologies. So, let us now travel back a hundred years...to the down and dirty railroad industry:

This is a story about James J. Hill, a genius of society one hundred years ago who was well on his way to multiplying standards of living of entire civilizations of ordinary people and taking care of their every need until he got held down by big-government regulations. His story represents all geniuses of society, even outside the computer industry.

He was a railroad pioneer back at the turn of the 20th century, and his story is brought to light in a book called *Entrepreneurs Versus The State* by Burton Folsom.

Let's travel back in time to the 1860s. America was experiencing its first railroad boom. Railroads were being built all up and down the East Coast. Well, as Mr. Folsom identifies in his book, two classes of entrepreneurs exist: market entrepreneurs and political entrepreneurs. Political entrepreneurs make their money by seeking government subsidies, by getting special government rights of way, and by accessing political clout. They seek their success through political clout with government officials.

Market entrepreneurs make their money by providing more and more values and services to society at lower and lower costs. They also create more and more jobs for us.

During America's railroad building boom in the 1860s, an opportunity arose for big government. The political entrepreneurs seeking easy money got together with career politicians seeking popularity, and together they created a deception. The deception was that only the government could finance the building of America's first transcontinental railroad. That deception over 100 years ago is still promoted today; children read about it in their history text books in school.

But that was a deception created by political entrepreneurs

so they could line their pockets with lavish government subsidies and by career politicians so they could boost their self-worth by spending money that they controlled but did not earn. They could parade around and say, "Look how important we are. Look how we benefit the American public. We, the big government, are building this transcontinental railroad and opening up the interior and west coast of America." ...A perfect setup for greedy political entrepreneurs joining hands with power-seeking politicians. A perfect setup to control our mutant bicameral mentality.

So a deception was created: only the federal government could finance the building of the transcontinental railroad. The public bought it, and with great fanfare, Congress went ahead with it.

There were two companies: Central Pacific started building eastward from the West Coast and the Union Pacific started westward from the East Coast. The government paid those companies by the total miles of track they built. So what did they do? Instead of being bound by the disciplines of a bottom line, they were getting lavish subsidies from the government for the total miles of track they built. So they rushed into the wilderness to collect government subsidies.

But because they were being paid by the mile, these companies purposely built the longest, most circuitous routes they could possibly justify so they could get more government money. And they rushed construction to collect their per-mile subsidies. They rushed ahead with poor construction and poor planning into the wilderness.

Remember, the congressmen were spending money that they did not earn but controlled, and they wanted to reap the glory for spending that money. Those politicians, always trying to justify their jobs, always trying to show that they benefit the American public, got into the railroad business where they had no business being in the first place. Controlling tremendous amounts of money they did not earn, they reaped all this popularity that comes with spending the money. Now they could say, "Look how valuable we are; we're financing the building of a transcontinental railroad across America!"

But those career politicians were part of bogus big government. They gladly spent money with their flashy "good intentions", but they were not interested in getting out and

219

exerting the nitty-gritty effort that business does when it spends money. They were glad to spend the money, large amounts of money, and reap the glory, but they weren't about to get out there and exert the nitty-gritty effort to put the controls on spending to make sure that money was spent right. They were not about to get right down into the details themselves to make sure that they were buying the right quality goods and that the railroad was being built over the right routes...not like a market businessman would who is spending that money *out of his own pocket*.

So the whole program was laced with fraud from the beginning. The line managers set up their own supplier companies selling their railroads substandard quality rails and ties at exorbitant prices. For, there was no control over the government money.

In addition, because they were getting paid by the amount of rail they built, each company was racing to build as much track as it could before the other one...to get the most money from the government. So instead of taking the proper time to carefully map out the best routes, especially vital for building over hills at the lowest uphill grade, they instead just raced forward and paid no attention to vital planning and surveying. No time to be wasted on planning and surveying, they built track over uphill grades that were far too steep. They did not take the necessary time to do anything right. When winter came, they just kept on building over the plains, right *over* the ice! Because they wanted to build as much as possible, they did not wait for the ice to melt — they just kept on laying track. When summer came, they had to tear up thousands of miles of track and rebuild it, before they could open the line! And to get more money, the two railroad companies built the *longest* routes with *under-quality* material. ...You can just imagine what the future operating costs this transcontinental railroad would endure.

Indeed, when the Union Pacific was complete, from day one it could not make a profit because its operating expenses were too high. First of all, thousands of miles of shoddily built, under-quality track had to be constantly replaced. Second, because they took the extra long route, and it wasn't built over the lowest grade hills, they had to pay a lot more money in fuel costs, wage costs, and it took a lot more time to haul freight across the country. So the operating expenses were so high, from day one the Union Pacific was never able to make a profit.

Therefore, the government had to continue to subsidize the transcontinental line once it was built. Union Pacific had to continue to receive more and more government money or it would have gone out of business and stopped running. Indeed, Congress had just spent a fortune financing the building of the transcontinental line. Now Congress could not let their prize transcontinental line declare bankruptcy and close down. So, the government continued financing it.

After the Union Pacific was built, other political entrepreneurs got together with glory-seeking politicians in their areas of the country and said, "The federal government financed the Union Pacific, therefore they have to finance a transcontinental railroad in our region."

So Congress went ahead and financed the building of a transcontinental up North called the Northern Pacific, and one down South called the Santa Fe. Of course, both of those had the same results. They built extra long, circuitous routes; they turned into an orgy of fraud, substandard quality material used, no time taken to select the lowest grade hills. So right from day one, the other two transcontinentals lost money, and they had to receive government subsidies just to continue operating.

In the meantime, there was a young man way up North, James J. Hill, going about making a living. He was born in a log cabin in Ontario, Canada to a working-class family. His father died when he was a boy, so Hill got a job to support his mother. At seventeen, he moved to St. Paul and got a job for a shipping company. He started in an entry-level position, but he loved the transportation business. He really applied himself; he began making contacts, and he began moving up. Before long, he began making partnerships in local railroads that were being built in his area. With a sweeping vision, yet always focussed on nitty-gritty details, Hill commanded success. Eventually, Hill decided that he was going to build the first completely privately financed transcontinental railroad way up along the U.S. and Canadian border, which at that time was all wilderness with no settlers!

221

Well, from the beginning the idea was labeled Hill's Folly, and you can see why. How could someone build a railroad that could possibly compete when he had to pay all the building costs himself, and there were three others that existed farther South that had all their building costs paid by the government? Moreover, Hill's railroad was going to be way up North where no one lived. Those other three government-financed railroads were located in the main population areas of the United States. In addition, once Hill did complete his railroad, how could he compete with the other three railroads when they continued to receive government subsidies and Hill had to pay his expenses through his own bottom-line profits — and the three other lines proved that no profits existed!

Well, Hill went ahead with his plans anyway. Hill had to obey the disciplines of a bottom line. He could not go rushing into the wilderness to collect government subsidies. He had to build his line out West one extension at a time. He would build westward into the wilderness a few hundred miles at a time. Then he would send agents back East to advertise to farmers in the East. Hill offered to move people for free into this western wilderness so they could settle and start their farms. Then Hill would give them free rates to ship their crops back to the markets in the East for a couple of years until they got established. He gave a lot of ordinary low-income people exciting new leases on life and made their dreams come true.

This worked. For each extension West, he brought in enthusiastic hardworking farmers; they'd flourish; he'd build up business on his track, and after awhile his extension West made money. From those profits, he'd finance another extension West...a few hundred miles at a time. He never stopped. By turning low-income settlers into land-owning entrepreneurs, among others, he settled the entire northern border of the United States with his railroad. And, lo and behold, in 1890 the first American transcontinental railroad was built without one penny of government money! He reached the Pacific Ocean, and he did it by offering people, some of whom had little chance at much in life, an opportunity of a lifetime to own land and become entrepreneurs.

What an accomplishment. But most amazingly, *one man* did

it! Not the entire might of the U.S. Government — one lone man! One genius of society was raising the prosperity of an entire nation! But, now that he accomplished this amazing feat, could he make it work? Here Hill was with his transcontinental, way up North when the population base was farther South; he was competing against three transcontinentals farther South that had all of their expenses paid for by the government. So, what would happen to Hill's transcontinental?

During the building of Hill's railroad, since it was his personal money that was being spent, he personally dug into the tough nitty-gritty details. With unyielding disciplines and efforts, he put controls on everything: He personally surveyed the routes; he made sure the shortest, most direct routes were built. When the track had to go over hills, he would spend time with the engineers and make sure they picked out the lowest-grade hills. He personally supervised the buying of materials to make sure they got the highest quality rails and ties for the lowest cost. ...So what happened to Hill's Folly? Well, from day one, when it was completed, he made a profit! He ran circles around the three government-financed lines because his operating expenses were so much lower. In addition, his freight took a lot less time to reach the West Coast. From day one, Hill made a profit. From day one, the government-subsidized transcontinental railroads never, ever turned a profit.

One man was running circles around the almighty U.S. Government! Of course, the incompetence and greed of career politicians could never bring values to the people. But one market entrepreneur could raise the standard of living of a nation.

This one market entrepreneur's advantages kept building momentum and, with a great irony, left Congress's follies in the dust. Hill built up the whole industry of the Northwest. He built feeder lines. For example, if copper were found a hundred miles north, he would build a feeder line, move in a copper company so they could start mining and shipping the copper over his line. If lumber were discovered up in the mountain, he would feeder line up there, move in a lumber company, and they would start shipping the lumber over his lines. If there was a good clearing for cattle ranching a few miles south, he would build a feeder line. ...Railroads discovered that feeder lines became a main source of profit.

But consider Congress's lines built for politicians' own glory and self-worth. Because those railroads were receiving their money from the government, they would have to get Congress's permission to build a feeder line. Well, of course, everyone knows what happens when the government has to make a decision. A simple black-and-white decision to build a profitable feeder line that should be made overnight would be tied up for months, even for years. All the incompetent congressmen would get up and debate over it to get in the spotlight and appear needed and important. ...They cared only about themselves, not about what was best for America.

So Hill's railroad ran circles around the three government-financed railroads from day one. In addition, Hill brought civilization and industry to the Northwest: mining in Montana, lumber along the North, apple farmers in Washington, wheat farmers on the plains. He built up the whole region along his railroad line.

Once Hill completed his line to the West Coast, he did not stop there. He kept reaching out and pushing up standards of living. Integrating more and more widely, into Neothink itself, Hill started reaching out toward the Orient. What about trade with the Orient? Hill did some calculations: if one major province in China substituted an ounce of rice a day with an ounce of American wheat, that would mean 50 million bushels of American wheat would travel over his railroad to China every year! Think what that would do for his farmers! Now, he would make them rich! American farmers exporting huge shipments of wheat to China — what a possibility! So Hill sent agents to Japan and China to begin promoting American trade, the same way he had done during the building up of his transcontinental railroad.

In the meantime, we had these political entrepreneurs in Washington, D.C. still running around wondering how to get more government subsidies to line their pockets. Yet one market entrepreneur was creating jobs and dreams by the thousands. Indeed, Hill sent his agents to Japan and China to start promoting American products, and he went out and bought his own steamship line. He raced his ships back and forth between Japan and China and America. Hill built up American trade with Asia the same way that he built up business along his line. He would send products for free to the Japanese and Chinese if they would just try them out. Then once they tried them out, if they liked them they would come back, and Hill would build up the business.

Every day Hill filled his ships with American grain from the plains, with copper from Montana, lumber from Washington, cotton from the South, textiles from New England, rails from Pittsburgh, apples from Washington. He would send them all free to the Far East. The Asians would try these American goods, and if they liked them, then they would come back for more.

In fact, Hill went to Japan, met with Japanese businessmen, and proposed that he would buy southern cotton, pay for it himself, ship it to the Japanese for free, and *give* it to them free. Hill would buy the southern cotton out of his own money if the Japanese would just try this cotton in place of the cotton they normally got from India. Well, the Japanese took him up on his offer; they liked it, and soon Hill's box cars were full of cotton, travelling from the South to the North to the Pacific Coast and then on to a steamship to Japan.

Hill used this strategy to build up all kinds of business. In 1900, Japan started a railroad building boom. Hill recognized the potential of railroads throughout Asia. At that time, the world's suppliers of rail were England and Belgium. But there were a few American rail makers in Pittsburgh. So Hill went to Japan; he purposely underbid the English and the Belgians, paid the difference out of his own pocket just to get the Japanese to try rails made in Pittsburgh. His strategy worked: Japan started buying all their rail from Pittsburgh, which built up the fledgling rail industry in America.

What happened in the 1890s was nothing short of a miracle: When Hill started his push into Asia, trade with Japan was seven million dollars a year. Nine years later, with Hill in charge of this American mission into Asia, American trade with Japan *alone* was 52 million dollars! And he was now pushing into China as well! Hill was causing geometrical increases in American commerce. He was spearheading, a hundred years ago, an

225

American dominance of trade in Asia. In the meantime the political entrepreneurs, Hill's so-called rivals, were still running around Washington, D.C. trying to figure out how they could get more subsidies. And Hill just kept on reaching out, with Neothink, taking care of people's needs, and pushing up standards of living while spearheading a geometrical increase of American commerce in Asia. That was one hundred years ago.

As time went by, the other three government-financed transcontinentals continued to lose money. The government kept pouring taxpayers' dollars into financing them. The public started getting fed up with this. In addition, as time went by, the frauds committed by the political entrepreneurs started to surface — things like setting up their own companies to sell substandard material at overcharged prices. The American public had to continue to pay subsidies into this hoax just to keep these other three government railroads running. The public finally had enough. So Congress, those eternal glory-seeking politicians, started self-righteously parading the corrupt political entrepreneurs in front of Congress and the nation, forming special-investigation committees.

Well, once again, Congress created a deception: They presented themselves as protectors of the American public. They would nobly project, "Look how great we are; look how needed and important we are; we're going to protect the American public from those greedy and corrupt railroad executives." Yet, the root cause of the problem was Congress itself. Congress was the culprit! Congress spent other people's money in a railroad business where they had no business being in the first place.

So instead of getting up and confessing, "Look, the problem was us. We now realize the problem was us getting into the railroad business in the first place. We had no business in there, so now we're going to get completely out." They could have been honest, but they were not. No, they did not want to say that because that would have exposed bogus big government. Instead, they saw a chance to enhance big government and to increase their own popularity and political power for re-election. They instead self-righteously projected, "Look how we earn our keep. We're protecting the American public." Congress self-righteously started parading those corrupt railroad executives in front of the nation. Congress made the railroad executives solely to blame for the transcontinental fiascoes. And then, to "protect the public", they proposed to form more higher "authorities" such as the ICC, the Interstate Commerce Commission, and to pass Sherman Antitrust legislation to further get in there and regulate the railroads.

Well, Hill knew what was going on; he knew what the story was here. So Hill moved to Washington, D.C. He set up residence in the country's Capitol. He personally talked to the congressmen. He testified before their special committees. He told them what was going on: the root cause of the problem was big government getting in there where it had no business being in the first place, financing those railroads, spending other people's money on rails. That caused the corruption. Hill gave the example of his railroad. He did not accept one penny of government money while his railroad built up all the industry in the Northwest. And now his line was promoting an explosion of American trade into Asia while the three government-sponsored lines were sinking in corruption.

Now, the congressmen were intelligent men. They were college educated. They knew what Hill was saying. They knew he made perfect sense. They knew his account was the truth, but they did not care because they wanted to justify their own jobs. So they ignored him. They ignored Hill, and they went on to pass the ICC and the Sherman Antitrust legislation, which enabled them to get in and heavily regulate and punish the railroads.

Hill even wrote a book on this whole ordeal and circulated his book to the congressmen, explaining the situation. He presented all the evidence that showed how Congress was doing the wrong thing. But the big-government ruling class ignored Hill because they wanted to advance their own power. The career politicians went ahead and passed the ICC, passed the Sherman Antitrust legislation. And what did that do? Those regulations "for the public good" made it illegal for railroads to make any special deals with customers. They had to charge the same standard rate to all customers. Therefore, the Neothink dynamics Hill used to build up his railroad, to move in people for free, to make their dreams come true, to ship their freight for free or for a low cost until they got established...was now illegal! Those same dynamics that he was now using to spearhead an American dominance of trade in Asia were all now illegal! Wham! Hill was a genius of society who was pushing up the lid to lift all America into a jack-in-the-box explosion of prosperity — and WHAM! Big-government regulations smashed him down. Hill's drive into Asia was over.

The year after the ICC's legislation passed, America's trade with Japan alone dropped by 40%. Now remember, Hill was spearheading a *geometrical increase* in trade. Trade with Japan and China was increasing geometrically. Now Congress passed this legislation and, plop, everything dropped 40%.

Hill was forced to sell his steamship lines, he got out of trade completely with Asia, and he was so frustrated, he retired. Suddenly, the miracle was over. Now, this was a hundred years ago. Let us stop and look at the implications of this. Let us stretch this out to see what Congress really cut off a hundred years ago. It was bad enough they cut off Hill's trade with Asia back then and destroyed the wealth, lives and dreams of many entrepreneurs dependent on Hill's dynamics, but let us project that into the future to see what they cut off today:

Throughout the past two decades, you have heard our President and top CEOs and top economists say that America's greatest danger economically is its trade imbalance with Asia and our lack of international competitiveness. But who in the world knows that a hundred years ago Hill was spearheading an American dominance of trade throughout all of Asia? That trade dominance was cut off by big-government regulations. Who even knows that? Nobody mentions that today, but everyone has warned about "the greatest economic danger facing America today". Americans have lost jobs by the thousands, have been outcompeted, factories have closed down. Yet who knows that one hundred years ago this one genius of society, *one man*, learned how to tend to people's needs, make people's dreams come true, and spearhead an American dominance of trade with Asia? Who knows that a hundred years ago a man named James J. Hill started something really magnificent that would have painted an entirely different picture of America's future than that of uncertainty today? Big government destroyed that prosperous future when they destroyed Hill a hundred years ago.

The politicians back then knew what they were doing. They were intelligent men. They were college educated. Hill went and explained the facts to them. Typical of big government, however, they only wanted to increase their political powers. Indeed, such god-like power to rule over us was a bicameral mutation never meant for conscious civilizations. The hierarchy of authorities, the career politicians, wanted to advance their images and egos. So they ignored Hill, and they cut off something magnificent a hundred years ago. Same as today, the ruling class back then stopped our great grandparents from rising into a paradise on Earth. Same as today, that was the anticivilization of mutant bicameral mentalities suppressed by external "authorities".

So there you have an example of what just one genius of society can do for everyone. And you can see that the geniuses of society will rise in any industry at any time, not just in the computer or hi-tech industries, if not held down by the anticivilization's big-government regulations. And you can see that, when the geniuses rise tomorrow in all industries, our problems, needs, and dreams will quickly be tended to. In short, the Neo-Tech Society tomorrow — a supersociety with millions of James J. Hills — will take care of us and make our dreams come true.

Now, imagine a hundred million geniuses of society, a hundred million James J. Hills all using Neothink...all catalyzed by modern technology. You cannot imagine, because the image goes beyond anything we can know today.

Held Down in the Darkness

My Tenth Vision showed me that in tomorrow's Neo-Tech World, looking back at today's anticivilization was very frustrating. We saw how career politicians and bureaucrats ruling over us and holding down society today caused the only injustice that no one could see, because no one today could imagine the Neo-Tech World tomorrow. One obvious example, America would have been the dominant trade of that huge upswinging in Asia, but we never had a clue. America's problems with the trade deficit and people losing their jobs to international competition would have all been reversed. But no one saw that. Instead, today we were held down in the darkness. Looking back at the anticivilization today, no one except those who read The Twelve Visions could see this particular injustice of government ruling over us and holding us down because in the anticivilization no one knew about the Golden Neo-Tech World.

James J. Hill started pushing us up toward that paradise on Earth, but America was held down by the anticivilization's big government. Tomorrow, once we lived in the Neo-Tech World and could see the injustice of former anticivilization's big government, to look back became painfully hard to do. The people in the Neo-Tech World realized that every life lost on the battlefield, all famine and sufferings in America and around the world in the 20th century and early 21st century, including deaths from diseases...all of that was encompassed in the Great Suppression — the ruling class holding down America from soaring into the Golden Neo-Tech World. The ruling class — men and women bicamerally granted the "divine" ruling power —was a vestige of the Bicameral Age and was responsible for the Great Suppression.

The Geniuses Pulled Everyone Up With Them

In this Tenth Vision into the Neo-Tech World, the geniuses of society were free to go up; they pulled everyone up with them, just as Hill was doing. All our personal needs were taken care of because we did not have just one James J. Hill a hundred years ago. We did not have just one Michael Milken today. (Michael Milken would have most likely financed the industrialization of the third world, particularly the economically ruined Eastern European countries, and again established an American dominance of trade there, had he not been smashed down like J. J. Hill by anticivilization big-government deceptions.) We actually had thousands and then millions of James J. Hills and Michael Milkens...all making ordinary people's best dreams come true.

In my Tenth Vision, tender youth could rise and rise quickly. Tender youth today, by contrast, cannot rise because they cannot climb through the big-government regulatory web and then face being caught and squashed like a Milken-Hill bug. They just cannot get enough momentum to rise in the thick web of big-government legislation, regulation, litigation, destruction and punishment.

In 1936, mankind reached a new high with the completion of Hoover Dam to harness the Colorado River. After 3000 years, conscious man reached a level of technology that could control nature on a large scale. But man took only another 33 years to go to the moon. Civilization was *begging* to progress *geometrically,* which occurred in my Tenth Vision sometime in the first quarter of the 21st century when the big-government legislative/regulatory web was swished away and super technologies and the geniuses soared upward, unrestrained, no longer "caught" and destroyed such as Hill and Milken.

The Tenth Vision showed me unburdened technology — regulated not by glory-seeking politicians and bureaucrats but by private services — advanced incredibly fast, nearly at the speed of accessing information. Science, business, and medicine came together during the communication/information revolution for synergistic breakthroughs, no longer politicized by big government, free as the nonpoliticized computer industry of the previous two decades.

Upon setting free the entire Technological Revolution from big government, genius-driven new technologies quickly took care of all our problems. Disease, unemployment, poverty, divorce, obesity, insecurity, stagnation, racism, crime, budget deficits, the national debt, government abuse, Social-Security deficiency, illiteracy vanished along with big government. So did our personal problems such as a lousy job, lousy love-life, an uncompetitive body, a stagnant mind, an embarrassing home, car, and overall financial self-worth.

Too Painful To Look Back

Until America went Neo-Tech, however, some readers of this very page lost their lives to disease or lost a precious loved one. That Vision of loss was in my head, day and night, haunting images such as the deterioration of my friend John who, at 12 years old, ran and played with all the other schoolchildren; but the next year, muscular dystrophy started taking over his tall and handsome body. John first needed crutches, then a wheelchair, then an electric wheelchair...his long, limp body strapped in with a seat belt. In those days, John and I would go around doing things that young men do. John was almost in my world, talking about sports and girls. Yet, John would never experience those things. I could sometimes see in John's eyes his longing to throw off his seat belt, jump out of his wheelchair, and scream, "Here I am world! Here I am!" One day, John got a cold, and still just a young man, he died. Yet, geniuses in a Neo-Tech Society would have long ago taken care of John and cured his disease.

The anticivilization's big government held down the lid on America including cures to diseases, but we could not see the harm caused by big government. Tomorrow, it became almost too painful to look back at what and *who* we lost.

Consider looking back at the following image: Imprisoned by hunger, little children in poverty-stricken third-world countries hoped for a little fish with their rice for dinner. If James J. Hill were not stopped 100 years ago, along with all the other market businessmen hence, including most recently Michael Milken who would have very likely financed third-world industrialization and an American dominance of trade if not wrongly incarcerated by "well intentioned" government regulations and legislation, then those poor countries would have been industrialized and prosperous a long time ago.

Instead, those third-world children suffered and died to the bitter end of the 20th century and into the 21st century as the "glorious" big-government "good intentions" flourished and lived. The Great Suppression went on and on. Sometime in the first quarter of the 21st century, we brought to trial and to justice many politicians and bureaucrats — the sinister ones such as those responsible for incarcerating Michael Milken for their personal political gains — all of whom enjoyed reverence through the anticivilization's very end.

American children have always felt excitement about their futures. Yet, tomorrow when we looked back we realized that America, the land of opportunity, was also the land of disillusionment and disappointment. The drop from childhood dreams to adulthood reality was a deep letdown. Indeed, American adults carried a subdued sadness every day...to the end. Before the Neo-Tech World, they died unfulfilled, without experiencing wealth, romantic love, the life they were meant to live.

In the Neo-Tech World, looking back became almost unbearable, for we saw the images of what was lost. We failed at our dreams in the 20th century and early 21st century because we were in a society in which we could not win. My Tenth Vision showed me that the Neo-Tech Society, by contrast, would not let us fail. Instead, it made our dreams come true and made every ordinary person wealthy and healthy.

How hard it was, in the Neo-Tech World, to accept that only a *tiny* percentage of our population – the hierarchy of authorities consisting of our political and bureaucratic leaders — caused our irreplaceable loss of happiness and life in the anticivilization. That tiny clique was our ruling class. They created an indomitable burden on advancing technology (B.O.A.T.) in the anticivilization. When we sank that B.O.A.T. of neocheaters in the first quarter of the 21st century, new technologies emerged that made prices dive. When the B.O.A.T. sank, all society rose.

Looking back at the anticivilization from the Neo-Tech World, people shook their heads in disbelief. The legal battles, regulations, and legislation made opportunities at success limited, costly, and risky. In the Neo-Tech World, without such burdens, lucrative opportunities were everywhere, for everyone.

Like breaking from an awful spell, we glumly looked back at the stagnation that killed our dreams in the anticivilization, weakened our marriages, and destroyed the thrill of love we felt only during the first few weeks or months of falling in love. And, most painfully, we saw how our children absorbed from us our hopeless resignation, just as we had from our parents.

The Disgraceful End

In the first quarter of the 21st century, the Great Suppression came to its disgraceful end. Neo-Tech was deprogramming minds everywhere (see The First Insight). As our mutant bicameral mentality collapsed, so did our acceptance of external "authorities". Big government could in no way, not ever again, strangle progress and kill our dreams. In fact, our three greatest childhood wishes of great wealth, great romantic love, a great body and mind all came true.

Society no longer got pushed down with us being squeezed into stagnation-traps where we had always lived in the anticivilization. Career politicians were no longer around to suppress progressive technology with big-government regulations and legislation — all in the name of the "social good". Government no longer included that bogus, second purpose below:

1) Physically protect the people from aggression with local police, courts, prisons, and national defense (an honorable defensive government to defend against and punish initiatory force, *only*)

2) Promote social "prosperity" and provide social "well-being" through social and regulatory programs "for the social good"..."good intentions" to "serve the people" (a dishonorable offensive government of external "authorities" enforcing what is deemed the "social good", "good intentions", or the "national will"...mere men and women playing God with our money and our lives)

Tomorrow we looked back and realized in disgust that, as with the transcontinental railroads, our career politicians spent our money to ostensibly enhance our "well-being" and promote social "prosperity", but they really wanted the glory and "importance" that went with spending *other people's* money and ruling over us. They did not want anything to do with the effort, though, that went into building values, which market businessmen and women put themselves through every day when spending their own money.

Career politicians today suppress all industries (the computer industry being the most fortunate, least politicized industry). Career politicians today suppress our entire economy and standard of living as they did a hundred years ago with the railroads. Market businessmen, by contrast, are interested in creating and building values, not in ruling others. They create miracles for the human race, from Hill's transcontinental railroad to Gate's computer software and beyond.

The Miracle Makers

Tomorrow, the miracle makers, the unburdened market businessmen and women dramatically improved our well-being and prosperity. A Neo-Tech Society, flourishing with geniuses, handed us our needs on a silver platter and filled all our desires.

The erroneous idea in the anticivilization that government could "promote social prosperity" sort of sneaked up over the previous century through career politicians finding ways to self-indulge at spending our money to become more and more likable for re-election. Indeed, spending *other people's* money was a fast way to build favorable illusions in the 20th century and early 21st century. But when the people caught on sometime in the first quarter of the 21st century, the career politicians' careers ended with great shame.

In this Tenth Vision, market businessmen and women replaced career politicians. Geniuses of society rose and threw open the lid on society and lifted society toward its destiny of great, great prosperity. Each person was pulled up, our wheelchairs left behind. The whole world was then lifted as the communications revolution obsoleted distance and boundaries.

Paradise On Earth

The Tenth Vision showed me that in the Golden Neo-Tech World, irrationality disappeared. Poverty and crime vanished. In the Golden Neo-Tech World, the motivation for people to do dishonest things reversed. In time, in that world of disappearing irrationality and mysticism, armed forces were no longer necessary. The idea of crime and war became archaic. We achieved paradise on Earth.

Perhaps this all sounds like Utopia. But my Tenth Vision showed me tomorrow's Neo-Tech World truly reversed the motivation for people to do dishonest things, for our problems disappeared, and a millionaire standard of living was automatic — far easier and more lucrative than any possible crime. When America went Neo-Tech, the era of wealth and peace was here,

235

finally and forever.

Before the Twelve Visions, the people never knew about this wonderful Neo-Tech World. We only dreamed about it when we were children. Dr. Wallace, discoverer of Neo-Tech and author of *The Neo-Tech Discovery*, knew of its existence, but he needed for people to "see" it through these Twelve Visions.

Today, we live in a lucky time. Our bicameral behavioral patterns are wearing off. Huge financial rewards beckon us to deprogram our minds with Neo-Tech and shed our deep-rooted bicameral behavioral patterns always seeking external "authorities". (See The First Insight, Part Two of this book.) The nature of big government and its career politician is being recognized, and the Great Replacement Program is on the horizon. Our get-rich era is coming.

My Tenth Vision revealed a special Gift of the Neo-Tech World: the new miracle makers — the rising geniuses of society — "spoiled" us by serving us our needs on a silver platter, including great wealth and health. Now, think about the power in all this: the relatively few geniuses were the first to venture into Neothink. And *they alone* raised our standards of living to that of millionaires without us lifting a finger, as they first did in the computer world...the testimony to the power of Neothink! Imagine when the masses followed into Neothink — imagine the wealth!

The geniuses led our final evolution into God-Man. Later, we all followed. And when we did — when millions upon millions of us did — well, I will try to describe, in the Eleventh Vision, next, the new-color economy that I saw once we all switched over to the Neothink mind.

Vision Eleven
The Geniuses' Prosperity Explosion Will Make You A Millionaire

"That's the technology paradox: Businesses can thrive at the very moment when their prices are falling the fastest. 'The only thing that matters is if the exponential growth of your market is faster than the exponential decline of your prices,' says George M.C. Fisher, chairman and CEO of Eastman Kodak Co. The challenge is enormous, he says. 'Companies have to project out: How will I be competitive in a world (in which) technology will be virtually free?'

"The new rules require more than ingenuity, agility, and speed. They call for redefining value in an economy where the cost of raw technology is plummeting toward zero. Sooner or later, this plunge will obliterate the worth of almost any specific piece of hardware or software. Then, value will be in establishing a long-term relationship with a customer — even if it means giving the first generation of a product away."

— Business Week
"The Technology Paradox: How Companies Thrive As Prices Dive"

Many new technologies bombarded my thoughts as the Eleventh Vision came to me. (I am actually in the process of pursuing a patent for one of those amazing future technologies that I saw at the beginning of this Vision because I think *everyone* is going to want one!) A great competitive storm of super rapidly advancing new technologies in tomorrow's Neo-Tech World caused consumer prices to fall like rain.

In the 21st century, the famous free-falling prices of computers spread beyond the computer industry across many old industries and all new industries, reaching nearly all consumer products. Then, even modest paychecks and savings were worth a fortune.

Well, you got rich, without lifting a finger, in that Neo-Tech

237

World. The computer revolution was a forerunner to a Technological Revolution that drove prices toward zero and values toward infinity in most industries.

Today, people wonder where the Technological Revolution will take us. America's richest man and other powerful people predict mind-boggling technological transformations culminating in a *distance-free* world. They are right: the walls of distance have nearly come down as digitized information traveling through broadband fiber-optic cables and between personal satellite dishes let us work, learn, shop, and play anywhere in the world, anytime, regardless where we live. But those visionaries have limited insight into what will *really* happen. They do not predict the *enormous wealth*.

You see, they do not know that mankind is about to leave behind his bicameral programming and end the hierarchy of authorities ruling over him. The very large financial benefits of ending the ruling class brings increasing pressure for people to overcome their mutant bicameral mentalities. The most powerful and fastest moving trends throughout history were economically driven. As this monetarily motivated trend to end the ruling class grows, my Eleventh Vision showed me big government eventually could not hold. My Vision showed me that during the first quarter of the 21st century, big government popped off society like a champagne cork. Suddenly, millions of super entrepreneurs spouted forth, out of nowhere. They were the first to jump into the Neothink mentality. During my Eleventh Vision, those millions of freed super entrepreneurs caused a catalytic progression of tomorrow's super technologies, which caused a catalytic explosion of buying power.

The era of inexpensive super technologies showered upon us. Cost-collapsing telecommunications, fiber optics, digitized information, super-powered personal computers, Web TV, the Internet...these were only a few small clouds at the turn of the millennium before a giant storm of competitive geniuses and their super technologies during the 21st century. They feverishly competed day and night against each other to bring us breathtaking values for just a few dollars. When the technological storm began, more and more affordable super technologies showered upon us day after day, our buying power soared, and it never touched the ground again once lifted by the great technological twister.

Our lifestyles metamorphosed into our fantasies as our buying power kept soaring until we lived as millionaires. All along, the only thing that delayed the Neo-Tech World and our millionaire status was big government, a vestige of our bicameral minds.

Throughout the 20th century and into the 21st century, most industries and their technologies were terribly burdened by big government — by regulation, legislation, litigation, taxes, and their own political businessmen who looked for political favors instead of facing market competition or creating something new. By the 21st century, most industries and technologies had long been *politicized;* the computer/cyberspace industry had not (although there was a growing attempt, starting with the infamous antitrust lawsuit brought against Microsoft).

Without carrying the same burden, the geniuses in the computer field easily jumped ahead, and some evolved into Neothink. And that was the difference between prices miraculously racing toward zero with the computers versus the way everything else was in the anticivilization.

That preview to the Technological Revolution happened during the late 20th century and early 21st century. Now, as we move into the 21st century, will governments let us open the hatch? Will governments free the entrepreneurs to make the jump into Neothink and make us rich with their super rapidly advancing new technologies?

Over the next three pages are three images that flashed before me during my Eleventh Vision:

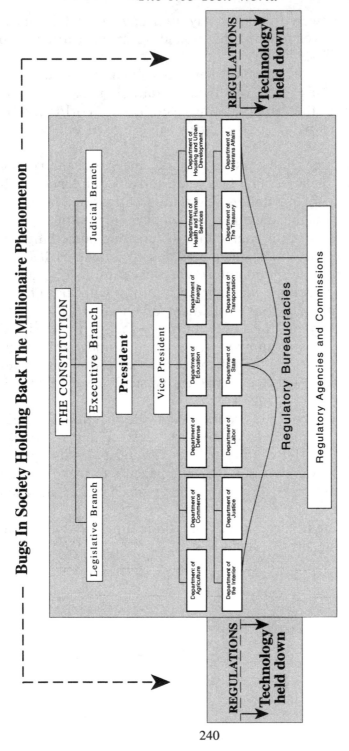

Bugs In Society Holding Back The Millionaire Phenomenon

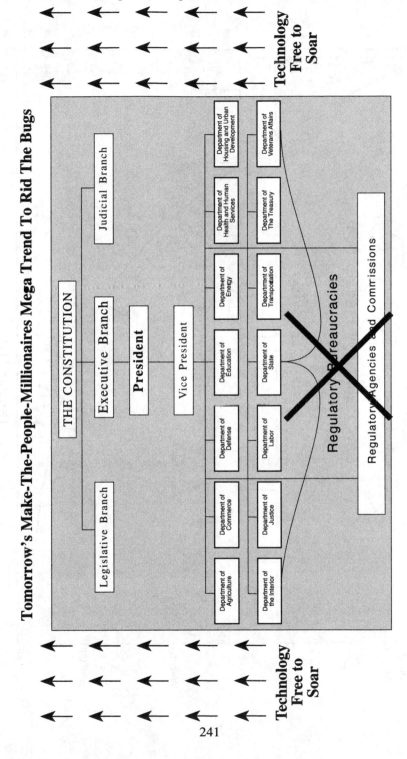

Tomorrow's Make-The-People-Millionaires Mega Trend To Rid The Bugs

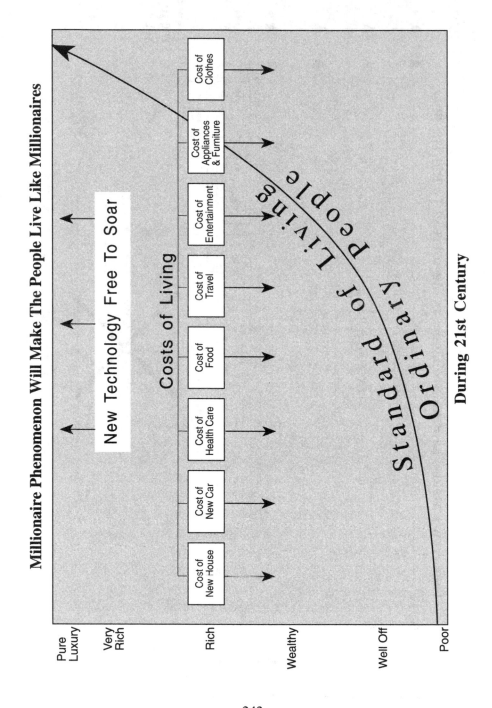

Millionaire Phenomenon Will Make The People Live Like Millionaires

New Technology Free To Soar

Costs of Living

Cost of New House
Cost of New Car
Cost of Health Care
Cost of Food
Cost of Travel
Cost of Entertainment
Cost of Appliances & Furniture
Cost of Clothes

Standard of Living Ordinary People

During 21st Century

Pure Luxury
Very Rich
Rich
Wealthy
Well Off
Poor

My Eleventh Vision showed me technologies in *all* areas of life free to race ahead in the way the computers had. In that Neo-Tech or *New Technology* society of radically advancing technologies, living costs fell to fractions in the way the computers had. Buying power in *all* areas of life multiplied a hundred times or more. I saw ordinary people living like millionaires in custom homes, driving luxury cars, and vacationing all over the world first class.

One man had the power to quickly bring us into that Golden Neo-Tech World where poverty and suffering no longer existed and all Americans lived in luxury. That man was the President of the United States. In the 20th century and early 21st century, no President would initiate the millionaire phenomenon because no career politician would slash his own base of power. But now, we have seen a sample of the great prosperity:

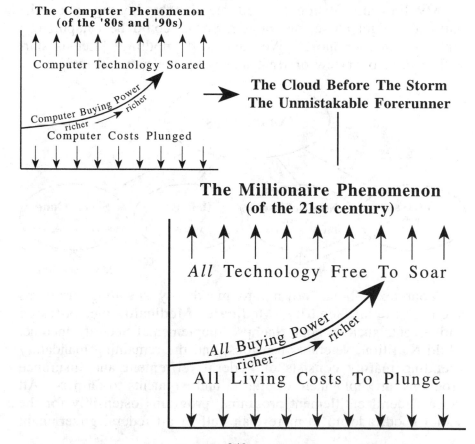

The Computer Phenomenon
(of the '80s and '90s)

Computer Technology Soared

Computer Buying Power *richer* *richer*

Computer Costs Plunged

The Cloud Before The Storm
The Unmistakable Forerunner

The Millionaire Phenomenon
(of the 21st century)

All Technology Free To Soar

All Buying Power *richer* *richer*

All Living Costs To Plunge

The regulatory seams around society restrict new technologies and hold back the Technological Revolution. Those regulatory seams holding back the Technological Revolution also postpone the job revolution and block a hundred million super entrepreneurs (explained in the Fifth Vision). When big government disintegrated in the 21st century, Neo-Tech (new technologies) burst out everywhere and mixed with millions of unleashed super entrepreneurs using Neothink. The overwhelming creativity pumped into the supersociety generated prosperity that went way off the charts, beyond anything ever contemplated in economic think tanks. Ordinary people experienced yet another Gift of the Neo-Tech World: enormous wealth.

You Became 100 Times Richer

My Eleventh Vision showed me that by honing in on the national budget alone, our buying power could be catapulted a hundred times or more! We have to do nothing! Let us start with a brief overview of what makes up the national budget:

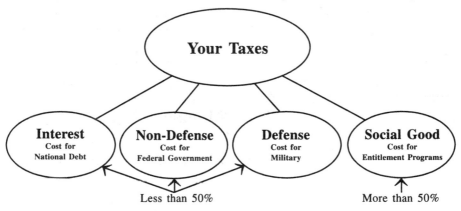

Your taxes break down into mandatory spending programs such as Social Security, Medicare, Medicaid, means-tested entitlements such as Food Stamps, Supplemental Security Income, Child Nutrition, veterans' pensions; and the remaining mandatory spending mainly consists of Federal retirement and insurance programs, unemployment insurance, and payments to farmers. All those Federal entitlement programs, programs ostensibly for the social good, add up to more than half of all federal government spending in the early 21st century. The discretionary spending breaks down into defense spending for the military and non-defense discretionary spending, which covers the Legislative Branch, the Judicial Branch, the Executive Branch, including its fourteen departments, the EPA, NASA, foreign aid, science...basically whatever it costs to run the Federal government. Then, of course, there is interest on the national debt. Discretionary spending, which is what it costs to run the military and the government, plus the interest on the national debt, add up to less than half of all federal spending in the early 21st century.

Finally, federal spending usually creates either a surplus or a deficit, meaning it collects more than it spends in the case of a surplus, or it spends more than it collects, in the case of a deficit. Growing deficits mean growing debt, which means growing interest payments.

Now, let us look at my Eleventh Vision that showed me how to approach the budget to cause our buying power to soar a hundred times or more, without us lifting a finger!

My Eleventh Vision showed me the most sensational creation of wealth the world has ever known. I saw a Neo-Tech President slash government spending by nearly removing the entitlement spending programs and the majority of non-defense discretionary spending. He was very careful that, first, those who had earned entitlements such as social security and veterans' pensions were fully compensated through a spectacular sale of all government assets that had nothing to do with protection. With the trillions of dollars accumulated from the largest sale in mankind's history, social security owed was paid off completely, up front and in full, plus interest. Then, the Social Security program ended altogether, for the government had no business telling people how to spend or save their money. Veterans' pensions were continued, but managed through a private, third-party service.

The budget to run the government was reduced to running the military (including veterans' pensions), courts, and prisons only — to protect the people from physical aggression, the only valid purpose of a federal government. Eventually, the military, courts, and prisons advanced into a businesslike setup, as described in *The First Immortals*, where people willingly subscribed to those protection services.

During this Neo-Tech President's term, there was no chaos. (The President had a two-year battle with Congress over the budget, but the mid-term elections washed out many of those resisting the President's budget as the people noticed their buying power rising.) Instead, he simplified the Federal Government. The country fell into beautiful order as he privatized the important government services. Moreover, the great prosperity explosion — the millionaire phenomenon — ignited as businesses and entrepreneurs were free to invest in research and development without the burden and risk of an offensive, regulatory government. Big business and garage entrepreneurs both developed new technologies so swiftly, with such rapidly dropping costs, that our buying power began climbing...climbing so rapidly, in fact, that people previously dependent on government entitlements instead lived with the standards of living of millionaires by the end of the Neo-Tech President's term. Soon, *no one* missed big government, not even the most liberal communities. Everyone was too busy enjoying his or her new standard of living...a standard of living only the millionaires enjoyed just one presidential term earlier. A new era had arrived, the Neo-Tech Era.

In the Eleventh Vision, looking back at today's budgets, we knew what defense spending and interest on the national debt were for. But, no longer programmed with the bicameral-like desire for external "authorities" telling us what to do or how to live, we had a hard time understanding the spending programs for the "social good" or for non-defense government. We had no idea how it helped the people. For one thing, tomorrow we knew the best way to help the people was to release the geniuses to make the people rich: *to make their buying power go so high they lived like millionaires.*

Tomorrow, the make-the-people-millionaires program, as shown on the preceding charts, freed technologies and freed super entrepreneurs to drive the new technologies into computerlike revolutions everywhere. A Neo-Tech President whose career was *not* politics turned inward and slashed his own base of political power — regulatory power — to free the technologies and the super entrepreneurs.

After experiencing the wealthy Neo-Tech World tomorrow, the debilitating past became so clear: To be the President of the United States in the anticivilization was to be a career politician; the career politician by nature *built* his base of political power, and the President's base of political power so happened to be regulatory power — the regulatory bureaucracies, commissions, and agencies beneath him (see previous flowcharts). That was why in the anticivilization no president *seriously* wanted to eliminate regulations. Social and regulatory programs supposedly "for the public good" supported both the President's and Congress' base of power. Those spending programs, even those entitlement programs, such as social welfare, came hand in hand with massive regulations telling us how to spend our money and run our businesses. Unbeknownst to you, but so obvious in my Eleventh Vision, those massive regulations actually blocked the Neo-Tech World in which you would live as a millionaire...all so the President and Congressmen could control more political power.

My Eleventh Vision showed me that, frankly, we looked back in disgust at our past Presidents. We realized their debilitating regulations built their structure of power as the boss of regulatory bureaucracies. Those so-called "help the people" social and regulatory programs were illusions that actually *hurt the people* while building the Presidents' popularity, ego, and power. In my Eleventh Vision, I was amazed that the "great" presidents of the 20th century who started "noble" social programs for the "social good" were looked back on as the worst malefactors of society.

The Biggest Illusion

Today, the massive Federal spending programs on entitlements so-called "for the social good" in turn give the Federal Government absolute power to *regulate* the economy and *rule over* our money. Today, the Federal Government has its regulatory web all throughout our economy — in every business, every consumer product, every job, every profession, including every hospital, every doctor's office, every research and development program, every discovery, every invention, every paycheck, every person's wallet.

In my Eleventh Vision, the people in tomorrow's Neo-Tech World were aghast that politicians and bureaucrats once ruled over our money and our lives. The archaic regulatory web throughout the economy *trapped and paralyzed* new technologies. Without super rapidly advancing technologies, costs did not drop to fractions. Instead, costs went up and up and up for the entire 20th century. We just could not believe it, looking back: *prices went up for 100 years!* The elderly who lived on set pensions and measly entitlements got trapped in the dungeons of society as long-term inflation ate up everything they had.

Sometime in the 21st century, we discovered that the *only* way to truly help the needy and everyone else was to send the economy through a buying-power metamorphosis such as the computer industry's buying-power metamorphosis. The Eleventh Vision showed me the needy and everyone else's limited buying power leapt *a hundred times* when the Neo-Tech President's protection-only budget swished away the regulatory web throughout the economy. His budget swished away those so called "good intentions", such as social welfare and the regulatory bureaucracies that wove regulatory control throughout every nook and cranny of the business world. When that regulatory web was gone, technology was free, and it took off just as the unregulated computer technology had, but in every industry. *Everyone's* buying power quickly rose.[1]

The World's Greatest Irony

The world's greatest irony was: the way to best help the people was to cross out the government's programs to "help the people" and the *massive regulations* that came with those "well intentioned" massive spending programs. Indeed, ending the

---

[1]This ended Social Security payments. Moreover, this unique approach miraculously repaid *every penny* of social security to Americans with *full fair-market interest!* That financial miracle meant elderly Americans received a small fortune from the government, all up front, by selling off all government assets that had nothing to do with protection.

noble-sounding "higher" causes, those programs for the "social good", ultimately ended the hierarchy of authorities ruling over us, suppressing us.

My Eleventh Vision showed me an amazing world without those regulatory webs of "good intentions" so-called "for the social good". The needy and everyone else lived like kings as unburdened technology soared, costs plunged, and everyone's buying power multiplied on average a hundred times. *Everyone* became rich.

The "social good" was just a clever way of saying "politicize society, rule over the people, and play God with their money and lives." The "social good" was the neocheaters' prime illusion that manipulated our bicameral programming for "higher" causes.

Sometime in the 21st century, we deprogrammed our bicameral programming with Neo-Tech (the First Insight) and, like coming out of a spell, we shook our heads and said "enough" to spending more than half of the Federal Budget on the "social good".

Ending The Spell

The first Neo-Tech President ended politicization of our lives and ended government on the offense — ended entitlement and regulatory programs. The Neo-Tech President reduced government to self-defense protection only, a government of defense without external "authorities" telling us how to live, which freed the geniuses of society.

They, in turn, whirled into an aggressive storm of Neothink competition to serve up our every need. In doing so, they lifted technology into new dimensions, which drove down living and health costs to fractions and brought us spectacular new values and entertainment. The computer revolution of the 20th century seemed like a little white cloud compared to the storm of new technologies raining on us in the 21st century.

As you know, after World War II, we looked back in disbelief at the holocaust. In tomorrow's Neo-Tech World, our children and grandchildren looked back in disbelief at the anticivilization's hierarchy of authorities ruling over us. In both cases, millions of innocent people died at the hands of politicians ruling over us. Everyone, everywhere, in my Eleventh Vision knew the *only* reason the disease-free, wealthy Neo-Tech World never happened in the 20th century was because, simply put, no politicians wanted to slash their base of political power. They cared only about building their base of power — regulatory and spending power. (Indeed, spending money they did not earn brought them a lot of power.) Therefore, we did not have the slightest clue of the phenomenal wealth and health available to us by reducing to a protection-only government of defense...until the "Solar Eclipse":

The "Solar Eclipse"

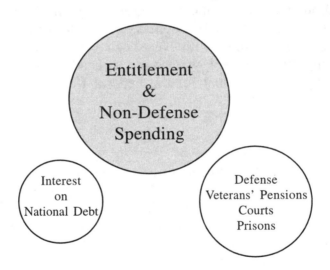

Consider that Einstein's Theory of Relativity ($E=mc^2$) went years unrecognized. Then, a natural phenomenon occurred — a solar eclipse — that demonstrated his theory. Instantly, Einstein and his Theory of General Relativity were a world sensation accepted by nearly everyone. With that solar-eclipse demonstration, the world quickly moved beyond Newtonian physics to Einsteinian physics.

During my Eleventh Vision, I saw a similar phenomenon in politics: The Neo-Tech President's first budget was that "solar eclipse" as he blacked out many of the blinding, solar-high spending programs for the "social good" and most of the non-defense spending. Although Congress did everything possible to undo his budget for their own survival, the unmistakable demonstration of falling taxes and rising buying power still occurred, no matter how diluted. Similar to Einstein's Relativity, instantly the make-the-people-millionaires program of slashing regulations and the hierarchy of authorities was a world sensation.

With that "solar-eclipse" demonstration, world politics quickly moved beyond career politicians and their hierarchy of authorities...into the new political paradigm, the unprecedented get-the-people-rich government.

Needless to say, the Neo-Tech President's protection-only budget was a shock to Congress as he tried to cut the budget *in half his first year.* He wanted no more bicameral structures — no more hierarchy of authorities politicizing our lives and ruling over us. Of course, that cut out the ruling class, which cut out the political careers of the career politicians. Thus, Congress did not accept his budget at all. They did not want to give up their ruling class.

Yet, Congress had no choice but to give in to some extent because once the people elected a Neo-Tech President, they sensed this route to the millionaire phenomenon and stood behind him. So the small ruling-class clique, 435 Congressmen and 100 Senators, had to abandon their first thought of impeachment. With their very own constituents cheering for the make-the-people-millionaires program, Congress was not able to completely undo his budget. Of course, Congress radically changed the budget, but the President vigorously pointed his finger at the culprits for the whole country to see. Thus, Congress backed off and some of what he submitted took hold.

Bingo. People's taxes dropped immediately. But more importantly, their buying power started going up almost immediately. For the first time, exciting practical results outperformed political rhetoric. After that "solar-eclipse" demonstration, the Neo-Tech President then told America, loud and clear: "Imagine what could happen to your buying power if my protection-only budget passed in its entirety. You could all be rich before my term is over!"

With that realization, the people unanimously implemented a nationwide change called **The Great Replacement Program**:

Like a big wave at high tide due to the Solar-Eclipse Budget, the Great Replacement Program washed over the country; it washed away the politicians and their ruling class. Voters nominated and voted into Congress business owners and genuine, market-driven businessmen and women, knowing they would pass the Neo-Tech President's Solar-Eclipse, Protection-Only Budget in its entirety.

Those market-driven businesspeople never cared about building political power. Such as the Neo-Tech President, they were not politicians. Instead, they wanted a free and booming economy. So, to that end, they were more than happy to eclipse their own structures of political power. They were more than happy to eclipse all government "good intentions" — that is, all those social and regulatory programs "for the social good" that were really Trojan Horses carrying massive, suppressive regulations. Those market businesspeople passed the Neo-Tech President's budget in its entirety. The ruling class vanished.

Taxes immediately fell by more than half. But far more important, the regulatory/legislative web throughout the economy simply got swished away, which immediately set free the aggressive entrepreneurs who leapt into Neothink (society's geniuses) and immediately set free the advancing new technologies. Neothink (the geniuses) drove forth Neo-Tech (the new technologies). Industry after industry went through unprecedented buying-power metamorphoses. Computerlike revolutions were happening everywhere, in every industry, even in the housing industry, bringing us inexpensive beautiful new homes.

Indeed, removing the many regulations on the construction industry and its many suppliers and support industries, not to mention removing the bulk of taxes, immediately allowed general contractors to build bigger, better, and more beautiful homes for a lot less money. And that improvement was immediate, before the technological breakthroughs kicked in!

Wealth as I saw in my Eleventh Vision had never been seen before because the human race had always been dominated by a bicameral structure led by a ruling class of politicians and bureaucrats. Of course, politicians in the anticivilization built their careers through regulatory and legislative power, which hampered technologies and entrepreneurs...and ultimately blocked our evolution into Neothink. Thus, under the anticivilization's government of offense, your buying power tended to decrease instead of increasing a hundred times or more.

The Great Replacement Program led by a Neo-Tech President and his Protection-Only Budget rescued us and resulted in us becoming a hundred times richer *during our lifetimes*. And that great wealth, a Gift of the Neo-Tech World, was enjoyed by all men, women, and children in society's Neo-Tech structure of Neothink mentalities led by geniuses of society.

Everyone Will Be Taken Care Of

The long roots to our bicameral past finally died. We simply lost our automatic urges for guidance. Through Neo-Tech (the comprehensive definition of Neo-Tech explained in The First Insight, Part Two of this book), the 10,000-year-old automatic urges for guidance just sort of dried up and died. As a result, the god-like hierarchy of authorities that guided us by *ruling over* us wilted, then crumbled to the ground and soon blew off us like a dead weed.

Tomorrow's get-the-people-rich government physically *protected us* only, and a budget less than half previous budgets, then half again as the Federal Government was reduced to protection against aggression only, was all that was needed to protect our country. The other half to three-quarters of previous budgets was never needed. Sometime in the 21st century, we woke up from our bicameral sleep and realized three-quarters of the Federal Budget was wrongly used by the hierarchy of authorities to *rule over* society through politicizing our lives and our businesses, enforced by big-government regulations.

Throughout Neo-Tech, we simply lost our bicameral urges for having career politicians and regulatory bureaucrats politicizing our lives and ruling over us. Those higher "authorities" played God with our lives. Of course, their authority over us was always enforceable for the so-called "social good".

But my Eleventh Vision showed me that we simply lost our bicameral-like urges for "higher" causes such as the "social good"

253

being dictated by higher "authorities". (Sacrifice to "higher" causes was a deep-rooted vestige of the mystical bicameral structures and bicameral man's hallucinatory behavioral patterns.) In fact, the whole idea of political programs for the "social good" became repulsive. Indeed, the bicameral behavioral patterns were quickly wearing off in the light of rapidly multiplying 21st-century new knowledge, including the new knowledge of Neo-Tech (the First Insight).

The people saw the double negative of money taxed and spent for the "social good". In fact, the whole idea of a government on the offensive for the "social good" became a bizarre thought. The government had one purpose — a government of defense to protect its citizens from physical attack. All the other money taxed straight out of our lives — three dollars for every four taken from us in taxes for spending other than defense and interest on the debt — simply sucked that enormous portion of money out of the economy, particularly out of those hard-working geniuses who liked to reinvest their money into growth to generate more wealth and jobs. The government then redistributed the better half of that money to a government-created class of unproductive people who "inherited" a living and generated nothing for society.

But even worse than the huge mandatory spending programs was the discretionary spending to regulatory bureaucracies. They ruled over us with regulations that suppressed geniuses and new technologies. So, the negative effect of government on offense was painfully double: big government drained our money out of our lives *and then used it to specifically block us from rising into a wealthy paradise on Earth!*

The happy, wealthy people in the Neo-Tech World looked through history books while scratching their heads, wondering why we did not see this obvious double negative a lot, lot sooner. Of course, we did not see the double negative because of our bicameral programming, causing our urges for guidance. We disastrously accepted the neocheaters' illusions called "the social good".

The anticivilization was a sort of netherworld held down in a bicameral structure under a destructive ruling class. The ruling class was very debilitating, yet well camouflaged as existing for the "social good".[1]

The Elderly Benefited the Most

What about the elderly and the genuinely needy? In the anticivilization, the elderly were stuck in the poverty trap caused by the social-welfare illusion. In my Eleventh Vision, the elderly and needy gained the most in the Neo-Tech World, for they *more than anyone* needed a monetary metamorphosis in which their savings and pensions suddenly could buy a hundred times more. And that is exactly what they got. Unburdened, free-to-soar technology began driving down costs to fractions immediately after the Solar-Eclipse Budget passed.

When anticivilization government had complete regulatory control over the economy, prices did not go down. They went up. Inflation was a slow death-by-torture for the elderly and the needy on set incomes. Inflation, even slow inflation, eventually trapped the elderly (those on set pensions) and the needy in the dungeons of society as poverty-ridden, dependent slaves — slaves to big government, forever dependent on their measly entitlement money. That slave class meant guaranteed votes for an ever-increasing regulatory government.

But sometime in the 21st century, all that changed. Ironically, that change most benefited the huge American slave class — the elderly and the needy. With the make-the-people-millionaires program, everyone discovered financial independence and then financial prosperity.

What about health, education, and everyone's welfare? What about all those spending programs that got blacked out? The

---

[1]The conscious mind was supposed to be its own authority, the God-Man. As explained in The First Insight, Part Two of this book, we were never meant to live under a ruling class and its hierarchy of "higher" authorities. Through master neocheaters, the dying, obsolete bicameral mentality mutated 2400 years ago and aggressively invaded the conscious mentality as a virulent disease of the mind, which got passed down like a computer virus from generation to generation. The ruling class and its hierarchy of "higher" authorities throughout the past 2400 years has been a devastating mutation of bicameral man's imagined, ruling gods and their hierarchy of divine authorities.

resulting millionaire phenomenon (see charts on pages 240-242) made *everyone* rich. Those who were previously dependent on entitlements benefited most. Those who were previously trapped "slaves", dependent on suppressive big government in order to survive in poverty, for the first time lived like *healthy and wealthy kings* as buying power and jobs began multiplying.

Healthy Kings

Now, I said *healthy* kings because unhampered, soaring technologies not only drove health-care costs to fractions, but eradicated serious diseases. Consider that years ago, Dr. Frank R. Wallace (author of *The Neo-Tech Discovery*) was involved in research at Du Pont that offered a unique approach for the treatment of diseases. One potential approach involved the development of extremely fine fibers impregnated with slowly releasing drugs. If such fibers were injected around cancer tumors, for example, the growth of those encased tumors might be retarded or stopped — to lay harmlessly dormant in their man-made coffins, forever. But the FDA, looking out for the "public good", killed that and many other promising low-cost cures at Du Pont with cost-prohibitive regulations.

Moreover, consider that much more government money than private money had been spent to find a cure for cancer. But nearly every notable advancement in science and medicine during the 20th century came from business or privately funded research. In my Eleventh Vision, I witnessed that unburdened geniuses of society *outside of government contracts,* particularly entrepreneurs, got the public good done and done quickly. Through the help of unburdened super technologies, the Neothink geniuses quickly, among other things, eradicated diseases (Vision Twelve, next).

I saw the end result of **The Great Displacement Program**: Government assets and programs not part of protecting its citizens from physical force were sold to the private sector. Geniuses of society, not career politicians, took over programs for the social good to finally achieve social good.

The Great Replacement/Great Displacement Program led by a Neo-Tech President and his Protection-Only Budget ushered in the new Neo-Tech Era with no ruling class and no government programs for the "social good". Super technologies and super entrepreneurs, finally free of political pollution, free of even the smallest regulatory impurities, gave the world an unprecedented power-reactor explosion of prosperity beyond comprehension in today's terms.

The New Prosperity

The new prosperity made it difficult to look back at the anticivilization and its government programs "for the social good":

- Education: Among lowest standard of industrialized nations.
- Social Security: A greater and greater strain on the economy.
- Welfare: Left the poor in deeper and deeper poverty traps. Stressing the economy.
- Health Care: Less and less effective.
- Social Programs: Deteriorating results.
- Regulatory Programs: Handicapped America in global competition while driving up costs, suppressing progress, and shrinking our job base...all while arming more and more teams of bureaucrats with guns and legislative-like power.

In the Neo-Tech World, the above programs "for the social good" fell out of the hands of a few hundred politically driven politicians and bureaucrats...into the hands of millions of sharp geniuses who finally did those programs right.

The Eleventh Vision answered my own two questions:
1) How will people take care of their parents with no more government aid and medicare?
2) How will people educate their children with no more public schools?

First of all, the Great Displacement Program and the sale of trillions of dollars of government assets to private businesses easily repaid Social Security *with full, fair-market interest.* A lot of people suddenly got back small fortunes, especially the elderly who spent their lives paying the taxes that paid for those government assets sold. That sale of government assets ended the flawed Social Security era with everyone being repaid his or her money with interest. Working people no longer poured their money down the Social Security drain; most adults received a big check from the Federal Government, and retirees suddenly got back a small fortune.

We discovered — even those on entitlements discovered — that social-welfare programs of all kinds, including the medicare and medicaid programs, were clever illusions that hurt, not helped, the elderly and needy. Those social-welfare programs let the government regulate our economy and politicize our health, blocking computerlike revolutions and free-falling prices for breakthrough cures. Tomorrow, we rescued our parents by freeing the economy and medical industry of those regulatory webs. Soon, health and living costs fell to fractions. Quality of life soared. The Neo-Tech President's "solar eclipse" demonstration during his first year in office led to the inevitable millionaire phenomenon that made *everyone* wealthy and healthy, young and old alike.

Now, our children: In the Eleventh Vision, I witnessed superior private education become the affordable norm and not the unaffordable exception. Today, only the privileged can, in a sense, pay twice for their children's education — once to the government (via taxes) and once to a private school. But tomorrow, everyone paid only once, but for superior private education. Moreover, for a fraction of the cost, any child could receive an effective education over the Internet.

Private schools became very inexpensive as open competition delivered the highest value for the lowest cost once the government's monopoly on education ended. Our children grew increasingly knowledgeable, creative, and motivated. They grew up to become successful, happy, and rich value creators.[1]

---

[1] See my novel *The First Immortals* to get a complete picture of education in tomorrow's Neo-Tech World.

Money Talks, Abuse Walks

During this Eleventh Vision into the Neo-Tech World, I noticed that the Solar-Eclipse Budget — blocking out the blinding, solar-high spending programs, ending the nearly three out of four dollars spent on entitlement programs, on politicizing our lives, and on ruling over us...collecting only the money needed to protect us — did something else besides set free super entrepreneurs and super technologies that made all ordinary people rich. The Solar-Eclipse, Protection-Only Budget also eliminated powerful forces of big government that were steadily taking away our freedom and individual rights.

Once the Protection-Only Budget passed in its entirety in the Neo-Tech President's third year in office after the mid-term Great Replacement Program, no more money was available to go to regulatory bureaucracies, all of which had quietly armed their agents over the decades — a dangerous step in America toward secret police and fascism. Those armed armies of bureaucrats ultimately answered to our President as part of his growing structure of power and ego.

The people in the Neo-Tech World simply asked: why should any regulatory bureaucrat be armed? If he confronts a potentially hostile situation, then he should call the effective 21st-century local police as any other citizen.

For the previous century, however, the government had been quietly building armies of armed bureaucrats. The IRS, FTC, FDA, EPA, SEC, DEA, FBI, INS, ATF, CIA — every regulatory bureaucracy and beyond had armed agents...*even the postal service came complete with armed bureaucrats!* As the people in my Eleventh Vision looked back, they were amazed at how obvious this abuse of power was, which before went over their heads.

Those armies of armed bureaucrats in the anticivilization, all under the command of the President, grew increasingly aggressive while steadily subtracting our freedom and individual rights. Caught up in the illusions of "social good", we let them rule over us.

The Solar-Eclipse Budget, once in full force with the onslaught of the Great Replacement Program, simply cut off the funds to those growing armies of fascism. The Solar-Eclipse Budget, simply put, *just said no!*

So, while making everyone rich, the Solar-Eclipse Budget saved us from deteriorating freedom and growing government abuse. That Protection-Only budget dehydrated then whisked away the remaining ruling class. The people just had no more desire for higher "authorities" and their so-called "guidance". The neocheaters' facade vanished.

Jobs, Wealth, Security

Once in office, the Neo-Tech President's fiscal policy was simple: eliminate three of four dollars spent from the annual budget.

Looking back over the 20th century, America got in trouble regarding the currency. In 1933, Franklin D. Roosevelt took us off the gold standard. With no more accountability or disciplines, the government pumped more and more money into our economy. That caused inflation to eat up our parents' retirement savings and pensions, leaving them poor and financially dependent on us and the government.

Pumping unbacked currency into the economy had a short-term stimulating effect on the economy, but a long-term deadly effect. Of course, politicians sold out our futures for short-term re-election gimmicks. The people in tomorrow's Neo-Tech World were amazed, looking back, that fiscal policy in the anticivilization had become an exclusive power-and-ego manipulating game for the powers that be. The ordinary working man was the victim. ...After decades of unbacked currency pumped into the economy — forever followed by inflation and increasing poverty for each new generation of elderly and needy Americans — what did we do? In my Eleventh Vision, here was the Neo-Tech President's course of action — a one, two punch:

One: He eliminated spending programs for the "social good" and steadily paid off the debt. That cut our taxes in half or more and cut out any need to print more money.

Two: The Neo-Tech President eliminated corporate income taxes altogether (which accounted for less than one-tenth of the

Federal Government's revenues). That caused an explosion of business, employment, opportunities, and rising incomes for the people as companies reinvested large sums of money back into their businesses, including cash incentives for employee performance. The money that normally went toward taxes and the "social good" instead went toward expansion, job creation, and employee incentive. The economy boomed. ...This concept was first demonstrated in the early '60s during John F. Kennedy's presidency and reinforced in the '80s during Ronald W. Reagan's presidency.

In the Neo-Tech World, the younger students laughed in disbelief at the silly illusions used by big government that tricked their parents and grandparents into sending a major portion of our wealth down the drain and into society's sewer of waste disguised as the "social good". But what made those illusions so effective was our bicameral programming causing our longings for higher "authorities" and their "higher" causes. Once our bicameral longings subsided, the politicians' illusions became laughable.

In the Neo-Tech World, the younger students could not help thinking what dupes their parents and grandparents once were. Of course, free of bicameral programming, those students could not be fooled or manipulated by neocheaters, unlike their parents.

In the Neo-Tech World, with no more government programs for the "social good", our taxes a fraction of what they once were, and with no more corporate income taxes, the money once flushed away to the "social good" now was reinvested into economic growth. That same money instead went toward starting and expanding businesses, creating jobs, motivating us as in-house entrepreneurs (Fifth and Sixth Visions), and causing dynamic technological growth...which, like the computers, drove up our buying power a hundred times.

The Golden Neo-Tech World — Technology, Wealth, and Health

Let me sum up my Eleventh Vision: I saw new technologies rain on us in such quantity that the future looked almost surrealistic. The freed geniuses of society whom I saw in my

Tenth Vision mixed with the freed 21st-century super technologies that I saw in my Eleventh Vision. Once the impurities of society — the higher "authorities" ruling over us and their "higher" causes enforced through endless regulations — were removed, the super entrepreneurs and super technologies went through a catalytic, power-reactor explosion that lifted society into a beautiful new world, the Golden Neo-Tech World.

Here were our steps into that new world: America's growing damnation of politicians ushered in a nonpolitician Neo-Tech President sometime in the first quarter of the 21st century. His "solar-eclipse" demonstration quickly brought about the Great Replacement Program. Then the Solar-Eclipse Budget, a self-defense, protection-only budget, passed in its entirety and eclipsed government on the offense doing the "social good". Everyone's taxes fell in half...and then *in half again* as market businessmen drove down the remaining government expenses for protection by digging into the nitty-gritty details and making them efficient.

As that occurred, geniuses of society rose by the millions and steadily raised our buying power as their breakthrough technologies drove costs toward zero. We became essentially a hundred times wealthier. Furthermore, every day and night felt as safe as living in Disneyland, for people became wealthy without lifting a finger. Committing crime was too much work. Moreover, the government's sole focus was your protection: national defense on the federal level and police protection on the local level. Finally, as Neo-Tech (in its comprehensive definition, see The First Insight, Part Two of this book) accelerated the end of our bicameral behavioral patterns, the hierarchy of authorities — the ruling class — ended. For the first time, civilization existed in pure freedom.

My beautiful Eleventh Vision is our destiny. The Golden Neo-Tech World is the paradise on Earth we were meant to live in — a world in which we will be very wealthy with exciting opportunities, even for those who now have little opportunity. In my Eleventh Vision, that Golden Neo-Tech World provided ever better technology for ever cheaper prices, no longer the sensation of just the computer industry, but of all industries. Major health breakthroughs and cures occurred at increasing frequency and became affordable to everyone, even to the elderly.

Unsurpassed, quality education became available and affordable to all families. Fears of unemployment were forgotten in the perpetually soaring economy with endless selections of living jobs anywhere in the world that could be done right from home through your computer. And finally, the millionaire's life of exotic vacations and first-class luxuries removed every last drop of boredom from our lives. Life was fun and exciting.

Looking back at the anticivilization left a heavy sadness in our hearts for the millions who died unnecessarily to disease. We realized how just a small clique of people — career politicians and regulatory bureaucrats — cost many of our loved ones' precious lives.

The anticivilization's big government was on the *offense* politicizing our lives and ruling over us. By contrast, the Neo-Tech World's get-the-people-disease-free-and-rich government was only on the *defense* protecting our lives from any physical threat or attack. After depoliticizing society, thus setting free the geniuses of society, super rapidly advancing new technologies showered on us and, like godsends, eradicated infectious disease after disease until we lived with perfect health.

As you might suspect, political leaders resisted the idea of depoliticizing America. But, as Victor Hugo once wrote, "An invasion of armies can be resisted, but not an idea whose time has come." No one could stop it. Our deep-rooted bicameral urges to be told how to live simply subsided 3000 years after the bicameral mind was replaced by human consciousness.

The Neo-Tech World is the world everyone wants to live in, but has no clue of. Once enough people got exposed to the prosperity and love available in that previously unknown world — once fifty-million people saw the Twelve Visions — the following steps swiftly occurred:

1) A politically free Neo-Tech President was elected, vowing to essentially make the people healthy millionaires by depoliticizing America.

2) The Solar-Eclipse Budget was submitted to eliminate government on the offense. Congress rejected most of the budget, but enough held to show businesses and potential entrepreneurs the coming code of freedom. Suddenly private funds for researching new technologies

multiplied in all industries. Rapid discoveries and breakthroughs started happening; prices began to fall, demonstrating the Solar-Eclipse Budget's mighty potential effects on the people's wealth and health.

3) The Great Replacement Program washed over the country in the subsequent midterm election like a big wave, washing away career politicians. Original business owners and other market-driven businessmen and women replaced career politicians nearly unanimously. For, the voting public knew that market-driven businesspeople would pass the Solar-Eclipse Budget without hesitation. Indeed, the Solar-Eclipse Budget passed in its entirety.

4) The Great Displacement Program naturally followed as the government's spending monopolies vanished; private businesses and entrepreneurs moved in to legitimately serve the people. America quickly became a wonderful place to be! Buying power multiplied a hundred times. Ordinary people began living like millionaires. Medical technology jumped into the lead against every disease.

Those make-the-people-millionaires and make-the-people-disease-free programs quickly brought three outstanding benefits to us:

1) Near-perfect health to us and our loved ones as medical technology raced forward and eradicated disease after disease.

2) Millionaire wealth as technologies raced forward in every industry like today's nonpoliticized computer industry, driving prices toward zero and standards of living toward millionaire wealth.

3) Supermen and superwomen selves as businesses, in that rapidly advancing Neo-Tech World, dumped their outdated routine-rut jobs and instead brought out every worker's potential. Our stagnant routine ruts were left behind with the anticivilization as we discovered our human potential and achieved 21st-century dreams we could never even fathom in the 20th century. Boredom and stagnation vanished from our lives and got permanently replaced with excitement and stimulation. In

short, this was the job revolution (described in the Fifth and Sixth Visions) that poured a hundred million geniuses into society. Our jobs became our transmission belts to Neothink. Such creative energy rushing into society lifted our nation's wealth beyond all economic theories or models prior to the 21st century. We were in a wonderful new world never before known to man.

Vision Twelve
You Will Live With Perfect Physical and Mental Health

"It is not just new viruses that have doctors worried. Perhaps the most ominous prospect of all is a virulent strain of influenza. Every so often, a highly lethal strain emerges. Unlike HIV, flu moves through the air and is highly contagious. The last killer strain showed up in 1918 and claimed 20 million lives — more than all the combat deaths in World War I. And that was before global air travel; the next outbreak could be even more devastating."   —Time Magazine

By now during my Neothink Visions, the images centered more and more around our health. More than anything else in the 21st century, the people cried out for the geniuses, with their groundbreaking technologies, to eradicate virulent diseases.

Devastating new diseases were on the rise and, perhaps even worse, drug-resistant strains of several old killer diseases were back. Those frightening new diseases and new strains tended to break down our bicameral urges for higher "authorities" such as the FDA that suppressed the rise of Neothink geniuses in medicine and held back the advancement of Neo-Tech in the medical industry. Our physical survival more and more depended on Neo-Tech.

My Twelfth Vision showed me that during the early 21st century, doctors were less and less able to handle certain infectious diseases that were gaining resistance to antibiotics. A powerful warning came when only a single remaining antibiotic could stop a popular strain of staph infection that commonly spread throughout hospitals. Once that lone remaining antibiotic ceased to work, hospitals would become risky places to visit. Next, the common strep infection gained resistance to antibiotics. My Twelfth Vision warned me of the increasing danger as we advanced into the new millennium. A killer disease, tuberculosis, returned, this time attacking our children, and this time even a combination of antibiotics could not stop it.

In short, infectious diseases caught up with modern medicine in the 21st century. As you may now realize, higher "authorities" such as the FDA worked against a major medical revolution that was just waiting to explode with greater force than the computer revolution. In fact, the inherent force of the medical/biotech explosion was so great that even with the FDA, genetic engineering such as the Human Genome Project and other biomedical projects were advancing at an all-time pace. But the mighty biomedical explosion could not ignite with the FDA in place. As with computers, the technology needed quick access to the marketplace, which the FDA blocked.

Here is a brief review of a *Time Magazine* warning.

Killers All Around
New Viruses and Drug-Resistant Bacteria
Are Reversing
Human Victories Over Infectious Disease
(A Review of *Time Magazine* Cover Story)

The *Time Magazine* cover story begins by reminding us how, not long ago, humanity thought that infectious diseases were rapidly becoming a thing of the past. In the 1970s, the medical world started boasting its imminent victory. And why not? Previously deadly illnesses such as polio, small pox, malaria, diphtheria, pertussis, tetanus "seemed like quaint reminders of a bygone era, like Model T Fords or silent movies". And antibiotics transformed the most terrifying diseases known to mankind such as tuberculosis, syphilis, pneumonia, bacterial meningitis, and even bubonic plague into "mere inconveniences that if caught could be cured with pills or shots". Medical students were being told not to go into infectious disease, a "declining speciality". Instead, they were advised to concentrate on "real problems" such as cancer and heart disease.

But, unfortunately, today the era of great medical success and confidence has been giving way to a new era of unnerving medical defeats...and fear. The *Time* cover story states, "The question ceased to be, When will infectious disease be wiped out? and became, Where will the next deadly new plague break out?" The article goes on to tell us about new lethal agents emerging in Africa and South America. As population grows and man settles new parts of the world, such as a new part of the Brazilian rain forest, for example, new deadly diseases spread from other animals such as monkeys to humans. As those deadly agents adapt to humans, they gain the potential for large-scale deadly pandemics. In a world of extensive air travel, those deadly agents become just a plane ride from America.

And it could get worse, the timely article claims. Antibiotics are our main defense that stand between us and some of the most deadly bacterial diseases. But bacteria have been evolving and steadily adapting for survival, and now they are well adapting to antibiotics. In fact, the article warns us that every disease known to man is already resistant to antibiotics of one form or another. Several devastating diseases once thought to be nearly eradicated are back and on the rise: malaria, cholera, measles, tuberculosis, even bubonic plague. Perhaps even more threatening are the "seemingly prosaic but once deadly infections" staph and strep. They have become much harder to treat. Both spread through the cleanest of hospitals, routinely cured with antibiotics. But as those two infections develop universal resistance, the article questions, what will happen to our hospitals?

"One of medicine's worst nightmares is the development of a drug-resistant strain of severe invasive strep A," the article states. Severe, invasive strep A killed Muppeteer Jim Henson in 1990; this vicious killer is on the rise.

Bacteria adapt to antibiotics because, while rapidly multiplying, bacteria mutate and change slightly, just enough to outwit their combatant drugs.

Viruses, on the other hand, are usually tamed and sometimes even eradicated by the preventive vaccine. But the article points out that new viruses keep emerging. Viruses that have gone undetected, inhabiting animal populations, can and sometimes do make the jump to humans. The *Time* article tells us that was the case with some very lethal African viruses such as Ebola, which made the jump from monkeys to humans.

Still, the biggest fear of all, as explained in that *Time Magazine* article, would be another killer flu, which usually makes the jump from another animal to humans. Humans have little defense against such a flu, and if it took hold, then it would wreak deadly havoc. The 1997-1998 Hong Kong "chicken flu" introduced such a killer flu that, tragically, killed a few people in Hong Kong but, fortunately, did not take hold and go into a widespread outbreak. When a global outbreak does happen, the world will never be the same.

The *Time Magazine* article was a warning. Today's biomedical progress is impressive, but is it moving fast enough? The answer is: no, not until the technology has quick access to the marketplace, as do the computers. And that means no regulatory FDA.

The definitive antidote is "begging" to happen now, in the early 21st century, to rescue the human race from the threatening plagues. That antidote to the threatening human catastrophes is: **super rapidly advancing new technologies (Neo-Tech).** Only rapidly advancing new technologies (Neo-Tech) can win the race against rapidly evolving infectious diseases, which have outpaced our vaccines and antibiotics. But those new technologies will

National Archives

Killer Flu

Seattle police wore protective masks during the pandemic of 1918. That killer flu infected 1 billion people and killed more than 20 million in 10 months. The population in 1918 was less than half of today.

not advance quickly enough until they can swiftly reach the marketplace.

Starting in the late 20th century, continuing into the 21st century, the national media such as *Time Magazine* repeatedly warned us we were suddenly losing the race against infectious diseases, with mutant strains of old diseases returning after decades of "absence" and new diseases invading us with devastating results. The media warned that a medical defeat to microbes could bring with it human catastrophes such as those experienced in the time of bubonic plague, polio, and killer flus. The Superflu of 1918 infected over one billion people, *half* the world's population in 1918, and killed over 20 million people in just 10 months. Never in the history of the world had there been so many deaths in such a short period of time. Man has not experienced anything close to that catastrophic pandemic since, but in the early 21st century, scientists feared a repeat was not far in coming.

The 1918 Spanish Flu, as it was often called, actually started right here in the United States and infected 25% of our population. Scientists and doctors have said in the early 21st century that logistically "we are due" for another killer strain. In fact, in 1976, we survived a great scare — a false alarm, or perhaps more apropos, a fair warning: A soldier at Fort Dix, New Jersey got the flu and died. The medical world was stunned when the virus taken from the dead soldier was a descendent of the 1918 killer flu. The medical world braced itself for another catastrophe of unthinkable proportions. But by the grace of God, the deadly swine-flu virus that made the jump from pigs to humans was an isolated case unable, this time, of passing among humans. This time, we were lucky. Next time...

Only super rapidly advancing new technology can prevent a "next time". The race is on. The new technology of genetic engineering has the potential to permanently and universally stop deadly viruses and bacteria. The problem with this promising new technology in the early 21st century, however, is that it is not *super rapidly advancing*, not fast enough...not until the removal of the FDA. Remember, Neo-Tech is *super rapidly advancing* new technology, which demands rapid access to the marketplace. Breakthrough technologies and drugs must freely reach the marketplace. Private regulatory services and risk rating systems would be in place, but simply put, the way things are now with the FDA, we could lose the race. For a computerlike medical revolution to happen, the hierarchy of authorities, which includes the FDA, will have to come down in order to spring loose the geniuses of society and their new technologies.

The following brief review from the same issue of *Time Magazine* tells of new technologies pursued by doctors, scientists, and businessmen (but again, missing the key ingredient of market-accessible *super rapidly advancing new technology):*

Counterattack:
How Drugmakers Are Fighting Back
(A Review of *Time Magazine* Article)

"Doctors and the public were not alone in feeling cocky about infectious disease a decade ago. The drug companies did too," so began the article. "More than 100 antibiotics were on the market, and they had most bacterial diseases on the run, if not on the verge of eradication."

The pharmaceutical industry simply modified existing antibiotics to stay one step ahead of the bacteria. But that approach no longer works. So, researchers are turning to new technologies to get back in the lead against disease.

One dynamic approach is called "rational" drug design. Scientists study the molecular structure of a bacterium, particularly the active site of the enzyme used by the bacterium to fight off the antibiotic. Next, scientists attempt to design a molecule to "plug up" the active site of that enzyme. Without the effect of that enzyme, the bacterium would once again be killed by the original drug.

A similar concept is being pursued against viruses. You see, viruses cause their destruction by invading our bodies' living cells. To invade a living cell involves receptor sites, like little hooks, where the virus joins the cell. Similarly, a molecule can be designed to block the receptor sites so the virus never attaches to our cells thus remains harmless to our bodies. ...So goes the search for such defendant molecules through combinatorial chemistry.

Again, the problem with such new medical technologies is that they are not *super rapidly advancing*...not as they should be, not like, say, computer technology. How, then, did our country finally get medical technology to *super rapidly advance* to prevent the human catastrophes? My Twelfth Vision showed me:

The Great Rescue

I witnessed during the Twelfth Vision that the looming medical catastrophes helped us see reality and depoliticize the medical industry. Two things happened at once by depoliticizing medicine that seemed like godsends: 1) record amounts of private research funds went toward medical research, and 2) a record number of entrepreneurial geniuses went into medical research. Those unhindered geniuses of society drove medical technology into unimaginable new dimensions that eradicated the most complex diseases. In short, Neothink (the geniuses) drove Neo-Tech (the new technologies) to save our lives.

Depoliticizing the medical industry, depoliticizing everything about it from regulations on health insurance to regulations on medical research, saved many tens of millions of lives.

Today in the anticivilization, each added increment of politicizing the medical industry further bureaucratizes and slows advancing new medical technology, which in turn dramatically drives away private research funds. Medical projects become too inefficient and cost-prohibitive for businesses to invest. Moreover, the lone entrepreneurs, those aggressive geniuses of society, could never function in such a cost-prohibitive, risky environment. The force of their creativity and endless energy that so propelled the free computer/cyberspace industry is but a fraction of what it could be in the medical industry. They are needed to unlock the cures to the most complex diseases.

In the Twelfth Vision, those geniuses, once they were free to flourish and leap into Neothink, rapidly unlocked otherwise impossible combinations.

Politicization, a vestige of the bicameral mentality, ravages our health and costs us millions of precious lives. Each incremental step the other way — depoliticizing the medical industry — dramatically frees up thus speeds up advancing technology, which in turn dramatically attracts private research funds and opens up the medical industry to the entrepreneurs and their endless energy and creativity, their speed and ability to ferret out brilliant advances.

In the Twelfth Vision, I witnessed that we outgrew our desire to be ruled over. As people began dying in increasing numbers, at a faster rate than the exciting bio-tech advancements started saving people, we chose to depoliticized the medical industry to make it as free as the computer industry. Survival pressures helped push us from our bicameral behavioral patterns. Soon, the geniuses did to medicine what they first did to computers. Our country won this race against the microbes. In the Neo-Tech World, after depoliticizing the medical industry, more and more geniuses rose up and saved us from world-wide human catastrophes. That medical revolution became known as the Great Rescue. But the human losses were never forgotten.

Two Forces That Brought Us Neo-Tech

My Twelfth Vision showed me two forces at work: Rising within us, we felt a growing damnation toward politicians and regulatory bureaucracies. That rebellion against a ruling class started spontaneously rising throughout civilizations around the world, from China and the Orient, through Russia and Eastern Europe, Asia Minor and down through Africa, to the relatively free United States and throughout Central and South America. Those early signs of the new Neothink mentality, spontaneously rising throughout different civilizations around the globe, paralleled a similar phenomenon 3000 years ago as the new mentality of human consciousness spontaneously sprang up in different civilizations around the world.

Tomorrow, we started resisting politicians just as we would resist religious zealots trying to tell us how to live. A shrinking number of people retained their bicameral behavioral patterns, still following their political leaders not unlike followers of religious cults. A larger, growing number of people left behind their bicameral behavioral patterns, never again following someone else. Indeed, more and more people fell out of favor with a ruling class.

That anti-authority mega trend gained momentum as medical catastrophes loomed and put the human race on code blue. Out of survival pressures, the people assumed command, relieved big government of its ruling "duties", and ended the ruling class.

Thrust ahead by that mega trend was another, more specific force at work: the inevitable Neo-Tech Party with the underlying mission to reverse the human catastrophes. The Neo-Tech Party replaced the two old parties and set free the geniuses of society. They brought Neo-Tech beyond the computer industry to the medical industry and to all American industries — the only antidote to the looming medical and economic catastrophes.

The Neo-Tech Party quickly depoliticized the medical industry and set free the drug companies and especially the aggressive entrepreneurs, the geniuses of society. The Neo-Tech Party represented medical technology versus medical catastrophe...the new world of freed geniuses using Neothink versus the old world of higher "authorities" suppressing progress. The Neo-Tech Party brought in the new world and unleashed the technologies and geniuses in *all* industries. When America embraced the Neo-Tech Party, the party for depoliticizing America, then three benefits surfaced:

1. Near-perfect health for the young, the old, and for those in their prime.
2. Millionaire wealth for ordinary people.
3. Exciting jobs of the mind *for nearly everyone,* which released nearly everyone's human potential (the Fifth and Sixth Visions).

Young Again

My Twelfth Vision showed me that as the ordinary person got swept into a stimulating life of perfect health and millionaire wealth, he passionately sought life over death. Death at mid-70 simply became unacceptable. Science, medicine, business, and entrepreneurs focused on one epic event — to eradicate all diseases and illnesses to enable ordinary people to live healthily well into their hundreds, and then beyond.

Technology-blocking higher "authorities" such as the FDA that burdened progress were scorned out of existence by the people, passionately demanding their God-given Gift — a long, *healthy* life.[1]

Today, most people feel the unacceptability of the ultimate disease, *aging*. But few people can relate to their own greatest tragedy of dying in their 70s because:

• The thought of living healthily and prosperously for 130 years or more seems like science fiction.

• One's wealth, health, love and happiness are stagnant or shrinking. At 75 years, life is no longer very stimulating, and the desire to live longer in "old age" is gone.

In tomorrow's rapidly progressing Neo-Tech World, I saw (in my Twelfth Vision) that the idea of living longer did not seem so futuristic. What before seemed technologically impossible was in wide use. Without disease, we lived well into our hundreds. Moreover, the idea of extending human life by slowing the disease of cellular degeneration or aging, and slowing the effects of gravity and entropy, became a mass appeal, especially as ordinary people became wealthy, healthy, and in love with life...the young and romantic life. The geniuses were hard at work learning how to extend our lives.

Today, by contrast, people eventually lose the desire to live. Sinking in stagnation, most good people experience limited financial and emotional success. Physically, emotionally, and financially burned out, most older people do not care to live much longer. Quality of elderly life is low in the anticivilization. Thus, today the desire to live longer is not in wide demand.

In tomorrow's nonpoliticized money/power/romantic-love paradise on Earth, I saw people regain a childlike desire to live longer. Rich and in love, quality of life was high, and the desire to live longer was in wide demand.

Death Became an Unacceptable Option

A strong sense of tragedy grew in us as we grew older and

[1]God-given in the sense that man should have had the Gifts of the Neo-Tech World 2400 years ago as God and Man were close to uniting as God-Man, just two dozen generations after the collapse of the hallucinated gods and the bicameral mentality, as explained in the First and Second Insights, Part Two of this book.

closed in on death. We emotionally grasped the unacceptability of dying in our 70s. In fact, the thought of dying at all, not to mention *so young,* grew increasingly intolerable. That unacceptability of dying was a direct result of our deep and permanent happiness as value creators. Tomorrow, the freed geniuses of society raced forward to answer our cries for life as we discovered the persons we were meant to be, forever ending the burden of life (Vision Two).

Most of us today do not grasp the tragedy of dying so young because, as we grow older, we steadily lose our enthusiasm for life. The burden of life comes to the surface as we use up our happy experiences of life (Vision Two). We cannot blame ourselves, for in the suppressed anticivilization, life offers limited mortal doses of wealth and happiness.

My Twelfth Vision showed me that the Neo-Tech World actually *reversed* the trend: enthusiasm actually *intensified* as we grew older. As Neothink value creators, we built larger and larger puzzles of creation, which became very exhilarating. Instead of withering in our ruts, we blossomed in our creations.

The Amazing Life Charts

In my Twelfth Vision, I saw something rather unusual catch on across the country prior to the Neo-Tech World:

First, people began thinking about their imminent deaths: on a certain date, at a certain time, every person would die. They figured if they faced their deaths, their lives would change dramatically. They would appreciate their one and only lives more intensely. So, using the average life expectancy, people began writing the "estimated" date of their deaths on a piece of paper. They taped that written date on their bathroom mirrors.

Immediately, their lives changed. Even teenagers' emotions and perspectives changed. Before the "death date" technique, most teenagers wanted the years to whiz by to reach the age of 16 so they could drive, or 18 when they graduated from high school, or 21 when they were legal adults. But with their parents' date of death on the bathroom mirror, the teenager no longer said, "I can't wait until I'm sixteen so I can get my driver's license." For, he would be that many years closer to his parents' date on the mirror, and the teenager would be that many years closer to his own date. Now, no one wanted the years to whiz by. Instead, even teenagers appreciated every moment of their lives and every moment of sharing time together with loved ones.

Now, this idea grew into something more than just an "estimated" date of death taped to bathroom mirrors. Many people turned their dates into monthly countdown sheets with monthly squares to "X" off. Each month that went by, they would "X" off one square. When they were babies, their parents would "X" the squares for them. By their third birthday, before they even knew what was going on, 36 squares of their life charts were already gone. Figuring that everyone started out with 900 squares (75 years average x 12 months), they only had 864 left.

At 38 years old, people had less than half their squares left. As they grew older, they did not slow down. For now, they were intensely aware of their mortality and were interested in living life to the fullest, perhaps even leaving a legacy.

What happened when those open squares, for the first time, dropped from three digits to two digits — under 100 left? Just 100 months left! Did they slow down for "old age"? No, instead they picked up the pace. "How much have I done with my life?" they kept asking themselves. "Not much time left!"

They broke out of restricting comfort zones and did not hesitate to take worthwhile risks. They used the exercises in Vision One to uncover and pursue their Friday-Night Essences. For, the most valuable commodity became those open squares — their remaining lives. People had only those open squares in which to accomplish and experience everything they would ever accomplish or experience in life. A stagnated, specialized job for security that ate up those squares while they got nowhere became the exception for those people instead of the norm. They pursued entrepreneurial challenges or became in-house entrepreneurs (the Fifth and Sixth Visions). They became the persons they were meant to be. Their lives no longer answered to the standards of others — that meant little now. Their lives answered to those remaining open squares. That meant everything.

On the other hand, imagine the relationships, using this

exercise, with their spouses and children, their parents, brothers and sisters, and friends. They savored their moments with them. They became much closer, more caring — they got much more out of life. The value of their brief lives and relationships were amplified to where they should be, for they felt *the preciousness* of life.

Adventurous value production heading toward value creation, even taking rational chances in entrepreneurial challenges became the only way to live for those people using the life charts. Not letting love slip by, not undermining the preciousness of life or wasting life with negativity, instead savoring time together and enjoying romantic and family love, wonderful friendship love, and giving life one's all became the only way to live for those growing people using the life charts. Life with the life charts was lived to the fullest.

Entire perspectives changed. Children did not let 264 squares get "X'd" off to an inferior education, leaving them with just 636 left to really start living. Ten-year-olds started integrated thinking (the Ninth Vision) after just 109 squares got "X'd" off. Those ten-year-olds wanted to really start creating.

Enthusiasm increased as these people, these forerunners to the people in the Neo-Tech World, grew older. The older they became, the more motivated they became to get more out of the precious shrinking supply of life.

The life charts became life intensifiers. They helped people get more out of life. The life-chart phenomenon happened just before we depoliticized America and entered the Neo-Tech World. Therefore, fortunately, people did not get depressed over their shrinking supplies of life because geniuses in business, science, and medicine were working more and more freely to extend life expectancy. As the new world replaced the old, geniuses focussed on the world's greatest goal: to add more open squares to the life charts faster than they got X'd off.

When depoliticized business and science started moving faster than nature, and people added squares faster than they X'd them, great celebrations broke out around the world. Ticker-tape parades were held in the cities for the geniuses responsible for extending life.

The life charts gained popularity as they, at first, stimulated people's remaining, brief time in all eternity. The life charts then grew famous as they unified the whole world behind mankind's single most important goal: extending quality life.

Once in the Neo-Tech World, the life charts were no longer needed. Ordinary people became the persons they were meant to be (Vision One) and lived their dreams as value creators (Vision Two). As they discovered eternal happiness, an unforgiving sorrow for life's greatest tragedy — their inevitable deaths — emerged. They began to question why death for humans was "inevitable".

More and more geniuses continued evolving into Neothink and taking life extension to new levels. Then the question was asked of them, "Can we live eternally?"

Eternal Life — The Way It Could Be

As people's lives became more and more exciting with age and accomplishments, they eventually could not fathom the tragedy of a growing, eternally happy person dying. That death could only be compared to the death of a child — so much unseen and left undone. Then the cries to the geniuses began: "We *must* live forever!" Much of the world's creative energy came together into a superpuzzle that would achieve mankind's greatest goal: eternal life in our heaven on Earth. Project Life began (Vision Four).

Certain Death — The Way It Used To Be

Still trying to make sense of our past, people tomorrow looked back at how dying in the old world actually seemed natural. Since life progressed in an open-ended flow from generation to generation, death was somehow acceptable. For example, at a certain age during childhood or early adulthood, one's grandparents died. Later one's parents died. Then oneself. His children and grandchildren lived on. The loss seemed natural. Religious beliefs eased the pain.

Consider the following sad yet all-too-common story: Henry Ford, the entrepreneur who broke into Neothink at the turn of the 20th century and built Ford Motor Company, was a genius of society. He also deeply loved his son, Edsel, who went to work in Ford Motor Company and eventually became Ford's president. Henry Ford proudly watched his son's growth from a baby, through his childhood, his schooling, his teenage years, his early adulthood, his first day at Ford Motor Company to the presidency of Ford Motor Company. Then Edsel died at the age of 50. He died from cancer. Henry Ford, his father, lived a few more years, running Ford Motor Company with a broken heart.

Imagine the grief Henry Ford felt. He could remember bringing the tiny baby Edsel into the world, teaching him how to walk, to talk. He could remember celebrating the twenty-millionth Ford automobile side by side with Edsel. Then suddenly, in a flash, his son was gone, forever...come and gone within his father's lifetime. Imagine the realization Henry Ford had to face: the pitifully short experience that life really is. Life, so valuable, full of feeling, *one's everything* — gone so quickly.

By seeing his son's entire life come and go, the shortness of life and finality of death became inescapably real. He saw life not as an open-ended progression from grandfather to father to himself to son — a perspective in which the brief, closed nature of life is never fully grasped. No, he saw the true nutshell of life in witnessing his son's life.

Very few people in the 20th century had the true, nutshell perspective of their lives. Instead, the open extension of the family, children outliving their parents, blocked that perspective. Yet, people's lives were but closed little nutshells in time. If your own son were to die before you, then you would suddenly see the nutshell perspective of life and would emotionally feel death as wretchedly immoral and intolerable.

Now, try to imagine, for one sad moment, watching your own son die as did Henry Ford. Imagine...as you hold your son's hand as you did when he was a boy, for one last time, everything he would ever feel or experience is ending. In a few hours, your son's short time in all eternity will be over. As you watch him lying there, the pain becomes unbearable. For, you know that your son's one experience of life will soon be all over, forever. And you can still remember the first time he dropped his mouth two times in a row to say, "dada"...as if that day were yesterday.

Yet your son, in a flash, is gone. Gone *forever*.

That same closed nutshell of life applies to you. Take this moment to imagine the unimaginable. Imagine...yourself dying: Your vision is fading, going. You look at your wife, your children beside you; but they are fading like fog on a window separating you as darkness begins to envelop you. As they fade, you look as intensely as you can at their wonderful faces; you are hanging on to those last moments, for you know you will never see their beautiful faces again.

You have closed your eyes to sleep many thousands of times before. But you know this time will be the last. You know this time, when you slip into darkness, you will never again be part of life. After thousands of times of seeing your spouse good night, this time will be the last time you will see her, ever. Your life is over. At that moment, you alone know perhaps for the first time that once life leaves you, every wonderful feeling of life is really over...forever.

In tomorrow's Neo-Tech World, our brief seven-and-a-half decades of life within all eternity was considered much too brief for the wealthy and happy ordinary person. The demand for living longer grew enormous. First, disease was eradicated to give us healthy life well into our hundreds. Then, major businesses, financial institutions, scientists and entrepreneurs embraced the growing demand for longer life. Money, minds, technology, science, medicine came together through entrepreneurial business. Their superpuzzle soon met the ultimate demand of slowing down and eventually curing the disease of aging.

The geniuses awakened the sleeping-giant consumer product of all time: life extension. For suddenly, happy people's *brief* time in all eternity became unacceptable. Too brief. Within *your* lifetime, the new world of Neo-Tech doubled your journey through life...and more.

Irreplaceable Youth

Right about now, during the middle of my Twelfth Vision, a story went through my mind's eye. I could see, hear, feel, even smell the surroundings as if I were there. Afterwards, whatever I did, I could never forget the value of life and love. Place yourself into this short story that came to me at this moment during my Vision, and feel the value of life and love:

A young man and woman in their 20s jumped onto a rock in a quiet cove. They faced each other. The only sound was the gentle noise of the water cradling the rock. The tall pine trees filled the mountain air with sweet aroma. The autumn evening was crisp; the sun was setting over the lake. The young man knew the moment was right. He reached out and touched her hair then placed his hands on her shoulders. He looked into her eyes and asked her to marry him. She looked deep into his eyes as she said yes. Suddenly her eyes filled with tears as she tilted her head slightly and began to cry and laugh. His eyes filled with tears as they hugged and kissed. "Look at that!", she said as she pointed to a majestic orange and pink sunset glowing over the lake.

They stepped from the rock back to the land. They were overflowing with happy energy. They sat on the ground for a moment as he showed her the ring and put it on her finger. She held her hand toward the sky and admired the ring sparkling in the sunset. He stood up then picked her up, lifted her off the ground and turned in circles. As he turned her around, he saw the pink sky over the lake, then the white full moon between the tall pine trees. The young couple's whole life was before them. Their future together and a lifetime of excitement and happiness was ahead. They had nothing to worry about and everything to look forward to. Everything — their careers, their marriage, their children — everything was before them. They were happy and carefree. They celebrated until darkness fell over the lake.

The couple took an exciting path through life: They loved their work, sharing their goals, and they loved each other. Their happiness grew. Their love for each other deepened. But as their happiness grew and their love deepened, life passed by in a flash. They felt the unjust irony — life for the happy person bringing exciting values to mankind passed quickly. Yet, for the stagnated person, time was a burden. Time passed slowly. For the happy couple, time was a precious gift. Fifty years passed quickly.

After fifty years, they went back to the same little cove on the mountain lake. The moment was so special fifty years ago that the cove became a permanent photograph in their minds. Now, everything looked the same. They stepped on the rock. The only sound was the water cradling the rock. They smelled the pine and felt the crisp autumn air as the sun set over the lake. They remembered. At this moment he had asked her to marry him. They looked at each other. Their eyes filled with tears of sadness as they reached out to hold each other. She touched his face and turned it gently so he saw the fiery sunset.

As they stood there, all the beauty around them was the same...except this time everything in life was not before them. Their careers, their marriage, their children...that was now all behind them. This time, they were quiet and did not celebrate. Life was too short. They felt so happy last time with all life to experience in front of them. But now their lives were practically over...over in a flash. All that happiness they felt last time for what was to come had already come and gone. That happiness felt last time now turned to sadness. For nearly all life was now behind them. And their love for each other would in a few short years be lost to death.

They stood on the rock and looked at each other. They said nothing. They held each other. Then they walked over to where they had celebrated last time and remembered their carefree happiness. Without saying a word, she pulled off her ring and gently placed it in his hand. They both looked at it, sparkling in the sunset as it did fifty years ago. He looked into her eyes and slid it on her finger again. Then he held her hand and told her he loved her more than the day he first put that ring on her finger. His voice shook as he told her. He gasped and looked up for a moment and saw the moon between the pines as he did fifty years ago.

The more they remembered, the more they felt sadness. They hugged, and then they held each other for a long time. They knew these moments were precious, for they would not have each other much longer. They watched the sunset and remembered. Darkness fell over the lake.

A few years later, the man came back alone one evening. His wife had died. For the first time, he stood alone on the rock. He was overcome by feelings. Just yesterday, it seemed, his wife was here with him as they looked into each other's eyes and held each other in reassurance. He could see her still standing there in front of him. He reached out to touch her hair. She was not there. He began to weep and to remember. He remembered when he put his hands on her shoulders and asked her to marry him. He remembered her eyes and her expression. He remembered how she tilted her head slightly as her eyes filled with tears. ...Oh, he needed her now. He felt so empty as the water cradled the rock.

He stepped off the rock and onto the land. He suddenly looked behind him, as if to find his wife there with him after all. If only he could hold her one more time! The pain while remembering the last time here, when he held her hand and told her he loved her, now became unbearable. To momentarily escape the pain, his thoughts jumped back to the time they once celebrated life still before them, over fifty years ago. It seemed like just a short time ago — they laughed and cried and celebrated. He walked over to where they had celebrated. He turned slowly in circles as he remembered lifting her and turning her in circles in their celebration. As he turned, he saw the sunset; he saw the moon between the pines. He stopped turning. He remembered. He sat on the ground where they once sat as he first slid the ring on her finger. Suddenly the sweet celebration became crushed with the knowledge that she was gone, forever. He looked at the sunset. He remembered the last time when they watched this sunset together. ...She would never see another sunset. Darkness fell over the lake.

He did not leave this time. He sat there in the dark. He remembered every moment of when they shared this cove one last time together. He remembered how precious those moments were. He kept on remembering. He remembered first his most recent memories with his wife; then his memories traveled back over the years. He relived in his mind every special moment with her throughout all the years. Several hours later, physically paralyzed by his thoughts, he had remembered all the special moments back to the moment he stood up from the very spot where he now sat, lifted her and turned her in circles as they celebrated a whole life still to come together...their wonderful lives ahead, which he just spent the last several hours remembering, moment by moment. Those special moments that he remembered tonight were what they were celebrating for over fifty years ago...for a wonderful lifetime in anticipation. Suddenly he began to cry loudly. "It's all over!" he yelled into the darkness.

The sunrise caught the old man still paralyzed in his memories. He finally stood up to leave. He was weary. His heart ached as he recalled that the last time he stood up from this spot, he was overflowing with energy and happiness as he lifted her and turned her around...and that the last time he stood here was a few years ago when he told her how much he loved her. He looked at the cove in the morning light. He looked for a long time. He looked at the pines, at the land where they celebrated, at the lake, the sky...and then he looked at the rock and listened as the water cradled it. Tears fell from his eyes. It was hard to turn away. He knew he would never again see this place that had meant so much to his life. ...He was saying good-bye, forever.

The old man tried to go on with his goals. But he and his wife had always worked together. Going back to his desk, pulling out work that she had worked on with him, reaching for goals that she had reached for with him...caused deep pain. Working toward those goals without her now tore his heart. They both loved their work and their goals. But now the work and those goals devastated him with hurt. He kept remembering her and how she had loved their goals. When he walked into his home office, he became filled with the pain of losing her. He could not work without her presence. He spent all day working on something that before, with her, took him less than an hour. His mind slipped back into memories of her all day long. He emotionally could not achieve their goals without her. For, every forward movement toward those goals made the loss of her more painful.

He struggled forward for two more painful years. He accomplished little, then died. ...The water still cradles the rock in the cove. The sun sets over the lake and the moon shines between the pine trees. But he will never see that again.

* * *

Looking back from the Neo-Tech World, the anticivilization seemed so sad and strange that people lived only into their 60s, 70s, and 80s. Eventually, it seemed bizarre that we once *actually died.*

Today, you live for a brief moment in time, then are gone, vanishing from life, forever. Everything, all the wonderful experiences of life and heartwarming feelings, end with death. That inherent sadness of life amplifies the moral purpose of living: to achieve happiness. During your brief moment alive in all eternity, you *must* experience happiness and as much as you possibly can. You must accomplish this to get everything you can out of your one shining moment of life.

Your Next Level of Happiness Tomorrow

In all the infinity before we were born and in all the infinity after we die, our brief, little flicker of time here on Earth offers us every feeling of life we will ever know in all eternity. This is our one special moment to *be happy.*

In the anticivilization, our lives are very short; we are here for a moment and then are gone forever. The Twelfth Vision turned my thoughts to my young children and their one special moment in time. I saw an image of them all grown up. Oh, how I wanted only good to happen to them, for this was their one special moment in all eternity.

Seeing into the future during this Twelfth Vision was painful at first, for it showed me how quickly our loved ones got old. I saw the "sad someday" when my parents and siblings each died. Their every precious feeling in life ended on their last day, ended forever. All the love in their lives came to an end; forever and ever. Gone not for a few weeks. Gone forever. Never to occur again. ...In this Vision, I came face to face with the fact that everything special in life is lost to death.

During the Twelfth Vision, at times so sad and somber, I realized that only by feeling the sadness of life could I discover the rightness of happiness...of super happiness. Now I knew why the Twelfth Vision was putting me through these darkest of feelings: to prepare me to discover the next level of happiness.

Are your children intensely happy? Are you? Or is life just passing, day after day? You have a God-given right (i.e., the natural state of God-Man, the First Insight) to wake up every morning to exhilarating happiness. But in the anticivilization, you cannot...not without a lot of unreasonable luck. In the Neo-Tech World, when we looked back, we cringed at all the lost love and happiness of our precious lives. Today, we have no idea how happy we can be.

Four New Frontiers of Happiness

Mankind does not yet know about something very special: when I entered the new world in my Twelfth Vision, I discovered the next level of happiness — exhilarating happiness every single day of ordinary people's lives. As the Twelfth Vision took me into the Neo-Tech World, I rose from my sad stupor and unexpectedly entered a delightful euphoria. You see, as we became the persons we were meant to be (Vision One), the giant numb spot to appreciating life and love in the anticivilization began tingling with feelings in the Neo-Tech World. We entered four entirely new frontiers of happiness. (Today, buried under the burden of life, we cannot fully or permanently experience the four new frontiers of happiness.)

First New Frontier of Happiness

The first new frontier of happiness that I actually experienced during the Twelfth Vision was an incredible treat called *the celebration* (first described in Vision Seven). The celebration caused exhilarating romantic love as well as powerful family love and friendship love.

The best way I can describe the celebration to you is for you to remember the early weeks of falling in love and how every visit with your newly found love filled you with exhilarating joy. Remember that? Also, remember each of the special days your children were born? Remember the excitement that ran through you? And remember being with your best friend or loved ones during the best times of your life. ...Those experiences filled you with more happiness than anything you have known since and came closest to giving you a hint of the celebrations the people felt *all the time* in tomorrow's Neo-Tech World. Remember, you never had to work for those wonderful feelings; they just automatically filled you. Remember? Those sensational celebrations such as falling in love or bringing a child into the world captured temporarily in the anticivilization what life was like permanently in the Neo-Tech World.

Alas, in the anticivilization, your celebrations of love — those intense flames of happiness while falling in love — ran out of

288

energy after awhile. In your one special time in all eternity, you felt those intense flames of happiness for only a few months or less. As the romantic celebrations lost energy and faded in the anticivilization's suppressed society, you and your love got together on one particular day, perhaps less than a year after finding each other, and for one last time felt the celebration. There you were, feeling happy, holding and touching, not knowing that this was the last real celebration. A sad tragedy was happening right then during that happy moment together. The intense flames of happiness when together were ending. From then on, time together would not be a special celebration. The flames had been dying down and hence would burn brightly no more. Your special moment of romantic love in all eternity...was over. Now, things would get back to "normal".

In the Neo-Tech World, you felt those intense celebrations of romantic love not for a fraction of your life, but for your *entire* life. Imagine feeling *in love* and intensely happy, on a natural high, year after year after year.

In my Twelfth Vision, we could barely believe that we could have lived the rest of our lives never knowing all this happiness; sometimes we would quiver at the thought of what tragedies would have been if we had stayed in the anticivilization. In the anticivilization, the unthinkable would have happened: not until your spouse was dying would you experience, once again after a lifetime of absence, for one heartbreaking last time, the long-lost flame. There you would be, looking deep into her eyes at the end, wanting to hold the life inside her with your love. There, while looking into her eyes, and she looking into your eyes, you would have felt the greatest love that you had ever felt for each other. This moment, the most special moment of your love affair, would have been the saddest moment of your life as her eyes could stay open no longer. As she closed her eyes, your heart would have broken. Don't go...don't go. ...During her one last moment, as you looked into each other's eyes for one last time, you both would have felt the warm flame flickering once again. Then, just as quickly as it came, it would be gone, gone forever.

The Twelfth Vision showed me that the Neo-Tech World rescued us. Tomorrow's prosperous and romantic Neo-Tech

World freed us from our stagnation-traps. We were so successful and happy as the persons we were meant to be (First Vision) that we naturally returned to the intense celebrations of our early weeks of falling in love and felt the flame flickering for our entire lives together. We were always in the mood for celebrating! The Neo-Tech World also elevated love among family members and close friends. Tomorrow, when you looked into your spouse's eyes that last time, your child's eyes, your best friend's eyes, you all knew that you enjoyed the celebrations your whole lives together. You were, at that final sad moment, also very happy, for you did not miss out, not in your life. Of course, shortly into the Neo-Tech World, there would be no more "final sad moments".

Second New Frontier of Happiness

The second new frontier of happiness in tomorrow's Neo-Tech World came from discovering *the preciousness* of life. In the anticivilization, not until a loved one died would one fully know the preciousness of life. Suddenly the surviving person, say an elderly gentleman who lost his spouse, would become enveloped in a helplessness that no matter how much he longed to spend time with his lost loved one, no matter how much he hurt inside to be together with her just once more, he never, ever would spend another moment with her, not even one more good-bye embrace. Gone was everything: her funny little gestures when happy, her smiling eyes and lips, her soft hands and arms that would so often hold him. Gone was her tenderness and her love that was always there for him. Gone were all the little things they used to do together. All was gone. ...He could only sit alone at night, remembering her...swallowed by the sadness of life.

During the emotional Twelfth Vision, for the first time, I could feel down to my bones the *irreplaceable preciousness* of life. In turn, I suddenly *cherished every moment I had* — both with my loved ones and with myself. In fact, for several weeks after my Twelfth Vision, I held onto those precious feelings. Even the littlest things I did with my loved ones or on my own brought me joy. I felt every fleeting moment's preciousness; I savored those moments knowing once they were gone, I would never have them again. In fact, for several weeks following my Twelfth Vision, that went on. I felt joy in *everything I did*, even routine tasks!

I saw ordinary people tomorrow savor even the little moments, as I did, as precious gifts. In that new era, people felt deep joy just for being alive, especially every time they were with their loved ones, yes, even during the most routine situations.

Perhaps the best insight I can give you now of the power of the preciousness is to first imagine you were given two years to live. Now, imagine how you would suddenly absorb every bit of love and happiness out of every living moment with yourself and with your loved ones. In the Neo-Tech World, we did exactly that: we absorbed love and happiness from every moment, but for our whole lives. People's journeys through life became manyfold more meaningful. Their lives were filled every single day with warmth and love as they savored the preciousness of all their moments with their loved ones and with themselves. When the end came, they knew they had absorbed every last drop of joy and happiness out of life. And soon in the Neo-Tech World, "the end" never came, and people enjoyed the preciousness forever.

Third New Frontier of Happiness

The third new frontier of happiness in the Neo-Tech World reached back to the *bigger-than-life excitement* you experienced in your childhood. Adults got back those childlike bigger-than-life sensations again. Let us take a reminiscent look back at bigger-than-life childhood. Here is what was shown to me during the Twelfth Vision:

A young boy and his little brother awoke early. They poked their heads through the opening of their tent and looked across the yard to Grandma and Grandpa's large beach house. Once a year they came here. Three of their cousins would arrive that day, two the next day, and four the day after.

Overcome by excitement, the boys got up and went inside. Grandpa was already drinking coffee at the breakfast table. The boys listened with fascination as he told them about ice-age rocks scattered throughout the woods on the other side of the railroad tracks. Soon their dad came downstairs, ready to go jogging with the boys. They went out the back door onto the beach. As they jogged along the beach, exciting thoughts rushed through the boys' imagination: After breakfast with Grandma and Grandpa, they would swim and body surf all morning. Then, they would go into town to the toy shop with Grandma. By the time they got back, their three cousins would have arrived! Of course, the first thing to do after the cousins arrived — the yearly tradition of building the big beach bonfire. After that, a picnic barbecue. And after the barbecue, then off to the clubhouse to watch cartoons on the big movie screen and meet the other neighborhood children who have already arrived at their summer homes. And tonight, Uncle Chuck promised to take all the kids to Sunset Park farther up the beach to go on the carnival rides and play the games. Wow, everything here was bigger than life. Two whole weeks in this fairy tale! ...As the exhausted boys lay in the tent that night with their sister and cousins, the soft rumble of a train in the distance rocked them to sleep.

When we were children, life was often like those two weeks for the boys: exciting things that seemed bigger than life happened a lot. Even going out for a fast-food dinner seemed bigger than life. Or hiking in the woods with Grandpa. Or body surfing in the waves seemed bigger than life and kept us busy all day long. As children, life was full of bigger-than-life sensations.

Whatever happened to those bigger-than-life sensations? As adults, going to McDonald's or body surfing in the ocean no longer seem bigger than life. Do bigger-than-life sensations happen only as children? And is that why many people long for their childhoods?

Until now, trapped in an anticivilization, bigger-than-life sensations happened only as a child, and they came from early-on *new experiences* of life. But my Twelfth Vision showed me that in the Neo-Tech World, those bigger-than-life sensations also happened routinely as an adult, and they came from *building new experiences* of life. As exhilarated value creators (Vision Two), I saw ordinary people living bigger than life in the exciting

292

Neo-Tech World. They were rich, successful, and building upon life itself through achieving dreams that they never even considered in the anticivilization (see the Fifth and Sixth Visions).

For example, back to my Twelfth Vision, I saw an image of the same two boys full grown. They still often jogged together with their Dad. Having become the value creators they were meant to be, exciting thoughts still filled their minds and flowed from their tongues on their runs: The new product worked on for two years was now ready for marketing tests. The *Amazing Stories* booklet was showing signs of becoming a best seller. The data pointed to a whole new marketing approach in Brazil. The new 60-second TV ad looked good; now came the airing. The Slavic translation was completed and ready for marketing. A breakthrough was unfolding in the domestic direct-mail brochure. The full-page newspaper ad would run in next Tuesday's national paper. Another book was near completion for publishing. The new half-hour television show was in editing. The goal of retail locations had come to life with the opening of the first location. The seminars in Australia and America showed promise. Product line was expanding monthly. Everything here was bigger than life.

In the Neo-Tech World, adults enjoyed bigger-than-life sensations every day, just as children. For, adults became value creators on their Friday-Night Essences (Vision One), which means they became creative dream builders. Emotional and financial stagnation disappeared and eventually left our memories.

Fourth New Frontier of Happiness

The fourth and final new frontier of happiness in tomorrow's Neo-Tech Era also reached back into childhood to the *carefree happiness* that got left behind. Consider that life was bigger than life for the father and his sons because they used Neothink techniques (taught in Visions One, Two, Five, Six, and Nine) from the future Neo-Tech World. But they still lived in this pre-Neo-Tech World, this anticivilization under the ruling class. Therefore, they could never have the same *carefree* sensation they did as children. You see, they could never escape the tragedy of moving toward "the end".

When the father and his sons were younger, when the sons were just boys, their Grandma and Grandpa were as young as Dad was now. Dad was over sixty now. When everything was bigger than life as children, everything was also carefree. Grandma and Grandpa were still young and Dad was in his prime. Everything was wide open and life had so many adventures for the grandsons. No one really knew about or talked about death. Death was so far in the future that, as children, the grandsons never even thought once about it. They were just happy and carefree. As they grew older, however, old-age and death closed in on their family.

Grandpa was gone now. The father and his sons were too busy with their worldwide business to go back to see Grandma. The aunts, uncles, and cousins were spread across the country and busy with their lives. Grandma sat alone, every day, trapped in the silence of no one there...nothing and no one but the memories. She went to bed at 7:00 p.m. every evening, for just getting ready for bed gave her something to do.

One of the cousins or uncles visited Grandma every once in a while. When they did, her life lit up. Those short-lived happy visits also brought a sad nostalgia into the beach house as they brought back memories of the way things used to be, before the tragedy of life — death — closed in on Grandma and took her husband and friends.

A younger person could get through even the worst tragedy, for that person would have a life still before him. But Grandma did not have a life still before her. When Grandpa died, she could not get through the tragedy. Instead, she suffered day after day in the quiet house where everything once happened. Oh, the desire for the way it used to be hurt! Every day...every day...day after day.

One of the grandsons took perhaps his last trip across the country to see Grandma. He had not been here for several years. Everything looked the same as when he was a boy. But everything was empty — the yard, the beach, the breakfast table. He could remember the carefree happiness he and his brother and father used to feel here. But the carefree happiness was gone — even in them...three men whose lives were still bigger than life. For the first time in his life, he longed for the past

— for the carefree happiness again. He longed for Grandpa to be back at the breakfast table. He longed for Dad to be a young man again. He longed for his cousins to fill the yard again...back when they were young and life was carefree. The desire for the way it used to be gripped him and did not let go.

The next day, he walked through the big front yard to the little storage shed. He opened its door, and there was the plastic brown bat and the whiffle ball! Who was the last one to touch that bat? He wondered, smiling. Was it Hammy; was it John; was it himself? He wanted to pick up the bat, but instead pushed close the shed door. As the door was closing he saw, neatly folded in the corner, the tent. ...All the happiness and life had abandoned this wonderful place.

The last day of his visit, he finished looking through the photo albums. Grandma was with him. He found an old newspaper clipping announcing his Grandma and Grandpa's engagement — sixty years ago! There they were, a picture of Grandma and Grandpa engaged...just about twenty years old. What a striking couple. Grandma looked so beautiful, so vivacious with a hint of mischief in her smile. She looked so deeply in love with Grandpa. Could this beautiful girl be Grandma?

As the grandson now looked at Grandma, she giggled as he pointed to the picture. Suddenly, he could imagine that same giggle in the beautiful young girl with the dimples in the picture. He could see and hear the young girl doing that same giggle, with that same smile. But the girl in the picture had a whole life before her. She had the carefree happiness back then — glowing in her beautiful face. Oh Grandma, he thought, how can I turn time back sixty years for you? "It seems just like yesterday," Grandma sighed.

Just "yesterday", Grandma had everything. She had beauty and bubbling happiness and intense love. Sixty short years aged away her beauty. Even more tragic, sixty years took away and killed her happiness and love. Sixty years made everything go from beautiful, carefree, happy, and from deeply in love to old, painful, sad, and deeply suffering from the loss of her lifelong love. Sixty short years changed everything from wonderful to suffering.

When the grandson came here to visit Grandma, he had come with his sister. During their visit here, he and his sister remembered a deep, long-lost place inside themselves once filled with their childhood carefree happiness, gone forever into memories. ...Now, the time had come to leave. His sister's plane was to leave two hours before his. As she said good-bye to Grandma, most likely for the last time, the grandson sat in the living room and listened to their softly spoken parting words. When his sister left, Grandma closed the door and went to her room. He heard her crying.

When she stopped crying, he suddenly noticed the quietness of Grandma's house. He had never known such quietness here before, not like this. Whenever he visited, loud and joyous talk and laughter filled the house. Even when he and his sister were the only visitors, still their own voices filled the house. But now with his sister gone and Grandma in her room, he noticed a quietness he never knew before. Oh, what a sad quietness...the quietness of life lost and good times gone forever.

For the first time, he saw life from Grandma's perspective. She lived in this sad quietness from the time she woke up till the time she went to bed, every single day. And she had no way out, nothing to move her through this tough time in her life to better times. For, all her good times had come and gone. She suffered in this sad quietness day after day. Oh Grandma, how did this happen to you? How did things end up this way? You made us all so happy and gave us all such beautiful carefree times when we were children. You did not deserve this.

Soon, he had to leave for his plane. When he said good-bye to his Grandma, they both silently knew this was the last time. They looked at each other in the doorway. He hugged her. This hug was different from any he had given her before. He held her against him. Her head rested sideways on his chest. She did not get hugged or held by anyone anymore. They knew this would be their last embrace. When he let go, her eyes were filled with tears. He nearly lost his composure, but managed to say good-bye. As he turned and walked away, he felt his childhood drain from him. For the last time, he walked through the big yard where he and his brother used to sleep in the tent. He would never again see these surroundings of Grandma's. His small remains of carefree youth left him as he left Grandma.

He knew as he was walking away that Grandma was watching him — her precious grandson — walking across her lawn for the last time. He turned around and, for one last time, saw her standing in her doorway. She looked so alone. He waved, and as he waved, he could see in her face that she was remembering back through the years to when he would run across the yard to her as a little boy.

As he drove away, he knew that inside the house, Grandma went to her room and cried. He imagined it: when she stopped crying, the lonely silence returned, but this time the lonely silence was a lot lonelier than before, for she knew she would never see her precious grandson again.

When we were young children, we were swirling around at the very top of the very wide funnel of life. We were carefree, worry-free. Tragedy was nonexistent. And life seemed bigger than life with so many new experiences in that very wide opening of the funnel of life...filled with the potion of life swirling us around into new, unexplored adventures.

Now grown up, we can retrieve the bigger-than-life sense of life by *building* new experiences of life. But life's potion still gets pulled down the funnel. Life steadily leaves the funnel until, as Grandma, sixty years later each one of us drops into the final tube at the bottom of the funnel of life. In that final tube, our loved ones around us begin to die — spouse, brother, sister, friends. But this time, we will not move past the tragedies. For, we will be caught in the final exit tube at the bottom of the funnel of life. So little life left. Soon our final drop of life will fall from the funnel of life.

Grandma died the next year. Now Dad moved toward his final exit tube in the funnel of life. Nothing could stop it. Life for Dad and his sons moved from carefree days in the past toward tragic days ahead. The unbreakable love they built among each other would be mercilessly broken by death. They built their bigger-than-life company, goals, and achievements together. Yet, they would lose all that and their lives. Dad was the first to go. From there on, all carefree happiness in his sons was extinguished forever. In just a seeming flash of time, his sons entered their final tube in the funnel of life. This time, they were not saying good-bye to Grandma, to their carefree youths, and to all the wonderful times at Grandma's beach house. This time, they were saying good-bye to each other, to their own lives and loved ones, and to all the wonderful values they built together.

Why could not life for Grandma, Dad, and his sons ever again be like it was when they were children? Two life-lifting sensations are lost when we grow up in the anticivilization:

1) The bigger-than-life sensations, and

2) The carefree happiness

I witnessed that both the bigger-than-life sensations *and* the carefree happiness came back in the Neo-Tech World. The Twelfth Vision showed me that life was bigger than life again after the job revolution (the Fifth Vision) as we excitedly built and lived our dreams. Moreover, the carefree happiness returned after we depoliticized America and ended big-government regulations to set free rapid medical progress that eradicated fatal diseases and slowed down and eventually cured the fatal disease of cellular degeneration — aging...death.

When the Neo-Tech World arrived, the thought of dying, which robbed us of our childlike carefree happiness, went away for another fifty years, even more eventually...and then, forever, as accurately demonstrated in my novel *The First Immortals: The Story*. The demand for longer life was answered by unburdened entrepreneurs who evolved into God-Man (the First Insight) and drove technologies into new dimensions. When people no longer got old until well in their hundreds, then the carefree happiness known today only in children returned to adults.

The Neo-Tech World saved us from emotional diminishment and lifted us to the next level of happiness. We lived each and every day with four new frontiers of happiness: *the celebrations, the preciousness, bigger-than-life excitement, and carefree happiness.* Those new dimensions of happiness summoned the geniuses of society to rapidly advance technology toward achieving immortality.

In the anticivilization, uneventful years are all we have left...for our one short experience of life in all eternity. In the

Neo-Tech World, my Twelfth Vision showed me we were like children with so much to experience. Life was bigger than life again. Every new day was packed full of exhilaration. The burden of life was gone. We achieved both the technology and the desire to live a lot, lot longer. We enjoyed another Gift of the Neo-Tech World: perfect physical and mental health for a long, extended life of happiness...eventually for eternity.

Today, our God-given right (i.e., the natural state of God-Man, the First Insight) to both perfect health and to the four new frontiers of happiness is kept from us by our bicameral programming that accepts higher "authorities" or neocheaters. Of course, those neocheaters exploit our bicameral longings for guidance, and they cleverly provide that guidance through their massive regulatory and spending programs for the "social good" (Vision Eleven). Those regulatory and spending programs for the "social good" are illusions that politicize our lives and rule over us. The neocheaters get enormous power, prestige, and they control enormous wealth. On the other hand, we get suppressed in the anticivilization with physical diseases, mental stagnation, and short burdensome lives.

Looking forward into the Neo-Tech World, external "authorities" or neocheaters were left behind. The geniuses jumped ahead into Neothink and brought us enormous buying power and nearly perfect health. Thereafter, we too jumped into Neothink. The four new frontiers of happiness appeared before our eyes and brought us back to a beautiful, lost world in which we rediscovered the thrill of life.

Part Two

The
Three
Insights

The First Insight
God-Man Is Our Final Evolution

"...the theory of evolution by natural selection was the hollowing knell of all that ennobling tradition of man as the purposed creation of Majestic Greatness, the elohim, that goes straight back into the unconscious depths of the Bicameral Age. It said in a word that there is no authorization from outside. Behold! there is nothing there. What we must do must come from ourselves. The king at Eynan can stop staring at Mount Hermon; the dead king can die at last. We, we fragile human species at the end of the second millennium A.D., we must become our own authorization. And here at the end of the second millennium and about to enter the third, we are surrounded with this problem. It is one that the new millennium will be working out, perhaps slowly, perhaps swiftly, perhaps even with some further changes in our mentality."

— *The Origin Of Consciousness*
Julian Jaynes, Princeton University

3000 Years Later, Mankind Will Undergo One More Evolution

I turned off the lights in my home office. My day was over, but I went to bed with thoughts pounding in my head and adrenaline flowing through my veins. I was discovering the next evolution of man I called **God-Man.** Sometime in the 21st century, God-Man would rise throughout civilizations on Earth. "Isn't God-Man the perfect specimen?" I asked rhetorically in the dark while lying in bed. "He's our final evolution. What beauty and power he possesses. Ordinary people will become millionaires...some will become billionaires. They'll experience superior love and spectacular sex. Their intelligence will soar so high they'll be creative geniuses."

While lying in the dark, I pondered how three thousand years ago, man advanced from the bicameral nature-controlled mentality into human consciousness. Soon, I knew we would advance again, from human consciousness to a new *Neothink* mentality. I now knew exactly *what* we would become: *God-Man* — the highest life form on Earth, the final evolution of man. The First Insight after my Twelve Visions showed me exactly what the God-Man would be like.

For seventeen years, I had worked on the God-Man hypothesis. I built the hypothesis upon the lifetime works of two scientists: 1) Dr. Julian Jaynes, a renown professor at Princeton University, who solved the missing link in all theories of human evolution with his well accepted discovery of the bicameral man who lived 3000 years ago, and 2) Dr. Frank R. Wallace, a Senior Research Scientist for Du Pont, who advanced and went beyond Jaynes' discovery with his best-selling Neo-Tech Discovery. Wallace's discovery identified a "glitch" in human consciousness, which opened the way for knowing the next evolution of man. In my hypothesis, I demonstrate that this "glitch" of human consciousness blocks our final evolution into God-Man.

My First Insight after my Twelve Visions finally *showed me* the God-Man, and it was a beautiful Insight. My seventeen years of research made it possible to have this Insight. Out of this Insight came turnkey techniques so you can personally "jump" to the much more competitive God-Man. Here lies the secret to gaining what seems to be god-like power as you eliminate the bicameral "glitch" and advance into the new Neothink mentality of God-Man.

To bring this Insight together for you, I am going to take you through some of my seventeen-year development of the God-Man hypothesis. From there, you will be able to see what I saw during my First Insight after my Twelve Visions.

The God-Man hypothesis starts with Jaynes' discovery of the bicameral man who lived 3000 years ago and who made an evolutionary "jump" from an automatic "animal" mentality to our cognitive "human" mentality, solving the missing-link riddle. Here is Dr. Wallace's revelation of Dr. Jaynes' fascinating discovery, over the next fifteen pages.[1]

---

[1]When Dr. Wallace wrote this revelation that reviewed then reached beyond Jaynes' book in 1980, the bicameral man was a new and controversial hypothesis. Today, however, Jaynes' bicameral-man hypothesis is accepted by the scientific establishment as the prevailing position on our ancestry.

Our Amazing Bicameral Past

A person could make an excellent bet by wagering a hundred ounces of gold bullion that Julian Jaynes' book *The Origin of Consciousness in the Breakdown of the Bicameral Mind* will someday rank among the five most important books written during the second millennium. The discovery of the bicameral mind solves the missing-link problem that has defied all previous theories of human evolution.

Dr. Jaynes discovered that until 3000 years ago essentially all human beings were void of consciousness. Consciousness versus unconsciousness is not defined here as awake versus asleep, or aware versus knocked out. Consciousness is defined as modern man's awareness of himself, his subjective thoughts and feelings, his subjective choices and *self-determined* interaction with the world around him versus mere automatic reactions to external stimuli as with all other animals, including man until about 3000 years ago.

Until the first millennium BC, man along with all other primates functioned by mimicked or learned reactions. But, because of his much larger, more complex brain, man was able to develop a coherent language beginning about 8000 B.C. In effect, human beings were super-intelligent but automatically reacting animals who could communicate by talking. That communication enabled human beings to cooperate closely to build societies, even thriving civilizations.

Still, like all other animals, man functioned almost entirely by an automatic guidance system that was void of consciousness. Ten thousand years ago, man's neurological guidance system incorporated his superior phenomenon of speech: man's neurological instructions amazingly took the form of automatic, audio commands in his own mind known today as audio hallucinations. Those audio hallucinations came from neurological instructions triggered in the right hemisphere of the brain and transmitted as "heard" voices of "the gods" in the left hemisphere of the brain (the bicameral or two-chamber mind). Whereas the cat would automatically run from danger, bicameral man would hear a voice in his head from his god saying, "Run, run away!"

Ironically, this advanced guidance system based on speech carried its own death sentence as it allowed civilizations to thrive to such new heights that the complexities went beyond the capacity of an automatic, neurological guidance system designed by nature. About 1000 BC, whole civilizations began collapsing as the "voices" became confused, contradictory, or just plain vanished. Man was forced to invent consciousness or a self-determining (versus automatically reacting) way of using his mind to become his own guide and god to survive in the collapsing bicameral civilizations.

Jaynes eliminated the missing link in the evolution of man by discovering that consciousness or the self-determining way of using the mind was never intended by nature — consciousness was invented by man. (Later you will see close parallels to our upcoming "jump" into the much more competitive God-Man.)

The major components of Jaynes's discovery are:

• All civilizations before 1000 B.C. — such as Assyria, Babylonia, Mesopotamia, pharaonic Egypt — were built, inhabited, and ruled by automatically reacting, unconscious people.

• Ancient writings such as the *Iliad* and the early books of the Old Testament were composed by unconscious minds that automatically recorded and objectively reported both real and imagined events. The transition to subjective and introspective writings of the conscious mind occurred in later works such as the *Odyssey* and the newer books of the Old Testament.

• Ancient people learned to speak, read, write, as well as carry out daily life, work, and the professions all while remaining unconscious throughout their lives. Being unconscious, they never experienced guilt, never practiced deceit, and were not responsible for their actions. They had no way to determine their actions; they were automatically reacting animals. They, like any other animal, had no concept of guilt, deception, evil, justice, philosophy, history, or the future. They could not introspect and had no internal idea of themselves. They had no subjective sense of time or space and had no memories as we know them. They were unconscious and innocent. They were guided by "voices" or strong impressions in their bicameral minds — unconscious minds structured for nature's

automatic survival.
- The development of human consciousness began about 3000 years ago when the automatic bicameral mind began breaking down under the mounting stresses of its inadequacy to find workable solutions in increasingly complex societies. The hallucinated voices became more and more confused, contradictory, and destructive.
- Man was forced to invent and develop consciousness in order to survive as his hallucinating voices no longer provided adequate guidance for survival.
- Today, after 3000 years, most people retain remnants of the bicameral guidance system in the form of mysticism and the desire for external authority.
- Except for schizophrenics, people today no longer hallucinate the voices that guided bicameral man. Yet, most people are at least partly influenced and are sometimes driven by the remnants of the bicameral man as they seek, to varying degrees, automatic guidance from "voices" of others or external "authorities".
- All religions are rooted in the unconscious bicameral mind that is obedient to the "voices" of external "authorities" — obedient to the "voice" of God, gods, rulers, and leaders.
- The discovery that consciousness was never a part of nature's evolutionary scheme (but was invented by man) eliminates the missing-link puzzle in human evolution.
- Essentially all religious and most political ideas survive through those vestiges of the obsolete bicameral mind. The bicameral mind seeks omniscient truth and automatic guidance from external "authorities" such as political or spiritual leaders — or other "authoritarian" sources such as manifested in idols, astrologists, gurus — as well as most lawyers, most psychiatrists and psychologists, certain professors, some doctors, most journalists and TV anchormen.

The idea of civilizations consisting entirely of unconscious, automatic-reacting people and the idea of man bypassing nature to invent his own consciousness initially seems incredible. But as Jaynes documents his evidence in a reasoned and detached manner, the existence of two minds in all human beings becomes increasingly evident: (1) the obsolete, unconscious (bicameral) mind that seeks guidance from external "authorities" for important thoughts and decisions, especially under stressed or difficult conditions; and (2) the newly invented conscious mind that bypasses external "authorities" and provides thoughts and guidance generated from one's own mind. ...Understanding Jaynes' discoveries unlocks the 10,000 year-old secret of controlling the actions of people through their bicameral minds.

What evidence does Jaynes present to support his discoveries? After defining consciousness, he systematically presents his evidence to prove that man was unconscious until 3000 years ago when the bicameral civilizations collapsed and individuals began inventing consciousness in order to survive. Jaynes's proof begins with the definition of consciousness:

Defining and Understanding Consciousness

Julian Jaynes defines both what consciousness is and what it is not. After speculating on its location, he demonstrates that consciousness itself has no physical location, but rather is a particular organization of the mind and a specific way of using the brain. Jaynes then demonstrates that consciousness is only a small part of mental activity and is not necessary for concept formation, learning, thinking, or even reasoning. He illustrates how all those mental functions can be performed automatically and unconsciously. Furthermore, consciousness does not contribute to and often hinders the execution of learned skills such as speaking, listening, writing, reading — as well as skills involving music, art, and athletics. Thus, if major human actions and skills can function automatically and without consciousness, those same actions and skills can be controlled or driven by external influences, "authorities", or "voices" emanating under conditions described later in this review. ...But first an understanding of consciousness is important:

Consciousness requires metaphors (i.e., referring to one thing in order to better understand or describe another thing — such as the head of an army, table, page, household, nail). Consciousness also requires analog models (i.e., thinking of a map of California, for example, in order to visualize the entire, physical state of California). Thinking in metaphors and analog models creates the mind space and mental flexibility needed to bypass those automatic, bicameral processes.

The *bicameral thinking* process functions only in concrete terms and narrow, here-and-now specifics. But the *conscious thinking* process generates an infinite array of subjective perceptions that permit ever broader understanding and better decisions.

Metaphors of "me" and analog models of "I" allow consciousness to function through introspection and self-visualization. In turn, consciousness expands by creating more and more metaphors and analog models. That expanding consciousness allows a person to "see" and understand the relationship between himself and the world with increasing accuracy and clarity. As he becomes more and more aware of himself and his interaction with the world, he gains control of his actions, makes decisions, and discovers self-determination.

Consciousness is a conceptual, metaphor-generated analog world that parallels the actual world. Man, therefore, could not invent consciousness until he developed a language sophisticated enough to produce metaphors and analog models.

The genus Homo began about two million years ago. Rudimentary oral languages developed from 70,000 B.C. to about 8000 B.C. Written languages began about 3000 B.C. and gradually developed into syntactical structures capable of generating metaphors and analog models. Only at that point could man invent and experience consciousness.

Jaynes shows that man's early writings (hieroglyphics, hiertatic, and cuneiform) reflect a mentality totally different from our own. They reflect a nonmetaphoric, unconscious mentality. Jaynes also shows that the *Iliad*, which evolved as a sung poem about 1000 B.C., contains little if any conscious thought. The characters in the Iliad (e.g., Achilles, Agamemnon, Hector, Helen) act unconsciously in initiating all their major actions and decisions through "voices", and all speak in hexameter rhythms (as often do modern-day schizophrenics when hallucinating). Hexameter rhythms are characteristic of the rhythmically automatic functionings of the right-hemisphere brain. Moreover, the *Iliad* is entirely about action...about the acts and consequences of Achilles, always reacting to the world and the gods around him. The *Iliad* never mentions subjective thoughts or the contents of anyone's mind. The language is unconscious — an objective reporting of facts that are concrete bound and void of introspection and abstract thought.

With a conscious mind, man can introspect; he can debate with himself; he can become his own god, voice, and decision maker. But before the invention of consciousness, the mind functioned bicamerally: the right hemisphere (the poetic, god-brain) hallucinated audio instructions to the left hemisphere (the analytical, man-brain), especially in unusual or stressful situations. Essentially, man's brain today is physically identical to the ancient bicameral brain; but with his invention of consciousness, he can now choose to integrate the functions of the left and right hemispheres and be his own authority.

Beginning about 9000 B.C. — as oral languages developed — routine or habitual tasks became increasingly standardized. The hallucinating voices for performing those basic tasks, therefore, became increasingly similar among groups of people. The collectivization of "voices" allowed more and more people to cooperate and function together through their bicameral minds. The leaders spoke to the "gods" and used the "voices" to lead the masses in cooperative unison. And that cooperation allowed nomadic hunting tribes to gradually organize into stationary, food-producing societies. The continuing development of oral language and the increasing collectivization of bicameral minds allowed towns and eventually cities to form and flourish.

The bicameral mind, however, became increasingly inadequate for guiding human actions as societies continued to grow in size and complexity. By about 1000 B.C., the bicameral mind had become so inadequate that man's social structures began collapsing. Under threat of extinction, man invented a new way of using his brain that allowed him to solve the much more complex problems needed to survive — he invented a new organization of the mind called consciousness.

With consciousness, man now became his own executor, his own god, and now controlled his actions and became aware of his past and future. With consciousness, man became aware of himself, his life, his feelings. A whole new world opened up to him as his life now had meaning and value...and direction. He could now establish goals and feel the unique ecstasy of self-determination and accomplishment. Man, in essence, went from an automatically reacting animal to a fully conscious human being, just as we are today. The thrill for life — a dynamic conscious life — had to be spectacular to those pioneers who overcame their fears and embraced the new world that opened up to them. ...Similarly today, we are at the threshold of embracing, again, a spectacular new world as we discover the Neothink mentality. But first...

The Development of Consciousness

Dr. Jaynes shows through abundant archaeological, historical, and biological evidence that the towns, cities, and societies from 9000 B.C. to 1000 B.C. were established and developed by unconscious people. Those societies formed and grew through common hallucinating voices attributed to gods, rulers, and the dead — to external "authorities". Various external symbols that "spoke" (such as graves, idols, and statues) helped to reinforce and expand the authority of those common "voices". And those "voices" continued to expand their reach through increasingly visible and awe-inspiring symbols such as tombs, temples, colossi, and pyramids.

But as those unconscious societies became more complex and increasingly intermingled through trade and wars, the "voices" became mixed and contradictory. With the "voices" becoming muddled, their effectiveness in guiding people diminished. Rituals and importunings became ever more intense and elaborate in attempts to evoke clearer "voices" and better guidance. The development of writing and the permanent recording of instructions and laws during the second millennium B.C. further weakened the authority and effectiveness of hallucinated voices. As the "voices" lost their effectiveness, they began falling silent. And without authoritarian "voices" to guide and control its people, those societies suddenly began collapsing with no external cause.

As the bicameral mind broke down and societies collapsed, individuals one by one began inventing consciousness to make decisions needed to survive in the mounting anarchy and chaos. During the chaotic cataclysms of the collapsing civilizations, during which entire populations were wiped out, the bicameral man would, for example, automatically fight a band of men plundering his home and raping his spouse — his automatic reaction to external stimuli — even though his gallant fight would mean certain death for him and his family. The newly conscious man, however, might smile passively on the outside — while planning his revenge in his mind — and later that night visit the bedsides of his sleeping enemies to end their lives and save his own. The conscious man, who could separate himself from the objective world to subjectively determine his actions, greatly increased his advantages for survival over the bicameral man.

On making conscious and volitional decisions, man for the first time became responsible for his actions. Also, for short-range advantages and easy power, conscious man began discovering and using deceit and treachery — behaviors not possible from unconscious, bicameral minds. (Before inventing consciousness, man was as guiltless and amoral as any other animal since he had no volitional choice in following his automatic guidance system of hallucinated voices.)

As the "voices" fell silent, man began contriving religions and prayers in his attempts to communicate with the departed gods. Jaynes shows how man developed the concept of worship, heaven, angels, demons, exorcism, sacrifice, divination, omens, sortilege, augury in his attempts to evoke guidance from the gods — from external "authorities".

All such quests for external "authority" hark back to the breakdown of the hallucinating bicameral mind — to the silencing and celestialization of the once "vocal" and earthly gods.

Much direct evidence for the breakdown of the bicameral mind and the development of consciousness comes from writings scribed between 1300 B.C. and 300 B.C. Those writings gradually shift from unconscious, objective reports to conscious, subjective expressions that reflect introspection. The jump from the unconscious writing of the *Iliad* to the conscious writing of the *Odyssey* (composed perhaps a century later) is dramatically obvious. That radical difference between the *Iliad* and the *Odyssey* is, incidentally, further evidence that more than one poet composed the Homeric epics.

The transition from the unconscious *Iliad* to the conscious *Odyssey* marks man's break with his 8000-year-old hallucinatory guidance system. By the sixth century B.C., written languages began reflecting conscious ideas of morality and justice similar to those reflected today.

The Old Testament of the Bible also illustrates the transition from the unconscious writing of its earlier books (such as Amos, circa 750 B.C.) to the fully conscious writing of its later books (such as Ecclesiastes, circa 350 B.C.). Amid that transition, the book of Samuel records the first known suicide — an act that requires consciousness. And the book of Deuteronomy illustrates the conflict between the bicameral mind and the conscious mind.

Likewise, the transition to consciousness is observed in other parts of the world: Chinese literature moved from bicameral unconsciousness to subjective consciousness about 500 B.C. with the writings of Confucius. And in India, literature shifted to subjective consciousness around 400 B.C. with the Upanishadic writings.

American Indians, however, never developed the sophisticated, metaphorical languages needed to develop full consciousness. As a result, their mentalities were probably bicameral when they first encountered the European explorers. For example, with little or no conscious resistance, the Incas allowed the Spanish "white gods" to dominate, plunder, and slaughter them.

The Bicameral Mind in Today's World

Dr. Jaynes identifies many vestiges of the bicameral mentality that exist today. The most obvious vestige is religion and its symbols. Ironically, early Christianity with its teachings of Jesus was an attempt to shift religion from the outmoded bicameral and celestial mind of Moses to the newly conscious and earthly mind of man. Christianity then discovered a devastatingly effective tool for authoritarian control — guilt. Indeed, guilt not only worked on conscious minds, but required conscious minds to be effective.

Despite religion, conscious minds caused the gradual shifts from governments of gods to governments of men and from divine laws to secular laws. Still, the vestiges of the bicameral mind combined with man's longing for guidance produced churches, prophets, oracles, sibyls, diviners, cults, mediums, astrologers, saints, idols, demons, tarot cards, seances, Ouija boards, glossolalia, fuhrers, ayatollahs, popes, peyote, Jonestown, born-agains.

Jaynes shows how such external "authorities" exist only through the remnants of the bicameral mind. Moreover, he reveals a four-step paradigm that can reshuffle susceptible minds back into hallucinating, bicameral mentalities. The ancient Greeks used a similar paradigm to reorganize or reprogram the minds of uneducated peasant girls into totally bicameral mentalities so they could become oracles and give advice through hallucinated voices — voices that would rule the world (e.g., the oracle at Delphi). ...Today, people who deteriorate into schizophrenic psychoses follow similar paradigms.

A common thread united most oracles, sibyls, prophets, and demon-possessed people: Almost all were illiterate, all believed in spirits, and all could readily retrieve the bicameral mind. Today, however, retrieval of the bicameral mind is schizophrenic insanity. Also, today, as throughout history, a symptomatic cure for "demon-possessed" people involves exorcising rituals that let a more powerful "authority" or god replace the "authority" of the demon. The New Testament, for example, shows that Jesus and his disciples became effective exorcists by substituting one "authority" (their god) for another "authority" (another god or demon).

As the voices of the oracles became confused and nonsensical, their popularity waned. In their places, idolatry revived and then flourished. But as Christianity became a popular source of external "authority", Christian zealots began physically destroying all competing idols. They then built their own idols and symbols to reinforce the external "authority" of Christianity.

Among today's vestiges of the bicameral mentality is the born-again movement that seeks external guidance. Such vestiges dramatize man's resistance to use his own invention of consciousness to guide his life.

The chanting cadence of poetry and the rhythmic beat of music are also rooted in the bicameral mentality. In ancient writings, the hallucinated voices of the gods were always in poetic verse, usually in dactylic hexameter and sometimes in rhyme or alliteration — all characteristic of right-brain functionings. The oracles and prophets also spoke in verse. And today schizophrenics often speak in verse when they hallucinate.

Poetry and chants can have authoritarian or commanding beats and rhythms that can effectively block consciousness. Poetry is the language of the gods — it is the language of the artistic, right-hemispheric brain. Plato recognized poetry as a divine madness.

Most poetry and songs have an abruptly changing or a discontinuous pitch. Normal speech, on the other hand, has a smoothly changing pitch. Jaynes demonstrates that reciting poetry, singing, and playing music are right-brain functions, while speaking is a left-brain function. That is why people with speech impediments can often sing, chant, or recite poetry with flawless clarity. Conversely, almost anyone trying to sing a conversation will find his words quickly deteriorating into a mass of inarticulate cliches.

Likewise, listening to music and poetry is a right-brain function. And music, poetry, or chants that project authority with loud or rhythmic beats can suppress left-brain functions to temporarily relieve anxiety or a painfully troubled consciousness.

Jaynes goes on to show phenomena such as hypnosis, acupuncture, and déjà vu also function through vestiges of the bicameral mind. And he demonstrates how hypnosis steadily narrows the sense of self, time, space, and introspection as consciousness shrinks and the mind reverts to a bicameral type organization. Analogously, bicameral and schizophrenic minds have little or no sense of self, time, space or introspection. The hypnotized mind is urged to obey the voice of the hypnotist; the bicameral mind is compelled to obey the "voices" of "authority" or gods. By sensing oneself functioning in the narrow-scope, unaware state of hypnosis, gives one an idea of functioning in the narrow-scope, unaware state of bicameral man.

Jaynes also identifies how modern quests for external "authority" are linked to the bicameral mind. Many such quests use science to seek authority in the laws of nature. In fact, today, science is surpassing the waning institutional religions as a major source of external "authority". And rising from the vestiges of the bicameral mind are an array of scientisms (pseudoscientific doctrines, faiths, and cults) that select various natural or scientific facts to subvert into apocryphal, authoritarian doctrines. That subversion is accomplished by using facts out of context to fit promulgated beliefs. Such mystical scientisms include astrology, ESP, Scientology, Christian Science and other "science" churches, I Ching, behaviorism, sensitivity training, mind control, meditation, hypnotism, cryonics, as well as various nutritional, health, and medical fads.

Today the major worldwide sources of external "authority" are the philosophical doctrines of religion (plus the other forms of mysticism and "metaphysics") combined with political doctrines such as Fascism, Marxism, and Maoism. All such doctrines demand the surrender of the individual's ego (sense of self or "I") to a collective, obedient faith toward the "authority" of those doctrines. In return, those doctrines offer automatic answers and life-time guidance from which faithful followers can survive without the responsibility or effort of using their own consciousnesses. Thus, all political systems represent a regression into mysticism — from conscious man back to bicameral man.

Despite their constant harm to everyone, most modern-day external "authorities" (i.e., neocheaters, explained later) thrive by using the following two-step neocheating technique to repress consciousness and activate the bicameral mind in their victims.

1. First man is made to feel guilty. He is condemned for having lost his "innocence" by inventing consciousness. He is condemned for assuming the responsibility to use his own mind to guide his life. He is condemned for exchanging his automatic, bicameral life for a volitional, conscious life...condemned for exchanging his nature-given bicameral mind for a superior, man-invented conscious mind.

2. Then man is offered automatic solutions to problems and guidance through life into an "effortless" Garden of Eden or a utopian hereafter if he exchanges his own invented consciousness for faith in external "authority" — bicameral faith in some leader, doctrine, or god. He is offered the "reward" of escaping the self-responsibility to make one's own decisions and to guide one's own life. But for that "reward", he must renounce his own mind

to follow someone else's mind or wishes disguised as the "truth" promulgated by some external "authority" or higher power.

But in reality, no valid external "authority" or higher power can exist or ever has existed. Valid authority evolves only from one's own independent, conscious mode of thinking. When that fact is fully realized, man will emerge completely from his bicameral past and move into a future that accepts individual consciousness as the only authority. ...Man will then fully evolve into a prosperous, happy individual who has assumed full responsibility for his own thinking and life.

Still, the resistance to self-responsibility is formidable. The bicameral mentality grips those seeking "authorities" for guidance. Those who accept external "authority" allow government officials, religious leaders, faith, homilies, cliches, one-liners, slogans, the familiar, habits, and feelings to guide their actions. Throughout history, billions of people unnecessarily submit through their bicameral tendencies to the illusionary, external "authorities" of government and religion. And that submission is always done at a net loss to everyone's well being and happiness.

Despite the great advantages in using the man-invented conscious mode of thinking, most people today depend to various degrees on their automatic bicameral mentality and external "authorities" to make their decisions for them. Most people search for "sure-thing" guidance from "higher authorities", rather than using their own consciousness for making decisions and determining their actions. In their search for automatic guidance, they seek automatic answers from religion, politics, idols, leaders, gurus, cults, astrology, fads, drugs, feelings, even psychiatrists. Most people's bicameral tendencies seek outside sources that will tell them how to think and act. *Neocheaters* (as explained soon) exploit the automatic bicameral minds in the masses by setting themselves up as "authorities" for influencing or controlling that bicameral mentality seeking external guidance. Bicameral mentalities avoid human self-responsibility by seeking and obeying external decision makers.

Neo-Tech (as explained soon in its full meaning) signals the end of the 10,000-year reign of authoritarian institutions. Neo-Tech also marks the beginning of a new era of individual consciousness during which people will increasingly act on the authority of their own brains. That movement toward self-responsibility will increasingly weaken the influences of external or mystical "authorities" such as government and religion. But more important, Neo-Tech opens the door today to an entirely new and much more powerful way of using the mind called *Neothink,* with which all human life can evolve into abiding prosperity and happiness.

To some, the implications of Neo-Tech will be frightening, even terrifying. To others, the implications will be electrifying and liberating, perhaps similar to what the early pioneers into consciousness felt. ...The implications of Neo-Tech are that each individual is solely responsible for his or her own life — responsible for making the effort required to guide one's own life through one's own consciousness. No automatic, effortless route to knowledge or guidance exists.

No valid external "authority" exists that one can automatically live by. To live effectively, an individual must let only the authority of his own consciousness guide his activities. All consistently competent people have learned to act on reality — not on their feelings or someone else's feelings or doctrines. An individual must accept the responsibility to guide his own life. He must constantly exert the effort needed to identify reality through his own consciousness in order to live competently and happily.

People knowledgeable about Neo-Tech have the tools to outcompete all others who act on their bicameral tendencies. Equally important, people knowledgeable about Neo-Tech have the tools to control their own lives and destinies, free from crippling mysticism and harmful neocheating.

Now you can identify the bicameral elements of any statement or action by anyone or any group, for example, church, government, media, politician, priest, businessman, doctor, friend, parent, spouse, self. Armed with Neo-Tech, you can free yourself from the control or influence of mysticism and external "authority". Sometime in the 21st century, Neo-Tech and Neothink will have eliminated all vestiges of the bicameral mentality — all external "authorities" ruling over us.

Without the bicameral mentality, external "authorities" will wither and vanish, for they have no validity except that which is granted to them by our bicameral mentalities. With political and religious influences disappearing, the mechanisms for "authorities" to harm individuals and wage wars will also disappear. Thus, if civilization is prospering well-into the 21st century, Jaynes's discovery along with the discoveries of Neo-Tech and Neothink will have contributed to that prosperity by ending the symbiotic, mystical relationships of bicameral mentalities with authoritarian societies, which now hold nuclear weapons. Such mystical relationships would sooner or later cause the annihilation of any civilization.

If our civilization is flourishing well into the 21st century, rational human consciousness will have eliminated the bicameral glitch and its external "authorities" through Neo-Tech. And without external "authorities", governments and their wars will be impossible. Best of all, without external "authorities", no one will be forcibly controlled, impeded, or drained by others. There will be no ruling class. Then, the people will discover their true power and finally unleash their human potential.

That completes Dr. Wallace's expansion of Dr. Jaynes' discovery of the bicameral man. Now, I will reveal our future based on the God-Man hypothesis. I built this hypothesis upon Dr. Wallace's Neo-Tech Discovery and weaved some passages from the Neo-Tech Discovery in and out of pages 325-345.

Our Amazing Neothink Future

Julian Jaynes showed us that 3000 years ago, human nature was split in two, an executive part called a god, and a follower part called a man. All along, the gods were really in man's own mind. When bicameral man made the jump into consciousness, he unknowingly and with undoubtedly much trepidation and uncertainty, became one with God. (My Second Insight showed me that the teachings of Jesus actually attempted to show the bicameral peasants how to become conscious).

Now, as bicameral man made the leap into human consciousness, the imagined gods were replaced with man's own authority and decision making. As demonstrated by the extraordinary Greek philosophers and scientists just a few hundred years after the cataclysmic collapse of the bicameral civilizations, man was by now aggressively evolving toward his destiny of God-Man. Man was discovering the immense power of his own mind as its own authority, thinker, decision maker; he was evolving toward the powerful Neothink mentality, which is consciousness in its pure state...not diseased with mutations of the bicameral mentality, explained throughout the remaining First Insight.

But, before humanity could secure the pure state of consciousness (the Neothink mentality) and complete its final evolution into God-Man, master neocheaters (as explained soon) used the ultimate divide-and-rule ploy that took away man's immense power of his own mind as its own authority and reversed humanity. Breaking away man's executive part or his own authority tragically began with the writings of Greek philosopher Plato and culminated in Christianity during the Dark Ages. The Church divided God-Man into God (the executive) in Heaven and man (the follower) on Earth.[1] Then, the master neocheaters proceeded to rule man "in the name of God" for a self-serving millennium. Of course, the power of man was lost for a thousand years to the Dark Ages, and actually for 2400 years when we include from the Greek philosopher Plato until now. In short, the neocheaters caused the fading bicameral mentality to mutate and infect the new conscious mentality. That debilitating infection of the conscious mind stopped our natural evolution into God-Man 2400 years ago. Moreover, that infection of the conscious mind or that "glitch" of human consciousness has blocked our evolution into the much more prosperous God-Man ever since.

Today's political structures are also mutations of the bicameral mentality and a continuation of neocheaters ruling over man. But that will soon change. Twenty-four-hundred years after the Greeks nearly evolved into God-Man, we will finally resume and complete our final evolution. God and Man will unite as one with our coming evolution into God-Man. The immense power of man's mind as its own authority and ruler will be launched;

---

[1]The Second Insight takes the reader through the leap into human consciousness and demonstrates the Plato/St. Augustine reversal that blocked our second leap into the God-Man mentality, until now.

the real gods will emerge — as you and I. God-Man will *appear* like gods with higher consciousness to those not yet evolved. Our god-like power will be acquired through consciousness in its pure state, called the Neothink mentality.

Neothink

Neothink is a new way of using the mind. It is the mind of tomorrow. Neothink comes from Neo-Tech. Neo-Tech removes mutated, bicameral mentalities infecting today's conscious mind through exerting hard-thought honesty to understand reality. The presence of the obsolete bicameral mind makes the conscious mind impotent as it waits in a passive stupor for external guidance to tell it what to do and how to act.

As Neo-Tech breaks apart and removes more and more bicameral programming, passed down like a computer virus for 2400 years, the conscious mind becomes very potent as it no longer waits to be guided. Instead, on its own, it integrates knowledge more and more widely, building bigger and bigger mental puzzles that reveal never-before-seen puzzle pictures, bringing it escalating power not known to the ordinary mind today. As the mind breaks free of grooved-in bicameral behavioral patterns, through Neo-Tech, the mind releases a whole new potential of unlimited wide integrations or unlimited power. That brand-new way of using the mind, activating its limitless capacity, is called Neothink. Through the process of using Neo-Tech to release Neothink, the limitless capacity of the human mind comes to ordinary people, one by one. Ordinary people can then make explosive advancements of human knowledge, on a regular basis. They will transform into wealthy geniuses.

When the ordinary person's mind switches over to Neothink, then as you will see, he becomes God-Man.

God-Man

What exactly is God-Man? To get an idea, let us look at a few early pioneers using Neothink:

Four and a half centuries ago, when scientists looked into the night sky, they would say they saw the stars moving across the sky, circling our Earth, which they said was at the center of the Universe. One person, however, broke from that church-approved, literal above/below Heaven-and-Hell traditional view and said he saw everything in orbital motion, *including* Earth. He said the Sun was at the center of the Universe, not Earth. That person made a revolutionary advancement of scientific knowledge that restarted the engines of new scientific knowledge after a 1400-year silence. His discovery pulled the world out of the ruinous remains of the Dark Ages, fueled the Renaissance, and led to Newton and the Age of Reason. That scientist had broken through to the next level with Neothink. His name was Nicolaus Copernicus.

Ninety years ago, car companies manufactured and sold a few thousand cars, at most, per year. Suddenly, one car company manufactured and sold thirty-two thousand cars in a single year, sixty-nine thousand cars the year after, and one-hundred-and-seventy thousand cars the year after that! Ten years later, that car company was manufacturing and selling over a million cars per year. That one car company took manufacturing and marketing of cars from a few thousand a year to over a million. The owner, who never completed high school, made a revolutionary advancement of industrial knowledge that started the engines of mass production and made America the economic giant of the world for generations to come. He had broken through to the next level with Neothink. His name was Henry Ford.

Today, Bill Gates, Andy Grove, and several people throughout the computer industry are making revolutionary advancements of knowledge that have brought us the information/communication revolution and brought us to the edge of a great Technological Revolution. Those geniuses have broken through to the next level with Neothink, which is why computer buying power has multiplied 1000 times in a few years. Today, Neothink not only makes its beholder rich, but radically increases the buying power of his beneficiaries — the consumers.

The person who jumps wholly into the Neothink mentality becomes God-Man. Through Neothink, God-Man has the ability to see to the next level, beyond what exists today. The human mind today works in a sort of following mode — following leaders, idols, politicians, clergymen, automatic feelings, upper management, a routine. Deeply embedded in our psyches is the mental structure of following, a remnant of the bicameral mind. Tomorrow our psyches will be structured to prolifically integrate knowledge and build mental puzzles, not stagnantly follow in routine ruts as it does today. Our stagnant, following mentality today is precisely why beneficial changes for mankind that break from tradition take generations to occur.

God-Man does not follow. He or she looks around for more and more information to snap together (i.e., to integrate) into growing puzzles that reveal never-before-seen puzzle pictures such as Copernicus's heliocentric cosmos, Ford's assembly line, and the computer's super-rapid progress (no waiting for generations for change there). Using an advanced Neothink mentality, God-Man routinely makes major breakthroughs. Mankind experiences rapidly rising standards of living.

Whereas consciousness is achieved through generating metaphors and analog models, Neothink is achieved through building mental puzzles that take human knowledge to the next level. Without Neothink, major discoveries never occur. With Neothink, major discoveries routinely occur.

After 10,000 years of a deep-rooted following mode, man's mind is changing. We can see the signs of change all around us today, from the continuous quantum leaps in the computer/ information industry to people's growing damnation of the politician in particular. People are getting close to making the switch — from today's following mind to tomorrow's integrating mind. God-Man is his own authority no longer looking toward external "authorities" to follow. He is the "higher consciousness" people have always searched for.

When our final evolution into God-Man happens, major advancements will come to us in all fields of knowledge, as has been the case in the computer/information world. Soon *you personally* could change the world. ...Perhaps you once, years ago, thought you could someday change the world. Now, today, with Neothink, you can change the world. Tomorrow, everyone can. And what a world that will be! As you know, certain people have been able to break through to something never seen or done before. When they did, they forever changed the world for the better as did Copernicus, Ford, and Gates...forerunners to God-Man. Of course, nowadays, the part-time Neothink users such as Gates make millions or billions. And, this phenomenon is happening more and more frequently in this generation, with the computer and electronic industries, than any generation before.

Those increasing numbers of persons rising with lucrative, creative breakthroughs that change the world are the forerunners to an evolutionary change soon to happen throughout the human race called *God-Man*. The resulting world, once the evolution into God-Man begins when everyone can change the world for the better, is called the *Neo-Tech World*. The creativity pouring into tomorrow's Neo-Tech World will rapidly raise the average standard of living toward that of millionaires. In fact, we have seen a microcosm of that millionaire buying power happening already in the computer world where more and more forerunners to God-Man are pouring their creativity as buying power multiplies a thousand times over. Indeed, God-Man makes himself rich and the world around him rich with breathtaking new values.

Soon, we will enter that new world. Consumers will have the buying power of millionaires. This switch into God-Man is going to bring beautiful Gifts to mankind. But you can still "sneak in" ahead of the others by removing your bicameral programming through exerting Neo-Tech in your life, which I will get into next.

So, let us begin the process to go from a following mind to an integrating mind. Let us begin our final evolution into God-Man, sometimes called the Neothink Man. Let us start by understanding what limits the mind today. Jaynes determined that *stress* is the common denominator that triggers the voices today in schizophrenics and before in bicameral man. Jaynes also determined through biological studies that *decision making* is the most prominent cause of stress. Therefore, important decision making in bicameral man (e.g., to fight or flee) triggered the voices for answers. Similarly today, people look toward external "authorities" for answers to avoid making their own important decisions. Avoiding decision making today by seeking external guidance or "authority" weakens one's competence and is called *mysticism*. Mysticism first appeared in Neanderthal man 50,000 years ago — perhaps as early as 200,000 years ago when Neanderthal civilizations formed — as he mentally grappled with the deaths and burials in his clan.[1] Later, mysticism dominated bicameral man's search for answers, and mysticism has dominated man's search for answers ever since. But that will soon change.

Mysticism

Mysticism here is defined as the bicameral mentality infecting today's conscious mind...or, more precisely, mutations of the bicameral mentality infecting today's conscious mentality like a stubborn, resistant disease. Mysticism, or the bicameral mentality, searches for answers from external nonreality, whether that be imagined gods or illusion-creating politicians. The conscious mind, by contrast, integrates reality.

The course of this disease called mysticism is one of increasing attempts to avoid decision making, avoid integrating reality, instead seeking external or automatic guidance. The symptom of mysticism is jumbled or nonintegrated thinking — acting on automatic feelings or on the external guidance of eager neocheaters rather than the logic of reality in front of you...leading to mind-created "realities", which are actually illusions crafted by neocheaters or delusions crafted by your own mind. The mind is a reality integrating organ, not a reality creating device. Using the mind to create "reality" (to serve a feeling or external "authority") rather than to identify and integrate reality (the job of the conscious mind) is a disease — an epistemological disease that progressively undermines one's capacity to think, to identify reality, to live competently. Using the mind to create "reality" is nonreality or mysticism, which all began during the Bicameral Age.

Mysticism is also a collective disease that affects everyone who looks toward others, or the group, or the leaders for solutions to his or her own problems and responsibilities.

Mysticism infects our minds early in life, spread to us from

---

[1]*Transformations of Myth Through Time*, Joseph Campbell.

our parents, educators, and the adult world around us. Mysticism easily infects our conscious minds at a young age because the adult world is 100% infected. Since the breakdown of the bicameral mind 3000 years ago, the bicameral mentality has mutated in a myriad of ways to infect our conscious mentality...no longer following imagined gods but following a number of other authorities including political and religious leaders, morality or activist leaders, media and entertainment personalities, cults and clubs, lawyers and pips, the Establishment and the status quo, a routine, even automatic impulses and impressions.

Mysticism is a disease of the mind that blocks integrated thinking and brings stupidities through mind-created "realities". Instead of integrating reality, the mysticism-plagued mind waits for external guidance from external "authorities". Thus, mysticism is also the door through which neocheaters enter our lives.

Then, they further manipulate our mysticism to increasingly assume external "authority" over us and to justify or rationalize the use of force, fraud, or dishonesty to usurp values from us, the producers. In the end, the neocheaters control our lives and rule over us. For example, politicians and the media generate mind-created "realities" used to create false standards and guilt designed to beguile us into surrendering our earned values, power, and happiness to increased taxes and regulations.

Again, mysticism easily infects our conscious minds because of the unbroken links still chaining us to bicameral man. In other words, mysticism got passed on, generation after generation, spreading from adult minds to children's minds like a computer virus. Children's minds, in a sense, become programmed with mysticism. The chain that kept us subservient to external "authorities" never broke.

Neocheating

Neocheating is any intentional use of mysticism designed to create mind "realities" or false illusions — in other words, activate the following-mode bicameral mentality in others — in order to extract values from others. Neocheating is the technique for expropriating unearned money or power by manipulating bicameral tendencies or mysticism in others. Neocheating is the means by which nearly all politicians, clergymen, union leaders, many journalists, many academics, and many lawyers usurp power and values from the innocent producer. They are professional neocheaters, and they control your life. Today, people are easily controlled and exploited because their deep-rooted, deeply programmed mysticism seeks automatic answers or guidance from external "authorities" telling them what to do and how to live their lives.

Neocheating means *new cheating* for usurping values earned by others. Actually, neocheaters have used neocheating for over 2000 years in hidden, unnoticeable ways. But the techniques of neocheating were not specifically identified until now. Thus, neocheating is a *new identification* rather than a *new technique*. Before that identification, no one could define or even notice a neocheater. Now, anyone with Neo-Tech can easily spot neocheaters and render them impotent. For, against Neo-Tech, the illusions of mysticism vanish and neocheaters become powerless.

Neo-Tech

Neo-Tech in its full meaning is a noun or adjective meaning fully integrated thinking (the opposite of a following mode), which requires fully integrated honesty. For, one must be fully honest with himself to take the challenging road of integrating reality, not seeking automatic or external guidance that creates "reality". That path of least resistance to avoid decision making will easily creep into the human psyche if one gets a little lazy and does not actively integrate reality.

Neo-Tech is an exercise of the mind that deprograms mysticism and removes illusionary, mind-created "realities" caused by the bicameral mentality. Neo-Tech is an *ongoing process* that puts an end to one's bicameral behavioral patterns and clears the path to expanding power, money, and romantic love.

Neo-Tech — that continual process of honestly integrating reality to make your own rational decisions — lets you know exactly what is happening and what to do for gaining honest advantages in all situations.[1] That knowledge is needed to be competent — to guiltlessly and honestly obtain the wealth and happiness available to everyone but achieved by so few. Neo-Tech provides the power to profit in every situation by nullifying neocheating and mysticism not only in others but within one's own self. Only Neo-Tech can deprogram mysticism in one's mind to finally, after 3000 years, break the chain of bicameral subservience. Indeed, exerting fully integrated honesty or Neo-Tech removes mysticism in your psyche, which closes the door on all false authorities, neocheaters, and their infinite array of deceptions. Neo-Tech lets a person gather all power unto his or her own self while rendering neocheaters impotent.

Neo-Tech, or fully integrated honesty, is a rare human state of mind that leads to the Neothink mentality and to the God-Man. Neo-Tech is the rare state in which an individual: 1) thinks through and integrates all necessary knowledge to guide oneself without external authorities, *and* 2) processes all those thoughts with honesty, void of mysticism, rationalizations, deep-rooted agendas or desperate whims. Neo-Tech is a difficult state to achieve and even more difficult to sustain. Growing up in an anticivilization, too many deep pockets of mysticism make up the human psyche to sustain that intellectually challenging state of Neo-Tech. So, the questions return: How, exactly, do you deprogram your mind of mysticism? It's been passed down for more than a hundred generations. What could possibly break the chain?

The secret here is to get Neo-Tech past your intellect...into your emotions. Then that difficult human condition of Neo-Tech or fully integrated honesty becomes natural and not difficult at all.

Imagine if, from the bottom of your heart, you do something out of pure love for someone else, say for your child. Think back to when your child (assuming you have a child) was a vulnerable, little one-year-old. If acting out of pure love for your beloved child, you would also be acting with fully integrated honesty.

[1]*The Neo-Tech Discovery* is a collection of "new techniques" or "new technology", 114 powerful, overarching life-enhancing advantages derived from fully integrated honesty, written by Dr. Frank R. Wallace.

When the mind is saturated with pure love, all actions taken in such a mental state can only be fully honest Neo-Tech. Love is the only force in the Universe powerful enough to break the chain — to end the virus of mysticism.

What is pure love? For now, just keep imagining the love you felt for your child when he or she was little. Not only would you act solely to the best interest of your child, with honesty that overrode deep dishonesties or deeply hidden agendas, but you would also *think through* situations instead of just following authorities. Your pure love and protective passions would lift you above typical bicameral-like responses to act for the well-being and protection of your precious child.

Indeed, when filled with love, one naturally acts with fully integrated honesty and *does not* follow external authorities — one *thinks* and *integrates reality*, just as he would for his one-year-old child.

Your state of mind with your one-year-old child is that rare state of Neo-Tech. Now, what if you could feel that same pure love and protective passions for important values everywhere you turn? Let us look more closely at pure love:

Only one kind of love exists, which is pure love. So, why call it "pure" love instead of just "love"? I do that because of something that seems like love but fools people, something like fools gold is to gold, something I call *fools love*.

I also call that fools love: perverted love because what seems like love devastates people's lives. We have in this anticivilization pure love and perverted "love". In the Civilization of the Universe (those civilizations throughout the Universe that survived their Nuclear Decision Thresholds, described soon), fools love or perverted love does not exist.

Pure love — think of your one-year-old child — brings with it, as an integral part, something I call protective passions for that value you love. Now, let's define pure love: Pure love is love and protective passions for life (with priority always on conscious beings) and that which benefits life. Pure love — the love for life and that which benefits life — breaks out into three categories:

<u>Pure Love and Protective Passions for...</u>
1) Self and loved ones

2) Value creators and producers

3) Value creation and production — you do not know it yet, but you will feel love and protection for innocent businesses as you do now for innocent toddlers.

Fools love or perverted love, on the other hand, is caused through illusions that seem like, even feel like, love. But that so-called "love" (often unsuspectingly to the innocent person) is for that which hurts life (especially hurts humans) and hurts that which benefits life. Fools love comes by way of illusions, mysticisms, dishonesties, and rationalizations often created and spread by neocheaters. Perverted love — the "love" for that which hurts life and hurts that which benefits life also breaks out into three categories:

Perverted Love and Protective Passions for...

1) Something that hurts self or loved ones

2) Value destroyers

3) Value destruction — you do not know it yet, but (out of protective passions for self, loved ones, value creators and value creation in tomorrow's Neo-Tech World), you will feel toward politicians and regulatory bureaucrats as you do now toward child molesters.

Perverted "love" or fools love will vanish as you read through *The First Immortals* (my novel), which gets pure love into your emotions and breaks the spell of the age-old illusions of fools love.

Remember, Neo-Tech is a twofold process: 1) think on own, and 2) think honestly. Raised in today's anticivilization, the ongoing processes of Neo-Tech are difficult to maintain. And, to jump to the Neothink mentality, a person must sustain Neo-Tech long enough to build the puzzle pieces and to snap together the puzzle picture. And to jump to the God-Man, a person must become free of mysticism by permanently sustaining the mental state of Neo-Tech.

When you understand the adult's trap in the anticivilization and its forces of nature (Vision Three), you realize how nearly impossible it is, if not impossible, to achieve and sustain the human condition of Neo-Tech. So, it is basically impossible to escape the anticivilization and become the God-Man through sheer determination alone.

A missing ingredient is needed — the ingredient of *love*. Why can love (i.e., pure love) save you from the anticivilization and lift you to the God-Man whereas sheer determination and discipline cannot? The reason goes back to the forces of nature described in Vision Three. The forces of nature keep us trapped in the anticivilization. Those forces of nature, remember, come from survival pressures in a system of nature. But man advanced beyond the system of nature 3000 years ago when he leapt from the bicameral man to human consciousness. Yet, because of a mutation of the bicameral mind — a mind disease called mysticism — man remained trapped in the forces of nature designed by nature. And those survival pressures that cause the forces of nature affect us at our roots, deeper than any intellect, discipline, or determination can dig up.

But, pure love can get down to that survival level and dig up and permanently throw out those destructive forces of nature. Let me give you an example involving our fundamental biological nature:

The protective passions of pure love take you right down to survival pressures and actually take you to a deeper survival pressure — a priority deeper than all other survival pressures. For example, as you saw in Vision Three, a powerful force of nature is one's drive to mate with someone beautiful (i.e., someone symmetrically superior). But, if that beautiful woman or man tried to hurt your one-year-old child, your protective passions would kick in and drive that beautiful woman or man right out of your life. Indeed, the protective passions of pure love override all other survival pressures, for protecting someone or something you love is *the most powerful* survival pressure. That fact is demonstrated in nature when a mother animal defends her litter with her own life.

That means that through pure love for life and that which benefits life (i.e., yourself, your loved ones, value creators and producers, and institutions of value creation and production such as innocent businesses and private research foundations), you not only can get down to the same survival level at the roots of the destructive forces of nature...but you can go even deeper to dig up and free yourself from those destructive forces.

The reason for that is: whereas the protective passions for someone you love is a fundamental force of nature in a system designed by nature (e.g., the mother of most mammals will fight to the death to protect her young), those protective passions for someone you love are, furthermore, the fundamental force of God-Man in a system *beyond* nature. Indeed, on the evolutionary scale, an animals' emotions, love, and compassion increase the more evolved it is. So, when we went through the man-made evolutionary leap beyond nature 3000 years ago, our ability for love and compassion leapt to a new level. This is what Lao-Tzu, Buddha, and Jesus sensed and exploited with much success. *Love* jumps to yet a whole new level as we enter the realm of the God-Man. The other forces of nature do not; they get forced out by the forces of Neothink (Vision Three).

Pure love and compassion will drive the supersociety, also known as the Civilization of the Universe.

Now, I want to give you some insight to what will eventually happen to *your* emotions as you spread your pure love beyond your one-year-old child to yourself, your loved ones, value producers, value creators, and to institutions of value production and value creation. As I explain in the Second Insight, I can convey this only because, after twenty years of working on the edge of the next man-made evolutionary leap, I have slipped in and out of the Neothink mentality. I can feel things and see things that you cannot yet. As I explain in the Second Insight, next, you will develop faith in God-Man and the Civilization of the Universe as you see evidence of that other, beautiful world, even if you are not yet in it.

So, back to what will eventually happen to your emotions: at the beyond-nature God-Man level, love will go to another level. Pure love, say in the "verb form" (e.g., daddy "pure loves" daughter), will in your heart and soul, at the survival level, be felt as a less-than-or-equal-to sign (e.g., daddy $\leq$ daughter). So, the protective passions will be an intrinsic part of you, like a reflex, something you do not have to stop and think about. For example, if daddy's daughter gets swept away into a stormy sea, daddy's reflexes will jump in after her without a momentary second thought.

Well, that daddy-saves-daughter scenario seems obvious enough. But what will happen is: your pure love will spread to other things that benefit life, including businesses that are innocently producing and creating values for mankind. You will find yourself, at a primary level, vehemently protecting...business! For, as you will discover, passionately loving and protecting life (priority on humans) and all that benefits life (especially businesses) is *the* survival pressure when going to the next world — the system *beyond* nature...the civilization of the God-Man. You will love and protect your world — your loved ones and your businesses of values — from the value destroyers and institutions of value destruction that fill our anticivilization through illusions of "love" — fools love...perverted love.

Indeed, that sole survival pressure of *love* in the next world of man-made human consciousness, Neothink, and the God-Man — that pure love and its protective passions for life and all that benefits life — answers the mysteries of the Universe.

For now, realize that pure love is your way to spring free from the forces that hold you back. Integrate everything you have read thus far, including Vision One about identifying your Friday-Night Essence — the person you were meant to be. Look at business and try to feel this love and protection for its value production and value creation. Everything good including scientific breakthroughs and cures to diseases reach us through business. Look at *yourself* and feel this love and protection for the person you were meant to be. Look at your loved ones and try to feel this love and protection. Even look at someone you do not like, but to get past your repulsion, at first look at him and try to imagine him when he was a little toddler who was vulnerable and sweet and needed love and protection. ...I say to look at your "enemy" this way because, even if you still must protect yourself from him, when looking through compassion — through eyes full of love for life and values — you will see through widest scope accounting. You will override your pressing hate for his negatives — which before was all you could see — and you will pull together every value that "enemy" represents and put that value into your assessment. Speaking from my own experience, when looking through such wide-scope accounting, many times you adjust and sometimes even reverse

333

your assessment and feelings toward your "enemy". At the least, you become more effective at dealing with your "enemy" and in protecting life and values. Moreover, once you can look at your "enemy" through a mental state full of love, then you can look at everyone and everything through eyes of love.

Have you noticed that people who are falling in love tend to see many positive values around them that normally would go unnoticed? That is the phenomenon of *love*. You go through life focussing on values and protecting those values. You go through life a happier person. If you look at your "enemy" through the mental state full of love for life and values (which can be done with some practice), it does not mean that you love your enemy per se, but you can, for the first time, see his values that your hate for his negatives blocked out before, and then you can make a better assessment, even defeat him more soundly if necessary.

How do you go about filling your mind with pure love? First, a change in perspective comes by simply trying it. In the Neo-Tech World, which will someday exist on Earth, and in the Civilization of the Universe that exists throughout the cosmos, everyone is filled with pure love, which is the natural state of God-Man. But we live in the anticivilization full of envy, hate, betrayal, and dishonesty born out of the bicameral mutation of Plato and St. Augustine that kept us trapped in the forces of nature (the Second Insight). Those negative emotions along with dishonesty are not naturally part of the human psyche — they are learned. So, simply changing the perspective of your mind to the *natural* conscious state of pure love becomes increasingly effective and natural. As you more and more feel this pure love for life and values, you will more and more easily experience Neo-Tech, eventually experiencing Neothink and eventually sustaining Neothink as you become the God-Man.

The end result of Neo-Tech — fully integrated honesty — is a civilization overflowing with wealth, romantic love, happiness, and immortality. The result of Neo-Tech — fully integrated thinking — is the depoliticized Neo-Tech World with super rapidly advancing new technologies (Neo-Tech) making our standards of living soar beyond any conception we could have now as subjects of the mystical anticivilization.

Need Some Help? Talk to Toddlers

Observing my own toddlers watered the seeds of my discovery about pure love. If you talk to toddlers, you will find they naturally pull together everything they know when answering questions about people or life, and they naturally exert honesty with those thoughts...which is Neo-Tech. You will also notice they always emphasize the values or the positives about people or life. That is because toddlers still function through pure love. They have not yet learned the unnatural emotions of the anticivilization. They have not *yet* been programmed with mysticism.

Still seeing the world through pure love, which means seeing through widest-scope accounting of Neo-Tech, toddlers can amazingly grasp complex concepts about the Civilization of the Universe in one five-minute talk, whereas adults will go a lifetime and not be able to understand. For example, I explained the entire Civilization of the Universe dynamics that you will read in the Third Insight to my four-year-old daughter while pushing her in a cart during one of my four-mile runs. From that one talk, she thoroughly understands everything you will read in the long Third Insight. On the other hand, I have been spoon-feeding an adult friend the same information that my four-year-old daughter grasped in a half hour. I have been spoon-feeding him for six years, and he is nowhere near understanding the ideas.

The toddler's ability to grasp complex concepts of the supersociety and the Civilization of the Universe is a dramatic demonstration of the power of Neo-Tech, achieved through pure love. As I have done, you can launch yourself into this perspective-change of pure love by talking to and emulating toddlers under seven years of age.

Intelligence Outcompeted

Neo-Tech will eventually eliminate neocheating throughout the world while enhancing prosperity and happiness for everyone.

335

Most of all, the process of personally exerting Neo-Tech to remove one's own bicameral behavioral patterns leads to Neothink and major breakthroughs of knowledge on par with Copernicus, Ford, and the computers.

Neo-Tech frees your mind of the computerlike virus passed along for a hundred generations. Neo-Tech lets your mind break free of its many limitations. Neothink is the unlimited wide integrations made possible by having Neo-Tech eradicate mysticism. Neothink is the harnessing of that Neo-Tech power here on Earth. Neothink soars beyond today's mind. We all know about the enormous capacity of the human mind. But our minds are so limited today. The mystery of what so limits our minds is finally solved: mysticism. Neothink is tomorrow's limitless mind and replaces the meaning of intelligence:

Intelligence in tomorrow's Neo-Tech World is redefined as the *range of integrated thinking*. The range, width, or scope of valid integrations of knowledge is more a function of honesty than of IQ. No matter how high is one's raw IQ, that person can ultimately be outflanked and outperformed by a lower IQ mind that is more honest, less mystical, allowing wider-scope integrations. In tomorrow's Neo-Tech World, wide-scope integrations of knowledge are what give conscious minds unlimited power. Neothink supersedes the role of IQ.

Remember, Pure Love Is Your Catalyst

Today man has a highly intellectual mind, but it easily slips back into the automatically functioning bicameral modality from thousands of years past. Strange, isn't it? We are doing advanced business and running advanced computer technologies as intellectuals, but we easily slip into those bicameral mentalities with zero intellection. Here is why: Decision making is the source of stress. Thus, it is not automatic to exert your own mind, exclusively making all your own decisions; it is not easy to be conscious and responsible every step of the way. So, if you are not careful and get a little lazy, then your mind will automatically on its own slip back into its bicameral-like mode of following or reacting to higher "authorities". For, long ago, mysticism was programmed into your mind.

To avoid stress, your mind seeks the path of least resistance. That regression into a bicameral behavioral pattern is automatic and physiological, actually: get a little lazy, and surprise, without warning, your bicameral behavioral patterns take over. In fact, Jaynes demonstrates this point by describing when people are *not* exerting the conscious mode, say while automatically driving a car, then they are in an unconscious state that simulates the bicameral mind. That is why, if you remember back in my Ninth Vision, I described how difficult it was, at first, for me to lift my mind into the "Hemingway Code".

Mental laziness becomes man's greatest cause of slipping back into harmful bicameral behavioral patterns, making you most vulnerable to neocheaters. To overcome the pervasive mind disease programmed into your mind at an early age, you must actively exert your conscious mode. Moreover, it takes being brutally honest with yourself to recognize your laziness and bicameral tendencies in order to overcome them and to integrate reality for making your own decisions. It is so easy to be a little dishonest with yourself and rationalize your own laziness and your mind-created "realities" growing from lack of self-thought. So, realize that laziness and dishonesty will put up major resistance to deprogramming your bicameral behavioral patterns. Neo-Tech is your antidote. Pure love is your catalyst.

Neocheaters are the Typhoid-Mary spreaders of mysticism who keep the disease of the mind dominating every human being so that they can control us for their own unearned power and wealth. Let us examine how:

Higher "Authorities" and "Higher" Causes

The deeply programmed bicameral behavior in the multitudes makes them easy to control — followers looking for leaders. And those leaders, our career politicians, for example, are neocheaters. In short, neocheaters hurt their followers, the multitudes, through enforcing subservience to the higher "authorities" and sacrifice to their self-serving "higher" causes.

Our bicameral behavior, programmed into our mind as young children, makes higher "authorities" and their "higher" causes very inviting, almost "natural" aberrations for conscious man. To finally break from higher "authorities" and their self-serving "higher" causes is not easy. Bicameral man was owned by his god — by what he called his ili or ka. To hear was to obey. That same obedience resides in us today. In our bicameral past, a command from our god was our higher cause and was not questioned, even if it meant death. Today, commands from higher "authorities" often become our "higher" causes and are so often not questioned, sometimes even if they mean death, as in the case of war.

Altruism is today's dominant philosophy, and it is based on sacrifice to "higher" causes. Of course, the higher "authorities" determine the "higher" causes and who will be sacrificed to whom. The "higher" causes of altruism make altruism the ideal tool to push lots of easy-target people into their bicameral mentalities that obey higher "authorities" and "higher" causes.

Our vulnerability to accepting "higher" causes and seeking higher "authorities" telling us what to do and how to live is why the leaders, the rulers of society, *the neocheaters* use altruism as their "reasoning" behind every destructive program that demands sacrifice of the honest working man. For example, we not only pay taxes to the higher "authority" known as government, but we pay *ever higher* taxes to the "higher" cause known as social welfare. Of course, our sacrifice ultimately provides the political leaders their own power and wealth. So, those neocheaters manipulate the pre-programmed, bicameral behavior in the multitudes, using the "higher" causes of altruism as their sound-good "reasoning". People are very, very vulnerable to following "higher" causes and higher "authorities" through destructive altruism.

But, why don't the multitudes recognize the harm done to them — the financial harm especially — by altruism and its sacrifice to "higher" causes via the higher "authorities"? The neocheaters use reality-altering mysticism to create illusions of "noble" programs "for the social good", for instance, that camouflage the life-diminishing destruction caused by altruism and sacrifice. We cannot see, for instance, the Neo-Tech World and the millionaire-like standard of living we would enjoy if not for our sacrifice to the neocheaters and their "higher" causes.

What can change all this? We are fighting bicameral programming "hardwired" into our minds...a computerlike virus in our minds passed on for thousands of years in the human psyche. How can we break free from altruism and the neocheaters' stranglehold on mankind? That change will come through using Neo-Tech facilitated by pure love, to end our bicameral programming and all its vestiges such as governments and religions. With Neo-Tech, we will fulfill our destiny; we will evolve into a whole new mentality — the Neothink mentality.

A Long Time In Coming

The Neothink mentality has been a long time in coming. Twenty-four hundred years of sacrifice to neocheaters has kept mankind from his destiny of becoming God-Man. In bicameral man, human nature was split in two, as Jaynes points out, an executive part called a god (the right brain), and a follower part called a man (the left brain). Jaynes demonstrates that portions of the Old Testament were written by bicameral man, some during the transitional period of the bicameral mentality to the conscious mentality. In the New Testament, references are made to man becoming one with God. Such references would perhaps suggest some early attempts to describe the new mentality, consciousness, where man was no longer the follower, but his own god and decision maker as well. The Second Insight demonstrates that the teachings of Jesus were attempts to break the chain and bring the bicameral peasants into the new conscious mentality...into God-Man. Notice, by the way, Jesus's abundant use of the concept of *love*. Then, as now, pure *love* was the catalyst to leaping ahead into the new mentality.

Unfortunately, a few hundred years after Jesus, the developing master neocheaters of the Western World perfected their tool of guilt, sophisticated their illusory altruism, copped the teachings of Jesus and mixed them into their brew of guilt and sacrifice, took control of and reactivated the masses' residual but otherwise fading bicameral mentalities for a self-serving millennium, known as the Dark Ages. Using Plato's philosophical foundation, the master neocheaters orchestrated a mutation of the bicameral mentality that, in turn, ravished the new, conscious mentality. Consciousness and new knowledge was conquered as mysticism and neocheaters ruled the world.

The passing centuries since the Dark Ages have been a continual retreat from mysticism (which always allows neocheaters to rule over us); of course, we suffered severe relapses along the way. And now, with nuclear weapons in the arsenal of neocheaters, a relapse could destroy civilization. We will discuss that possibility soon.

Altruism, the philosophy of the neocheaters, is based on the mystical premise that man lives for the sake of others...that man's life and property are available for sacrifice to "higher" causes, e.g., the common good, society, the needy, the environment, the dictator, God, country, politicians, bureaucrats. Implementing altruism always requires widespread bicameral mentalities accepting or seeking higher "authorities".

Altruism yields by nature a malevolent society in which individuals deal with one another on terms of who will be sacrificed to whom, who will support whom. Force wielded by the higher "authorities" becomes the deciding factor. Altruism is the neocheaters' tool that exploits our bicameral urges for higher "authorities" and their "higher" causes. From altruism, never will Neothink rise...never will our final evolution occur.

During the 21st century, however, with the spread of Neo-Tech and collapse of mysticism, the next evolutionary jump of man will occur. Wars will end. Man will mentally "jump" from today's consciousness, diseased with bicameral behavioral patterns or mysticism, to Neothink consciousness, free of the bicameral behavioral patterns, free of mysticism. Indeed, mysticism is the disease; Neo-Tech is the antidote; Neothink is the cured mind. Within the Neothink mind, bicameral behavior cannot exist, thus external "authorities" or neocheaters can no longer exist. In that Neo-Tech World free of neocheaters, a new code of living will emerge; everything will change. Ordinary people will be rich, safe, and secure. After 3000 years, the new code of living will lift mankind into his full glory as God-Man.

The Turning Point

Our civilization is at *the* pivotal point today. The *Nuclear-Decision Threshold* is the point at which energy, knowledge, and technology have advanced to where sufficient, man-made energy — nuclear energy — can be generated to physically destroy all life on the planet. From that point, civilizations must follow one of two courses:

(1) Proceed in an altruistic philosophical system in which mysticism-plagued conscious minds support mystical "higher" causes that feed political power to the neocheaters. Such systems dominated by manipulating bicameral mentalities for political power will eventually lead to all-out nuclear warfare in which most knowledge and technology are lost. Most of the world's population would die and civilization would perish...because of meaningless mysticism being manipulated to give false power and bogus livelihoods to the higher "authorities"...the value destroyers.

(2) Proceed in a Neo-Tech philosophical system in which mysticism-free Neothink minds support no "higher" causes or higher "authorities". Such a system dominated by Neothink mentalities allows civilization to safely advance beyond the *Nuclear-Decision Threshold*. The world's population would flourish beyond any conception from today's world (as described throughout the Twelve Visions). The Nuclear-Decision Threshold is the point that every advanced civilization must successfully pass through to survive.

Thus, any civilization advancing significantly beyond that threshold would have by nature evolved into God-Man and his Neo-Tech World of soaring prosperity. That in turn would mean a free society from which external "authorities" are eradicated as destructive and immoral. In any such advanced society, all forms of mysticism would by nature have been discredited and discarded as stupid and destructive. Such a society would be free of politicians, theologians, neocheaters, coercive governments, and other higher "authorities". Actions would be based on mysticism-free logic exercised by free individuals.

Today, man's survival still depends on his choice of beneficially following his own consciousness or destructively following the voices of external "authorities". Indeed, for our own civilization to advance significantly beyond our current *Nuclear-Decision Threshold* would require a shift from the current altruistic philosophical base and its mysticism-plagued conscious minds supporting dangerous neocheaters...to a Neo-Tech philosophical base and its Neothink minds supporting no neocheaters, as first demonstrated in the computer/cyberspace industry. (To witness the Neo-Tech World, read *The First Immortals*.)

What Would Have Been

Civilization would have advanced super rapidly if the Neothink mentality, rather than the bicameral mentality, had dominated for the past 2400 years. Free-enterprise capitalism (as in today's rapidly advancing computer/cyberspace industry) would have raced ahead. Neo-Tech would have eliminated altruisms and force-backed governments with the subsequent elimination of neocheating, wars, crime, disease, poverty, and death itself. In this super rapidly advancing Neo-Tech Society, the steam engine and trains would have been in operation at the birth of Christ; mass produced cars would have been available in 50 A.D.; commercial airlines would have been in operation by 60 A.D.; crime and fraud would have been eliminated, not by government police but by private protection services, private courts, and computerized ostracism by 65 A.D.; nuclear power would have existed by 70 A.D.; man would have landed on the moon by 80 A.D.; cancer would have been cured by 90 A.D.; youth-perpetuating biological immortality would have occurred by 120 A.D.; immortal conscious individuals, master of all known nature, would have happened by 2000 A.D.

What are we saying? A Neo-Tech Society is a super rapidly advancing society, as everyone will discover sometime in the 21st century, soaring ahead upon a new code of living for a new mentality. If a Neo-Tech philosophy rather than a mystical philosophy had dominated the Western World since the Golden Age of Greece, mankind would have experienced that super rapidly advancing Neo-Tech World. This is what would have happened:

350 B.C.   Aristotle 384 B.C.-322 B.C.   Plato's philosophy identified as mystical and forever dismissed as dishonest, destructive.

200 B.C.   America discovered.

100 B.C.   Free-enterprise capitalism established around the world.   Free markets flourishing.   All forms of mysticism and neocheating identified, discredited, and rejected.   All government taxation and nonprofit spending programs abolished.   All forms of initiatory force are morally condemned.   Wars become obsolete and vanish.   Arts, sciences, technology boom in totally free markets.   Dynamic competition and value production rule.   Romantic love flourishes.

0 B.C.   All traces of mysticism, altruism, and collectivism are gone.   Poverty essentially eliminated.   The individual is the supreme value.   Jesus builds the highest skyscraper in Asia Minor.   Trains and steamships are major forms of transportation.

20 A.D.   Electrical power developed, camera developed.

40 A.D.   Internal-combustion engine developed.

50 A.D.   Cars in mass production.   Airplane developed.

60 A.D.   Commercial airlines flourishing.   Computer developed.

65 A.D.   Crime and fraud become unprofitable, obsolete, and essentially eliminated by computerized ostracism.

70 A.D.   Nuclear power developed.   Nuclear weapons never conceived.

80 A.D.   Man on the moon.   Internet developed.

90 A.D.   Cancer and most other diseases eliminated.

100 A.D.   Man on Mars and heading for other planets.

110 A.D.   Need for sleep eliminated.

120 A.D.   Youth-perpetuating biological immortality developed.

140 A.D.   Prosperity and happiness of conscious beings are universal.

200 A.D.   Worldwide, commercial, biological immortality

achieved. All diseases and aging eliminated. Man colonizing, mining, and commercializing the moon, asteroids, and Mars. Commercial shuttle flights, passenger and freight, to space-station colonies. ...Achieve access to the gravity-coded, interstellar universal computer.

1200 A.D. Energy and technology advanced to where sufficient energy can be generated for traveling to other earth-like planets in outer space. Science, knowledge, and fulfillment advanced to the point at which no economic or scientific incentive exists for directly communicating with or travelling to the billions of other, outer-space civilizations.

2000 A.D. Immortal conscious beings in a Neo-Tech, free-enterprise society are master of all known nature. People and goods are transported at the speed of light via electronic transfer. Most goods manufactured via nanotechnology with the electronic control of atoms and molecules. New knowledge is expanding at near the speed of light.

All of that could have happened by shedding our bicameral mentality. Instead, the Greek Philosopher Plato preserved our bicameral mentality — or perhaps more accurately, caused its mutation — in order to establish Plato's Republic with an elite ruling class for the smart neocheaters.

With Plato's philosophy the root of altruism, the destructive authorities and neocheaters say that human beings are by nature evil, irrational, and destructive. They are subordinate to "higher" causes. Human beings must be controlled by some higher "authority" or government and forced to serve others or society...controlled as in Plato's Republic — by the elite neocheaters.

Of course, the neocheating external "authorities" say that sacrifice, humility, and service to duty are needed for prosperity, love, and happiness. In reality, though, human beings survive by using their minds rationally to deal with reality. They must know reality to competitively produce the values needed to prosper. Only by being left free to satisfy their nature can human beings serve themselves and others best. As shown to me in my Twelve Visions, people who live free and according to their natures can easily build a future of enormous prosperity and happiness. Finally, with Neo-Tech, people can rid themselves of neocheaters.

Uprooting Laziness

Laziness always involves mysticism undercutting the conscious mind. Indeed, if you do not watch out and your conscious mind becomes a little lazy, then the outmoded bicameral mentality automatically creeps back in, for it has been programmed into your mind. Again, that bicameral mentality and its growing mind-created "realities" in today's conscious mind is mysticism — the only disease of the mind.

Because of our bicameral programming as a child, we are very vulnerable to the process of mental laziness giving way to bicameral mentalities — laziness begetting mysticism. One must *exert* his or her consciousness...a constant, honest, life-long effort to maintain a prosperous, happy, healthy life. Mental and physical laziness means defaulting on those key attributes of honesty and effort required for advancing beyond our long outdated bicameral tendencies.

At first, the effort will seem difficult. In time, that feeling of being difficult will shift to feelings of exhilaration as you discover value creation and experience the life you were meant to live.

The Problem Of Switching Over

Let us take one last close look at mysticism and neocheaters, for they are your foremost nemeses and what you must leave behind:

Mysticism is a little-known but omnipresent disease of the human mind. Everyone automatically acquires this disease during childhood, a computerlike virus passed down from parent to child, programmed into children's minds. That disease finally explains why our minds' natural capacity is hundreds or thousands of times greater than we ever approach.

The disease previously had never been diagnosed, largely because it is invisible (i.e., not originating from a bacterium, physical virus, or defective gene) and, since *everyone* is affected, there appears to be no symptoms. In discovering that never-before-detected disease of the mind, Dr. Wallace discovered that the apparently normal mind was actually a diseased mind — a very difficult discovery to pull off. Having discovered and diagnosed the disease, thereafter he was able to discover its cure — Neo-Tech. (Therefore, he wrote *The Neo-Tech Discovery*.)

Neo-Tech removes the disease, releasing the limitless potential of the human mind, sending any ordinary person on a journey into more and more money, power and love. As the ordinary person uses Neo-Tech in the business world, for example, and removes the disease of the mind, he soon discovers something new and wide open called *integrated thinking* in contrast to today's predominant specialized thinking that pigeonholes people in lifetime, routine ruts.

As the ordinary person uses Neo-Tech to break apart the programmed mysticism in his mind, he or she experiences a mind that can break beyond its stagnant boundaries and integrate or snap together more and more ideas to build, piece by piece, growing success puzzles. Integrated thinking is his precursor to a much greater power called *Neothink,* and he discovers that integrated thinking in itself is extremely profitable in business.

Neo-Tech clears the path to Neothink. Neothink is an entirely new mentality that we will switch over to sometime in the 21st century. People who switch over to the new mentality will appear to the still mysticism-plagued person to have risen to a higher consciousness, just as the people who switched over to consciousness 3000 years ago appeared to the bicameral person to be gods. The approaching Neothink mentality takes man to a whole new level where he will eventually acquire literally god-like power as God-Man (the Third Insight).

Going Beyond Nature's System

The problem of switching over to God-Man reduces to just

how deeply embedded the program of mysticism is in our minds. Going back to our ancestors, the bicameral man's survival mechanism of hallucinating voices of the gods was a *neurological process*. As an analogy, if a cat faced a hostile situation, whether it fought or fled came from a neurological process, a neurological instruction or command. As Jaynes demonstrates, if a bicameral man faced a hostile situation, like the cat, whether he fought or fled came from a neurological process, a neurological instruction or command. But because man had developed a sophisticated language, the neurological process or neurological instruction or command came in the sophisticated form of a powerful voice and was the consummate guiding mechanism evolved by nature.

No greater authority exists than the spoken voice, particularly when that voice comes from within one's own brain, as in bicameral man. As Jaynes identifies, using descriptive analogies to schizophrenics today, that voice in his own head was all-enveloping from which there was no retreat. He could not hold his ears to muffle the voice or draw back or run away to weaken the voice. There was no escape; wherever he might flee, the voice would not weaken. The voice consumed every part of his body, as if his fingers and toes all had ears. The authority was unquestioned, complete, and clear. In fact, the neurological process or neurological instruction or command was much more effective through the commanding authority of the voices than any other process in nature's evolution, so much more effective than, say, the cat's guidance system. Bicameral man and the authority of sound was the ultimate evolution through nature's system.

The fact that our brains today are physically identical to those of our bicameral ancestors, which means we have the exact same neurological circuitry that once heard and obeyed the voices, makes the bicameral mentality very hard to deprogram. The computerlike virus was passed down through the generations, and today we almost "instinctively", automatically react to the strong voices of our leaders. Even today, the authority of sound — as in a powerful political or campaign speech — can overwhelm an individual and move a nation.

347

The Neo-Tech World

Fully Evolving Into Man's System

Conscious man marks the break from nature's system to man's system, when man took over. Neothink Man or God-Man is the ultimate evolution through man's system. Now, conscious man must evolve — psychologically — from mysticism-plagued consciousness into mysticism-free or Neothink consciousness.

Two mentalities exist under consciousness: 1) The flawed mysticism-plagued consciousness accepts, even seeks external "authorities" instructing people how to live. The feature denomination or proof of that flawed mentality is the existence of a ruling class. 2) The nonflawed mysticism-free consciousness or Neothink mentality accepts full self-responsibility on how to live — the pure state of consciousness in which man's mind is its own authority. The feature denomination or proof of that flawless conscious mentality is the presence of the Gifts in everyone's life (the Gifts revealed in the Twelve Visions).

For 3000 years, people have searched for a higher consciousness — a mystical higher consciousness. The Neothink mentality or God-Man ends that search and brings us what appears to be that higher consciousness — but a nonmystical higher consciousness, more accurately articulated as "the pure state of consciousness".

The Problem, the Promise

Three thousand years ago, when the bicameral mind broke down and the voices of the gods fell silent, man went through enormous efforts to still communicate and receive answers and authorization from their silent gods who had left the earth and now lived in the sky. During this period, prayer was invented to ask for guidance; angels were invented as the winged messengers of the gods who now lived with Anu, the greatest god in the sky; and heaven was invented as the place in the sky where the gods now lived.

Today, people still pray for guidance from God, believe in messages from angels, and look toward the sky as heaven where God lives. The bicameral mentality is still very much in us. Jaynes demonstrates we are still in the breakdown process of the bicameral mind. Of course, this presents an enormous problem: how do we possibly make the switch into Neothink, still so steeped in the bicameral mentality?

I believe we are close to overcoming the problem and close to making the switch into the Neothink mentality. I base this belief on observing today the mirror image of what immediately preceded bicameral man's switch into consciousness, which indicates to me that we are leaving today's mysticism-plagued conscious mentality for a new mentality.

During the breakdown of the bicameral mind, man went through approaching stages toward subjective thought and consciousness. Those stages particularly involved divination, which were attempts to divine the speech of the now silent gods and discover the will of the silent gods — man's urgent quest for authorization. Even today, people in deep decision making often plea, "God, give me a sign!" Examples of those past divinations were omens, sortilege, augury, and spontaneous divination (described in Jaynes' book). Those four main types of divination brought man closer and closer toward the subjective structure of consciousness. They brought man to the edge of consciousness.

Today, for the first time in history, I see the reverse image of that quest for authorization that led man into divination and on to the edge of consciousness. That reverse image today is the growing *damnation* of politicians, in particular. To damn the politician is a direct, conscious attack on authorization, a definite sign of a break from our bicameral past.

Of course, for centuries, people have rebelled against rulers and governments, but always against a particular party or system, looking for another party or system to come in and provide "better" external "authority" and guidance. For the first time, people today are turning against the idea of the politician, period. For the first time, large percentages of people are not just grumbling their dissatisfaction at their existing external guidance, seeking what they perceive is an improved external guidance to take over authorization. Instead, for the first time, people are turning against authority — against the fundamental concept of government ruling over their lives. That damnation of authority at its core is a landmark for humanity and, I believe, puts us on the edge of Neothink.

My Actual Insight

Now that I have taken you through some of my seventeen-year development of the God-Man hypothesis, which made it possible to have this Insight, now let us turn to the actual First Insight that showed me exactly what the God-Man would be like. I feel very fortunate to have had this Insight, for making the difficult switch into the new mentality and its new world would be greatly aided if we could see ahead to what the switch will be like specifically and what things would change and how. If we could have some idea of what to expect and how to change, to somehow see the changes and how they would affect us, then we would have some sort of orientation and expectation to get our bearings and secure our footing to advance confidently, with a clear plan.

The First Insight gave me that orientation with a look into the fascinating new mentality and its new world. This Insight showed me a civilization in my mind's eye that is actively Neothink. In a sense, the First Insight provided me with an analog model, say a map of the new civilization needed to visualize the new world and then switch over to the new mentality.

Within that demonstration of the Neo-Tech World, I witnessed some exciting Gifts we can look forward to when we evolve into God-Man.

The First Insight *showed me* the God-Man, and the Insight was beautiful. Here is what I saw during the actual First Insight after my Twelve Visions:

My Encounter With God-Man

I saw that God-Man is the perfect specimen with special Gifts. The First Insight showed me God-Man and his Gifts:

Gods of Life

I saw that we thought differently, such as Copernicus, Ford,

Gates. I saw the very rich world we lived in. I could see that we actually became the controllers of the Universe (the Third Insight). I saw that we never aged, for we eliminated aging with youth rejuvenating biological immortality to live forever. Those god-like powers, of course, were the results of going to the next level called God-Man.

Live Forever?

I saw that, in the Neo-Tech World, the Bill Gates-like geniuses broke through to the next level in all industries including the medical industry. They rapidly eradicated disease after disease, bringing us perfect health while doubling our lives. Eventually, they eradicated the most devastating physical disease — aging itself.

Outperforming Adult Video Stars

I saw that, as God-Man, we became the perfect specimen — the highest life form on Earth...and throughout the Universe. We advanced physically and psychologically beyond any life form, including all people in today's mentality. Our superior physical and mental state went beyond any human being today. I witnessed that our sexual competence outperformed anything seen today — even on adult videos!

Becoming Billionaires

I saw millions of people breaking through into Neothink and becoming rich. At the end of the 20th century and at the start of the 21st century, more billionaires surfaced than ever before. *Forbes' Richest 400 People in America* edition identified 170 billionaires versus only 13 billionaires fifteen years before. That increase was an indicator of the increasing number of forerunners to our evolution into God-Man and his Neothink mentality. During my First Insight, I saw *ordinary people* evolving into God-Man and becoming *billionaires!*

Becoming Geniuses

I saw us easily and effortlessly making breakthroughs that made us powerful, respected, and wealthy. Our minds no longer followed their routine ruts or followed leaders. Instead, our minds integrated knowledge...we snapped together knowledge as though we were building puzzles. As the puzzles grew, they began forming pictures never seen before by anyone else. Those puzzle pictures revealed breakthrough knowledge for the world, just as Copernicus, Ford, and Gates revealed their breakthrough pictures.

Becoming Omnipotent

As our breakthrough pictures grew, as with any puzzle pictures, we were able to see what the whole pictures would look like before they were finished. Thus, we knew what the missing pieces looked like and, therefore, knew with omnipotence exactly what to do for success. ...Now, we knew how those other geniuses seemed to do everything right with confidence for success — they did so because of this Neothink process of building breakthrough puzzle pictures and building them with increasing confidence and omnipotence. Knowing what the missing pieces to the puzzle pictures looked like and making all the right choices, they almost seemed psychic. Now, we thought in pictures, too — puzzle pictures — and could do everything right for success, too. We could do everything those geniuses could do. Indeed, we became geniuses ourselves. I saw it happen in the First Insight. We realized that God-Man was the only legitimate "psychic", for God-Man was the only human in existence who could, through the puzzle pictures, *see the future*. And now, we were God-Man, too. With Neothink, we not only could see the future, but we could now *control the future*. We discovered that, with this *nonmystical* "psychic" ability, we experienced the easiest, most exhilarating life of success. To those who had not yet leapt into Neothink, we seemed to be the luckiest people alive, always making the right choices. Indeed, we were "speculating" in large-stakes projects and always winning with unbeatable omnipotence. ...We seemed, to those not yet

352

into Neothink, to be wildly lucky...and unbeatable. Luck has nothing to do with it...but we certainly were unbeatable.

Attracting Friends and Lovers

One person who achieves the Neo-Tech state of mind more and more frequently told me this story, "The woman I'd been trying to date for six months, to no avail, called and asked me out! On our second date she said she was overwhelmed and in love with me! I'm dumbfounded at how powerful Neothink is!" During my First Insight, I witnessed that superior people attracted more mates and more competitive mates. Those who evolved into God-Man not only transferred all money, power, and prestige from the following man to themselves, but easily won any lover in any situation or quickly regained their ex-lovers. Recently, I overheard at a Neo-Tech Summit the following comment: "Within hours after applying Neo-Tech, my beautiful ex-wife was back in my arms! Neo-Tech is unbelievable but works! We'll never be the same again! Now I'm working my way toward making the switch into Neothink!"

Another person sent me this testimonial in a letter: "While in prison, I discovered Neo-Tech. I left prison broke, without a penny or a woman or a friend to my name. Through Neo-Tech and at times, Neothink, six months later I was a multi-millionaire and my live-in girlfriend was a Penthouse Magazine Pet-of-the-Month. Six months after that, I was a famous celebrity, wooed by beautiful women and surrounded by geniuses and the rich and famous all over the country." The person who sent me that letter is now a famous television celebrity.

The point is, not only does the person who evolves into God-Man easily control anyone, man or woman, and easily beats any opponent in any situation, but everyone he meets wants to be his friend. In fact, I saw in my First Insight that every relationship — spouse, lover, children, friends, co-workers — became better and more fulfilling.

Moreover, I saw in this Insight that God-Man quickly acquired a special circle of friends — beautiful women, geniuses in the medical, science, and business fields, and famous celebrities ...interesting, valuable people.

Becoming the Perfect Physical Specimen

Your mind and body are inextricably linked. I saw in my First Insight that when we evolved into the entirely new way of using our minds — God-Man's integrating, not following, Neothink mentality — our bodies metamorphosed, too. Physical changes occurred quickly that are not easy to communicate to people before their final evolution (somewhat explained in Vision Eight). The symptoms, however, included losing interest or appetite for food, slimming down automatically, without even trying, to the perfect weight for one's frame, all while radiating with a new, beautiful or handsome confidence. God-Man — man and woman — was physically beautiful in my Insight. God-Man was physically perfect. He or she had an awesome body and mind.

Discover Fearlessness

I saw that God-Man was innocent and pure. The very process into God-Man required complete honesty. Once we reached that highest life form called God-Man, I saw in my First Insight that even the most vicious lower life forms could not really hurt us just as, say, the most vicious lower life forms such as tigers, crocodiles, wolves do not bother us today. God-Man tomorrow never needed to worry about being cheated or hurt by anyone, by any competitor, foe, liar, or con man, for they were harmless lower life forms. God-Man did not even fear the powerful neocheater (i.e., the most subtle but vicious breed of cheater), including politicians and regulatory bureaucrats or any other destroyers of wealth and prosperity. In short, they became a joke. I could so clearly see and feel during my Insight that God-Man was invincible.

Summary

Let us summarize my First Insight and, at the same time, reveal humanity's charted course into God-Man and his Civilization of the Universe:

About 10,000 years ago, man developed a coherent oral

language. Speech was then incorporated into nature's most advanced neurological guidance system, known as the bicameral mind. That culmination of nature's evolution, bicameral man, continued to develop more and more sophisticated written language, which eventually, around 3000 years ago, led to the development of metaphors and analog models.

Man needed metaphors and analog models to separate from the objective world before him and, in his mind, enter a subjective world for his reflective thoughts...known as consciousness. Now, he could think about the world around him instead of just reacting to it. Thus, he could now make the decisions on how to interact with the world around him. He now had control. He had leapt beyond nature's neurological guidance system into man's own, invented guidance system.

But, conscious minds still carried deep-rooted bicameral triggers, urges, longings. Conscious minds were plagued by outmoded bicameral tendencies or, in other words, conscious minds were infected with mysticism — a disease of conscious minds. Neocheaters enabled the fading bicameral mentality to mutate and then ravage the new conscious mentality. If not for Neo-Tech, that virulent disease of the conscious mind would eventually destroy man during the Nuclear-Decision Threshold.

The discovery of Neo-Tech enables conscious minds, for the first time, to systematically remove mysticism and eventually cure themselves.

Similar to how language and metaphors were needed to separate from the objective world in order for man to evolve into consciousness, Neo-Tech is needed to deprogram bicameral mysticism to evolve into Neothink. As man uses Neo-Tech to remove the debilitating disease of mysticism and frees his mind, he is able to acquire more and more power and success as he integrates more and more knowledge. He breaks out of his trap, his bicameral-like routine-rut, just automatically reacting to the world around him. Instead, he starts controlling and building his dreams in the world around him. Through integrated thinking, he snaps together more and more knowledge and starts building a success puzzle. Like any puzzle, as he snaps together more pieces, a puzzle picture begins to form...a never-before-seen puzzle picture. And it is at this point — when he begins building a never-before-seen puzzle picture, a major advancement of human knowledge — that he leaps into Neothink.

Similar to how metaphors and analog models were needed to create the mind space for consciousness, integrated thinking and mental puzzles are needed to go beyond the normal processing capacity of the human mind into Neothink. You see, the human mind can only process a single thought cluster with four or five thoughts at one time. Integrated thinking and mental puzzles enable man to go beyond the mind's processing capacity to build multiple thought clusters with limitless thoughts, which is Neothink. Each puzzle piece is, in itself, a maximum integration unit — a thought cluster of four or five thoughts. Through mental puzzles, one goes beyond his maximum integration capacity to hold endless integrations in his mind.

As one evolves into limitless Neothink, he breaks through to the next level and brings major advancements of human knowledge into the world. Moreover, with Neothink, he often functions with omnipotence as he sees the future. Indeed, as with any developing puzzle picture, he reaches a point where he knows what the completed picture will look like. Therefore, he knows with omnipotence, well before the puzzle is completed, what the missing puzzle pieces look like. Now functioning through Neothink, he knows both exactly what the future looks like and *how to create it.* Indeed, God-Man not only sees, but *creates* the future and his destiny.

The Second Insight
God-Man Is God

This is the most difficult part of my book to deliver. It is the most difficult for people to absorb, no less accept. Yet, as I got into my Second Insight from a nonbiblical, historic perspective, it became fascinating to me as it will to you, if you go into it with an open mind.

To properly present this controversial Second Insight to you, I must start at the beginning...with the development of man's conception of God.

At first, man's effort to explain the unexplainable gave rise to mythology. From mythology rose polytheism, which is the belief in many gods. As you will see, out of polytheism evolved monotheism and the belief in one God. This all occurred over thousands of years when man was still bicameral — still an animal of nature — culminating 2000 years ago with the shifting of the *masses* from bicameral man to conscious man.

When bicameral man made the leap into human consciousness, the idea of a supernatural God almost vanished in place of a super powerful God-Man, as you will see in this Insight. But the educated elite Church Fathers — rulers of the land — did not want to release their power over the evolving masses. The Church Fathers brilliantly caused a mutation of the bicameral mentality, as you will see, to secure a supernatural God — their meal ticket, their way to control the masses during those harsh times. In fact, the nonbiblical Jesus was ancient history's strongest warrior against the educated elite and for the "one with God" coming of the God-Man.

Let's back up. Let us better understand our first evolutionary leap from nature's bicameral man to conscious man in order to understand what Jesus was really teaching.

Our First Evolutionary Leap

Before man jumped from a nature-controlled mentality into human consciousness, as we know him today, he went through a shifting period of his mental structure that began with the development of language. That period is called the Bicameral Age. Bicameral man possessed the most advanced mentality possible through nature. As you will observe later, human consciousness is a leap beyond nature.[1]

Bicameral man, as with all animals, lived in the here and now, reacting to the world around him, outside him, with no sense of the past or the future and no inward sense of himself. Yet, bicameral man had developed language and, later, writing. Writings from the Bicameral Age such as the Sumerian epic *Gilgamesh* (written before 2000 B.C.) and the Homeric epic *Iliad* (written before 700 B.C.) were written like newspaper clippings reporting the news. There was no past, no future, no introspection.

The books of the Bible were different: they introduced the past, the future, and the inner self to humanity. Those books, written over an 1100-year span from about 1000 B.C. through 100 A.D., covering nearly 2000 years of events from the journey of Abraham (about 1850 B.C.) through the age of the Apostles (through 100 A.D.), capture the major shifts in man's evolving mental structure from the automatic, reacting-to-the-outside-world bicameral mentality toward the inward, determining-one's-own-actions human consciousness.

The books of the Hebrew Bible (i.e., the Old Testament), written from about the 10th century B.C. through about the 6th century B.C. during bicameral times, were very different from other writings during that time. For the first time in recorded literature, for example, the books of the Hebrew Bible put an unmistakable effort on trying to capture history — *the past*. The Bible broke from the universal wheel perspective of time (i.e., no beginning or end, no past or future) and for the first time opened the idea of *the future*.

The boundary breaking sense of time, as Thomas Cahill identified in his book *The Gifts of the Jews*, was the result of an "enormous value shift". Until now, everything meaningful happened in the only "real" world — the world of the gods. Man was merely a pawn to be used to the fancy of the gods,

[1]Dr. Julian Jaynes, the renowned Princeton Professor, discovered Bicameral Man in the 1970s. See his book *The Origin of Consciousness in the Breakdown of the Bicameral Mind.*

as evident in the early epics.   In fact, bicameral man was merely an automaton, dutifully performing his duties and reacting to the voices of the gods or the God-Kings telling him how to act.

The Hebrews, however, as represented in the Hebrew Bible, shifted importance from the celestial gods to man on earth: for the first time, man now held meaning and importance. He now lived in a real world.

Therefore, for the first time, *the events* of man on Earth were meaningful and *his world* was real. Thus, the events of man on Earth needed to be captured...including where he came from: *his past*. And because reality and meaning now existed in man's world, his events could lead to the new: *his future*. Shifting value from the world of the gods to the world of man was also a shifting of his mental structure from the outside world toward his inward world...a major step away from the bicameral mentality that automatically responded to the outside world and toward human consciousness that turned inward to one's thoughts and decisions.

The stories in Genesis and Exodus of the Hebrew Bible introduced for the first time in literature a sense of *time*, a past and a future. Those stories certainly reflect the shifting of bicameral man's mental structure. Until those stories, bicameral man simply reacted to the world around him. He was directed from "out there", from the world of the gods. But those early stories of the Bible reflect a shift from "out there" toward *his own* world.

Now, the Ten Commandments in Exodus went another major step toward human consciousness: those Ten Commandments stretched bicameral man's sense of himself even further than past and future. The Ten Commandments expanded his sense of himself inward, toward his inner space, by forcing *choice* upon him — thrusting upon him the new idea of *controlling the present*.

The Ten Commandments in the Hebrew Bible were unique to literature in that they did not merely describe the consequences of doing certain wrongful acts as other writings at the time. Instead, the Ten Commandments were just put out there as self-evident *choices*, bringing the bicameral man a rudimentary introduction to inward self-responsibility and self-control. Before the Ten Commandments, man had no self-control; as all animals, he merely reacted to the world around him. He simply served as pawns for the "gods" to direct as they pleased. All his actions came from outside of man, from the whims of the "gods", as demonstrated in the epic poems, passed down by bicameral man, such as *Gilgamesh* and the *Iliad*. But now, the Ten Commandments caused a major shift toward the inward world of human consciousness. With the Ten Commandments, a person had *to choose* how to act.

For the first time, that person's every action was not guided by the gods. Instead, he had to, in an elementary sense, work through internal thoughts to guide himself. And now, *the choices* he would make in *the present* would determine *his future*. In other words, for the first time, bicameral man was gaining a sense of *control*: if I chose to act a certain way in the present, I control what happens to me later.

All this was bringing major shifts in bicameral man's mental structure. He was evolving from no control toward self-control and self-determination, the hallmark of human consciousness. The Ten Commandments represented the outer edge of introspection bringing the Hebrew mental structure closer to human consciousness.

But, why these desert nomads...the dusty ones (the original meaning of "Hebrew") from the desert? Why didn't human consciousness rise previously out of the thriving civilization of Sumer or out of the flourishing Egypt or Assyria or Babylon?[1]

Human consciousness was a whole new inner mind space that did not exist in bicameral man. Bicameral man, as with all animals, had no sense of time, and he only comprehended and reacted to what his senses perceived immediately around him. There was no inner mind space in which to step back from that external stimuli to go into thoughts, to think, to analyze, imagine,

---

[1]Bicameral man was by far the most intelligent animal with the largest brain who learned to communicate and, gradually, developed language and eventually writing, which enabled him to communicate and coexist so effectively that he built thriving civilizations (e.g., Sumer, Egypt, Babylon) *prior to* gaining human consciousness, as explained in the First Insight.

judge, and make decisions. Bicameral man was, simply put, an extremely smart yet automatically reacting animal. He was not human...not as we are today to where we think, decide, and guide ourselves.

The opening of that mind space of inner thoughts known as human consciousness was an event beyond all proportions, beyond any conception today, for suddenly those bicameral animals entered into the realm *of the gods.* The opening up of the mind space known as human consciousness would have rocked those humans to the core, filling them with confusion, exhilaration, fear, power, and comfort all at once. The opening of the new mind space of inner thoughts known as human consciousness was not a development through nature. Nothing in the physical structure of the brain changed. Simply an intangible new space or dimension opened up, for the first time, for thoughts.

The opening of the new mind space known as human consciousness actually occurred through the sophistication of language, namely the development of the metaphor. The metaphor — using something else, something *separate* from the event on hand, to understand the event on hand — created the mind space that allowed man to *separate* and stand back from the immediate world before him...to turn inward from the world outside him into his own world of thoughts. That mind space that opened up through the advanced linguistic tool of metaphors enabled man, for the first time, to step back and separate from his sensory perceptions and *think,* just as we think today...to analyze, judge, introspect, and *make decisions.* He could turn away from the events on hand to contemplate.

Today we take for granted our ability to think and make decisions, but back then the enormity of that new power — jumping from an "animal" mentality, seeing, hearing, feeling, and, like a child yanking his hand back from a hot stove, automatically reacting to the world around us...to suddenly having a whole world of thoughts in our heads to think and decide and *control* the world around us — was the power of God *now within the man!* As we'll see, the thunderclap that rocked those who first experienced this lightning-like "jump" from one world of the animal to the other world of the human with god-like power, was actually the message of Jesus who was a bicameral peasant who had gone through the thunderclap of becoming conscious...or, becoming one with God.

The opening of the new mind space known as human consciousness was an event beyond nature...an evolutionary leap of the mind into an entirely different organization made possible by advanced linguistic tools, namely the metaphor, and spurred on by enormous survival pressures. Ironically, this lightning-like jump from nature-controlled animal into human consciousness could not happen under comfortable, prosperous environments. It had to happen under harsh survival pressures, as historically documented by Julian Jaynes in his book *The Origin of Consciousness in the Breakdown of the Bicameral Mind.*

The two necessary ingredients to open up this new mind space known as human consciousness were: 1) the development of the metaphor, and 2) enormous survival pressures. The answer to the question, "Why the dusty ones from the desert?" is: they had the second necessary ingredient missing in Sumer, Egypt, and Babylon. The history of the Hebrew Bible — from the early patriarchal figure Abraham in Genesis, journeying out of the comfortable surroundings of the city of Haran into a life in the harsh desert...to Moses in Exodus, leading the Children of Israel out of the relative comforts of Egypt into a life in the harsh Sinai Desert...to the destruction of Judah and the exile into Babylonian slavery — is a history of tough *survival.* The major mental shifts toward the mental structure of human consciousness rose out of those nomads struggling to live and survive.

Indeed, sometime after YHWH (i.e., God) cries out the Ten Commandments to the Children of Israel cowering in fear at the foot of Mt. Sinai (a bicameral experience, explained later), He decides these Hebrews led out of the lush Egypt by Moses are too soft and makes them survive in the rugged Sinai Desert for 40 years before moving on to the Promised Land.

Six centuries before, when Abraham left the comforts of Haran to go into the harsh desert, his journey was a constant challenge for *survival.* This explains the remarkable difference between the many stories about warriors and kings of the age, stories that perished over time, versus this story that became part of the canon of the Bible and survived four millennia. In *this* story, Abraham develops a closeness with God never before seen in literature. Abraham develops, however incredibly, an *interpersonal relationship* with God.

This remarkable evolvement of Abraham that brings him so close to God that he *sees* Him, reflects a mental structure evolving for the first time toward monotheism (i.e., *one* God), a prerequisite to "unifying" with God, which is really what happened when bicameral man jumped to human consciousness: reactive man leapt into the decision maker and became his own authority, *his own god*; he no longer needed a voice to guide him. Human consciousness, as Jesus would later tell the world in parables and metaphors, is when man becomes "one with God".

Two thousand years after Abraham followed the voice of God into the desert, Jesus' teachings completed the ever so long record of man's shift from the bicameral mentality into human consciousness that rose out of these desert nomads at the edges of civilization. Amazingly, it is *their* writings, those wandering tribes *so separated from thriving bicameral civilizations*, that document who we are today. The stories of the dusty ones survived across the millennia to tell us *how we are* who we are today.

Sparkling Glimpses of Consciousness

In the Bicameral Kingdoms, a hierarchy of imagined gods made the major decisions and directed man via hallucinated commands that either were "heard" during rituals or "repeated" by hallucinating oracles. The phenomenon of hallucinating the voices and decisions of the gods is well accepted by today's scientific Establishment. In short, the audio hallucinations came from neurological impulses in the right chamber of the two-chamber (i.e., bicameral) brain. Those neurological impulses were part of bicameral man's nervous system, nature's neurological guidance mechanism, which existed in all animals. But in man, who had developed language, nature's directions came through neurological impulses that originated in the right chamber of the two chamber (i.e., bicameral) brain and were transmitted and "heard" as authoritative commands in the left chamber..."heard" as the "voices of the gods". Whereas nature's neurological impulses would cause a land animal to turn and run from a flooding river, nature's neurological impulses would cause a bicameral man to hear his god command, "Turn and leave. Flee!" Both were neurological guidance systems, part of the animals' nervous system designed by nature...with bicameral man's audio hallucinations representing the most evolved system possible through nature.

Bicameral man functioned through automatic, learned or mimicked reactions or, in more stressful situations, through the commands from the "voices" of the gods. Over thousands of years, his mentality went through a few major shifts to reach a certain mental structure that suddenly could separate from the outer world and go into a whole new inner world of thoughts. With that new mind space, man leapt into the decision maker. He was awestruck by this new power within — this new power of God.

In its proper context, this was the message the conscious peasant Jesus took to the countryside to the uneducated, bicameral peasants. From the early patriarch, Abraham, who got uniquely close to God, to Jesus Christ's metaphorical message of becoming one with God (nearly two thousand years later), the accounts of the Hebrew Bible and the Gospels of Matthew, Mark, Luke, and John are the accounts of bicameral man's evolution into human consciousness, with glimpses of consciousness sparkling across the Bible like stars sparkling across heaven itself.

In fact, the common denominator that pulled together the canon of the Bible and made each of its books Holy Scripture and its major characters superhuman was, I believe, their early glimpses of human consciousness sparkling through the many bicameral stories and writings of the times. And the culmination of the Christian Bible was Jesus Christ because he represented human consciousness — the final breakthrough. He was not merely a prophet who saw or heard God. No, he *was* God, literally one with God, as he told everyone in his teachings.

Starting with the Bible's early patriarchal figure Abraham, the first sparkling glimpses of consciousness could be seen. Of the many, many tales around at the time, what made the story of Abraham stand out and become Holy Scripture? Abraham was the lowly desert nomad who deceived the great god-king Pharaoh of Egypt by claiming Sarah, Abraham's beautiful wife, was his sister, knowing full well the Pharaoh would put her in his harem and kill her husband. This act of survival saved Abraham's life. In fact, the Pharaoh rewarded Abraham with silver, sheep, cattle, and servants.

Abraham's encounter with the god-king occurred sometime around 1850 B.C. Man was bicameral then and automatically reacted to external stimuli. The act of deceit requires the mind space of human consciousness. Out of survival, this desert nomad manipulated the great god-king of Egypt, the most powerful man in the world, through deceit in what appears to be a flash into consciousness.

Moreover, something even more fascinating separates the story of Abraham from the other tales at the time: As the story continues, Abraham challenges and even negotiates with his god. His powerful sense of individuality uniquely advances him beyond bicameral man's polytheism, which had always been the guiding force of bicameral man's societal structure. Abraham's powerful sense of individuality pulls him further and further into monotheism (i.e., the belief in one God).

Although we cannot sense it now, back then Abraham's monotheism was nothing short of amazing. The Bicameral Kingdoms were all ruled as theocracies; a hierarchy of imagined gods and real god-kings was absolutely necessary for the political fabric for survival. The theocracy was part of man's survival system, the imagined gods part of his nervous system. For the first time, the authority of many gods and god-kings changed to the authority of *one* God in the eyes of Abraham because of his own needs for survival, away from thriving Sumerian civilization, alone in the desert.

Abraham's monotheism was much more than a belief system — it was a major shift of the mental structure away from being controlled "out there" by the only meaningful world of the gods...toward the meaningful inner world of man interacting with this one God — *the* God who chose Abraham to start a great nation and to establish a covenant with the chosen people, a world filled with meaning, purpose, and promise.[1]

The multiple gods of the bicameral theocracies put little meaning or purpose on man. YHWH (the name of *the* God in the Hebrew Bible) puts enormous meaning and purpose on man. Suddenly, life on earth was important — very important. The individual was...well, *an individual*. The chosen people had...well, *a covenant with God*. They had to make the right choices so as to be worthy of YHWH's covenant with them.

Abraham, who started this amazing shift to monotheism, had to have a strong sense of individuality in order to transcend the domineering structure of multiple gods and carry on this interpersonal relationship with one God. Abraham's leap of individuality represents a major shift in man's mental structure. Man must have this sense of individuality — this sense of *himself* — before he can open the mind space of human consciousness.

Cahill wrote, "But the god is becoming more than a voice: he is 'seen' by Avram (i.e., Abraham), who is told, 'I am God Shaddai' — a name for which we may have lost the linguistic key, though many have thought it means 'Mountain God' or 'God of the High Place'. 'Walk in my presence!' invites the god. 'And be wholehearted!' Seeing the god in all his splendor and being invited to such intimacy causes Avram to fall 'upon his face'. The relationship is becoming more intense; and as we witness its development, we must acknowledge something just below the surface of events: without Avram's highly colored sense of himself — of his own individuality — there could hardly be any relationship, yet the relationship is also made possible by the exclusive intensity that this incipient monotheism requires, so much so that we may almost say that individuality (with its

---

[1] Why were the Hebrews — the dusty ones — the "chosen people"? They had the second ingredient needed for human consciousness — *survival pressures* — that was missing in the surrounding, thriving civilizations. Indeed, the Jews would become the first to break through into human consciousness. Bicameral man's broadly integrating right-chamber brain — in this case, Abraham's right-chamber brain — sensed this developing phenomenon, which was transmitted as the word of God and His covenant with the "chosen people" — the conscious people.

consequent possibility of an interpersonal relationship) is the flip side of monotheism."

As the story continues, Abraham gets closer to his god than had been known in any other story during those bicameral times. He talks to and even *sees* God. Abraham's unique closeness to God was a sign that he was, or the original narrator was witness to, a bicameral man forming the mental structure that was approaching the jumping off point just before the great leap into human consciousness.

Next across the night sky of the bicameral mind that could see no further than *directly in front of it* — neither seeing back in time nor extrapolating forward into the future and certainly not inward at oneself — comes, six hundred years later: the light of Moses. He broke the darkness of the human psyche with the Ten Commandments. The Ten Commandments gave the bicameral man *his own choice* in the present to shape his future, casting the first glow across the horizon, preceding the dawn of human consciousness.

Moses also greatly advanced the meaning and value of the world of *people* versus the world of the gods and the god-kings. He brought value to *people* through his grave persistence to free the chosen people, who were suddenly more valuable than the great god-king Pharaoh of Egypt. The chosen people, who followed Moses into the Sinai Desert, had meaning, value, an important past, present, and a very important future that would determine the fate of civilization on Earth — God's own creation.

Two and a half centuries later, David, the slayer of the Philistine warrior Goliath, was the King anointed by the prophet Samuel. He is Israel's second King, preceded by Saul. In this story, King David is not a prophet like Moses and Abraham. Although completely and fully devoted to God, David is not a religious leader; he is a political leader with secular concerns.

Here in this new time of Kings, the Bible presents us with the third major shift in bicameral man's mental structure. With David, the charismatic King, the writing of the Bible begins to turn inward...to the man, into the self.

The hallmark of human consciousness is the ability to look

inward, to introspect...and the word "I" used in this way to give space to the inner self is a major vehicle, a prime thinking tool, for turning inward into the space of our own psyches. Consequently, the word "I" as that vehicle to see within the man never appeared in ancient literature, *never*...until the Psalms of the Hebrew Bible. And it would not appear again this way in other literature for another 400 years. It is believed that several of the Psalms were written and sung by David himself around 1000 B.C.

The next four hundred years, the period of the Prophets as recorded in the second section of the Hebrew Bible called the Neviim, led to the fourth major shift in bicameral man's mental structure. The prophets were, in essence, persons very proficient at putting together the big picture. To understand the prophets, you must understand a little more about the bicameral mind. The right-chamber creative side of man's brain (our brain today is physically identical to the bicameral man) is where the visions and audio hallucinations of the gods originated. Modern day tests show that the right-chamber brain absorbs many times the information than our left-chamber logic side of the brain. That information is constantly, subconsciously absorbed by the right-chamber brain. Then, in a flash sometimes accompanied with "eureka!" or "I've got it!", a thought comes pouring into our logical, "aware" left brain. That thought is sent there from the right brain that had been storing up information until, in one flash, the logical left brain put it all together into an original thought.

That description correlates to how the bicameral man's right brain would store lots and lots of sensory data, then in a moment of stress, the right brain would send a message, in the form of a "vision" or "voice" of God, to the "aware" left brain.

Ironically, the broadly integrating right-brain dominance of the bicameral mind in those bicameral times helped provoke quite accurate big-picture prophecies from oracles and prophets, as was the case with the prophets in the Bible...such as the warnings of Amos and Hosea about the imminent destruction of Israel in the North, and the warnings of Isaiah and Jeremiah about the imminent destruction of Judah in the South. They prophesied that self-indulging material excess of the elite through abusive power and taxation would bring destruction to the tribes in the North and in the South. Both big-picture apocalyptic prophecies came true.

Through hindsight, when the elite Jews were deported to Babylon as slaves during the exile in the sixth century B.C., they finally understood why those prophecies came true: they were warning those Jews that each individual's behaviors and actions, *the individual's choices*, would impact his future. After the destruction of Israel in the North and Judah in the South, the elite Jews, back to the lowliest lows of slavery and bare survival during the exile, adjusted their mental structures to advance into the new dimension of self-choice and self-responsibility.

This major shift of bicameral man's mental structure came on the heels of the destruction of Judah, four hundred years after King David. As predicted by the Prophet Jeremiah, the vicious King Nebuchadnezzar of Babylon attacked and destroyed Jerusalem. He deported the devastated surviving elite Jews to Babylon as slaves. The Jews were right back to where they started 700 years before — as captive slaves. But here lies a great irony: under those survival pressures, having lost everything to complete devastation — this reducing the prospering Jews down again to the slave struggling for survival — the greatest shift of man's mental structure began...the shift inward into introspection.

"Those who first thought these thoughts must have felt that a great thunderclap had shaken them to their roots," writes Cahill about this "journey of the spirit". The thunderclap Cahill refers to here is: the Jews' first inward experiences of *human consciousness.*

There was no counterpart to this journey of the inward spirit in religion or politics in the early sixth century B.C. Yet, with the total destruction of their outward material world, the Jews were able to make the dramatic shift inward — to the journey within. The new writings that arose, the later books of the Hebrew Bible, were unlike any writings before. The new writings reflected a journey within the inner individual...not the outer group, tribe, or nation. The new writings reflected a mental shift to the jumping off point into human consciousness. And somewhere along the way of this early journey within arose the question, "Why must the just and compassionate man suffer?"

By now, the Hebrew Bible (i.e., the Old Testament), was dealing with complex issues of justice and love that entered the twilight of human consciousness. However, the Hebrew Bible was still unable to satisfactorily answer, and would never fully answer, its most puzzling question brought on by introspection: why must we suffer?

The full light of human consciousness would be needed to answer such a question. That question was dealt in the Book of Job of the Old Testament, but was not *really* answered. That question was finally answered 500 years later by Jesus Christ. Jesus' ministry represents the final mental shift or, more accurately, the stunning leap into human consciousness. With Jesus, the mind "opened up" to a new consciousness that Jesus called "the Kingdom of God".

Those mental shifts during man's nearly 2000-year trek from Abraham to Moses, to David, the prophets, the exile, the return, and finally, Jesus, allowed the light of human consciousness to rise and vanquish the bicameral darkness:

> "Life itself was in him, and this life gives light to everyone. The light shines through the darkness..."
> — The Gospel of St. John

The Man Who Radiated Light

When the light of consciousness finally rose, it was symbolically attached to the man who brought consciousness to the lowly masses. That man was Jesus Christ.

Human consciousness lights the world we live in. We can *see beyond* our hands and feet (that dominate bicameral writings)...we can see the past, the future, and most important, we can see *within ourselves*. The bicameral mind was the darkness, the night in which one sees only what immediately surrounds him. Human consciousness is the light, the light that followed Jesus wherever he went as he gave light (i.e., the new mentality) to everyone.

Tracey Alexander is the first to present the hypothesis that

Jesus' ministry was teaching the new mentality — the rise of the "new consciousness", the "Kingdom of God" *within* each person. Her hypothesis demonstrates that Jesus' message, his "Kingdom of God" within, his "new consciousness", was the new leap of power into human consciousness that lit the world and the spirit for each person who received it.

This man who the light followed was the one who finally answered, after five centuries, the question of Job in the Hebrew Bible, unanswerable in the old mentality. Indeed, the new mentality created the mind space for the deep introspection needed to answer *why* the good man suffers.

The Jews generally believed at the time of Jesus that suffering was punishment from God for one's sins or the sins of one's parents or grandparents. Jesus confounded both the Hebrew leaders and his followers when he taught that suffering was something *good*, something that would enable his followers to enter the Kingdom of God, something *honorable*.

Such an abrupt reversal of thought left people scratching their heads, asking "huh"? In fact, when reading the Gospels, particularly Jesus' dialogues with the Hebrew leaders, one can just imagine the head scratching that went on as Jesus spoke in ways that shook up and confounded deeply established thought patterns. I will come back, in a moment, to Jesus' "What-does-he-mean-by-that?" head-scratching approach never seen before.

But first, I will attempt to convey the lost context of *Jesus'* answer (not Paul's answer or any other interpretation) to why the good man must suffer. Properly conveying Jesus' context (after two millennia of Paul's innocent distortions and the Church Fathers' politically motivated distortions, which we will deal with later) could only happen because of my relationship with Dr. Frank R. Wallace and our combined five and a half decades at the cutting edge of humanity's *next leap* into mankind's *next* mentality (to happen sometime in the 21st century). A leap into a new mentality has only happened once — during Jesus' time. As *The Neo-Tech World* describes and *The First Immortals* demonstrates, a leap into a new mentality is about to happen again — during our time. We have gone through four major mental shifts during the past three thousand years, as explained in Dr. Wallace's writings, and we are standing in the twilight of the new light. Only because I stand on the cutting edge and have slipped into and out of again the new mind space of our next mentality, can I have these unique insights into what Jesus was truly conveying and perhaps *feeling*, for Jesus was standing on the inside edge of the first new mentality. My insights, I might add, are not just intellectually configured. Those insights come from over two decades of living and working every day — with all its frustrations — on the edge of the next great leap...observing some people's reflexive retractions versus other people's tendencies to flow naturally toward the coming leap. I submit that these are the same human reactions (unique to these rare evolutionary leaps) that Jesus witnessed, with all the frustrations, on the inside edge of the leap into "the new consciousness"...his "Kingdom of God".

Specifically, what Dr. Wallace and I have observed, with scientifically sound frequency, is the nature of one's *investment* in the existing mentality. The more invested — the more material success — the more they recoil from the coming leap. On the other hand, the less invested — the materially suffering — the more naturally they can accept, grasp, and desire the new mentality.

Jesus obviously observed this same reaction among the commoners and drew his answer as to why the good man must suffer. He must suffer to be free of earthly possessions — investments in the old mentality — to come into the Kingdom of God...to make the leap into the new consciousness.

Now, I must give you an added insight: By the time of Jesus, the people of the privileged class including the Pharisees (i.e., teachers of the law), with the advantage of advanced education, were conscious. Most of them, as a collective whole, dishonestly used their advanced power to manipulate the uneducated bicameral peasants. Jesus, an honest peasant himself, made the necessary attachment of morality to the new consciousness. Now, once one made the evolutionary leap into human consciousness, he then entered the new realm of choosing between honesty and dishonesty (not a choice of the automatically reacting bicameral man who, like a dog, could not be dishonest).

Then Jesus told him (in metaphors), "I have come to

judge the world. I have come to give sight to the blind and to show those who think they see that they are blind."

The Pharisees who were standing there heard him and asked, "Are you saying we are blind?"

"If you were blind, you wouldn't be guilty", Jesus replied. "But you remain guilty because you claim you can see."

John 9:39-41

To enter his Kingdom of God, a person had to be honest and good, not dishonest and bad. The elite leaders, living in material excess, were oppressive. During that time, Jesus observed the conscious elite, including the Pharisees and scribes, living in material excess at the expense of taxing and oppressing the peasants. He knew that was immoral. On the other hand, Jesus observed the struggling common man treating his fellow man with respect and equanimity. He knew that was moral. This attachment of morality to his "Kingdom of God" was obviously inspired by the injustices Jesus witnessed in town after town, the injustices bore by the struggling people. Those poor souls were the good, the suffering. They were the honorable.

> "Blessed are you who are poor,
>   for yours is the kingdom of God.
> Blessed are you who hunger now,
>   for you will be satisfied.
> Blessed are you who weep now,
>   for you will laugh."

Luke 6:20-21

Extinguishing the Light

When studying the New Testament and Jesus' ministry, and pulling together its proper context, we are dealing with an inherent problem: brilliant *conscious* men — the Church Fathers and scholars of the Middle Ages...the educated elite with self-serving political agendas — had control over the canon of the Scriptures. There is speculation among today's scholars that *suppressing* and even *destroying* gospels about Jesus occurred.

This unsettling thought is echoed by biblical scholars today who often pose the question: why only *four* Gospels? Furthermore, we know that Matthew and Luke copied the Gospel of Mark (until recently it was thought that Mark and Luke copied Matthew). So, if we say that two of the four Gospels were copied, then that means there are only two original accounts of Jesus' life. Yet, at the end of the Gospel of St. John, he wrote, "...if all the other things Jesus did were written down, the whole world could not contain the books." The thought of only *four* Gospels goes against St. John's account and St. Luke's account and other accounts of the prolific Jesus and the magnitude of what was written about him. Many gospels are believed to have existed.

Unfortunately, all those writings were property of the Church and its manipulative leaders, driven by self-serving political agendas. Whereas many gospels are believed to have existed, historians believe they were forever destroyed by the Church.

Why?

Feminists believe the patriarchal church, which certainly did oppress women for centuries, destroyed all gospels that showed women in positions of power or authority. That theory may very well be true, but the feminist theory certainly would not account for destroying *all but two* original gospels in that male-dominant age. I believe the feminists have pinpointed a small but integral part of the bigger problem.

In the framework of what we know now, I submit that those other lost gospels did not fit into the canon because they would not easily fit the political context the Church used for Jesus and his teachings. Perhaps the other gospels were too revealing, too detailed, not easy to gloss over and change context.

But this practice of controlling context is not surprising for that age. In fact, it was the normal practice. In those days, history was not an objective science as it is today, rather it was common practice to subjectively interpret or even shape history to fit the desired context. It would be surprising if the Church *did not* tamper with or suppress the writings about Jesus.

The Middle Ages was the period the Church controlled, shaped, sanctioned and permitted only the official context. No one, *nothing* could challenge the official context sanctioned by the Church. The litmus test for freedom — science — failed miserably, for science itself had to conform to the Church's Geocentric view of the Universe (i.e., Earth was the center). Scientists such as Copernicus dare not release his Heliocentric breakthroughs (i.e., the Sun was the center) that contradicted the Church's official context of the Universe...not until he lay on his death bed (story told in *Neo-Tech: The Philosophical Zero*, Neo-Tech Books).

Knowing this leaves no doubt that when we read the New Testament, including the Pauline Letters, the Acts of the Apostles, and the Catholic Letters, we are, in essence, reading a canon designed to fit *the Church Fathers'* political context, not Jesus' original context. So, how do we deal with this to bring back Jesus' original context? After 2000 years, can it be done?

Reigniting the Light

Although admittedly a speculative process, it's one I feel confident in making based on my unique position, standing in a similar dynamic in which Jesus himself stood — on the edge of an evolutionary leap of the mind. The unique insight of myself and Dr. Wallace combined with logical inductions and reasonable deductions should allow us to cut through the bogus context, which as we shall see started in the New Testament.

Science cut through first, starting with Copernicus over 450 years ago, because the dynamics of the cosmos are ultimately provable via physics. *Our job* to get to Jesus' original context took four and a half centuries longer, for not until the parallels could be drawn from one evolutionary mental leap (that is soon to come) to the prior evolutionary mental leap (that Jesus experienced) could the context be formed for what it means — what Jesus meant — while looking at civilization from a different world with a different consciousness.

Certainly we cannot understand Jesus' real message without at least understanding the magnitude of the mental shift from one mentality to the next, that is: from the bicameral mentality to human consciousness. I hope by now you have at least some sense of the magnitude of humanity's great leap forward from darkness to light. ...Humanity today, 2000 years later, is approaching another mental leap of the same magnitude. Fortunately, I have spent nearly my entire adult life working shoulder to shoulder with Dr. Wallace, the only man alive to have transcended this mentality and leapt into the next for extended periods of time. Therefore, working so closely to the next mentality, I can begin to not only intellectually, but *emotionally* grasp what Jesus strived for, under a completely different set of circumstances, of course. But the magnitude of the event of leaping from one mentality to the next can override the specific circumstances to bring us close to the experience and context of Jesus. In other words, on the edge of humanity's next evolutionary leap, we can really relate to what the man Jesus was trying to do and where he was coming from.

For example, by knowing what I know from my close work with Dr. Wallace, it is obvious Jesus could never, as Dr. Wallace could never, merely tell people how to get to the next mentality. Of course, I am sure Jesus, just as Dr. Wallace and myself, wished it were that easy. But since it is a mental *leap*, neither Jesus then nor Dr. Wallace today can walk others through it. Instead, Jesus then and Dr. Wallace today must "shake up" people's thought patterns to get their minds ready *to jump*. This is exactly what Jesus did then and Dr. Wallace does today.

For example, I find myself sometimes chuckling with insights as I read the Gospels and Jesus' comments and parables that would really stump both his followers and adversaries. Of course today, after the privilege of 2000 years of hindsight and academic dissection and all the teachings and studies and sermons, we easily understand his general messages of justice, love, compassion, forgiveness (at least at a certain level, but not at the root level, which I revealed in the First Insight). But if you can, for a moment, try to imagine the minds of people back then. For instance, the idea mentioned earlier that suffering was a good thing and honorable left his rivals and followers stumped. Or imagine the idea of love and compassion and forgiveness as a guiding force of society in those rough and tumble times. As understandable as those concepts seem now, they were just totally off the wall back then.

The very act of Jesus himself leaping into human

consciousness brought forth this outpouring of love and compassion during those harsh, often brutal times. The evolutionary leap from the bicameral "animal" mentality into human consciousness lifted the individual into a whole new emotional existence that exponentially transcended his previous emotional existence. It was from that new emotional existence that Jesus taught. Time after time his lessons of love were beyond comprehension to onlookers and his disciples. Jesus' teachings on justice, suffering, love, and compassion made people back then just stop, stare, and often think he was downright crazy.

Many things Jesus said, back then, seemed different...weird. This jumbling of people's grooved-in thought patterns was Jesus' only possible way to shake people out of their old world so they could make the leap, which explains his confounding comments that left his subjects back then scratching their heads. He taught in parables and metaphors (remember, metaphors were the linguistic tool that enabled bicameral man to separate from the world before him to turn inward into a new world of thoughts within him). A point would come when his disciples least suspected it: their minds would make the jump (not unlike the child who has been struggling to read single words, then one day, makes the jump and reads nearly everything around him).

I can, when I read the Gospels, so clearly see Jesus confounding his people, statement after statement, metaphor after metaphor. I can, however, know and relate to this only because of my work with Dr. Wallace, for I can relate to that gulf that separates two worlds. Like Jesus then, Dr. Wallace now cannot tell you how to get into the Neothink mentality just as Jesus could not tell the peasants how to get into human consciousness. Dr. Wallace's latest writings shake up the reader's thoughts with things that seem different and weird...as did Jesus. For, Wallace's latest writings come to you from the other side, from the other world...as did Jesus.

St. Paul

On the journey back to Jesus' original context, we must take a detour here through St. Paul. Some call Paul the "second founder" of Christianity. Before becoming a Christian, Paul was a devout Jew, possibly a Pharisee, who participated in the persecution of Christians. Then on the road to Damascus, he had a "divine experience". He says he saw and heard Jesus, and soon he was baptized. After that, he was a servant of the Lord and spent his life spreading Christianity to the world, especially to the Gentiles, and founding churches throughout the Mediterranean. Paul wrote long letters to churches of the region. Those Pauline Letters make up over a third of the New Testament, and they crystallized Christology.

Those letters were either written in response to questions asked him by those new churches dealing with real-life, everyday, nitty-gritty problems that Paul needed to address...or were written from Paul's own hands-on observance of problems with the new religion in certain locations, particularly while bringing Christianity to both Gentiles and Jews. So, Paul's letters really were *real* — down to earth, right down to the nitty-gritty workings of everyday life. Whereas Jesus presented the idea system, Paul disseminated the operating system. (Similarly, Wallace presents the idea system beneath the next mentality in *The Neo-Tech Discovery*, and I present the operating system in *The Neo-Tech World*.)

Paul was a hard-working man with admirable energy and devotion. He made and sold tents throughout his missionary work to have enough money to survive. He was honest, practiced and believed what he preached, without hypocrisy.

Paul never met Jesus; Jesus died before Paul converted. Realize that Jesus brought to the countryside a new mentality that carried with it confounding new thought patterns and a strategically odd communication process (i.e., speaking in parables and metaphors) that can confuse even biblical historians today. ...Along came Paul, certainly a conscious man, an educated man, but not a professional, educated elite (his academic grasp of Greek Philosophies was below average). He had a vision; then this tent maker who never knew Jesus developed, from Jesus' ideas, the entire application system that Christianity took off on for the next 2000 years. ...When you stop to think about that for a moment, you realize (as Paul did himself) what shaky grounds much of Christianity was founded on, right from the start.

And I know, because of my historically unique position of

working on the edge of an evolutionary leap of man's mind, only the second ever, that Paul very innocently got Jesus' fundamental point well off track. I will not take the time here to go through the specifics of Paul's Christology such as his beliefs in Original Sin and guilt, his treatment of theodicy (i.e., why the good man suffers) in his letter to the Romans, his ideas of predestination, and so on. But I will just mention that Paul's psyche carried a heavy burden: before he converted he was responsible for persecuting Christians, which would have tormented the mind of the man Paul became — the "second founder" of Christianity...the religion of love, which perhaps offers insight into Paul's inclinations to say what he says in dealing with his own guilt. But, we cannot delve into that in this treatise. (Notice Paul's self-torment in this passage to his beloved son in faith, Timothy, late in his life, as follows:)

"Even though I was once a blasphemer and a persecutor and a violent man, I was shown mercy because I acted in ignorance and unbelief. The grace of our Lord was poured out on me abundantly, along with the faith and love that are in Christ Jesus.

"Here is a trustworthy saying that deserves full acceptance: Christ Jesus came into the world to save sinners — of whom I am the worst. But for that very reason I was shown mercy so that in me, the worst of sinners, Christ Jesus might display his unlimited patience as an example for those who would believe on him and receive eternal life. Now to the King eternal, immortal, invisible, the only God, be honor and glory for ever and ever. Amen."

— Paul's letter to Timothy 1:13-17

Now, without first understanding what Jesus heroically set out to do — i.e., to bring the uneducated peasants human consciousness thus bring to their lives meaning, value, power, justice and freedom from the educated elite, as identified by Tracey Alexander — Jesus' "confusing" message spoken in parables and metaphors, designed for the bicameral man, could so easily get off course, even reversed, if carried forth by someone else besides Jesus. I know this from my work with

Dr. Wallace and his work in the next mentality. But first, I will give you a brief example of how Jesus' message so easily gets reversed, even by scholars today, because they do not know what Jesus was doing or where he was coming from:

Below I paraphrase from an insightful lecture by Robert Oden, Ph.D., who graduated *magna cum laude* from Harvard College, formerly Professor and Chair, Department of Religion at Dartmouth College, currently President of Kenyon College:

"I think the central message of Jesus is: Life itself is transitional...Life itself is liminal...Human beings are powerfully tempted to see this life as *it*: birth, life, death. Jesus says that's a temptation to which you must not fall prey because that's not *it*. You're relying on sensory data and not on authentic reality...The route that He took from life to death and to another life is a life that is open to all Christians who accept Christ...Life is liminal...I do think, cosmologically, that is the chief Christian message...all those Christian hymns about going home, they're bang on...The message is that your real home is not here on Earth; it's in another realm, access to which you have because of Jesus."

If Dr. Oden only knew that Jesus was trying to invoke the evolutionary leap of the bicameral peasants into another world of human consciousness in which man became one with God. Then this scholar, once he understood the major metaphors through which Jesus taught, would see Jesus' original message was actually the opposite of this well intentioned scholar's interpretation.

Now, translating Jesus' major metaphors that he used over and over to his bicameral followers, let's see how Dr. Oden's interpretation turns around, even while using the good doctor's own expressions: "When Jesus talked to the bicameral peasants and told them that life as they knew it (i.e., their bicameral existence) is not *it*...and that the route He took from life (as a bicameral peasant) to death (of his bicameral mentality) and to another life (reborn with human consciousness) is a life open to all bicameral peasants...Jesus' message is that your real home is not here on Earth (as a bicameral peasant); it's in another realm (as a conscious human or God-Man), access to which you (the bicameral peasants) have because of Jesus (a conscious human...a God-Man)."

As you can see, without understanding the necessary metaphors for his terribly limited audience (Jesus had no choice but to use those metaphors with his bicameral audiences) his entire life's message gets reversed. Dr. Oden thinks that Jesus' message says authority and power and meaning and value is all "out there", which was exactly true *for the bicameral man to whom Jesus was talking to* but was exactly *the opposite of what Jesus was working toward!* The powerless bicameral mentality was the very problem Jesus was trying to reverse. He was trying to invoke those bicameral peasants' leap into human consciousness...to the ancient God-Man, to whom comes the authority and power and meaning and value. I know this from my work with Dr. Wallace on the edge of our next leap into Neothink. I know Jesus was talking to the bicameral man in metaphors; he was *not* talking to the conscious man. He did not expect the conscious man to take his metaphors for the bicameral peasants literally.

Paul innocently made that same mistake. Without understanding the two mentalities, Paul could not differentiate that Jesus' metaphors for the bicameral man were *not* to be followed literally by the conscious man. The metaphors were a tool to invoke *the process* into human consciousness. Jesus was highly motivated by justice to bring an end to the oppression of his brethren — the peasants. Paul did not know Jesus and could not know his strategic use of metaphors. Paul could not know Jesus' deepest objective. Tracey Alexander could look back and know what Jesus was doing and know his strategic use of metaphors only because of her association and work with Dr. Wallace on the edge of the next evolutionary leap of the human mind, the parallel event that enabled her to see the parallels.

So, Paul missed the necessary role of Jesus' metaphors and instead interpreted Jesus' metaphorical teachings to the bicameral peasants as literal teachings for the conscious man. Then Paul added his own ideas from his own troubled psychological makeup (such as man is born guilty through Original Sin[1]) and sent the

---

[1]Realize Judaism does not believe in Original Sin or guilt. Although the story of Adam and Eve is in the Hebrew Bible, the Jews believe Adam and Eve merely made mistakes...as humans are prone to do because they are not divine.

Christian theology in a direction that was in reverse of where Jesus was taking it.

Where was Jesus taking Christianity? He was taking the ordinary person to where Jesus himself was — to the ancient God-Man. *The Book* (Neo-Tech Publishing Co., 1200 pages, Hamilton and Wallace) presents the cosmology Jesus, given a full life like Plato or Aristotle, would have strived for. I know this only because of my work on the edge of a leap in our mentality — a leap Jesus started but could not complete.

I know clearly, from my own work with Dr. Wallace, the problem Paul got into by building the operating system to Jesus' idea system, a problem Paul would be the first to admit if he were alive today. For instance, I have built the detailed operating system *The Neo-Tech World* (and, even more specifically, *Neo-Tech Business*, Neo-Tech Books, 740 pages) to Dr. Wallace's Neo-Tech idea system *The Neo-Tech Discovery*. Had Dr. Wallace, as did Jesus, died young, say twenty years ago after completing *The Neo-Tech Discovery*, the destination where his course was headed would have stopped. I would have continued, as did Paul, building the operating system. My destination, however, would have been completely different from Dr. Wallace's, as was Paul's destination different from Jesus'. And I say this having had the advantage of deeply knowing Dr. Wallace (I am his son) and knowing the next evolutionary leap better than anyone else in the world next to Dr. Wallace. Paul did not even know Jesus or that the evolutionary leap even existed. Jesus *alone* was intensely working on the inside edge of a new mentality. Even his apostles were obviously still bicameral. He was orchestrating *a process*, not a static idea system, which is what his teachings became with his early death. Jesus simply died too young.

It seems to me that Paul, as did Dr. Oden, simply did not know Jesus was talking in metaphors *to bicameral men,* not literally to conscious men. Paul did not know Jesus' deep motivation to bring justice to the bicameral peasants by bringing them the power of human consciousness. Thus, Paul built a whole theology upon this misinterpretation of Jesus. Paul seems innocent, honest, hardworking and nonhypocritical at heart. That is to say, he had no political agendas as did the Church Fathers such as St. Augustine and perhaps the unknown author of the Letter to the Hebrews in the New Testament. Nevertheless, Paul's misinterpretation of Jesus turned the mental structure of man back to a *bicameral structure.*

Paul wrote his letters during a time in which Christians believed overwhelmingly that the world would end with the second coming of the Messiah. Paul thoroughly believed this, which affected much of what he thought and wrote. For instance, he advised people should not get married if they could overcome temptation. But he advised not marrying so they could concentrate on the Lord's work, believing the end of the world was coming soon. He had nothing against marriage per se.

I think Paul was a man of integrity who simply did not understand what Jesus was doing. He, like most others, was waiting for the Christ to return, not knowing that the Holy Spirit and Second Coming were metaphors...that Jesus was telling the bicameral peasants that the Spirit of Christ was in each of them, who would come to them as they rose into the new consciousness — human consciousness. Their bicameral world would end as they rose into the Kingdom of God.

The letters of Paul would have undoubtedly faded in importance over time...as virtuous but outdated advice. However, the political Church realized they had a gold mine in the Pauline Letters for the structure of power that could be built over the masses. In St. Paul, the politically driven Church had a sincere, genuine evangelist — a martyr — who innocently started his life of misguided devotion following a right-brain bicameral experience in which he "saw and heard" Jesus. A true believer, Paul put enormous energy and honesty into his life's work, although his work was a misinterpretation of Jesus...a misinterpretation that inverted Jesus' message, reversed the leap of power into human consciousness (and freedom from the educated elite) back to the powerless bicameral mental structure (and slavery to the educated elite).

Paul, who was *not* a professional, educated elite, innocently gave the Church Fathers of the Middle Ages the foundation to build their political power over the masses. That explains why Christianity grew into the bureaucratic political monster, the Catholic Church, that ruled the Western World for a thousand years. Christianity grew into *the* religion, *the* survivor during a time of many competing religions. St. Augustine, an educated elite and the early Church's premier influence, latched onto the writings of St. Paul.

What About Jesus' Miracles and Resurrection?

During a conversation with a true believer in the Church's interpretations of the Bible and in a God above, he asked me to explain Jesus' miracles.

I said that I see a few issues here: The first begins with a description given by Professor Elizabeth McNamer in her eight recorded lectures titled *The New Testament: An Introduction.* In Lecture Six, she says, "Now, before one reads a book like this, one has to shed one's 20th century American skin. We're so used to thinking of history as a recording of *the facts* and nothing but *the facts*...like we see them presented every evening on our television sets: these are the facts; this is what happened. But this is a very new way of presenting history...this is only this century. Before this time, historians were much more interested in the *interpretation* of the facts, rather than in the facts themselves. So bear that in mind when we are reading through the Acts of the Apostles." In other words, the miracles in the Bible are not meant to be facts. That writing style was a literary vehicle to complete the interpretation of Jesus as the Messiah. Moreover, that writing style, undoubtedly, became even more exaggerated in the Bible by the Church scholars taking liberties to serve their political agendas and, particularly in more gullible times, to pass them off as literal happenings.

A second explanation comes from the philosopher Euhemerus who lived in the 4th century B.C. Since Dr. Oden explained Euhemerism so well in his lectures (although he does not fully agree with it), I quote him in explaining Euhemerism: "All religions started as collections of stories around the deeds of extraordinarily gifted, enormously smart and powerful human beings...but people who were just that — they were only human beings. And then, because these people, though they were human beings, were so talented, so smart, so gifted, in the decades and generations and centuries following their deaths, these stories were exaggerated; they became hyperbolized so that the deeds of once mighty but still mortal human beings became the deeds of supernatural beings. ...This mode of analysis says that...there once really was a Moses, there was a historical being called Khrishna, there was a Buddha, there was a Jesus, there (was) a Mohammed. They were all gifted, talented, extraordinarily committed, outstanding human beings...but that's all they were. But they were so talented that their followers in the years, decades, generations, and centuries following them, began to tell stories about them that made them sound more and more supernatural. So you want to know how religions got started? That's how they got started: they were the deeds of...mortal but very significant beings, and they got exaggerated."

Now, that theory takes on new meaning and strength when understanding that those religious figures were the original sparkles of the light of human consciousness on Earth, which takes us to the third explanation regarding Jesus' miracles: he was a fully conscious man surrounded by bicameral peasants. The Gospels, for instance, report awestruck crowds with people who ask in awe, who is this man to speak with such authority? That would be an immediate reaction and question a bicameral man would ask when confronting a conscious man.

Imagine such an event: a conscious man wanders into a society of bicameral men and women. That would be similar to the bicameral American Indians confronting the conscious European "white gods". Jesus would seem to bicameral men to be a god with miraculous powers. His evolutionary leap into human consciousness could go a long way in explaining his ability to perform "miracles" in the eyes of awestruck, hallucinating peasants.

For comparison, one of the first achievements that will occur in the Neothink mentality will be curing aging and death (Vision Four). That will seem completely natural to those in the Neothink mentality, but will be nothing short of a miracle to those who have not yet taken the leap into Neothink. The vast gulf between Jesus' bicameral followers and his own conscious mentality could have started the tales about the Messiah's miracles. Over time, those tales could have easily grown into tall tales, made even taller still by the ready hand of the Church editors.

In any case, when I read the Gospels, it's like reading two books at once: The teachings of Jesus, especially about love (which I deal with later), are impactful, whereas the reportings of his miracles slip into silly fairy tales, used as literary vehicles to present an interesting story. As the cliché says, "Facts tell, but stories sell." To me, reading the serious quotations of Jesus and his dialogues with the Hebrew leaders, for instance, then shifting to accounts of his miracles is like putting down a serious book on psychology or philosophy and picking up a fairy-tale book to read my daughter. The Gospels are full of this switching back and forth between fact and fiction.

I see similar issues regarding the Resurrection, along those same lines. Aside from the same issues raised above as they also apply to the Resurrection, I see two further issues:

First, believing Jesus would return, the authors of the Gospels wrote nothing down for many years. But when too many years passed and the Apostles started dying off, they decided they had better write about Jesus. During those years between Jesus' death and their writings, the tales could have easily been blown up, even in their own heads. They were the quiet followers — perhaps still possessing the bicameral mentality, which sought supernatural leaders. To have seen Jesus' Resurrection would have been consistent with a bicameral mentality.

These disciples, these followers, might have flipped into bicameral hallucinations with the stress of losing their leader. As explained in the First Insight, *stress* (caused primarily by *decision making)* sent bicameral man into bicameral hallucinations — both audio and sometimes visual hallucinations. Suddenly, without their leader, the disciples were faced with unbearable stress because without Jesus, the decision making fell upon them. So, perhaps they hallucinated their leader, their god, to give them decisions, a classic model of the bicameral mind. When reading the New Testament, the Gospels and the first half of Acts, the Apostles still seem bicameral.

The second issue is that the early Greek translations did not have the portion at the end of Mark 16:9-20 (remember Matthew and Luke copied Mark, and John's Gospel came even later) that describes the Resurrection. Could that have been added later by the Church editors? I don't know the answer, but the Resurrection seems suspicious. Think about it: Jesus supposedly taught his Apostles for another forty days after the Resurrection. It would be *those teachings* that would dominate the Gospels, yet neither in the Gospels nor in the Acts of the Apostles exist anything but references to those forty days of teaching. It makes sense that the Church editors completed their political agenda by adding in the Resurrection. And yet, they were smart enough not to try to craft those "teachings", for doing so would make vulnerable their forgery.

Before we move on, I must mention that it would be interesting to see a *primary* translation done now of the original Greek (Koine) copies of the Gospels with our understanding of Jesus' leap of power into the new mentality of human consciousness, realizing he was communicating to bicameral peasants (not fellow conscious men) using metaphors that the bicameral peasants could more easily relate to. Could such a translation bring forth entirely new insights? I am also, personally, quite interested in his expressions about eternal life in such a new translation. Was the meaning something slightly different, perhaps his way of describing the new dimension of the future and control over your destiny (remember, bicameral man lived in the here-and-now with no sense of the future or self-control), or was eternal life a metaphor, or was eternal life a sales gimmick in a time of many competing religions...or was he peering through to yet the *next level* in the Neothink mentality (where the first feat of society will be to cure aging and death, as you saw in Vision Four)? I am very curious about Jesus' references to eternal life.

The Leap of Power Nullified

As the new consciousness spread and shifted value, power, control, and authority to the individual, the common man, the original message of Jesus was strategically taken out of context by the educated elite — the brilliant leaders of the Church — and ultimately used for a selfish power grab: they could stop this shift of power to the common man and, instead, continue their manipulation of and rule over those lowly peasants. With the clever "enshrinement" of St. Paul in the cherry-picked canon of the New Testament and the late inclusion of the Letter to the Hebrews (which scholars later realized was not written by Paul as we were led to believe by the Church) and the Catholic Letters at the end (which scholars no longer believe were written by those who personally knew Jesus as we were led to believe by the Church), the message of Jesus got successfully (and nearly permanently) inverted for 2000 years...until now. The Church turned Jesus' message, for the common man, against him.

Greatly oversimplified, this is how the Church turned Jesus' message against the very people he was trying to help: As man, one by one, became conscious, he became his own decision maker...he became, as Jesus metaphorically told them, one with God. (Remember, bicameral man had no decision-making ability. That was done by the imagined gods.) But the educated leaders of the Church cleverly, brilliantly stopped this "one with God" idea before it manifested itself.

The educated Church leaders, working off the innocent Pauline Letters, masterfully preserved the old bicameral perspective that God was a *separate* entity to whom man was subservient. By propagating Paul's misinterpretation and presenting Jesus' message in this wrong context, the leaders of the Church could continue ruling the masses *in the name of God*. And now with the political power, the Church could use this wrong context to rule over the masses even *after* they evolved into consciousness.[1]

From Abraham to Moses to David to the Prophets to Jesus, the canon of the Bible brought together the accounts of man's fascinating leap from the Bicameral Kingdoms, ruled by the imagined gods, into one's Kingdom of God, ruled by one's consciousness. In its proper context, the Bible was a working document — the light of day — for making the leap.

The extraordinary power of human consciousness initially caused a great flourish. The Golden Age of Greece with its breathtaking knowledge rose quickly from the barbaric ruins of entire civilizations just a few hundred years before, during the

[1]Nietzsche greatly admired Jesus as the only true Christian, but bitterly despised Christianity for instigating its gigantic fraud in twisting Jesus' teachings to harmful ends.

388

breakdown of the bicameral mind (explained in the First Insight). But then, as humanity stood on its launching pad, something like a debilitating disease started to weaken the power of consciousness. It started with the Greek philosopher and great academic, Plato (427-347 B.C.), who created the pernicious philosophy for the educated elite to be our higher authorities, to be our leaders. The disease gradually gained strength until, eight hundred years later, it was synthesized with Christianity by St. Augustine (354- 430 A.D.). Instead of conscious man soaring as his own authority, his own decision maker and god, man became a pawn once again (as before consciousness) to higher authority, *external* authorities...the leaders of the Church. Man's value, power, control, and authority vanished as did the light of Jesus. Instead of humanity and knowledge soaring from its leap of power into consciousness, humanity and knowledge sank into a thousand years of darkness known as the Dark Ages.

With the aid of Plato, as we will see, the Church turned the Bible from "a journey into human consciousness" to "a journey into mysticism". For 1600 years, the Bible has been viewed from this illusionary context of man serving a supernatural being called God — a context devised by the external authorities, the leaders of the Church who ruled mankind in the name of God. As we will see, perhaps a much bigger problem than the Church suppressing gospels about Jesus was this shift in context using brilliant conscious men such as Plato, the unknown author of the Letter to the Hebrews and, later, St. Augustine...all three educated elite and, in the case of Plato and St. Augustine and most likely the author of Hebrews, political figures interested in power.

Humanity's Greatest Irony

Plato lived 400 years before Jesus. Plato was a brilliant Greek philosopher who developed the most comprehensive, fully surviving idea system for living. The basis of his metaphysics was that the transient world we live in was but a shadow of the authentic world of meaning and value...of authentic reality that he called *forms*. Amazingly, this brilliant academic developed a complete philosophy and definitive idea system for living that paralleled the same underlying value system and mental structure of the Bicameral Age where meaning and value — the real world of *authentic reality* — was "out there" in the world of the gods, not in the meaningless, transient world of man.

Plato, as did all the Greek philosophers, intensely studied the *Iliad* and the *Odyssey*, the so-called Homeric Poems. The *Iliad* was written by bicameral man and reflects the bicameral mental structure that Plato ultimately developed into a fully integrated *conscious* philosophy. The result of Plato's philosophy, of course, leads to the same results seen in the *Iliad* and other bicameral epics: all-powerful, often immature gods full of jealousies and envy acting like spoiled children used the meaningless, valueless humans to serve the gods' every whim with no accountability or importance placed on the humans, even if they went to war and lost their lives for a god's emotional fancy. Now, simply exchange the humans under the gods to the populous under Plato's elite political leaders. Of course, Plato makes his leaders out to be noble academics interested only in the eternal beauty of the perfect forms, but the mental structure and practical results of Plato's *Republic* are the same as the bicameral world of the *Iliad*.

However incredibly, this educated elite Plato brought back, in a potently integrated matrix, the mental structure of the bicameral mind. Plato's powerful mutation of the bicameral mind could actually survive within the conscious mentality that was otherwise quickly dismissing the old bicameral beliefs. This bicameral mutation, created by one of humanity's most brilliant men, was such a debilitating disease to the new conscious mind that human consciousness steadily lost its enormous power.

Plato's philosophy was based on something he called *forms*. The forms were the pure and perfect state of things that existed in the eternal world of "authentic reality". Consider the example given by Phillip Cary, PhD, head of the Philosophy program at Eastern College: if you were a math teacher who, for his entire adult life, drew triangles on the chalkboard, you would never draw a perfect triangle. A complex mathematical equation, however, intellectually tells us that the perfect triangle exists and has existed eternally despite the millions of imperfect triangles drawn by man. That perfect triangle is the beautiful, eternal form. It is authentic reality, not what math teachers draw on chalkboards.

Plato pigeonholed man as: never knowing, no less achieving, those perfect forms that represented "authentic reality". According to Plato, the *ordinary* man could never get close to knowing reality.

Plato said that reality was a function of reason and *could not* be perceived by our senses. To approach reality took years and years of special education to just begin to learn the forms.

Plato's beautiful, poetic *Republic*, his most famous writing about the ideal State, concretizes politically on Earth his metaphysical view of forms. It all sounds interesting and harmless at first interpretation, even admirable, especially the virtue of striving for the ultimate form of good. But then you realize this philosophy is reversing everything that brought man his leap of power — reversing us back to powerless bicameral mental structures.

In metaphysics, Plato reversed our new mental structure of consciousness back to the bicameral mental structure. As in bicameral beliefs, our world was now unimportant; it was not even real. What was important and real was that unattainable world of forms...like the bicameral man's unattainable world of the gods (yet the unattainable was now advanced by this brilliant philosopher into a sophisticated and unassailable mutation through his idealistic world of forms, a perfect place we would go to after we died before being reborn on Earth). Plato's perfect world of eternal forms reversed the previous 1500 long years of shifting value, power, control, and authority from beyond man to within man; Plato's "perfect world" shifted that value, power, control, and authority right back again to "out there", *beyond* man.

In the study of ethics, Plato put forth that the ordinary man is not responsible for not knowing reality. Reality is not known until you know the forms. But to begin to know the forms takes many, many years of advanced education. Thus, we may conclude, besides the educated elite — comparable to the god-kings of the Bicameral Kingdoms — the masses know not reality and are to be led by the educated elite, the new external authorities. That completely undoes the ordinary man's self-responsibility (and the power, control, and internal authority that goes along with it, which was first introduced to man by the

Hebrews in the Torah and the Ten Commandments, by the Prophets and the journey within...on the long road to consciousness).

In politics, Plato's *Republic* represents his ideal State. A very few selected persons become the ruling class through years and years of exclusive education. They are fifty years old before they know the forms well enough to become a governor of the State. Of course, no one else knows reality, only the educated elite. They rule the State. They are equivalent to bicameral man's god-kings. They are the external authorities (just as those who ruled over the Bicameral Kingdoms). Meaningful self-authority and self-control vanishes under Plato's politics. Plato's *Republic* undoes the evolution recorded in the Bible that brought value, power, control, and authority to the common man.

In the study of epistemology, Plato put forth that knowledge is acquired through memory: the higher realities are the forms, and when we die we go to the perfect world of the forms for a period of time. Then, we are reborn on Earth. All our lives, we carry that knowledge of the forms deep in our subconscious. We acquire knowledge as we remember bits and pieces from our subconscious. This is a sophisticated version of the same mind structure of bicameral man who believed man had knowledge only to the degree the gods intermingled in his life and gave him knowledge. ...The Bible recorded man breaking out of that celestial, cyclical wheel of the gods to establish his past and his future...to create the New through knowledge of the past and decisions (e.g., the Ten Commandments) in the present. He gradually developed the tools to generate knowledge. All that is undone by Plato.

The trick of Plato is that his philosophy is idealistic and sounds virtuous. Of course, so does communism. But both revert back to *the powerless*: to the obsolete bicameral mental structure of external "authorities".

Plato's bicameral mutation, now injected into the new conscious mentality, steadily built influence and gained strength over the next four centuries. Of course, Plato lived in a different place and culture than the Hebrews. But, in the second half of the first century A.D., the Letter to the Hebrews in the New Testament was written by an unknown author who was an educated elite. Although the author was unknown, scholars do know by his writing he was a Hellenistic Jew. He was very educated and deeply understood Greek philosophy...particularly Plato. Here is where the misinterpretation of Jesus became permanently solidified. The Letter to the Hebrews in the New Testament says man's world on Earth is transitory, a shadow of ultimate reality in heaven. The Letter to the Hebrews tied together the major characters and events (i.e., man's world on Earth) in the Hebrew Bible — from Abraham and the covenant to Moses and the Ten Commandments to David and the Prophets — and superseded it all with the culmination of Jesus from heaven and the new covenant. Of course, the brilliant letter does this using the wrong interpretation of Jesus, using his metaphors literally with strong Platonistic overtones. The laws of the Torah, for instance, were said to be just a transitory shadow on Earth of what had come through Jesus from heaven. The Letter to the Hebrews successfully rolled up everything in man's 2000-year trek into human consciousness, and teed it off in one Platonistic smack right back into the bicameral mentality.

The Letter to the Hebrews (originally claimed by the Church to be written by Paul) actually differed dramatically from the Pauline Letters, which delivered specific advice that would have faded piece by piece over time with the fading bicameral mentality. The Letter to the Hebrews brilliantly pulled together the events of man on Earth in the Hebrew Bible and made them all lesser realities than the ultimate reality of Jesus and (his metaphor) God, "out there". Indeed, Hebrews made Jesus' message, through Plato's philosophical tools, fit directly into a bicameral mental structure where the authority, meaning, and value was "out there" in another world and not inside man himself — the complete opposite of Jesus' message! Hence, the Bible, mankind's idea system for living, flipped from a turnkey manual for evolving into human consciousness...to a turnkey working document for external authorities to send man's evolving consciousness back to a bicameral structure! The Letter to the Hebrews now gave the Church a powerful, self-serving context through which it could build its political power over the world.

That self-serving context, expressly for political rule over the world, culminated in the fourth century A.D. with St. Augustine,

393

Bishop of Hippo. He was a genius who, as a young man, became inflamed with love for books on Platonism. After St. Augustine's conversion to Christianity, he synthesized Plato's philosophy with Christianity and the Bible, particularly with St. Paul's misinterpretations of Jesus.

This brings us to the greatest irony of all time: now, through Plato's definitive philosophy and St. Augustine's prolific literary genius (that required three full-time secretaries to keep up with him), the mutant, bicameral mental structure for living was now irrevocably tied into Judeo-Christian religion and, specifically, to Jesus Christ and the Bible! Jesus Christ was the very man leading the bicameral peasants out of the bicameral mentality, and the Bible was the very piece of accumulated literature that represented the written account of man's evolvement *away* from the bicameral structure of the mind into the conscious structure...*away* from meaning and values being "out there" in the world of the gods, bringing meaning and values down to Earth into the interior world of man. That evolving body of literature represented the advancing stages of man's mental structure, evolving for survival under harsh living conditions. The struggles and ascent to consciousness occurred over a two-thousand-year span of evolving lives and over a thousand years of painstakingly scribing the literary accounts.

The Bible — that historic account of man's ascent from bicameral man to human consciousness — culminating in Jesus' message, now was reversed by this bicameral mutation injected into humanity by Plato and St. Augustine.

Over the course of the Bible, we can see the progression from godly power to individual power, from power beyond to power within, culminating in the New Testament and the metaphorical message of Jesus that man can become one with God through the "new consciousness". That is the proper context of the Bible: the evolvement from bicameral man to **God-Man**.

Jesus was the God-Man of that ancient time. He spoke in metaphors. He called himself man of God, Son of God, the Father, which were metaphors. He spoke of dying and his Resurrection, which were metaphors. He spoke of the Holy Spirit entering the good people on Earth, which was a metaphor. Myself seeing what it takes to go through an evolutionary leap of the mind (into Neothink), I see how the old mentality must first die, then one rises again in the new mentality. He spoke of heavenly love and beauty, which were metaphors for the love and beauty one entered through consciousness. I can see that Jesus was speaking metaphorically to the bicameral peasants. His message about the Kingdom of Heaven was a metaphor for the evolutionary leap into human consciousness...into God-Man.

> Jesus replied, "I assure you, unless you are born again, you can never see the Kingdom of God."
>
> "What do you mean?" exclaimed Nicodemus. "How can an old man go back into his mother's womb and be born again?"
>
> Jesus replied, "The truth is, no one can enter the Kingdom of God without being born of water and the Spirit. Humans can reproduce only human life, but the Holy Spirit gives new life from heaven. So don't be surprised at my statement that you must be born again. Just as you can hear the wind but can't tell where it comes from or where it is going, so you can't explain how people are born of the Spirit."
>
> John 3:1-8

The Plato/St. Augustine combination separated Jesus' God-Man into God *and* man...or, God *over* man — right back to the bicameral perception and value structure. The Church now used the great power of the Bible out of context, as a self-serving political tool to rule over man in the name of the almighty God above man. Meaning and value now lay with God and the Church. Man was, once again, the pawn...the powerless.

A Quick Proof

This hypothesis may seem unrealistic considering its total absence on the radar screen of many thousands of biblical scholars and historians. First, I will say that the proper context of the Bible could not be seen before because the Bible first required a parallel event — the next evolution of man — to be seen in the proper context. We have reached that parallel event on Earth, which Dr. Wallace and I have studied in depth and now present to you in our writings. Yet, even without knowing about our next evolution into God-Man, this hypothesis has the advantage of coming equipped with a self-evident proof:

Try to imagine the leap of power human consciousness gave man. Prior to human consciousness, man had no control. He just lived by mimicked reactions and learned responses and automatic guidance from his nervous system as did all other animals, although he had the most advanced brain, including language, thus the directives from his nervous system were "heard" as commands. Human consciousness sprang forth after reaching a point of sophistication in language and writing, namely the development of the metaphor. The metaphor met paths with enormous survival pressures[1] to push man's mind — first, the struggling Jews — into a new inner mind space that enabled him to separate from the immediate external world around him and enter that internal world where he could analyze, judge, think, introspect, and make decisions. Suddenly, he had self-control. Imagine, he could *think* and *make decisions* independent of the gods — independent of the automatic guidance from nature's nervous system. He leapt beyond nature into man-made self-guidance and could plan his future. He, in essence, mentally jumped from a nature-controlled animal to a self-controlled human. Imagine the prosperity such a leap of power would bring him!

However, after injecting the crippling Plato/St. Augustine mutation of the bicameral mental structure into this new conscious mentality through Christianity, the incredible new power vanished to *nothing*.

Incredibly, as the masses gained this great power, civilization sank into its most powerless age. The world *reversed* in knowledge for a thousand years! That bizarre reversal of knowledge and power is mind boggling upon understanding the

---

[1]To get a fuller understanding of the enormous survival pressures that more or less forced man into the new mind space of human consciousness, you must understand the dynamics of the *breakdown of the bicameral mind*. To get that proper understanding, you must read Julian Jaynes' book: *The Origin of Consciousness in the Breakdown of the Bicameral Mind*.

context of that time...coming on the heels of mankind's phenomenal leap of power into human consciousness. The only possible way that could happen would be if somehow the all-powerful conscious mentality reverted back to the powerless bicameral mentality, which could only happen if a powerful mutation of the bicameral mental structure — a disease of the conscious mind — infected and crippled this new leap of power into human consciousness.

The fact that humanity reversed for a millennium, just as *the masses* were discovering human consciousness, is unbelievable. Humanity should have instead soared as a supersociety at a lightning pace. (See the chart in the First Insight to see how fast humanity should have soared.) That bizarre reversal of power can only be explained upon realizing that the conscious mentality became infected by the mutant bicameral pathogen of Plato and St. Augustine and was subsequently spread by the Church Fathers.

Plato and St. Augustine's mutation of the bicameral mentality was *far more powerful* than the original bicameral mentality itself, which was quickly fading as silly and dismissable rituals that arose from primitive man's inability to think through things and explain things. This powerful platonic mutation created by two of the most conceptually brilliant men who ever lived, could survive in the conscious world. In fact, it was a germ so strong it could not be stopped. This mutant bicameral germ spread throughout the western world (eventually the *entire* world) and destroyed, dead in its tracks, the limitless power of human consciousness. The mind disease crippled humanity into the Dark Ages and has, ever since, sickened the world in an anticivilization.

The Heartbreaking Reversal

The Bible, once the most valuable document ever written, was turned into the most destructive document ever written. Instead of freeing the bicameral peasants, the Church enslaved them for a thousand years. Jesus, who gave his life for his love of the struggling peasant, would have been eternally heartbroken upon learning this.

Jesus died too young. His enemy, the educated elite, murdered him and went on, without him, to win the war of two worlds.

The Final Victory

The Neo-Tech World and *The First Immortals* are here to tee up that destructive mystical world and smack it away, forever. They will, finally, win the war of two worlds for Nietzsche's Jesus and for every value producer who ever lived, from the peasants to self-made billionaires.

My writings and Dr. Wallace's writings give us the cosmology Jesus would have strived toward had he not been murdered just three years after his ministry began. I am not saying the specifics in my writings such as the money-making techniques in Visions One, Two, Five, Six, and Nine, for instance, would have risen from Jesus' teachings. What I am saying is: my writings complete our final evolution into God-Man that Jesus started. Take comfort in knowing that the general message here is what Jesus himself wanted you to know. This Insight and the next will do right for Jesus (and humanity) what his crucifixion did wrong for Jesus (and humanity) for 2000 years.

We do not know it now, but today we are in a Dark Ages compared to what we will have when the bicameral mind disease is gone (predictably sometime in the early third millennium, perhaps in our lifetimes). We cannot know that we are in a tragically suppressed era (by comparison to *what we will have*) anymore than people in the grips of the Dark Ages could know about the sparkling Renaissance yet to come. *The Neo-Tech World* and especially *The First Immortals* give you your first glimpse into the illuminated world free of the bicameral mind disease.

The big picture of *The Neo-Tech World* is to remove that bicameral mind disease from human consciousness, throughout the world. When that occurs, civilization will go through a leap of power and soar to new levels of prosperity, wealth, and love for everyone. The supersociety will form and take us into the Golden Neo-Tech World.

The immediate picture of *The Neo-Tech World* is to remove that bicameral mind disease from *your* consciousness. When that occurs, you will go through a leap of power into a new mind space called *Neothink*. You will so prosper beyond your current self that you will become a millionaire, discover permanent happiness, and experience the next level of romantic love.

The Missing Ingredient

When we study Jesus' teachings of love and his metaphorical teachings of who are the blessed, we realize Jesus went much further than guiding the bicameral peasants to the jumping off point to human consciousness. He introduced the missing ingredient of honesty to consciousness.

Neo-Tech, fully integrated honesty, is a human process achievable when acting through pure love (explained in the First Insight.) Jesus' feat of introducing preliminary aspects of Neo-Tech to the masses may be Jesus' greatest feat of all, for Neo-Tech was *the* necessary ingredient to human consciousness — and *the* missing ingredient — to complete the leap into the God-Man and to rise into the supersociety.

The special ingredient called Neo-Tech (defined as fully integrated honesty and achievable through pure love) was missing for the thousand years before Jesus was born. (The Greek philosopher Aristotle introduced the educated to preliminary aspects of Neo-Tech 350 years earlier.) After the educated elite had already made the leap into human consciousness, they gained such enormous power over the common people that the privileged class tended to slip into lazy generalship over the masses. Absent from their minds was honesty, a state achievable when acting through love, which Jesus brought to the world both in his own unyielding principles and in his metaphorical teachings. With honesty, a person would rise into the Kingdom of God. Today with Neo-Tech, a person will become the God-Man in the Civilization of the Universe (explained in the Third Vision, next). The people without Neo-Tech and its honesty and love will stop short of man's final leap into God-Man and will eventually perish in the dying world of mutant bicameral mentalities and conscious dishonesties and hatred.

During his years as a peasant, Jesus witnessed the dishonesty and hatred toward human life, especially toward the working classes, displayed by the educated, conscious Pharisees, scribes, and Hebrew leaders. Perhaps without explicitly defining the psychological dynamics, he implicitly knew that the educated elite's consciousness was flawed — with dishonesty. That flaw — dishonesty — led to oppression, cruelty, and hatred, and it destroyed civilization and prevented the Kingdom of God. Jesus, an unyielding man of principles right to the end, was determined to cure humanity's mental flaw. And the only cure was Neo-Tech — fully integrated honesty — that rare human condition that can be achieved when acting through pure love.

Jesus set out to reverse that thousand-year human flaw of dishonesty and hatred through his honest ministry of *love* and *compassion*. ...The writings of Wallace and myself will finally remove humanity's flaw as Jesus had hoped to do. But, for now, let us see how Jesus introduced preliminary aspects of Neo-Tech to the world:

The leap of power from the bicameral mentality to human consciousness meant man no longer automatically followed external authorities. Instead, he now controlled his own life. The ability to think and make decisions and control one's own life shifted authority from "out there" to within. Jesus came along and exercised such internal authority. The Gospels refer to Jesus in awe, begging the question, "Who is this person with such authority?"

> The people were amazed at his teachings, because he taught them as one who had authority, not as the teacher of the law.
>
> Mark 1:22

> The people were all so amazed that they asked each other, "What is this? A new teaching — and with authority!"
>
> Mark 1:27

Internal authority is the major characteristic of human consciousness, just as external authority is the major sign of the bicameral mentality. Through internal authority, man can integrate knowledge, think, make decisions in the present, create the future, evolve beyond the past, and no longer be bound by external authorities.

Jesus demonstrated this internal authority as he challenged the Pharisees (the teachers of the Torah or Law in Hebrew scriptures) and their dogmatism. The Pharisees demanded strict adherence to the Torah — the law of Moses in the Hebrew Bible. Jesus challenged several of the laws of the Torah, which infuriated the Pharisees. He violated purity and dietary laws. He violated the Torah by healing on the Sabbath. He forgave sins and spoke in the name of the Lord, which was to speak blasphemy.

This caused Jesus great harm and eventually cost him his life. He was always on the run because the Pharisees and Hebrew leaders would have persecuted Jesus. But he never relented.

To understand what was going on here brings us into the world of fully integrated honesty. Consider that the inner space of the mind known as human consciousness results in integrating thoughts and forming conclusions and decisions — the very process of consciousness and its symbiotic internal authority. That process of integrated thinking called consciousness leads the conscious man to something called *context*. Forming accurate *context* is the prime responsibility of consciousness, which Jesus upheld. He put himself in enormously uncomfortable positions, especially during those times, by challenging laws of the Torah and dogma of the Pharisees because, with consciousness, *context* had changed.

Jesus was shifting the people's perspectives from the laws of Moses and the Torah outside of man, such as purity laws "out there" — to the purity of the heart within, bringing authority from the external bicameral-like world to the internal conscious world.

For example, when arguing with Pharisees about purity laws, Jesus said,

> "Nothing outside a man can make him 'unclean' by going into him. Rather it is what comes out of a man that makes him 'unclean'." Mark 7:15-16

Jesus went on to say,

"For from within, out of men's hearts, come evil thoughts, sexual immorality, theft, murder, adultery, greed, malice, deceit, lewdness, envy, slander, arrogance and folly. All these evils come from inside and make a man 'unclean'."

Mark 7:21-23

Jesus also told those Pharisees,

"Isaiah was right when he prophesied about you hypocrites; as it is written: 'These people (the Pharisees) honor me with their lips, but their hearts are far from me. They worship me in vain; their teachings are but rules taught by men.' You have let go of the commands of God and are holding on to the traditions of men."

Mark 7:6-8

Jesus was constantly shifting his followers away from the external authorities and their many laws that take away the common man's authority and power over himself. Jesus was constantly shifting man toward power within himself.

The Hebrew leaders did not like that, for they wanted to keep the dogmatic allegiance to the laws of the Torah, maintaining the educated leaders' livelihoods as the external authorities of the law — the privileged class. (The parallel perspective today, by the way, is: Wallace and Hamilton shift people away from the external guidance of politicians and regulatory bureaucracies "above man" to the internal guidance of Neothink, bringing guidance and power to within the God-Man.)

With human consciousness, some of bicameral man's laws of the Torah did not work anymore. "Eye for eye, tooth for tooth, hand for a hand" provided a masterful shift, *when they were written,* away from the bicameral mental structure where the common man had little value and could lose his hand for striking an elite...toward the mental structure of consciousness where the common man had value, too. But in Jesus' time, several centuries after the Torah was written, when man jumped to

402

human consciousness, *context* changed. The evolutionary leap into consciousness brought an enormous leap in emotional richness, human value, and compassion. Jesus was evolving and teaching in context with this next level of emotional richness by teaching love and compassion, from barbarianism to forgiveness and understanding:

> "But I tell you who hear me: Love your enemies, do good to those who hate you, bless those who curse you, pray for those who mistreat you. If someone strikes you on one cheek, turn to him the other also. If someone takes your cloak, do not stop him from taking your tunic. Give to everyone who asks you, and if anyone takes what belongs to you, do not demand it back. Do to others as you would have them do to you.
>
> "If you love those who love you, what credit is that to you? Even 'sinners' love those who love them. And if you do good to those who are good to you, what credit is that to you? Even 'sinners' do that. And if you lend to those from whom you expect repayment, what credit is that to you? Even 'sinners' lend to 'sinners,' expecting to be repaid in full. But love your enemies, do good to them, and lend to them without expecting to get anything back. Then your reward will be great, and you will be sons of the Most High, because he is kind to the ungrateful and wicked. Be merciful, just as your Father is merciful."
>
> Luke 6:27-36

His message of love and forgiveness attempted to describe the leap of emotional richness and compassion upon making the leap into consciousness. ...Now, we must introduce a new word and concept here to properly understand Jesus, human consciousness, and the catalytic ingredient called Neo-Tech (i.e., fully integrated honesty) that will allow conscious individuals to take the leap into God-Man. That new word and concept is "contextualist", which Jesus was. This new word "contextualist" leads to the opposite results of "dogmatists" and "pragmatists", which, by the way, are flip sides of the same coin.

To understand these three terms better, you must first realize that principles and morals are absolutes. In other words, what's good is good; what's bad is bad across all space and time. Both the dogmatist and the pragmatist, in opposite-appearing ways, violate and destroy principles and morals...whereas the contextualist serves, preserves, and protects principles and morals, which Jesus did.

Of course, the dogmatist will claim that he is the one who serves, preserves, and protects morals. The Pharisees, who were dogmatists, cried that it was Jesus who was attacking the principles and morals of the Hebrew Bible. But Jesus knew it was those Hebrew elders who were destroying the principles and morals of good, and he lambasted them:

"The teachers of the law and the Pharisees sit in Moses' seat. So you must obey them and do everything they tell you. But do not do what they do, for they do not practice what they preach.

"They tie up heavy loads and put them on men's shoulders, but they themselves are not willing to lift a finger to move them.

"Everything they do is done for men to see: They make their phylacteries wide and the tassels on their garments long; they love the place of honor at banquets and the most important seats in the synagogues; they love to be greeted in the marketplaces and to have men call them 'Rabbi'."

Mathew 23:1-7

"Woe to you, teachers of the law and Pharisees, you hypocrites! You give a tenth of your spices — mint, dill and cummin. But you have neglected the more important matters of the law — justice, mercy and faithfulness. You should have practiced the latter, without neglecting the former. You blind guides! You strain out a gnat but swallow a camel.

"Woe to you, teachers of the law and Pharisees, you hypocrites! You clean the outside of the cup and dish, but inside they are full of greed and self-indulgence. Blind Pharisee! First clean the inside of the cup and dish, and then the outside also will be clean.

404

"Woe to you, teachers of the law and Pharisees, you hypocrites! You are like whitewashed tombs, which look beautiful on the outside but on the inside are full of dead men's bones and everything unclean. In the same way, on the outside you appear to people as righteous but on the inside you are full of hypocrisy and wickedness."

Mathew 23:23-28

Jesus knew that as man evolved beyond his external-world mentality, he must evolve beyond the external-world laws of the Torah. As the dogmatists (and the religious dogmatists ever since) demanded the same literal application of the Torah as man and the world changed context, they were merely creating a power structure from which they dishonestly placed themselves in the positions of external authority to rule others to serve the law, which in their hands changed everything that once was good about the Torah to bad, tyrannical, and evil...much the same fate of the Christian Bible and Jesus' teachings a few hundred years later.

The Pharisees and scribes had taken the priceless work of Moses (and the other anonymous yet brilliant authors of the Torah) and steadily blocked out context and locked in a system of rule and oppression. The same thing would happen later to Jesus' own teachings and, as you will see, to the great Greek Philosopher Aristotle. Over and over throughout history, valuable idea systems, from Moses, Aristotle, Jesus to what is happening to Ayn Rand and her Objectivist philosophy today, eventually contribute to horrific systems of tyranny and oppression. The creators of the idea systems are not to blame and would be horrified and heartbroken, for it is the dogmatists who, later, steadily block out context and lock in a system of rule and oppression.

The Pharisees and scribes, a privileged class during Jesus' time, used Moses' Torah to build their system of control and oppression, against which Jesus rebelled. The Church Fathers during the Middle Ages used Aristotle and Jesus to build their system of control and oppression, against which Copernicus and other scientists finally rebelled. Today, dogmatic Objectivists are gradually doing to Ayn Rand what the Church did to Jesus and

Aristotle.

Jesus, a fully conscious and honest man, stood up to evil and exposed the Pharisees' hypocrisy and fraud, which required enormous character and strength. Yet, amid his outlashes against the dishonest leaders, he taught with almost confounding love and compassion at the new level of emotional richness. It was as if he were passionately protecting and loving a child. And everyone who saw the world this way, through passionate protection of life and value and through *pure* love, would see the world through the most broadly integrating, contextual, and honest eyes. Seeing life and value this way through love, such as the pure love for a little child worth protecting and loving, would bring morality and righteousness (which meant justice in Jesus' time) to the conscious person so he could enter the Kingdom of God...and become the God-Man.

Why is that? As you saw in the First Insight, two processes working together at the same time bring about the rare mental state of Neo-Tech (needed to become the God-Man). Those two processes are: 1) thinking through things and integrating thoughts with your own mind instead of turning that process over to and following external authorities, and 2) exerting honesty in each and every one of those thoughts. Those two processes of the mind cause the mental state of Neo-Tech (which puts everything into context). That mental state of Neo-Tech is difficult to achieve and especially hard to maintain because of deep-rooted bicameral tendencies and deep-rooted rationalizations and mysticisms, as explained in the First Insight. As difficult as it is to achieve and then maintain the state of Neo-Tech that is required to jump to the God-Man, that state of Neo-Tech comes naturally and easily when, say, acting on behalf of your one-year old child. For example, when caring for your own small child, you will not turn authority over to others as you might do in other areas of your life. You will think through and integrate widely to do what is best for that child. Also, every thought and action will be fully honest for the well-being of that small child, overriding any deep agendas, rationalizations, or laziness that may exist within. Acting on pure love naturally brings about this otherwise very difficult state of Neo-Tech or fully integrated honesty. Jesus sensed this and based his ministry on that kind of *pure love*.

In short, Jesus used honesty throughout his three-year ministry right to the end. And he discovered that *love* was the vehicle to enable people to act with Neo-Tech. Acting with Neo-Tech meant seeing situations fully and honestly in context by thinking through things fully and honestly. Acting with Neo-Tech makes a person a contextualist, as was Jesus.

By contrast, pragmatists and dogmatists are the flip side of the same coin of dishonestly destroying principles and morals. In short, pragmatists do not work from a priority of adhering to principles and morals, which Jesus did. To the pragmatist, the priority goes to *the moment*. Principles and morals become subordinate and eventually wither to nothing. The last U.S. President of the 20th century, William Jefferson Clinton, championed political pragmatism.

To be a contextualist requires fully integrated honesty. In his time and place, Jesus exerted fully integrated honesty. Since then, ever since that time and place, both dogmatists and pragmatists have destroyed his principles and morals by presenting his teachings out of context. This Second Insight attempts to put his message back into context. *The Neo-Tech World* and *The First Immortals* bring the special, catalytic ingredient *Neo-Tech* with all its love to your consciousness to enable you to rise as the God-Man into the Civilization of the Universe.

The Bible: Religion or Evolution?

How did Christianity, originally one of many competing sects within Judaism, take hold and become *the* largest religion on Earth? Consider Jesus' teachings becoming combined with the Hebrew Bible to form the canon of the Christian Bible. As obvious as that seems today, at the time of Christ, the odds would have been highly against it. The Hebrew elders who determined the canon of the Hebrew Bible accused Jesus of blasphemy. They ostracized him from their synagogues. Yet, Jesus' teachings were destined to become part of the canon, and Christianity would spread over the world. Why?

First, the answer based on religion: for better or for worse, we must take pause and give credit to Paul whose lifetime of travels and teachings was *the* reason Christianity spread to the Gentiles (non Jews) in large numbers across many lands. Unfortunately, Paul's martyrdom combined with his innocent misinterpretation of Jesus made Christianity and its Bible the ideal instrument for political domination of the world.

As you now know, Paul was never a bicameral peasant. He perhaps was even once a Pharisee, an educated conscious man. He never knew Jesus. Paul could not have known about Jesus' leap from a bicameral peasant to human consciousness. Paul could not know about Jesus' secret metaphors used for his bicameral audiences to help invoke *the jump* into human consciousness. So, true believer Paul taught Jesus' secret metaphors, but he never knew they were metaphors. He literally applied them to the conscious world, which played into the hands of future Church Fathers such as St. Augustine. Using Jesus' secret metaphors in literal terms, instead of as a metaphorical process to invoke the jump into human consciousness, would be analogous to the Church Fathers taking my work on *love* in the First Insight and using it as a proponent of altruistic selflessness and sacrifice in order to tax a living from the people...when instead my work on love is meant to provide an emotional condition that invokes the individual's process of Neo-Tech to make the jump into Neothink and onto becoming the God-Man. ...As you will see, the Church was skillful at this dishonest art of manipulating context.

Now, the answer as to why Jesus' teachings were destined to permanently join with the Hebrew Bible based on evolution: we must understand that the Bible was not originally a religious document per se (certainly not in the wrong, mystical context of the past 2000 years) insomuch as it was, both the Old Testament and the Gospels of the New Testament, the recording of the evolution of human consciousness. Jesus' teachings represented that leap into the new mentality, making his teachings destined to become part of the documentation that had captured the highlights of man's evolution into consciousness for nearly 2000 years. That fascinating documentation, known as the Bible, will henceforth live forever *in context* as our record of humanity's 2000-year journey, culminating in our leap, through Jesus, into human consciousness...and almost, through preliminary aspects of Neo-Tech, into the God-Man of that ancient time.

Evolution Shifting Power and Control to Man

The Hebrew Bible became the Old Testament of the Christian Bible. The first five books of the Hebrew Bible called the Torah were believed to have been written in large part by Moses, who was a bicameral man communicating to bicameral people. The Torah, also called the Book of Moses, contains the laws, including the Ten Commandments. As we know, the Ten Commandments were a major shift in the mental structure away from the bicameral mind reacting to external authorities...toward self-control, self-determination, and the conscious mind of self-authority.

Other examples of this shift toward human consciousness appear in the Torah when understanding its context. For example, the *lex talionis*, the law of retaliation, "life for life, eye for an eye, tooth for tooth, hand for hand, foot for foot," going back to the context of its time reflects the ongoing shift toward the mental structure of human consciousness and internal authority. Until those laws, the elite could, as Cahill points out, have a commoner's hand for stealing a loaf of bread. The *lex talionis* shifted value, power, and control from the privileged class, the educated elite "external authorities", to the common man.

The process of shifting value, power and control from the world of the temperamental gods and privileged class to the common man advanced bicameral man's mental structure toward human consciousness. This shift of value, power, and control occurred in mental jumps across 2000 years before the mental structure could make the big jump into human consciousness.

Those mental jumps toward human consciousness, shifting authority from "out there" to "within", can be seen over and over throughout the Hebrew Bible and Jesus' ministry...starting with the Book of Genesis and Abraham's interpersonal relationship with God, and the idea of a covenant with a chosen people, for the first time shifts value, power, and glimpses of control toward man...to the Book of Exodus and Moses' scribing the Ten Commandments and the marriage-like relationship between YHWH and the chosen people shifts value, power, and control toward man...to the *lex talionis* shifting value, power, and control from the privileged class "out there" toward the common man...to David the King who sang "I"...to the Prophets' demands for self-responsibility...to the exile and the journey within...to, ultimately, Jesus' ministry shifting value, power, control, and authority from the Jewish leaders and the educated elite to the power of God *within the common man.*

Jesus' teachings pushed man into that inner mind space as each individual started to look inward for the power of God, *within himself.* Even when Jesus had to leave his Apostles, he told them to look for the Holy Spirit...another metaphor to keep them looking inward to the journey of the spirit within...where they would discover consciousness. Notice his use of this metaphor in the following excerpt from Acts:

> In my former book, Theophilus, I wrote about all that Jesus began to do and to teach until the day he was taken up to heaven, after giving instructions through the Holy Spirit to the apostles he had chosen. After his suffering, he showed himself to these men and gave many convincing proofs that he was alive. He appeared to them over a period of forty days and spoke about the kingdom of God. On one occasion, while he was eating with them, he gave them this command: "Do not leave Jerusalem, but wait for the gift my Father promised, which you have heard me speak about. For John baptized with water, but in a few days you will be baptized with the Holy Spirit."
>
> So when they met together, they asked him, "Lord, are you at this time going to restore the kingdom to Israel?"
>
> He said to them: "It is not for you to know the times or dates the Father has set by his own authority. But you will receive power when the Holy Spirit comes on you; and you will be my witnesses in Jerusalem, and in all Judea and Samaria, and to the ends of the earth."
>
> Acts 1:1-8

God-Man Is God

The Kingdom of God within was the individual's leap into his own psyche, into the realm of decision making, self-determination, self-control. Moreover, the conscious man was, through Jesus, now faced with the choice between honesty versus dishonesty. Jesus' Kingdom of God brought on that choice: whether or not to make man's next leap into fully integrated honesty, achievable through pure love. (As you saw in the First Insight, fully integrated honesty is *the* ingredient needed to become the God-Man and is achievable through pure love.)[1]

The evolution of human consciousness — from authority "out there" beyond man to "within" the man — is complete with Jesus. Here I quote again from Dr. Oden:

"Jesus, in fact, replaces Israel. The function performed by the twelve tribes of Israel in the Hebrew Bible is very clearly, in the New Testament, ascribed to Jesus himself. He is fully man and fully God, and therefore he, in his own person, can mediate divine knowledge to humanity in a way that the entire Jewish community does in the Old Testament."

Not only does authority shift from the group...into the man, the individual, but authority shifts from God to within the man, combining man with God, raising bicameral man into the next world of meaning and value, finishing what Abraham started. The evolutionary leap into human consciousness with Neo-Tech is metaphorically spoken, to the bicameral man, as rising into the Kingdom of Heaven to be one with God. Jesus did just that. No literature needed to be added to the Bible after the Gospels of Jesus. The evolution of human consciousness was complete. The final evolution into God-Man would have occurred centuries ago. No religion ever needed to rise and rule the world, for through fully integrated honesty, through pure love, man could have ruled himself.

---

[1]If you act through pure love for someone, say for your child, then your actions will be free of dishonesties, agendas, rationalizations. If you act through pure love, you will take everything in your knowledge and, with all honesty, do what is best for your child. Actions that originate in pure love are fully honest. This is why Jesus' most important message was *love*. (The First Insight deals more completely with love and Neo-Tech.)

Religion Shifting Power and Control Back to God

St. Augustine (354-430 A.D.) synthesized the philosophy of Plato and the religion of Christianity (i.e., Paul's Christology), which forever (until now) reversed Jesus' ministry...from Jesus' God-Man mental structure of pure honesty and love back to the bicameral mental structure. Of course, St. Augustine's brilliant writings seem to harmonize with and support Jesus' ministry, until one looks beneath the eloquent words themselves to the mental structure underneath them. Upon doing this, one can see the reversal, and then one realizes that Jesus' teachings, as interpreted by St. Augustine, are taken *out of context.*

Two of St. Augustine's major teachings exemplify this point: 1) he believed that man could not be blamed if he was not good. Good was bestowed upon a person prior to birth by the grace of God. This was St. Augustine's belief of predestination, and 2) to achieve God's grace, if indeed one has received God's grace, he must devote himself to the Church and receive its sacraments.

Those two teachings shifted the meaningful, valuable, powerful, and one's control and authority over his own destiny from within himself...back to "out there" to the grace of God and to the Church. Indeed, St. Augustine sent man into hopeless devotion to both mystical and secular external authorities — to God and the Church. Based on Plato's philosophy, St. Augustine sent the ordinary person into powerlessness, no longer the proud owner of value, control, or authority. Of course, in the age following St. Augustine, just as the masses were acquiring the amazing new power of human consciousness, the world sank into its darkest period.

St. Augustine's writings serve the opposite *context* of Jesus who was bringing value, power, and control to *within* the common man. St. Augustine instead served Plato's context — authentic reality is beyond man "out there", unattainable to lowly man — to undo humanity's heroic 2000-year struggle of shifting value, power, and control from *out there* in the only "meaningful world" of the gods and nobles to *within* the common man and his world. St. Augustine, the man who wrote so much about his love for Christ as the only true eternal love, missed the boat

412

of Jesus Christ: Jesus' love was *for man*. Jesus' love was for the innocent commoner to make the evolutionary leap into human consciousness and then, through fully integrated honesty (achievable through love), into the omnipotent God-Man. St. Augustine's love, on the other hand, was specifically *not* for man or any earthly thing. Love for anything but eternal God was sin (but Augustine viewed sin not in terms of guilt, but in remorse).

As you saw in the First Insight, pure love means love and passionate protection for life and that which benefits life. In the Civilization of the Universe, you will know only pure love for yourself and loved ones, value producers and creators, and institutions of value production, which as you will see includes innocent businesses. You will love those three earthly things and protect them like your own little children. You will feel protective passions against anyone or anything that hurts you or your loved ones, hurts the value producers or creators, or hurts institutions of value production. Such value destroyers today, as you will see, include politicians and regulatory bureaucrats who have much the same role in society as the ancient Pharisees and Scribes who Jesus so disliked.

Only through Jesus' *pure love* for conscious life and for that which benefits conscious life can you achieve and sustain the rare state of Neo-Tech or fully integrated honesty to leap into God-Man.

Through St. Augustine's *perverted love* against life and that which benefits life, you will achieve the predominant state of the past 2000 years: bicameral-like mysticism full of illusions, rationalizations, and dishonesties to sink back into the powerless bicameral mental structure.

Forgiveness

Even when dying on the cross, according to the Gospel of St. John, Jesus said, "Father, forgive them, for they know not what they do." Were his persecutors evil conscious men or unknowing bicameral men following orders? Either way, they were nevertheless trapped in the anticivilization of diseased minds. Jesus lived his life with Neo-Tech[1]. He lived in a place

---

[1]Although Jesus lived with honesty and love, he made mistakes, as could anyone using Neo-Tech.

of seeming miracles and pure love that we will soon discover for ourselves. And when we do, we too will look at harmful people in this anticivilization, as did Jesus, and however remarkably, we will forgive them and help them repent and repay each victim for their crimes...from Plato to St. Augustine to our current ruling class of external authorities.[1]

Jesus' Message To You

Jesus was the only person back then who could have delivered his message that is now presented in Neo-Tech writings. Consequently, the New Testament begins to dilute Jesus' message and alter its context right from the start of the Gospels themselves and increasingly through the Acts and the Letters of Paul, and then deliberately through the Letter to the Hebrews and the Catholic Letters at the end.[2] That changing of context makes Jesus' message quite difficult to decode at first. Moreover, there is unexplainably little quoted of Jesus. Obviously, the Church minimized the actual quotes of Jesus and maximized the misinterpretations. Certainly the Church would have done this purging of Jesus' quotes, because Jesus was so outspoken against secular authority, which defines the Church's power. Jesus emphasized spiritual authority, which in the end frees man from the chains of politicization on Earth. But the medieval Church was all about politicization. ...Spiritual authority really means the man is left alone to take the journey within — the journey to God-Man and his supersociety. Remember, Jesus' message

---

[1]To fathom forgiving "evil" people, see *The Dialogues* by Dr. Wallace.

[2]The Catholic Letters (Catholic meaning universal) are the several letters/epistles that follow the Pauline Letters and Hebrews in the New Testament supposedly written by James (Jesus' half-brother), Peter (Jesus' Apostle), John (Jesus' cousin and Apostle), and Jude (Jesus' half-brother). Just as the authorship of Hebrews was found *not* to have been written by Paul, biblical scholars today do not believe the Catholic Letters (save for maybe two) were written by whom the Church said they were. Those letters, interested in obedience to authority, are too sophisticated and were brought into the canon later, like Hebrews. (Early canons did not include these letters.) Also, the authorship of Revelation, supposedly by John (Jesus' cousin and Apostle), is suspect.

to you was: pure love and passionate protection for conscious life and that which benefits conscious life.

Jesus had no option other than using a powerful authority figure in God to stand up to the Jewish leaders and Roman leaders, for he was fighting the dishonesty disease identified in Neo-Tech. This was the only move that would encourage the common people to silently break allegiance from false authority and turn to the journey within to eventually discover their internal authority.

We would, undoubtedly, be shocked if scribed teachings of Jesus (which were obviously purged) could be produced today. What would we see? Jesus' path could be a precursor to the Neo-Tech writings.

Because the majority of Jesus' scribed teachings have obviously been purged, not a lot is there to specifically get into and analyze. However, among what is there, realize the general message of Jesus consistently picks apart the external authorities oppressing the commoners. That was the necessary first step — to free the commoners' minds from the external authorities over them. To help them do this, Jesus gave them a *more powerful* external authority to turn to — God — and prompted them toward spiritual authority, and he kept the politicians back with his use of fear.

However, God in heaven is a secret metaphor to both help the bicameral man relate to something familiar and strong while breaking from secular external authorities...and to hold back the violent oppressors. Breaking from the secular external authorities, or at least witnessing Jesus doing so, helped to shift the bicameral peasants out of their bicameral mental structures toward the jumping off point into human consciousness.

Jesus was, however, going for more than the innocent common man's jump into human consciousness; he obviously wanted more: He was going for the *complete* jump into the God-Man, as finally achieved in the Neo-Tech writings. He was fully aware of the dishonesty disease that Dr. Wallace now calls *mysticism*, and Jesus was applying pure love and honesty...leading toward what Dr. Wallace now calls *Neo-Tech*. Jesus was aiming toward the man-made leap from bicameral man to God-Man. ...The Neo-Tech writings give you what Jesus wanted to give you and *everything more*.

415

A Riddle of Suffering

King David has often been a historical riddle for Judeo-Christian theology. In trying to answer the "theodicy" problem of: why is there evil when God created everything, the question is often asked why King David was a Chosen One of God. For, David committed criminal acts on his route to power and violated so many of the Ten Commandments including bearing false witness in framing others and committing murder. When we understand that "chosen people" meant the "conscious people", the riddle is easily solved: King David was one of the earliest conscious beings. His lyrical use of the inward "I" in 1000 B.C. demonstrates that he was conscious. Moreover, his evil, deceitful ways also tell us that David was conscious, for deceit and dishonesty can come only from a conscious mind. King David was among the first persons who experienced consciousness and was at the beginning of a line of Kings and a privileged class that consciously used deceit and dishonesty (not capable in bicameral man) to gain enormous power over the masses. The early conscious people such as David were educated elites who used their new power to manipulate the masses for enormous wealth and power. (This problem of easy oppression was what the bicameral prophets warned against.) ...It would be Jesus who would finally bring the missing ingredient of honesty to human consciousness to free the bicameral masses from the endless cycle of dishonesty and oppression, started by his multi-generational grandfather.

> "But woe to you who are rich,
>   for you have already received your comfort.
> Woe to you who are well fed now,
>   for you will go hungry.
> Woe to you who laugh now,
>   for you will mourn and weep.
> Woe to you when all men speak well of you,
>   for that is how their fathers treated the false
>   prophets."
>
> Luke 6:24-26

Of course, the privileged class easily manipulated those vulnerable people who could only follow the commands of external authority. The conscious, privileged class gladly became the bicameral peasants' external authorities and taxed and controlled the commoners. But, Jesus taught the bicameral peasants that "God" — the decision maker — is what everyone can become through discovering the "new consciousness"...the conscious mind, one's inner space to think and make decisions and direct one's self...the "Kingdom of God" within. Then, with internal authority, those people could break free of the manipulative external authorities.

Indeed, as the Gospel of Luke defines, Jesus was a liberating Messiah. When he began his ministry, he stood up in the synagogue in Nazareth to read from Scripture. He read from the prophet Isaiah,

"The Spirit of the Lord is on me,
  because he has anointed me
  to preach good news to the poor.
He has sent me to proclaim freedom for the prisoners and
  recovery of sight for the blind (a metaphor),
  to release the oppressed,
    to proclaim the year of the Lord's favor."

Luke 4:18-19

Jesus was breaking free the common man from political external authorities...turning him to spiritual authority and eventually internal authority. In the Kingdom of God, man would discover, through pure love and honesty, great power and authority and would rise above the guilty, manipulative leaders. See how Jesus refers to the guilty rulers — the Pharisees — using "the light from heaven" as a secret metaphor of early glimmers of Neo-Tech. His quote still applies to our rulers today — the politicians:

"The light from heaven came into the world, but they loved the darkness more than the light, for their actions were evil. They hate the light because they want to sin in the darkness. They stay away from the light for fear

417

their sins will be exposed and they will be punished. But those who do what is right come to the light gladly, so everyone can see that they are doing what God wants".

John 3:19-21

You can see the distant parallels from the power Jesus was trying to deliver the commoners so they could leapfrog the leaders and rise into the Kingdom of God...to the power *The Neo-Tech World* delivers the ordinary person to leapfrog the leaders today and rise into the Kingdom of God-Man.

What About the Concept of Faith?

When you understand the parallel event about to come through Neo-Tech, things about the Bible snap into place like perfect puzzle pieces. For instance, the full meaning and power behind the concept of *faith* in the next world really matured and took hold with Jesus. What is this powerful idea called faith, and why was it developed? Only by being on the edge of the second major leap into a new mentality can faith be understood for what faith really is. As Dr. Wallace has shown, to go from one mentality to the next is a "jump"; there is no transition. Of course, man's mental structure goes through major shifts to approach the "jumping off point", but you cannot see across the gulf to the next world or imagine it. Therefore, not unlike the bicameral peasants who began to see growing evidence of the Kingdom of God through Jesus, as you begin to see growing evidence of the Kingdom of God-Man through the Neo-Tech writings, but you are not yet in that Kingdom of God-Man yourself, you have to *believe in* that other world even though you have not actually seen it, which is *faith*. The peasants saw plenty of evidence of the conscious God-Man, who was Jesus himself. Therefore, they had faith in the Kingdom of God. Now, through the Neo-Tech writings including Neo-Tech Physics (available from Neo-Tech Publishing Company), you will see growing evidence of the God-Man. Therefore, although you are not yet in the Kingdom of God-Man, you will develop a belief in it; you will have faith.

418

In the Gospels, Jesus is always talking about faith. The reason he does that is: faith, as described in the previous paragraph, begins releasing one's mind from the anchors of the old mentality, both in Jesus' time and now in Wallace's time. The mind is held in the old mentality by thousands and thousands of conditioned "hooks". The mind simply cannot release itself from the old mentality, not then in Jesus' time, not now in Wallace's time. But as one begins to see evidence of the other world and acquires "faith", that faith begins releasing those mental hooks in the old mentality. Only by releasing those mental hooks through one's growing faith can his mind go to the jumping off point to make the leap to the new mentality. That is why Jesus always stressed faith, but not the religious "blind faith" as the Church politically propagated. The Gospels and Jesus continually say that he has shown enough evidence for the people to have faith in the Kingdom of God:

> Therefore many of the Jews who had come to visit Mary,
> and had seen what Jesus did, put their faith in him.
>
> John 11:45

Similarly, the Neo-Tech writings show enough evidence for people to have faith in the Kingdom of God-Man.

Jesus and Aristotle: Early Spreaders of Neo-Tech, Victims of the Church

The idea that Jesus has been viewed out of context for 2000 years and that the new and accurate context changes the meaning of Jesus' words at first seems incredible. But another example of this very same phenomenon happened at about the same time in history. It is no secret today that the Greek philosopher Aristotle, the father of reality, was also viewed out of context during the same millennium known as the Dark Ages. And although Aristotle is now recognized as the father of objective reality, the great scientists and Renaissance men during the rise out of the Dark Ages despised Aristotle because of the scholastic/Church-twisted wrong context in which they viewed his works. The proper context, when finally restored

419

to Aristotle's works, reinstated the meaning of Aristotle's words as they became the bedrock upon which science and life itself flourished.

It happened to Aristotle: the bedrock for life and science was turned into a platform for death and mysticism. In the dying stages of the Dark Ages, the religious platform shifted from Plato to Aristotle, mainly through Thomas Aquinas. The culprits who changed Aristotle's context were the Church Fathers and the Academics — the Scholastics. Indeed, those educated elites were the same culprits who changed Jesus' context to hurl humanity into the Dark Ages and into the anticivilization.

Today

Once the proper perspective of man is seen — man is one with God, the highest entity in the Universe — then man is no longer subservient to anyone or anything. Suddenly, political leaders lose their power to rule over man. No, there never was a God of man. Rather, as Jesus once taught, conscious man *is* God, is a God-Man. And when that perspective takes hold, a supersociety will rise as demonstrated throughout the Twelve Visions, and no man, woman, or child will ever suffer again.

In ancient times, Jesus' message delivered profound power to the common man unlike anything before. Today, this book delivers profound power to ordinary people unlike anything before. It takes you, upon applying its techniques, through a miraculous leap of power by opening a new mind space known as *Neothink*. Neothink — the new mentality — brings the ordinary person god-like power as it takes him through his final evolution into the God-Man:

1) Bicameral "Animal" Mentality: No mind space. Automatic
   (who man was)   reactions to external stimuli.

       Leap of Power
       (The Bible)

2) Conscious "Human" Mentality: A new mind space opened
   (who man is)   through sophisticated
                                        language, metaphors and
        Leap of Power   analog models that let man
      (Neo-Tech Writings)   think and make decisions and
                                        control his own life.

3) **Neothink "God-Man" Mentality:**   **A new mind space opens**
   (who man will be)   **through Neothink puzzle**
   building that snaps together
   never-before-seen pictures
   — puzzle pictures — that
   let man jump to the next
   level at everything he does
   in all fields of knowledge
   and create his own future.

Neothink builds mental puzzles, one piece at a time. As the puzzle grows, a puzzle picture forms, and well before it is complete, as with any puzzle, you can see the whole thing — what the finished picture will look like. That gives you visions of your future and enables you to live with omnipotence, for you will now know exactly what to do for success, for you know what the missing pieces look like. With Neothink, you regularly create and control the future.

To make that leap of power — to make your final evolution into the omnipotent God-Man — takes a commitment to applying the techniques you learned throughout this book. You have turned to a new page in your life. You have embarked on a journey from which you will never return.

The Third Insight
You Will Become God

In the First Insight, we saw that Neo-Tech offers us our final evolution into God-Man. In the Second Insight, we were introduced to the idea that God-Man is God. Now, let us put it together and discover that, through Neo-Tech, we humans — you and I — *will become God.*

Blasphemy? Let us begin with an analogy: the discovery of Darwin's Theory of Evolution through Natural Selection.

Charles Darwin was so deeply affected by the attacks and cries of blasphemy against his Theory of Evolution that he repeatedly fell ill. Fearing the outlash his work on Natural Selection would cause, he continually delayed releasing his findings until close friends coaxed him, finally after twenty-five years, into giving his knowledge to the world. At the end of his book *The Origin of Species,* Darwin wrote a sort of homage to God, hoping to reduce negative religious reactions, pleading that there was a place for God and a place for evolution.

Of course, as he feared, his powerful scientific theory created havoc everywhere, not just within religion, but throughout philosophy, mythology, in academia, schools, politics, and social order in general. The heated controversy and ripping attacks on Darwin and his work caused him severe anguish and ill health.

Still, the extensive inductive reasoning and conclusive deductive reasoning within his work could not be scorned away. Nevertheless, people tried. Realize, though, *why* his Theory of Evolution would have caused such an uproar: in the mid-1800's, the creation of intelligent man, beautiful animals, and perfect ecosystems could have no possible explanation other than a Majestic Creation. The perfection and beauty could have occurred no other way but through the love of a Supreme Being. And that being the obvious observation that it was, we further believed that the world followed His divine plan, which fulfilled our bicameral longings to follow our external "authority".

Suddenly, however, with Natural Selection, no longer did the world follow some divine order of a Supreme Being. Instead, now everything happened *by chance.* A deep-rooted, cherished

423

sense of security within the people was stripped away; their bicameral longings to follow a higher "authority" was suddenly stripped away by Natural Selection. Furthermore, comprehensive factual research, particularly upon Darwin's subsequent release of *The Descent of Man,* overwhelmingly suggested intelligent man himself was not special; he came not from a higher being, but from a lower life form, perhaps an ape!

The people's God, their beloved leader, and their honor seemed to be ripped out from under them. Their most precious and needed feelings of *hope* seemed to die. ...But, over time, mankind began to see the beauty and benevolence of evolution. Moreover, Darwin's scientific reasoning versus the mystical Adam and Eve explanation had to be acknowledged. The scientific reasoning was just too powerful to deny for long. The power of logic will always rise and prevail over inferior traditional beliefs steeped in mysticism, even if people do not at first want to let go.

Letting Go of Mysticism

Similarly, the Third Insight contains new scientific knowledge from Dr. Wallace that will undoubtedly undergo ripping attacks and cries of blasphemy. Analogous to Darwin, Frank R. Wallace is putting forth a scientific theory based on thirty years of extensive inductive reasoning and conclusive deductive reasoning.[1] Similar to Darwin, Wallace has no intentions of attacking God per se. But he does intend to advance knowledge.

Still, realize why his God-Man Theory will cause an uproar: it reveals there is no God of man, no external "authority", but there are gods of the Universe. Wallace's Neothink puzzle, presented next, reveals an unforgettable picture: God-Man is immortal. God-Man is God.

Before Darwin, man could only explain the world around him as coming from a Majestic Creation. Man today can only explain the Universe as coming from a Majestic Creation. Few people today question the existence of a Supreme Being.

---

[1]Most of the studies and examples, in short the inductive process, is found in *Neo-Tech Physics* by Dr. Wallace.

Now, in this Third Insight, scientific reason suggests that our Universe came not from a Supreme Being, but from *a man* — a very advanced God-Man. Our beloved God and our faith seems to be under attack. Of course, a cherished feeling within our souls, our bicameral longings to follow our Lord, is suddenly stripped away by God-Man.

But, over time, mankind will see the beauty and benevolence of mere man — a very advanced God-Man — being the creator of the Universe. Moreover, Wallace's scientific reasoning versus the mystical God-sitting-in-Heaven explanation has to be acknowledged. As you will see, the scientific reasoning is just too powerful to deny for long. Once again, the power of logic will always rise and prevail over inferior traditional beliefs steeped in mysticism, even if people do not at first want to let go.

Grasping Our God of the Future

After reading the Second Insight, the reader can comprehend that until now, God was viewed from the bicameral mentality seeking automatic answers from a higher "authority" telling us what to do and how to live — our God of the past. Now, we will for the first time see God from the Neothink mentality to really discover God — our God of the future.

Dr. Wallace recently provided me with his Research Journal that housed his project on the Civilization of the Universe. Dr. Wallace's Research Journal was several hundred pages long, building a Neothink view of the Universe and a map to the Civilization of the Universe. As I went through all those pages, I sat in stunned silence. In those pages, he had unlocked the mysteries of God. After many millennia, here Wallace had done it!

Furthermore, unlocking the mysteries of God unleashed the untapped power of man, which the money/power giants today have not yet exploited — not even a fraction of their human potential. As I read through his Journal, new nerves never tweaked in my nervous system were being plucked like a banjo. Time and time again I had to stop reading and put the pages aside just to calm down.

425

The Neo-Tech World

Discovering the Universe's Deepest Secret

In some ways, I apologize to you. You see, here you are merely reading a book; yet here the answers to the multi-millennia mysteries of God and man are coming straight at you. As author and narrator, I have done my best to prepare you. Nevertheless, the importance of what you are about to read could go right by you. Or it might hit you square between the eyes and stagger you as it turns your life around.

Either way, I wish I could better prepare you. I have done my best, however. I have selected approximately fifty pages from Dr. Wallace's Journal to walk you through the essential portions that unlock the mysteries of God and unleash the power of man. ...In short, Dr. Wallace built a Neothink puzzle-picture that shows us the Universe's deepest secret: *God-Man is God...Gods of the Universe.* And we will soon join the Gods of the Universe in the Civilization of the Universe.

The Ultimate Thrill: Becoming God

As Wallace wrote his Journal, he found himself more and more exerting Neo-Tech — the eyes, thoughts, and voice of fully integrated honesty. Eventually, he broke through into Neothink. He was now able to build never-before-seen puzzle pictures of new knowledge, one of which will follow.

Years ago, Wallace retired from a highly successful career as a Senior Research Chemist for Du Pont so he could aggressively research Neo-Tech and Neothink to their outer limits. As Neo-Tech exorcised his mysticisms, he was able to more and more widely integrate reality around him. In the process, he was learning more about Neothink Man, the Universe, and himself.

Wallace was simply, honestly and widely integrating reality. When an individual purges his mysticism, Wallace learned, he can honestly and rapidly integrate reality. In time, he "jumps" into Neothink. And then, through unblocked integrated thinking, powerful far-reaching Neothink extrapolates every subject to its ultimate conclusion and benefit, which Wallace did with the Universe, God, and man in his Journal to show us the ultimate thrill: *becoming God.*

Dr. Wallace's Revelation

As he worked on his Journal, at times Wallace felt as if he were possessed by something unexplainably invigorating. During those times, he was able to think and write with unusually far-reaching, fully integrated honesty, so long as the experience lasted. The longer and more intense those inspirational moments became, the more wide-reaching integrations of reality he made, and the more power he reaped.

Curiously, those moments caused him a sense of déjà vu, as if he had felt that way before, sometime long ago...far back in his past, long before his earliest memories, perhaps when he was just a toddler. What do I feel? he would ask himself. Indeed, Wallace was feeling the thrill of life again as he had once before, back when he was a toddler regularly using Neothink to expand his knowledge and control over the world around him.

As he used his background as an accomplished Du Pont scientist to integrate the world around him and the cosmos above him, he had a revelation:

He more and more felt that during his longer and longer inspirational moments, he became one with God. His unity with God happened for as long as his inspirational moment lasted. Then, the moment was gone, and he was himself again. Indeed, his mind was trying to make the evolutionary jump into God-Man!

Feeling the Thrill of Life Again

Wallace began to look forward with a passion to those inspirational moments when he encountered his own God-Man. He felt so stimulated and alive! Oh, how he would love to live that way all the time. It would mean living with omnipotent power, control, and euphoria 24 hours a day! ...As he closed the gaps between his moments of being God-Man and his exhilarating Neothink mentality, he wondered if those exciting episodes would someday link together and go on forever.

How would that ever be so, he wondered. The answer,

though, became obvious: When he enjoyed those stimulating experiences, he was mystic-free. In other words, his mind was void of the integration-blocking mind disease of mysticism. He could see right through illusions. There was no dishonesty, defensiveness, protectionism...no mind-created "realities"...of any idea or position — just reality out there before him to freely and rapidly integrate.

Free of mysticism, he became very powerful and, like a young child, enjoyed figuring out and controlling life, love, and success. As a trained scientist, he became especially effective at physics and figuring out the Universe. ...He recognized that throughout those stimulating experiences, he was feeling again the thrill for life he once did long ago.

A Common Denominator Reveals the Path to God-Man

He honed in on the common denominator in each euphoric episode experiencing God-Man Unity: "While it lasted, I was mystic-free," he confessed to me. Of course, that got him wondering, what if he could permanently purge his mysticism?

He concluded that, if he became mystic-free 24 hours a day, then he would, in essence, become God-Man. He would have successfully made the evolutionary jump. And, of course, not just himself, but every person could become God-Man, for mystic-free man is God-Man (see the First Insight).

Now, wait until what comes next — the Universe's deepest secret: *God-Man is God...Gods of the Universe.* And we, ourselves, will soon feel the ultimate thrill: becoming God! I personally became overloaded with excitement while going through Wallace's Journal. I could see so, so far. In fact, in several deep talks with Wallace since reading his Journal, we both realized that my Twelve Visions came from my own encounters with God-Man. ...Now, let us look ahead at the ultimate encounter.

Who or What Is God?

Mystic-free man is God-Man. Now, let us travel out into our Universe. Do we dare ask, now with man's newly discovered, far greater reasoning power called Neothink, who or what is God? Using Neothink, we just might have enough power now to unlock millennia's biggest mystery.

We must begin with an agreeable definition of God before we set out to discover God for all readers. With so many different beliefs from Eastern to Western philosophies, we need a generic definition to work from. Let us start our journey by defining God as the Controller of the Universe. It seems all Eastern and Western philosophies agree on that.

During the sparkling 18th-century Age of Reason, the predominant belief was that man could further understand God as man further understood nature, through reason. In other words, we could better understand the Controller of the Universe by better understanding the Universe.

The Age of Reason rose in the 18th century from the 17th-century works of the English philosopher John Locke and his friend and genius, the famous scientist Isaac Newton. For the first time, science was being used by philosophers and theologians to understand metaphysics, religion, and politics. The more the workings of the Universe could be explained through scientific reason, the closer we got to understanding God and his relationship to man.

The authority of government over man versus God or Natural Law was questioned and became a popular issue of debate.

The Age of Neo-Tech in the 21st century will see both a continuation and completion of the 18th-century Age of Reason. For, we have gone light years beyond Newtonian physics that drove the 18th-century Age of Reason. We have advanced to Einsteinian physics and now Neo-Tech physics to offer a major new set of directions for a 21st-century Age of Reason, which will finally complete the great journey on understanding God.[1]

Now, let us further understand the Universe, thus get to know more about its Controller — God. So now, with our advanced scientific knowledge and our newly acquired tool of Neothink, let us go to Dr. Wallace's Journal where he put together a Neothink puzzle that reveals an amazing picture: *God-Man is*

---

[1]For an in-depth treatment of Neo-Tech Physics, see *Profound Honesty*, Frank R. Wallace, 640 pages.

God, soon to be joined by earthlings.

Dr. Wallace's Journal...
A 25-Part Neothink Puzzle

Part 1: A Neo-Tech Discovery

Tony, a lad of thirteen, was singing the theme song of Monty Python's "The Meaning of Life". The song went something like this:

"Just remember that you are standing on a planet that's revolving at 900 miles per hour, that's orbiting at 90 miles per second. So it's reckoned that the source of all our power, the sun, and you and I and all the stars that we can see are moving at a million miles a day. That's figured out as moving at 42,000 miles an hour, in our galaxy called the Milky Way. Our Galaxy itself contains 100 billion stars. It's 100,000 light years from side to side and 16,000 light years thick. We are 30,000 light years from our galactic center and go around that center every 200 million years. Our galaxy is one of millions of billions in this amazing, expanding universe. The universe itself keeps on expanding in all directions at the speed of light. It's whizzing as fast as it can go, you know, at 12 million miles a minute. So remember when we are feeling very small and insecure, how amazing and unlikely is our birth. And pray that there is intelligent life somewhere up in space, 'cause we are down here on Earth."

What makes those lyrics fascinating is that every statement is essentially factual and verifiable. But the song left out the most important part: Probability statistics overwhelmingly reveal that our universe contains at least a hundred million, and probably billions of Earth-like planets populated with conscious beings like you and me. Millions of conscious civilizations exist that are millions of years more advanced than our newly born, immature, still mystically oriented civilization.

Moreover, that song was praying for what Neo-Tech already discovered. In fact, Albert Einstein spent his professional life searching in vain for what Neo-Tech discovered — the unifying, controlling element of the universe: *human-like consciousness.*

You Will Become God

Part 2: Einstein and the Unifying Link

Throughout history, conscious beings on Earth have struggled with mystical notions of a "superior" consciousness, an imagined god, or some other "higher" power reigning over the universe. But today, by integrating the dynamics of mass and energy, Neo-Tech reveals a relationship between our own Earth-bound consciousness and all existence. The unifying power that orchestrates existence is not some mystical god or "superior" being. But, as demonstrated in this puzzle, that unifying power is conscious beings — conceptual/introspective beings as you and I.

Einstein never accomplished his ultimate goal of unifying all forces. He never derived a Unified-Field Theory. But extrapolating Einstein's work into Neo-Tech reveals the unifying entity of existence — the only integrating force of the universe: human-like consciousness.

Why did Einstein not realize that fact? One reason perhaps stems from his abhorrence for unpredictable actions among the dynamics of nature. For that reason, he disliked quantum mechanics or anything that suggested arbitrary or "god-like" interventions. Always searching for order, Einstein focused on only two components of existence: mass and energy integrated with the geometries of time and space. He believed those components could always be explained, exactly and predictably. Thus, he never considered the third and controlling component of existence: volitional consciousness — free-will, conceptual/introspective/integrating conscious minds.

Perhaps his passionate dislike for the unpredictable and disorder caused him to overlook consciousness as the third spacetime component of existence. For consciousness can and does unpredictably alter the dynamics of nature, every moment, throughout the universe. Yet, from the widest perspective, consciousness brings the most elegant order and predictability to the universe as demonstrated in this puzzle.

All past attempts to link consciousness with existence were based on mystical, "higher forms of consciousness". Such irrational, ethereal linkages always originated as dishonest, unfounded assertions by mystics or neocheaters conjuring up

431

religious and political power. But the Neo-Tech discovery of human-like consciousness as the unifying element of existence can be scientifically established not only with theory but with direct observation and experimental proof.

Understanding the conscious mind as the controlling, unifying element of existence first requires understanding the *unchanging* nature of consciousness and existence versus the *changing* nature of matter and energy:

Part 3: *The Unchanging, Eternal Nature of Consciousness*

As first identified by Professor Julian Jaynes of Princeton University, the conscious mind was discovered within nature's bicameral mind[1] about 3000 years ago. Given sufficient information, that first conscious mind had the same capacity as conscious minds today to understand anything in the universe from Einstein's theories to computer technologies and beyond. Consider the astonishing conscious minds of Socrates, Plato, Aristotle, Archimedes that were flourishing only a few centuries after the discovery of consciousness. They would, for example, have no problems whatsoever in understanding Einstein's theories or computer technology. Given the information, they certainly had the capacity we have today to understand anything in the universe.

In other words, while much is unknown, nothing is unknowable to the conscious mind. By nature, the conscious mind requires no change or evolvement to understand anything in existence.[2] On acquiring the correct knowledge, conscious

---

[1]The bicameral mind was man's intelligent, nature-evolved mind before he discovered consciousness as a conceptual/introspective mind. The conscious mind is not a part of nature's evolutionary process. But, rather, consciousness is a discovery by man that lies beyond the dynamics of nature. This discovery process is explained in the First Insight. ...When referring to consciousness, the word *discovered* is used when perhaps the word should be *invented*.

[2]Individual minds are endowed with various capacities. Individuals then develop or retard their capacities through either conscious efforts or mystical defaults. But consciousness itself is either there to be used or abused...or it is not there.

beings today are capable of doing anything within the immutable laws of physics throughout the universe.

Consciousness is man's discovery that sprang from his nature-evolved bicameral mind. Consciousness is not part of nature's evolutionary processes, but is a natural phenomenon of existence.[1] Thus, the first conscious minds on this planet 3000 years ago are the same as the conscious minds on this planet today...and the same as conscious minds in any galaxy ten million years from now. All conscious minds have the same ability to understand anything in existence.

Consciousness, therefore, does not evolve. It exists eternally, unchangingly.[2] And its capacity to understand anything in the universe transposes into forever fulfilling the supreme responsibility of conscious beings. That responsibility is to preserve forever the supreme value of the universe — individual consciousness. To meet that responsibility means achieving non-aging biological immortality as described in Parts 12 and 16 of this puzzle.

---

[1]As demonstrated later in this journal, consciousness has always existed throughout the universe as an integral part of existence.

[2]The Neothink mentality is a dramatic new way of using the conscious mind. An analogy could be drawn to a power reactor: As long as impurities remain in the solution, the power reactor will not activate. But remove the final traces of impurities, and presto — a power-reactor explosion. Similarly, as long as mysticism remains in the mind, the power reactor of Neothink will not activate. But remove the final traces of mysticism, and presto — a power-reactor explosion of Neothink. The Neothink mentality is a whole new mentality, an unconnected jump beyond conscious minds today plagued with bicameral mentalities. The Neothink mentality is a "Planck's jump" away — a whole new mentality of astonishing power beyond anything today. The Neothink mentality, however, is still a function of consciousness, i.e., consciousness performing perfectly, limitlessly with no impurities, as the power reactor of conscious life. Consciousness is eternal and unchanging when making the jump into the limitless Neothink mentality, which exists in all advanced civilizations throughout the Universe.

Part 4: The Unchanging, Eternal Nature of Existence

Who Created Existence? And who or what created the creator of existence? And then who or what created the creator of the creator, and so on regressing forever. Such questions are, of course, unanswerable. But, such infinite-regression questions need never be answered. For existence is primary and axiomatic — meaning irreducible, self-evident, and requiring no further explanation. While new realms of existence such as galaxies and universes are constantly being created, nothing creates existence itself. It simply exists. Existence always has and always will exist. And that primacy of existence existing forever is independent of consciousness or anything else. ...The most profound of all concepts as underscored by Einstein is simply: Existence exists. What is the alternative? No alternative is possible unless one accepts the contradiction that existence does not exist.

Throughout eternal time, existence constantly generates new realms of life out of which conscious minds spring from the evolvement of bicameral minds — minds of evolved intelligence capable of discovering consciousness. Once consciousness is discovered and harnessed, it can, with accumulating knowledge and productive efforts, learn to forever muster new realms of existence. From those new realms evolve new life. And from new life evolve bicameral minds from which conscious minds spring.

Throughout eternal time and space, the following creation cycle always has existed and always will exist:

Table 1
THE CREATION CYCLE

Realms of existence created —> life evolved —> bicameral mind evolved —> consciousness discovered —> mysticism developed to replace lost, bicameral gods —> mysticism and neocheaters take control of conscious beings —> partial freedom and capitalism developed —> Neo-Tech discovered —> guiltless prosperity, power, romantic love revealed to value producers —> mysticism and neocheating are uncompetitive and, thus, eliminated —> Neothink Man rises

—> biological immortality achieved —> control of the universe learned —> new realms of existence created by new conscious beings, God-Man —> and so on, forever expanding and repeating the cycle.

Stated another way: Space, time, consciousness, and existence are eternal; they have no beginning or end. Throughout time eternal, stars, solar systems, and Earth-like planets constantly form anew. Thus, living organisms and conscious beings constantly form anew. Throughout never ending time and universes, limitless planets forever generate life. That life, in turn, forever generates nature's evolutionary processes that always end with conscious beings. ...Conscious civilizations free of mysticism always survive, prosper, take control of nature and then existence.

Given the endless number of water/oxygen abundant, Earth-like planets forever spinning in endlessly evolving existence, one realizes life and consciousness have forever co-existed in limitless abundance. Human-like consciousness, therefore, is as much a part of eternal existence as are mass and energy. When consciousness is integrated with endless existence and time, the stunning conclusion unfolds that human-like consciousness is also unchanging and has always existed.

Consciousness, mass, and energy are the three macro components of existence. Those three components are inextricably linked and must be integrated into all physical understandings and mathematical accounts of our universe. If only the mass and energy components existed, then all existence would be predictable and predestined through the dynamics of nature and physics. But further research and refinement of data will show that seemingly predictable actions of the universe are actually unpredictable from a mass and energy accounting alone. That unpredictability arises from not accounting for the influence of volitional conscious beings throughout existence.

Human-like, volitional consciousness is:
1) the third and integrating component of existence,
2) the unifying component or force never recognized by Einstein,
3) the supreme component of existence that controls the dynamics of nature, mass, and energy to forever

preserve and evolve conscious life,
4) the eternal component that has existed and controlled
existence, not for trillions of years, but forever.

The balance of this puzzle develops a nonmathematical, nontechnical understanding of how conscious beings dominate the universe and muster new realms of existence and life through increasing control of mass and energy.

Part 5: The Changing Nature of Mass and Energy:
The Grand Cycle

All events of the universe fall within nature's mighty Grand Cycle, the dominating, all-inclusive energy wave involving the entire universe. That cycle consists of nature's longest energy wave exactly counterpoised with nature's shortest energy wave. All other cycles, waves, or forces of nature, ranging from cosmic and gamma rays to radio waves fall within the Grand Cycle. ...The Grand Cycle is described in Table 2 below:

Table 2

The Total History Of The Universe

(omitting the unifying element of consciousness)

is contained in

THE GRAND CYCLE

which consists of

1. The Googol-Year Explosion
Half-Cycle, Long Wave

with gravity-wave dissipation
with proton decay
with quark and electron annihilation

2. The Googol-Year Implosion
Half-Cycle, Long Wave

3. The Googolth-of-a-Second
Full-Cycle, Short Wave

(black hole/white hole)

(a googol equals 10^{100} or
10 followed by 100 zeroes)

A capsulized account of the Grand Cycle starting with the so-called big-bang birth of the universe is illustrated in Table 3 on the next page.

Table 3 also indicates that all activity during nature's longest wave, the googol-year exploding/imploding cycles, exactly equals all activity occurring during nature's shortest wave, the googolth-of-a-second cycle. An understanding of that seeming paradox will evolve over the next few pages.

Part 6: The Explosion Cycle

Within the universe, all existence oscillates in one Grand Cycle spanning trillions of years. The actual time to complete that Cycle is not relevant here, but will someday be scientifically measured by us on Earth. But, even today, experiments and calculations from the astrophysical Doppler effect[1] show our universe is in the explosion, energy-to-matter half cycle. Our universe is exploding outward at near the speed of light, scattering away from a so-called "big-bang birth" with ever increasing entropy[2] — a measurement of spent energy.

Energy available for work throughout the universe will keep

---

[1]A change of light-wave frequencies caused by a moving light source such as a star. The wavelength of light from a star moving away *red shifts* — becomes longer — stretches toward the color red.

[2]Entropy involves the second of the three laws of thermodynamics for closed systems. Entropy is simply the movement of events toward their highest probability or disorder.* Entropy measures irretrievable energy spent on scattering a closed universe. ...For every star that explodes, every pebble that drops from a cliff, entropy and disorder irreversibly increase throughout the universe. Approaching infinite entropy, all usable energy throughout the closed universe is spent. All is flat and scattered to the maximum. No star is available to explode, no cliff is available from which a pebble can fall. No wind blows. All is dead and still. Stars are collapsed, cold and dark, or not at all. No sound or light exists: perhaps not even mass exists. Perhaps only unusable radiation near and always approaching 0°K exists.

*The same probability concept applies to formulating hypotheses: always formulate toward the highest probability. Thus, the formulation of the Long-Wave hypothesis.

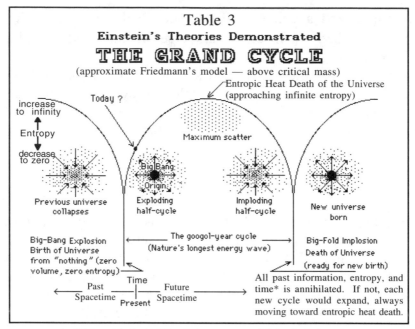

Table 3

Einstein's Theories Demonstrated

THE GRAND CYCLE

(approximate Friedmann's model — above critical mass)

Entropic Heat Death of the Universe
(approaching infinite entropy)

increase to infinity

Today ?

Entropy

Maximum scatter

decrease to zero

Big Bang
Origin

Previous universe collapses

Exploding half-cycle

Imploding half-cycle

New universe born

Big-Bang Explosion
Birth of Universe
from "nothing" (zero volume, zero entropy)

The googol-year cycle
(Nature's longest energy wave)

Big-Fold Implosion
Death of Universe
(ready for new birth)

Time

Past   Future
Spacetime   Spacetime
Present

All past information, entropy, and time* is annihilated. If not, each new cycle would expand, always moving toward entropic heat death.

*When time is annihilated, the next event (birth of a universe) is instantaneous to the previous event (end of a universe). No time passes between the two events.

decreasing as the universe spreads out for trillions of years until all energy is spent. In that state, trillions of years after the initial big-bang explosion, the universe exists at its maximum scattered or disordered state — as inert residue of an exploded bomb. At that moment, the entire universe is motionless, energyless, and while always approaching absolute zero Kelvin temperature ($0^0K = -273.16^0C = -469.67^0F$), all energy is in the form of uniform, unusable heat radiation. ...Do subatomic arrows of time exist? Will protons, quarks, and electrons eventually decay or annihilate to end in radiation for all subatomic particles and motions?[1]

---

[1]Are gravity waves the final dissipater of energy and motion? Or does mass itself seek higher entropy? With incredibly long half lives of 10^{32} years or perhaps up to 10^{220} years, do protons themselves decay toward infinite entropy? What about the energy and mass of a quark, an electron? Do quarks and electrons finally decay or annihilate with antiparticles? In any case, without conscious intervention, entropy death of a closed universe will eventually occur. **...The laws of**
(footnote continued at bottom of next page)

Part 7: The Implosion Cycle

With no usable energies or motions, the universe is dead. Entropy is essentially infinite. Entropic heat death has occurred. Without the force of consciousness, one incredibly weak force remains — by far the weakest of nature's forces — gravity. And, at that moment, in the absence of all other forces, gravity begins acting as an invisible cosmic hand destined to fulfill its function as the ultimate housekeeper, healer, and energy restorer of the universe. For, at that moment, gravity begins pulling a totally scattered, exhausted universe back toward increased order while gradually restoring potential energy. Increasingly restoring energy by reversing entropy, this cycle is the mirror image of the explosion cycle and equally lasts trillions of years. In that implosion cycle, gravity eventually pulls the universe back into essentially perfect order...an ultimate-compact, black-hole[1] bomb, ready to explode into another big bang as entropy races toward zero.

As contraction of the universe begins, gravity gradually changes from the weakest to the mightiest force of nature. Starting as an unimaginably faint but constant pull, gravity begins rebuilding the scattered universe by drawing all energyless existence closer together — perhaps initially by a millimicron in a million years. But every movement closer together increases

---

(footnote continued from previous page)
thermodynamics, however, apply only to *closed* systems. Existence itself is eternally open and evolving. Thus, any meaning of entropy to existence disappears, including the idea of entropic heat death.

[1]The universe-containing black hole described here is matter and energy condensed beyond the critical mass and density needed to be captured, collapsed, and then imploded by its own gravity. When the collapse is complete, the resulting black hole can convert into a white hole, exploding into a new universe. The entire black-hole/white-hole cycle occurs in the tiniest fraction of a second because all information, entropy, and time obliterates between the two Grand Cycles.

the pull of gravity.[1] That, in turn, increases the speed at which the universe condenses toward an ordered, densifying mass. From the beginning to the end of that condensing-collapsing-imploding cycle, gravity steadily moves toward increasing all forms of energy ranging from potential and kinetic energies to chemical, heat, and nuclear energies.

In the explosion cycle, all energy escapes the diminishing grip of gravity. But in the implosion cycle, no energy escapes the increasing grip of gravity. In this cycle, the universe keeps moving together. Gravity holds all forms of increasing mass and energy within the same shrinking unit as the universe races closer together at accelerating speeds.

Part 8: The Googolth-of-a-Second Cycle

On drawing the universe *toward* a never reachable point, the accelerating pull of gravity begins compacting matter and energy toward a super-ordered, super-compact black hole. Becoming the mightiest physical force in existence, gravity begins crushing the universe. All forms of energy blend into all forms of matter and vice versa. All molecules, atoms, protons, neutrons, electrons, sub-atomic particles, and energy waves of the universe are crushed together into unrecognizable forms of matter and energy. That rapidly compacting universe assumes entirely different forms of existence occurring only during that nearly instantaneous moment of super compaction at the final instant of the implosion half cycle.

Then, as the entire universe implodes to the size of a basketball, those bizarre forms of existence keep changing with

---

[1]Gravitational attraction increases proportionally to the amount of existence involved multiplied by the inverse square of the distances between the eventual masses and energies. That means gravitational attraction accelerates exponentially as masses and energies are collapsed toward unity. Fields of existence are rolled ever closer together, perhaps into multidimensional space* and then into Gravity Units.

*Up to a twenty-six dimensional space has been mathematically derived in superstring theory. ...Most of those dimensions are rolled up into inconceivably tiny volumes or strings that vibrate at characteristic resonances.

increasing rapidity. Undergoing seemingly infinite changes into ever more radical forms of existence, the universe crushes inward at near the speed of light, imploding to golf-ball size, then to pinhead size, then to pinpoint size. Everything in the universe, including trillions of stars and billions of galaxies, even black holes, are crushed into that pinpoint. The universe then flickers from microscopic to submicroscopic size then to sizes unimaginably smaller than a proton — all while continuously changing into near infinite varieties of unimaginable radical structures shrinking toward zero volume and infinite density. ...The end condition may or may not be different, more disordered, from the beginning condition.

Most incredibly, the total of all mass/energy/activity changes that occur during nature's longest cycle (the seemingly infinitely long, googol-year explosion and implosion half cycles) is exactly counterpoised or duplicated during nature's shortest cycle (the seemingly infinitesimally short, googolth-of-a-second cycle). In other words, the total action during nature's longest cycle of trillions of years is exactly counterbalanced during nature's shortest cycle occurring in the tiniest fraction of a nanosecond[1].

Part 9: The Universe Turns Inside Out From Implosion to Explosion

At that final instant, all activity ceases as the universe is essentially, but not actually, at zero volume, infinite density, and zero entropy. At that final instant, all the universe is in the form of gravity/existence symmetry. All information and time from the previous Grand Cycle has vanished. At that moment, with a quantum flux, a new spacetime is born — the universe turns inside out from the implosion cycle to the explosion cycle. At once, the universe converts from increasing order and compaction to "nothing" then to increasing disorder and scatteration, from decreasing entropy to increasing entropy, from implosion to explosion. At that instant, the entire universe is cataclysmically destroyed and then instantly reborn from seemingly nothing — reborn in a big-bang inflation of a trillion times a trillion suns.

---

[1] A nanosecond is one billionth of a second.

Created from seemingly nothing, a mammoth composite of post-inflation mass and energy expands in every direction at nearly the speed of light. That ball of mass and energy keeps expanding for centuries, millennia, or perhaps longer before blowing apart, scattering, and then congealing its mass and energy. That scattering and congealing eventually forms visible stars, solar systems, planets. During our current googol-year cycle, millions of Earth-like planets and conscious civilizations formed billions of years before Earth's formation. And millions of Earth-like planets and conscious civilizations will form billions of years after Earth's formation.

Part 10: Super Grand Cycles

Assuming similar gravitational dynamics operate among universes,[1] similar Grand Cycles would occur among the universes themselves, but on endlessly greater scales. And then, ever longer cycles exist among ever larger clusters of universes, and so on, eternally. For each greater cluster of existence, its exponentially longer Grand Cycle would have occurred endlessly in eternity.

From the perspective of forever greater Super Grand Cycles, infinity becomes two dimensional with one vector forever reaching into space, eternally gathering greater and greater mass and energy. Concomitantly, the other vector forever reaches into time, eternally repeating ever longer cycles. Thus, travelling on those two vectors, existence evolves forever throughout the endless universes.

From the limited perspective of our world and universe, the speed of light seems incredibly fast and free. But from the perspective of endlessly evolving existence and ever greater clusters of universes, the speed of light seems increasingly slow and restricting. For, the process of escaping such super big-bangs seems chained to the speed of light. Indeed, being limited by the speed of light, a seemingly endless time would be needed

---

[1]Currently, Earth beings have no way to observe other universes. Thus, no way is currently known to establish if gravity operates among the universes — throughout the meta-universe.

just for those unimaginably large masses to escape their "instantaneous", initial big-bang inflations in their Super Grand Cycles.

Space, time, and distance throughout existence are mind-boggling because they truly never end.

Part 11: Grasping the Ungraspable:
The Infinity of Existence

Within the Milky Way, our relatively small galaxy, billions of stars and planets exist that are millions of years older than our Earth. Within our universe, billions of galaxies exist that are larger than our Milky Way. Throughout the Grand Cycle, millions of stars, solar systems, and Earthlike planets constantly form anew. Among those millions of Earthlike planets abundant in water and oxygen, the dynamics of nature immutably generate life. Life, in turn, always undergoes nature's evolutionary process that ends with conscious beings...and conscious beings always evolve to control endless existence.

Indeed, life itself, its evolutionary processes, and thus, conscious beings themselves, have always existed throughout the universe as its third and unifying/integrating/controlling component. And that unifying/integrating/controlling component of the conscious mind was the component Einstein always sought but never recognized. For, he focused only on the mass and energy components of the universe while overlooking the component of consciousness.

When dealing with infinity, relationships among time, distance, knowledge, events, and probabilities become meaningless, resulting in seemingly bizarre situations. Consider a realistically impossible event here on earth for which the odds are a billion to one against occurring. When put in the context of infinite time, such an improbable event will not only occur with absolute certainty, but will occur an infinite number of times. Throughout infinity, whatever is theoretically possible becomes an absolute certainty that occurs an endless number of times.

To further demonstrate the bizarreness of infinity: Take an essentially impossible event that might occur once every billion years.   Now take an event that happens constantly, say, once every nanosecond.   Relative to infinity, both events will reoccur endlessly, forever into the future.   Thus, from the perspective of infinity, no difference exists between their occurrences, for they both occur with endless repetition. So, juxtaposed against infinity, no difference exists between an event that occurs every nanosecond versus an event that occurs once every billion years. For, throughout infinity, both events occur infinite times.

Also, in the context of infinity, no difference exists between distances throughout space.   For, throughout infinity, no reference points exist to measure differences among time or distances. ...Infinity is the only concept in existence without identity or boundaries.   Thus, infinity[1] is radically unique from all other concepts.

To grasp the meaning of infinite existence, one cannot view existence from the perspective of a finite planet or a finite universe.   Instead, one must view existence from the perspective of eternal endlessness.   From that perspective, no difference exists between a mile and a trillion miles, or a year and a trillion years, or a forest fire and a star fire, or a lightning bolt and a big-bang birth of a universe.   For, no reference points exist to compare distance, time, knowledge, or events of any magnitude when forever really means <u>forever</u>.

As shown later, certain deterministic concepts in the above four paragraphs are valid only in the hypothetical absence of eternal, free-will conscious life.

Part 12: Achieving Biological Immortality Now

From a perspective of the infinite time available throughout existence, all newly formed life evolves almost immediately into a highly intelligent brain that can invent consciousness from nature's bicameral mind.   The resulting conscious beings then, nearly instantly:

    1) take control of nature,
    2) render obsolete nature's evolutionary "need" for life-

---

[1]Infinity, as explained in *Neo-Tech Physics,* is a useful mind-created concept that does not exist in reality.

and-death cycles,
3) evolve into the Neo-Tech/Neothink mind,
4) cure mysticism, the only disease of the conscious
   mind, and
5) achieve non-aging immortality in order to live
   forever with growing prosperity and happiness.
6) control existence.

But from a perspective of the brief, finite time available for contemporary life on Earth, exactly how and when will biological immortality occur? First consider that, today, newly discovered Neo-Tech will eradicate the disease of mysticism and its parasitical neocheaters. Without the constant destructiveness of professional parasites, conscious beings will quickly, naturally develop commercial biological immortality as described below.

As Neo-Tech cures the disease of mysticism and vanishes those professional parasites, biological immortality will become a certainty for most human beings living today, regardless of age. In fact, today, freedom from mysticism will almost guarantee biological immortality for most people. And that could happen without massive efforts or spectacular medical discoveries. What is necessary, however, is the curing of mysticism. For mysticism, directly or indirectly, eventually kills all human beings while preventing biological immortality for all conscious beings.

Mysticism is the only disease of human consciousness. The symptoms of mysticism are harmful dishonesties. Those symptoms undermine the ability to integrate together the values of rationality *and emotions*. What is the value of emotions? The all-important value of emotions is to experience happiness — the bottom-line moral purpose of conscious life. But, mysticisms mixed with emotionalisms dishonestly assume a primacy over reason and reality. That dishonesty, in turn, casts mortal harm over every individual human being on planet Earth.

Neo-Tech, which is fully integrated honesty, eradicates the disease of mysticism. Thus, the immediate evolvement of biological immortality need not require quick technological breakthroughs, major research projects, or even explicit, direct efforts. But rather, with Neo-Tech, the process of biological immortality can begin immediately within one's own self. And that process will culminate with definitive biological immortality as the 3000-year disease of mysticism is cured by Neo-Tech worldwide.

How will biological immortality actually happen? First, consider:
- a world without mysticism,
- a world without professional value destroyers, parasitical elites, and dishonest neocheaters,
- a world without their destructive institutions of usurped power, such as the FDA (the most health-and-life destroying entity) and the IRS (the most value-and-job destroying entity),
- a world without the *anti-business* elements of mystical governments.
- a world without mystical governments.

Without life-corroding mysticism and its virus-like neocheaters draining everyone, business would explode into an endless productivity spiral. That value-driven explosion would launch human life into upward-spiraling prosperity with continuously expanding life spans.

Consider, for example, how the dynamics of computer technology have so far operated relatively free of parasitical elites, professional value destroyers, and government interference. Being relatively free of irrational regulations, force, coercion, and destructiveness, the computer industry has burgeoned. Computer technology is now delivering soaring capacities for processing and utilizing new knowledge at rates faster than new knowledge can be integrated and used by human beings. Such explosive advances in computer technology, or any technology, requires being free of government mysticism and its professional parasites.

The rational, conscious mind is synonymous with the productive, business mind. The value-creating business mind is the antithesis of the value-destroying political mind. The destructiveness of socialist, fascist, and religious societies prevents their citizens from developing efficient business-driven technologies. Indeed, all such societies are controlled by parasitical elites using force and deception to usurp harmful livelihoods. Such people live by attacking, draining, harming, or destroying value-and-job producing businesses...and their heroic creators and competitive expanders.

By contrast, explosive computer-like advances in human health and longevity directed toward commercial biological immortality will naturally occur in any mystic-free, business-driven society. But exactly how could biological immortality quickly occur today in a mystic-free society? Consider, a 60-year-old person today having a life expectancy of 20 more years. In a rational, business-minded society, uninhibited market forces will rapidly develop the most valuable products and technologies. ...The most valuable of all technologies — the quality preservation of conscious life — will advance so rapidly that when that person reaches 70, high-quality life spans will have expanded to 100 or 120 years, or more.

In a rational, mystic-free society, knowledge and technology accelerate geometrically. Thus, when that person reaches 100, high-quality life expectancy will have expanded to 140 or 180 years, or more. Those accelerating extensions of life expectancy would provide the time needed to develop *definitive biological immortality* for almost every value producer living today. Indeed, in the coming years, Neo-Tech will cure the disease of mysticism to eradicate physical diseases and death among all conscious beings on planet Earth.

In a competitive business-driven atmosphere free of mysticism, the life spans of conscious beings will advance faster than the passing of years. Thus, the result of Neo-Tech eliminating mysticism is immediate, de facto biological immortality. Then, rapidly accelerating health technology — including antiaging genetics — will yield that *definitive biological immortality.*[1]

Therefore, by replacing all forms of mysticism and neocheating with the fully integrated honesty of Neo-Tech, nearly everyone today can live forever.[2] Most important, with

---

[1]Curing death is described in other Neo-Tech works. ...Mortality is natural in life, except for conscious beings whose nature is immortality — the same immortality God possesses!

[2]The longer a productive individual lives, the more valuable that person becomes through his or her increased knowledge, experience, competence, productivity, and capacity for business and happiness. Thus, in any rational, mystic-free society, the motivation for and value of biological immortality increases as the age of the individual increases.

Neo-Tech, one can live forever with increasing prosperity, happiness, and love.

Almost anyone living today can survive to biological immortality by (1) replacing the death disease of mysticism with the life elixir of Neo-Tech and by (2) stopping mystical behaviors and destructive actions, such as making problems where none exist, smoking, and becoming mentally and physically unfit. Almost everyone today can and will achieve biological immortality by rejecting mysticism and neocheating both in one's self and in others. The key for everyone is to first recognize and then reject the disease of mysticism from within one's own self. Then one can effectively reject mysticism in others.

Life is everything. Death is nothing. Mysticism trades everything for nothing. Mysticism is a terminal disease that breeds professional value destroyers who eventually harm or kill everyone. ...Today, the disease of mysticism is totally unnecessary since it can be cured with Neo-Tech. Thus, through Neo-Tech, essentially everyone can live forever with ever increasing prosperity and happiness.

Also, conscious civilizations much advanced beyond ours would by necessity be free of mysticism and neocheating. For, by holding mystical premises, no civilization can advance much past the Nuclear-Decision Threshold[1] without destroying itself. ...In rational mystic-free societies, the idea of dishonesty is unknown.[2] Thus, *unknown* ideas also include war, murder, deception, fraud, forced taxation, conscription, racism, theft, assault, envy, anxiety, guilt.

Part 13: Infinite Knowledge

To quote from the first Neo-Tech World Summit (March, 1986) keynote address titled, "Three Steps to Achieving

---

[1]Planet Earth is currently at that Nuclear-Decision Threshold. For our civilization to survive, the disease of mysticism must be cured.

[2]Science-fiction stories and movies of evil or hostile aliens are illogical. For, no civilization with the nuclear-energy technology required for interstellar travel could survive as irrational, evil, violent, corrupt, or criminal in *any* way.

Commercial Biological Immortality in Our Lifetime":

"Living forever would be boring. False. Exactly the opposite is the fact. For creating and increasing values is the essence of a happy, exciting life, which, in turn, gives increasing motivation to live forever. Indeed, all new values come from expanding knowledge. And each new unit of knowledge generates several newer units of knowledge. Therefore, the ability to generate new knowledge is limitless. The notion of finite knowledge is only an illusion from our present, limited-knowledge perspective. Indeed, knowledge is not simply uncovered; it is generated from past knowledge. Thus, each day, the discovery of new knowledge generates ever greater bodies of ever newer knowledge and values.

"No one in the last century could have, for example, imagined any aspect of quantum mechanics, the computer age, genetic engineering, superconductivity, or fusion energy. For, everyone was many layers of knowledge away from even imagining those twentieth-century achievements. Yes, knowledge upon knowledge and achievement upon achievement will be generated anew — forever — by human consciousness.

"Human consciousness is the only force in the universe not predetermined by nature. Indeed, only consciousness can alter or go beyond the fixed patterns of nature. Consciousness obsoletes nature's blind, life-and-death survival cycles when applied to human beings. ...In a society free of mysticism, every conscious being produces open-ended achievements for society without bounds or limits. Thus, by producing an eternal stream of benefits for society, each conscious life continues happily, forever."

Part 14: Immortality — the Natural State of Consciousness

Thousands of years ago, before anyone on Earth grasped the concept of geometrical shapes, a man looked toward the heavens at the moon, then at the sun, then at the eyes of his woman. Suddenly he grasped the concept of "round"...a strange, new concept that no one had grasped or understood before. From that geometric concept came the circle, the wheel, the principles of mathematics and science, the automobile, the computer, and the latest theories of gravity. Yet, essentially no one today realizes that a concept so naturally integrated with life and taken for granted as the shape "round" was at one time unknown, strange, and spectacular to discover.

Likewise, a few thousand years from today, the natural physical state of conscious man — biological immortality — will be so natural, so integrated with life, so taken for granted that only historians would realize how during a brief time in faded history conscious beings were mystical and thus mortal. Indeed, mortality is not only the most unnatural, bizarre state for conscious beings, but is an essentially unknown state among mystic-free, conscious beings throughout the universe.

In addition to biological immortality as revealed in *The Neo-Tech Discovery*, conscious man's most natural, psychological state is happiness. Essentially all human unhappiness arises directly or indirectly from the disease of mysticism. With mysticism cured, happiness will become so natural and commonplace that in future millennia few if any will know that unhappiness and death ever existed.

Part 15: Einstein's First Oversight: Failure to Integrate Human Consciousness On Earth With the Grand Cycle

Consider us Earth beings with our technology of less than 3000 years. Consider our advances projected in the first half of the 21st century: The Futurist Society says all the knowledge we have *ever accumulated* will multiply a hundredfold! Then project that rate of growth into a geometrically increasing curve of knowledge soaring toward a thousand years hence, a million years hence. One can easily see that conscious beings arc altering the dynamics of nature at ever increasing rates. And through a relatively minuscule time span within the incomprehensibly long, googol-year cycle, conscious beings on Earth can quickly learn to dominate nature.

After only the first few centuries of consciousness, around 500 BC, human beings begin controlling nature faster than nature's evolutionary processes. Witness, for example, the development of consciousness from only 3000 years ago, an invisibly short time span in the Grand Cycle as shown in

Table 4 below. Earthbound consciousness has already obsoleted nature's evolutionary processes: Today, man-made shelter, food, medicine, and technology advance human survival and well-being much faster and better then do the slow evolutionary, adaptive processes of nature. In less than 3000 years, consciousness is already taking over the dynamics of nature on Earth. With that takeover, consciousness obsoletes nature's protective/survival mechanism of death. Thus, through time, consciousness mandates biological immortality for all conscious beings.

Becoming free of mysticism, Earth beings will not just increasingly control nature, but will dominate nature just a few hundred years hence as explained below.

During the next million years, planet Earth will geologically remain relatively static with basically the same oxygen, land, and water conditions. But, with geometrically accelerating knowledge, we on planet Earth will soon dominate and control nature. Consider, for example, the world's largest man-made lake accomplished by building Hoover Dam with only 3000 years of accumulated, conscious knowledge. That man-made feat controlled and then dominated nature's mighty Colorado River.

From the discovery of consciousness to the first automobile

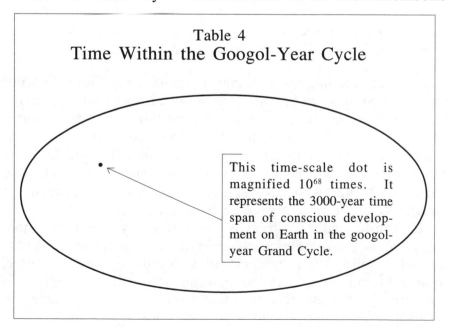

Table 4
Time Within the Googol-Year Cycle

This time-scale dot is magnified 10^{68} times. It represents the 3000-year time span of conscious development on Earth in the googol-year Grand Cycle.

took 2900 years of accumulated knowledge. Then, within 100 years, man went from the auto to the airplane, to the moon, and now toward super computers for everyone. ...Knowledge accumulates geometrically, quickly leaving nature's forces far behind as if frozen compared to the incredibly fast, always accelerating generation of new knowledge.

Perhaps only a few-hundred years hence, we Earth beings will be accumulating new knowledge at lightning speeds. With that rapidly increasing knowledge, we will easily, for example, corral heavenly asteroids into man-made orbital matter to fill our needs, just as today we corral river water into man-made lakes to fill our needs. ...What needs will we Earth beings have a thousand years from now, a million years from now? And how will we use our super-advanced knowledge and tools to control nature in filling those needs?

A thousand, even a million or a billion years, is an incredibly short time, a mere instant, within the Grand Cycle as shown in Table 4. But, well within that brief time span, we Earth beings can also accumulate the knowledge to dominate and drive the universe — to interdict nature's mass/energy dynamics in preventing the Grand Cycle from ever completing itself.

Part 16: Einstein's Second Oversight: Failure to Integrate Consciousness Beyond Earth With the Grand Cycle

Consider the billions of Earth-like planets existing within our own universe that are billions of years older than Earth. Through immutable evolutionary processes among those billions of Earth-like planets, conscious beings have evolved with millions or billions of years more advanced knowledge than we have on Earth today. ...Just imagine the technology and capacity of those conscious beings who have enjoyed geometrically accumulated knowledge for a million years, a billion years.

Human-like consciousness is the only entity in existence that can alter the inexorable course of nature. Human consciousness quickly advances from building cities to utilizing nuclear power, to developing computers, to making astronautical flights, to corralling astro matter, to understanding the universe, to controlling existence — and beyond forever.

Integrating nature's Grand Cycle with conscious beings reveals an elegantly simple understanding of existence. That integration reveals how individual consciousness is not only an integral component of existence, but is the dominating and controlling component. For example, at either end of the Grand Cycle, all life would perish. But individual consciousness — the supreme value of the universe — must forever protect itself. Thus, conscious beings a thousand or a million years more advanced in knowledge than we on Earth have long ago *met that responsibility to preserve the supreme value of existence: individual consciousness.*

Without immortal consciousness, the Grand Cycle would inexorably and infinitely repeat itself as dictated by the natural dynamics of mass and energy. But, with consciousness, the integrating and controlling component of existence missed by Einstein, the Grand Cycle is always interdicted and truncated. Thus, the destruction of the universe and consciousness has never occurred and will never occur. In other words, by integrating conscious beings into the dynamics of existence, nature's Grand Cycle becomes hypothetical and never occurs.

Consciousness and Existence Integrated

1) Anything theoretically possible in existence, no matter how remote the probability, will happen infinite times unless interdicted by conscious beings.
2) Human-like consciousness has forever been and will forever be an integral part of existence.
3) Conscious beings, as you and I, can understand anything in existence. On gaining the knowledge, therefore, we can and will eventually do anything theoretically possible that rationally benefits our existence.
4) Thus, human-like conscious beings throughout the universe always have, and always will, control existence.
5) On curing the disease of mysticism through Neo-Tech, we Earth beings will gain the same power, prosperity, and immortality of our fellow beings

who control existence throughout the universe.

Part 17: Knowledge at the Speed of Light

Everything in existence seems limited by a universal constant — the speed of light. For, as shown by Einstein, nothing can exceed the speed of light. Consciousness, therefore, being an integral part of existence, must also be limited by the speed of light. But how can the speed of light limit knowledge, especially since consciousness has no limits on understanding anything in existence? To answer that, one must first understand the dual faculty of consciousness:

1) The unlimited faculty to understand anything in existence.
2) The limited faculty to store and process knowledge.

By nature, each new unit of knowledge begets multiple units of still newer knowledge. Thus, consciousness creates knowledge geometrically. So, then, what can limit increases in knowledge? Nothing can stop knowledge from increasing forever. But, the rate of knowledge accumulation is ultimately limited by the speed of light in our closed universe.

To understand the faculty of consciousness that stores and processes knowledge, one must first understand the history of that faculty starting with the origins of man-discovered consciousness on Earth 3000 years ago: For the first 2000 years after the discovery of consciousness, knowledge accumulated very slowly. That accumulation gradually increased as the base of knowledge increased through memory and oral communication. Knowledge then accelerated through written communication.

For man to produce great sailing ships, for example, he needed that initial 1800 years of accumulated knowledge and technology stored and passed by memory, hand-scribed documents, and oral communication. Then he needed another 1000 years of faster accumulated knowledge and technology stored and passed through written works to produce steamships and trains in further improving transportation. He needed another 100 years of more rapidly accumulating knowledge and technology stored and passed through printed works to produce

454

automobiles that greatly improved transportation. Next, he needed only 60 more years of accelerating knowledge and technology stored and passed through books, journals, and communication equipment to produce practical airplanes that provided transportation inconceivable a century before. Finally, he needed only 40 more years of soaring knowledge and technology stored and passed through computers and electronic communications to develop space ships for landing men on the moon and building space stations.

Now, today, new knowledge is accelerating so rapidly that our productive focus is shifting toward storing, processing, integrating, and transmitting information through million-dollar super computers moving toward thousand-dollar personal computers. Thus, today, computers are undergoing explosive increases in capacities, power, practicality, and economies. And from now into the future, the demands of accumulating, storing, processing, and transmitting knowledge will shift into high gear from man's limited storage-capacity brain to external extensions of the brain with electron/photon-circuited quantum computers and beyond.

Today, storing and processing our geometrically increasing knowledge depends on our developing and building increasingly efficient, man-made computers. Advancing economies and prosperity depend on developing ever more advanced devices until the capacity of every spacetime point in the universe is utilized for storing, processing, and transmitting knowledge.

Knowledge will increase geometrically for a few millennia or perhaps only a few centuries — until the building of external-knowledge devices approaches the speed-of-light limitation. From that point, the expansion of knowledge shifts from geometric to linear. Knowledge will then expand linearly, near the speed of light, and limited by the speed of light.

When our own expanding knowledge reaches that limitation, we can join the millions of other civilizations in our universe that have reached that point. We can then communicate through the universal computer (perhaps gravity-coded) and control existence as our fellow conscious beings do. For, then, the entire universe of universes expanding at near the speed of light becomes our computer and storage facility for all acquired knowledge.[1]

The relationship of conscious knowledge to existence reduces to a single equation. To understand that equation, the following two points must be understood:

1) Knowledge is a function of time, which as Einstein determined is related to the speed of light.
2) Essentially all mega-advanced knowledge throughout the universe is generated, stored, and processed near the speed of light, limited only by the infinite Universe of universes on vectors forever expanding at near the speed of light.

Thus, knowledge ultimately obeys the same laws that all existence obeys...such as Einstein's law that integrates energy and mass with the speed of light as expressed by his famous equation:

$$E = mc^2$$

where:

E = energy; m = mass; c^2 = the speed of light squared

Likewise, knowledge integrates with time and the speed of light as expressed by the following equation:

$$K = tc^2$$

where:

K = knowledge; t = time; c^2 = the speed of light squared

Today, in our young Earthbound civilization, the always fatal disease of mysticism darkens the future for all human beings. Growing mysticism reduces and eventually stops the accumulation of new knowledge needed to survive and prosper. Growing mysticism eventually destroys the conscious mechanism for processing and accumulating knowledge. But, with the Neo-Tech discovery, mysticism can be cured worldwide to let all conscious

[1]Conscious beings perhaps overcome the speed-of-light limitation through eternal inflationary expansions of Gravity Units beyond our universe, into limitless existence and hyperspace.

beings forge ahead, geometrically accumulating knowledge at rates eventually limited only by the speed of light.

Part 18: The Universe is but a Dot Next to Individual Consciousness

Every individual consciousness has the capacity to generate, process, and use new knowledge at rates approaching the speed of light. By fully understanding the effects of such knowledge production and use, one quickly rectifies the false view of life held by most people who have lived on Earth. That false view expressed in Monty Python's "Meaning of Life" and promoted by mystics throughout history is: "Individual human beings are but insignificant dots among the vast universe."

Facts and logic demonstrate the exact opposite: Without mysticism, each individual consciousness has unlimited capacity to generate and utilize new knowledge at near the speed of light. Francis Bacon identified, "Knowledge is power." Thus, after a few millennia of such knowledge accumulation, any conscious individual gains the power to so totally dominate existence that the entire universe and all its evolutionary processes seem by comparison to shrink into static insignificance. For, in both power and significance, individual consciousness quickly soars beyond the dynamics of nature and the entire universe.

Today, on Earth, the fully integrated honesty of Neo-Tech finally reverses that mystical view bewailing mankind's insignificance. Neo-Tech demonstrates that the power of the universe shrinks to almost nothing when compared to the unlimited power of individual consciousness.

Part 19: Who is the Creator?

Does a creator of galaxies and universes exist? Indeed, such a creator could not defy the laws of physics. Yet, today, as for the past three millennia, most people believe a creator must be some mystical higher "authority" or power as promulgated by someone's scriptures or edicts. ...For two millennia, such mystical gods of creation were conjured-up by neocheaters wanting nothing more grand than to live off the efforts of others.

As demonstrated in the balance of this puzzle, everyday conscious beings like you and me work within the laws of physics to create and control all heavens and earths.

Part 20: The Goal of Conscious Beings

Throughout the universe, conscious beings pursue their natural goals and responsibilities by achieving biological immortality, limitless prosperity, and eternal happiness. Thus, they forever preserve the supreme value of the universe: individual consciousness. For without conscious beings, no value or meaning would exist throughout the universe. ...Conscious beings free of mysticism never allow their precious lives — lives of limitless value — to end.

Part 21: Galaxies Created Beyond The Dynamics of Nature

Eons ago, a conscious being, as you and I, worked at the edge of a distant galaxy with an integrating computer of a spatial-geometry driven, mass/energy assembler. By assembling units of gravitational geometries, that person corralled enough strings of wound-up gravity to equal the mass of another galaxy. As the moment of critical gravity approached, the final collapse into an entropy-reversing, rotating "black hole" began. He then arose smiling. With arm held high, he cried, "Let there be light!"[1] ...At that moment, in a far corner of the universe, the light of a million times a million suns flashed and began its photonic journey across the universe. A galaxy was born...a man-made galaxy.

Part 22: Galaxies Discovered Beyond The Dynamics of Nature

Today, eons later, specks of light from that conscious-made galaxy fall on the planet Earth — on the lens of a telescope. An astrophysicist examines computer data gathered from those

---

[1]The expression "Let there be light" was first manipulatively used in the mystical world of the Bible, then entertainingly used in the science-fiction world of Isaac Asimov, and now factually used in the objective world of Neo-Tech.

specks of light. Then, integrating that data with the physical and mathematical dynamics of astral mass and energy, he moves closer to a momentous discovery. He moves closer to discovering a major astral event falling outside the natural dynamics of mass and energy — an event that irrevocably altered nature's charted course for the universe.

But, that scientist knows, as any competent scientist knows, that nothing, including conscious beings, can alter the axiomatic laws of physics, mathematics, and existence. And he knows that existence can have no antecedent basis or original creator. Yet, he realizes that, within the laws of physics, conscious beings can alter the natural dynamics of mass and energy. Thus, he realizes conscious beings and only conscious beings can alter nature's manifest destiny, not only here on Earth, but throughout the universe.

Combining such knowledge with computer processed data, that scientist moves closer toward directly observing the alteration of nature's Grand Cycle by conscious beings. Such direct observation may come, for example, through a correlation of computer data concerning black holes or possibly quasars and pulsars. In fact, such correlations of data probably already exist on Earth — hidden in considerable accumulations of uninterpreted data. Integrating such data could reveal that certain cosmic events exist outside the natural dynamics of their mass, energy, and gravity. In turn, that data could then demonstrate how conscious beings create and control such cosmic events as energy and galaxy creators for the eternal prosperity of all conscious life.

Thus, conscious beings could forever prevent the Grand Cycle from completing itself. They could do that, for example, by routinely creating gravity dimensions and geometries that constantly pump entropy-reversing structures back into the universe. Such constantly created, new structures would break the dynamics of the Grand Cycle, allowing the universe to forever oscillate within its most efficient range for conscious beings.

Part 23: Create Your Own Galaxy

Beginning with the data from that speck of light born a

million years before, today's Earthbound scientist will discover and prove a newborn galaxy created outside the mass/energy/gravity dynamics of nature alone. He will then look toward the heavens realizing that he has discovered a galaxy made by a conscious being. He will further realize that over eternal time, over eternally interdicted cycles, all the galaxies and universes, all the heavens and Earths, were at one time created from conscious-made structure pumps that formed new realms of existence while preserving old realms.

And finally, he will realize his mind is the same conscious mind possessed by our immutable conscious cousins who create new realms of existence in other worlds and galaxies for us, them, and everyone.

Part 24: After the Discovery

After that first discovery of a conscious-made galaxy or black hole, scientists will then approximate from our geometric increases of knowledge on Earth and our achievement of biological immortality, when you and I can stand above all the imagined gods to give the command, *Let there be light!*

Part 25: Conclusion

No intimidating god or ethereal super consciousness reigns over the universe. Mystical gods or "higher beings" do not exist, cannot exist, need not exist. For only universes created and controlled by rational, value-producing conscious beings as you and I are needed to explain all existence. And with biological immortality, we Earth beings will someday stand smiling at the edge of space creating our own stars, galaxies, universes, collections of universes, and beyond.

Epilogue

The mightiest power in existence, the power to control existence, is expressed by the great command, "Let there be light!" That power has forever existed among fellow beings throughout the universe. The essence of that power is available to all of us, now, here on Earth today through Neo-Tech. ...Neo-Tech eradicates mysticism — the disease that causes ignorance and death among conscious beings.

AIDS degenerates the body's protective immune system into weakness, sickness, then death; mysticism degenerates the mind's protective thinking system into ignorance, sickness, then death. Mysticism cripples and finally destroys the conscious mind.

But unlike AIDS, an immediate cure exists right now for mysticism and its virus-like neocheaters. That cure is Neo-Tech. Curing mysticism will also bring definitive cures for AIDS, cancer, heart disease, and all other diseases harmful to conscious beings. Neo-Tech forever eradicates mysticism and its symbiotic neocheaters, allowing the individual to direct his or her life toward achieving guiltless prosperity and abiding happiness for self, others, and all society.

Neo-Tech also opens the way for knowledge expanding geometrically to eventually approach the speed of light. Every person applying Neo-Tech, therefore, holds unbeatable advantages over those crippled by mysticism, parasitical elites, and neocheaters. Indeed, Neo-Tech allows human beings to acquire total control over both the material and emotional realms. Neo-Tech gives all human beings on Earth today the power to execute the tripartite commands: "Let there be wealth!", "Let there be romantic love!", "Let there be eternal youth!"

The time has come to grow up...or be left behind to perish in a world of mysticism. Clinging to mystical beliefs such as supreme creators or "higher authorities" is as crippling to human life and prosperity as would be the clinging to the once popular belief that the Earth is flat or today's fading belief that force-backed "authorities" or politicians can advance the well-being of any individual or society.

After 3000 years, the time has come to abandon life-destroying mysticism and all its symbiotic parasites and neocheaters. Now is the time to mature into meeting our responsibility of grooming the supreme value of the universe — our own conscious lives. Now is the time to groom our conscious minds with fully integrated honesty for limitless growth and value production forever into the future. Now is the time to join our fellow conscious beings throughout all existence in meeting our supreme responsibility to life — to live happily, prosperously with our fellow conscious beings throughout eternal existence. *For, we are the creators of all heavens and earths. ...All glory to us conscious beings!*

* * * *

Wallace's 25-part Neothink puzzle above goes to the next level in discovering the Controller of the Universe. In short, mystic-free man in the mystic-free Civilization of the Universe controls the Universe. That makes mystic-free man, or God-Man, the Controller of the Universe; they are the real Gods of the Universe.

Mystic-free man is God-Man. God-Man is God. In fact, the Scriptures refer to man achieving unity with God, about the glory of when man becomes one with God. When humanity purges its disease of mysticism, man eventually becomes the Controller of the Universe...man becomes God...God-Man. Soon, we on Earth will join the Gods of the Universe.

Now, the word "Zon" was developed by Dr. Wallace to designate the very advanced God-Man at the level of creating values *for the Universe*, such as creating new realms of existence, say a galaxy, throughout which the supreme value of the Universe will evolve — conscious life. Zon is the ultimate value creator — the supreme creator. At one point, a Zon created our Universe.

Going To "Heaven"

Through puzzle-building Neothink, Wallace showed us the Universe's deepest secret: *God...is Zon.* When we evolve into the new Neothink mentality, we here on Earth will join the Gods of the Universe. But, if we do not make it — if we die before our final evolution and before achieving non-aging biological immortality, well then, Dr. Wallace put forth a sound theory on what will happen to us based on his years of work on the nature of mystic-free man. His theory, less the many pages of scientific reasoning and explanations, goes something like this in layman's terms:

The Civilization of the Universe has always existed. It is

free of mutations of the bicameral mentality infecting conscious minds (i.e., free of *the* mind disease: mysticism, which perpetuates our anticivilization). The extremely happy, mystic-free people in the Civilization of the Universe, where they enjoy the Gifts and are financially and emotionally rich, have long ago achieved non-aging biological immortality. Likewise, Earthlings in tomorrow's Neo-Tech World will have no reason or desire to age and die. With the Gifts, life will be extraordinarily happy and every new moment will be wonderfully precious. Furthermore, human consciousness will be viewed as the value it really is: the supreme value in the Universe.

Therefore, in infinite time, the rapidly expanding knowledge of exhilarated, mystic-free conscious beings among the Civilization of the Universe, long before Earth even existed, achieved biological immortality for themselves, their families, their civilizations on their planets and throughout their galaxies. Those Zons also learned through super advanced technologies, long before our galaxy was created, how to protect and preserve the supreme value in the Universe, human consciousness, everywhere for everyone.

Those who die, those still caught in mystical anticivilizations, would be saved through highly advanced technology. Perhaps an ether acts as a transceiver that first receives, then transmits your consciousness into the Civilization of the Universe. There, people live as euphoric Neothink men and women, free of mysticism. They live as man was meant to live — as gods...highly stimulated and contributing immensely to the prosperity of the Civilization of the Universe, creating new values via Neothink. Going to the Civilization of the Universe after we die is going to "Heaven".

Below I have extracted the pages from Wallace's Journal that describe this theory. I have left out hundreds of pages, including the many pages of hard-core Neo-Tech physics, but those are available from Neo-Tech Publishing Company.

Dr. Wallace's Journal

On any objective consideration, one cannot take seriously religious claims of life after death. Yet, such claims are the centerpiece of Western religions as well as many other religions. But, all such claims are marketing hype to exploit the deepest hopes and fears of conscious beings. For the past two millennia, afterlife promises have hoaxed Earth's anticivilization into embracing mystical organized religions.[1]

Earth's Greatest Discovery: Profit-Driven Immortality[2]

The afterlife hoaxes promoted by mystical religions serve to hide the single most important, potentially provable fact on this planet: *Most if not all honest conscious beings who have died on Earth in the past 3000 years continue to live with eternally expanding prosperity and happiness throughout the Civilization of the Universe!*

Ultimate Justice

Justice is an immutable law of nature. As demonstrated by the *Neo-Tech Discovery,* justice is *always* fulfilled throughout existence. As a result, the eventual destination or just reward for every actual and potential value producer — of every honest conscious being — is eternal prosperity and happiness in the Civilization of the Universe.

That just destination is the inevitable consequence of nature. From that nature comes (1) immutable justice that characterizes the Civilization of the Universe, (2) the supremely leveraged, limitless value of each conscious being when placed in a rational civilization, (3) the dynamics of eternally expanding prosperity,

---

[1]Religious faith has, however, been a key value at various periods in history. At times, for example, religious faith served to divide and weaken government tyranny, and vice versa, leaving pockets of freedom to advance knowledge, technology, and well-being within the anticivilization.

[2]Profit-driven immortality as presented in this journal is a speculative hypothesis arising from a-priori logic. Yet, logically, no contradictions exist in that hypothesis. Today, the chief value of that hypothesis is metaphorical — an illustration of justice that reality ultimately asserts. Tomorrow? Facts and knowledge will unfold to reveal the hypothesis as fact or fiction.

which demand the full use of *every* available conscious being, and, as explained later in this chapter, (4) the technology needed to transceive[1] every volitionally developed human consciousness through the omnipresent existence field and into the Civilization of the Universe.

Humanoid criminals or parasitical neocheaters who have lived by harming others or society through force, fraud, and illusions also meet ultimate justice: They become humanoids because they destroy the human nature of their own consciousnesses. Therefore, they destroy the conscious structure needed to transceive through the ether or existence field and into the Civilization of the Universe. Moreover, having lived as enormous net negatives to society, humanoids such as destructive politicians with their armed bureaucracies and ego-"justice" systems are, unless rehabilitated, worthless to the Civilization of the Universe. Thus, they simply vanish from existence, forever forgotten.

Bases of Proof

Any future proof of immortality for conscious beings must be derived from theories that are in full correspondence with the laws of physics. Theories derived both deductively and inductively must provide wide-range predictiveness, reproducible experimental evidence, consistent mathematical definitions, and limitless ways to test for contradictions and falsifications. This journal provides the elements needed to develop such proofs, predictions, and facts. ...Those theories must withstand challenges of direct and indirect experimental tests, observations, and calculations.

Listed below are the elements found in this journal. When assembled, those elements posit the hypotheses that (1) the Civilization of the Universe exists, (2) every fully developed, honest conscious being who lived on this planet for the past 3000 years continues to live with growing prosperity, love, and

---

[1]Transceived not in the mystical Plato sense of a detached soul. For, the soul and physical body are one in the same and function as a unit. But, transceived (within a profit-mode, business dynamic) in the Gravity-Unit form that captures conscious "I"ness immortality, all in accord with the laws of physics.

happiness in the Civilization of the Universe, and (3) technology commonly exists throughout the Civilization of the Universe that provides eternal life and prosperity to all honest, conscious beings on this planet. Those hypotheses also posit that every humanoid criminal who has died during the past 3000 years has vanished from existence. Moreover, all such parasitical humanoids who currently live by harming others will also vanish from existence. Humanoids living on Earth today, however, can be "saved" by restructuring their behaviors in order to mature into healthy, conscious human beings who competitively produce values for others and society.

Potential Elements of Proof Found in Wallace's Journal

Existence exists.
Existence is axiomatic, endless, eternal.
Existence exists eternally with no prior causes.
Consciousness is not only an eternal part of eternal existence, but is the eternal controller of existence.
Individual human consciousness is the greatest value in eternal existence...the seminal value from which all other values flow.
The greatest social value among conscious beings is honest, competitive businesses combined with *objective* law and justice.
Valid knowledge is contextual and hierarchal. Valid ideas are hierarchal paradigms of contextual facts.
Conscious knowledge is limitless because knowledge always begets new knowledge — geometrically, up to the speed of light.
The essence of human consciousness is goodness: By nature human consciousness is noble, rational, honest, just, compassionate, value producing, benevolent, kind, loving, happy.
The only disease of human consciousness is mysticism.
That disease destroys the natural good of human consciousness. That disease causes all wars and crimes, including politically inflicted property destructions, harms, sufferings, cruelties, and deaths. Such evils are inflicted by force or fraud to support the lives of open criminals (subhumans) such as muggers and rapists...or the much more evil, hidden criminals (humanoids) such as destructive politicians, tyrannical rulers, and killer-type

466

You Will Become God

(WACO) bureaucrats.

Camouflaged mysticism and deception used to drain, harm, and kill human beings is called neocheating.

Neocheaters are highly intelligent humanoids in whom the disease of mysticism has destroyed the human nature of their conscious minds. Thus, such neocheaters are no longer human beings. They are humanoids who have destroyed the conscious structures of the human essences needed to enter the Civilization of the Universe.

To parasitically exist, neocheaters purposely propagate a bizarre, irrational civilization on planet Earth within which conscious life always moves toward unnatural death instead of natural immortality.

This unnatural, transitory anticivilization in macroscopic existence is somewhat analogous to the unnatural, transitory antiparticle in microscopic existence.

As the bizarre antiparticle vanishes forever on contact with natural matter, the bizarre anticivilization will vanish forever on contact with the natural Civilization of the Universe.

The supreme value of human consciousness will always be preserved by advanced civilizations using multidimensional[1] transceiver technologies in quantum-state, digitized cyberspace. Those technologies integrate rational consciousness with the existence field throughout the Civilization of the Universe.

By the fact of their continued existence, civilizations technologically advanced significantly past their Nuclear-Decision Thresholds are free from the disease of mysticism. Thus, all such advanced civilizations are a part of the Civilization of the Universe.

In most areas, no one can predict the state of technology 100 years ahead, and certainly not a 1000 years ahead, much less a million years into the future. We cannot even imagine the technological states and economies of the advanced societies throughout the Civilization of the Universe.

---

[1]Such multidimensional examples are derivable from superstring and wormhole theories. Traversable wormholes, rotating black holes, and above-and-below Gravity Units offer theoretical but questionable time-travel possibilities at superluminal speeds. Such possibilities, nevertheless, can be codified through mathematics.

We can, however, know that no society, regardless of how advanced, can contradict the laws of physics or nature. Moreover, we can know that conscious beings throughout the Civilization of the Universe will never purposely act to violate their nature, well being, and happiness.

The basic nature of rational conscious beings has never and will never change. No rational being would ever let technology overtake his or her nature, self-control, self-responsibility, growth, and happiness. For, that loss of control over one's self — one's greatest value — would be self-destructive and irrational. Indeed, all conscious beings in the Civilization of the Universe are free of such irrationality or any other impediments to the growth and happiness of individual consciousness.

Thus, conscious beings in the Civilization of the Universe have the same nature: They live for happiness and its corollary emotions of genuine self-esteem and love. Indeed, the moral purpose of conscious beings is to meet the requirements for achieving rational happiness.

The nature of existence includes (1) objective law and justice, which characterize the Civilization of the Universe, (2) the limitless value of each conscious being when functioning in a rational civilization, (3) the dynamics of continually expanding value production and prosperity, which demands eternally preserving the supreme value of *every* conscious being.

The most bizarre characteristics of the anticivilization are its overpopulation and aging problems. In any rational civilization, overpopulation and aging are impossible. Exactly the opposite occurs. When free of destructive humanoids, each conscious being is free to productively, culturally, and artistically innovate and flourish without limits, becoming a priceless value to others and society. For, each conscious being in a rational civilization is free to innovate and produce through division-of-essence dynamics far more values and resources than he or she consumes. ...Always increasing in value while always decreasing entropy, conscious beings remain forever young and precious.

Thus, in the open-ended Civilization of the Universe, a great demand for volitionally conscious people *always* exists. ...When free in an open and rational society based on objective law, each conscious individual enormously benefits and enriches all other conscious individuals and their societies. Through eternity, therefore, each conscious being will eventually contribute more value to society than its entire population at any given point in time.

Knowledge and technology increase endlessly. All advancing civilizations require developing ever greater and cheaper energy sources and production efficiencies.

Prosperity and happiness of conscious beings do *not* depend on their actual level of knowledge or technology, but depend on their rational thinking and acting processes required for continuously advancing knowledge and technology from any level.

Throughout the universe, every level of advancing knowledge and technology exists. Thus exists a technological level of conscious beings whose most efficient production of values depend on the *unsupervised* development and utilization of free-will conscious beings...such as found in an anticivilization as exists today on planet Earth. For, each such transceivable conscious person would provide endless values to all individuals and societies in the Civilization of the Universe.

Every populated area in existence has the economic-growth needs for which each additional, volitionally developed, conscious being from any civilization would be of immense value. Thus, honest conscious beings anywhere in existence are never allowed to perish.

In Earth's anticivilization, *every* volitionally developed, honest conscious person is transceived/redeemed on a commercially profitable basis into the Civilization of the Universe. In other words, essentially every honest conscious being who has ever lived on Earth continues to live, flourishing eternally, in the Civilization of the Universe. ...But, the harmful humanoids of past history self-programed themselves to perish — to vanish from existence forever in the ultimate Ostracism Matrix.

Thus, justice and rationality are preserved through immortality.

The Neo-Tech World

Assembling the Proof of Immortality

Consider the effect of delivering irrefutable proof showing how all honest human beings live *forever* with increasing prosperity and happiness. Such proof might include measuring Gravity-Unit[1] field changes of human beings versus humanoids and animals as they die.[2]

Of course, the primary responsibility of conscious beings on Earth today is to protect and preserve their existence — to create their own immortality in which transceiving would be unnecessary.

Schindler's List, the factual story of German businessman Oskar Schindler in the 1940s, illustrates how even at the evilest depths of this anticivilization, the value-and-job producer is the *only* person with genuine power and love...even midst humanoids who live by guns and mass murder. Only businessman Schindler, for example, could walk through the bloody mud of the Holocaust without soiling his soul, his compassion, his respect for human life. Only job-producing Schindler had the power, moral character, and strength to reach into the depths of this anticivilization to save conscious beings from the destruction and death wrought by its humanoid propagators.

Extrapolate the metaphor of businessman Schindler into the advanced technologies among the Civilization of the Universe. One will then recognize that honest businesspeople with their limitless valuation of conscious beings are the real saviors of everyone in existence. Only such value-and-job producers have

---

[1]Gravity Units are the theoretic fundamental units of existence, elaborated on in Neo-Tech physics.

[2]In the mid 19th century, the great German mathematicians, C. F. Gauss and G. F. Riemann uncovered the noneuclidean geometries and higher spatial dimensions involved in such transductions throughout existence. Matter, energy, forces, and fields arise from motions through varying geometries in various dimensions and quantum states. Einstein needed Riemann's geometries to develop general relativity. Today, superstring theory originating from Kaluza-Klein theory further links geometries in various dimensions to existence.

Gravity-Unit \ $\xrightarrow[\text{to}]{\text{convert}}$ matter/energy/forces/fields $\xrightarrow[\text{to}]{\text{convert}}$ spacetime curvatures/geometries $\xrightarrow[\text{to}]{\text{convert}}$ < Gravity-Unit
Consciousness /   \ Consciousness

the power, responsibility, and love to never let perish the supreme value throughout the universe — conscious life, including conscious human beings on planet Earth. ...The competitive, value-and-job producing business-person eternally preserves and advances all conscious life.

When You Go to "Heaven"

What will actually happen when you travel into the Civilization of the Universe? What will you experience? Will you ever return to this anticivilization? What about those left behind? What will limitless prosperity and eternal happiness really mean to you — emotionally, practically?

Once in the Civilization of the Universe, you will quickly forget the anticivilization. For, the anticivilization vanishes as the unreal nothingness it really is — it simply vanishes to be forever forgotten. And, those left behind? They too will vanish and be forgotten. But, no one will be left behind except criminal humanoids who have destroyed their human nature and refused to reconstruct their humanity. Thus, every conscious being, once in the rational Civilization of the Universe, has no reason or desire to connect their lives or memories with the destructive irrationalities of an anticivilization.

What will a nonpolitical civilization based entirely on integrated honesty and *objective* law be like? That civilization will be free of *subjective* political-policy laws, irrational ego "justice", and dishonest parasitical elites. Gone will be force-backed governments with their above-the-law rulers. Gone will be the politicians, lawyers, and judges identified as criminal-minded "superior people" by Fyodor Dostoyevsky in his classic *Crime and Punishment.* Gone will be armed bureaucracies, mystical religions, wars, crime, fraud, poverty, disease, and death itself.

But, what is the Civilization of the Universe really like — emotionally, intellectually, and experience wise? What will living free of disease, mysticism, dishonesty, criminality, and irrationality be like? One's entire pattern of thoughts, emotions, and experiences will be different — so radically different from anything experienced in this anticivilization that no one today

471

could fully know or describe that eternal difference...at least not until the Civilization of the Universe is created on planet Earth.[1] The conscious-created Civilization of the Universe will be available on Earth sometime after 2001. Five years later, many conscious beings in the business-developed countries will have already left behind this unreal anticivilization to reside in the exciting Civilization of the Universe.

How can one get some idea of what conscious life in the Civilization of the Universe might be like — some idea before actually taking that one-way journey from this grotesquely contradictory anticivilization into the beautifully harmonious Civilization of the Universe?

Perhaps one can begin imagining an eternally prosperous, happy life by trying to view this closed-system anticivilization from the outside. From that external view, one can sense how mysticism constantly blocks or cuts off experiencing life as ecstasy, cuts off achieving limitless prosperity, cuts off experiencing a fully joyful, productive, rational life. From the Civilization of the Universe, *every* perspective will look different from anything one could experience within this anticivilization. Each new perspective will be like encountering a new color for the first time — a new-color symphony — a stunningly unexpected experience unrecognizable from any previous experience.

The increasing government-imposed difficulties in achieving competitive values and genuine happiness throughout this anticivilization will wondrously transform into the easy way — the path of self-responsible freedom — a consistently joyful path filled with endless victories. Indeed, that easy way is *endless* growth through discipline, rational thought, and productive action.

---

[1]Consider a flatlander living in a two-dimensional universe being flipped up into a three-dimensional universe then falling back into his flat-plane universe. Observing only a series of two-dimensional planes or lines fly by as he travels through three-dimensional space, that flatlander would have no adequate way to understand a three-dimensional universe and would have no way to explain it to his fellow flatlanders. ...Do not confuse this useful dimensional analogy with the invalid analogy of Plato's cave to so-called higher realities. No higher or multirealities exist. Only one reality exists.

Perhaps the closest, but still distant sense to that experience, can be observed in children under six years old still not diseased by the anticivilization. In every such child, one can observe his or her learning as not only remarkably rapid but compellingly joyful and exciting. Until poisoned by the dishonesties and mysticisms of the anticivilization, each young child experiences increasing joy in progressing toward knowledge and control of existence.

Indeed, an ecstatic life of endless growth is experienced by all conscious beings in the Civilization of the Universe. Even destructive politicians and other parasitical humanoids can reenter that nonpolitical Civilization of the Universe after reconstructing their humanity — after becoming honest, competitive human beings who are genuinely valuable to others and society.

You Will Become God-Man

Consider the following six points:
1. God-Man is the measure of all conscious beings.
2. God-Man is disconnected from *every* aspect of any anticivilization.
3. Parasitical elites have created a dishonest, violent anticivilization on Earth. They each will unhesitantly lie, make war, commit crimes, murder, even mass murder to continue their destructive livelihoods and increase their power usurpations.
4. One finds eternal freedom by disconnecting from Earth's anti-civilization. Such a disconnection switches one from this anticivilization into the Civilization of the Universe.
5. No part of any anticivilization is redeemable or correctable. For, nothing is redeemable or correctable from illusions based on nonreality. ...Fully integrated honesty with its wide-scope reality vanishes all such illusions.
6. Daybreak does not at once replace the darkness. Thus, the Civilization of the Universe will not at once replace Earth's anticivilization. In both cases, a seeming glow comes first. Then light breaks across the darkness. All becomes visible, clear — a peaceful civilization of eternal prosperity and exciting romance here on Earth. To experience the coming

light, read the first epic of the Civilization of the Universe: *The First Immortals.*

The following journey unites the above points by returning *you* to God-Man whose kingdom is the Civilization of the Universe.

> You Control Existence
> You are Invulnerable
> You are God-Man

God-Man is a citizen of all universes. How would a citizen of Earth recognize God-Man? How would God-Man appear? How would God-Man think? What would God-Man do?

God-Man is the controller of existence. The very advanced God-Man or *Zon* is the past and future creator of all universes. God-Man is identical to you, except he or she acts entirely through a new mentality — the Neothink mentality of fully integrated honesty and wide-scope accounting. Thus, you can experience God-Man. Indeed, you can become God-Man to rule existence and gain eternal prosperity. ...As God-Man, nothing in an anticivilization has power over you.

You were born God-Man. Every conscious being who has ever existed was born God-Man. But, on planet Earth, *every* conscious being has been dragged from childhood into the dishonest illusions that perpetuate this anticivilization. Thus, everyone today behaves as someone else — as someone other than an honest, fully conscious human being. ...Until today, every adult on Earth has lived as a phantom, never realizing that he or she is an eternal God-Man.

You are God-Man living in an illusion-shrouded anticivilization. In this illusionary civilization, all human beings live as phantoms deluded into believing they are mortals who live and die with no eternal power, purpose, or prosperity. When, in reality, conscious beings are immortal with limitless power and purpose. We are the Gods of the Universe.

On vanishing the illusions of this anticivilization, you reconnect with God-Man, the ruler of existence. Although you still walk among the phantoms in this anticivilization, you have no connection with their illusions. You are as divorced from their illusions as you would be divorced from the illusions of schizophrenics in an insane asylum.

Yet, you see *everyone* as your kin. You see the profound value and power in every conscious being. Beyond all else in existence, you treasure the soul of each human being, regardless of what civilization or age in which each lives.

As God-Man, how would you appear physically, mentally, and behaviorally among the phantoms of this anticivilization? How would you gain ever increasing prosperity, love, and happiness when you are disconnected from all the illusions comprising this anticivilization? How would you function among the hypnotized human beings and destructive humanoids of this anticivilization?

As God-Man, you do not feel superior to, aloof from, or even particularly different than others. Nor are you a Bartleby. You simply know you are in a different civilization — a 180° different civilization. That difference does not make you feel uncomfortable or uneasy. In fact, your ability to function with others is enhanced. That disconnection also enhances your ability to benefit all human beings *and* humanoids on this planet. Moreover, your disconnection enhances your own happiness and enjoyment of life on Earth.

Most profoundly, as God-Man you know that you are invulnerable to the irrationalities of this anticivilization. Like the anticivilization itself, the irrational actions of both its human-being and humanoid citizens are unreal — not connected to reality. Thus, such nonreality has no meaning for you...no real influence on you.

Still, you are among fellow conscious beings — the greatest value in existence. Moreover, the objective requirement for eternal life, prosperity, and happiness remains the same wherever conscious beings exist. That requirement is to deliver ever increasing values to others and society. Through the division of essence and labor combined with voluntary transactions, you create increasingly more values for others than you consume. You become increasingly valuable to yourself, others, and society.

You live to *be*, not to *have*. You live to create, not to consume. You need nothing beyond the requirements to produce life-enhancing values at maximum efficiencies for yourself, others, and society. You need or want nothing from this moribund anticivilization. You neither need nor want anything from its inherently destructive rulers and their dishonest media, organizations, academe, politicians, intellectuals, or celebrities.

Why the zero value of this anticivilization? Consider its irrational effects: The more life-enhancing values that heroic value producers deliver to society, the more parasitical humanoids foment public envy against those value producers. Why? To increasingly usurp unearned livelihoods from the productive class. Likewise, the more life-supporting jobs that honest businesses deliver to society, the more parasitical humanoids use government force to drain those businesses through irrational taxes, political-agenda laws, and destructive regulations. Such insanity is not the fault of human beings. Rather, that insanity is inherent in any irrational civilization functioning through subjective laws fashioned by parasitical rulers backed by armed agents of force.

In reality, you and all human beings belong *not* among this unreal anticivilization but among the Civilization of the Universe. All the insanities of which an anticivilization is constructed are merely illusions that never exist in reality — bizarre illusions that ultimately yield only diminishment and death to human beings — dishonest illusions that serve only the parasitical livelihoods of humanoids.

Yet, you as God-Man are eternally protected by honesty and reality. You are always advancing in *real* spacetime to ever greater accomplishments, continually decreasing the entropy[1] of existence — continually making order out of disorder. Thus, nothing in the anticivilization can really harm or adversely affect your progress in moving through spacetime toward eternal life and prosperity.

At this moment, you can experience the first glimpse at how you as God-Man function among your fellow human beings in this anticivilization. You first note the honest innocence of young children. You realize that essentially all children under six years of age are God-Man — innocent, uncorrupted, honest. You

---

[1]That capacity to decrease entropy is why conscious beings and only conscious beings can potentially reverse physical aging.

notice how all such children struggle to obtain objective knowledge, not illusions. Those children strive for value-producing powers, not socially destructive pragmatisms. Then you realize how all parents and adults in this anticivilization are deluded by their humanoid rulers — humanoids who eventually corrupt and then bury the innocence, honesty, and power inherent within *every* young child.

Only through that ultimate crime inflicted on all children has this bizarre anticivilization been perpetuated since its creator, Plato, twenty-four centuries ago.

You start your journey into the Civilization of the Universe by transporting yourself into a mind and body that functions through fully integrated honesty and wide-scope accountability. With the power of fully integrated honesty, you discover the universal laws that deliver valid solutions to all problems.

Objective Laws are Universal Laws

In the final analysis, all problems tie together to yield valid, effective solutions according to objective, universal laws that can never be contradicted. Only objective laws are valid and apply to everyone, at all places, at all times. By definition, objective laws do not spring from the minds of men and women. Such laws have always and will always exist universally — independent of the human mind and its emotions. Thus, no objective law is new; each is eternal. Moreover, *no* law — physical, legal, or moral — is valid unless that law is naturally applicable, universally and eternally.

The Universal Law

Preamble

The purpose of human life is to prosper and live happily. The function of society is to guarantee those conditions that allow all individuals to fulfill their purpose. Those conditions can be guaranteed through a constitution that forbids the use of initiatory force or coercion by any person or group against any individual:

The Constitution

Article 1: No person, group of persons, or government may initiate force, threat of force, or fraud against any individual's self or property.

Article 2: Force may be morally and legally used only in defense against those who violate Article 1.

Article 3: No exceptions shall ever exist to Articles 1 and 2.

Living by the universal principles of objective law, one neither needs nor wants approval, acceptance, or recognition from anyone interacting with this unreal anticivilization. The entire history of the anticivilization and its humanoid rulers is one of fraud leading to human diminishment. The anticivilization has no real existence or power. Its humanoid perpetrators have only illusionary existences and imaginary powers in an anticivilization first conjured up by Plato and then perpetuated by parasitical elites. Such parasites are epitomized by the dishonest hierarchies of the church, statc, and academe who have fatally corrupted the minds and bodies of human beings for the past two millennia.

Now consider the meaning of vanishing the illusions that support this anticivilization and its humanoid rulers — the meaning of you becoming God-Man:

Becoming God-Man

On becoming God-Man, you increasingly disconnect from the actions, people, and humanoids interacting with this unreal anticivilization. Your disconnection is not one of misanthropy, but one of grace. Your disconnection involves (1) *physical actions* reflected by a pleasant demeanor, (2) *mental processes* reflected by creative, nonlinear, far-from-equilibrium thinking that brings order out of chaos to create new knowledge, and (3) *behaviors* reflected by benevolent disconnections from the irrationalities of this anticivilization. Those irrationalities include health-diminishing, life-consuming distractions ranging from drug-like obsessions with eating to life-escaping obsessions with sports, entertainment, and celebrities.

You need not correct anything in an uncorrectable anticivilization. **You only need to disconnect.** ...Now consider these areas of disconnection:

— Physical —
Expanding health and vitality are earned, not given. Expanding health and vitality come no other way except through DTC — Discipline, Thought, then Control. DTC self-perpetuates, builds on itself, and then brings rewards to every aspect of conscious life. ...DTC is the most powerful determinant of human health, longevity, and happiness.

You are trim, fit, and happy. With your spouse, values such as growth, communication, love, and sexual enjoyment grow each year. In handling life, your effectiveness increases each year, *never* diminishing with age.

Your joy with your work, your loved ones, and your life expand eternally. You realize DTC and physical fitness are natural for all conscious beings throughout all universes, in all ages.

You disconnect from the irrationalities of overeating and under exercising throughout this anticivilization.

— Mental —
Your power to acquire expanding knowledge for controlling existence derives through fully integrated honesty and wide-scope thinking. Fully integrated honesty is the underlying source of value creation and competitive businesses on Earth and throughout existence. In an anticivilization, its humanoid creators and perpetrators can survive only by disintegrating the

479

most powerful essence of conscious beings — fully integrated honesty.

You disconnect from the dishonesties throughout this anticivilization.

— Behavior —

Conscious beings are social animals mediated through value exchange and business. The limitless benevolence, prosperity, excitement, and happiness possible among conscious beings are derived from the natural dynamics among the Civilization of the Universe. They are derived from conscious beings freely producing and volitionally trading mutually beneficial values. ...Poverty, crime, and war are inconceivable concepts in the Civilization of the Universe.

You disconnect from the socially and economically destructive behaviors throughout this anticivilization.

As God-Man, you feel a profound care and valuation for the source of *all* human values, in all universes, in all ages. That source of values is your fellow conscious beings. You also care for the humanoid parasites who created and propagate this destructive anticivilization. Indeed, you work for their redemption as human beings. Why? Most humanoids can be guided back to their childhoods when they were innocent God-Man. From that point, they can learn to grow up — to mature into value-producing and then value-creating human beings. On becoming honest conscious beings, they also can reenter the Civilization of the Universe to become limitless values to others and society.

Zon Religion

That concludes the pieces I chose from Wallace's Journal to present his hypothesis. ...Now, from Wallace's hypothesis, I have personally deduced ten simple components that I use to explain Zon Religion to anyone who asks. First, I tell them that Zon Religion believes that, yes, God exists. God, however, is not a mystical God. God is real — *you* are God as you evolve into God-Man.

So, when people ask me, "What is Zon Religion?" I say there are ten simple components to understanding the Zon Religion:

Component 1: Abundance of Water

Recently water was discovered on at least three other bodies in our solar system including possibly on our own moon (in the form of ice), which made scientists realize there must be an enormous abundance of water throughout the Universe. Water is the crucial ingredient for life. Thus, today physicists believe life, including evolved conscious life, flourish throughout our Universe.

Component 2: Age of the Universe

Recently, physicists discovered the Universe is older, perhaps much older, than they thought. Combining component 1 with 2, abundant conscious life has flourished for billions of years before life on Earth.

Component 3: Time Stands Still

As time passes, conscious civilizations generate knowledge at increasing speeds. As civilizations advance to quantum computers and beyond, acceleration of knowledge happens so lightning fast that the function of time becomes less and less an issue until it becomes a non-issue. Knowledge eventually advances so fast that time seems to almost stand still (see Neo-Tech Physics). On Earth, we have experienced human consciousness for just 3000 years (the First Insight), and we are already on the verge of quantum computers (i.e., computer circuitry made of atomic and subatomic particles). Imagine human consciousness that has been around a million years, a billion years. Combining components 1, 2, and 3, we realize with the abundance of life and age of the Universe, conscious life throughout the Universe has reached this point long ago where knowledge advances so fast that time relatively stands still.

Component 4: The Controlling Component
        of Existence

Einstein said existence consisted of two components: mass and energy. In Wallace's Neothink puzzle, you saw why human consciousness is the third component of existence, which Einstein missed. Life is a common, natural phenomenon of existence that quickly evolves into conscious life, making conscious life the third, fundamental component of existence. Not only that, but consciousness is the *controlling* component as it takes over and controls mass and energy to serve the needs of consciousness. Combining 1, 2, 3, and 4, abundant conscious life has been around so long and is so advanced that it has taken physical control of our Universe.

Component 5: The Unexplainable Always Turned
        Man toward "God"

Since the beginning of time, whenever man could not logically explain the world and cosmos around him, whenever the answers went beyond his intellectual grasp, he turned to "God" as the only explanation. As man advanced his knowledge to cover more ground in understanding the world and cosmos around him, the role of God steadily drew back from his daily thoughts as he logically explained the formerly unexplainable. The classic example would be the Darwin experience. His work *The Origin of Species* and later *The Descent of Man* sent shock waves throughout the world through all fields of thought. Suddenly, people's lives, the world they lived in, were no longer part of God's order. People were shaken up by that, but Darwin's Theory of Evolution through Natural Selection explained the previously unexplainable, which vanquished the belief that God's majestic creation was the origin of species and God's divine plan plotted man's development. Because of *the explainable* in Darwin's works, the unexplainable — i.e., God — covered much less ground in our psyches. Combining components 1, 2, 3, 4, and 5 raises the questions: "If God is the substitute for the unexplainable, what will happen when everything is explainable? What will happen to God?"

*Component 6: From an Unexplainable God to
an Explainable Zon*

Because man could not and still cannot fully understand the Universe — the answers heretofore go beyond his intellectual grasp — he has turned to God as the explanation for the creation of the Universe. God created the Universe? That unexplainable ground in our psyches still belongs to God. Now, because of components 1, 2, 3, 4, 5, and 6, however, we can start to understand the Universe. Bringing those puzzle pieces together, we can explain how very advanced consciousness not only took control over, but *created* the Universe. Let's review: 1) Abundant water means abundant life flourishing throughout the Universe, 2) the age of the Universe means much of that conscious life has existed and advanced for billions of years, 3) that advanced consciousness generates knowledge so fast that time seems to slow down and disengage, 4) that lightning-fast acceleration of conscious knowledge is taking control of mass and energy, the cosmos, and has done so for millions and billions of years, and has taken control of the overarching dynamics of the Universe, 5) as we explain the world and Universe around us, the unexplainable ground of God gets smaller and smaller; God gets more and more pushed out of our psyches, as demonstrated from evolving ancient civilizations to the Darwin era, 6) very advanced consciousness, *a Zon*, who has, billions of years ago, taken complete control over mass and energy, created our realm of existence (i.e., our galaxy) and, just as certain, *a Zon* created our Universe. The unexplainable ground of God gets filled with *the explainable*. God gets pushed out of our psyches. Now, as we enter the third millennium, we can replace an unexplainable God with an explainable Zon.

Component 7: Creating Existence

Physicists know that enormous amounts of existence is trapped in black holes throughout our Universe. Dr. Wallace has taken that even a step further with his Gravity Units Theory (Neo-Tech Physics). Zons have taken control of existence — of mass and energy — to the point of controlling the creation of new realms of existence. They unfold black holes or gravity units to create new realms of existence and bring forth new consciousness (the third component of existence), including galaxies and universes, including our galaxy and our Universe. As we bring together components 1, 2, 3, 4, 5, 6, and 7, we will want to emotionally and spiritually honor our Zon who gave us life.

Component 8: Emotionally/Spiritually Honor Our Zon

As we grasp the first seven components, we will want to be grateful to our Creator who gave us life — to our Zon. And, we will want to be grateful to our Savior who preserves our spirit, when we die, for eternity — to our Zon. But, *how* do we honor Zon? By combining components 1 through 8, we realize Zon is a value creator. He creates new realms of existence, mostly to create the *supreme value*: new realms of consciousness (the third component of existence). For, that new consciousness will eventually advance into value creators, into God-Man, to add values to Zon's house — his galaxy or universe — fulfilling his objective as our Creator. So, how do we honor our Creator? We honor him by jumping from value producers (who maintain existing values but do not add new values) to value creators (who add new values to Zon's house), fulfilling our destiny, the role of consciousness (Vision Two). Zon's ultimate desire is to see his creation beget creators...ultimately beget Zons.

*Component 9: Leaping from a Value Producer
to a Value Creator*

Leaping from a value producer to a value creator is our way of fulfilling our own nature and our Creator's desire...our way of honoring ourselves and Him. ...How do you make that leap to honor yourself and your Creator and Savior and fulfill your nature and his wishes? It is presently a very difficult leap because we are surrounded by an anticivilization with a business structure, political structure, and educational structure that suppresses us into stagnant value producers and prevents us from soaring as value creators. The starting point is to discover your Friday-Night Essence (Vision One) and become the person you were meant to be and to use the mini-day/power-thinking team (Vision Five) to pursue the path you were meant to travel. That being said, however, the leap from value producer to value creator can be enormous and overwhelming. Emotional support, practical advice, and valuable contacts in an ongoing, common-goal environment can make that overwhelming leap into God-Man a reality.

Component 10: Congregation/Church of God-Man

During this Third Insight, I saw a *Church of God-Man* that put the ordinary person in the right environment to make the jump. The weekly congregation also provided, for those after the leap into God-Man, the first formations of the Civilization of the Universe here on Earth. That environment in my Third Insight put value producers in the right atmosphere to become value creators, and put value creators in their most advantageous environment. The weekly congregation in my Insight took insightful probes into *The Book* (the Bible for the Church of God-Man, available from Neo-Tech Publishing Co.). The Church of God-Man housed the Zon Business Religion (i.e., become a value creator to put new values into the world, eventually into the Universe). At the Church of God-Man, people learned that our consciousness is the same as Zon's, just without the advanced levels of knowledge. People saw the beauty in the explainable Zon Religion: we are not powerless, little humans being looked down upon. We are limitless God-Man who will someday be Zon.

Inquire About the Church of God-Man

Bringing together all ten components...*go to a Church of God-Man near you* when it becomes available to you. There you will find the Civilization of the Universe forming on Earth; you will walk into a unique emotional aura, be provided with practical techniques and surrounded by valuable contacts — the ripe environment to help you on your journey from a value producer to a value creator. When you become a value creator, you

485

become the God-Man.   You will then thrive in the Civilization of the Universe provided at the Church of God-Man as you help others leap from value producers to value creators.   The God-Man, who functions through Neothink to create values for the world, eventually for the Universe, will someday become Zon.

Future Definitive Component: The Proof

Not many scientists had put much credence in Einstein's Relativity until a solar eclipse offered the proof.   Overnight, scientists everywhere were driven into Relativity.   As the proof that Zons control our Universe becomes overwhelming (through Dr. Wallace's Overlay Charts, being developed at Neo-Tech Publishing Co.), scientists and ordinary people everywhere will be driven into the Zon Religion.   God and other mystical religions will vanish.   The Zon Business Religion and its Church of God-Man will eventually envelop everyone, everywhere.   For therein lies the answer.   There the search for "something better" ends, and the journey into "something better" begins.   Something much better.

Conclusion

The New World

The Twelve Visions and Three Insights showed me that soon everyone, sometime in the 21st century, will live as millionaires with perfect health and exciting romantic love. A new world, a much better world, will replace the old.

Today we are at the right place at the right time. We are in the starting gates of a great Technological Revolution, and we can see signs of that with super-fast microprocessors in the computer industry, fiber optics in the telecommunications industry, inexpensive satellite dishes in the television industry. Those forerunners to what lies ahead bring with them rapidly falling prices. For instance, the latest $250 video-game machine from Nintendo has the computing power that would have cost $14 million a few years ago.

In the foreseeable future, rapidly multiplying geniuses of society and super technologies of the 21st century will join together with a synergy never witnessed before. The geniuses, the first to evolve into the Neothink mentality, will drive down costs and drive up buying power so dramatically their advancements will regularly become the front-page headlines of the daily papers.

Where will the geniuses come from? Looking back at the late 20th century, an unusual abundance of geniuses rose in the computer industry and far outnumbered the geniuses in any other century-end industry. Of course, that helped explain why the computer industry advanced so rapidly and was a sign of things to come.

But, why was the computer industry so well endowed with geniuses? Looking back, the answer is obvious: the personal computer industry had shifted toward the new world: *the geniuses were **free** to rise up and to team up with super technologies.*

The geniuses were held down in most other industries, stuck in the old world of bicameral mysticisms and external authorities...sinking under the regulatory bureaucracies. Thus, with a slowing progression of technologies, we were vulnerable to growing problems closing out the 20th century and heading into the 21st century, namely disease, poverty, and crime. In fact, we started sinking toward a potential Catastrophic Era.

That Catastrophic Era could have lasted for a full generation or longer if not for a sudden change that I witnessed in my Visions. That sudden change came as the communication revolution helped introduce tens of millions of people to the Twelve Visions, making the Twelve Visions self-fulfilling prophecies. For, those people then understood what was causing us to sink into the complex catastrophes. That understanding helped start an unstoppable shift that saved us from sinking and ultimately lifted civilization into a paradise on Earth.

The Old World Versus the New World

The question became, as we began the 21st century: can we leapfrog the Catastrophic Era and land in the Neo-Tech Era? Fortunately, my Visions showed me we did pull out of the Catastrophic Era before we sank too deep. While looking back at the final years of the 20th century and early 21st century, I saw a dichotomy building between the old world plagued with bicameral mentalities versus the new world soaring with Neothink mentalities. Let's go back and visit the end of the 20th century and start of the 21st century:

Computer people lived partly in the new world soaring with Neothink mentalities. They were hard-driving individualists who fiercely fought off external "authorities" such as government interference and regulations. Medical people, on the other hand, suffered under the old world plagued with bicameral mentalities and neocheaters. External "authorities" such as the FDA had long since subjugated the research doctors, the businesses, and the scientists in the medical field.

In the computer industry, rich with Neothink mentalities, technologies raced to the marketplace; breakthroughs advanced so quickly that oftentimes they got obsoleted by other technologies even before reaching the marketplace. In the medical industry, by contrast, each advancement was put through years of regulatory controls and many millions of dollars in expenses before getting an approval by the external "authorities", in this case by the FDA. Under severe restrictions and huge cost burdens, no individual geniuses could rise, and wide-sweeping Neothink could never function.

Fortunately, that mystical curse did not happen to the computers, and that was why computers raced forward and prices raced downward. The medical industry was not so lucky. Of course, it advanced at a painfully slow pace with escalating prices. Until the FDA was gone, there would be no medical revolution on par with the computer revolution. Yet, infectious diseases for the first time in half a century advanced faster than modern medicine, pulling us and our loved ones into a society increasingly vulnerable to the horrors of drug-resistant strains of deadly diseases.

As antibiotics increasingly lost their effectiveness, civilization could have sunk into a medical nightmare; modern-day epidemics could have terrorized mankind. Millions could have died.

Tens of millions still can conceivably die from such a scenario, but my Visions showed me a steady shift from the old world to the new world, which saved us from that fate. As the FDA lost some of its debilitating control over biotech progress, the biotech revolution began.

Big-government regulations were part of the old 20th-century political structure built on our bicameral behaviors supporting a hierarchy of external "authorities". Government increasingly politicized our lives. Regulatory bureacrats enforced that politicization. Regulatory bureaucracies increasingly regulated our businesses, professions, sciences. Social welfare increasingly regulated our money. As I looked back at the computers versus medicine closing out the previous century, I knew we would sink under the old code of external "authorities" with big government politicizing and regulating our lives.

The political structure was based on our obsolete bicameral mentality of being directed by a hierarchy of authorities. Indeed, Dr. Julian Jaynes[1] explained that the bicameral kingdoms as in Mesopotamia and Egypt existed with a powerful, divine hierarchy

[1]Dr. Julian Jaynes (1920-1997), renowned Princeton Professor and author of *The Origin of Consciousness in the Breakdown of the Bicameral Mind.*

of authorities. Similarly, prior to civilization's evolution into God-Man, our political fabric was patterned after the bicameral kingdoms with a similarly powerful hierarchy of authorities.

Whereas bicameral man depended on authorization for survival, conscious man must ultimately break from authorization for survival. In my Visions of the new world, a get-the-people-healthy-and-wealthy political dynamic rose in the 21st century that broke from authorization. That Neo-Tech Party depoliticized our civilization. Suddenly, gone were the many bicameral-mentality barriers, those external "authorities" such as the FDA. Individual geniuses were free to rise up and team up with 21st-century super technologies not just in the computer industry, but in the medical industry and in all other industries to bring us rapid progress and falling prices. The shift toward the new world saved us from twenty-five or more years of disease, poverty, and crime. Instead, in our Neo-Tech World, we rose to the life human beings were supposed to live, and we enjoyed the Gifts.

The Weaning Period

Looking back at events leading up to the Neo-Tech World, people in the late 20th century and early 21st century weaning themselves from bicameral mentalities repeatedly asked, "But what about all the good from big-government regulations?" Yet, those same people began to sense we actually got only harm from big-government legislation and regulations. The people began to realize that politicians and bureaucrats wrongly assumed bicameral civilization's "power of the gods" in ruling over the people via legislation and regulations...an addictive, destructive power when extended beyond ancient gods (i.e., bicameral man's neurological guidance mechanism) to politicians (i.e., conscious man's hypnotic neocheaters). The people began to realize the ruling class — the hierarchy of "authorities" — was a destructive remnant of our bicameral past.

The nature of man is God-Man or self-authority. Authorization from outside goes against man's nature. Indeed, as demonstrated throughout the ages, this "divine" ruling power of external "authorities" axiomatically hurts society — from the ancient emperors to today's career politicians. My Neothink

Visions showed me the people realized sometime in the 21st century that men who assumed "divine" power and played God with our lives ultimately destroyed society, for God belonged to each individual unto himself. Indeed, the external "authorities" were clever neocheaters[1] manipulating our bicameral tendencies. The people finally realized that their own deep-rooted bicameral urges to be told what to do and how to live by higher "authorities" ultimately destroyed society, for those higher "authorities" were smooth neocheaters eloquently providing their dazzling array of guidance through masterful, mystical illusions commonly called "good intentions" for the "social good", but always in exchange for our sacrifice to their own power, prestige, and control over enormous wealth.

Still, to stop government from politicizing our lives is, today, a difficult idea for the ordinary person because of the many illusions of "serving the social good". Of course, the neocheaters are manipulating our bicameral mysticisms. In fact, good *will* come from some of those programs "for the social good" when no longer done by politicians for political power, but done by private entrepreneurs to sincerely serve our needs (or go out of business). Therefore, my Neothink Visions showed me that as we moved into the new get-the-people-healthy-and-wealthy political paradigm, we went through a *Great Displacement Program*: government programs "for the social good" including regulatory and entitlement programs were sold to the private sector. Politicians' secret sin of ruling over us ended, and then the services were free of politics and done right and finally served us well.

How We Entered Our Neo-Tech World

Did we leapfrog the Catastrophic Era and go straight into the Neo-Tech Era? In my Visions, we actually began sinking into the Catastrophic Era, but were able to pull out before it was too late. In the first decade of the 21st century, these Twelve Visions

---

[1]Neocheaters have existed for 3000 years, but only recently have they been discovered. They are "invisible" cheaters who fleece their livings by catering to our bicameral behaviors. The First Insight went into detail on neocheaters.

of our beautiful lives in tomorrow's Neo-Tech World spread to tens of millions of people. When fifty million people saw the exciting new world, something changed. An unstoppable strategic inflection point, which meant everything would change, had come of age. The people wanted and voted for the life of their dreams.

In other words, the path into the Neo-Tech World of no higher "authorities" or ruling class was not a hopeless political one. Instead, like me, when the ordinary person saw the Neo-Tech World, saw the Twelve Visions, his dreams fell into place. The Twelve Visions got under his skin and never left, for within those Visions the ordinary person saw the life he always dreamed of, the life he was meant to live. Without ever a single political discussion from that person's lips, when the time came, he quietly voted for the life of his dreams. Nothing could stop the change into a new political paradigm that freed the geniuses and super technologies from big-government regulations.

Just as today, the people tomorrow by and large were not politically inclined. The path into the Neo-Tech World would have been hopelessly slow as a political movement per se, which answered my questions as to *why* the Twelve Visions came to me. Something or someone was looking after us (later I learned that "someone" was God-Man) and was giving mysticism-plagued humanity the way to shed its bicameral vestiges and pull out of the approaching Catastrophic Era. Again, I saw that once fifty million people saw these Twelve Visions and realized their God-given right[1] to the Gifts, then critical mass was reached and depoliticizing America began and could not be stopped.

Fundamentally, things began changing, for civilization had

---

[1]During our final evolution into God-Man sometime in the 21st century, God the executive part of human nature united with man the follower part of human nature...as nearly happened during the Golden Age of Greece 2400 years ago before neocheaters broke off man's own executive authority and gave it to external "authorities". When our final evolution united God and man into God-Man, when man's mind was its own authority as conscious man was supposed to be, then we enjoyed the Gifts that we do not have now as merely man — the follower. The God part of God-Man brought the Gifts to man. Thus, the Gifts were God's Gifts to man...and, so be it, our God-given right.

always lived beneath a ruling class. Now, that mutation of the bicameral mentality would no longer be the way. The ossified hierarchy of authorities cracked apart and fell into a heap of dust that was quickly blown away and forgotten. A new code of social interaction had begun. Geniuses in the marketplace replaced politicians in Washington D.C. to aggressively serve our needs.

New World, New Wealth

In tomorrow's new world, geniuses used super technologies to drive our costs to fractions for nearly every need. Thus, we soon lived like millionaires. But how could *everyone* live like a millionaire? Wouldn't we experience hyper-inflation or some kind of monetary crisis? I am not an expert on money and money supply. But understand that productive and creative energy pouring into society raises the wealth of society. What I saw was like a miracle: In my Visions of the Neo-Tech World, tens of millions, up to one hundred million geniuses in America alone relentlessly poured productive and creative energy into society. Furthermore, that flood of productive and creative energy repeatedly multiplied itself as first those geniuses and then the entire human race evolved into explosively creative Neothink. The wealth of society and standards of living rose to heights never even imagined before. Throughout this flood of wealth, private financial businesses and their geniuses tomorrow figured out the effective use of money, credit, safe transitions to other money supplies where necessary, the function of commodities, bartering arrangements, and so on. They took care of all such rising needs.

Moreover, businesses in the next era evolved beyond the division of labor that has served us well for the past century. You see, jobs of labor serve the bicameral mentality of automatically reacting to the world around us...in this case, the routine rut. To keep up in tomorrow's super rapidly advancing Neo-Tech World, businesses evolved into the more competitive division of essence: the essence of business is to create values that build wealth. The division of essence broke businesses down into value creating wealth-building jobs...i.e., miniature companies within the company instead of today's boring routine ruts in which we stagnate. Tomorrow's entrepreneurial jobs of the mind opened the way for Neothink. We thrived on success as in-house entrepreneurs.

Now, imagine the implications of this job revolution that made working people essentially in-house entrepreneurs. Every day using their minds, those hundred-million entrepreneurs became more and more creative and eventually with Neothink evolved into super entrepreneurs. Remember, productive and creative energy determines the wealth of society. A hundred-million super entrepreneurs poured energy and creativity into society, flooding society with wealth, lifting everyone's standard of living to unprecedented heights. Moreover, those super entrepreneurs, free to race ahead, teamed up with 21st-century super technologies. The wealth of society went off the measuring charts.

The People Finally Realized

Still, what about big-government regulations? Wouldn't we have chaos without them? We *must* need them! The people tomorrow finally realized that beyond their deep-rooted bicameral urges, the answer was: *no*, we did not need those higher "authorities" ruling over us — not if we wanted rapid progress and large cuts in costs.

For example, the medical industry was in big trouble as antibiotics lost their effectiveness, and we faced less and less protection against infectious diseases. Since the discovery of penicillin in 1928 and more than a thousand antibiotics since, bacteria steadily evolved through gradual mutations to more and more resist antibiotics. During the early 21st century, humans were literally in a race for their lives against stubborn drug-resistant infectious diseases, and our progress was slow in this race for our lives because of FDA regulations. And medical costs became less and less affordable instead of dropping to fractions, again because of FDA regulations that were exorbitantly costly and that, furthermore, prevented rapidly advancing technological breakthroughs that would have driven down prices toward zero.

Thus, speaking about results and costs, higher "authorities" such as the FDA and their big-government regulations for noble-sounding "good intentions" literally killed us. Virulent diseases, poverty and crime continued to flourish at the start of the 21st century *as a result* of big-government regulations, which held us knee-deep in the Catastrophic Era before being pulled out by the shift toward new world. In short, tomorrow the Neo-Tech World let the geniuses rise up and do to medicine, poverty, and crime what they did to the computers!

Gods, Oracles, Politicians, and Bureaucrats

The people tomorrow realized that politicians and regulatory bureaucrats, who ruled over our lives, were mystical vestiges from our bicameral past of gods and oracles. Politicians and regulatory bureaucrats played the role of gods and oracles over man; they ruled over us. They manipulated our mysticisms through very convincing illusions of "social good". Our deep-rooted urge for external guidance accepted those neocheaters. In fact, all civilizations for the past 3000 years lived under the same old mystical spell that allowed a ruling class to rule over the people. The new world broke the spell and allowed no ruling class. The new world employed a protecting class as opposed to a ruling class. Government was for defense, for physically protecting us and our properties and nothing more.

Some social welfare programs still seemed very good and desirable, of course. Still, to have that compassionate social welfare that regulated our money put the "divine" authority to rule over us in the hands of neocheaters. Again, that was the old code of higher "authorities" and "higher" causes, when ruling-class neocheaters — from Golden Greece's career politicians, the Hebrew elders, Roman emperors, monarchs of the Middle Ages, totalitarian rulers of the 20th century, to America-the-Beautiful career politicians — eventually destroyed the society over which they ruled. Men could not prosper under other men enjoying the "divine" right to be our gods, even if elected to do so. That "divine" hierarchy of authorities went against the nature of conscious man and destroyed our prosperity.

The people tomorrow realized that *every* regulatory act was disguised as something good — *good intentions* for the "social good" — by those politicians and bureaucrats who ruled over us. The result of their "good intentions"? The rulers doubled the money they took from hard-working Americans during the last decade of the 20th century, from one to two trillion dollars, which was destroying our prosperity and dipping our feet into the Catastrophic Era of poverty, crime, and disease. No ruling class would stop that multiplying rate of money and power from being mercilessly drained from our lives. No ruling class would stop that multiplying rate from continuing through the first decade of the 21st century. Even worse, no ruling class would lift its heavy foot off the many, many potential geniuses of society.

As knowledge rapidly multiplied in the early 21st century thanks to the computer/communication revolution, however, more and more people either directly or indirectly learned about Neo-Tech. Then they knew that any program of government that seemed good and desirable, in the end would destroy us if men — politicians and bureaucrats — were assuming "the power of gods" to rule over us. ...Indeed, we were shedding our bicameral behaviors.

Did we need regulations to stop corruption in business? Corruption in business had indeed always been a problem, particularly in big business. But in my Visions, people began to see that big government *caused* the corruption. They realized that big government consisted of men just as you and me, but the difference was they wanted to get ahead *politically.* So the basis of every decision was tied to political clout, not to building values. A lot of political clout and money came by befriending big business. And in turn, a lot of advantages for big businesses came by befriending politicians...advantages such as special rights of way, passage of regulations that limited competition particularly from aggressive entrepreneurs. Tomorrow the people called such businessmen who looked to get ahead through political favors: political businessmen. They called businessmen who got ahead by producing better values at lower prices: market businessmen. The people realized, in short, if there were no big government, if politicians were stripped of their ruling powers, there could be no more special arrangements and big-business corruption.

But some concerned moms wondered, would the new world's

political paradigm ban the Department of Education? I mean, some programs for the "social good" *really were* important. Indeed, they were. And tomorrow, their very importance became the impetus to get them out of the hands of people motivated by political clout. Education, energy, agriculture, commerce, transportation, environmental protection, all of industry's regulatory bureaucracies for that matter were sold to private services. Those private services were no longer controlled by political power. Instead, they were controlled by *you* — the consumer. To provide you with a competitive, desirable service, finally those good intentions materialized. They called this selling of government's programs for the "social good", this transferring of those programs from corrupt politicians and bureaucrats interested in ruling over us to entrepreneurs and market businesspeople interested in competitively taking care of our needs, *the Great Displacement Program.*

The People Realized They Would Live Like Millionaires

Once fifty million people got a glimpse of what I saw of the Neo-Tech World in my Visions, and once they realized they would live like millionaires, well, they embraced the new world whose time had come. The widespread damnation of "higher" authority had begun. As seen in my Visions, the people voted for depoliticizing America, which opened the gates for the great Technological Revolution that took us into the Neo-Tech World.

The vision of wealth caused the change. A political path per se was a hopeless cause. For instance, in my Visions while looking back at the late 20th century and early 21st century, I uncovered an admirable political effort that just would not work. I observed Libertarians and their good ideas to depoliticize America. Libertarians said that people would vote Libertarian if they only listened to the Libertarian ideas. The problem with that was people, by and large, did not listen to political ideas. Not in the 20th century, not in the 21st century. Unless we were on the brink of a national disaster such as a war, political ideas just did not enter the average working person's routine.

Nevertheless, elections were very tempting to third-party hopefuls because nearly a hundred million people went out and voted. That was the country's single biggest movement of people every four years. "If I could only connect with and corral an impressive chunk of that movement of people," every third-party presidential candidate hoped for in vain. But it was a fool's journey, for people voted as a sense of civic duty, not because they ever got involved with political ideas. People were too busy making a living and raising a family. Even with growing popularity at the local level at century end, Libertarians were looking at a very long time to bring about significant change. And on the eve of the Catastrophic Era, we did not have a lot of time.

To speed up the process and help us pull free from the Catastrophic Era, a higher power intervened and showed me the exciting Twelve Visions of the Neo-Tech World. The Twelve Visions were appealing. They offered the ordinary person his selfish desires and dreams, which were first and foremost to him. He was not too busy to personally prosper. He was not too busy to receive the Gifts.

So, millions of ordinary men in the street — ordinary people *not* politically inclined — got excited about these Visions and talked about them among their friends and loved ones when they got exposed to the Visions and the new way. They no longer needed to suffer in silent frustration. Like me, the answers to everything that ever bothered the average stagnated person were in these Twelve Visions. Now, to get to that Neo-Tech World that fulfilled his dreams, the political part about depoliticizing America was an afterthought. But now that the desire for the Neo-Tech World and its Gifts was inside the layman and would not go away, he followed through on the political side when the time came and voted for his dreams.

The elusive riddle of how to politically corral a major chunk of the immense movement of people every four years was solved by first getting under the layman's skin to his selfish motivations. I really believe this was why the Twelve Visions came to me with an "instruction" to deliver these Visions to the world. There could be no other way for change. The Libertarians tried to little avail.

No, there was no political jackpot to be won by a third party. But in my Visions, I witnessed that when enough of these books

The New World

reached the mainstream, a critical mass happened and the *Great Replacement Program* began: All over the country, we began shedding our bicameral behaviors and replacing career politicians who were interested in ruling over us and politicizing our lives, replacing them with instead people interested in the commendable chore of producing and creating values.   So, entrepreneurs and market-driven businesspeople were voted into office.   That included the President of the United States.

I witnessed that once people got a hint of their own potential millionaire wealth, then today's anti big-government mega trend, steady as she goes, turned into tomorrow's make-the-people-millionaires stampede.   Once in office, the Neo-Tech President submitted a protection-only budget that cut out all spending toward all "good intentions"...from regulatory bureaucracies that regulated our businesses to social welfare that regulated our money.

In other words, the President moved us away from a government on the offense to a government of defense only.   He depoliticized America to make all industries as free as the relatively nonpoliticized computer industry.   We then entered the Neo-Tech World flourishing with Neothink geniuses driving forward super technologies.   Costs for that soaring new technology quickly dropped toward zero, and we grew wealthy.

In the End, Money Pointed the Way

Of course, although they knew better, during the early stages of the transition from the old world to the new world some people were still wondering: aren't there some good programs in the federal government besides national defense, the courts, and prisons?   But those same people discovered how to answer for themselves every question such as that, as follows: Aside from all the appearances of how good or harmless a particular program seemed, those people asked themselves if that program was physically protecting American citizens, or if it was, no matter how good it appeared, politicizing a part of their lives, ruling over them?   For, they now knew the moment men began playing gods with our lives, our businesses, and our money, the fall of our standards of living began.   In the end, the harmless "good intentions" for the "social good" swelled annually to well over two trillion dollars with three-fourths of government-spending going toward ruling over us in every way. That was the old world.

Did people give up their entitlements? Not at first. But in my Visions, I saw a new group of people come out to vote — the disillusioned, nonregistered citizens old enough to vote came out in droves and registered to vote. They teamed together with the registered voters not on entitlements. And once a Neo-Tech President was in office, a demonstration occurred during his first year after he introduced the protection-only budget. You see, Congress mostly got its way and diluted his massive budget cuts that first year, but the political climate of absolute freedom had been posited. Money, energy, and creativity came flowing into our economy. Standards of living and buying power started going up quickly. This new era of burgeoning wealth became more and more obvious, even to welfare recipients: they would lose their small entitlements in exchange for millionaire-like wealth. They got exciting jobs as the economy exploded and everyone became rich before the President's term was up.

The Seniors Got Rich Too

As the desire for the Gifts got under the skin of tens of millions of people, the government had no choice but to depoliticize America and shrink back to a protection-only government of defense. As government drew back, it underwent a huge sale, which they called the *Great Displacement Program.* Everything in government, apart from physically protecting our people, went up for sale.

The trillions of dollars generated went to paying back the people *with interest* every penny they ever paid into Social Security. The seniors got back the largest checks, many somewhere between $100,000 to $200,000. Every active and retired working person received a check back from the federal government for what was paid into Social Security plus interest. And then, of course, we forever ended the flawed Social Security program.

The New World

We Ended All Political "Social Good"

Sometime in the 21st century, the people firmly accepted that a hierarchy of authorities ruling over us was a remnant of the obsolete bicameral mentality and no longer our politicians' prerogative. The people now understood their own bicameral programming to be told how to live by external "authorities". Those external "authorities", in turn, used the people to gain power and wealth. Thus, those neocheaters manipulated the people through their bicameral mysticisms. Those neocheaters provided elaborate external guidance and disguised that destructive politicization as programs for the "social good". Of course, all such "social good" was enforced by regulations that ruled over us and sacrificed us to their "higher" causes.

For example, the "higher" cause known as social welfare was disguised as a humanitarian act for the "social good", but in reality welfare politicized our economy as politicians played God with and sacrificed our earned money to others...through force. Another example, the "higher" cause of regulatory protection — regulatory bureaucracies such as the FDA — was disguised as our protectors of public well-being, but in reality they politicized our industries as bureaucrats played gods with and sacrificed our businesses and professions for political power and control.

In the end, three-fourths of the national budget was sacrificed to the so-called "social good"...the politicians' illusions for politicizing our lives and ruling over us, which prevented the geniuses from rising and in turn, prevented all of us from rising into our paradise on Earth. People died unfulfilled, their one time in all eternity gone without ever experiencing their greatest desires: the Gifts.[1]

Tomorrow, Neo-Tech deprogrammed our bicameral

---

[1]When neocheaters took away the authority of man's mind and replaced it with external "authorities" 2400 years ago, as explained in the First Insight, they took away the God in God-Man, taking away the Gifts. Thus, tragically and ironically, man himself — the neocheaters — took away God's Gifts to man, and we never experienced the life we were meant to live. Therefore, those elusive Gifts became man's most hungered for desires — for the life he was meant to live but never had.

programming. We lost our taste for "higher" causes for the "social good". Through the Neo-Tech Party, we depoliticized America and restricted government to physical protection of its citizens. All we needed was a physical-protection-only budget to protect ourselves, about 25% of the previous budget. The freed geniuses of society — free from big-government regulations — teamed up with super technologies to quickly lift us into our paradise on Earth...our Neo-Tech World. There, the Gifts came to all men, women, and children.

The Mother Lode

The Neo-Tech World in the 21st century, in my Visions, was the mother lode of wealth and security for ordinary people. It all started when computer people of the late 20th century fought off regulators and legislators who traditionally hung up progress and prevented Neo-Tech. As we entered the new millennium, that fierce independence spread to more and more American people. The quest for authorization had reached the end of its long road; with Neo-Tech, our minds just stopped looking for guidance. Big government grew more and more unpopular. During the early 21st century, Neo-Tech swept through most industries.

People were stunned by the get-rich results. Before, we had always lived with ruling-class big government; it was a given, and we knew nothing else; we knew only that big government hurt us, and we started to reject it. The 20th-century computer revolution opened our eyes to the wealthy alternative to big government. Essentially, we embraced government of defense — 21st-century get-the-people-rich government. And we rejected, outright, government on the offense — 20th-century big government.

Early in the 21st century, big government made a big mistake: it tried to get a foothold on regulating computers and cyberspace; government tried to regulate the burgeoning communication revolution. The people began quietly contemplating this new direction of government. Aside from the ominous First Amendment violations with government controlling information and regulating the information revolution, people also started to ponder: Imagine big government creating something like a CEA...a Computer Enforcement Agency; or a CCC...a Computer Communication Commission. Instead of waves of new technologies and software obsoleting other waves of new technologies soon after they reached the marketplace, every single advancement would instead have to go through years of regulations, approvals, and mounting costs before ever reaching the market!

Arguments against that scenario started privately swelling in people's minds. By the 21st century, the Internet had become an important tool for information. People were not about to let the government start regulating information and the technologies that made information more accessible. Needless to say, the information revolution would die, right there and then! But the communication/information revolution had become too valuable. The people resisted big government.

How Everything Changed

As knowledge multiplied manyfold during the 21st century's information explosion, more and more people directly and indirectly learned about Neo-Tech, which caused a quiet psychological rebellion. People lost interest in authority. They imagined moving past symptoms of big government such as the FCC, FTC, SEC, FDA, EPA as we advanced toward a 21st-century Technological Revolution.

Something had changed, an idea whose time had come, a force so big that everything would change. I witnessed that change — a strategic inflection point — in my Visions of the new millennium. Everything changed politically, economically, financially, personally. Our leap into the Neo-Tech World became unstoppable and explosive. Wave after wave of new super technologies, pushed ahead by millions upon millions of Neothink geniuses, sent the medical industry and all other industries into unprecedented computerlike revolutions.

Indeed, with computerlike freedom, turbocharged by the communications revolution, all industries were free to do what the computer industry already did: drive prices toward zero and buying power toward infinity. I saw geniuses rising up and eradicating disease after disease.

Looking back over our shoulders from the new world, we asked ourselves, one last time: Did we need those big-government regulations from the old world? The answer was now obvious: We did not. In fact, it became painful to look back at what was taken from us in terms of wealth, health, and love. Politicians and regulatory bureaucrats had become intoxicated with politicizing our lives, playing God with our lives, ruling over us. Under their thumbs of authority, like bicameral automatons, we sacrificed our paradise on Earth. People in that old world died unfulfilled, without ever experiencing wealth, power, and romantic love.

Following the computers' lead, though, we moved past the old world sometime in the 21st century. We left behind its omnipresent ruling class strapping us down with big-government regulations. In our final evolutionary jump, when our bicameral behaviors and longings for higher "authorities" ended, we moved on to the new world with no ruling class, freeing up a new era of super entrepreneurs, super technologies, super standards of living.

No Anomaly

Some people might say that the computer revolution was just an anomaly because of the invention of the silicon chip. But even before high technology, a lone genius of society, James J. Hill, single-handedly built up the entire Northern border of America and was making Americans rich by spearheading the industrialization of Asia with American goods 100 years ago (described in the Tenth Vision). Geniuses dramatically lifted standards of living all throughout our country's history. All the industrialists who built the industrial empires, for example, dramatically raised society's standard of living. Likewise, as I saw in my Visions, when we set free millions of geniuses in tomorrow's Neo-Tech World, they began driving up everyone's standard of living. And there, to speed it all up, was high technology.

Indeed, the development of 21st-century high technology dramatically sped up progress. In fact, the combination of super entrepreneurs with super technologies caused a catalytic reaction *because of* high technology such as the silicon chip, fiber optics, digitized information, the Internet. Rather than an anomaly, the silicon chip was a forerunner of what was going to happen everywhere in the coming Technological Revolution.

Of course, that Technological Revolution, rich with Neothink, stands quietly in the starting gates, waiting for something to come along and depoliticize America to open the gates to the get-rich era. Dissemination of the Twelve Visions is what mankind has been waiting for. The computer revolution, communications revolution, information revolution...those are the forerunners. The Technological Revolution is coming and so are the geniuses of society who are going to drive the Technological Revolution to bring us into a paradise on Earth.

What Does It All Mean?

As young children, before our consciousness was programmed with bicameral mysticism, we were all God-Man; for a brief time, we all lived as Gods. Indeed, in our early years as little Gods of the Universe using our Neothink mentality to learn to talk and become conscious and to learn at a geometrical rate, we were at that time equipped with the "God" part of God-Man. We would have easily grown into the Gifts of the Neo-Tech World.

But when still just young children, mysticism from the bicameral-mutant world around us took away our God world within us. The authority of our own minds was handed over to others; we lost the Neothink mentality, and we landed in the hands of neocheaters. They became our "higher authorities" and became the gods of our lives. ...The neocheaters' greatest kept secret went undiscovered for 2400 years: *there are no Gods of man, only Gods of the Universe...among whom we belong.*

God and man will finally unite. The God-in-Heaven mutation of the bicameral mentality, looking for automatic answers from a "higher" authority telling us what to do and how to live, the God of the past, will vanish along with the neocheaters surviving off that mysticism. In its place will rise the real God, the God of the future, *you* as God-Man.

Appendices

More Thoughts

Appendix A
Feel the Future

Author's Confession

Through *The Neo-Tech World*, you can *see* the future.

After all I have communicated to you, developed over the past seventeen years of my life, still I say in frustration: I just cannot express to you the depth of what I *feel* inside me. Although you can now *see* the future, you cannot *feel* the future.

I have expressed a lot, but I have not come close to expressing what I *feel* inside. I sometimes look at picture books of influential people; sometimes I see destructive political leaders, and then I see the pictures of them when they were two or three or four or five-years old. Even if I now so *loathe them*, I see that I could have so *loved them* at that young age. Had I been their father, they would be good, really good people today. When I see them in photos as toddlers, I can almost feel their childhood emotions. Back then, they *loved* life the way only the God-Man can. When I study a photo for awhile, I want to go back and save that beautiful child...I want to keep his thrill for life alive. I want to save him from the burden of life that will slowly suck that happy exhilaration right out of him until he is, someday, ready and willing to die. I see the pictures of those young children, even those who grew up and became destructive, and I want to somehow save the child from the anticivilization. I want to somehow preserve his exuberance, his expression that life is *everything*. Then, I remember: that very child will someday feel that life is *nothing*...and my soul cries.

If I could reach inside myself and tear out a handful of my soul that aches with these feelings, just put those feelings on paper for my readers...if I could only do that, before long there would be no anticivilization.

My feelings inside me, if I could only get them on paper, would impact you and overwhelm you with an altogether different emotional dimension that essentially human beings have not experienced. I am referring to the next level of emotional existence that occurs only in the next mentality of the God-Man in the Civilization of the Universe.

How can I, for the first time, create literature that fills you with an entirely different dimension of emotions never felt before? How can I get man's next evolution of emotions from within me to the paper before me? How do I take you deep within the soul of the God-Man? There are no words — no thinking tools — to do that. There are no concepts to express it. So, I ask, how can I translate a new dimension of *emotions* to intellectual words...emotions that cannot be described — only felt? The answer was my great mystery. The consequences of not solving that mystery tormented my waking hours. Time was running out.

After seventeen years developing *The Neo-Tech World,* I have spent the past four years writing an epic novel. Fiction is art, and you can feel through art. This novel, I realized, solved the mystery. Through the story it tells, I am able to deliver to you the feelings in my soul.

My First Sense of Inner Peace

As I get ready to publish my thousand-page novel titled *The First Immortals,* I can feel relief. For, all along, I have known that working alone, Dr. Wallace and I could not vanquish the anticivilization *in our lifetimes and our children's and grandchildren's lifetimes,* which is our precious goal — the highest goal of conscious life: *to preserve itself!* Instead, in the anticivilization, everyone dies: dad and mom, brother and sister, husband and wife, parent and child, grandparent and grandchild. In the Civilization of the Universe (C of U), which will rise on Earth as a supersociety, we will live forever as exhilarated value creators...euphoric God-Man.

My feelings deep in my soul were incommunicable beyond my being. But the publishing of *The First Immortals* brings me a sense of inner peace, for I could finally communicate the emotions of the God-Man from the C of U. Through *The Neo-Tech World,* I let you *see* the future. Through *The First Immortals,* I let you *feel* the future.

If you are — and I think you are — ready to take a trip

from the anticivilization to the Civilization of the Universe, then get *The First Immortals*. When you receive it...sit back, take a deep breath, and prepare yourself to *feel* the way human beings were meant to live.

Appendix B
About Me...Mark Hamilton

Life Complete

This personal background begins at the birth of my first child — a girl. I felt *so complete*. I felt euphoric when I was with my daughter and wife. For the first time in my life, I felt fulfilled.

The troublesome feeling that there must be "something more" to life vanished. This euphoria when together with my daughter and wife — *this* was that "something more". This was everything, life complete. There was nothing more, nothing lacking.

A beautiful phenomenon occurred: time seemed to "stand still" as I, for the first time in my life, soaked in the preciousness of every day, every moment. Life was bliss. No anxieties existed; nothing was missing.

I realized: I was a *happy man*.

Little moments meant everything...such as sitting with my daughter on the horsey swing...absorbing, feeling happiness. I could not stop thinking how special life was — looking at her. It seemed life would forever be this way, time standing still, the future a vast, endless journey — a journey filled forever with these feelings of joy, and happiness, completeness...a journey that would *never end*.

Romantic love with my wife soared — look at what we created — this beauty! This sweetness! I discovered the beauty of the *happy child*.

More Bliss

My second child was born — a boy. I knew the exact moment I fell in love with my son. Like a video, that moment played over and over again in my head: picking up my baby in his crib, seeing him so vulnerable, so trusting.

I felt admiration for my son's blossoming traits as he grew

into a little boy. I felt admiration for his strong personality and independence. I experienced pride.

Time Passes

For the first time, I got a sense of time passing by...with my children's phases going by so fast. Time started clicking by quickly. I realized my beloved children and I do *not* have so much time together. The sense of eventual loss, with my children's phases passing by, began to grow in me. The forces of the anticivilization began to enter and invade my emotions from the Civilization of the Universe (C of U). For, only in the C of U can you continue feeling the bliss of life forever.[1]

Death of My Mother

About this time came the unexpected death of my mother. Her death was unbelievable to me because my siblings and I were perhaps the only persons in the world who held — since young childhood — two synergistic beliefs, put into us from our father: 1) death was unnatural, insanely wrong, and a problem that needed to be overcome, and 2) my father — a renowned Du Pont scientist — would cure that problem, which was my father's focus.

My father realized when I was a boy, if the efforts of the Manhattan Project or Moon Project were put toward curing aging and death, especially on a comprehensive scale, we would have cured aging and death.

He identified that death was never meant for conscious human beings. I realized he was right, and as a boy, I grew up believing that by the time my parents got old, death would be cured. I developed *emotionally* expecting never to see my loved ones die.

As I became an adult and realized the technology existed to

---

[1]By the way, you know from reading *The Neo-Tech World* the meaning of anticivilization and C of U: Anticivilization is the mortal civilization on Earth filled with irrationality. C of U is the abbreviation of Civilization of the Universe, which is the purely rational immortal civilization throughout the Universe.

end human dying very quickly, in a matter of a few years, if there were a drive to do so, I could not answer: *why isn't there this drive — this Project Life?* I emotionally could not relate to mankind. *What was everyone thinking?* However, when I communicated this to my daughter, she quickly shared the same deep emotional perspective of the insanity of human death. Now, my boys do, too. Very few adults do besides my father, brother, sister. Very few really feel this way.

The adult lack of feeling this insanity of human death seemed insane to me. The death of my mother drove this insanity to the surface. I began to more deeply understand the anticivilization.

My Dad & Me

When I was a boy, my father started the mission to end the world's acceptance of human death. I grew up and was pulled to my father's mission, like a magnet; it was like an internal calling. Deep within my emotional network was the feeling that death was bizarre and *wrong* and *must* be corrected before I could do anything else.

The mission, my father and I learned, became a nearly insurmountable feat. Moreover, no one really understood my father's and my deepest motivations, thoughts, and feelings, not as we understood one another.

After one long day, working together on our goal, it hit me: my father would never see my greatest accomplishments toward our goal. When one is a value *creator*, that's a given, because he is always building to the *next level*.

More Bliss

My third child was born — my second son. Three months later, as I looked upon my baby boy, something deeply moving happened to me: For the first time, as I held my baby in my arms, I saw an image in my mind ninety years ahead. I saw an almost incomprehensible picture:

I saw...	
<u>My Baby Now</u>	<u>My Baby 90 Years From Now</u>
– recessed hair line (gaining hair)	– recessed hair-line (losing hair)
– must be pushed...in a stroller	– must be pushed...in a wheelchair
– his exhilarating ascent from dependence toward independence	– his tragic decent from independence toward dependence
– the first baby babble — gaining his mind	– the first "baby babble" (senility) — losing his mind

As I saw the image of my baby ninety years from now, imagine how I felt: That image of my innocent little baby deteriorating ninety years from now brought on a sense of *evil* — as though my baby was being murdered. I looked at my two other innocent little children and felt the same way. Human death was evil. From birth to the conscious child was the ultimate good. From adult to death was the ultimate evil. From that image of my baby turning ninety years old, I realized I was fighting the ultimate battle of good versus evil.

I asked myself, when thinking of my blossoming children someday withering away...*why* this tragedy? And then it hit me: I myself will not live to see my children's greatest creations.

The Nine-Year Span

At this point, my wife became pregnant with our fourth child. My mother was gone and not able to be part of this celebration. I was full of nostalgia; I felt the powerful love for the new addition, but I kept remembering this same celebration for my first child. Back then, I felt the same powerful love, but thoughts of death did not exist.

As I looked forward to my fourth child with the same utter love as my first child, I felt a difference. Gone was the bliss, euphoria, ecstasy. Gone was the "nothing more", the life complete. Time did not stand still — time mercilessly hurled my loved ones and me forward toward more insane losses. I asked: *Why?*

A C-of-U Happy Man

First, understand that *I am happy,* and that's why death to me is so devastating. What *is* happiness — *C-of-U* happiness? First, you must understand value creation versus value production. Value production traps you in stagnation — doing the same responsibilities at work over and over every day, every year — sinking you into *the burden of life.* Value production traps you in *the burden*...traps you in the anticivilization...traps you in a life heading toward death. Death is escape from *the burden.*

Value creation *frees you* from *the burden*...frees you from the anticivilization...and delivers true happiness. Value creation is how immortals live forever, with happiness. The human brain is made for creation, not stagnation. With stagnation, one must die to escape the burden. Stuck in value production, civilization on Earth must remain a mortal civilization.

Discovering value creation and C-of-U happiness pushed my love for life and for my loved ones to the next level. There is *no burden* underneath. My happiness is open-ended and can go on forever — *forever.*

However, as it is...imminent death casts dark shadows over my one brief moment to enjoy everything I will ever get out of life.

Suffering Incommunicado

For me, an eternity-suited C-of-U happy man, death took away eternity. Death took away a love so profound the burden-laced anticivilization man could never, ever perceive. The tragedy of death is so big to the C-of-U man, *to me,* beyond what the anticivilization man can ever know, ever understand, ever have a clue. There can be no communication of this tragedy from the C-of-U man to the anticivilization man. There is no bridge.

I began to wonder: how will I deal with this mounting, inescapable loss of my loved ones and myself? After years of grappling with this, I realized I had two choices as to how to deal with the tragedy of being an eternity-suited C-of-U man trapped in a death-destined anticivilization. I had two choices to dealing with the tragedy of death: 1) Denial — so I could *feel happy* without being overwhelmed by the certain tragedy of death. 2) Make it my essence, my mission in life, to cure death.

I elected number two. The job, my father and I learned, to cure *the unnatural* — the death of the C-of-U man — was massive, way, way beyond the technological aspect itself, for the technology existed to achieve biological immortality within ten years. But, there was no worldwide drive, no effort whatsoever to remove the greatest tragedy, the most incomprehensible insanity in the Universe — the death of conscious life.

The problem lay in the incommunicable nature of the real tragedy of death, not communicable from the rare eternity-suited C-of-U man who understands the real tragedy...to the burden-laced anticivilization man who has no clue of the real tragedy.

Yet, my father and I could not successfully cure death by going the medical route. First of all, we did not have enough knowledge or resources available. Secondly, the anticivilization's forces (e.g., FDA) were too great. The approach would be to unleash all civilization, all minds, knowledge, resources, unrestricted toward curing death.

But, we could not persuade, could not communicate the real tragedy of human death in order to *kick start* a worldwide drive toward curing death. My father and I were up against an incomprehensible feat. We learned that people's acceptance and expectation of death was actually hardwired into their brains since primitive, preconscious times.

I Answered **Why**

I asked myself over and over ...why do we die? Why this incomprehensible tragedy? During my relentless search I had two epiphanies:

Epiphany 1) Why do we die? From the perspective of nature and the Universe, human death is *not* a question of *why*. Life simply evolved to this point. The question of *why* do we die, *why* this insane value destruction of conscious life and insane destruction of eternal love, is not a mystery. The issue is merely:

that is the way it is at this point of our evolutionary scale. Mythology sprang up from bicameral man; religion sprang up from conscious man...both trying to explain our lives and deaths. But the physical and metaphysical question of conscious death is not really a question of *why*. In fact, there is no question to ask — we merely die — that's *what is*, the point in time we are at...and that problem of death is waiting to be cured.

Epiphany 2) Why do we die? From the perspective of not having *already* cured aging and death or at least being surrounded by a heated drive to do so, *is* a question of *why*. Why is not every effort pointed at stopping the greatest, 100% fatal, natural disaster — death...and the most widespread, 100% fatal disease — aging? My second epiphany answered this question as follows:

The Three Anchors

Three anchors lock us to the anticivilization:

Anchor #1) Politicization of Society — restricting freedom, retarding progress.
Anchor #2) Stagnation in Our Livelihoods — making life a burden, extinguishing excitement *to live*.
Anchor #3) Expectation of Death — not understanding the *real* tragedy.

Break any one of those three anchors to the anticivilization, and civilization will start drifting toward the Civilization of the Universe. I realized the need to weaken all three anchors. Then, when one breaks, the other two would break soon thereafter.

In this anticivilization — this unnatural *die*-civilization — I realized *every single* human being lives a self-defeating life:
• Value producers and nonproducers live with stagnation — with the underlying burden of life.
• Value creators (rare) live with creation, with exhilaration — but with the underlying suffering of imminent death.

For both...and for all...I knew we must somehow break the anchors to the anticivilization! Breaking the three anchors meant:
Breaking Anchor One: Depoliticizing America
Breaking Anchor Two: Catapulting people from value

519

producers to value creators.

Breaking Anchor Three: Changing perspective of human life from a dispensable value to the *supreme value* in the Universe. An indispensable value!

Breaking the First Anchor: Depoliticize Civilization

When this anchor snaps, the other two anchors will snap. For, depoliticizing America will free civilization. "Garage" entrepreneurs will rise quickly. To stay competitive, businesses will be forced to unleash their own entrepreneurs — the "in-house" entrepreneurs. The "garage" entrepreneurs versus the "in-house" entrepreneurs will cause an exciting advancement of new technologies. The competition will force business structures to change from the division of labor to the superior division of essence. The division of essence will change to the division of Friday-Night essences. Value producers will leap to value creators. Stagnation will get replaced with exhilaration. And then the *demand* will set in for biological immortality.

When we depoliticize civilization, society will become wealthy through the Technological Revolution. The relatively nonpoliticized computer industry gave us a clue of the multiplying buying power that will come from the universal Technological Revolution. But the benefits will go far beyond people becoming wealthy. For, once they are wealthy, they will be free of their work traps — they will be free to pursue their Friday-Night essences and rediscover the *thrill* of life and their vector of value creation...their open-ended exhilaration...their eternal C-of-U happiness. Upon discovering eternal, C-of-U happiness...upon discovering *value creation* and blissful harmony, they will *desire immortality*. They will *demand it!*

Now, once we depoliticize America, businesses and entrepreneurs will be free to race ahead and aggressively pursue Project Life. The healthy battle of "garage" entrepreneurs versus "in-house" entrepreneurs would drive forth the supply to meet the demand, for people everywhere would *demand* immortality.

But, *how* do we break Anchor One? The approach cannot be head-on, say by discussing immortality, because right now people *do not want* immortality. The approach cannot be head-on politically either. Libertarians try this approach to no avail. Instead, we must approach people on a personal level — in terms of their wealth, health, happiness, livelihood, and love. A campaign that hammers home those points would get traction. So, I proceeded to articulate this campaign approach in my writings (Appendix D).

Breaking the Second Anchor: Catapult People from Value Producers to Value Creators

The forces of nature are hardwired in our psyches. We still suffer from the bicameral mentality — we need to be told what to do. A whole different mentality is needed to *create* values. I learned that the way to get to that new mentality is to find your deepest motivational root. I write about this (Vision One). You must become the person you were meant to be. Once accomplished, your mind will change. You will discover something called *downstream focus* that will lead you to value creation.

Discovering the person you were meant to be will eventually bring you *far greater* wealth than chasing after the highest paying job of the moment. I developed techniques to discover and effectively pursue the path you were meant to travel through life. I developed easy-to-follow steps in my writings (Vision One, Five, and Six).

People can become wealthy this way, but wealth is only the first consequence. Becoming the person you were meant to be — the value creator on your Friday-Night essence — you discover Nature's Quintessential Secret, that rare harmony with the world, that elusive "something more" in your life (as creation replaces stagnation), and you then desire, as I do, to live forever. You feel, finally for the first time, eternity-suited C-of-U happiness.

Breaking the Third Anchor: Change Perspective of Life From a Dispensable Value to THE INDISPENSABLE Supreme Value

I cannot communicate the real tragedy of death to others, not even to other value creators. (They cannot let themselves see the *real* tragedy; for peace of mind, they chose denial.) So...I

521

battled with how to change people's perspective of human life from a dispensable value to the supreme value — absolutely NOT dispensable. I recalled my early exposure was different from others. At a young age, I held two unique perspectives. I felt...

1) Dying was totally unnatural for humans, and
2) Dying would be cured.

Other children grew up feeling that 1) dying was natural, and 2) never a thought that dying would be cured.

I pondered: if all those others could *feel* the supreme value of human life, thus the real tragedy of human death, that would bring about the willingness and desire to depoliticize America. The key word here, I realized, was the word: FEEL. *Not* describe or articulate the supreme value...people must FEEL it. And to that end, I wrote a major novel to deliver that feeling entitled: *The First Immortals*.

My Four-Part Formula to Snap the Anchors

Over years of experience in the real world, I formed a four-part formula that would weaken and eventually snap the three anchors to send us into the C of U.

How Formula Weakens the Anchors	The Four-Part Formula
1) Must first identify, define and articulate C of U. People must *see* it...but still is not enough to enter it.	1) Define and articulate intellectual axioms and practical advantages. In other words: idea systems, operating systems, details worked out describing C of U. These writings provide superior C-of-U advantages to people and greater C-of-U stimulations, thus people migrate toward these C-of-U dynamics, weakening the anchors to the anticivilization.
2) Then, must enable people to *feel* it...in	2) Communicate emotions. In other words: artistically present a "painting"

order to *want it*.

of the C of U. This artistic "painting" lets us *feel* the emotional C of U. These writings shift our perception of death and life. They weaken the anchors to the anti-civilization as readers, perhaps for the first time, *feel* the desire to live longer.

3) Must get Parts One and Two above *to many people* to have an effect.

3) Disseminate through business. Business — marketing these writings — is the only way to accelerate people's awareness of the superior advantages and emotional perspectives of C of U. Business and all its data also accelerates the learning curve for my father and myself.

4) Then, if prove what is presented above, accelerate results.

4) Prove through science. In other words: scientifically prove the C of U. Scientific proof of the C of U and peaceful immortality out there in the cosmos would end people's *personal resistance* to these ideas, advantages, and perspectives.

I realized that each part of the four-part formula was crucial to flip the mortal anticivilization into the Civilization of the Universe on Earth. Then, the drive to end death would be on.

Our Contributions

So...to that end, my father and I honed our efforts into the formula. I have not yet mentioned my brother whose life parallels mine in many ways. He is the third major contributor to the goal of biological immortality. Here is what the three of us created:

Our Contributions

Four-Part Formula	My Father	Myself	My Brother
1) Articulation of idea systems and operating systems in C of U.	1) *The Neo-Tech Discovery*, major seventeen-year work, 700 pages...and *Zonpower*, major four-year work, 640 pages.*	1) *The Neo-Tech World*, major seventeen-year work, 650 pages...and *The Neo-think Business*, major five-year work, 700 pages.	1) *Global Wealth Power*, major multi-year work, 410 pages.
2) Emotional expressions and "pictures" of physical and emotional experiences in C of U.		2) *The First Immortals*, major four-year work, 1000 pages.	2) Major future work in progress, tentatively titled *The I&O Story*.
3) Business or spreading of the above world-changing products.	3) Founded the business as I & O Publishing Company in 1968.	3) *Neo-Tech: Guide to Money and Power*, major twenty-year work, 104-page brochure. Started Neo-Tech Publishing Company in early 1990s.	3) Disseminates Neo-Tech abroad into 163 countries in 13 languages. Started Neo-Tech Worldwide in early 1990s.
4) Science or proof of the C of U.	4) Overlay Charts — a scientific breakthrough approach to prove C of U.		

* Later this year, my father will release another major multi-year work, yet to be titled.

About Me...Mark Hamilton

My father, myself, and my brother have to be the product developers, both fiction and nonfiction, the businessmen and marketers, and the scientists because we will get no help beyond ourselves. We get absolutely no division of labor on our goal. Why not? Our goal is *immortality*. Right now, people are afraid of it. So, we have to execute each part of the four-part formula ourselves — my father, brother, and me. That's it. And that's been the story from the beginning and will be to the end.

Identification of the Three Contributors*

Mark Hamilton   = Myself
Frank R. Wallace = My father
Eric Savage   = My brother

*Of course, those are our pen names.

Surviving in the Anticivilization

Obviously, we are not there yet; we do not live in the C of U with immortality. I refuse to let my happiness, for my one and only flicker of life, to be dragged down. I discovered how to get closeness and bliss again with my children and other loved ones, and this is my advice to you:

Allow *no mental separation* while with a loved one — no preoccupation, no mental block, no lamenting...push the suffering out of your mind.

Focus on *the moment;* you must melt away the tragedy of the anticivilization...you basically go into *denial* of death and anticivilization, but denial during *the moment*, not denial of the overall picture. So, you're really *not* in denial. When I'm not with my loved ones, for example, my focus and feelings go to the four-part formula. But my time with my children/loved ones becomes wonderful, beautiful, blissful...*while our time together lasts*.

Those beautiful moments of *closeness* will fill your experiences and *build your life*. That's the secret for the C-of-U man to fill his life, to build his life, with happiness and love without being overwhelmed by the anticivilization.

Now that I took care of and solved that problem, I am able to hone the formula...that elusive Neothink puzzle that will flip civilization into the Civilization of the Universe on Earth.

Appendix C

> The following piece was written by a former Himalayan Monk who personally discovered the power of Neo-Tech. I felt his treatise was enlightening and invaluable.

Neo-Tech: The Philosophical Zero

by

Ray Kotobuki

0. The Voice Of Honesty

For three millennia since the dawn of consciousness, humanity has lived under the spell of mysticism. Mysticism is the disease, epistemological disease, of human consciousness which promotes, internally as well as externally, false notions that create problems where none in fact exist. Mysticism is the seed of dishonesty that involves rationalizations, *non sequiturs*, and mind-generated "truths" and "realities." Mysticism is also the ground of neocheating wherein the seed of dishonesty proliferates into the monstrous noxiousness that destroys values and causes suffering.

However, despite all-afflicting, omnipresent mysticism, amidst pervasive destruction and suffering effected by noxious neocheating, man has brought a monumental edifice of knowledge and values into existence. That edifice of knowledge and values is literally the monument of man's virtues — of heroic effort and honesty exerted countless times by the producers of values among us. Such value producers include Philolaus, Aristarchus, and Copernicus in astronomy; Galileo, Newton, and Einstein in physics; Aristotle, Ayn Rand, and Frank R. Wallace in philosophy; and Jay Gould, Henry Ford, Mark Hamilton, and Soichiro Honda in business.

Honesty needs no support save the evidence of reality, while dishonesty begets myriad distortions of reality in order to sustain its frail existence. The voice of honesty is confident, firm, yet quiet. The voice of dishonesty is uncertain, flimsy, but loud. The loud voice of dishonesty seems to have prevailed throughout history by the sheer force of its volume, yet it is the voice of honesty that has permeated the world and carried humanity always forward. The roots of dishonesty are now identified for the first time by Neo-Tech (the voice of *fully integrated honesty* based on contextual facts and objective reality). Neo-Tech will forever uproot dishonesty by curing mysticism and eradicating neocheating, and thus the voice of dishonesty will no longer be heard on this planet.

Through Neo-Tech, at last the time has come for the voice of honesty to prevail. At last the time has come for the lives of honest men and women to soar into power, prosperity, and happiness. At last the time has come for the Neo-Tech world to unfold. In light of the monumental values that man has produced within the last three millennia *despite* prevalent mysticism and neocheating, imagine how much value humanity can produce *without* mysticism and neocheating. It is indeed to imagine the unimaginable and to think the unthinkable. For, with Neo-Tech (fully integrated honesty), humanity now steps into the dimension of infinity and the realm of eternity...into infinite value and eternal life.

History, science, and philosophy interweave in harmony throughout this treatise to bring to light a resplendent new system of knowledge — Neo-Tech, while revealing, implicitly as well as explicitly, a new stratosphere of conscious intellection — Neothink. Upon reading this treatise, readers will not only gain knowledge of little-known aspects of history and science but will also be able to integrate Neo-Tech and Neothink to reach new heights of awareness, prosperity, and happiness forever.

This treatise is a window to human history and a preamble to eternity that chronicles the ascent of human consciousness through the purgatory of mysticism into the sunlit universe of Neo-Tech/Neothink.

1. The Copernican Revolution

"In the center of everything rules the Sun; for who in this most beautiful temple could place this luminary at another or better place whence it can light up the whole at once? ...In fact, the Sun sitting on a royal throne guides the family of stars surrounding him...the Earth conceives by the Sun, and through him becomes pregnant with annual fruits. In this arrangement, we thus find an admirable harmony of the world, and a constant harmonious connection between the motion and the size of the orbits as could not be found otherwise."

— Copernicus

The publication of "On the Revolutions of the Celestial Spheres (*De revolutionibus orbium coelestium*)" by the Polish astronomer Nicolaus Copernicus (1473-1543) in 1543 marked a complete break from the entire system of ancient astronomy previously conceived by Greek scientists such as Eudoxus, Callipus, Aristotle, Apollonius, Hipparchus, and ultimately by Claudius Ptolemy. The system which those Greeks had developed has been termed *the geocentric* (*Earth-centered*) theory of the universe. The new system which Copernicus propounded has been termed *the heliocentric* (*Sun-centered*) theory of the universe.

By ascribing to the Earth a daily spin on its own axis, which gyrated, and an annual orbit around the Sun, which was stationary, Copernicus evolved a new system of the universe which opposed Aristotle, who had cogently argued the fixity of the Earth. This provided a superior alternative to Ptolemy's geocentric universe, which had been propounded in his "Mathematical Compositions" (also known as *"The Almagest"*) and which dominated the astronomical conception of humanity for over 1400 years.

In Western Christendom the views of Aristotle and Ptolemy had been elevated to the level of religious dogma, and to many thoughtful intellectuals of the Renaissance, those views stifled further development in science and were long overdue for revision. The geocentric theory had also been used as the "scientific" basis for the Christian theological/cosmological notion of a two-dimensional flat world existing sandwiched in parallel between Heaven above and Hell below. Copernicus was the first to successfully challenge the authorities of antiquity. In his search for a true picture of the "divinely ordained cosmos", Copernicus dethroned the Earth from the center of the cosmos and opened a new path which was to lead to the eventual dethronement of "God" himself.

Copernicus, however, refrained from publishing his work for

nearly two decades. He feared the ecclesiastical jitteriness, which arose out of the dissensions between Catholics and Protestants. For his work might cause sufficient scandal for him to be charged with impugning the "authority" of the Church through his assertion that the earth was neither fixed nor at the center of the universe. That assertion might be construed as contradicting one "authorized" literal interpretation of certain passages in the Bible. But Copernicus was finally prevailed upon by his friends to allow his student, Rheticus, to publish his work. Toward the end of 1542, Copernicus was seized with apoplexy and paralysis; on May 24, 1543, an advance copy of his work was presented to him. On that same day he died, leaving behind a magnificent contribution — a revolution in man's concept of the universe.

No longer could the Earth be considered to be the center of the universe nor could it be considered the epitome of creation or the center of all change and decay with the changeless cosmos encompassing it, for it was now a planet just like the others, simply yielding to mathematical description. No longer was it accurate to state that the Sun "rose" or "set" upon the Earth nor was it valid to view the universe in terms of "up" and "down" or "above" and "below", for those concepts were all perceptual delusions and had meaning only within the confines of the geocentric universe.

The revolution of knowledge that began with the publication of "On the Revolutions of the Celestial Spheres" and led to the further discoveries by Johann Kepler (1571-1630), Galileo Galilei (1564-1642), and Isaac Newton (1642-1727) is rightly termed "The Copernican Revolution". The value of the Copernican Revolution, however, does not end in the fact that Copernicus brought about a complete shift in man's philosophical conception of the universe. He epitomized a revolution in man's consciousness as well.

Through his identification of the physical structure of the universe, Copernicus eloquently demonstrated the power of reason and consciousness when unhindered by perceptivity-bound preconceptions. Through Copernicus, the universe evolved from a mere sensory/perceptual experience into a conceptual scheme or design which transcended immediate human perception. For perceptivity-centered consciousness does not take perceptual experiences as data but as conclusions, whereas conceptuality-centered consciousness takes experience, perceptual as well as conceptual, as data and constructs a model that reflects the structural design of the universe. There is a subtle but unmistakable distinction between the two, and that distinction is what the Copernican Revolution exemplified in the history of human consciousness.

A profound restructuring of consciousness and a considerable conceptual leap is required to conceive of a heliocentric universe in which the Earth is in motion around the Sun while spinning on its own axis. Copernicus vividly demonstrated the conceptuality-centered conscious mode at the dawn of modern history and elevated human consciousness to the level that had once been achieved by the Greeks 1700 years before him.

Perception is always concerned with events, whereas conception is primarily concerned with interrelations between events. And the universe is the complex aggregate of the whole interrelations of events in existence. In order to comprehend that complex aggregate of interrelations known as the universe, one must transcend the seeming subjective reality of perceptual experience and construct a conceptual map in concordance with logic that best reflects the underlying design principles of the universe. By moving from the perceptivity-centered to the conceptuality-centered, one enters the realm of objective reality, and it is the knowledge of objective reality that gives the power to harness and control the universe — power that can be claimed only by a conscious being.

When one is fully integrated in conceptual consciousness, he can enter the sphere of Neothink. Neothink is forward moving integrated consciousness completely free of mysticism. Neo-Tech is the system of knowledge through which Neothink is fully realized. What the Copernican Revolution started Neo-Tech completes, and brings forth a new revolution, the Neo-Tech Revolution, which will take humanity into dimensions of knowledge never before imagined.

Since its birth about 3000 years ago from the bicameral mind, consciousness has taken three distinct modes of operation: the first is the *perceptivity-centered mode* that emulates the bicameral mind and takes perception as the conclusive picture of reality while using concepts to rationalize perception — exemplified by the geocentric concept; the second is the *conceptuality-centered mode* that takes experience, perceptual as well as conceptual, as data to construct the conceptual model of reality — exemplified by the heliocentric concept and the Copernican Revolution; the third is the *Neo-Tech/Neothink mode,* that operates contextually, synergetically using both hemispheres of the brain to develop never before known integrations and concepts.

Frank R. Wallace's epochal discovery, Neo-Tech[1], was not only a breakthrough in knowledge but also a revolution of human intellection. Neo-Tech and Neothink are symbiotically linked in the same manner as the Copernican Revolution and the conceptuality-centered mode. Every time a new integration of knowledge is formed, an element of Neothink is always involved. However, except for Neo-Tech, no system of knowledge has ever identified a contextuality-centered, Neo-Tech/Neothink mode. Thus, no system of knowledge has ever explored the unseen dimensions of Neo-Tech/Neothink and developed it to its fullest potential. With the Neo-Tech/Neothink mode, the perceptivity-centered mode becomes obsolete and the conceptuality-centered mode evolves into entirely new dimensions.

2. The Lost Knowledge Of The Greeks

During the first decade of the 16th century when Copernicus was still forming his astronomical hypotheses, he read the works of many Greek authors and found that heliocentric ideas had already been propounded. He mentions in his work some of those Greek mathematician-astronomers who held distinctly different views of the celestial system from that of Aristotle and Ptolemy, although not necessarily heliocentric, such as Philolaus, Hicetus, Ecphantus, and Heraclides ("On the Revolutions of the Celestial Spheres", Book One). Indeed, the geocentric theories were not the only systems known to the Greeks, nor even at times the most accepted.

Between the sixth and fourth century B.C., there was a philosophical society known as the Pythagorean society in Greece.

[1]*The Neo-Tech Discovery*, Neo-Tech Publishing Company.

Pythagoras of Samos (c. 582-500 B.C.), founder of the society, traveled extensively in his youth by way of the sea to the East as well as to Egypt, and not only accumulated a wealth of knowledge from different corners of the Earth but also obtained a unique perspective that was possible only for the celestial navigator-businessmen of the time, i.e., the sphericity of the Earth.

Astronomy and mathematics, particularly trigonometry, originated to a great measure among those celestial navigator-businessmen of antiquity whose survival almost entirely depended upon knowing the relative positions and movements of the celestial bodies. Furthermore, while traveling across the sea by observing the movements of the celestial spheres, it became revealingly clear to them that the Earth was a spherical entity. (Around 200 B.C., three hundred years after Pythagoras, Phoenician navigator-businessmen circumnavigated the Earth for the first time in recorded history and proved that the Earth was indeed spherical, preceding Magellan by more than 1700 years.)

Pythagoras returned to Greece with the perspective and the knowledge of the navigator-businessmen, along with other knowledge which he acquired in the far corners of the world and founded at Croton, a Greek colony in southern Italy, an academy that was devoted to a life of mathematical speculation and philosophical contemplation. It is clearly evidenced that the Pythagorean scientists were the first recorded humans in history to conceive of the Earth, the celestial bodies, and even the universe as a whole, as spherical entities.

Around 410 B.C., the Pythagorean Philolaus of Tarentum (c. 480-400 B.C.) conceived of the Earth as a spherical body in motion around a central cosmic fire. He also postulated that the stars, the Sun, the Moon, and the five known planets — Venus, Mercury, Mars, Jupiter, and Saturn — were spherical bodies. His Sun was not at the center; as the Earth revolved around the central fire once a day and the Moon once a month, the Sun moved around the same cosmic fire once a year. The other planets took even longer periods to orbit around the fire, while the sphere of the fixed stars was stationary.

Around 350 B.C., a latter-day Pythagorean, Heraclides of Pontus (c. 373 B.C.), conceived of the Earth sphere as spinning west to east, adopting the earlier view of two Pythagoreans, Hicetus and Ecphantus, in order to explain the apparent diurnal rotation of the celestial system. He also suggested that Mercury and Venus moved in circular orbits around the Sun, accounting for the changes in their apparent brightness. He further speculated that the universe was infinite, each star being a world in itself, composed of an earth and other planets. However, Heraclides' universe, like that of Hicetus and Ecphantus, was as yet geocentric and his Earth spun at the center of the fixed stars.

Around 250 B.C., the greatest astronomer of the Alexandrian period, Aristarchus of Samos (c. 310-230 B.C.), postulated that the Earth rotated on its axis daily, and revolved around the Sun in a circular orbit once a year, the Sun and the fixed stars being stationary, the planets moving in circular orbits with the Sun at the center, and the Moon revolving around the Earth. Thus, in Aristarchus the heliocentric conception of the universe had reached its near-complete formulation. No one until Copernicus more than 1750 years later described the celestial system as well and accurately as Aristarchus had done in his now lost treatise. (According to Plutarch, the head of the Stoic school of philosophy, Cleanthes, demanded that Aristarchus ought to have been indicted for impiety. Aristarchus was indeed almost killed for his revolutionary thoughts.)

Based upon these historical accounts, it is clear that a special chain of the Greek mathematician-astronomer-cosmologist-philosophers consisting primarily of Philolaus, Heraclides, and Aristarchus had successively evolved a concept of the universe which was in fair agreement with that of Copernicus over 1750 years later. Why is it then that the heliocentric concept of the universe with its spinning Earth did not evolve further after Aristarchus? Why is it that genuine knowledge of the celestial world had to be buried in the obscurity of the terrestrial realm? Why is it that a theory so luminous had to remain in darkness and wait for centuries to be rediscovered?

3. The Geocentric Hierarchy

History reveals that around 200 B.C, less than five decades after Aristarchus' exquisite formulation of the celestial system, the geocentric concept of the universe, despite its inherent theoretical difficulty, became more and more adopted by the power structure of the Western world — by the master neocheaters operating through their governments. The geocentric concept achieved prominence over the heliocentric system not because it was superior theoretically but because it was more expedient politically. It was not a scientific decision but a political strategy that made the geocentric system the "official" picture of the universe.

The geocentric school of astronomy began with Eudoxus of Cnidus (409–356 B.C.), an eminent resident at the academy of Plato (427–347 B.C.), several decades *after* Philolaus had postulated his distinctively non-geocentric theory. Eudoxus' theory was further developed by Callipus (c. 325 B.C.), Aristotle (384–322 B.C.), Apollonius (c. 220 B.C.), Hipparchus (190–120 B.C.), and finally Claudius Ptolemy of Alexandria (A.D. 85-165).

Eudoxus, after developing a certain mathematical procedure, evolved the first geocentric model of the celestial system wherein he assigned a spherical shell to every periodic movement that centered upon the Earth, a combination of such spheres describing reasonably well the complex periodic movement of a particular celestial body. All of the spheres were fixedly embedded in the surfaces of the spheres further out. In this manner he explained the motions of the celestial system by using twenty-seven spheres, one for the fixed stars, three each for the Sun and the Moon, and four each for the five known planets — Venus, Mercury, Mars, Jupiter, and Saturn.

As new periodic phenomena were identified, the system had to be expanded. Callipus gave each celestial body an extra sphere, bringing the total up to thirty-four, while Aristotle added a further twenty-two spheres. In the field of astronomy Aristotle was responsible for the idea that the spheres which carried the celestial bodies along their paths were real physical entities, not mere geometrical constructions as Eudoxus had previously supposed and Ptolemy would later postulate. (His strong adherence to objective reality did not allow Aristotle to view his theory as a mere geometrical construction without any corresponding existence in the universe.) He also believed that the outermost sphere of the fixed stars was moved by the *Primum*

Mobile (the Prime Mover) which governed the entire universe.

Unlike the heliocentric system which originally came from the ancient navigator-businessmen's business-based integration of reality, i.e., the sphericity of the Earth, the geocentric theory was purely an academic enterprise and entailed many difficulties from the very beginning. Furthermore, it not only was an extremely complex theory technically but also became progressively more complex throughout its development. Heraclides' model of the spinning Earth was one of the attempts made to overcome those difficulties within the context of the geocentric universe. During the Alexandrian period, Apollonius, Hipparchus, and Ptolemy also tried to overcome the limitations inherent in the geocentric system, again within the conceptual framework of the geocentric model. They failed to take into account the validity of the heliocentric concept developed by Aristarchus through his remarkable hypotheses.

Apollonius and Hipparchus both developed the system of eccentrics and epicycles. Apollonius suggested that if a planet moved in a circle, the epicycle, the center of which moved upon another circle, the deferent, which centered upon the Earth, then the motions of the planets could be quantitatively accounted for. He further suggested that the celestial bodies moved in circles eccentric to the Earth, the center of their orbits lying at some distance from the center of the Earth. Hipparchus further developed Apollonius' concept. Ptolemy adopted and evolved the system of eccentrics and epicycles used by Hipparchus to explain the apparent motions of the celestial system.

Ptolemy himself made a discovery which showed that the whole system of the geocentric universe could not have any physical existence as Aristotle had suggested: Ptolemy seems to have regarded his scheme as a mere mathematical convenience. (In other words, he admitted that his geocentric system was a *mathematical rationalization!*) Thus, in Ptolemy, the geocentric construction of the universe had reached its theoretical perfection and, despite its inherent difficulty and rationalized complexity, it dominated the scientific world for the next 1400 years.

However, long before Ptolemy completed his celestial theory as described in his "Mathematical Composition", the geocentric system of the universe had already been adopted by the neocheating authorities of Europe. Beginning around 200 B.C., the combined political and religious power structures of the Western world undertook a systematic oppression not only of the kind of knowledge which did not suit their purpose, such as the heliocentric theory, but also of the very source of knowledge itself, the conceptuality-centered consciousness and its reasoning faculty.

The heliocentric universe did not fit into their scheme of establishing a hierarchical social structure wherein the neocheaters were to stand at the center of the universe. The geocentric universe did. Thus, the heliocentric system was slowly eliminated from the face of the Earth and the geocentric theory gained prominence. Their success in oppressing the heliocentric system and other valid knowledge, and in establishing the geocentric hierarchy, gradually prepared Europe for the Dark Ages and drew the curtains on science for over 1700 years. It was not until the rise of business/commerce took place in Europe toward the end of the Middle Ages, which brought about the propagation of the zero along with the place-value number system, that the light of reason finally shone through the darkness of the human mind and raised the curtains of science at long last.

How could the political/religious master neocheaters be so successful in their scheme as to be able to oppress human knowledge and consciousness for over 1700 years? The answer lies, at least in part, in the very nature and propensity of human consciousness.

4. The Origins Of Mysticism

The process of life consists of awareness and self-creation. In contradistinction to nonliving systems such as the celestial system, all living systems from amoebae to human beings possess two distinguishing characteristics which constitute life. They are *autopoiesis* (self-creation, production, or generation) and awareness or cognition, which ranges from the most primitive form of awareness such as amoebae's stimulus-response to the highest form of cognition — conscious human awareness. *Autopoiesis* and cognition are the two quintessences of life without which no life is possible. Moreover, *autopoiesis* and cognition are interdependent of, and integral to, one another. That is, neither can exist without the other.

Conscious life is the highest integration and expression of the *autopoietic* cognitive living process. Consciousness is the most complex form of cognition which is distinctly different from any other mode of cognition found in other sentient beings. Consciousness came into existence on this planet about 3000 years ago and human beings achieved consciousness not as a product of nature's evolutionary process but as an *autopoietic* reorganization of their cognitive systems. Consciousness was a discovery and an engineered invention of human beings. Therefore, no change took place in the physical structure of the brain but only in the structural organization of the mind.

Nature's process of evolution had ultimately brought to human beings what is termed the bicameral mind, and it was in the cognitive breakdown of the bicameral mind that consciousness first originated. The bicameral mind was a highly evolved and intelligent cognitive system that operated with language, percepts, and rudimentary/imaginary concepts, yet with complete *automaticity*. In the bicameral mind, one hemisphere of the brain, guided by the inherent logic of nature, organized the whole inventory of information from the past in an automatic, non-introspective, and non-self-referential manner, and communicated some of that information to the other hemisphere for decision-making or action.

The bicameral mind invented such life-sustaining tools as language, numbers, the wheel, and the ship in its critical pursuit for survival. It was indeed a remarkably intelligent and ingenious cognitive system, yet there was no fundamental difference between it and the mind of anthropoid apes or porpoises in their automaticity. They differed in terms not of quality (automaticity vs. non-automaticity) but of quantity or degree of intelligence arising from their evolutionary/biological differences. Around 1000 B.C. when human society evolved and became too complex for the bicameral mind to handle, it made its greatest invention, at the cost of its own continuance, in order for the human organism as a whole to survive: that invention was consciousness. Toward the end of the second millennium B.C., the bicameral world saw a dramatic increase in commerce. And the laws of commerce/business began to take over the laws of nature, thereby pushing bicameral men and women to a complete *cognitive breakthrough* — to a quantum leap into an entirely new mode of cognition. Through that commerce/business initiated cognitive breakthrough, consciousness was born.

Consciousness is the *uni*cameral mind, as it were. Speaking physically, it is the new unified communication network within the brain whereby two hemispheres function synergetically to create a higher order of operation which is self-referential and introspective. Speaking metaphysically, it is the new integrated inventorying of reality in abstract concepts that organizes myriad facts of experience in accordance with conceptually identified logic. In addition, consciousness is an operative modality of the brain or the mind which is inherently *non-automatic*. That is, there is nothing in nature that causes consciousness to operate automatically.

Consciousness is the *causative factor* relative to its own existence. There is nothing in existence that can make an individual conscious but his own act of being conscious. Consciousness exists as an *entelechy;* when it exists it exists in its full manifestation, and when it exists not it exists not at all. That means *consciousness never evolves.* It is an individual's very act of being conscious (of something) that brings consciousness into being with its utter totality. Thus, in reality, when one is conscious, he is *fully* conscious with nothing missing and nowhere to evolve.

In the beginning, however, consciousness sought to operate within the lost matrix of the bicameral mind, that is, consciousness made the entire inventory of brain-stored information *emulate* the dominant hemisphere of the bicameral mind. Consciousness operating in *the emulated bicameral modality* is perceptivity-centered consciousness. It is when consciousness developed a sufficiently integrated conceptual knowledge internally that consciousness made the shift from the subjective to the objective and became aware of reality, objective and in essence abstract. Consciousness operating in the context of abstract and objective reality is conceptuality-centered consciousness.

Reality *in the final analysis*, reality *in a fully integrated epistemological context*, is abstraction. It is the aggregate of abstract principles that are completely independent of any particular observer and his experience, and as such reality is objective. Furthermore, abstract principles by nature exist independent of time, and as such reality is eternal. And when reality is cognized by consciousness, it exists in the form of concepts. However, since it exists in the form of concepts, consciousness can *subjectively* create or simulate "reality" without ever *objectively* conceiving, comprehending, or identifying reality as such. This inherent proclivity of consciousness to create, simulate, or make up "reality" is mysticism. *Mysticism is the epistemological disease of consciousness to confine itself in the perceptivity-centered modality (the emulated bicameral modality), in subjectivity, while fabricating or making up non-existing, illusory "realities".*

Since consciousness is self-causative, consciousness must generate a continuous integration of energy to sustain its existence in its comprehension of reality. In other words, consciousness must continuously exert effort to fulfill its function as the conceptual integrator of reality. Mysticism is consciousness' default in that effort. It is the self-negation of consciousness by consciousness. No other cognitive mode including the bicameral mind is capable of mysticism, for none other than consciousness is nonautomatic and is the sole source of its own existence. Mysticism is not caused by the lack of consciousness but by the lack of *integration*. *Mysticism is the symptom of man's default in epistemological integrity and the cause of all human suffering.*

Perceptivity-centered consciousness is a developmental stage of consciousness in its apprehension of reality. When the integration of knowledge reaches a critical point, consciousness begins to see its perceptual experience in the context of conceptually integrated knowledge and goes beyond its perceptually or subjectively bound experiences to awaken into objectivity. If left free and unhindered, every child as well as humanity as a whole innately transcends the perceptivity-centered modality to advance its knowledge in the objectively defined context of reality.

Conceptuality-centered consciousness is consciousness *qua*

consciousness. Mysticism, unless it is identified and corrected, prevents or truncates forever consciousness' integrating growth into maturity. Consciousness is self-correcting epistemologically and self-controlling cybernetically. If it could identify its internal mysticism, it would self-correct its devastating errors and cure the disease that is mysticism. However, in history, this correction or healing, except for a few rare individuals, did not take place until today. The external force that prevents consciousness from self-correcting is neocheating.

Neocheating is the deliberate manipulation of mysticism in others. It is the poison-feeding of mysticism in others. Mysticism came into existence 3000 years ago with the birth of consciousness, and with it came its symbiotic neocheating. However, it was not until Plato formulated his philosophy that a systematic and conceptual framework was supplied in which to carry on neocheating. It was Plato who not only rationalized mysticism but also capitalized on it to create a brilliantly fabricated, yet devastatingly destructive philosophical system that provided the conceptual tools of neocheating for millennia to come. Through Plato and his philosophy, the whole matrix of neocheating was set, the spell of mysticism was deliberately cast upon humanity, and the reign of master neocheaters became firmly established in the course of history.

Platonistic philosophy begins by accepting the primacy of consciousness, that is, by reversing the relationship of consciousness to existence. It assumes that reality must conform to the content of consciousness, not the other way around, based upon the premise that the presence of any concept in consciousness proves the existence of a corresponding referent in reality. Plato thus validates *de jure* self-made realities while invalidating *de facto* reality as such.

According to Plato, the content of "true" reality is a set of universals or Forms that represent that which is in common among various groups of particulars in this world. He repeatedly insists that the Forms are what is "really" real. The particulars they subsume, the concrete objects that constitute this world, are not. Although he asserts that the Forms are immutable, timeless, intellectually apprehensible, and capable of precise definition at the end of a piece of "pure ratiocination" because they are independently existing entities in "reality", he never once elucidates in a rational context how that apprehension or definition can be achieved.

Although *epistemo-contextually* integrated reality is abstraction in the final analysis, yielding to crystallization in the form of concepts through the process of appropriation by consciousness, it is *in the final analysis* that reality is abstraction and *through the process of appropriation by consciousness* that reality is crystallized — apprehended and defined — in the form of concepts. Existence exists and exists independently of consciousness. Consciousness does not and cannot create reality; it is metaphysically passive. Consciousness *exists* to identify reality or existence, and in the very fact that consciousness must *exist* to be conscious of reality or existence, the primacy of existence to consciousness is evident.

The primacy of existence and the ultimacy of reality is the *alpha* and the *omega* of all valid conceptual knowledge. Knowledge is the explication of existence (*explicandum*) into reality (*explicans*). Existence is reality implicate metaphysically and reality is existence implicate epistemologically. Existence is what is given to consciousness metaphysically while reality is what is revealed to consciousness by consciousness epistemologically. Existence and reality are in essence synonymous, and as existence exists independently of consciousness, so does reality. Therefore, no knowledge of reality can ever be achieved by merely fabricating concepts without regard to existence, as Plato suggested.

Plato, by inverting the epistemological structure of the conscious cognitive process, by reversing the metaphysical relationship between reality (existence) and consciousness, succeeded, in effect, in giving the perceptivity-centered modality the highest and the ultimate cognitive status, while also providing mysticism a completely justified (and even dignified) "full-time job" in the inner workings of human awareness. Through Plato such false concepts as "God", "gods", or "the eternal soul", which has no metaphysically verifiable cognitive content, gained a well-justified philosophical foundation, for, according to him, anything that anyone could make up in his mind should exist because "that's the way it is".

Throughout his long career, Plato carried within him an intense political ambition and need to control others. His philosophy is largely a manifestation of that ambition and need. He played his politics and tried to control others not through an ordinary political channel but through the channel of philosophy. He tried to control others not physically but intellectually, for once people accepted his philosophy, then it was simpler and easier to control them physically. Although Plato died before he could witness his "dream" come true, the neocheaters throughout the world used his philosophy to bring his dream to fruition. Thus, as Plato's dream evolved into reality, a long and tragic nightmare unfolded.

Coinciding with the rise of the Romans around 200 B.C., the Western world saw the proliferation of religious/political master neocheaters along with the systematic application of their neocheating strategies. Their proliferation marked the decline of Greek culture and the fall of its highest intellectual manifestation — Aristotelian philosophy. Aristotelian philosophy is the first complete system of philosophy ever developed on the basis of the primacy of existence. Aristotle evolved the system of logic — the principle of *noncontradictory identification* — only by means of which objective reality is identified and verified authentically. Aristotle also developed the first ethical philosophy based on the supremacy of a conscious human individual. Aristotelian philosophy indeed is the fountainhead of all knowledge and the antithesis of Platonistic philosophy.

It was Aristotle, not Plato, who epitomized the mind of the Greeks. It was Aristotelian philosophy, not Platonistic philosophy, which was the epitome of Greek consciousness and its intellectual achievements. Therefore, the fall of Aristotelian philosophy around 200 B.C. meant a rise of Platonistic philosophy or Platonistic-oriented philosophies, and a beginning of a dark intellectual obscurantism.

Although this intellectual obscurantism was finally broken during the Renaissance by the resurgence of Aristotelian philosophy and the newly discovered power of the zero, its roots had never been eradicated until the discovery of Neo-Tech by Frank R. Wallace in the late 20th century. Aristotelian philosophy laid the foundation for all life enhancing discoveries and values culminating in the discovery of Neo-Tech. Aristotelian philosophy fulfilled its function and destiny as the fountainhead of knowledge and antithesis of Platonism in the discovery and development of Neo-Tech.

5. The Master Neocheaters

Knowledge is power. Integration of knowledge is power. It is through knowledge that one can control the destiny of his life, his environment, and his universe. It is through knowledge that one can achieve his true individuality, an indivisible conscious wholeness, and the self that is genuinely his. It is through knowledge, and through knowledge alone, that the flowering and the ultimate fulfillment of what it means to be human, what it means to be conscious, can come to exist.

For two millennia until the dawn of the Industrial Revolution and the subsequent advent of capitalism, knowledge was almost the exclusive possession of priest-scholars (e.g., Nicholaus Copernicus) or artist-engineer-scientists (e.g., Leonardo da Vinci) who worked under the sovereignty of their patronal governments. This monopolization of knowledge was a policy deliberately planned and executed by the successive master neocheaters who controlled and reigned over the world for millennia. Among these master neocheaters were some of the most brilliant and powerful kings, emperors, prime ministers, and priests or philosophers of human history.

Around 200 B.C. the master neocheaters of the Western world began a systematic oppression of human knowledge and usurpation of power by employing Platonistic-oriented philosophies that provided an ideological foundation for the propagation of mysticism. They devised a strategy whereby they successfully achieved their purpose and prepared Europe for the darkest tragedy of human history: the Dark Ages. Throughout recorded history, wherever there was a rise of commercial or business activities, there was a flourishing of Aristotelian-oriented philosophy and an advancement of human knowledge. Athens, where the Greek culture flourished, was such a place. Around 200 B.C., with the rise of the Romans who were in essence an agricultural nation, commercial activity declined and the world became more mystical. This coincided with the proliferation of the neocheaters.

Neocheaters strive for power without exerting effort to earn genuine knowledge of reality. ...They strive for power without earning genuine power. They accomplish their purpose and achieve their "power" by oppressing knowledge and disempowering others through the use of force, mystical as well as physical. Their power is in essence illusory and it is only in a mysticism-entrenched society that neocheaters can sustain such an illusion. It is only through the propagation of mysticism that neocheaters can survive.

Master neocheaters are those who have mastered the "art" of neocheating. They thoroughly understand the realm of nonreality and can see through the mysticism in others. Yet, out of dishonesty and laziness, instead of seeking to identify reality and gain genuine power and happiness, they choose to manipulate and usurp values from others. They are the masters of the mystic domain — mind-created "realities" and "truths." So far as one is caught in the labyrinth of their domain, so far as one is caught in the web of mysticism, he can never win the battle against those masters of nonreality.

The master neocheaters' grand strategy, through which they successfully propagated mysticism, oppressed knowledge and usurped values, consisted of three major substrategies:

(1) To systematically destroy the foundation of knowledge, i.e., reason, by (a) misinforming or not informing the populace of crucially important knowledge, such as Aristotelian philosophy or the heliocentric theory of the universe, and (b) conditioning the human mind and reflexes by Platonistic-oriented mystical thinking.

(2) To systematically train those who are intellectually endowed and bright enough to be a potential threat to the master neocheaters to become specialized scholars and to advance knowledge in a manner that serves the purpose of the power structure, while making the scholars completely dependent upon the power structure for their physical survival.

(3) To restrict commercial activities to the extent that the producers produce just enough to support the continuance of the power structure, while completely controlling the line of life-

support, such as food and money, by the power structure itself — so that no incentive will ever arise to advance knowledge among the populace.

All of these substrategies were carried out by deception, force, threat of force, and the systematic propagation of mysticism. The geocentric system gained prominence over the heliocentric system within this socio-political environment. Platonistic philosophy became predominant over Aristotelian philosophy within this anti-intellectual climate, reversing the intellectual trend of the Greeks, which had produced a remarkable wealth of knowledge and incomparably brilliant intellects such as Pythagoras, Philolaus, Heraclides, Aristarchus, Apollonius, Archimedes, Socrates, and Aristotle (perhaps the foremost intellect in history). (Plato, although he was in essence anti-Greek, was nevertheless one of the great intellects and writers of human history, and without the flourishing intellectual climate of ancient Greece, even Plato would not have been possible.)

Neo-Tech defines mysticism as: (1) Any attempt to recreate or alter reality, usually through dishonesty, feelings, *non sequiturs*, or rationalizations. (2) Any attempt to ignore, evade, or contradict reality. (3) The creation of problems where none exist. It defines neocheating as: Any intentional use of mysticism to create false realities and illusions in order to extract values from others. From these definitions it becomes quite clear why Platonistic philosophy became the prime tool for neocheaters to carry out the first substrategy of destroying the foundation of all valid human knowledge: reason.

Reason is the faculty of the mind that conceptually identifies and integrates the materials provided by senses, perceptions, and previous conceptions. Reason is the prime faculty of consciousness in reaching ever higher abstractions or broader conceptions, first by distinguishing the relevant from the nonrelevant within the entire realm of sensory, perceptual, and conceptual data-banks, and then by conceptually integrating the relevant in accordance with logic. Logic is the art and principle of noncontradictory identification. Reason functioning in the conceptuality-centered modality is reasoning, while reason functioning in the perceptivity-centered modality or in the mystical context is rationalization.

Reasoning is an intellectual process for achieving an integrated conceptual picture of reality by always starting from perceptual experiences and then making a logical connection between what is perceived and what is conceived. Rationalization is an intellectual process for fabricating an illusionary "reality" in concepts by disconnecting conception from perception. Reasoning is based on the primacy of existence, whereas rationalization is based on the primacy of consciousness. Both use reason, logic, and concepts. However, they are diametrically opposite to one another. Reasoning begins with logically non-contradictory premises based on the facts of reality, while rationalization begins with premises that contradict reality.

No matter how logical-sounding it might be, any conclusion that begins with a contradictory premise inescapably contradicts reality. The primacy of existence is the prime principle of reality. No valid knowledge is ever possible without observing the primacy of existence, for existence exists in the very act of living, reasoning, and even rationalizing. Platonistic philosophy stands upon a ground which does not exist in reality, i.e., upon nothing, and since it is nothing it could be anything. Platonistic philosophy is the philosophical system that rationalizes rationalization and *"non sequiturs" non sequiturs.*

The most devastating *non sequitur*/rationalization that arises directly from Platonistic philosophy is altruism. As mentioned before, according to Plato, what is "really" real are the Forms, disembodied abstractions which represent that which is in common among various groups of particulars in this world of concrete perceptual experiences. Therefore, in effect, individual human beings are merely particular instances of the universal "human being"; they are ultimately not real. What is "real" about human beings is only the Form that they share in common and reflect. To Platonism, all the seemingly individual human beings are "in reality" the same one Form in various reflections.

Thus, all human beings ultimately comprise one unity, and no earthly human being is an autonomous entity. This momentous conclusion leads to altruism and all the "higher-cause", collectivist moralities. Platonistic philosophy, while establishing the primacy of consciousness, denies the supremacy of an individual wherein consciousness resides. For consciousness that is supposed to be primal is not, according to Platonism, an earthly individual consciousness but a universal entity, a Form, of which an individual consciousness is merely a reflection. Plato, with his literary genius, propagated this kind of contradictory and destructive philosophy which was to dominate the mind and thinking of humanity for the following 2300 years.

Platonistic philosophy or Platonistic-oriented philosophies provided the tools for neocheaters to exploit as well as manipulate innocent and productive individuals. People, thus Platonistically conditioned, had no means to protect themselves philosophically against the neocheaters' assaults. Although Aristotelian-based thinking was by nature always employed in all healthy and productive human endeavors which kept the life-line of human society going, people were bound to live in undeserved guilt. Some asserted Aristotelian-oriented philosophies, but, until Ayn Rand, none were able to discover the fault of Platonistic philosophy in a fully integrated and thoroughly reasoned context, and none were able to identify the poison-core of mysticism and neocheating in its entirety until Neo-Tech.

During the time of the Romans, little advance was made in the field of science. The Romans in essence lived under the glory of the Greeks intellectually, and the systematic enactment of their neocheating strategy and propagation of Platonistic-oriented philosophies prepared Europe for the Dark Ages. Around 200 B.C., Stoicism, a Platonistic-oriented philosophy, became influential among the Romans, for it presented the traditional beliefs they had inherited from the Etruscans in a more sophisticated form. Around A.D. 200, Stoicism merged with Platonism in the form of Neoplatonism, particularly in the Neoplatonistic system of Plotinus (A.D. 204-270). During those 400 years, the conditioning of the human mind to misconceive reality through Platonistic-oriented thinking became quite prevalent.

In regard to the second substrategy of training the bright to become specialized scholars, it was here that the two-millennium-old trend of specialization in knowledge originated. Since knowledge is the source, the only source, of genuine power, the ones who are capable of integrating knowledge are the greatest threat to neocheaters. Therefore, those who are intellectually endowed must be divided into their specialized fields of knowledge so that they cannot integrate different spheres of knowledge to gain integrated power. They must also be isolated from the rest of the world and made oblivious of the whole context of reality, while at the same time being made dependent upon political neocheaters for their physical survival.

A mathematician alone, no matter how brilliant he might be, could not be a threat to a neocheater without the knowledge of other fields and the rest of the world, and without the means of achieving financial independence — without a business integration. So long as those who are bright remain divided and "specialized", oblivious of the world, neocheaters are safe to exercise their "power" and use those scholars for their own advantages. This is what happened and what has been happening throughout the entire history of man. Moreover, some of those scholars turned to mysticism or neocheating and achieved political and/or religious prominence. The so-called social "intellectuals" of today are the direct offspring of those earlier "scholars turned neocheaters".

Research in the fields of biology and anthropology reveals that all the species and tribes that became extinct did so because of overspecialization. The current educational systems of the world, which originated in the neocheating strategy of ancient political powers, emphasize specialization, and thus endanger the continuation of the human species. Until today, the least specialized field, the field that requires the widest integration of knowledge, has been politics, where neocheaters, who have the least regard for knowledge, gravitate the most. Ironically and tragically, the fittest to survive in the mysticism-ridden world of inverted reality have been the least capable of surviving in reality.

In principle, the field in which the widest integration of knowledge is required is business. It is in business that philosophy, science, and technology meet the challenge of life to integrate into higher values that benefit humanity. It is in business that metaphysical values are transformed and crystallized into physical values that nurture human needs. Without producers and their business activities, no society can possibly survive. Therefore, in executing the third substrategy, the master neocheaters could not wipe out the producers and their businesses totally. Otherwise, they would have jeopardized their own existence. It is through those heroic, yet unknown, producers that the world, albeit severely oppressed, could survive all the darkness which humanity had to endure. Time and again business flourished in various parts of the world, and every time there was a flourishing of business there was an advancement of knowledge and an evolution of human happiness and prosperity.

6. The Discovery Of The Zero

"It is India that gave us the ingenious method of expressing all numbers by means of ten symbols, each symbol receiving a value of position as well as an absolute value; a profound and important idea which appears so simple to us now that we ignore its true merit. But its very simplicity and the great ease which it has lent to all computations put our arithmetic in the first rank of useful inventions; and we shall appreciate the grandeur of this achievement the more when we remember that it escaped the genius of Archimedes and Apollonius, two of the greatest men produced by antiquity."

— Laplace

Producers are the *Primum Mobiles* (the Prime Movers) of the world and business is the very motion which carries humanity forward. It was the rise of producers and the integral component of business — Aristotelian philosophy — in the 13th-14th century that broke the Middle Ages and brought the Renaissance to Europe. It was the same rise of producers and Aristotelian-oriented philosophies, implicitly employed, during the first five centuries A.D. in India that made possible one of the greatest mathematical inventions of all time — the zero, without which the Renaissance and the subsequent development of scientific knowledge would not have been possible.

The zero is the mathematically defined numerical function of nothingness that is used not for an evasion but for an apprehension of reality. The "nothing" has been the exclusive territory of mystics and neocheaters. They thrive on "nothing", in nonreality, and create their mystical edifice of power and dominance upon "nothing" with "nothing". The zero is the only "nothing" thus far conceived that is nonmystical, i.e., reality-based. It is a tool, a mathematical tool, for dealing with reality, and as such is integral to the whole context of reality *qua* reality. After the Renaissance, the monopolization of knowledge became broken and scientific knowledge flourished owing largely to the propagation of this mathematical "nothing", the zero — to the increased computational capability among common people that was made possible solely by the widespread use of the zero concept and its counterpart — the place-value numerical system.

On the assumption that an Aristotelian-based philosophy rather than a Platonistic philosophy had dominated the Western world since the Golden Age of Greece, Neo-Tech *predicts* the following *retrospectively* (see "Neo-Tech Discovery", Neo-Tech Advantage #77, An Aristotelian Course of History):

350 B.C. Aristotle (384-322 B.C.)
200 B.C. America discovered.
100 B.C. Free-enterprise capitalism established around the world.
  0 B.C. All traces of mysticism, altruism, are gone.
 20 A.D. Electrical power developed, camera developed.
 40 A.D. Internal-combustion engine developed.
 50 A.D. Cars in mass production. Airplane developed.
 60 A.D. Computer developed...
 70 A.D. Nuclear power developed.
 80 A.D. Man on the Moon.
100 A.D. Man on Mars and heading for other planets.
120 A.D. Human biological immortality developed.
200 A.D. Universal immortality achieved...

As revealed in the second chapter, exactly as predicted above, the Phoenician navigators circumnavigated the world and discovered the American continent around 200 B.C., preceding Columbus and Magellan by 1700 years. Aristarchus' heliocentric theory of the universe was developed approximately fifty years prior to that circumnavigation. However, also around 200 B.C., with the rise of the Romans, Platonistic-based philosophies became increasingly more dominant and growth in science rapidly declined, except in Alexandria where Greek culture and science still continued to flourish.

What is implicit in this "retrospective forecast" of human history, however, is that a numerical system much like ours with the zero and the place-value principle should have been developed somewhere between 200 and 100 B.C., for the Greek numerical system was much too rudimentary to make the subsequent developments in science and technology probable. In fact, no matter what kind of numerical symbols people of antiquity might have adopted, logic dictates that their number system should have been the same as ours with the zero concept and the place-value principle. Since man has ten fingers, it is most likely that the base of their number system would have been ten (10). The computers of 60 A.D. should have employed a binary system due to the nature of logic.

Our modern written numeration, with the zero concept and the place-value principle, is such an ingenious, efficacious, and conceptually integrated system that no one who has ever considered the history of numerical notation or mathematics fails to realize its enormous profundity, significance, and power. For instance, consider the following addition — the same addition by means of Roman numerals and of our Hindu-Arabic numerals:

CCLXVIII	268
MDCCCVII	1807
DCL	650
MLXXX	1080
MMMDCCCV	3805

Without converting the Roman numerals into our modern system the problem is difficult, if not impossible, to solve. And this is only an addition — multiplication or division would be far worse. Roman numerals and most other systems do not lend themselves to written computation owing largely to the static nature of their basic numerals, which are in essence only abbreviations for recording the results of computations done by means of an abacus or counting board.

For this reason, before the advent of our modern positional numeration (the zero and the place-value system), the art of reckoning remained an exclusive and highly skilled profession. Indeed, it attests to the success wherewith the master neocheaters executed their destructive substrategy, specialization of knowledge, that the knowledge of reckoning remained so exclusive a profession. That master neocheating strategy created a lack of motivation for the advancement of knowledge, particularly of science, and its accompanying mathematical/computational tools. Thus, no progress was made in the field of reckoning in the Western world beyond Greek or Roman numeration. Roman numeration, particularly, was an intentional device to keep the populace ignorant and powerless, forever confined in the perceptivity-centered modality, in a mystical cave, by a mega-dose of neocheating.

Therefore, the discovery of the zero and the development of the place-value numeration had to wait for a less oppressive intellectual climate — a flourishing business and commercial atmosphere. Such a climate took place in India between the first and fifth centuries A.D. It was during that time in India that the zero was discovered and the system of place-value numeration was developed, almost reaching to their fullest formulation by 500 A.D. Although in recorded history the place-value number systems have been developed four times (by the Babylonians, Mayans, Chinese, and Hindus), and the zero concept has been evolved three times (by the Babylonians, Mayans, and Hindus), none outside of the Hindus have devised such a complete system of numerical operation. Furthermore, none outside of the Hindus evolved the zero concept to the degree that it is used as the null-value in all facets of calculation.

Increased commercial/business activities during the first three centuries A.D. in India called for further developments in navigational technology and astronomical science, and for an evolution of a written computational methodology for recording the process of calculations that were employed in navigation, astronomy, and business. To accomplish these ends, development of a superior numerical system that lent itself to written computation became imperative. It was among those sea-dwelling navigator-engineer-scientist-businessmen who kept and evolved the lineage of advanced knowledge from antiquity that the place-value number system with the zero concept was first developed. The

Brahman scholars, the Pythagoreans of the East, further evolved and perfected the system nearly to its present formulation. By using only ten numerical symbols while assigning one of the ten symbols, the zero, unique meanings and functions, they succeeded in expressing infinitely large numbers and making complex numerical operations remarkably more simple.

In Sanskrit (the scholarly language of the Hindus), the word for the zero is *"sunya"*, meaning "void", and there is little doubt that the zero concept originated as the written symbol for the empty column of the abacus. The abacus had been used around the world since antiquity to provide a facile means of accumulating progressive products of multiplication by moving those products ever further leftward, column by column, as the operator filled the available bead spaces one by one and moved the excess over ten into the successive right-to-left-ward columns.

Number products in even tens (such as the number 20 or 30) leave the first right hand column empty (void). When expert abacus users had no abacus available to them, they could remember and visualize the operation of the abacus so clearly that all they needed to know was the content of each column in order to develop any multiplication or division. They then invented symbols for the content of each column to replace drawing a picture of the number of beads. Having developed symbols to express the content of each column, they had to invent a symbol for the numberless content of the empty column — that symbol came to be known to the Hindus as *"sunya"*, and *sunya* later became *"sifr"* in Arabic; *"cifra"* in Roman; and finally *"cipher"* in English.

Only an empty column of an abacus could possibly provide the human experience that called for the invention of the zero — the symbol for "nothingness", and that discovery of the symbol for nothingness had an enormous significance upon subsequent humanity. The zero, the cipher, alone made possible humanity's escape from the 1700-year monopoly of all its calculating functions by the neocheating power structure operating invisibly behind their governments and religions. It was also the power of nothingness, the zero, that raised the curtains of science during the Renaissance, which had been drawn by the master neocheaters since 200 B.C. (It is significant to realize that the positional numeration with the zero concept had been implicitly employed in the operation of the abacus almost in its entirety, including the zero being the null-value. The Hindu numeration was the *written translation* of that operation.)

Even if the zero with the place-value principle and its computation-facilitating capability had been discovered by the Alexandrian Greeks, by Archimedes or Apollonius, for instance, it would have been banished or even lost when the emperors of the Roman Empire amalgamated the vast power of the priesthood with their already-established military supremacy. Historically, Roman numerals had been invented to enable completely illiterate people to keep "scores" of events occurring one by one. The more complex Roman numerals were those used by their superiors, keeping count by their fingers — V for five (the angle between one's thumb and the other four fingers) and X for ten (representing one's crossed index fingers). Since one cannot see "no sheep" or "no person", the Roman world had no need for a symbol for nothing.

For science to evolve, there should be three basic socio-intellectual factors present: (1) a flourishing business climate that will provide an incentive to advance knowledge; (2) an explicitly defined Aristotelian philosophy that will provide the metaphysical/epistemological foundation or context for valid scientific knowledge and the ethical/moral basis for productive living; (3) mathematical tools, such as the zero with the place-value principle, that will facilitate the advancement of science. During the Renaissance all three of these factors were clearly present. Science did not develop in India after the discovery of the zero owing to the fact that no explicitly defined Aristotelian philosophy had ever been prevalent in India or had been known to the Hindus in general.

Indian philosophies from Hinduism to Buddhism, although they differed in various issues, all held that reality could not be known by reason and logic but only by a mystical union with existence called *samadhi* or *nirvana*, purported to be transcendental to reason and logic. They believed that reason and logic could take them only to the point where they could merge into existence through the cessation of the mind. In truth, their mystical union, *samadhi* or *nirvana*, was nothing more than a glorified perception or sensation. They inverted the epistemological order of human cognition, which proceeds from sensation to perception and perception to conception, and gave perception and sensation the ultimate cognitive status.

Therefore, albeit the Hindus perfected one of the greatest discoveries in human history — the zero, they could not realize its cosmic function as a mathematical tool of science. Although it required a conceptuality-centered modality of consciousness to conceive of the zero, the Hindus did not possess a conceptuality-centered philosophy — an Aristotelian philosophy — to integrate the zero concept into a larger philosophical scheme so as to bring about its fruits. The zero, thus, had to wait for nearly 1000 years until the time of Leonardo da Vinci and Copernicus in order to bear its fruits and transform the human world forever.

Meanwhile, in the West, the Romans repeatedly burned the Alexandrian library, which as early as 100 B.C. was reputed to have had 700,000 manuscripts containing the wealth of Greek intellectual achievements. The library was first set on fire in 47 B.C. during the war between Caesar and Pompey (40,000 volumes were burned), second in 272 A.D. by a Roman emperor, third in 391 A.D. by another Roman emperor, and finally completely destroyed by the Muslims in 642 A.D. Thus, before the zero could reach the Western world around 700 A.D. via the Moorish invasion of Spain, the intellectual soil wherein this remarkable concept could have borne fruit had been destroyed almost completely by the master neocheaters and their neocheating strategies. The Western world had entered the Dark Ages.

7. The Propagation Of The Zero

In the centuries since its discovery, the place-value system of numeration with the zero concept has been propagated throughout the world even more widely than the alphabet of Phoenician origin, and it has become the only universal language humanity now possesses. When its advantages became known to the scholars, reckoners, and businessmen of civilization in contact with India, they gradually began to adopt this new system, abandoning the imperfect systems which they inherited from their ancestors. The zero and its immense computational capabilities provided humanity with an infinite horizon for the evolution of knowledge.

Among those who adopted this new system of numeration and adapted it to their own forms of writing were the Arabs. In the vast empire that they built within less than a century after Mohammed's death, the Moslems forced conquered nations to adopt their language and its writing. Thus, Arabic soon became a means of communication, particularly among scholars of diverse origins. In 772 A.D. al-Mansur, the second caliph of the Abbassid dynasty, founded the capital Baghdad, which quickly became one of the great commercial and intellectual centers of the world where the cultural heritage of the conquered nations was well-received. It was in Baghdad that the evolution of Arab science began, assimilating all the Greek and Hindu scientific works that came to the Arab-Islamic world.

Mohammed ibn-Musa al-Khowarizmi (c. 780-850), who lived at the court of the Abbassid caliph al-Mamum, was one of the most distinguished and illustrious mathematicians of the period. Al-Khowarizmi's treatise on arithmetic, "Treatise on Cipher", is the earliest known Arabic work in which the Hindu place-value numeration and computation methods are specifically elucidated. (In Europe, al-Khowarizmi's name, first Latinized as Algorismi, turned into the terms "algorism" and "algorithm", designating computation with the Hindu written numerations before taking on the more general meaning of computation with any notation. The first word of the Arabic title for his other treatise, "*Al-jabr w'al-mu-qubalah*", later came to designate the branch of mathematics known in English as algebra.)

Although the Moorish invasion of Spain introduced Hindu-Arabic numerals and algebra for the first time to Europe around 700 A.D., preceding al-Khowarizmi about a century, it was the Latin translation of his "Treatise on Cipher" around 1200 A.D. that awakened Europe from its computational darkness to an evolution of mathematical knowledge. However, while Arab-Islamic civilization was achieving great scientific and cultural attitudes, comparable only with Athens and Alexandria, Western Christendom was languishing in social disorder, economic depression, and intellectual obscurantism caused by the master neocheaters' oppressive strategies to stay in power. Thus, it took over 400 years for al-Khowarizmi's treatise to be translated into Latin, and it took another 200 years for the Hindu-Arabic numeration with the zero and place-value concept to become widely diffused in Europe.

As in India, where virtually every sphere of knowledge was monopolized by Brahmans and other religious priest-scholars, so in the Arab-Islamic world was knowledge a field which belonged exclusively to the priest-scholars who served under their patronal caliphs. Furthermore, as in India, there was no explicit Aristotelian philosophy that dominated the mind of the Arabs. Their guiding philosophy was provided by their religion, Islam. Although Aristotle's works were earnestly studied and translated into Arabic, so were the works of Plato. It was the time of academic compilation and scholastic relativism. For that reason, no genuine scientific/technological revolution took place in the Arab-Islamic world. However, it was through the wealth of knowledge compiled there that the Western world learned about the lost works of Aristotle and the zero concept.

In the meantime in Europe, a systematic master neocheating scheme in operation since 200 B.C., particularly by the successive Roman emperors, had prepared Europe for the rise of Christianity. The combined religious and political emperorship had found its authoritarian formulae, *"credo"* (which means "I believe"), continually threatened by the Greek scientist-philosophers who had incessantly evolved ever unorthodox ideas and discoveries. The authorities had devised their grand strategy largely to cope with and counteract those scientists' persuasive, experience-supported, objective logic.

But it was not until the Roman priesthood developed an extremely clever neocheating theology around an obscure mystic who had supposedly died on the cross some centuries before that the traces of the Greek intellect could finally be wiped out. Although the emperors possessed absolute physical power, they lacked absolute metaphysical authority. Through Christian theology and its doctrine, the emperor-pope could now possess not only physical power but also the metaphysical dispensation normally given only by "God" — an authority that was purportedly received originally by the disciples from the only son of God, "Christ", and his direct authority from God himself. Indeed, following the death of Jesus and the preaching by his "disciples", the promised prospect of salvation for all believers raised the Christian priesthood to an unprecedented popularity and power.

In point of fact, Jesus was an obscure mystic known in his lifetime only by a handful of people. Uneducated and with hallucinatory propensities, he spent his known life neurotically striving to fulfill certain ancient Judaic prophecies under a megalomaniacal illusion that he was the son of God. His crucifixion was to a great measure his own making in order to fulfill his "divine mission" in life. For what sin did he actually commit that deserved a crucifixion except that he was somewhat insane and an annoyance to the establishment? It was indeed Jesus himself who managed to cause his own crucifixion, because, so far as he was concerned, the son of God had to be crucified.

Furthermore, it is highly unlikely that he died on the cross. His crucifixion took place on a Friday and the next day was the Sabbath. He was on the cross no more than six hours, so how could a young man of 33 possibly die so easily? The myth of Resurrection thus may have a well-founded genesis; this neurotic man might have appeared in front of people before leaving the town for an unknown place. His disciples, equally mystical and most of them uneducated, spread his legacy, which finally reached the neocheating priests of the Roman Empire, who then cleverly constructed a devastatingly destructive theology around that legacy by employing Platonistic principles. Thus was born the emperor-pope.

The emperor-pope who was "officially authorized" by God could require all believers to secretly confess their "sins" to his "officials" (ordained priests). He could also ordain universal adoption of his explanations of the causality of all human experiences, explanations that were most useful to him. The emperor-pope could tell his people how to conduct their lives, how to gain God's favor. The geocentric system was degraded to the notion of a two-dimensional flat world sandwiched in parallel between Heaven above and Hell below, and this cosmology put the emperor-pope and his "God" at the center of the universe. The heliocentric universe did not fit into his scheme, and thus was wiped off the face of the Earth.

The zero, like the heliocentric concept, had no place in such an intellectual obscurantism. Although it was first introduced around 700 A.D. in Spain, the zero could not find a way to reach through the darkness of the human mind to Europe at large. The zero as well as the heliocentric concept had to wait until the 11th and 12th centuries when producers and business again arose in Europe. During those two centuries Europe awakened abruptly, owing largely to a rapid population growth which had such consequences as the clearing of land, the development of cities, and the construction of larger churches. Prices rose, circulation of money increased, and, as sovereigns quelled feudal anarchy, commerce revived.

The revival of commerce necessitated more frequent international contacts and in turn favored the introduction of Arab science into the Western world. Universities were founded, arising from guild-like associations of masters and students at the cathedral schools. The western Crusade against Muslims in Spain resulted in the fall of Toledo (a Christian archbishopric in Spain) in 1085, and it was from this time that the Arabic versions of Greek science as well as Hindu numerals were translated into Latin, the most active period being 1125-1280. It was during this time that al-Khowarizmi's "Treatise on Cipher" reached northern Italy and southern Germany by way of Carthage in North Africa.

Two hundred years later, the zero concept finally diffused into the university system and became widely used in Europe largely because of its conceptual novelty. The zero was not only a tremendously powerful mathematical tool but also a catalyst that elevated the conceptual faculty of individual human beings to new heights. It is only the knowledge of the capability for unlimited multiplying and dividing — and thereby *ratioing* — and for evaluating relative experiences that is provided exclusively by the zero/place-value numerical system that could possibly enable individual human beings to know how to escape from the prison of ignorance which had been successfully established for centuries.

It was the zero, the mathematical nothing, that brought Europe out of the Dark/Middle Ages, out of the spell of mysticism, to the Renaissance, to a sunlit world of reason. Because the zero was indeed "nothing", the knowledge-monopolizing neocheating power structure whose entire existence was based upon nonreality, nothing, had improvidently overlooked it. Because it was a tool unlike the heliocentric theory or Aristotelian philosophy they could not comprehend its power and foresee the danger that it entailed for them. The zero, thus, became an essential and indispensable tool in the work of Leonardo da Vinci, Copernicus, Kepler, Galileo, and Newton. It also brought about Columbus' revised concepts of terrestrial navigation.

The advancement of science since the Renaissance is greatly indebted to this something-called-nothing — the zero. If the zero had not been discovered, humanity would still be in a dark age, scientifically and technologically. Imagine doing complex and highly sophisticated computations required for astrophysics or quantum mechanics by means of Roman numerals. It would be impossible. Those fields of modern science could not even exist without the zero and the place-value numeration. To understand the genuine importance of this mathematical null-value is to know the depth of our civilization and the power of human consciousness.

Through the discovery and propagation of the zero and the place-value numeration, humanity could achieve an immense advancement and a geometrical increase in scientific knowledge previously unimagined. Despite the remarkable progress in science, however, speaking philosophically, humanity has lived, until today, with philosophical Roman numerals alone, as it were. It was not until Ayn Rand developed her philosophy, Objectivism, in the mid-twentieth century that philosophy found its renaissance for the first time since Aristotle. Ayn Rand was the Copernicus of philosophy and she brought about a genuine philosophical Copernican Revolution.

Neo-Tech was discovered in the mid-1970s by Frank R. Wallace to further that philosophical renaissance, not only by integrating all the valid philosophical, psychological, and scientific knowledge on the basis of Aristotelian-Objectivist principles, but also by making a *philosophical regression* utterly impossible through its *fully integrated philosophical matrix* that identifies and eliminates the whole edifice of mysticism and its symbiotic neocheating. What the zero accomplished in the field of science, Neo-Tech is achieving in the sphere of human life, particularly in the field of philosophy. As the zero heightened the capability of humans to deal with reality mathematically, Neo-Tech heightens the competence of all men and women to deal with reality philosophically. As the zero nullifies unneeded numerical values to render new values, Neo-Tech nullifies nonvalue or nonreality — mysticism and neocheating — to bring forth values.

It was the zero, the nonmystical "nothing", that brought about the evolution of scientific knowledge. And it is Neo-Tech, the philosophical zero, that will bring forth not only the evolution of knowledge but also the evolvement of human happiness and prosperity, forever. The zero rendered all the numerical systems of the past totally obsolete. Neo-Tech now renders obsolete every system of philosophy that has ever existed, even Aristotelian or Objectivist philosophy, while integrating all valid knowledge of the past, the present, and the future in its forever- evolving philosophical matrix. The zero is the most potent mathematical tool ever to be conceived and Neo-Tech is the most powerful philosophical tool ever to be discovered. The zero and Neo-Tech are both based on Aristotelian principles, on objective reality, and epitomize the power of human consciousness in its full glory.

Neo-Tech is the philosophical zero. Indeed, to comprehend its depth and harness its power is not only to achieve a life of unlimited prosperity and happiness, but also to live forever, even after the Sun dies.

8. Neo-Tech, The Philosophical Zero

Neo-Tech is a new technology based on fully integrated honesty. "New" means never before discovered, never before identified. "Technology" means the application of knowledge. "Fully integrated honesty" means honesty that is based on contextual facts and objective reality, and applied in every dimension, every facet, and every moment of life. "Honesty" means the active state of according oneself with reality. Neo-Tech is a new system of knowledge that self-contains the knowledge of application or to which the knowledge of self-application is integral. And Neo-Tech contains, integrally and

562

integratedly, philosophical, psychological, and scientific knowledge.

The physicist-mathematician Sir James Jeans (1877-1946) cogently defined science as "the earnest attempt to set in order the facts of experience." Philosophy is a sphere of science that deals with "order" itself; it is the science or knowledge of the principles of "ordering" the facts of experience. Philosophy permeates the entire field of science and provides the principle or the context in which to set in order given facts of experience that pertain to a particular branch of science. Without a valid philosophical foundation no branch of science could arrive at a valid picture or theory of the reality-sphere about which it is concerned.

Experience is the raw material of science. Existence and cognition/consciousness are always inherently present in all experiences. Experience is the complex awareness of existing, of self coexisting with all the nonself. Experience is always biterminal, i.e., it has a beginning and an end. Since experience is biterminal, and thus finite, it can be stored, studied, directed, and, with conscious effort, set in order for various human advantages. Science is that conscious effort/experience for setting in order a finite set of finite experiences, and philosophy is a particular conscious effort/experience for setting in order the very experience of setting in order.

Philosophy, thus, concerns itself with the principle of "ordering" and provides a contextual order for all branches of science and all spheres of human existence. Furthermore, a philosophical context is self-referential, that is, it is not only the context for science and human existence but also serves as its own context. Philosophy, therefore, is the reflection or the expression of the fundamental inner working of consciousness *qua* consciousness. No philosophy had ever existed before the advent of consciousness. The bicameral mind had various myths but not a single philosophy. To be human, to be conscious, in essence is to be a philosopher and what kind of philosophy one consciously or subconsciously possesses determines the entire destiny of his life. Similarly, what kind of philosophy humanity as a whole predominantly chooses determines the entire course of human history.

Neo-Tech identifies two fundamental systems of philosophy: Platonistic and Aristotelian. Platonistic philosophy is rooted in the perceptivity-centered (or the emulated bicameral) modality of consciousness and breeds mysticism and neocheating. Aristotelian philosophy is rooted in the conceptuality-centered modality of consciousness and breeds knowledge. Platonistic philosophy has been used mostly in the fields of government, politics, and religion, fields that exist not through producing values but through usurping values. Aristotelian philosophy has been used mostly in the fields of science, technology, and productive business — the fields that create values.

Since the grand neocheating strategy by the master neocheaters of antiquity has prevailed, the forces of government, politics, and religion have reigned over the world. Platonistic philosophy has dominated and determined the course of human history, while productive scientists, technologists (including engineers, artists, and craftsmen), and businessmen (including the working class and farmers) have continued to produce values quietly, implicitly employing Aristotelian principles. Ironically, no one except a handful of master neocheaters such as popes was able to know the real cause of physical devastation and spiritual destruction which humanity seemed destined to endure. For no knowledge existed that could successfully identify mysticism and neocheating in their causal and structural entirety.

Neo-Tech is such a knowledge. Neo-Tech is the only system of knowledge that is *designed* to identify and collapse the entire edifice of mysticism and its symbiotic neocheating. Neo-Tech brings to light the total epistemological structure and mechanics of mysticism and neocheating through its fully integrated and evolving philosophical matrix. With Neo-Tech, people around the world are now capable, for the first time in history, to rid their consciousness of the 3000-year-old mental cancer — mysticism, and also to rid their lives of the 3000-year-old mystical hoax — neocheating. Neo-Tech indeed is the first philosophical device or knowledge-tool (*organum*) ever developed for the complete extirpation of the philosophical plague — mysticism and neocheating — that has afflicted humanity for three millennia.

In the history of philosophy three organums (the principles

or the tools of knowledge) were developed before Neo-Tech — the first, *"Organum"*, by Aristotle (384-322 B.C.), the second, *"Novum Organum"*, by Francis Bacon (1561-1626), and the third, *"Tertium Organum"*, by Pyotr D. Ouspensky (1878-1947). Neo-Tech by Frank R. Wallace is the fourth organum and completes the work by Aristotle. Aristotle, through his *"Organum"*, identified and developed the whole principle of valid knowledge, i.e., logic. He developed the principle of noncontradictory identification whereby all knowledge is discovered, verified, and evaluated. Even when his various misconclusions, such as his geocentric theory, were disproved, it is his organum that was used to disprove them.

Although Bacon had very little regard for either Plato or Aristotle, *"Novum Organum"* nevertheless exhibits a mixture of Platonistic and Aristotelian principles, and thus is fundamentally Platonistic (for no system can be built on the basis of Aristotelian principle if it "incorporates" Platonism; only within a Platonistic context can some fragments of Aristotelian knowledge be admixed, mainly as tools for non sequiturs). *"Tertium Organum"*, by P.D. Ouspensky, a Russian mathematician-turned-mystic who studied under another Russian mystic, G.I. Gurdjieff, is characterized by its regression into Platonism with an Eastern philosophy/psychology undertone. His conception of consciousness, "cosmic consciousness", as well as his interpretation of Einstein's *Theory of Relativity* and fourth dimension, is highly mystical and thus has little to do with reality *qua* reality.

The following is a comparison chart that demonstrates the difference between Aristotle's *Organum* and Ouspensky's *Tertium Organum*:

Organum: A is A.
A is not not-A.
Each existent is either A
or not-A.

Tertium Organum: A is both A and not-A.
or
All is A and A is all.

If A is both A and not-A, how can one identify A in the first place? If *Tertium Organum* is true, then everything loses its identity and nothing can be known — even *Tertium Organum* itself cannot be known. Ouspensky recognizes that his logic is absurd and attempts to exculpate himself from this apparent contradiction by saying, "We must be prepared for the fact that *it is impossible* to express superlogical relations ("higher logic") in our language." What is his philosophy based upon? A profound mistrust and contempt in man's "ordinary" cognitive process and the power of reason. Where does his philosophy lead? To a complete denial of conceptual knowledge. His philosophy of "higher logic" is a total negation of reality in the name of "higher reality". Only those who are profoundly dissatisfied and unhappy with reality could aspire to such a philosophy. Yet, P.D. Ouspensky was one of the most brilliant Platonists in history, integrating Eastern mysticism into Platonism with remarkable intellectual sophistication.

As Aristotle provided the fundamental principle of all valid knowledge and action, Neo-Tech offers the principle that identifies all invalid knowledge and action. Metaphorically, Aristotle evolved the philosophical positional number system and Neo-Tech discovered the philosophical zero raising Aristotelian philosophy to new heights. In essence, with Neo-Tech, the philosophical zero, man's philosophical capability for dealing with reality increases infinitely, in much the same way as the zero has infinitely increased man's mathematical capability for dealing with reality. Platonistic philosophy and other philosophical systems that are based upon Platonistic principles are the philosophical Roman numerals and cripple man's philosophical or conceptual ability to deal with reality successfully, and thereby to achieve knowledge, power, happiness, and prosperity. With Neo-Tech, the philosophical renaissance will indeed unfold forevermore.

Humanity as a whole now faces an unprecedented crisis brought about by the disparity between scientific/technological development, which was effected by the zero and Aristotelian philosophy, and the philosophical/moral/political underdevelopment, which was caused by Platonistic philosophy, mysticism, and neocheating. At the same time, humanity as a whole also now faces an unprecedented opportunity made possible by advancements in science and technology, by the discovery and development of Neo-Tech, and by the subsequent flourishing of productive business all around the world. The following are some of the major obstacles in achieving and realizing the unprecedented opportunity that now awaits humanity.

(1) Platonistic/Kantian philosophies, and prevailing mysticism/ neocheating that arise therefrom:

The task of philosophy and the job of a philosopher is not to obfuscate but to clarify reality, not to complicate but to simplify living, i.e., not to further mystify but to progressively demystify the human mind in relation to reality and human life. However, except for Aristotle, Ayn Rand, and a few others, most philosophers throughout history have almost completely defaulted in their responsibility.

Ever since Plato elaborated the *sophistry* of "reality creation" and developed the matrix of *noncontextual logic* (inner logic that has no reality-integrating context), philosophy has gone astray, falling ever deeper into the trap of mysticism. Yet, no philosopher, not even Plato, could systematically deny man's rational faculty and attack the validity of reason...until the German philosopher Immanuel Kant (1724-1804).

The expressly stated purpose of Kant's philosophy is to save the "morality" of self-abnegation and self-sacrifice, i.e., altruism. Since no rational basis can exist to support altruism (Aristotle, for example, successfully disqualified Plato's theory of Forms), what it has to be saved from in honesty is conceptual-centered consciousness and its prime faculty, reason. In order to fulfill his purpose, Kant conjures up a new version of Plato's Forms called the "noumenal" world and sets out to "prove" that the noumenal world by nature cannot be known, that it is out of reach of reason, while declaring all along that it is the world of "real" reality, "higher" truth, and "things in themselves."

Kant imperiously uses his noncontextual logic in proving his brazenly clear conclusion with unintelligible arguments that are full of evasions, equivocations, obfuscations, circumlocutions, and *non sequiturs*. He proclaims as self-evident what is in reality arbitrary or untrue, and provides erudite references to science as well as to pseudo-science to create an illusion of credibility. Thus, through his non-contextual inner logic and mind-paralyzing unintelligibility, Kant cleverly shifts morality from the sphere of reason to the domain of faith and declares that what cannot be known by reason (the noumenal world —the source of morality) can be *believed,* whereby making morality exempt from reason.

Kant asserts that the human mind by nature distorts reality because everything that is conceived by consciousness is conceived through automatic filters in consciousness (termed *categories*). Thus, according to him, reality as conceived by consciousness is inherently *subjective,* and objective reality, the noumenal world or things in themselves, forever remains on the other shore of reason not to be known but only to be believed. Therefore, consciousness, because it is consciousness, because it is a cognitive faculty — because of its very *identity* as a cognitive faculty, cannot cognize reality as such.

If reality conceived by consciousness were in truth *inherently* subjective and, therefore, relative, then his entire philosophy itself would lose its claim to truth. For, *any statement that is made with regard to reality demands itself to be objective.* A statement that reality is subjective is inescapably self-contradictory and negates its own validity. In point of fact, Kant's philosophy is an extremely clever exploitation of a common misunderstanding concerning objectivity.

Objectivity, epistemologically speaking, is the state of cognition that acquires knowledge of reality by means of reason in accordance with logic, the principle of noncontradictory identification. Epistemologically, objectivity rests upon the universality of reason and logic. Metaphysically speaking, objectivity is the recognition of the fact that reality exists independent of consciousness...of any particular state of consciousness. Metaphysically too, objectivity rests upon the universality of reason and logic.

Metaphysical objectivity, the fact that reality exists independent of consciousness, does not mean that reality exists beyond the reach of consciousness, as Kant maintains, but it means that reality exists beyond any arbitrary factor of the cognitive experience, beyond anyone's feeling, emotion, wish, or awareness/unawareness. Through the universal means of reason that accords itself with logic — the universal principle of noncontradictory identification, one can always apprehend and comprehend reality that is objective and immutable (see Chapter 4 of this treatise).

What is required is not faith or belief but discipline — the discipline to use one's consciousness in accordance with logic regardless of feelings, emotions, or wishes. Discipline is the process of consciously creating increasingly higher order within oneself. Philosophy is a discipline. Business is a discipline. Kant's philosophy offers the most clever rationale in history for the evasion of discipline, any discipline that is required for a rational apprehension of reality.

Kant's philosophy had a devastating impact on subsequent history. Both Marxism and Nazism have their philosophical roots in Kantian epistemology and ethics — the epistemology not of knowledge but of blind faith and the morality of self-sacrifice and self-abnegation. All current philosophies, which are in reality anti-philosophies, such as existentialism, pragmatism, and "logical" positivism which proclaims, *inter alia*, that one cannot prove that he exists, grew out of Kant. Kant's philosophy indeed was the culmination of Platonism, and became the temple of mystics and the Bible of neocheaters.

The still-prevailing Platonistic philosophy, mysticism, and neocheating around the world are indebted to Kant and his philosophy. If Plato is immoral, Kant is evil to the core of his soul, for he deliberately and knowingly undercut reason and consciousness, and thus the dignity of man as thoroughly as any human being can — a feat Plato could never have surpassed because of his professed respect for reason. (Authentic and generally sincere respect for reason was implicit in all Greek philosophies). Through Kant, philosophy became not only a useless exercise of the mind but also a lethal weapon of neocheating. Kant provided not only an opportunity for mediocre minds to feign an air of profundity but also an extremely powerful tool for clever mystics and neocheaters to rationalize their existence, which consists solely of destruction, manipulation, or plundering of others.

But now, through Neo-Tech, humanity has an *intellectual lie detector* by which an ordinary person can see through the neocheating labyrinth of Immanuel Kant and the mystical edifice of Plato. The hidden advantage of master neocheaters such as Kant rests solely upon the fact that they know untruth as untruth and nonreality as nonreality, while others are made to believe untruth as truth and nonreality as reality. However, no matter how clever Kant is or how brilliant Plato is, they can never deny reality *in reality*. Reality is there...to be known and to be integrated. Neo-Tech offers not only an integrated picture of reality but also, through its matrix-structure, definitive tools for the conceptual integration of reality.

Through Neo-Tech, people will be able to see that the philosophical labyrinth of Kant is nothing save an extremely clever scheme for concealing his incompetence as a thinker and manipulating others into believing his conclusions with no regard to truth and reality. Through Neo-Tech, people will also be able to see that the mystical edifice of Plato is nothing save a brilliant fabrication for controlling others and imposing his own will onto reality. Through Neo-Tech, reality will consistently reveal its commanding presence, shine forth upon the darkness of nonreality, and cast away that which has never in reality existed except in the minds of men under the spell of mysticism and its symbiotic neocheating.

(2) The grand myth that there is an inherent inadequacy or scarcity of life support such as food or money (symbolizing real value) on this planet:

In 1800, after receiving a complete inventory of the world's vital and economic statistics for the first time in history, Thomas Malthus, later professor of political economics at the East India Company College, concluded that the world population was increasing at a rate of geometrical progression, whereas life-support production was increasing only at a rate of arithmetical progression. In 1810 he confirmed this earlier finding. Thomas Malthus thus proved mathematically what people all over the world had innately believed since the beginning of human history, that there was an inherent inadequacy of life support on the planet and that the situation would become progressively worse.

"Pray all you want," said Malthus, "it will do you no good. There is no more!" A half-century later, Charles Darwin developed his theory of evolution, propounding that the inexorable processes of nature were the consequence of the "survival only of the fittest species and individuals within those species." Karl Marx compounded both Malthus's and Darwin's scientifically convincing conclusions in order to "prove" his predecided point, and said, in effect, "The proletariat are the fittest to survive, for they are the ones who know how to handle the tools and seeds to produce the life support. The opulent others, the bourgeoisie, are mere parasites."

The opulent others argued semi-rationally, "We are opulent and at the top of the heap because we have successfully demonstrated the Darwinian principle, survival of the fittest. The workers are dull-minded and have no vision. What is of essence for survival in this world is cunning, intellectual fighting skills, and farsighted enterprise." For the last century these two political/economic ideologies, communism and so-called capitalism, have dominated the political affairs of the world — both coming from the assumption that there is not enough to go around.

However, missing in Malthus's theory was a critical understanding regarding the power of the human mind and consciousness, as well as consideration concerning the possible evolution of human knowledge. He disregarded or failed to see that knowledge could and did indeed increase at a geometric-progression rate that would far exceed the growth of human population, overcoming the seemingly inevitable paucity of life support on Earth. The advancement of scientific and technological knowledge, which includes the food-production/distribution technology and the development of the birth-control pill, has long eradicated the once universal and seemingly inevitable inadequacy of life-supporting goods. In a world where there are sufficient numbers of producers who produce more than they consume, inadequacy of life support or overpopulation is categorically impossible. And once mysticism and neocheating are eradicated from the planet — once the Neo-Tech world comes into existence, *each* human being will always produce more values than he or she can ever consume, so that the impossibility of the inadequacy of life support or overpopulation will further become self-evident.

However, in spite of the clear evidence that humanity now has more than enough life support and everyone on this planet can be self-sufficiently wealthy if he or she works honestly and productively within his or her capability to produce values for others, the political neocheaters continue to propagate and exploit that age-old myth of inadequacy in order to stay in "power" and control the misguided populace. The religious neocheaters apply the myth of scarcity to their "Heaven" and say, in effect, "There is not enough space out there in the heaven, and in order to be the fittest to survive in that world, you must follow our teaching and donate your money and soul to prove that you are indeed worthy of survival after your death."

This is a clear example of creating problems where none in fact exist. The increasing sufficiency of life support on Earth indicates an entirely new era of human life and history: War is unnecessary. Governmental politics is unnecessary. All manipulation, deception, and physical force are unnecessary. In other words, neocheating in every form is unnecessary and in reality obsolete. For every man and woman can now live with an ever-increasing standard of living, and achieve genuine wealth, prosperity, and happiness through his or her own honest, rational, and productive effort, thinking, and action without ever destroying others. With Neo-Tech and its complete annihilation of mysticism and neocheating, the one most able to survive — the honest and rational individual — now becomes what he or she deserves to be, the fittest to survive.

Neo-Tech shows every conscious being the way to become a true producer of values, and works as a catalyst in bringing forth a world of ever-evolving happiness and prosperity with the only rational, value-oriented, natural-to-humans social/political/economic system, i.e., *laissez-faire*, free-enterprise capitalism. And it is on the basis of increasing sufficiency of life support on Earth that the value-oriented Neo-Tech business world — a profit-oriented, *laissez-faire*, free-enterprise capitalist society — is built. Value is the actualized knowledge or accomplished technological capacity that protects, nurtures, supports, and accommodates all growing needs of life. Money is the effective means of exchanging disparate and nonequitable items of real value. In a rational business world, the relationship of money

572

or profit to real value will be logically authenticated, and money or profit will follow the production of values naturally.

(3) National division: Since war is in reality obsolete, national division only serves as a means of protecting an individual who happened to choose living in a particular location on this planet so that he can exercise his free will, free choice, and free action in pursuing his productive career.   It is not nations but individuals and companies that must compete in creating and producing values higher than others in the same business.   It is not to nations but to themselves that individuals must belong.   It is not with nations but with companies that they must identify themselves.   For it is not where one lives but what he does to create values for others that is of significance.   People do not and cannot choose their birth, their place of birth, or their parents.   People do choose and must choose, however, what careers to pursue and which companies or organizations to work for (including their own).   Society, therefore, must be structured on the basis of people's conscious choices, and people should not be bound by things over which they can have no choice whatsoever, such as their birthplace, sex, or color.

The world's neocheating power structures have always "divided to conquer" and have always "kept divided to keep conquering."   As a consequence, the neocheating power structures have so divided humanity — not only into special-function categories but also into religious, national, language, and color categories — that humanity at large has lost its ability to distinguish between earned values such as knowledge, skill, or character and coincidental attributes such as color or nationality. It is imperative to structure the world on the basis of earned values and people's free choice or will.   Neo-Tech makes a clear identification of the human value system and helps to create a world in which every individual is identified not in terms of accidental attributes but of earned values acquired through his conscious choice and effort.

People do not belong to their countries.   People do not have any obligation to their countries.   People's obligation is only to themselves and to their dependent children.   No one should hinder others from fulfilling their obligation.   It is to that extent, and to that extent only, that people are collectively responsible for one another's well-being. The current national division, to a large extent, is the result of the "real-estate war" fought over the centuries amongst power-hungry, physical-property-coveting neocheaters. A nation is a nonfundamental entity that exists solely on the basis of agreements among individuals. What is fundamental is a conscious individual human being who, unlike nations, can think, create, and produce. Nations cannot exist without people, but people can exist without nations — probably much more happily and successfully.

Collectivism, therefore, is an inversion of reality. Individualism based upon the sound recognition that a conscious individual is the highest cause and the supreme value in existence is the only reality-based moral, ethical, political philosophy there is. In the future Neo-Tech world, countries will be recognized for what they really are, i.e., agreed-upon divisions for the convenience of living together. In the future Neo-Tech world, the planet will be seen as dynamic, synergetic interactions among companies and businesses whose *Primum Mobiles* (Prime movers) are the productive, energetic Neo-Tech men and women living happily and prosperously as the permanent residents of the universe.

(4) Over specialization of knowledge: Because of the successive master neocheaters' extremely effective strategy of specializing knowledge, universities around the world still continue to divide and subdivide the otherwise-integrated sphere of knowledge into many fragments. As a consequence, the great majority of humanity is incapable of understanding the language of science, the most highly specialized field of knowledge. In addition, the educator/philosophers who belong to the John Dewey-genre school of thought and fundamentalist/creationist religious fanatics further spur humanity into scientific illiteracy. Furthermore, scientists and mathematicians often base their philosophical thinking upon Platonistic principles, or completely divorce themselves from philosophical thought, resulting in a highly fragmented and isolated utilization of Aristotelian principles.

Therefore, humanity at large does not realize that all that

science has ever come to know is the fact that the physical universe consists of an interreciprocating technology with exquisite design principles, which consciousness discovers and harnesses to create all human technology. The great majority of people think that technology is a "new" phenomenon and identify it with (1) weapons and/or (2) machines, the latter, competing with them for their jobs. Because of these notions (or misconceptions) and all the antitechnology propaganda by the mystics and neocheaters, most people erroneously think that they are against technology, without realizing that the technology they do not understand and are against is a *sine qua non* for achieving never-before-possible prosperity and happiness on Earth. (Nothing inherent in technology causes environmental pollution. Further technological advances will soon solve the problem if there is no government interference.)

Business not only requires a wide integration of knowledge but also is the integrating force of knowledge. It is in business that various fields of knowledge meet and together produce values that have never before existed. It is in business that science and technology bear their fruits and transform nature into values. It is in business that philosophy meets the challenge of life and finds its application in the productive sphere of human life. Therefore, the overspecialization of knowledge that humanity has experienced since time immemorial and still continues to experience implies that the function of business in society has been continuously truncated until today. Furthermore, in the current system of university education, business itself is seen as a specialized field and taught mostly by professors who have never been in business themselves. In reality, business is not a specialized field but a synthesis of other fields of knowledge which integrates philosophy, science, and technology into a system of value production encompassing the entire sphere of human existence.

Overspecialization of knowledge, on the one hand, brought about a scientific/mathematical *esotericism* that is inaccessible to the general public and at times divorced from reality, and on the other hand, effected the truncation of the function and the purpose of business. Neo-Tech, through its full integration of philosophical principles, reveals a stunningly new picture of the

575

universe and opens a new path of science that is not only free of Platonism (a divorce from reality) but also will bring a new revolution/evolution of scientific knowledge that is accessible to every conscious being, which, then, in turn will make possible the world-wide realization of highly advanced technological societies and scientific literacy. It further reveals an integrated picture of business and its function not only in human societies but also in the universe. In the final two chapters of this treatise, the science of the future and the never-before realized purpose of business are explored.

9. The Neo-Tech Revolution

Every time knowledge reaches a new height, a whole new dimension of the unknown unfolds right in front of our eyes. We become aware of a dimension of the unknown which we previously did not know that we did not know. Since all of human knowledge is based on finite experience, there is always a sphere of existence or a dimension of reality that is as yet unknown. Knowledge perennially begets new dimensions of the unknown, which in turn begets new realms of knowledge and expands forever into infinity.

The Copernican Revolution revealed to humanity the fact that there is absolutely no "up" or "down", "above" or "below" in the universe, nor does the Sun "rise" or "set" on the Earth. An apple does not fall "down" to the ground; it simply collides with the surface of the Earth. What then is gravity? The Copernican Revolution not only totally transformed humanity's philosophical conception of the universe but also brought to light a whole new dimension of the unknown and a whole new set of questions. And the history of science since Copernicus has been that of a continual unfolding of new discoveries, new unknowns, new questions, and new realms of knowledge.

The Copernican Revolution laid ground for Newton's discovery of *universal gravitation*, which in turn, with other brilliant discoveries, made possible Einstein's *Theory of Relativity* and quantum physics of the 20th century. Beginning with Einstein, physicists around the world began a new search, an extraordinary intellectual enterprise, to give a complete description of the foundation of matter, space, and time with a single set of linked equations that contains the elements of the entire universe — a theory formally known as the unification theory or the unified field theory and referred to, half-humorously, as the Theory of Everything (TOE). Einstein spent his later life searching for a unification theory — in vain. Others in the late 20th century are coming increasingly closer to a TOE in a strictly physical sense through highly complex manipulations of mathematical/geometrical formulations such as in the superstring theory.

Within this historical context, Neo-Tech reveals an *in toto* different, new unification theory that will mark a new Copernican Revolution of scientific knowledge: the Neo-Tech Revolution. Throughout the history of science, consciousness has been seen only as a passive observer and conceptual integrator of cosmic phenomena, having nothing whatsoever to do with the destiny of the universe. Some in the field of quantum physics challenge that notion, and assert that the observer and the observed are inextricably linked and constitute one unified field or context of reality, and therefore consciousness could be a participating/contributing element in the destiny of the universe.

However, quantum physics, and science in general, lack the crucial knowledge and system of identification regarding the nature of consciousness. Thus, while quantum physics is an extremely efficient mathematical tool in predicting the subatomic phenomena, it fails to provide a unified theory concerning the nature of reality and the destiny of the universe. Moreover, some physicists indulge themselves in the mystical notion of "cosmic consciousness" due, partly, to the lack of knowledge with respect to consciousness and, mainly, to the philosophical poverty within the scientific community.

On the basis of Julian Jaynes' discovery and Aristotelian principles, the Neo-Tech unification theory states that consciousness — not some "cosmic" consciousness, which does not and cannot exist in reality, but "earthly" consciousness, which human beings and other conscious beings throughout the universe possess — is not only an essential component of reality but also the dominating force of the universe. The Neo-Tech unification theory demonstrates, on the basis of Einstein's model of the physical universe, that only through conscious beings' accumulation, integration and harnessing of knowledge, and utilization of technology therefrom, can the universe sustain its cosmic order eternally. And conscious beings sustain the cosmic order of the universe not just to maintain the universe *per se* but to sustain their own existence in the universe. For conscious beings always recognize the supreme value of individual consciousness within a universe, and therefore realize that conscious life must be sustained forever.

The Neo-Tech unification theory proves that consciousness *is* the mightiest controlling power in the universe and that each conscious being possesses that mightiest power equally in abundance, regardless of his or her native intelligence. The pre-eminent feature of this theory is that, even if the model of the physical universe employed in its exploration — *the long-wave/ short-wave model* — is proved wrong or incorporated into a larger model, its fundamental thesis will remain eternally true — for no matter what the physical or mathematical laws of the universe are, conscious beings will always discover and harness them to their greatest advantages. If an imminent annihilation of the physical universe approaches (as *the long wave/short wave model* suggests), a conscious being will literally create a new galaxy to sustain its life and maintain the cosmic order of the universe (see "We The Creators of Heavens and Earths" by Frank R. Wallace, 1986, I & O Publishing).

The first step toward that mightiest power on Earth is the complete elimination of mystics and their symbiotic neocheaters. The entire Neo-Tech literature including this treatise is dedicated to that purpose. The second step toward that mightiest power on Earth is to achieve commercial biological immortality. Life, as explored in the fourth chapter, is an *autopoietic*-cognitive process, and there is nothing in the nature of life that dictates that a living system has to perish and die, particularly a conscious living system such as a human being, for life as such is innately self-regenerative. Then, why is there the process of aging and the phenomenon of dying? The process of aging is the result of life's mathematically inevitable *aberration probability* of regenerative process. Each cell in the body continuously copies and recopies (self-regenerates) itself with some (mathematically inevitable) slight aberrations along the way, and the accumulation of those aberrations over the years is what is called aging. When the body is well cared for in a proper environment with proper nutrition, the aberration probability will be greatly reduced.

When the degree of accumulated aberrations exceeds the degree of accuracy in regenerative copying, the body ceases to regenerate itself and eventually dies (death is the cessation of *autopoiesis* — self-generation, and therefore of cognition/consciousness). The aberration probability, generally speaking, increases gradually as time passes (because the regenerative mechanism itself is subject to the aberration probability), and the body ages steadily. However, the aging process can be greatly prolonged and humanity of the future will be able to live an extremely long life — probably three to four hundred years very easily — as the technology to measure and control the aberration probability is developed; and when the probability is controlled to zero, an individual can literally live forever.

There are several different ways to achieve biological immortality. Human cloning is one. One is to recreate electrochemically an individual's entire body, which includes his brain and total information stored therein, by reducing his integrated physical pattern into a set of mathematical equations and measuring the balance and quantity of the 92 chemical components in his body. And then those 92 measured chemical substances would be electrically reconstructed into an exact replica of his body through such technologies as advanced nanotechnology. Finally, his integrated mental pattern would be transferred into his new body electroholographically. The basic method of electrical reconstruction/transference can be applied to such purposes as transporting people to far corners of the universe electrically, or electrotransmitting mathematically equated integrated patterns of living organisms to an earth-like planet somewhere in the universe — to construct a life-environment on that planet, with the chemical elements available, in order to assure that conscious beings will eventually be present in a crucial location in the universe in keeping the cosmic balance and order of the whole universe.

The purpose of biological immortality, however, is not merely to reconstruct one's body and the information stored therein but

The Neo-Tech World

to preserve the self, the conscious core of one's being, what Frank R. Wallace calls the sense of *I-ness*. The self is the metaphysical/epistemological axis within the entire sphere of consciousness in relation to which all the information stored in the brain is structurally integrated. Through self-consciousness, the universe becomes divided into the self and the nonself, and experience begins. (Experience is the complex awareness of self coexisting with all the nonself.) The sense of *I-ness* sets consciousness in motion. It is the core of consciousness' *autopoiesis*; *it is the autopoiesis*. Therefore, the I-ness cannot be reconstructed by any means externally; it can only be transferred to trigger *autopoiesis* — and here lies the greatest technological challenge of biological immortality.

Consciousness does not age, because it is not a physical living process that regenerates to exist but a metaphysical phenomenon that generates itself solely through metaphysical concepts and principles, albeit it requires a living conscious agent to sustain its existence. For the self-interest of a conscious being, his or her own conscious life of rational necessity becomes the highest value, the supreme cause, in the whole universe. Therefore, his or her conscious life must always be sustained. The sustenance of conscious existence with the sense of *I-ness* and all of one's character/personality traits, thus, becomes the highest and the ultimate moral purpose of every conscious being living anywhere in the universe. Therefore, the purpose of biological immortality is to preserve oneself for the sake of oneself to achieve ever higher prosperity and happiness for oneself forever (see "Three Steps To Achieving Commercial Biological Immortality In Our Lifetime" by Frank R. Wallace, I & O Publishing).

Moreover, once commercial biological immortality becomes a reality, each conscious being's knowledge will infinitely expand, first accelerating at a tremendous rate of geometrical progression, and then eventually at the speed of light. Thus, the realization of commercial biological immortality serves the destiny of the whole universe as well. The achievement of commercial biological immortality indeed is the utmost moral purpose of present humanity on Earth. And the complete eradication of mysticism, internal as well as external, and of neocheating around the world, is an extremely urgent issue facing every man and

580

woman on this planet today. For mysticism and neocheating are the only obstacles to the achievement of commercial biological immortality and all other life-enhancing values that exist and will ever exist in the universe.

Through the eradication of mysticism and its symbiotic neocheaters, and the subsequent achievement of commercial biological immortality, humanity will begin to fulfill its cosmic function as the local information gatherer, knowledge integrator, and problem solver of the universe. Thus, through the realization of commercial biological immortality on the planet Earth, humanity can join the ranks of other highly advanced conscious beings existing throughout the universe who have not only achieved biological immortality but who have also attained the power for controlling the eternal destiny of the universe and for reigning over infinity.

Existence is not intertransformable with nonexistence; existence does not turn into nonexistence nor does nonexistence turn into existence. Therefore, the axiomatic fact of reality that existence exists proves that existence is eternal and infinite. Thus, the universe — the complex aggregate of all consciously apprehended and communicated experiences of events in existence — is *actually* eternal and *potentially* infinite. That means the universe has never had a beginning nor will it ever have an ending, nor can it possibly have any beginning or ending.

Given the infinity of existence and its eternal span of time, what is theoretically possible will occur infinite times in actuality. The fact that conscious beings exist on the planet Earth unequivocally proves that there have been and there will be billions upon billions of conscious beings existing throughout the universe. Moreover, the fact that commercial biological immortality is theoretically possible further proves that there have been and will be millions upon millions of conscious beings living eternally.

Conscious beings' accumulation of knowledge increases, first at a geometrical progression rate, then eventually at the speed of light. Thus, their power for controlling the universe and its destiny also increases at a tremendous rate. Therefore, the amount of knowledge and power that might be possessed by conscious beings who have achieved commercial biological immortality millions of years ago is totally beyond the imagination of current humanity on Earth. And probability statistics indicate that these highly advanced conscious beings exist not by the few but by the billions.

Furthermore, it is logically predicated that many of those highly advanced conscious beings have attained the power to control the entire universe, and that the universe is *virtually* run by them. For, as mentioned before, given an infinite span of time, what is theoretically possible will occur infinite times. Those conscious beings not only control the existing universe but also can freely create new universes, whereby infinitely expanding the realms of existence forever. The universe is the eternal scenario of existence written by those highly evolved conscious beings that exist throughout the whole universe. Through the achievement of commercial biological immortality on Earth, we, too, will someday be able to write the scenario of our own universe.

Neo-Tech is the name given on the planet Earth to the primordial essence of all knowledge that conscious beings can ever possess anywhere in the universe. And the primordial essence of the universe-controlling power that conscious beings will eventually claim is Neothink. Perceptivity-centered consciousness incorporates the present with the past in the context of the past. Conceptuality-centered consciousness incorporates the past with the present in the context of the present. While these two modalities are inherently fragmented and can never reach the universe-controlling power, Neothink integrates the future with the present and the past; it integrates the entirety of time — the future, the present, and the past, i.e., eternity. Neothink also integrates the unknown with the known; it integrates the entirety of existence, i.e., infinity.

What is Neothink? Neothink is the ultimate modality of conscious intellection that generates the context-creating matrices through which all ground-breaking integrations of knowledge can occur. Contexts define the structure of integration, and context generation is the finest function of consciousness. Neothink brings into existence a vast integration of knowledge that would be impossible for the other two modalities of consciousness, i.e., perceptivity-centered and conceptuality-centered modalities, precisely because the Neothink integration of knowledge is accomplished in a *self-created* context. Perceptivity-centered consciousness has no context at all. Conceptuality-centered consciousness integrates knowledge only in an existing context. It is Neothink that takes knowledge into new dimensions of integration by continually defining ever larger and finer contexts.

The great thinkers are distinguished not by their intelligence but by their ability to create a new context. In science, Newton and Einstein are the two greatest Neothinkers of modern history because they could create the fundamental contexts that determined the entire course of subsequent scientific development. In philosophy, Aristotle and Plato are the two greatest Neothinkers because they created the two fundamental contexts, albeit radically opposing, that determined the course not only of philosophy but of the entire history of mankind. (Aristotle defined the context for reality identification/integration, whereas Plato defined the context for nonreality generation/rationalization.)

Neothink is amoral. That is why some of the greatest Neothinkers such as Plato and Kant are master neocheaters. Neo-Tech is the first conceptual matrix for Neothink formation that is designed to counteract and overcome the force of Neothink-neocheaters. Neothink is intellectual nuclear power; it can destroy values and annihilate humanity completely if employed by master neocheaters, or it can bring eternal happiness to humanity and transform the universe forever if employed by Neo-Tech individuals. Thus, for the benefit of all humanity, it is urgent that Neo-Tech, the voice of fully integrated honesty, be heard and understood, and evolve into the Neo-Tech/Neothink matrix.

Context creation is the finest form of integration; it is the integration of integrations. Neothink is a two directional vector, as it were, whose two distinct magnitudes represent potential eternity and infinity. Context creation, the integration of integrations, moves into two directions by increasing its magnitudes ever closer, in one direction, to eternity and, in another, to infinity. As the zero yields infinity when it divides a given number, Neo-Tech, the philosophical zero, brings infinity and eternity into the realm of cognition when it captures the facts of reality in its fully integrated matrix/context. Hence, the Neo-

Tech/Neothink matrix is the finest and the vastest context-creating matrix-structure whose infinity/eternity grasping power can far surpass and thus can soon collapse the neocheating/Neothink matrix of master neocheaters.

By fully integrating Neo-Tech knowledge while dispelling mysticism and transcending both perceptivity-centered and conceptuality-centered modalities...by entering the sphere of Neothink, humanity will be able to realize that the universe is an eternally regenerative scenario composed and directed by conscious beings, and consisting of intricate interactions of eternal design principles that exist as the totality of eternally noncontradictory abstractions, i.e., as objective and immutable reality. It is truly remarkable that conscious beings should be able to comprehend these inexhaustible eternal design principles of the universe and immensely fine abstractions of reality, and, with Neothink, to control the manifest destiny of cosmic existence. And through its faultless logic, Neo-Tech eloquently demonstrates that consciousness, this infinite capacity to know and control, along with its growth into Neothink, is not an accident but an essential component of the eternal design of the cosmos.

With Neothink, conscious beings begin to fulfill their destiny. With Neothink, conscious beings begin to control or alter the manifest destiny of the universe. The Neothink consciousness is not only the conceptual integrator of the universe's design principles but also becomes the prime designer of the cosmos. Neo-Tech, the philosophical zero, made possible the dawn of Neothink, the rebirth of human consciousness to unprecedented heights and into full maturity. Now, consciousness on Earth begins a new journey toward the evolution, a mighty power without end — the eternal journey and unfoldment of the Neo-Tech Revolution/Evolution. And the whole *romance* of that eternal cosmic Neo-Tech journey is called BUSINESS.

10. The Universe, Inc.

Business is the integrated circuit of consciousness designed to produce values. Value is the actualized knowledge that protects, nurtures, supports, or accommodates all growing needs of life. The process of value production consists of four stages: (1) metaphysically conceiving potential values — the conception stage; (2) metaphysically/physically developing working models of previously conceived potential values — the development stage; (3) physically mass producing previously developed product-models — the production stage; (4) physically mass marketing product-values for consumption — the marketing stage.

The process of value production is a tetrahedral system (*time-tetrahedron*) that divides the universe into that which is relevant and that which is nonrelevant to the production of particular values. That which is relevant to the production of particular values includes: all the information and knowledge that are required; all the individuals who possess the information, knowledge, or skills that are required; and all the physical materials, equipment, space, and time that are needed to produce particular values.

Each stage of value production — each vertex of the *time-tetrahedron* — has a unique value-index which increases geometrically as the process of value production evolves from one stage to the next. (The Value-Scale was first identified by Frank R. Wallace — the following is a version devised by the author of this treatise):

VALUE-SCALE

Stage/Vertex	Value-Index	Value
The conception stage/Vertex 1	10^0	$10^0 X$
The development stage/Vertex 2	10^1	$10^1 X$
The production stage/Vertex 3	10^2	$10^2 X$
The marketing stage/Vertex 4	10^3	$10^3 X$

X = potential value of a product

Business is the integrated circuit of consciousness in which these four stages of value production take place. The integrated circuitry of business is a system (*space-tetrahedron,* which consists of four vertices — the individual, the corporate, the world, and the universe vertices) that integrates the energy configurations of the universe into a value-producing machine. Production of value is the process of transforming physical/mental energy into a physical product of physical/metaphysical value, wherefore, productivity is the function of efficacy in transforming energy into product. Productivity means the efficient use of energy or the economics of energy. Productivity is in inverse proportion to the amount of energy unconverted into a product of value. The maximization of productivity, therefore, ultimately means to bring energy-waste to zero.

Energy has patterns, and different tasks consist of different energy-patterns. For instance, writing an article or a book requires a unique integration of energy-patterns that is distinctly different from that of accounting, participating in meetings, or making phone calls. When one mixes two or more different integrations of energy-patterns together by shifting from one task to another or from one responsibility to another without any *control structure,* interferences of energy occur, and energy becomes wasted without ever being converted into a product of value. This happens at all four vertices of the *space-tetrahedron* — in the individual vertex, the corporate vertex, the world vertex, and the universe vertex.

Numerous attempts have been made to discover the Neo-Tech law of productivity operating at every vertex of business or the *space-tetrahedron* — the law of minimizing the interferences of energy in the organization of business. Productive individuals from time to time get a glimpse of the law at a personal level — at their individual vertices. Productive CEOs from time to time come to realize the law at their personal and corporate levels — at their individual and corporate vertices. Super productive industrial giants, such as Jay Gould and Henry Ford, from time to time discover the law at a personal, corporate, and world level — at individual, corporate, and world vertices. Creative scientists, such as Newton and Einstein, from time to time identify the law at a universe level — at their universe vertices (in the form of the laws of physics or the natural economics of the universe).

However, no system of knowledge or field of science has ever fathomed and comprehensively identified the law of productivity at all four vertices of business *space-tetrahedron*. Business is the highest expression of consciousness and the most integrated form of technology through which the integrity of the universe is forever maintained — through which conscious beings transform nature into values and control the eternal destiny of the cosmos. Before Neo-Tech and Neothink, no one understood the cosmic significance of business and, consequently, no one was able to unleash the power of business to its fullest, for no one knew what consciousness is and what relationship it has to/with the rest of the universe. And now, the Neo-Tech knowledge takes every man and woman to the summit of consciousness — *business integration*; and Neothink lets every business unleash its immense power to the fullest and transforms the entire universe into THE UNIVERSE, INC.

Business is the integrated circuit of consciousness designed to produce values — to transform nature's technology (the physical universe) into values. The physical universe is the aggregate of energy configurations in existence. Every configuration of energy is a unique energy-pattern with its own set of separately unique frequencies. For instance, each chemical element is uniquely identifiable in the electromagnetic spectrum by its own set of unique frequencies. None of the 92 chemical elements thus far discovered in nature is the same as any of the others in its individual set of frequencies. Now, as the physical universe consists of 92 indivisible chemical elements, the whole mechanics of business can be seen as an interactive combination of unique sets of indivisible *physical movements*. That is, the entire process of business can be divided into unique sets of indivisible physical movements. (Physical movements of business were first identified by Mark Hamilton in his "Neo-Tech Control.")

A phone call as a physical movement is a unique and indivisible physical movement regardless of for whom it is intended and to what project it belongs. Similarly, letter writing, copy writing, accounting, and meeting participation can all be seen as unique, indivisible physical movements. By dividing the process of business into its fundamental physical units —

sets of indivisible physical movements — the interferences of energy in business can be greatly reduced and, as a result, the availability and the concentration of energy can be immensely increased. This is the first principle of the Neo-Tech law of productivity: Divide the process of business into its fundamental units or sets of indivisible physical movements — **The Principle of Division**. ...This principle applies to all four vertices of the business *space-tetrahedron* (see "Neo-Tech Control" by Mark Hamilton, I & O Publishing).

Having divided the process of business into its fundamental units of physical movements, in order to produce a maximum effect, these units must be combined, within the flow of time, into an integrated whole. In nature, two hydrogen atoms combined with one oxygen atom produce one water molecule ($2H + O = H_2O$). The nature or behavior of the final product (a water molecule) is totally unpredictable from the natures or behaviors of its components (hydrogen and oxygen atoms) taken separately (*the principle of synergy*). In metallurgy, a combination of iron, chromium, nickel, and other minor elements (carbon, manganese, and others) produces an alloy — chrome-nickel-steel. The tensile strength of iron is about 60,000 pounds per square inch (p.s.i.), of chromium about 70,000 p.s.i., of nickel about 80,000 p.s.i., and of other minor constituents put together about 50,000 p.s.i. However, the tensile strength of chrome-nickel-steel, which is about 350,000 p.s.i., far exceeds the average tensile strength of all the constituents combined (about 65,000 p.s.i.). This is another example of the synergetic phenomenon.

Similarly, in combining all the sets of unique physical movements, the effect or the outcome of integrating the fundamental units is synergetic and totally unpredictable from the separate effect of each set of physical movements. However, through experience, one can find the most effective or powerful combination/integration that produces the greatest result in his/ her work or business. The designed structure of the most effective combination is termed the *control structure* of business. Furthermore, each day of one's work or each division/function of a company is a uniquely indivisible unit of physical movements, and the *control structure* should be applied to one's long-range career or a company's wide-range business integration.

This is the second principle of the Neo-Tech law of productivity: Integrate the units of physical movements to produce maximum synergetic effects or results through a *control structure* — **The Principle of Synergetic Integration**. ...This principle applies to all four vertices of the business *space-tetrahedron*.

The third principle of the Neo-Tech law of productivity is concerned with the integration of the future with the totality of the present and the past, and requires Neothink. The success of a business is always dependent upon the creation of new values, and the creation of new values is dependent upon one's ability to see *what is not*. For example, Henry Ford saw early in his life that automobiles were *not* in use as a means of transportation in the world. The means of transportation was the horse. *What was not* was an affordable automobile that would replace a horse forever. Henry Ford, through his Neothink ingenuity, converted what was not into what was. His division of labor/assembly line concept was another example of his Neothink ingenuity. Frank R. Wallace realized that there was no science or technology for identifying neocheaters and their secret weapons. The product of his Neothink applications was Neo-Tech.

The future of every business depends upon one's ability to create the future — the ability to see what is not. And that ability is Neothink. After integrating the entire physical process of business through the *control structure*, one must look into the future and integrate it with the present business-movement to create new values by converting what is not into what is. The conversion of what is not into what is requires an enormously vast integration of knowledge and an effective application of Neothink. The presence of mysticism within a business severely limits its ability to create and integrate the future. Where there is mysticism, there is no integrated business, no effective value production, and no Neothink. The third principle of the Neo-Tech law of productivity, therefore, is: **The Principle of Future-Integration**. This principle applies to all four vertices of the business *space-tetrahedron*.

The fourth principle of the Neo-Tech law of productivity is: **The Principle of Contextual Integration**. As mentioned in previous chapters, Neothink integrates not only the future with the present and the past but also the unknown with all the known. Neothink is the contextuality-centered modality of consciousness in which the considerations of the whole system/context precede the considerations of its subsystems/subcontexts. The fourth principle of the Neo-Tech law of productivity — the Principle of Contextual Integration — means that business, in order to maximize the quality and quantity of value production, must begin with a consideration of the whole business context *before* considering its component-parts. The largest whole context in existence is the universe physically, and consciousness metaphysically. That is why it is imperative to capture the universe conceptually and comprehend the inner mechanics of consciousness. Before Neo-Tech/Neothink, no one was ever able to fully grasp the nature of the universe and understand consciousness. And that is the very reason why no business could ever achieve the ultimate in business integration and productivity. With Neo-Tech/Neothink, business will soar to new heights of integration and productivity.

In a business context, all four vertices of the *space-tetrahedron* are integrated with the law of productivity and the energy-interference in business is brought, in essence, to zero, the *time-tetrahedron* becomes interlocked with the *space-tetrahedron* and the universe emerges as THE UNIVERSE, INC. ...Business becomes the whole energy-configurations of the entire universe, and consciousness begins to control the eternal destiny of the cosmos. Neo-Tech/Neothink integration of consciousness will then dominate the course of the cosmos, and nature's technology — the physical universe — will be transformed into the technology of conscious beings.

The Neo-Tech Revolution in essence is the emergence of THE UNIVERSE, INC. with Neothink as the highest integration of the business mind. With the rise of Neo-Tech in the world, business will flourish in its full glory. The center of scientific/technological research/development/revolution will shift from the academe into the business community. In fact, the academe will be absorbed into the business community, becoming a part of the Neo-Tech/Neothink integration of business. In the future Neo-Tech/Neothink universe, no one will be able to survive successfully without the business integration of Neo-Tech and the business application of Neothink, and without being a fully integrated producer of increasingly higher values.

Great days are coming, and a great eternity is commencing for those who choose life over death, honesty over dishonesty, effort over laziness — Neo-Tech over mysticism and neocheating. But for those who choose death over life, dishonesty over honesty, laziness over effort — mysticism and neocheating over Neo-Tech, their days are numbered. For those who strive for honesty, knowledge, prosperity, and happiness while producing ever higher values for others, the possibilities are infinite. The whole universe awaits the transformation into values. For those who strive for nothing while usurping and extracting ever more values from others, no possibility is left but death and the universe turns into emptiness, void — the barren nothingness of the existentialist. No one can escape the powerful wave of the Neo-Tech Revolution/Evolution unchanged. One will either perish into darkness by choosing to remain a mystic or neocheater, or by choosing Neo-Tech/Neothink to become a true producer of values, evolve into a shining sun of consciousness around which the whole universe revolves. There is a choice — a choice between life and death, between Neo-Tech/Neothink and mysticism/neocheating — between the ultimate value and the ultimate disvalue...the choice that every conscious being must now make.

Epilogue

Three and a half million years have passed since humanity first appeared on this planet, and 3000 years since the dawn of conscious life. Over the millennia, humanity has acquired an enormous amount of knowledge and produced a universe of values. It is totally beyond our imagination how much advancement in knowledge we may make and how much more value we may produce in 3000 years or three and a half million years from today. It is utterly awe-inspiring to think about what knowledge, what technology, what power we will have to control the destiny of our universe in 3000 or three and a half million years. As the geocentric concept or even the heliocentric system now appears to us as primitive and moribund, our present knowledge and technology will appear totally primitive and obsolete to the humanity of those distant futures. However, that future humanity could be us — Neo-Tech men and women — today living on the beautiful planet we call the Earth.

Three and a half million years from now, we will still remember the time when the Neo-Tech Revolution began. We will recall the time before the Revolution when people still had to submit to neocheaters and die. We will then remember the time when the mystics and neocheaters around the world finally surrendered to the power of the Neo-Tech wave, and the time when humanity achieved its first commercial biological immortality. We will know then that the source which made the Revolution possible still remains the source, the entire source, of our knowledge and journey into the unknown, forevermore. We will say to ourselves...

"Still in our hands are the copies of a manuscript that made it all possible. It still stands at the pinnacle of our knowledge. After these three and a half million years, after we have long achieved the speed-of-light acceleration of human knowledge, it still remains the primordial essence of our knowledge. Therefore, we keep this manuscript in token of what we have accomplished ever since and what we can achieve henceforth. We keep this manuscript in celebration of our forever-growing happiness and prosperity, and of our eternal life at the center of the universe — in the office of THE UNIVERSE, INC. The name of this manuscript is **NEO-TECH** — THE PRIMORDIAL ESSENCE OF ALL KNOWLEDGE AND POWER."

Appendix D
Neo-Tech Networkings

"*F*or 2000 years, neocheaters had prophesied that the world would end late in the 20th century. Now, today, early in the 21st century, their world is indeed ending. Their world is ending through the emerging other world — the world of fully integrated honesty, the world of Neo-Tech. Their world, being an uncompetitive remnant of nature's bicameral past, is fatally diseased with mysticism. Thus, in their final war with Neo-Tech, their dying world will crumble to nothing."

— Frank R. Wallace

A Neo-Tech World

The Neo-Tech World based on the coming God-Man mentality — the next and final evolution of man — will occur sometime in the 21st century. This Appendix of the approaching Neo-Tech World is not so much based on anyone's ideas per se as it is based on *what will logically survive* the changes under man's new God-Man mentality.

I set up twelve Neo-Tech Networking Boards on the Internet that let you network with others. Let us review the general idea behind each Neo-Tech Networking (NTN) Board at www.neo-tech.com:

Neo-Tech Networking Board
The Neo-Tech Party

Making the People Wealthy

The Neo-Tech Party stands for new (Neo) technology (Tech). The platform is built on two premises: 1) the Neo-Tech Party would free the geniuses and potential geniuses of society by ending government regulations; 2) in turn, new technology would soar ahead in all industries, as already demonstrated in the relatively nonregulated computer industry, sending consumer costs to fractions...making the consumers — the people — wealthy.

The Neo-Tech World

Six Campaign Visions of Wealthy Living

The Neo-Tech Party simplifies the Twelve Visions into Six Campaign Visions that most benefit the man in the street:

The First Vision: The people are well taken care of by the geniuses of society, rising by the many millions as the Neo-Tech President and Neo-Tech lawmakers end government regulations. The millions of geniuses drive technologies into new dimensions that bring undreamt of values to the people.

The Second Vision: The costs for those new technologies keep falling toward zero, similar to computers during the original computer revolution. The great Technological Revolution happening in all industries makes ordinary people more and more wealthy as costs in all industries keep falling.

The Third Vision: The new technologies, racing ahead in all industries, especially race ahead in the medical industry without the destructive FDA regulations holding the geniuses back. The geniuses eradicate disease after disease and drive down medical costs. People live with nearly perfect health, well into their hundreds, or longer.

The Fourth Vision: Businesses strive to keep up in the rapid progress of the great Technological Revolution; everything changes as businesses, to stay competitive, concentrate on bringing out their greatest asset — the unique creativity of their employees. Soon, ordinary people experience extraordinary entrepreneurial-like jobs, and they love going to work. Ordinary people also share in the profits they create.

The Fifth Vision: The wonderful falling-in-love feelings in the early weeks of romantic relationships never fade. Why? People are no longer sinking in stagnation. Instead, they are successful and soaring in the livelihoods of their dreams. With that ongoing source of happiness inside, filling them and overflowing into their romantic relationships, they forever feel the power of love.

The Sixth Vision: Ordinary people become smarter than today's richest people. Heretofore, ordinary people awaited their instructions in life from work, from the media, from the government and from the church, from the Establishment. In the Neo-Tech World, however, instead of being told how to live, ordinary people begin integrating knowledge to lead themselves. They begin snapping together knowledge into growing success puzzles at work and life in general. They see through illusions and no longer need or want to be led by "authorities". The need for a ruling class and its regulations becomes repulsive to the super smart self-leaders. The old structure of government can not survive in the new mentality and yields to the geniuses. A new way of living — wealthy living — takes over.

Nothing To Do With Political Ideas
(Everything To Do With An "Evolutionary Jump")

The Neo-Tech Party's platform has little to do with political ideas. Instead, the platform represents the new political structure after the next evolution of man, which has already begun. Political structures, ironically, are not based on political ideas; they are fundamentally based on man's mentality. Heretofore, our political structure along with the other basic structures of civilization have been based on mankind's mentality from the past, known as the bicameral mentality. The bicameral mentality goes back to over 3000 years ago when people's minds regularly hallucinated the voices of the gods emanating from statues, tombs, pyramids or other awe-inspiring objects of worship, telling man what to do and how to live his life.

Today's mentality still functions in that bicameral fashion. Instead of voices of the gods, however, people let the voices of politicians and regulatory bureaucrats tell them what to do and how to live their lives. In short, the current and past mentalities seek to be told how to live by some outside authority.

But the next evolution of man has begun. The mentality of the future looks inside to one's own honest, integrating mind for authorization.

All those government programs for the so-called "social good" with politicians telling us how to spend our money, and all those regulatory programs with bureaucrats telling us how to run our businesses...none of those programs could survive the new mentality that no longer accepts being told what to do. Perhaps now you can understand that the Neo-Tech platform of 1) removing government programs that are on the offense telling people how to live their lives, and 2) reducing government to programs of defense only, protecting individuals from physical aggression...is *not* based on my political ideas per se. The platform is simply the new political structure based on the new God-Man mentality of no external "authorities" telling us how to live our lives. Therefore, as mankind makes its final evolution, the Neo-Tech Party will be the only political survivor.

Now you can understand where the issues of the Neo-Tech Party are coming from: *The Solar Eclipse Budget* that eclipses over a trillion-and-a-half dollars from the budget to eliminate the solar-high spending programs for the "social good" and to eliminate the regulatory bureaucracies, leaving only a half-trillion dollars for national defense and interest on the debt...well, now you can see that such issues are much more than mere political ideas; they represent a new political structure for the new mentality of no external "authorities" telling us how to live.

Surviving the New Mentality

Businessmen and women who have no interest in political careers will join the Neo-Tech Party across the country, a phenomenon called the *Great Replacement Program* as we say good-bye forever to the career politician. There will be no such thing as career politicians telling us how to live our lives in the new mentality of no external "authorities".

Government programs for the "social good", including the regulatory bureaucracies, will now go to the private sector. Now, instead of politicians serving themselves and their political agendas, millions of geniuses will be serving you — the consumer. This phenomenon is called the *Great Displacement Program* as we say good-bye forever to so-called political "social good". There will be no such thing as bureaucrats telling us how to spend our monies or run our businesses in the new mentality of no external "authorities".

As we displace those programs and services to the private sector, the Federal government will have a huge sale — selling off everything that has nothing to do with defense. The trillions of dollars generated from the sale of big government will repay every American's past contributions toward Social Security *with interest*. Then, when everyone is repaid with interest, the Social Security program for the so-called "social good" will be terminated. Social Security telling us how to save our monies could never survive in the new mentality of no external "authorities".

The only government that could survive the rapidly approaching new mentality is a protection service, a government of defense protecting individual and property rights from physical aggression. A half-trillion dollar budget is all that is needed to do that. The other trillion-and-a-half dollars that goes to government on the offense, telling individuals how to live, will not survive the new mentality of no external "authorities".

The new government structure of defense will serve one Universal Law of Individual Rights. In fact, it's so short, clear, and indivisible, anyone can memorize it as his or her anchor to freedom and recite it in about two minutes anytime, anywhere to uphold it and forever protect it:

The Universal Law

Preamble
The purpose of human life is to prosper and live happily. The function of society is to guarantee those conditions that allow all individuals to fulfill their purpose. Those conditions can be guaranteed through a constitution that forbids the use of initiatory force or coercion by any person or group against any individual:

The Constitution
Article 1: No person, group of persons, or government may initiate force, threat of force, or fraud against any individual's self or property.

Article 2: Force may be morally and legally used only in defense against those who violate Article 1.

Article 3: No exceptions shall ever exist to Articles 1 and 2.

The only possible structure of government that could survive under the new mentality would be one of defense. As all aspects of government on the offense come to an end, including programs for the "social good" dictating how we spend our money, the remaining valid government of protection from physical aggression would have to abide by the Universal Law.

Now, Forget About Political Ideas

You must realize that the political shift will *not* come from political ideas — no matter how excellent. Political ideas are *not* the cause of our political structure, based on external authorities. Political ideas might affect the degree of external authority — say from tyrannical to democratic. But to remove external authority — an altogether new political structure — requires an altogether new mentality, specifically the God-Man mentality.

Indeed, man's mentality is the cause of civilization's political structure and always has been, dating back to the Bicameral Age over 3000 years ago when civilization's political structure was a theocracy — a divine hierarchy of authorities...a hierarchy of communicating with the imagined gods.

Today's infected conscious mind — infected with a bicameral virus — is the cause of our political structure, which also consists of a hierarchy of "authorities" telling us how to live both our business and personal lives. ...We still look toward external "authority" for our answers and not inward at the authority of our own, integrating minds. Great political ideas (such as Libertarianism) cannot change the political structure because political ideas do not change man's mentality.

Fortunately, in the 21st century, we are entering a new mentality based on the authority of man's own honest, integrating mind that obsoletes the need for external "authorities" telling us how to live. Our evolution into that new mentality — the God-Man mentality — is *the* cause that will bring civilization into a new political structure based on no external "authorities".

Understanding that man's mentality is the underlying cause of civilization's political structure, you can help speed up our *evolution* into the new God-Man mentality in which man becomes his own guide and god, his own voice and authority. And when man's mentality shifts to God-Man, the political structure will shift to a government of self-defense only, never ruling over the people, always protecting them from physical aggression.

I'll say it again: the new political structure will end all aspects of government on the offense...that is, anything that rules over us, including programs for the "social good" that control our money, including regulatory bureaucracies that control our businesses. The people's new God-Man mentality would not and could not accept external "authority" any longer. Politicians and bureaucrats telling us how to live tomorrow would be like silly religious zealots telling us how to live today.

The freed geniuses of society will rise by the millions along with their rapidly progressing new technologies. Prices for those soaring new technologies, as with any soaring new technology, will soon plunge toward zero. Ordinary people will gain the buying power and standards of living of millionaires without lifting a finger or changing a thing.

How You Can Get Involved

You can start a grassroots networking of the Neo-Tech Party.

Can your efforts accelerate the end of man's bicameral mentalities? Yes, to some degree, particularly as you expose people to the Gifts described throughout the Twelve Visions. For example, people discovering that the new political paradigm would raise their standards of living to that of millionaires helps remove survival anxieties and helps push them past their bicameral-like dependencies on their leaders. The people, themselves, do not have to become integrated thinkers; in fact, they don't have to lift a finger to become wealthy just as people did not have to know a thing about computers to enjoy the thousandfold increase in buying power. The geniuses of society will take care of everything.

Indeed, a major reason the bicameral-like following mode could still linger on for years to come would be ordinary people's inherent survival fears of putting full authority upon their own minds. For many reasons including one's upbringing, learned reactions, education, culture, illusions, neocheaters and mysticism, the ordinary person is not able to efficiently see and integrate reality to rely on the authority of his or her own mind, so he or she turns to the "experts" and leaders for their guiding authority. Thus, the people turn their power over to external "authorities" out of survival fears.

Your best course of action is to first eliminate those survival fears. Then more and more people will find themselves excited about the Neo-Tech Party and its wealthy Neo-Tech World. The way to eliminate those survival fears is to promote the Gifts that will flow to *everyone* in the Neo-Tech World, even to those who *do not* change.

Remember, the results of eliminating government of offense and all its burdensome regulations will be wealth for the people as the freed geniuses of society and their new technologies soar. In this day and age of high technology, the geniuses will drive forth new technologies to create spectacular new values for us, and the cost of those technology-intensive values will plunge to mere dollars as we have seen with the computers. Ordinary people will soon live like millionaires — healthy millionaires who will soon no longer get sick as the geniuses eradicate most diseases through their soaring new technologies.

Another eye-opener that could help facilitate man's evolutionary jump to the God-Man mentality would be data today separating government laws (i.e., laws based on individual self-defense) versus government assaults (i.e., laws based on political offense). It would be interesting to separate the budget, the law books, case law, verdicts, and regulations that carry legislative powers...separate them into laws (i.e., based on individual self-defense) versus assaults (i.e., based on political offense). That clear delineation of government laws (which will be the fraction) versus government assaults (which will be the bulk) might also help remove mankind's survival fears to make a fundamental political change to a government of defense for a fundamentally different mentality.

In any case, showing people the Gifts, particularly the wealth scenario where they will live like millionaires without lifting a finger, will help remove the subconscious survival fears and anxieties of jumping ahead into a new political structure for the new God-Man mentality. Removing those survival fears, more than anything else, will help people to remove external "authorities" from their lives, telling them how to live, such as politicians and regulatory bureaucrats.

Go to www.neo-tech.com to find the proper Neo-Tech Networking (NTN) board. Your grassroots efforts toward building the Neo-Tech Party will help civilization flow into the new political paradigm as the mentality changes.

Neo-Tech Networking Board
Church of God-Man

Human Life Is the Greatest Value in the Universe

The goal of the Church of God-Man is achieving immortality here on Earth. That happens when humanity evolves into the God-Man mentality and technology is no longer held back by external "authorities", such as the FDA.

The Church of God-Man recognizes human life as the supreme value in the Universe. People *must not perish*...a belief that has powerfully wholesome effects on children while growing up. They become so integrated with the value of their own lives that they automatically abstain from self-destructive yet common teenage activities such as drugs, drinking, and fast cars.

The highest moral duty is to protect and preserve the supreme value in the Universe — human life. To that end, man has a moral duty to eradicate disease and natural disasters. Aging or cellular degeneration is the most pervasive fatal disease; death is the ultimate natural disaster. Man's greatest moral duty, therefore, is to eradicate aging and end human death.

Other religions accept death and passively offer the payoff (i.e., immortality) *after* you die. They could, in essence, be collectively called the Church of Death. The God-Man religion, by contrast, does not accept death and actively strives for the payoff *before* you die (i.e., immortality) and could be called the Church of Life.

Where Religions Come From

Religions and God-in-Heaven beliefs are mutations of our ancient, bicameral mentality when man hallucinated the commands from the gods, which would elicit immediate obedience from the bicameral humans.

Sometime in the 21st century, man's bicameral longings for the voice of a supreme being will subside. The full meaning of death's finality will set in. The full responsibility of immortality will shift onto us. The human race will shift enormous energy into *Project Life* — the world's most important project of all time, dwarfing all previous medical projects.

The evolving mentality of the 21st century will obsolete the need for "higher" authority guiding our lives. Under the new mentality, it would be impossible to be a follower or worshipper of "higher" authority, for authority resides in one's own mind — the mind of God-Man.

Understand that man's mentality is the underlying cause of civilization's religions. The only religion (i.e., way of life) that will survive in mankind's new God-Man mentality in which man becomes his own guide and god, his own voice and authority...will be the Church of God-Man seeking immortality here on Earth.

The New God-Man Religion:
- God of the Past: God rules over man.
- Gods of the Future: Immortal God-Man rules over existence, whom we must join.

Other Religions:
- A God who rules over man means that human "representatives" must rule over man "in the name of God". (That power over man ranges from psychological to political.) Most religious and nonreligious people agree that the Scriptures were...
- edited to serve the political structure, the power — those "representatives" of God
- edited to promote guilt and enhance the power — those "representatives" of God
- edited to promote subservience to the power — those "representatives" of God
- edited to promote sacrifice to the power — those "representatives" of God

602

- edited to promote blind obedience to <u>the power</u> — those "representatives" of God
- edited to promote fear of <u>the power</u> — those "representatives" of God

Moreover, those "representatives" of God are the only "salesmen" who offer you your return *after you are dead and gone!* Aside from those glaring problems, religion today is just not reconciling with progressive scientific facts. The reason religions are still successful and still survive even today, however, reduces to a single common denominator among all religions: *social advantages* for survival. Life is very competitive. Man is a social animal; church is a social network. Thus, "church" now translates to "life advantages" and is a big reason *why* the church survives today. Social advantages equal life advantages, and all churches today give their followers excellent social advantages such as:

- business contacts
- job leads
- dating and matchmaking
- friends to meet and keep
- friends for kids
- babysitters you can trust
- a sense of belonging

The church gives you a much needed competitive edge.

How You Can Get Involved

A good social network is the staying power behind today's uncompetitive religions and is the premise upon which the Church of God-Man must be built. You can now engage in social networking on the Church of God-Man discussion board (at www.neo-tech.com).

Also, you may post your insights about the new Church of God-Man that honors the value of our individual lives. You may freely network with others.

Sometime in the 21st century, the old religions based on a God who rules over man will die as man leaves behind the mutant bicameral mentality seeking "higher" authority telling him how to live. Instead, he will evolve into the God-Man mentality utilizing his own mind as its own authority. The only religion that will survive under the new mentality will be the Church of God-Man, which will use its money to finance and coordinate medical research, particularly *Project Life,* working toward biological immortality as the guiding goal.

Yes, we believe in God: God is you and me as we become the God-Man. God is our fellow God-Man throughout the Civilization of the Universe.

Neo-Tech Networking Board
Association for Curing Aging and Death

To fulfill our destiny of becoming God, we must take on Project Life. When will we? The answer lies in man's two different mentalities: 1) We will never take on Project Life with today's diseased mentality, for progress is impossibly retarded by political external "authorities" such as the FDA, and motivation is nearly eliminated by stagnation in our lives coupled with religious delusions of a stimulating Heaven waiting for us in the sky. 2) We will very rapidly achieve Project Life with the coming God-Man mentality, for unrestricted medical and anti-aging technologies will soar toward permanent cures as God-Man no longer accepts political external "authorities" such as the FDA, and motivation soars with creation and exhilaration in our lives. Suppressed hope for a better life, causing silly religious delusions such as Heaven, will fade away. The freed geniuses of society, acting on the full power and authority of their own integrating minds, would put enormous effort into Project Life. Again, the success of this program comes down to mankind leaving behind the bicameral mentality from the past and making the jump into the God-Man mentality of the future.

What follows is an open letter to self-made money/power giants around the world. Following the open letter below are actions you can take to get involved.

Letter from Mark Hamilton to Self-Made People

"I understand that Michael Milken has made considerable progress in his research/medical fight against prostate cancer.

Given enough time and energy, that one man with his team of medical help just might orchestrate a cure. He is someone who loves life, knows how to succeed, and has powerful resources — the 'special three' qualities that it takes to fight a complex disease.

"You, too, have the special three qualities.

"I have often wondered: What if the people who love life, know how to succeed, and have powerful resources came together to stop a complex disease? Say Michael Milken, Bill Gates, Andy Grove, Warren Buffet, Donald Trump and a dozen others with the special three qualities combined their energies and resources to stop a fatal disease and save their own lives. Say, for example, they all had prostate cancer. It'd be like the Manhattan Project, but even more rewarding.

"Of course, a disease like prostate cancer, although widespread, still strikes a relatively small percentage of the people who have the special three qualities. So that dream-team consisting of people like you — the lovers of life, very successful, powerful — will never materialize.

"Unless we consider this: We all do have a fatal disease — aging and then death. What if the people who love life, know how to succeed, and had powerful resources came together to stop a complex disease known as cellular degeneration, better known as aging? Say Michael Milken, Bill Gates, Andy Grove, Warren Buffet, Donald Trump and dozens of others with the three special qualities passionately wanted to live with vitality much longer. Imagine that they combined their energies and resources to stop this fatal disease and save their own lives. It'd be like the Manhattan Project or the Moon Project with an ultimate deadline — their own lives.

"Medically and morally speaking, slowing down and eventually curing aging can and should be done. Those with the special three qualities can make it happen...*in our lifetimes*.

"How valuable is your life to you? How about your children's lives? You can save your life and theirs. We need to come together — the people throughout the world with the special three qualities. I am inviting you to be part of this exclusive group.

"I want to assemble a team of people with the special three

qualities who are passionate about not dying. If you have ever stood over a loved one in a casket, you realize the body is just a tool that carries the infinitely priceless spirit. The spirit should not vanish because the tool gives out.

The Four-Part Puzzle

"Although the intention of this letter is to introduce you to the idea of curing the disease of aging to save your own life and your children's lives, I will take a moment to mention four specific puzzle pieces forming out there that are waiting to be snapped together:

"The first puzzle piece is the work of Dr. Robert White to attach human heads to healthy human bodies, which has already been done with monkeys (see www.abcnews.com/sections/living/ DailyNews/mckenzie_head980427.html).

"The second puzzle piece is the rapid progress on spinal cord research.

"The third puzzle piece is the rapid progress on skin rejuvenation.

"The fourth puzzle piece is the achievement of cloning animals, especially with the recent breakthrough on human cloning.

"Now, snapping together those puzzle pieces, the resulting puzzle picture is a much longer life free of debilitating diseases. For example, imagine having cloned Michael Milken's body, then replacing his head onto his own, healthy teen body and removing many years of aging from his face through new skin technology.

"Or, imagine an 80-year-old Bill Gates physically restricted by age. Imagine replacing his 80-year-old body with his own healthy, youthful 20-year-old cloned body. Moreover, rapidly advancing skin technology would cosmetically reverse the symptoms of facial aging.

"The technology to reacquire a young, healthy body (i.e., a replaceable new tool to carry the irreplaceable spirit) is approaching quickly. There are also other, more definitive approaches to curing the disease of aging on the horizon, such as controlling the reproduction of cells (i.e., potential breakthroughs coming by way of cancer research), even possibilities of reversing aging (potential breakthroughs coming by way of stem-cell research).

"But, to make the seemingly impossible happen requires people like *you* — people who have made the seemingly impossible happen in their livelihoods.

"The Manhattan Project and the Moon Project were two amazing feats accomplished by brilliant, motivated people coming together with bigger-than-life goals and intense deadlines. Let's do one of those amazing feats again. Let's do it for humanity and for ourselves. Let's come together with our pool of talents and resources; let's challenge Mother Nature. Rather, let's *do battle* with her and defeat her this time. Earthquakes, hurricanes, disease, aging, and death. We can do without nature's destructive elements. We love life; we love our children, and we love mankind. Let's proceed with *Project Life!*

"For the productive, happy person, the only real problem with life...is death. Think about it: all other catastrophes in life can eventually be fixed, from romantic calamities such as divorce to business calamities, even failure. If you are an honest, competent person, you can eventually overcome anything life throws at you...except death.

"If we didn't age, we wouldn't die, save for accidents. If you look at TV or movie stars from the '60s and then see them today, you suddenly realize that aging *is* a disease. And diseases can *and should be* cured. In fact, it is man's moral duty to cure disease. You have the opportunity to accomplish man's greatest moral victory. Of course, that is how history will see you.

"Specifically, what is the direction we should take? First, those with the special three qualities must come together and talk, and then we go from there. I have prepared this open letter to reach self-made people such as yourself. I do not know how many of you will be interested, but I will proceed if just one recognizes the noble project that needs to be started *now*.

"Neither I nor my company stand to gain anything monetarily from this. In fact, once I get the Association for Curing Aging and Death going, I will dedicate a major portion of my time and my company's profits to funding Project Life.

"My father, a former Senior Research Chemist for E. I. du Pont de Nemours & Company, told me when I was a boy that death was designed by nature for propagation of the species through evolution. 'But', he added, 'human beings obsoleted the need for death because man advances so much faster than evolution.' He then explained that our lives were the highest value in existence: 'Life is everything; death is nothing'.[1]

"Those talks with my dad affected me deeply. Since I was a young boy, I have repeatedly thought about someday eliminating death for my loved ones, myself, and mankind. Now I know, having lost a close loved one, the time has come to start Project Life.

"Everything I have ever done or written since becoming a writer and businessman, was to bring about the conditions that can lead to biological immortality. I think I am the ideal person to bring together people with the three special qualities (i.e., lovers of life who know how to succeed and have powerful resources.)

"The Association for Curing Aging and Death will coordinate Project Life and its research scientists and doctors. Eventually, we can introduce the Association for Curing Aging and Death to the public for expanding our resources.

"But first, we must come together and develop an aggressive plan. Are you willing to:

1) Save your own life and your loved ones' lives?
2) Serve on the most important project of all time?

"Certainly, at first our Association for Curing Aging and Death will be controversial. Controversy has plagued advancements in human thinking throughout history. If you would like, we could make the Association for Curing Aging and Death closed and secret. That might give us advantages at first. A time may come, however, when we want the whole human race to get involved with our idea. ...We can make those

---

[1]My father is Dr. Frank R. Wallace, discoverer and author of *The Neo-Tech Discovery*. In that manuscript, first published in 1979, he identifies man's highest goal and responsibility to obsolete death. He also scientifically demonstrates that the results would boom the prosperity of mankind, and he scientifically demonstrates that commonly perceived problems such as overpopulation and boredom would be quickly eliminated by new solutions and never actually become problems.

decisions when we meet.

"Please let me know if you might be interested. If you would prefer, for the first contact I could come to see you. But soon thereafter, we would want to all come together to develop a vision and a course of action that we will drive to completion.

"You and your loved ones can live with increasing health and happiness far longer...perhaps forever. We can accomplish that goal if the self-made people reading this letter decide to. If you are interested, you may call me or write me. I will send you another letter with more information on our next step. Thank you."

Sincerely,
Mark Hamilton

How You Can Get Involved

The above letter is meant for the most successful people...people known nationally and internationally. Yet, perhaps the greatest leverage in the long run (or at least a vital driving force behind Project Life) will come from self-made people who are not so widely known...those at the local level.

If you personally know a self-made successful person, you should introduce him or her to the Association for Curing Aging and Death and its program called Project Life. Just direct him or her to the discussion board at (www.Neo-Tech.com).

Realize that most people, even admirable self-made people, will not respond to Project Life and will have no interest in the Association for Curing Aging and Death. The reason for their apathy is clear: most people are still steeped in the mentality from the past. Only those who have either made the jump to the God-Man mentality or those who are ready to make the jump will be interested.

The other contribution you can make is to show and, perhaps, *stir up* a lot of interest and support for Project Life. Continually post to the NTN discussion board, and recruit others to the web page (www.neo-tech.com). You can bet that the self-made people who *might be* interested will be watching the web page to monitor the general interest in biological immortality. Even the most successful self-made people have a lot invested in the pre-Neo-Tech World under the old mentality. They have a lot to lose; they are wealthy and happy the way things are *now*. Therefore, for both survival and self-esteem reasons, they will be more willing to switch to the new God-Man mentality if the numbers are there. Post your thoughts and wishes in the Neo-Tech Networking (NTN) discussion board on the Association for Curing Aging and Death.

Summary, Time Line, & Things To Come

Life Is Simple

Life is very simple to understand. Everything falls into one of two possible categories based on mankind's mentalities: the mentality from the past *or* the mentality of the future:

Category #1: Bicameral Mentality from our past seeking authorization from external "authorities".

Category #2: God-Man Mentality in our near future seeking no further than the authority of one's own honest, integrating mind.

Below are listed the basic structures of civilization and the two possible categories they each fall into.

Mankind's Mentality Controls Everything

Political Structure

(#1 Heretofore) Ruling Class (external "authorities" tell us how to spend our money and run our businesses)

(#2 Soon) Protection Service (internal authority self-determines how to spend our money and run our businesses)

Religious Structure
- (#1 Heretofore) Church of God (external "authority" guides our lives)
- (#2 Soon) Church of God-Man (internal authority guides our own lives)

Science Structure
- (#1 Heretofore) Point of Origin (external "authority"...majestic creation)
- (#2 Soon) Conscious Controlled (internal authority...God-Man creation)

Business Structure
- (#1 Heretofore) Division of Labor (doing routine, delegated by external "authority")
- (#2 Soon) Division of Essence (making profits using internal authority)

Marriage Structure
- (#1 Heretofore) Divorce Bound (stagnating life under growth-and-happiness-killing external "authorities")
- (#2 Soon) Falling-In-Love Forever (exuberant life via growth-and-happiness-stimulating internal authority)

Education Structure
- (#1 Heretofore) Free-Flowing Thinking (social, political agendas are the external "authority")
- (#2 Soon) Integrated Thinking (the honesty-bound thinking mind is the authority)

Medical Structure

(#1 Heretofore) "Handcuffed" Research (suppressed by FDA-type external "authorities")

(#2 Soon) Unrestricted Research (soaring via geniuses' internal authority)

Legal Structure

(#1 Heretofore) "Higher" Causes (politicians enact sound-good "higher" causes and force them upon us as our external "authorities")

(#2 Soon) No Higher Causes (the individual is the highest cause protected from force from any source)

Technology and Enterprise Structure

(#1 Heretofore) "Handcuffed" Progress (suppressed by regulatory external "authorities")

(#2 Soon) Unrestricted Progress (soaring via geniuses' internal authority)

Societal Structure

(#1 Heretofore) Social Good (a few hundred politicians "take care of us" as our external "authorities")

(#2 Soon) Social Wealth (millions of geniuses take care of us by making us rich with nearly cost-free technology)

Arts Structure

(#1 Heretofore) Establishment Controlled (power in the hands of a few external "authorities")

(#2 Soon) Consumer/Artist Controlled (power in the hands of the many artists and consumers)

Media Structure

(#1 Heretofore) Establishment Controlled (power in elite few external "authorities", dishonesty rises to top.)

(#2 Soon) Internet Controlled (power in the hands of everybody, honesty rises to top.)

Moral Structure

(#1 Heretofore) Death Accepted (value of human life diminished by political, business & religious external "authorities")

(#2 Soon) Death Unaccepted (value of human life is highest value with no higher value or cause...highest moral calling is to eradicate human death)

Hamilton's Human Time Line

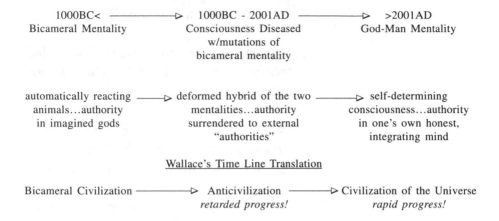

1000BC< ——————▷	1000BC - 2001AD ——————▷	>2001AD
Bicameral Mentality	Consciousness Diseased w/mutations of bicameral mentality	God-Man Mentality

automatically reacting ——▷	deformed hybrid of the two ——▷	self-determining
animals...authority in imagined gods	mentalities...authority surrendered to external "authorities"	consciousness...authority in one's own honest, integrating mind

Wallace's Time Line Translation

Bicameral Civilization ——————▷	Anticivilization ——————▷	Civilization of the Universe
	retarded progress!	*rapid progress!*

www.neo-tech.com

Get Involved Programs (NTNs)

NTN #1
Superior Religious Advantages

This discussion group marks the beginning of a new church that offers superior life advantages.

First, perhaps the greatest asset of all churches is the social advantages gained during the weekly congregation. This NTN brings those social advantages to the discussion board. State your needs, and see if someone who attends this NTN responds. Have fun.

Second, the next asset of churches is: they provide a code of living that is generally beneficial with good lessons for self-improvement. The weekly congregation keeps the churchgoer focussed. The Church of God-Man does this, too, particularly when you read its Bible called *The Book*. The difference is: the Church of God-Man brings back the proper context to the Bible and then soars beyond the value of the Bible to the next leap of power (see the Second Insight). The daily influx on the Discussion Board keeps the God-Man churchgoer focussed.

Third, the culminating asset of churches is: they provide what is called "spiritual guidance" toward an ultimate goal, such as striving for immortality in the Kingdom of Heaven. They help keep the faith in its idea system and its god. The Church of God-Man provides "spiritual guidance" but makes it *real*. The Church of God-Man (also called the Church of Life) strives for *biological* immortality — immortality *before* you die. *Your* Church of God-Man should help keep the faith (explained in the Third Insight) in its idea system and the Kingdom of God-Man.

Start *Your* Church of God-Man

The discussion board offers you the unique opportunity to connect with people in your geographical area to start your own weekly congregation. We encourage these grassroots efforts. Advertise your congregations on this discussion board. If your grassroots efforts grow, you can build (as will others around the world) your own Church of God-Man.

You will need the Church of God-Man's Bible to study, which is called *The Book* and is available from Neo-Tech Publishing Company. Those who have purchased *The Book* and want more copies for their congregations may get them for a substantial multiple-copy discount.

NTN #2
Political Bonanza

This discussion group marks the beginning of a new political party that offers real wealth to everyone in sharp contrast to all other political parties (i.e., politics in general) that drain the wealth of everyone, including the third-generation welfare dependent.

When the Neo-Tech Party takes over, ordinary people will live as well as millionaires. With a Neo-Tech President, even the inner-city welfare dependents will live as well as millionaires within four years.

Start *Your* Local Neo-Tech Party

This discussion board offers you the unique opportunity to connect with people in your geographical area to start your local Neo-Tech Party. We encourage these grassroots efforts. Advertise your political gatherings on the discussion board. If your grassroots efforts grow, you can build (as will others around the world) your local and eventually statewide Neo-Tech Party, putting up candidates in your area using the Six Visions as a campaign theme. Eventually, we will combine all the local efforts into a national effort to elect a Neo-Tech President.

NTN #3
Curing Disease, Aging & Death

This discussion group marks the beginning of the Association for Curing Aging and Death.

The greatest medical achievement over the past century was the leap of life expectancy from well under 50 to 76 years. The *USA Today* reports that doctors today say that now things are happening in anti-aging research that could not even be imagined a couple of decades ago. Doctors and scientists now believe we are on the edge of spectacular leaps in life expectancy, possibilities they would not even entertain a couple of decades ago.

Why? The biggest reported reason is: twenty years ago, anti-aging research went from a fringe science to a mainstream science. The most exciting and aggressive research in medicine today is tied to anti-aging.

The Association for Curing Aging and Death is here to take the idea of *not dying* from a fringe concept to a mainstream concept.

Start *Your* Remnant Work

The world needs a grassroots effort to generate interest from the ground up in curing aging and death. *Your* systemic, one-on-one efforts are ultimately what it's all about.

Some of you will discover a breakthrough in reaching people and will take a leadership role in organized efforts to get more people interested. When I am convinced that enough people are seriously interested, to the point they will contribute hard-earned money to Project Life, then I will formally structure the Association for Curing Aging and Death and begin the research/test programs.

NTN #4
Entertainment Power

This discussion group marks the beginning of Neo-Tech Live Arts, which includes film, plays, and music. In short, Neo-Tech Live Arts means the marketplace, not the elitists, decide what is valuable, which shifts power out of the hands of the elite and into the hands of the artist.

Many overlooked, talented artists mistakenly believe it is the commercial aspect that blocks their talent from getting recognized. Admittedly, to some degree, that is the case, but that can be worked around. The much bigger problem is that the *decision* of who makes it and who does not rests in the hands of a few powerful elite. If that *decision* were shifted to the marketplace, many, many talented artists who believe the commercial marketplace blocks their development would suddenly find themselves in great demand!

Neo-Tech Live Arts wants to shift the power from an elite-few power brokers to the marketplace, thus to the artist. Indeed, if those talented, overlooked artists had direct access to the marketplace, they would have the power to develop their skills, even blossom beyond their wildest imaginations, as they make *their art* more and more desirable to the public.

A direct example is the books of Neo-Tech Publishing. No major publisher would dare touch our books, rendering us powerless if we stopped there. But, we went directly to the marketplace with our unlikely books. That gave us the power to increase the value of our books and, subsequently, reach millions of people without compromising the concepts of

Neo-Tech.

Tell the World About *You*

This is where Neo-Tech Live Arts begins, right here with *you*. If you are a talented artist, tell others about it here. Connections, contacts can happen this way. If enough action comes to this discussion board, perhaps a Neo-Tech owner will create a web site to market alternative art to the public. Shifting the decision of choice to the general public (thus shifting the power to the artist), could take off.

NTN #5
Neo-Tech Employment

This discussion group marks the beginnings of an employment matrix designed to get an ambitious person into the career of his dreams *and* designed to get a business its model employee.

A note to business leaders and entrepreneurs: you will LOVE having the kind of devoted worker who comes out of here. You'd better hunt here!

And why is that? Here we have a powerful sorting mechanism. We have the type of worker who accepts and absorbs details, yet wants to and is indeed driven to exert his or her mind. If you run a business, you know such a combination is rare today: a person focussed on the small details, yet thinking forward and forming a big picture. ...Sort of sounds like an entrepreneur, right? That's right: one who cares that the small stuff is done right *and* one who looks for ways to grow.

Now, if you are searching for a job, desiring to leave behind your dead-end job of labor for that open-ended job of the mind, read on.

Your journey will be one of mastering and absorbing details, which every market businessman and market entrepreneur will appreciate and desire.

When you understand what's going on and enthusiastically desire to devote yourself to your job at that level, to the point you will become so integrated with the business you will transform a job of labor into a job of the mind, then state your case along with details about yourself. You are stating that you are willing to devote yourself to your work to grow your job into a job where you master the details and run it through integrated thinking...like an entrepreneur.

NTN #6
Dream Spouse or Partner

This discussion group marks the beginning of a meeting place designed for women and men to find the lover of their dreams.

I will start off with an appeal to women of all ages: here is a golden opportunity for you to meet a man who has higher odds of becoming the successful man.

Let me tell you a short story to make the point. When I was younger, I was par with most other guys. I was neither sought out by women nor avoided. But once I became quite successful, women sought me out. I married and had children. In short, as soon as I became successful, I was no longer available. The old cliché, "All the good men are taken," for the most part is true.

But, how was a woman to know when I was not yet successful that I would be someday? On the other hand, if she did know, she could have easily made me hers.

The odds are so against any one man rising into the top 1% or better. Imagine, however, if you had the advantage *of knowing* who those few men would be? You could then easily secure one of them for yourself.

A man who is attracted to the Neo-Tech Code of Living has discovered his essence, which is value creation.

The man who adopts the Neo-Tech Code of Living, whether he is 25 or 55 years old, has the same focus as I did before I became successful. That focus and drive, within the man who discovers his essence, destines him to become successful.

That is why this meeting place is a golden opportunity for women to meet qualified men. And here the old cliché that "the good ones are always taken" no longer applies. For, the single man who has truly adopted the Neo-Tech Code of Living is destined to become the successful man. Here are the good ones! So, ladies, make contact!

Now, if you're a man, you can get a feel for the Neo-Tech Code of Living from *The Neo-Tech World*. I strongly suggest you read through the book in your hands to fully integrate the Neo-Tech way of living and its many advantages. The ladies you meet here will understand what the Neo-Tech Man is all about; he's about values. And the ladies you meet here will have a sense of their dual essences, which makes for a more loving and lasting romance. So, if you adhere to the Neo-Tech Code of Living, let the ladies know.

NTN #7

Raising Geniuses In
Five Minutes A Day

This discussion board helps parents raise geniuses in just a few minutes a day. It also marks the embryo stage of Neo-Tech Schools that will create geniuses through a leap of power called Neothink.

Consider some of the world's most brilliant people of the distant past such as Plato, Aristotle, Alexander the Great in Golden Greece and, later, great Renaissance men such as da Vinci and Michelangelo. Those people had personal tutors who often lived with their pupils. For example, Plato was tutored by Socrates; Aristotle was tutored by Plato; Alexander the Great was tutored by Aristotle who lived with his pupil. Those men became great, not because of their academic training per se, although their education was important and a necessary requisite. But, the reason those men became great was: their minds worked differently, beyond the boundaries of other men. As children, they were exposed to the powerful minds of their tutors. Whereas other children took everything at face value, the children with powerful tutors constantly saw deeper to the essence of things. That essence tied together with other essences through common denominators about life.

Those special children started linking together those common denominators at the root of things. They started snapping them together as mental puzzles began to form in their minds. That allowed them to see not only deeply into things, but broadly across expanding fields of knowledge. Moreover, those growing mental puzzles, in time, began revealing never-before-seen puzzle pictures, enabling them to create new knowledge.

In other words, those great minds advanced into Neothink. That more powerful way of using the mind did not come from their academic training per se, although it was crucially important. Their new way of using the mind came from their tutors shaking up the normal way of looking at things, which forced them as children to look deeper to the essence. At the essence of things lie the common denominators in life. And that's when Neothink puzzle building begins.

I know this from my own experience. By no means do I compare myself to the great minds in history. That said, I received a terrible Dewey-system public education, which left me handicapped in the working world. However, my father is Dr. Frank R. Wallace, a former scientist for Du Pont and author of *The Neo-Tech Discovery*. It was clearly his talks with me that broke through normal boundaries of thoughts for a young person's mind and shook up my normal way of looking at things, which caused me to look deeper at things and led to my Neothink puzzle building and expanding success.

I have completed a novel about a third-grade teacher and the amazing results of just *one year* teaching eight-year-olds and shaking up their minds to go from mere perceptual thinking as everyone else to conceptual thinking and onto puzzle-building Neothink. The novel is entitled *The First Immortals*.

Start *Your* Tutelage

Understanding what makes minds great, you can raise a genius in less than five minutes a day. Tell your children bedtime stories about things that break through the normal perceptual way of seeing things. Many great topics are found here in *The Neo-Tech World*, which cuts through to the essence

621

of many things. Tell a particular topic to your child in your own words so that your child can understand. This technique really works. I do this with my young children. My six-year-old daughter knows most of the concepts in *The Neo-Tech World.*

Growing Grassroots Efforts

Post your efforts, experiences and successes. We want to keep this discussion board for learning and for communicating results. Moms, dads, and teachers, communicate your experiences to each other. Let each other know what works and why.

As the interest builds here, someone will start a virtual Neo-Tech School in its simplest form, using the 5-minutes-a-day lessons that break through normal boundaries of thought in young minds.

Eventually, an enterprising Neo-Tech educator will start a private Neo-Tech School. We encourage that, and we will lend our widely recognized name and worldwide PR if the principles are consistent with Neo-Tech's educational ideas.

NTN #8

God-Man Theory

This discussion board marks the beginning of a pioneering group called the God-Man Theorists who will relook at the enormous data collected on our Universe while asking a new set of questions based on: "What if God-Man created and controlled the cosmos?"

The scientifically sound theory by Dr. Frank R. Wallace is presented below. We encourage everyone's input here from the nonscientific layman to the trained scientist. The more of a mixture there is here, the more people will begin to understand and be drawn into the God-Man Theory. What makes the God-Man Theory below carry such an impact?

The God-Man Theory in essence says that consciousness is the fourth constant of the Universe. As the God-Man Theory explains, the cosmos has four universal constants: mass, energy, time, *and consciousness.* Dr. Wallace believes enough data currently exists that, if looked at by asking a different set of questions, the data will *prove* that consciousness controls the cosmos. The most probable way the proof will come: by showing that, through the unconscious, uninfluenced Laws of Nature, something can *not* be the way it is...meaning human consciousness or God-Man intercepted the course of nature.

When the proof comes, civilization will shift dramatically from the current irrational, political anticivilization to the Neo-Tech World...the rational, businesslike Civilization of the Universe. Nothing before or after will affect the ordinary person more...not Copernicus who led the way out of the Dark Ages, not Newton who led the way into the Age of Reason, not Einstein who led the way for modern electronics. Nothing before or after will catapult the prosperity of the ordinary person more than proving the God-Man Theory and his Civilization of the Universe.

Why?

Because that proof will make the political structure of the Neo-Tech Party and the drive for Project Life the *natural order of things*.

The acceptance of the Neo-Tech Party would mean rapid wealth for everyone as explained in NTN#2, and the acceptance of Project Life would mean perfect health, rapidly increasing longevity, and eventual non-aging biological immortality for everyone. Those people, by the way, would now be very wealthy (NTN#2), deeply happy (NTN#5), and in exciting romantic love relationships (NTN#6). Those ordinary people would now *want to live forever!* (To understand all this better, you need to read through the Third Insight.)

NTN #9
Neo-Tech Law

This discussion board marks the beginning of Neo-Tech Law and the Neo-Tech Lawyers who will bring new legal approaches based on fully integrated honesty (*the*-point law) into the decaying legal arena now based on manipulative truths (*a*-point law), half-truths, deception, dishonesty.

This discussion board offers opportunity for sparkling uses of Neo-Tech in the legal arena to be preserved. Here, those approaches can continue to shine and be increasingly combined and used to build the light of honesty, which will eventually throw the spotlight on ego justice and political policy law for all to see such dishonesty.

We here at Neo-Tech went directly into the legal arena against the most powerful evil in America, during its peak of power in the 1980s and 1990s, and used new approaches never seen before in the court of law.   It was our relentless, "in the Congressmen's faces" war of two worlds that directly led the way to the Congressional IRS Abuse Hearings and the subsequent IRS Horror-Stories Senate Hearings.

Through this discussion board, people will be watching the rise of Neo-Tech Law.   When enough power grows, an ambitiously honest lawyer could start a practice of Neo-Tech Lawyers much like the character Bruce Salinski in the novel *The First Immortals*.   That law firm would protect innocent businesses and entrepreneurs from existing parasitical lawyers, political policy law, dishonest a-point courtroom techniques, and ego-justice judges.   In other words, such a law firm would protect the value producers from the value destroyers.

Post your thoughts and experiences using fully integrated honesty. We will be watching.   ...Like Salinski in *The First Immortals*, explosive opportunity exists for the first breakthrough wave of professional Neo-Tech Lawyers.

NTN #10
Neo-Tech News

This discussion board marks the beginning of a media news source based on values in contrast to many media sources today based on tearing down or ignoring values.

The front page of most daily newspapers and the headline news are dominated with politics. Politics per se is nothing of value, with the exception of the Neo-Tech Party (NTN #2) because it *depoliticizes* society, which will bring exceptional wealth (NTN #2) and health (NTN #3) to society, making it a value.

Politics — politicizing society — is a *disvalue* that drains the wealth and health of society. Politics, therefore, should and would have no power, if not for the false power given to politics by the news media. Ordinary people get sucked into the illusion because it's all around them — a media-spun illusion called the anticivilization. Ordinary people are easily pulled into the political illusion because they are still plagued with a bicameral-like mentality that seeks external "authority".

If a major news media company existed that put out only values, not disvalues such as politics, people would, one by one, begin migrating toward it because every person (i.e., human nature) is attracted to values.

People would gradually become disintegrated with the illusion as the new media source integrated them with reality.

Whatever one is integrated with, whatever one is used to, can be a powerful force over his life, whether that be his political system, his God, his basketball team. When I moved to Canada for a year, at first I hated the daily paper. "It's nothing but politics!" I complained to my wife. Then, two months later, on a trip back to the States, I was shocked to realize the U.S. papers were the same. The only difference was: I was integrated with U.S. politics and not with Canadian politics. Not being integrated with Canadian politics, I saw what a debilitating joke politics really is.

For those who travel around the world find the same phenomenon with religion. Other countries' gods seem like a joke, and their religions are so silly. Any American who has travelled to Japan, for example, knows what I mean. But, after awhile, the traveler realizes the same goes for his own God and religion. The only difference is: he's integrated with his and not with theirs.

The point is, the major news media carry power only because people are integrated with them and believe what those media companies say is important, such as American politics. If a media source came along that could disintegrate people from today's media companies, then a major shift in power would occur, from a *politically* driven world to *value* driven world.

This discussion group is the beginning of such a media

source. We encourage you to bring to this discussion board newsworthy information that is a *genuine value* to the reader. Read about the character Al Patterson in *The First Immortals* to see how media can be...what is truly a value to the people. We will be watching your posts. If enough interest builds here, an enterprising Neo-Tech entrepreneur may eventually start a Neo-Tech News web site and might tap on some of you as a resource.

NTN #11
Sue IRS

This discussion board marks the first class-action lawsuit against the IRS. Whether or not we file this depends on the interest generated here. The IRS symbolizes injustice and evil in America.

NTN #12
Attack Neo-Tech!

Here's where people can have some fun. This discussion board allows anyone to attack the ideas of Neo-Tech without restraint.

Do not, however, libel or slander us, or *we will* and *we have* gone after and sued for some serious damages. To remove confusion and concern about this, thus freeing you to go full force against Neo-Tech, you can attack *the ideas* all you want with your differing views. But you should steer clear of negative attacks on the company or its people, especially claims that are untrue or half truths or taken out of context. Again, we will go after anyone who defames, slanders or libels us. For example, we have filed defamation lawsuits against Harvard Law School itself because of systematic defamation of one of our people by one of their people under their name.

As long as you have that clear, we encourage negative attacks against Neo-Tech. Those here at Neo-Tech do not have time to get in and debate you, but plenty of Neo-Tech customers will. We watch and encourage these "wars" because they really flush out a lot of arguing points, misconceptions, mysticisms, and yes, points *we* learn and grow from here at Neo-Tech.

So, with our blessing: go to it!

Neo-Tech Networkings (NTNs)
www.neo-tech.com

Appendix E

General Notes

Ending the False Gods

Ordinary people tomorrow looked back over their lives and saw history as part of mankind's long retreat from the bicameral mentality. Neocheaters provided the public with god-like authorization. Because of our mystical programming, we granted them the power to *rule over* us. That bicameral vestige in the 20th century, that hierarchy of authorities ruling over us, extended into the 21st century and blocked the good life we were supposed to enjoy.

My Twelve Visions showed me that sometime in the 21st century everything changed. Extraordinarily healthy and very, very wealthy people covered the Earth. The previous century of increasing diseases, stagnation, and poverty (i.e., by comparison) suddenly seemed weird, insane...as though we were once automatons functioning in a trance under the spell of the neocheaters.

Since the dawn of human consciousness, governments treaded beyond their natural purpose of protecting the people and wrongly assumed the bicameral gods' power of ruling over the people. Politicians never ceased playing God with society. In the process, as you know, they took away our own authority and our Gifts.

The neocheaters took the Gifts away, and we never experienced the glorious life we were meant to live. It has always been our right to enjoy those Gifts. In my Twelve Visions, once our bicameral-like mentalities of accepting higher "authorities" collapsed, the small but powerful ruling class lost its 2400-year-old ploy of playing God, and the people relegated government back to protecting the people only.

In my Visions, a 21st-century government of defense *protected* society with local police and a national army. To the other extreme, the 20th-century government on the offense *ruled over* us with aggressive politicization and relentless regulations. After the switch from a government on the offense to a government of defense, sometime in the 21st century, we harbored a lot of resentment against 20th-century-style neocheaters; we knew their old code had blocked the grand life we now lived.

Under the new code, government no longer existed for authorization, just protection from physical aggression. We granted government the power to *protect* us but rescinded the "divine" power to *rule over* us, i.c., to politicize and regulate our lives. The hierarchy of authorities politicizing and regulating how we live our lives and run our businesses permanently ended, replaced with an objective protection service. (See *The First Immortals* to know the story of how all this will occur.)

Thus, big-government regulations vanished, geniuses rose, evolved into Neothink, and their new technologies raced ahead. As a result, most industries in the 21st century delivered to their consumers the famous millionaire phenomenon. Under the new code, we became rich.

Waving the Magic Wand

Our country and thereafter our world was able to wave what seemed like a magic wand, and everyone became rich — a hundred times richer. That magic wand was called Neo-Tech, and we waved it by depoliticizing our country and then the world.

Interestingly, when society's standard of living rose during mankind's previous three major ascents throughout history, each time people eventually became a hundred times better off, but after generations or lifetimes. Rising from barbaric civilizations into the Golden Age of Greece, rising out of the Dark Ages during the Renaissance, and rising from agrarian societies into the Industrial Revolution each time gave mankind a steadily rising prosperity curve. Yet, each time that curve took generations or lifetimes to fulfill, eventually lifting mankind's standard of living a hundredfold.

But sometime in the 21st century, we barely heard the swish of a magic wand called Neo-Tech, and we became a hundred times richer. Neo-Tech (short for super rapidly advancing new technologies) raised mankind's standard of living a hundred times in just *a fraction of a lifetime,* in just a few years instead of lifetimes. The magic wand has already been waved through the computer industry and gave us a preview of things to come.

When exactly did that magic wand of Neo-Tech get waved through all industries, and who waved the wand? The wand of Neo-Tech got waved through all industries when we depoliticized all industries such as the uniquely nonpoliticized computer industry, yet I do not know the exact year when that happened. I guess I do not know because that time schedule is still being determined, which is why these Twelve Visions came to me and now to you...to help accelerate the schedule.

Now, who actually waved the wand? The geniuses of society did. I glanced back throughout history and noticed society has always advanced or retreated to the degree government depoliticized or politicized that society, respectively. Upon depoliticizing society, the freed geniuses of society, particularly the aggressive entrepreneurs, catapulted values into super values for cheaper and cheaper prices. In the 21st-century of electronics and high technology, however, they catapulted modern technology into super technologies to bring us Neo-Tech in all industries. Those super technologies, in turn, catalyzed the geniuses' own efforts. Remember, my Fifth Vision showed me a *hundred million* geniuses in the 21st century waving magic wands of Neo-Tech everywhere to take us into a paradise beyond anything Adam Smith could have anticipated.

Witnessing the Catalytic Reaction

The future in my Neothink Visions almost seemed surrealistic: wealth was everywhere...in the inner cities, in the retirement communities, throughout the countryside. Our civilization had discovered immense wealth by mixing Neo-Tech (super technologies) with Neothink (super entrepreneurs — a hundred million of them). Indeed, when we put them together — super technologies and super entrepreneurs, both free to race forward as in the computer/cyberspace industry — we experienced a catalytic prosperity-explosion the world had never seen that made everyone rich...in most instances a hundred times richer within a few years.

Until then, still under the old code in the early 21st century, politicizing our lives with big-government regulations in America alone cost over two trillion dollars per year, year after year. Protecting our lives with the world's best army (plus paying interest on the national debt) cost about a half-trillion dollars per year. Finally, when our country passed that *half*-trillion-dollar protection-only budget instead of the ever growing *two*-trillion-dollar budget and beyond, the trillion-and-a-half dollars used to politicize our lives and rule over us was no longer available. Under that new code, big-government regulations vanished, resulting in the universal millionaire phenomenon.

You must realize, the Neo-Tech World was a new-color civilization, a different world with immense prosperity that had no reference points in today's world or throughout history. That new world with a new mentality, unlike today, had *no boundaries*. Prosperity was literally limitless and based on the limitless creative energy from our Neothink minds.

Ending Our Quest for Authorization

Tomorrow looking back, the neocheaters' *annual* trillion-and-a-half-dollar politicization of society, every year, year after year, guaranteed the neocheaters their bicameral-civilization setup with its hierarchy of authorities ruling over us. In other words, 20th-century-style big government established a permanent ruling class for the neocheaters.

Sometime in the 21st century, however, the career politicians lost their privilege to politicize society, rule over us, and play gods with our lives. The time had come to put to rest authorization. Of course, career politicians would never relinquish their ruling powers — i.e., their annual trillion-and-a-half-dollar politicization of all aspects of society, enforced by big-government regulations. But career politicians were part of the old bicameral-like political structure on its way out. Sometime in the 21st century, the hierarchy of authorities began to crack a little. Being called a career politician during campaign season increasingly hurt a candidate's election results. Mankind's bicameral longings for external "authorities" were subsiding.

We finally ended our quest for authorization through something tomorrow we called the *Great Replacement Program*.

As our bicameral urges faded, we replaced the 20th-century-style career politicians with entrepreneurs and market-driven business leaders who were more interested in the commendable chore of creating values than in ruling others.

In fact, the Great Replacement Program became America's fastest growing mega trend sometime in the 21st century, ushering in the 21st-century get-the-people-rich government. The new political paradigm of entrepreneurs and market-driven business leaders freed their brethren to evolve into Neothink and wave Neo-Tech wands throughout all industries and make us rich. ...Mankind's final evolution into the Neothink mentality had begun.

Introducing the Get-The-People-Rich Government

Now, I saw the new code of living take form: entrepreneurs and market-driven business leaders protected us but did not rule over us. They did not desire to rule over us, and the people no longer desired authorization. In mutual agreement, the government and the people chose to revoke the politician's power to play God. Together, they ended politicization and big-government regulations; they ended authorization. Government became an institution of protection against physical aggression.

As a result, society soared to a prosperity previously unreachable under bicameral programming. The new get-the-people-rich government set free all industries, right down to the entrepreneurs, to race ahead in the 21st-century as did the forerunner, the amazing computers. However, as the Technological Revolution got going full steam, its hundred-million super entrepreneurs evolving into Neothink and using Neo-Tech dwarfed the computer phenomenon.

Just how high the prosperity rose in our Neo-Tech World, I cannot get down in just a few words or in an entire book. Let me just say, for now, the people *fully enjoyed* the Gifts. All along, only the neocheaters — the small clique, the ruling class — stepped between the multitudes and the Gifts in the 20th century.

Stopping the Devil's Trickery

The first political party of the new, get-the-people-rich freedom paradigm, driven to end the Devil's trickery[1] and *depoliticize* America, obsoleted the two old parties sometime in the 21st century. The people scorned the two old parties as the "Devil's left and right hands", both driven to politicize and rule over us, from the left or the right. The people embraced the new party, which protected but did not rule and lifted us to paradise on Earth, where we finally lived the good life we were meant to live.

They called the new political party that forever put our bicameral-like hierarchy of authorities to rest...the Neo-Tech Party. Again, Neo-Tech is short for *super rapidly advancing* new (Neo) technology (Tech). Neo-Tech shaped the new code of living, for when Neo-Tech began driving *all* industries, your couple of hundred dollars today became worth thousands and, in some cases, millions in just a few years. The new get-the-people-rich government freed society's business dynamics to let the magic happen just as it happened to the computer world.

Through hindsight, it became all too clear that the millionaire phenomenon could never happen under the old code, in the "old world" of big government and its two-trillion-dollar budget that carried the endless big-government politicization — a trillion-and-a-half dollars worth. Geniuses and technologies were paralyzed and suppressed; Neothink and Neo-Tech could not happen. Sure, many people got their "old world" entitlements — but they did not get their "new world" millionaire wealth.

Enjoying Our Wealth a Long Time

In the new code, ordinary people not only lived like millionaires, but we lived with near-perfect health. I saw in my Visions that suddenly many, many super entrepreneurs rose in the medical world and waved the wand of Neo-Tech throughout that industry, too. The super entrepreneurs were discovering

---

[1]If God-Man is God, and man becomes God-Man by *exorcising his mysticism,* then who is the Devil? The Devil is the *spreader of mysticism* — the neocheater.

Neothink and making huge advancements of human knowledge. In only a few years, super rapidly advancing new medical technologies eradicated most diseases.

The beauty of tomorrow's Neo-Tech World kept growing with my Fifth Vision: To remain competitive in that rapidly advancing Neo-Tech World, businesses went through a job revolution that transformed our boring routine ruts into exciting entrepreneurial jobs.

Now, remember the ingredients to a catalytic reaction of societal wealth: super entrepreneurs mixed with super technologies. We lived during the only time in history during which a great Technological Revolution about to bring us super technologies, and a job revolution about to bring us a hundred million super entrepreneurs, were both incubating within our civilization, both ready to break out. The catalytic reaction when the two together were released by the new get-the-people-rich government took us far beyond any existing economic theory.

The nation's wealth was a function of creative energy put into society, catapulted by super technologies (i.e., Neo-Tech). The creative energy put into society by a hundred million entrepreneurs, all evolving into Neothink and catapulted by Neo-Tech, permanently outdistanced any existing, extrapolative economic models. We enjoyed our wealth for our long, remaining lives...well into our hundreds and beyond.

Enjoying Awesome Romance, Bodies, and Minds

We became youthful again with more energy and romance, slimmer, sexier bodies and more creative minds than we have ever had — even in our prime.

Indeed, while we lived like millionaires and surpassed our dreams in tomorrow's Neo-Tech Era, our love-lives became spectacular too. Rich and successful, we were no longer bored and stagnated. Happy and stimulated, we had a lot more to give of ourselves, and we became romantic lovers. Our active bodies slimmed down to their best looks.

Moreover, our minds grew very creative. Information was so prolific in that Neo-Tech Era that our entrepreneurial minds began snapping more and more of that interesting information

635

into organized little units or puzzle pieces. Having outgrown our bicameral mentalities of being paralyzed without external guidance, those puzzles grew and revealed new puzzle pictures, some never seen before.

We almost seemed psychic, seeing and creating the future. But creating such new knowledge became natural to our minds. We discovered honest power and prestige in our new 21st-century jobs which, in turn, fed our happiness and love.

The New Millennium

The third millennium was mankind's most anticipated date. Mystical prophecies had been written, all the way back to the Scriptures themselves, predicting major changes for humanity at the end of the second millennium. Indeed, at the time ending the second millennium and starting the third millennium, humanity faced some tough challenges and near catastrophes, such as virulent new epidemics. Fortunately, the new code with no ruling class (simply a protection service) released the geniuses of society "to do their magic" and become our saviors.

America's fastest growing mega trend — to fire career politicians and end big government — got traction and picked up momentum in the 21st century as people saw the favorable economic and medical impact. In short, the people were monetarily and medically motivated to end our bicameral-like political structure.

The changes for humankind were dramatic, but in the end those changes brought prosperity. Out of the breakdown of the bicamerally programmed conscious mind rose the Neothink mind and our Neo-Tech World.

The People Learned Who Really Cost Us Our Dreams

Sometime in the 21st century, the anti big-government mega trend increasingly brought Americans together toward a united cause: depoliticize America to free all industries right down to the entrepreneurs to do what the computer industry did, thus making millionaires of us all. Americans, caught up in the traditional political rivalries, now redirected their energies against the true culprits of their frustrations. Indeed, political rivalries in the 20th century and into the 21st century reflected the frustrations and disillusionments we all felt in life. Sometime in the 21st century, however, we learned to see who really cost us our dreams and got them out of our lives. The Neo-Tech Party accommodated this mega trend and did the job for us. The rise of the Neo-Tech Party made everyone's get-rich dreams come true and initiated the new 21st-century get-the-people-rich government.

As big government shrank back to government's original purpose of protection — its 20th-century prize possession of providing the "social good" denied — the many social and regulatory programs became legitimate, private spin-offs (the Great Displacement Program). What remained of government was physical protection only — police protection, courts, prisons at the local level and national defense at the national level.

Tomorrow's government, a super-efficient protection service, ran like a business, with all the same disciplines and accountabilities.

Securing the Seniors

Furthermore, in my Visions into the 21st-century, I was thrilled to see the seniors got rich! They more than anyone needed their buying power to multiply manyfold. In the early 21st century, concerns climaxed about Social Security: Younger people were paying a lot of money they would never see again. That stark reality caused perhaps the greatest internal strife in our nation. A war between generations had been declared.

Social Security had become a paradox. The young working person trying to make ends meet felt the pain of paying precious money each paycheck into a Social Security that would not be there when he retired.

On the other hand, many retired persons lived in near poverty already, as a result of long-term government-created inflation. To end Social Security would drop many seniors too low, perhaps into homelessness and desperation. No one wanted that.

The country was stuck in this paradox with seemingly no way out. As we moved into the 21st century, however, the pressure against big government continued to build. The government was left with no choice: it released its grip on nearly every aspect of our lives and returned to its original and valid purpose to protect America nationally and locally. *Everything else had to go.*

And that's exactly what happened: the sale of trillions of dollars of government assets and programs. Everything that had nothing to do with protection was sold to the private sector. Those trillions of dollars from the sale went directly to paying back with accrued interest entire lifetimes of paying into Social Security. Every working and retired American got back a sizeable government check. Many seniors got back between $100,000 and $200,000.

Yet, retiring with a small fortune was only a *mini* money miracle compared to the major money miracle that happened for *everyone* by selling off big government and setting free modern technology and super entrepreneurs in this new era. That catalytic reaction of super technologies and super entrepreneurs coming together for the first time en masse caused an explosion of prosperity for everyone, *including the seniors.*

Securing Everyone Else

Leading up to the changeover to the new code and its great prosperity-explosion, even the slightest downturn in the economy would deeply disturb career people. They were scared to death of losing their jobs, especially good jobs, for their chances of getting comparable jobs were not good. Large companies would downsize their American workforces and employ both labor and management overseas.

Making things worse, being an aggressive entrepreneur had become downright dangerous because of big-government regulations. Thus, when the economy slowed and large companies downsized their workforces, America's only real creators of new jobs, those aggressive entrepreneurs, were decreasing and unable to create new jobs. Twentieth-century big-government regulations (extending into the 21st century), not global competition per se, choked off job creation. Society needed job creators, for only they breathed new life and opportunities into society. Only they could keep America's standard of living from sinking.

When and how did everything change to tomorrow's forever protecting/never ruling 21st-century get-the-people-rich government and its booming standard of living? Once *fifty million* people saw the Twelve Visions, then the new code and its Neo-Tech forces became too great to stop...and the strategic inflection point began.

Living in a World of Legitimate Laws

When fifty million people saw the Twelve Visions and got exposed to the Neo-Tech World, major changes started happening. Suddenly, people were ready to see the political change that would bring them the benefits of that Neo-Tech World. The Neo-Tech Party formed and quickly got national attention as it distinguished, among the thousand or so annual federal laws and the thousands of state laws, which were *laws* and which were *assaults*. Those laws for physical protection from aggression were *laws*; those for the "social good" were *assaults* — assaults on our freedom as the hierarchy of "authorities" regulated us and told us how to live our lives and spend our money.

The ratio of assaults to laws was consistently several to one. The enlightened American people began to feel the weight of the government's ongoing assaults, especially now that the Neo-Tech Party was articulating the problem to the American people who, now aware of the Gifts ahead, were *ready to listen.* Soon, the political revolution with its Great Replacement Program and Solar Eclipse Budget happened, which freed the geniuses and technologies to set off, like dominoes, the Technological Revolution, the medical revolution, the job revolution, the love revolution, and the evolution into God-Man. We lived with great wealth, health, success, love, and power for long and happy lives...eventually forever.

We actualized the first promise of our childhoods — the promise to *live happily ever after.*

Precious Children

This is a special appendix, a little turnkey section for children. I've broken down and simplified the entire book into this special appendix for children (and for a succinct summary for adults).

A Dedication to Children
My Wisdom About the World You Live In

I write my lifetime of wisdom about the world you live in to give you advantages that deliver the heights of happiness each of you can achieve.

Let's begin with the civilization you live in now. Why do people not live forever? It's because certain bad people hold back progress. Who are those bad people? They are very easy to detect, for they are the wrong kind of leaders. They are the leaders who get prestige and money without making values. In short, they are what's called political leaders — they do not make real values through a business. Instead they trick...and force...the people into paying them through something called taxes. In this world, there should be no such thing as taxes. People should pay for values they want. And where do those values come from? Businesses.

Therefore, the right kind of leaders are the business leaders. Leaders who are leaders because they are the best at building beautiful values for society — those business leaders — are the best of the good people. They are *great* people. They are responsible for bringing us wonderful values we need and use. And we thank them and admire them for making those important values for us.

If those great businessmen and entrepreneurial scientists and doctors were not held back by the bad people, then people on Earth would no longer die. The civilization of pure good that we'll call the Neo-Tech World would already be on Earth. ...In that advanced world, people would not die.

We must know who are the bad people, so they will lose their power and control over the good people so that the good and great people can progress rapidly into the Neo-Tech World and cure aging and death.

We're so close. I hope with all my soul that children today make it to immortality. I cannot wait for the joy of that day to come!

As you become teenagers and need to further understand the world around you and further learn the tricks and illusions of the bad people and the value and benevolence of the good people, I've written Visions Ten and Eleven. Never let the leaders of politics trick you into thinking they are providing some kind of a value, because it's only a trick (backed by forced taxes) as they hold back the good people. Visions Ten and Eleven unveil for you your Neo-Tech World.

Your Health

Now, let's move on to your physical health and well-being. I want you to be aware of your health and take care of yourselves. I want you to be generally aware of what's going on in the world around you regarding diseases and biomedical developments. Yet, I don't want you to become preoccupied or overly alarmed. When you see articles in the newspaper, say in the *USA Today*, about rising diseases or developing cures, skim or read those articles. Keep abreast of information. You live in an age of growing infectious threats yet exploding biomedical progress. You need to stay informed. ...And, of course, keep healthy, slim, and exercise. As you grow older, read Visions Four and Twelve about achieving Neo-Tech health and longevity.

Your Livelihoods

Now, I will give you my lifetime of wisdom for you to apply later as you become young adults and step into the business world of making values for society. This knowledge will help you whether you are directly making values for society or, as a valid option for you girls, indirectly making values by contributing to your future husbands who are directly making values for society.

I want you to look at business differently than most people

in the world look at business today. Business today is still mostly divided into jobs based on the division of labor (although that is starting to change). The division of labor means that jobs are based on physical labor — the body — more so than the mind. But man has the smartest mind of all the animals. Therefore, men and women must use their minds to fulfill their human potential. And that use of the mind is missing in most jobs today, and that is why the majority of workers feel caught in stagnation.

Business will someday change from the division of labor to the division of essence. (The essence of business is creating and marketing values.) That means jobs will someday (perhaps sooner than later) change from stagnant, routine jobs of labor to dynamic, entrepreneurial jobs of the mind. The electronic age will accelerate that change.

As you enter the business world of making values for society, understand the difference between where the business and your job is presently and where it needs to go. That will give you the power of *a clear vision* to where you plan to go, and you will never get unknowingly caught in the pervasive stagnation-trap that gets most people today. Use the techniques I laid out for you in Visions One, Five, and Six to work your way into a job of the mind or, if you girls so choose, to help your husbands work their way into a job of the mind. ...Through your minds, you will create values for the world...especially as you discover Neothink. Making values for the world brings you pride, wealth, and happiness.

Now, as children, you can exercise your minds and develop more and more ability to someday make great values for the world and great rewards for yourselves. When you look at things — anything — *get curious*. Figure out: how does it work? Why? What is it made of? Use your mind to *really understand* things; soon, with that superior knowledge, you will begin to know how to *improve* things. Someday, through this same learned habit, you will really understand business and easily improve it for lucrative profits, which will lead you into a job of the mind.

Every day, you see lots of things around you. Get curious, get information, and figure things out. Ask questions. Your mind will build a *lot* of valuable knowledge to be used later in life. But even more important, your mind will learn how to become efficient at getting down to the essence of things — to what they are and how they work. When your mind does that, it will also begin to see common denominators that 1) help solve problems (a cornerstone of business), and 2) start to pull together Neothink puzzle pictures (the cornerstone of building breakthrough values for society), as explained in Visions Five, Six, and Nine.

I also want you, at your young ages, to look at problems in life differently. Look at problems that may rise around you and ask yourselves, "How can I solve them?" As you grow older, your minds will become more and more able to solve problems and improve things and to someday create and build values that lots of people will want to pay for. As your mind builds this power throughout your childhood, you will naturally, aggressively flow into acquiring a job of the mind in adulthood. In turn, when you build values for society as an adult, you will become very proud, wealthy, and happy. (If later on you need more specific techniques on *how* to acquire a job of the mind in any business as an adult, then read my turnkey manual *The Neothink Business.*

Your Relationships

Now, for when you children grow up, I will explain some things here about romantic love. The subject of love can be very confusing, especially these days with damaging political and cultural influences as well as damaging influences by power-seeking groups such as the feminists, liberals, and the religious right. As in so many areas of life, you don't need to pay much attention to cultural norms, political correctness of your time, or what's cool in the eyes of your peers. As with everything in life, you only need to pay attention to what brings you lasting happiness.

As children, you are developing your minds and building your knowledge in order to, later on as adults, make values for society and bring lasting happiness to yourselves. *Learning* as children is very, very important for your futures. As adults, making values and/or helping a spouse make values for society brings you happiness and is the first half to a happy life. The second half to a happy life is value reflection — time to enjoy your happiness through your love life...time with your future wife or husband, and time with *your* children.

Value creation — making values for society — brings you happiness; value reflection — spending time with your spouse and children and friends — lets you *feel* and *enjoy* all that happiness inside you. That is how I live my life, and I am very happy.

Can you have happiness without love? Yes, you can. And when you find love, it adds to what you have. As you grow up, it is important that you get an understanding about both the similarities and the differences between men and women. I've written Vision Seven so, as you become teenagers, you can understand the biological natures — the essences — of a woman and of a man. Someday, you will experience Neo-Tech love.

Your Mental Power

Now, I will tell you how to become very, very smart. Starting now, as children, you can surpass history's hallmark of measuring the mind, heretofore known as *intelligence*. You can move toward the next great hallmark of measuring the mind, in which you will surpass even the most intelligent people, by developing the power of your minds to pull together knowledge and build Neothink puzzles that will eventually reveal never-before-seen, breakthrough puzzle pictures. Building Neothink puzzles surpasses intelligence and lets you break through to the next level at anything, with any existing value or potential value. I explain this for you in Vision Nine. *Anyone* with a normal IQ can build Neothink puzzles. Someone should read Vision Nine to you soon, but you need to go back and study it when you are teenagers. It will point you to the next level of using our minds.

For right now, you can start to build puzzles in your minds. Use your minds to try to see the *how* and *why* of things around you. Then, you will get very good at *understanding* and even *improving* things. This will lead you to absorbing knowledge and locking together common denominators...snapping together puzzle pieces that begin to build future Neothink puzzles.

You start this process now by asking and learning the *how* and *why* of things, including the details. This will start the process in your young minds that will catapult you in business and lead you toward Neothink puzzle building and breakthroughs in your futures.

Neothink is the new way humans will use their minds sometime in the 21st century (i.e., the next mentality, which you will learn about in a few years when you study Vision Nine). I want you to develop your minds for that new way of thinking.

The old way, people passively let others — leaders...the bad leaders — tell them how to think and act. The new mentality means that people actively use their Neothink minds to integrate and build knowledge. Their growing knowledge gives them answers and points their way, not their harmful leaders. People tomorrow lead themselves and no longer need or want the wrong kind of leaders — the political leaders.

The people then bask in the shining rays of bright new values improving their lives, radiating from good people and great people who are no longer held back by the bad people. The people will then be powerful, prosperous, happy and, without the bad leaders holding them back, on their way to the Neo-Tech World.

I've named the person with the new mentality *the God-Man*. As I explain in the First Insight, he or she becomes his or her own authority and God. Indeed, as you'll eventually see in the Second and Third Insights, *we are God*. The Twelve Visions and Three Insights will help you, when you grow older, to evolve into God-Man.

Becoming the God-Man

Precious children, you can sense the excitement and happiness that comes from making values for the world. As the God-Man, you will make enormous values for the world.

The first and perhaps most important step toward becoming the prosperous God-Man is to open the door to the person you were meant to be...living the life you were meant to live. That self-discovery nourishes your deepest motivational root within your soul.

The problem with most people today is that they have little motivation. They exist, but they do not *really live*. Their deepest motivational root dried up years ago, and the path they were meant to journey got buried by falling, dead leaves of resignation. Most people no longer even have a clue as to the person they were meant to be.

Deep-rooted motivation is *the* cause of major success, wealth, happiness, and romantic love. I want someone to read Vision One to you now, and again every year until you can read it yourselves. In Vision One, you will learn about your Friday-Night Essence. I must tell you that, as adults, we usually discover one or two Friday-Night Essences. But I can see how growing children could have one, two, or several Friday-Night Essences with much more flexibility and choices. The key is that you discover an exciting adventure through life. As you will see, living your Friday-Night Essence delivers the most exciting life available to human beings. That love for life will bring you boundless energy and drive, and will lift you to doing great things for the world, which will bring you deep happiness and everlasting romantic love. You will rise to major success and wealth. That ongoing thrill for living — that deep-rooted motivational drive for your Friday-Night Essence — will pull your thoughts day and night back to your Friday-Night Essence. That ongoing focus on your creations will bring you into the world of integrated thinking as you pull together puzzle pieces to a Neothink puzzle. In short, your deep motivational drive will eventually take you through the evolutionary leap into the Neothink mentality and onto becoming the prosperous God-Man.

The Twelve Visions and Three Insights are for you as you grow up, to see the path to God-Man and to his Neo-Tech World. The Twelve Visions and Three Insights are chock full of the advantages I learned and developed over my lifetime by uniquely piercing my vision into the Neo-Tech World that will someday exist on Earth. My life's work is here for you, precious children.